Time Out

Milan

www.timeout.com/milan

Time Out Guides
4th Floor
125 Shaftesbury Avenue
London WC2H 8AD
United Kingdom
Tel: +44 (0)20 7813 3000
Fax: +44 (0)20 7813 6001
Email: guides@timeout.com
www.timeout.com

Published by Time Out Guides, a wholly owned subsidiary of Time Out Group Ltd. Time Out and the Time Out logo are trademarks of Time Out Group Ltd.

Previous editions 2002, 2004, 2006, 2009.

10 9 8 7 6 5 4 3 2 1

This edition first published in Great Britain in 2015 by Ebury Publishing.
A Random House Group Company
20 Vauxhall Bridge Road, London SW1V 2SA

Random House Australia Pty Ltd 20 Alfred Street, Milsons Point, Sydney, New South Wales 2061, Australia

Random House New Zealand Ltd 18 Poland Road, Glenfield, Auckland 10, New Zealand

Random House South Africa (Pty) Ltd Isle of Houghton, Corner Boundary Road & Carse O'Gowrie, Houghton 2198, South Africa

Random House UK Limited Reg. No. 954009

Distributed in the US and Latin America by Publishers Group West (1-510-809-3700)

For further distribution details, see www.timeout.com.

ISBN: 978-1-84670-334-8

A CIP catalogue record for this book is available from the British Library.

Printed and bound in China by Leo Paper Products Ltd.

Penguin Random House is committed to a sustainable future for our business, our readers and our planet. This book is made from Forest Stewardship Council® certified paper.

MARIAE
NASCENTI
GIUGNO
MDCCCLIX

Contents

11

108

51

239

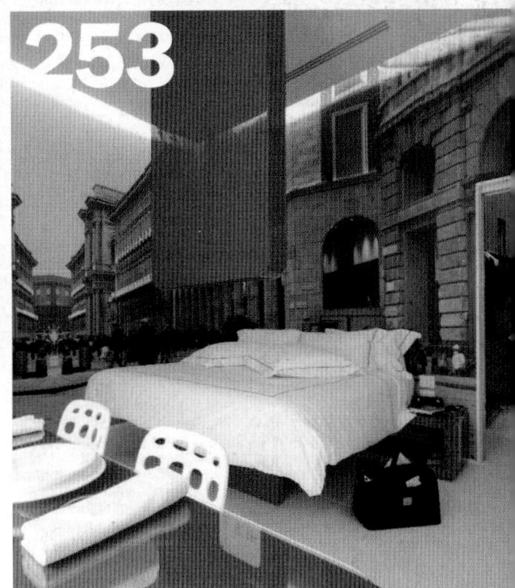

253

Time Out Milan

Editorial
Editor Valerie Waterhouse
Consultant Editor Roberta Kedzierski
Copy Editors Cath Phillips, Dominic Earle, Ros Sales
Proofreader John Watson
Indexer Annie Bishop

Editorial Director Sarah Guy
Group Finance Manager Margaret Wright

Design
Senior Designer Kei Ishimaru
Group Commercial Senior Designer Jason Tansley

Picture Desk
Picture Editor Jael Marschner
Deputy Picture Editor Ben Rowe
Freelance Picture Researcher Lizzy Owen

Marketing
Senior Publishing Brand Manager Luthfa Begum
Head of Circulation Dan Collins

Production
Production Controller Katie Mulhern-Bhudia

Time Out Group
Chairman & Founder Tony Elliott
Chief Executive Officer Tim Arthur
Chief Commercial Officer Kim O'Hara
Publisher Alex Batho
Group IT Director Simon Chappell
Group Marketing Director Carolyn Sims

Contributors
Milan Today, Expo 2015 Valerie Waterhouse. **Explore** Roberta Kedzierski (north, south, west), Valerie Waterhouse (centre, east, north). **Children** Valerie Waterhouse. **Film**, **Performing Arts** Roberta Kedzierski. **Escapes & Excursions** Roberta Kedzierski. **Fashion** Valerie Waterhouse. **Hotels** Christine Lee. **Getting Around**, **Resources A-Z** Roberta Kedzierski.

The Editors would like to thank Edoardo Cioccarelli, Silvia Bruno Ventre, Elisa Dal Bosco, Paola Augusta Dalla Valentina, Paola Deanis, Roberto Gallizia, Sarah Hardy, Giovanna Mori, Daniele Nathansohn, Vanessa Lopes, Elisa Losio, Marcello Lovagnini, Sara Migliore, Isabel Negri, Matteo Negri, Mike Snyder, Mario Zaccardi and all contributors to previous editions whose work forms the basis for parts of this book.

Maps JS Graphics Ltd (john@jsgraphics.co.uk)

Cover and pull-out map photography Galleria Vittorio Emanuele II by Getty Images/Lonely Planet Images

Back cover photography Clockwise from top left: miqu77/Shutterstock.com; Paolo Brignone; frozenlight.it; Andrea Scuratti; Fotostudio Jürgen Eheim

Photography pages 2/3 Bildagentur Zoonar GmbH/Shutterstock.com; 4 (top), 11 Alessandro Colle/Shutterstock.com; 5 (top), 51, 91 Lee Yiu Tung/Shutterstock.com; 5 (bottom left), 239 Alberto Moncada; 5 (bottom right), 253 Fotostudio Jürgen Eheim; 7 Anton_Ivanov/Shutterstock.com; 10 Image Broker/REX; 10/11 Simone Simone/Shutterstock.com; 12 (top) LHOON/Wikimedia Commons; 12 (bottom), 38/39 (bottom), 59 Qing Qing Wu; 13 (top left), 228 (bottom) Christian Mueller/Shutterstock.com; 13 (top right), 54, 70, 207 ValeStock/Shutterstock.com; 13 (middle), 117 Leonid Andronov/Shutterstock.com; 15, 18/19, 30/31 (bottom), 38/39 (top), 44, 68, 69, 81, 92/93 Alessandra Santarelli; 16/17, 24 (top) Paolo Bona/Shutterstock.com; 16 (bottom) andersphoto/Shutterstock.com; 20 Pier Marco Tacca/Getty Images; 23 Luca Bruno/AP/Press Association Images; 30, 44/45, 203 COLOMBO NICOLA/Shutterstock.com; 30/31 (top) Grzegorz Petrykowski/Shutterstock.com; 31 Paolo Brignone; 32 (bottom) Karol Kozlowski/Shutterstock.com; 33 (middle) Bruno Pulici; 34/35 (top) Adriano Castelli/Shutterstock.com; 34/35 (bottom) Marco Pieri; 36, 158, 235 Stefano Tinti/Shutterstock.com 41 ©hanninen; 42/43, 52, 57 Andrea Scuratti/Comune di Milano; 46, 210 umbertoleporini/Shutterstock.com; 53 Matteo Cirenei; 56 anArt/Shutterstock.com; 58, 95 (bottom) Claudio Giovanni Colombo/Shutterstock.com; 60 Alessandro Castiglioni; 65 Louis W/Shutterstock.com; 66 Matteo Valle; 70/71, 72, 77, 173 Claudio Divizia/Shutterstock.com; 85 (top and bottom left) Santi Caleca; 86 frozenlight.it; 95 (top) godrick/Shutterstock.com; 98 Manuel Scrima; 100, 107, 112, 166, 170, 243 (bottom) Olivia Rutherford; 101 Giorgio Majno; 103, 153 Gianluca Moggi; 105 Davide Barasa; 110 Albo/Shutterstock.com; 110/111 Mihai-Bogdan Lazar/Shutterstock.com; 113 Office of Metropolitan Architecture; 120 Carlo Furgeri Gilbert; 122 Massimiliano Pieraccini/Shutterstock.com; 125 Biffi Boutiques, Milano; 127 © Museo delle Culture; 129 Diego Rigatti; 130 MarkusMark/Wikimedia Commons; 130/131 Joymsk140/Shutterstock.com; 132 Tupungato/Shutterstock.com; 135 Renata Sedmaková/Shutterstock.com; 138 PHOTOCREO Michal Bednarek/Shutterstock.com; 139 Art Media/Print Collector/Getty Images; 141 Maurizio Mori/Wikimedia Commons; 143 Mondadori Collection/Getty Images; 146 ZRyzner/Shutterstock.com; 147 Elisa Locci/Shutterstock.com; 150 ETestori; 155 c.Magnolia/Everett/REX; 156 (top) Cineteca di Milan; 157, 159 Eugenio Marongiu/Shutterstock.com; 160 Marco Cannizzaro/Shutterstock.com; 161 (top and middle) Davide & Alessandro; 161 (bottom) Mercutio Chocolat; 164 Gionata Xerra; 169 Luca De Santis/Wikimedia Commons; 171 Nora Roitberg; 174 Santi Fernandez; 175 (top) Masiar Pasquali/Piccolo Teatro di Milano; 175 (bottom) Attilio Marasco/Piccolo Teatro di Milano; 178/179, 201 alteregostudio.it; 180 Philip Bird/Shutterstock.com; 181 Lennart Coopmans/Wikimedia Commons; 182, 206 Giancarlo Restuccia/Shutterstock.com; 184 Sam Strickler/Shutterstock.com; 185 Filip Fuxa/Shutterstock.com; 186 Frank Bach/Shutterstock.com; 188 Stefano Ember/Shutterstock.com; 190 Cristiano Palazzini/Shutterstock.com 192 Andrew Buckin/Shutterstock.com; 193 PerseoMedusa/Shutterstock.com; 194 Edita Piu/Shutterstock.com; 195 jehawe/Shutterstock.com; 198/199 Brykaylo Yuriy/Shutterstock.com; 200 (top) Rene Hartmann/Shutterstock.com; 200 (bottom) DavidYoung/Shutterstock.com; 202 Mor65/Shutterstock.com; 204 Capricorn Studio/Shutterstock.com; 211 Marco Rubino/Shutterstock.com; 212, 213 Skowronek/Shutterstock.com; 214 dolomite-summits/Shutterstock.com; 215 LianeM/Shutterstock.com; 216 (top) SusaZoom/Shutterstock.com; 216 (bottom) Khirman Vladimir/Shutterstock.com; 217 Yevgenia Gorbulsky/Shutterstock.com; 220 Anibal Trejo/Shutterstock.com; 222 Marzolino/Shutterstock.com; 224 The Art Archive/Alamy; 225, 227 De Agostini/Getty Images; 226 Monstrelet/Wikimedia Commons; 228 (top) vmedia84/Shutterstock.com; 231 (top) Oleg Senkov/Shutterstock.com; 232/233 miqu77/Shutterstock.com; 237 (top) ©Alessi SpA; 238 Andre' Lucat – SGP; 240 FeudiGuaineri.com; 241 kuvona/Shutterstock.com; 242 (top) Edward Westmacott/Shutterstock.com; 242 (middle) Only Fabrizio/Shutterstock.com; 242 (bottom) Matt Antonino/Shutterstock.com; 243 (top) bonchan/Shutterstock.com; 243 (middle) Jon Le-Bon/Shutterstock.com; 244/245, 248 GM Grimaldi; 246 Clizia Scapolan/Andrea Scapolan; 274/275 H.E./Shutterstock.com

The following images were supplied by the featured establishments: 4 (bottom), 13 (bottom), 16 (left), 17 (bottom), 24/25 (middle and bottom), 26, 28, 30/31 (middle), 32/33, 33 (bottom), 40, 62, 78, 82, 84, 85 (bottom right), 87, 88, 92, 99, 102, 108, 123, 124, 126, 128, 134, 142, 144, 148/149, 154, 156 (bottom), 163, 165, 167, 168, 172, 187, 191, 208, 218/219, 234, 237 (bottom), 247, 249, 250, 251, 254

About the Guide

GETTING AROUND

Each sightseeing chapter contains a street map of the area marked with the locations of sights and museums (❶), restaurants (❶), cafés and bars (❶) and shops (❶). There are also street maps of Milan at the back of the book, along with an overview map of the city and a transport map. In addition, there is a detachable fold-out street map inside the back cover.

THE ESSENTIALS

For practical information, including visas, disabled access, emergency numbers, lost property, websites and local transport, see the Essential Information section. It begins on page 244.

THE LISTINGS

Addresses, phone numbers, websites, transport information, hours and prices are all included in our listings, as are selected other facilities. All were checked and correct at press time. However, business owners can alter their arrangements at any time, and fluctuating economic conditions can cause prices to change rapidly.

The very best venues in the city, the must-sees and must-dos in every category, have been marked with a red star (★). In the sightseeing chapters, we've also marked venues with free admission with a FREE symbol, and budget restaurants and cafés with a € symbol.

THE LANGUAGE

Many Milanese speak English, but a few basic Italian phrases go a long way. You'll find a primer on page 269.

PHONE NUMBERS

The area code for Milan is 02. You must use the code, whether you're calling from inside or outside the area.

From outside Italy, dial your country's access code (00 from the UK, 011 from the US) or a plus symbol, followed by the Italian country code (39), then 02 for Milan (without dropping the initial zero) and the rest of the number as listed in the guide. So, to reach the Palazzo Reale, dial + 39 02 8846 5230.

FEEDBACK

We welcome feedback on this guide, both on the venues we've included and on any other locations that you'd like to see featured in future editions. Please email us at guides@timeout.com.

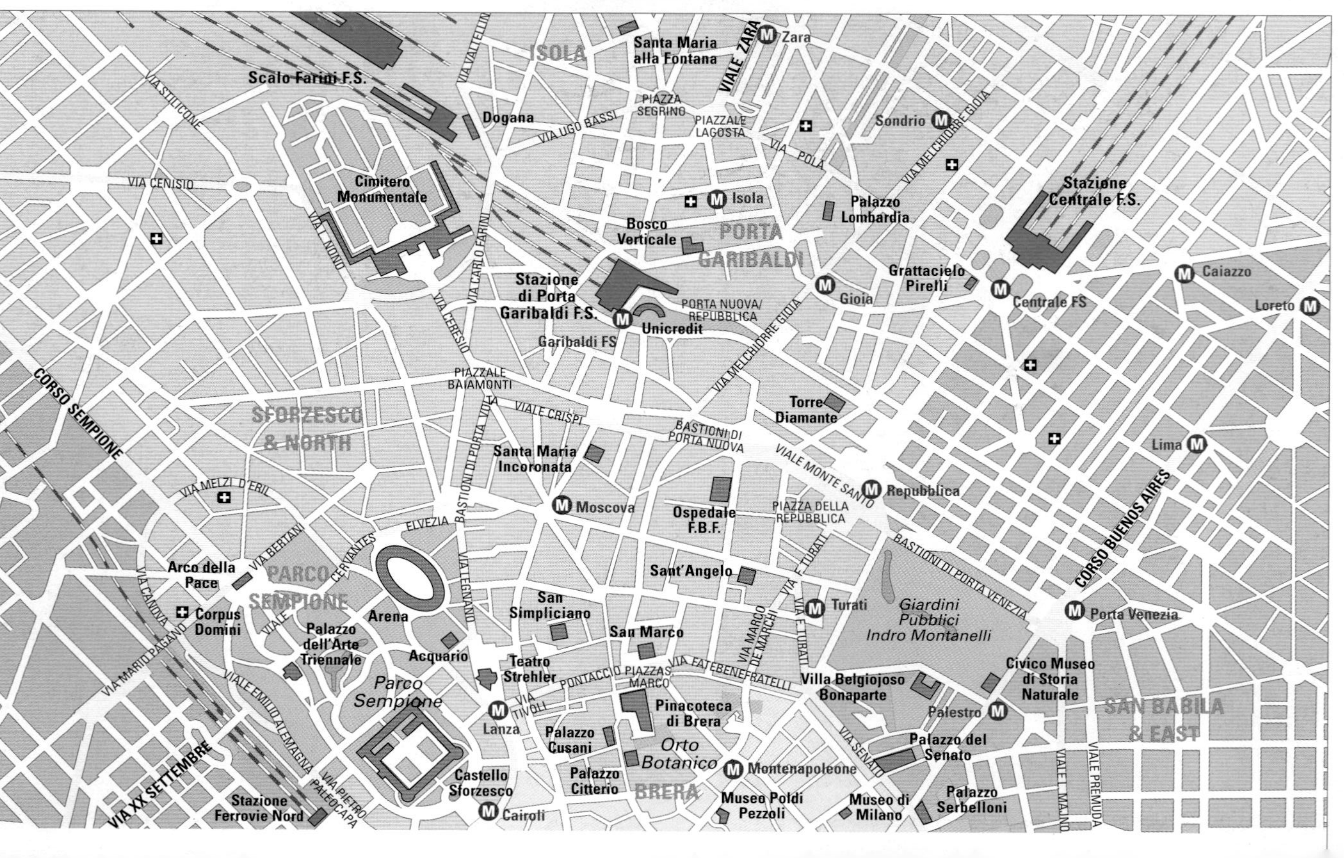
Scalo Farini F.S.
ISOLA
Santa Maria alla Fontana
VIALE ZARA
Zara
VIA VALTELLINA
VIA STILICONE
Dogana
VIA UGO BASSI
PIAZZA SEGRINO
PIAZZALE LAGOSTA
VIA POLA
Sondrio
VIA MELCHIORRE GIOIA
VIA CENISIO
Cimitero Monumentale
VIA L. NONO
Isola
Palazzo Lombardia
Stazione Centrale F.S.
Bosco Verticale
PORTA GARIBALDI
VIA CARLO FARINI
Stazione di Porta Garibaldi F.S.
Unicredit
PORTA NUOVA/ REPUBBLICA
Gioia
Grattacielo Pirelli
Centrale FS
Caiazzo
Loreto
VIA CERESIO
Garibaldi FS
PIAZZALE BAIAMONTI
CORSO SEMPIONE
SFORZESCO & NORTH
VIALE CRISPI
BASTIONI DI PORTA NUOVA
Torre Diamante
Lima
BASTIONI DI PORTA VOLTA
Santa Maria Incoronata
VIALE MONTE SANTO
Repubblica
CORSO BUENOS AIRES
VIA MELZI D'ERIL
Moscova
Ospedale F.B.F.
PIAZZA DELLA REPUBBLICA
ELVEZIA
CERVANTES
VIA BERTANI
Arco della Pace
PARCO SEMPIONE
VIA LEGNANO
Sant'Angelo
VIA F. TURATI
BASTIONI DI PORTA VENEZIA
Corpus Domini
VIA CANOVA
VIA MARIO PAGANO
Arena
San Simpliciano
Turati
Giardini Pubblici Indro Montanelli
Porta Venezia
Palazzo dell'Arte Triennale
Acquario
San Marco
VIA MARCO DE MARCHI
Teatro Strehler
PONTACCIO
PIAZZA S. MARCO
VIA FATEBENEFRATELLI
Villa Belgiojoso Bonaparte
Civico Museo di Storia Naturale
VIALE EMILIO ALEMAGNA
Parco Sempione
VIA TIVOLI
Lanza
Pinacoteca di Brera
Palestro
SAN BABILA & EAST
Palazzo Cusani
Orto Botanico
VIA SENATO
Palazzo del Senato
VIA XX SETTEMBRE
VIA PIETRO PALEOCAPA
Castello Sforzesco
Palazzo Citterio
BRERA
Montenapoleone
VIALE L. MAJNO
VIALE PREMUDA
Stazione Ferrovie Nord
Cairoli
Museo Poldi Pezzoli
Museo di Milano
Palazzo Serbelloni

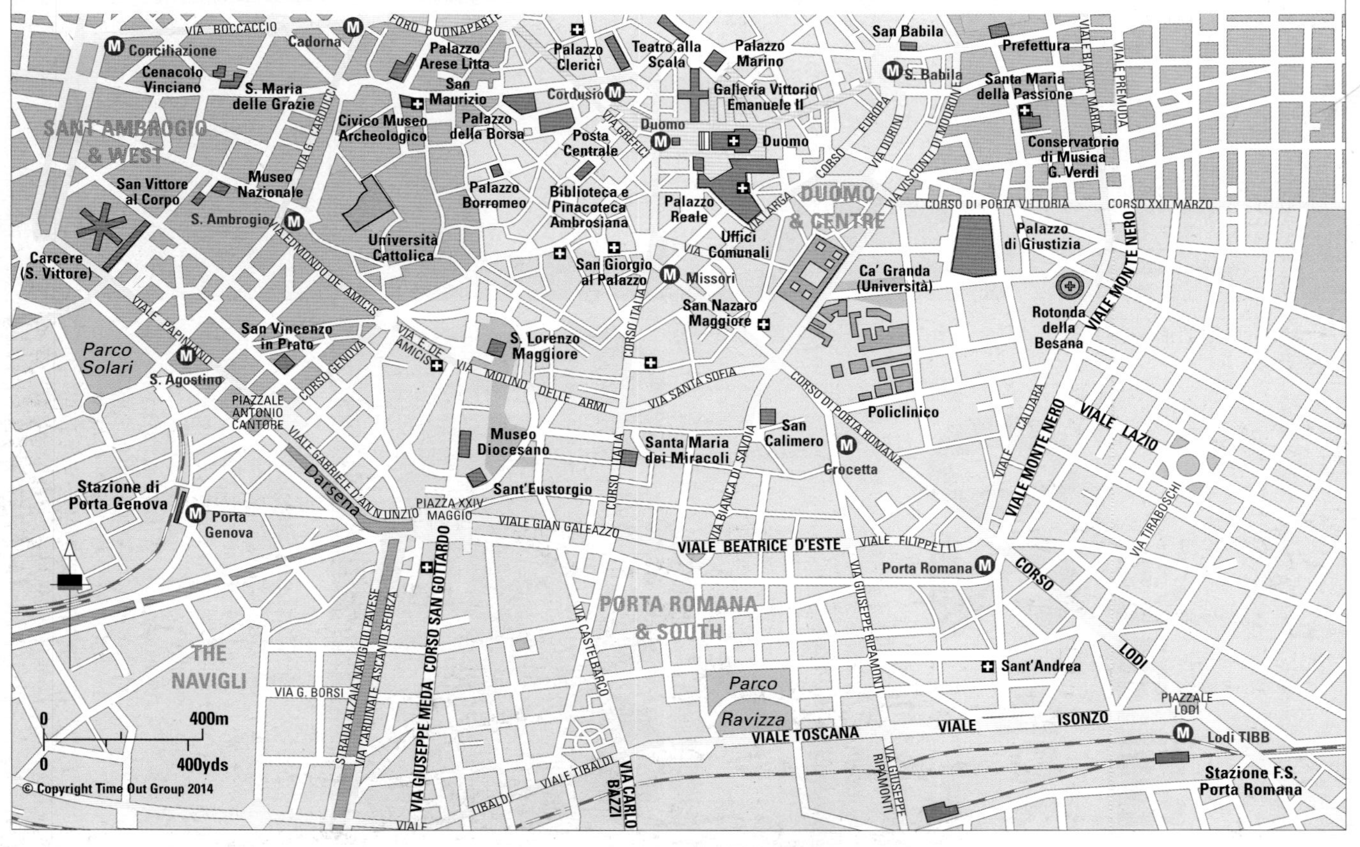

Conciliazione
Cadorna
Cenacolo Vinciano
S. Maria delle Grazie
Palazzo Arese Litta
San Maurizio
Civico Museo Archeologico
Palazzo della Borsa
Palazzo Clerici
Teatro alla Scala
Palazzo Marino
Cordusio
Galleria Vittorio Emanuele II
San Babila
S. Babila
Prefettura
Santa Maria della Passione
Conservatorio di Musica G. Verdi
Duomo
Posta Centrale
SANT'AMBROGIO & WEST
San Vittore al Corpo
Museo Nazionale
S. Ambrogio
Palazzo Borromeo
Biblioteca e Pinacoteca Ambrosiana
Palazzo Reale
DUOMO & CENTRE
Università Cattolica
Uffici Comunali
Palazzo di Giustizia
Carcere (S. Vittore)
San Giorgio al Palazzo
Missori
Ca' Granda (Università)
Rotonda della Besana
San Nazaro Maggiore
San Vincenzo in Prato
S. Lorenzo Maggiore
Parco Solari
S. Agostino
Policlinico
San Calimero
Museo Diocesano
Santa Maria dei Miracoli
Crocetta
Darsena
Sant'Eustorgio
Stazione di Porta Genova
Porta Genova
Porta Romana
PORTA ROMANA & SOUTH
THE NAVIGLI
Sant'Andrea
Parco Ravizza
Lodi TIBB
Stazione F.S. Porta Romana
VIA BOCCACCIO
FORO BUONAPARTE
VIA G. CARDUCCI
VIA GREFICI
CORSO EUROPA
VIA DURINI
VIA VISCONTI DI MODRONE
VIALE BIANCA MARIA
VIALE PREMUDA
CORSO DI PORTA VITTORIA
CORSO XXII MARZO
VIA LARGA
VIA EDMONDO DE AMICIS
VIALE PAPINIANO
CORSO ITALIA
VIALE MONTE NERO
VIA E. DE AMICIS
VIA MOLINO DELLE ARMI
VIA SANTA SOFIA
CORSO DI PORTA ROMANA
CORSO GENOVA
PIAZZALE ANTONIO CANTORE
VIALE CALDARA
VIALE LAZIO
VIALE GABRIELE D'ANNUNZIO
VIA BIANCA DI SAVOIA
PIAZZA XXIV MAGGIO
VIALE GIAN GALEAZZO
VIA TIRABOSCHI
VIALE BEATRICE D'ESTE
VIALE FILIPPETTI
CORSO SAN GOTTARDO
VIA GIUSEPPE RIPAMONTI
CORSO LODI
VIA CASTELBARCO
STRADA ALZAIA NAVIGLIO PAVESE
VIA CARDINALE ASCANIO SFORZA
VIA GIUSEPPE MEDA
VIA G. BORSI
PIAZZALE LODI
VIALE ISONZO
VIALE TOSCANA
VIALE TIBALDI
VIA CARLO BAZZI
0 400m
0 400yds
© Copyright Time Out Group 2014

Milan's Top 20

From flaky frescoes to fabulous film sets – and much, much more.

1

2

1 The Last Supper (pages 138, 139)

Tickets for Leonardo da Vinci's *Last Supper* are almost as hard to get hold of as front-row seats for a Prada fashion show. Those lucky enough to enter the hallowed refectory have 15 minutes to examine the consternation, hostility and despair on the faces of the disciples, just as Jesus reveals his imminent betrayal. The fresco is famously flaky, but that does nothing to detract from its impact.

2 Duomo roof (page 46)

Five hundred years in the making, the spiked Gothic cathedral has been compared to a wedding cake and a 'hedgehog' (by DH Lawrence). For a truly breathtaking experience, climb the 150 steps (or take the lift) to the roof to admire some of its 3,600 statues and 135 spires, many carved from pink Candoglia marble – and get a closer view of the famous gilded copper *Madonnina* atop the tallest spike. On a fine day, the view stretches far beyond the city to the snow-capped Alps.

3 Teatro alla Scala (pages 56, 172)

Typically Milanese, the discreet, neo classical façade of the world's most famous opera house belies its opulent interior – featuring acres of red velvet and gilded balconies. Tickets to world-class opera and ballet performances aren't as hard to get hold of as you'd think, if you're prepared to be flexible about seating. Look out for a superb programme of popular operas in 2015, under new musical director Riccardo Chailly.

4 Trams
(page 257)

Synonymous with the city, Milan's original yellow and orange 1920s and '60s trams have varnished wooden seats and iconic fluted-glass lampshades – a piece of living history. Today's rolling stock also includes '70s models and the newfangled, dark-green 'caterpillars' – but for a taste of the original, hop aboard the no.1; its route takes in some of Milan's most symbolic monuments. Or book an evening ride on ATMosfera, a vintage tram with dinner served, run by the ATM transport authority.

5 Villa Necchi Campiglio
(page 101)

This beautifully preserved 1930s villa transports visitors to another world – where glamour, good manners and immaculate taste reigned supreme. The backdrop to the 2010 film *I Am Love*, starring Tilda Swinton, the house contains original 1930s furniture by architect Piero Portaluppi, and wardrobes still crammed with the former owners' fabulous designer clothes. Take a tour, then relax in the garden café beside the outdoor swimming pool.

6 Classic art museums
(pages 59, 81)

Thanks in part to Napoleon, who dumped much of his northern Italian loot here, the Pinacoteca di Brera contains one of the most important art collections in Italy. Treasures include the eerily realistic *Dead Christ* by Mantegna, and Caravaggio's *Supper at Emmaus*. Smaller, but with works every bit as important, the Pinacoteca Ambrosiana houses *The Musician*, an early painting by Leonardo da Vinci, and a lock of Lucrezia Borgia's strawberry-blonde hair.

7 New art museums
(pages 50, 55)

Milan's oldest galleries have been around for centuries; but these days they have rivals in the form of the Museo del Novecento (*pictured*) and Gallerie d'Italia – both inaugurated since 2010. As its name implies, the Museum of the Twentieth Century houses 20th-century Italian and international artworks, by everyone from Modigliani to Matisse. The free, bank-owned Gallerie d'Italia displays works by the likes of Canova and Hayez in a sumptuous series of frescoed *palazzi*.

8 Galleria Vittorio Emanuele II
(page 50)

With its glass-and-iron dome, magnificent mosaics and marble floorways, this 1867 arcade is definitely one of the world's most glamorous shopping malls. Among its claims to fame is the planet's first-ever Prada store, here since 1913. Gucci, Louis Vuitton, Armani – and most recently, Versace – all have a presence, but most visitors come to spin their heels in the famous bull's testicles, part of a floor mosaic: it's said to bring good luck.

9 Castello Sforzesco

(page 73)

Its rounded turrets and spacious courtyards would be reason enough to visit this Renaissance castle – but it's also home to one of the city's most precious, yet often overlooked, artworks: Michelangelo's final, uncompleted sculpture – the *Pietà Rondanini*. A moving depiction of Mary holding the dead Christ, it's a lesson in how perfection doesn't come easily, even to a genius, but is reached year by year, chip by chip.

10 10 Corso Como

(page 88)

Since its opening in 1990 in a rambling converted garage, this whimsical fashion and design emporium – with bookshop, café, restaurant, B&B and gallery – has become an essential port of call for anyone with the vaguest of interests

in the fashion industry. Owned by former *Vogue* editor at large Carla Sozzani, its interiors feature swirling, organic furnishings and monochrome abstract patterns that add up to a magical take on fashionland.

11 Santa Maria presso San Satiro
(page 61)

Tucked between the ubiquitous chain stores on via Torino, this unassuming church hides another of Milan's unmissable sights. Walk through the door, and you might presume that the gilded apse at the end of the barrel-vaulted nave stretches back for at least a couple of metres. Get up close, and you'll see it's a trompe-l'oeil niche, with a depth of just 97 centimetres. The great architect Bramante is said to be responsible for this brilliant visual trick.

12 Sant'Ambrogio
(page 134)

The church's red brick exterior may not be eye-catching – but visiting Sant'Ambrogio's ancient interior is an illuminating experience. Look out for the Golden Altar, a ninth-century masterpiece of Carolingian goldwork, and the Stilicone Sarcophagus, a late-Roman funeral receptacle, said to have been made for a Roman general. Don't miss the grisly remains of Sant'Ambrogio, housed in a bronze and crystal casket along with two other saints, in the crypt.

13 Luini
(page 54)

At weekends, the queue for Luini snakes right down via Santa Radegonda. Come to this hole-in-the-wall takeaway at off-peak moments to try the legendary *panzerotti* – a fried pastry triangle stuffed with tomato and oozing mozzarella. It's originally from Puglia, but definitely one of Milan's most recognisable treats.

14 The Golden Rectangle
(page 68)

Purveying hot-off-the-catwalk clothes by the likes of Armani, Dolce & Gabbana, Prada and Versace, it's little wonder that Milan's upscale fashion-shopping district is known as the Quadrilatero d'Oro – the Golden Rectangle. Naturally, most of the merchandise is not for the budget-conscious, though it's worth having a look in Dmagazine Outlet, a discount fashion shop on via Manzoni. Otherwise, enjoy a bit of window shopping, while clocking the well-dressed local fauna.

15 Navigli
(page 125)

A network of canals, partly designed by Leonardo da Vinci, once stretched right across Milan, but these days the *navigli* are confined to two long waterways – the Naviglio Grande and the Naviglio Pavese – in the city's south. A welcome alternative to the fashion-obsessed centre, the bohemian

canals are lined with pavement cafés, vintage shops, and the occasional gallery. A popular antiques market is held on the Naviglio Grande on the last Sunday of every month.

16 Studio Achille Castiglioni
(page 79)

A hidden gem close to the Castello, this tiny museum was once the studio of legendary Milanese furniture and industrial designer Achille Castiglioni, who died in 2002. Shelves are crowded with gadgets, models and inventions; secret drawers and cupboards reveal some of the inspirations that led to his most ingenious ideas. Ask to see the miniature model of Castiglioni's iconic Arco lamp for Flos.

17 Salone del Mobile
(page 35)

With more than 350,000 visitors from 160 countries, April's Salone del Mobile (Furniture Fair) is Milan's biggest annual event. Designs from the 1,270 exhibitors at the main FieraMilano trade fair in Rho (open to the public at weekends) range from the understated to the bizarre.

But what makes the event worth coming to are the hundreds of exhibitions, cocktail evenings and parties at the Fuori Salone fringe back in town. Most are free and open to anyone.

18 San Siro Stadium
(page 146)

Built in 1925, and expanded for the World Cup in 1990, the San Siro Stadium is home to two of Italy's most famous football clubs: FC Internazionale and AC Milan. Watching a match here is an unforgettable thrill, but if that's not possible, take a tour of the museum and stadium on a non-match day. The highlight is a peek inside the dressing rooms – revealing the contrasting philosophies (both sporting and political) of each squad.

19 Unicredit building
(page 80)

For many residents, Cesar Pelli's Unicredit skyscraper is the new symbol of Milan. Erected in 2011, its illuminated spire evokes the Duomo, while stretching its height those extra few inches, making it Milan's tallest building at 231 metres. Some say the bank-owned building epitomises the city's spiritual emptiness and dependence on *dio denaro* (the money god), responsible for the crisis that has swept through the city over the past few years. Others feel it's a symbol of progress, displaying the city's reluctance to get trapped in history's sticky net.

20 Expo 2015
(page 24)

Mired by corruption scandals, chronic tardiness and escalating budgets, the build-up to Milan's Universal Exposition (1 May-31 October 2015) has been controversial, to say the least. Yet the high-minded foodie theme ('Feeding the Planet'), a wealth of creative ideas from the 144 participating nations and a rich programme of supporting events around the city promise to make this an event not to miss. Among the attractions: pavilions by Norman Foster and Daniel Libeskind; an installation by Wolfgang Buttress; and the largest exhibition of Leonardo's works ever held in Italy.

Milan Today

Sparked by Expo 2015, the city is reassessing its identity.

TEXT: VALERIE WATERHOUSE

Towards the end of 2014, Milan was gripped by Expo fever as the city prepared to host the Universal Exposition from May to October 2015 (*see pp24-29* **Expo 2015**). It wasn't clear, however, whether the raised temperature was caused primarily by excitement over the event itself and the prospect of it changing the city for the better, or by the corruption scandals, chronic tardiness and rising costs that had dogged the build-up to the fair.

Flashback to 2008, when the International Exhibitions Bureau (BIE) announced in Paris that Milan had won the bid to host the 2015 edition of Expo. A cross-party committee of politicians greeted the verdict with apparent ecstasy. 'A clear success for Italy,' declared the then prime minister, Romano Prodi, from the centre left. 'I'm happy for Milan – and for the whole world, because this will be an Expo for everyone,' said Letizia Moratti, then centre-right mayor of Milan. 'A reason for pride for the whole of Italy,' added Giorgio Napolitano, President of the Republic, then and now.

VERTICALE

HIGHS AND LOWS

Milan's victory over its main rival, Smirne in Turkey, was partly the result of its high-minded ambitions, which put food and nutrition centre-stage. From the start, Milan's Expo aimed to encourage debate around such concerns as how to feed the 9.7 billion people expected to populate the planet by 2050, how to tackle starvation when one in eight world citizens goes hungry, how to provide clean drinking water to the 800 million people without access, and how to halt the rising tide of obesity. 'Lombardy is Italy's leading agricultural region,' declared Moratti, putting the theme into context. An all-singing, all-dancing presentation showcasing the best of Milanese/Italian talent and innovation – and wheeling out international stars including architect Daniel Libeskind, environmental advocate Al Gore, musician Youssou N'dour and singer Andrea Bocelli – certainly didn't hurt.

The exponential sums of money associated with the win were also cause for smiles in many quarters. The Expo, it was hoped, would bring 20 million visitors to the city, investments totalling over €2.6 billion, and an 'added value' of €10 billion, kick-starting the flagging economy.

Flash forward to May 2014, a year before the start of the Expo, when a series of high-profile arrests challenged even the most optimistic of observers to reconsider their views. Angelo Paris, Expo's procurement manager, was accused of accepting bribes to smooth the path for lucrative contracts to go to the 'right' bidders; six other protagonists – connected to both sides of the traditional political divide – were arrested along with him, bringing back memories of Milan's 1990s 'Bribesville' scandal (Tangentopoli). Acting swiftly, Prime Minister Matteo Renzi appointed the former anti-Mafia judge and head of the Anti-corruption Authority, Raffaele Cantone, to put an end to such shenanigans – but the damage was already done.

The scandal couldn't have broken at a worse time. Already, works at the Expo site were running late and the fear was that the increased checks now rendered indispensible would slow things down. The first nation to start building its pavilion (in April 2014) was, predictably, Germany, which reportedly had to bring in its own generators as Expo could not guarantee constant electricity. In July 2014, newspapers quoted a letter from the European Union to Renzi, complaining that its pavilion had not yet been started, meaning that the original plans might have to be changed. And in August 2014, TV news programmes reported that the Expo's symbol – a sound- and light-enhanced fountain called the *Tree of Life*, adapted from a design by Michelangelo – might now not be constructed, due to escalating costs, estimated at €8.3 million. 'For that money, we could have planted 200,000 real trees,' commented Carlo Monguzzi, head of the Environmental Commission for the City Council of Milan.

Raffaele Cantone.

A BRIGHT NEW FUTURE?

While official surveys indicated that 80 per cent of Milan residents were in favour of Expo, an impromptu vox pop in May 2014 failed to turn up anyone who did not express reservations regarding the corruption scandals and costs. There was also scepticism about whether the event would be ready in time – and whether it would be a triumph, or an enormous flop.

Whatever the outcome, it was hard for inhabitants to ignore the ferment around the city, with construction sites, cleaning and conservation programmes, new skyscrapers, museums, shops, bars and restaurants popping up all over the place. Many of these projects pre-dated Milan's 2008 victory – but the Expo deadline provided new impetus.

Milan's controversial redevelopment plans had already seen skyscrapers shooting up faster than funghi in the northern Porta Nuova/ Isola areas, close to Stazione Garibaldi, including Pei, Cobb, Freed & Partners' **Palazzo Lombardia** (2010, *see p89*), Cesar Pelli's **Unicredit building** (2011, *see p80*), Kohn Pederson Fox's **Torre Diamante** (2012, *see p81*) and Studio Boeri's **Bosco Verticale** (ongoing in 2014; *photo pp18-19*). Now the race was on to see whether the new *grattacieli* (skyscrapers) commissioned for the CityLife development in the former city trade fair zone would be ready for the start of Expo. At the time of writing, it seemed that Arata Isozaki's soaring tower would likely make it, while Zaha Hadid's and Daniel Libeskind's would likely not.

A clutch of new museums and galleries has also opened around the city, in a burst of innovation and investment that puts even more tourist-oriented cities to shame. Among the most notable are **Museo del Novecento** (2010, *see p50*), showcasing 20th-century art; **Museo del Duomo** (2013, *see p50*), displaying artefacts connected to the cathedral; and the **Gallerie d'Italia** (2011-12, *see p55*), an art gallery owned by the Intesa Sanpaolo bank, spanning three *palazzi* on piazza della Scala/via Manzoni. Coming in time for Expo are David Chipperfield's long-awaited **Museo delle Culture** (*see p127*), opening in the Navigli zone in October 2014, and the private **Fondazione Prada** (*see p113*), exhibiting works from the fashion house's contemporary art collection in a former industrial complex restored by Rem Koolhaas. Its inauguration is scheduled for spring 2015.

Strolling around the city centre in late 2014, it was impossible to ignore the frenetically paced cleaning and conservation work taking place at some of the city's most visible monuments. Perched on scaffolding, a restoration team was sprucing up the interior of the Duomo, section by section; while in the Galleria Vittorio Emanuele II, an elaborate structure on wheels bearing clean-up experts was moving slowly down the arcade, financed by Prada, Versace and the Feltrinelli bookshop to the tune of a reported €3 million.

Transport around the city was also getting an Expo-related push, with ATM, the Milanese Transport Authority, opening nine stops on the new, driverless Line 5 (lilac), and a much-needed (lilac) link between Garibaldi Station and San Siro Stadium planned for May 2015, with intermediate stops opening successively. Other plans include the extension of the Malpensa Express train line from Cadorna station to Terminal 2 (not just Terminal 1) at

MILAN'S GOVERNMENT

National, regional, provincial and city rivalries.

Like all Italian cities, Milan's government consists of several layers, made up of the Comune (City Council), Provincia (Provincial Government) and Regione Lombardia (Lombardy Regional Government), each with its own remit. The Regione, for instance, is responsible for health and education, while the Comune looks after day-to-day administration and aspects such as city museums, galleries, the ATM public transport network and nursery school facilities. The Provincia's competencies, meanwhile, include agriculture, public works and tourism.

On top of these three layers is the Stato (State), which, in Milan, is in charge of sites of national importance, including the execrably managed *Last Supper* by Leonardo and the Pinacoteca di Brera. To further complicate matters, dialogue between the four strata is often non-existent, or severely strained, since different political parties govern each layer.

Since June 2011, Milan's incumbent mayor has been the left-leaning Giuliano Pisapia, while the Regione Lombardia is governed by Roberto Maroni of the federalist, xenophobic, centre-right Lega Nord. To further complicate matters, the Provincia was abolished by the national government in 2014. It is supposedly to be replaced by a new entity, the Città Metropolitana, in January 2015. It's to be hoped the Provincia's abolition will also increase efficiency, though this remains in some doubt. The tourist information sector, for instance, is in a state of flux.

Malpensa Airport, perhaps by the ubiquitous May deadline; though ATM's Line 4, a metro line linking Linate airport to the city and the Fiera, will not open in time for Expo. Then there is the site itself, of course, which may or may not be completed by the start of the show.

Yet many commentators remain optimistic. 'Expo has given Milan a new sparkle,' says Chiara Maffioletti, a young journalist for *Corriere della Sera*, and one of Italy's most popular bloggers. 'It's become the sexiest city in Europe. It's no coincidence that lots of the newest bars and restaurants now have long communal tables, encouraging conviviality. The city is opening up.'

Milan's centre-left mayor, Giuliano Pisapia (*see p21* **Milan's Government**), is also cautiously optimistic. 'It's like the World Cup in Brazil: everyone thought they'd never make it – and in the end it all went well,' he declared in August 2014. 'When we Italians get close to a deadline, we start running!' Somehow or other, Expo will be on time.

CRISIS OF IDENTITY?

With the eyes of the world upon them, it seemed that Milan's inhabitants were going through something of an identity crisis in 2014-15 – though the ongoing economic crisis and demographic changes over the past decade were as much to blame as the imminent advent of Expo. Perhaps sensing the zeitgeist, Pisapia commissioned a survey and report from the newly formed 'Milan Brand Committee' entitled 'Identità Milano'. 'Who are we? How did we get here? How are we seen?,' were some of the questions the report posed.

Significantly, it begins with a description of the city's shift from industrial to post-industrial economy over the past 70 years. Following heavy Allied bombing in World War II, large chunks of Milan were reduced to rubble, yet the famed hard work and creativity of the industrious Lombards transformed the city into a manufacturing centre, producing everything from Pirelli car tyres to Alfa Romeos, Lambretta motor scooters, bottles of Campari and designer chairs – and attracting migrant workers from all over Italy. In the late 1960s, the city began to shift its attention from material products to services connected to creativity, entertainment, communications and the fashion and design industries. By 2013, Milan's fashion and design businesses numbered 6,000, with 37,500 employees. Among them were well-known, Milan-based names like Armani, Prada, Versace, Dolce & Gabbana, Cassina and B&B Italia, although these days the city's offices mostly deal with aspects of design, image, commerce and communications, with production taking place elsewhere.

Having survived this first change of focus, the city now faces new challenges. Its identity – as the survey (of residents, native and non-, plus commuters and city users) highlights – is strongly based around work, but this has been far from a certainty for many Lombard residents over the past few years. As statistics from Milan's Chamber of Commerce show, unemployment has stabilised at around eight per cent over 2013-14, though 21 per cent of young people aged 15-29 were out of work. In the province of Milan, around 80,000 15- to 29-year-olds were neither studying, working nor undergoing training in 2013. While the number of Lombard companies (286,000) held steady, this was largely because foreign companies were moving in, supplying jobs in (among other sectors) telecommunications, information technology and energy. Meanwhile, the

CITY SYMBOLS

A recent exhibition on Milan's identity at the Triennale picked out the following multifarious symbols, some of which have survived for centuries.

1 **Il Gonfalone**: a banner with Milan's coat of Arms, featuring a red cross on a silver or white shield, a crown and laurel leaves.

2 **Il Panettone**: the famous raisin-studded Christmas cake.

3 **La Scrofa Semilanuta**: a half-woolly sow, supposedly seen in a dream by the Gaul prince said to have founded the city.

4 **Risotto alla Milanese**: saffron rice.

5 **La Madonnina**: the golden Madonna statue on the Duomo roof.

6 **La Cotoletta alla Milanese**: breaded veal chop.

construction, real estate and logistics industries, in particular, were suffering, with 1,278 businesses across these categories and others filing for bankruptcy.

That said, Milan's situation was far less gloomy than that of much of the rest of Italy, where unemployment was above 12 per cent in January 2014, and youth unemployment at an alarming 42 per cent. In irrepressible Milanese fashion, the city seemed to be showing signs of bouncing back. Just over a quarter of those surveyed by the Comune/ Triennale saw Milan as the city of start-ups, and a modest but significant total of 240 new businesses opened their doors in 2013. Meanwhile nine per cent of all Milan-based companies have owners under the age of 35, mostly in the hospitality, restaurant, rental, travel and professional services industries.

Milan's seven universities are also flourishing, with over 200,000 students studying for courses as diverse as new technologies, fashion, the sciences, music and choreography. A growing number of these students are non-Italian, accounting for around ten per cent of foreign students in Italy.

Not mentioned in the identity survey, except in passing, was the massive change wrought over the past 30 years by the influx of immigrants to Milan (and Italy). In the late 1980s, Milanese residents commonly boasted about the city's tolerance and lack of racism; no one would make those claims today. Starting with a trickle in the 1980s, Milan's non-Italian population now makes up 20 per cent of the total, arousing a mix of acceptance, consternation and downright intolerance among the natives, depending on points of view. Most non-Italians are from eastern Europe, especially Romania, followed by Asians and north Africans. There are the usual mumblings about jobs being taken away, but, in fact, most immigrants work in low-status areas in the construction or domestic service industries, which most Italian workers shun. Immigrant employment has also been badly hit, though. Many women from the Philippines, Sri Lanka, Peru, Ecuador and eastern Europe, in particular, work as *badanti* (private carers) for senior citizens – but over 2013, the number of available jobs shrank by two per cent. The immigrant population looks set to stay, though, soliciting a range of reactions, from the xenophobic policies of the Northern League, to the more embracing politics of Pisapia, who has been criticised for trying to establish an official mosque. Increased multiculturalism and ethnic diversity is just one more change the Milanese are slowly taking on board.

When it comes down to it, the influx of new inhabitants is nothing new. In Roman times, the city was known as Mediolanum, meaning mid-land, or 'land in the middle of the plains', where north, south, east and west converged. Piero Bassetti, first president of the Lombard Region, described it as a 'hybrid city, full of contradictions… more than anything… a cross-breed.' As one resident observed: 'We need to be like the statue of the Madonnina on the Duomo rooftop – looking out, beyond Milan.' Milan's Expo aims to encourage its inhabitants to do just that.

Expo 2015

What to see and do at Milan's Universal Exposition.

TEXT: VALERIE WATERHOUSE

Eight years in the making, Milan's Universal Exposition runs from 1 May to 31 October 2015. Based on the theme of 'Feeding the Planet: Energy for Life', Expo Milan 2015 hosts pavilions from 147 nations and organisations, showcasing edu-taining food-themed exhibitions, events, shops, cafés and restaurants. Its high-minded theme addresses the nutritional challenges facing the planet – starvation, the universal need for clean water, feeding the world's expanding population, and obesity – but there will be plenty of opportunities for entertainment, from fountain shows to open-air concerts and spectacular nosh-ups, along the way. The lead-up to the opening has been mired in controversy, however, with corruption scandals and chronic lateness generating no end of justified grumbling among locals and in the press. But with a rich supporting programme of cultural activities (including the city's largest-ever exhibition dedicated to Leonardo da Vinci) planned for 2015, Milan's Expo is already the most talked-about upcoming event in Italy.

THE LIE OF THE LAND

The heart of the Universal Exposition's action is the purpose-built Expo Milan 2015 site in the north-west suburban area of Rho-Pero, around 12 kilometres from the centre of Milan. A plethora of related events will take place within the city itself.

Designed by Milan-based architect Stefano Boeri, along with distinguished Anglo-American-Swiss team of Richard Burdett (of London Olympics fame), Mark Rylander and Jacques Herzog, the Expo Milan 2015 site occupies a roughly fish-shaped area of 1.1 million square metres. If Boeri & Co's plans come fully to fruition, by May 2015 the site will host over 65 pavilions – plus theatres, an auditorium, a biodiversity park, a children's play area, shops, bars and restaurants – by some of the world's most outstanding architects.

Close to the western entrance, visitors will be enticed into the **Zero Pavilion**, a launch pad providing an overview of the Exposition dreamt up by Davide Rampello, a former director of Milan's Triennale and of several editions of the Venice Carnival. Nearby is the **Expo Centre**, housing a 1,500-seat auditorium, a performance area and the Expo offices.

The visit proper begins when visitors head down the central, canopied avenue: the 1.5-kilometre **Decumano**, running west to east – from the fish's 'tail' to its 'head'. Just east of the site's centre, the Decumano is bisected north to south by another avenue, the 350-metre **Cardo**. The two routes mirror the historic layout of Milan and reference Ancient Roman city plans.

Along the Decumano, vistors can pop in and out of six of the nine **'cluster' pavilions** (shared-nation pavilions) , focusing on rice, cocoa, coffee, spices, fruit and legumes, and cereals and tubers. They will also be able to dip into the 50-60 self-built national pavilions, spaced at 20-metre intervals along the route. Among the most spectacular are structures and installations designed by Norman Foster and Wolfgang Buttress (*see p26*).

At the intersection of the Cardo and Decumano is the spacious **Piazza Italia**, forming a central meeting point. Heading north along the Cardo, visitors walk past the structures housing the Regions of Italy exhibits to **Palazzo Italia** (*see p27*), an exhibition space and place for institutional meetings between Italy and the participating countries. The remaining three **'cluster' pavilions** – dedicated to bio-Mediterranean food issues, arid zones and islands – and the striking **Venke Pavilion** by Daniel Libeskind (*see p27*), are located close by.

Water is an important feature of the site, which is to be surrounded by a canal, filled from a series of non-navigable underground and overground channels connected to the canal system and the Darsena dock area in southern Milan. Temporary wooden structures are to line the waterway's banks, housing bars, restaurants, services and shops.

The waters will also feed **Piazza d'Acqua** (the Lake Arena) at the end of the Cardo, a small artificial lake surrounded by a piazza large enough to hold 20,000 people – which can be used for fireworks, concerts and performances on floating platforms, art installations and fountain shows. The centrepiece of the arena is intended to be the *Tree of Life*, a 35-metre

Middle: **Kuwait Pavilion.**
Bottom: **Piazza d'Acqua.**

steel and wood structure, based on a design by Michelangelo, which can be switched on to emit a display of light and sound. However, the reportedly high costs (€8.3 million) have placed the monument's creation in some doubt.

Other attractions to watch out for include the 22-metre-high **Mediterranean Hill**, close to the site's western tip, which will host an agricultural display (think tumbling vines and olive groves) along with a Slow Food refreshment point. Made from soil excavated from the site, the hill will have stairways leading to a viewpoint from which visitors can check out the lie of the land. Not far from the hill, on the southern perimeter, the **Open Air Theatre** will host up to 11,000 people for outdoor concerts, theatrical shows and ceremonies. The **Biodiversity Park** is a 14,000-square-metre garden in the site's north-east, with 250 plant species, while the **Future Food District** in the south consists of two enormous pavilions where visitors can learn how the conservation, distribution, purchase and consumption of food will evolve in the future.

One of the site's most interesting structures is the **Cascina Triulza**, a pre-existing farm building in the site's north-western section, which is being renovated to host exhibitions and conferences connected to civil society and NGOs, with a restaurant.

Last, but far from least, families with kids can make for the site's northern **Children's Park**, with entertainment, educational experiences and services. Attractions include 'Drop by Drop', where kids collect water that drips from an installation on the ceiling and use it to bring flowers and plants to life, with spectacular effects.

FOUR MUST-SEE PAVILIONS

Naturally, in an exhibition this dense, it's impossible to visit everything. But these four pavilions promise to be among the attractions that everyone will want to see:

United Arab Emirates Pavilion by Foster + Partners

Representing the hosts of the forthcoming 2020 Universal Exposition, the UAE pavilion by British architectural legend Norman Foster, is among the largest at the 2015 show. Foster's main inspiration was the sand dunes of the UAE desert – along

UAE Pavilion.

with the sustainable, low-carbon Masdar City development near Abu Dhabi, which Foster + Partners also designed. From above, the pavilion recalls the wavy ripples of wind-blown desert sands, with undulating, parallel walls centring on a circular auditorium. Visitors enter through a 'canyon', surrounded by 12-metre-high, sand-coloured walls, leading them to films and presentations highlighting the UAE's experience of sustaining, caring for and sharing its more limited resources (including water). Above is the 'Oasis', with three floors of eateries. The top floor hosts a juice bar/roof garden with panoramic views of the pavilion. The edifice will be dismantled at the end of the show and rebuilt in the UAE, where it will be open to curious visitors. *www.expo2015uae.com*

UK Pavilion by Wolfgang Buttress

Buttress's highly conceptual design is inspired by the plight of the honeybee. Visitors enter the pavilion through a walled orchard with pear and apple trees, before climbing to an undulating wildflower meadow, referencing Britain's rolling hills. At the end of the meadow is a golden orb made of fine steel lattice, based on the design of a honeycomb. Recalling both the sun and a beehive, the orb will pulsate with the buzz of a bee colony. Bees won't actually be present, though, which may be significant in itself. 'A bee has pollinated every third mouthful of food we consume... yet the world bee population is currently... in poor

health,' Buttress has said. The design aims 'to create something quiet that says a lot with as little as possible'. It aims to be 'a place for contemplation within the Expo'.
www.wolfgangbuttress.com

Vanke Pavilion by Daniel Libeskind

The most striking of the corporate pavilions is the exhibition centre financed by Vanke, China's largest real estate company. The company has chosen Daniel Libeskind, the Polish-American architect behind the Ground Zero master plan in New York to design the unconventional, deconstructed edifice. A twisting, organic structure, covered in a rust-coloured, reptile-like skin, its exterior features a staircase leading to a rooftop viewpoint, overlooking the nearby Lake Arena. Inside, a 'virtual forest' with 300 screens – by museum exhibition design experts Ralph Appelbaum Associates– shows a series of eight- to ten-minute films. The Shitang – or communal table – features in each of them, highlighting the pavilion's theme of 'building community through food'. There will also be opportunities for devouring the real thing, with traditional and affordable Chinese food available in the dining zone.

Palazzo Italia by Nemesi & Partners (Rome)

Located close to the Lake Arena, the quadrilateral, four-storey Palazzo Italia is the symbolic heart of Expo 2015, and one of the few buildings destined to remain after the event is finished. Recalling a giant bird's nest, its façade is covered by an irregular network of interlocking, tree-like 'branches', made from high-tech, air-purifying cement, developed in Italy. Made from recycled materials, the cement filters out the damaging particles in smog. The network of branches is intended to resemble an 'urban forest', with the purifying cement performing a similar function to trees. The building also has a photovoltaic-glass rooftop, which generates energy used in the building. The exhibition area takes visitors on an 'allegorical journey' connected to 'Food, Man and Territory'. Video monitors link the pavilion to famous Italian markets, including the Vucciria in Palermo, Rialto in Venice and Campo de' Fiori in Rome, and the journey ends with contemplation of Renato Guttuso's original painting of the Vucciria market space.

FACT FILE 2015

Expo Milan in numbers

DURATION
184 days, from 1 May to 31 October 2015.

EXHIBITORS
147, including 144 countries and three international organisations; 13 NGOs will also take part.

PAVILIONS
50-60 self-built pavilions representing individual nations; nine themed 'cluster' pavilions showcasing groups of nations, covering 36,000 square metres; three corporate pavilions.

VISITORS
12 million from Italy and eight million from outside Italy expected.

VIPs
100 heads of state or high-profile national representatives expected.

EXHIBITION SITE
1.1 million square metres at Rho, north-west of Milan, between Rho Fiera and Malpensa Airport.

WORK FORCE
3,000-4,000 employed at the site by the end of 2014.

JOB CREATION
60,000 people expected to be employed directly or indirectly over 2015.

PUBLIC INVESTMENT
€1.3 billion.

PRIVATE INVESTMENT
€350 million.

INCOME
€1 billion estimated.

TICKET SALES
€500 million; 24 million tickets expected to be sold.

INCOME FROM SERVICES TO PARTICIPANTS, VISITORS, MERCHANDISING
€150 million expected.

BENEFIT FOR TOURISM SECTOR
€5 billion estimated.

ADDED VALUE (TO GENERAL ECONOMY)
€10 billion is the optimistic estimate.

IN THE CITY

Expo fever will spill into the city of Milan itself, with exhibitions, concerts and other events taking place before and during the show.

The Universal Exposition itself also has a presence in town, not least with its much-criticised **Expo Gate** (via Beltrami, North, open 10am-8pm daily), located opposite the Castello Sforzesco (*see p73*). The two transparent, pyramidical structures by local architect Alessandro Scandurra will serve as an Expo information and ticket sales point until 31 October 2015.

Another official city satellite is the **Art & Foods Pavilion** at the **Triennale** (*see p77*). Stretching across 7,000 square metres of building and garden, the exhibit is themed around dining, nutrition and food from the time of the first Universal Exposition in 1851 to the present day. Kitchen implements, laid tables, picnics, bars, restaurants and the effects on food of road, air and space travel will all be put under the microscope in a multi-disciplinary presentation, including everything from painting, sculpture and video, to music, literature and photography.

Milan's City Council and major institutions are also pulling out the stops during the Expo period with a range of special events. Exhibitions include an interactive display entitled 'Food' at the **Civico Museo di Storia Naturale** (*see p94*), and art retrospectives of the works of Leonardo da Vinci and Giotto at the **Palazzo Reale** (*see p50*). For dates, *see p29*.

Exceptionally, **Teatro alla Scala** (*see p56 and p172*) will stay open throughout the Expo period, forgoing its usual July-October summer break. The opera house's programme focuses on popular classics, from *Turandot* (conducted by the incoming musical director, Riccardo Chailly) to *Carmen*, *Tosca*, *The Barber of Seville* and *La Bohème*. There'll also be recitals by singers including José Carreras and Leo Nucci. For La Scala's complete Expo 2015 calendar and ticket information, see www.teatroallascala.org. *See also p173* **Scoring Tickets for La Scala**.

Following La Scala's lead, the **Giuseppe Verdi Symphonic Orchestra and Chorus** (directed by dynamic female Chinese conductor Xian Zhang) is also relinquishing its summer break, with a continuous season running from September 2014 to December 2015. Events at the **Auditorium di Milano** (*see p171*) – La Verdi's home – during the Expo period include a series of concerts entitled 'Around the World', devoted to composers from 14 participating nations, including Great Britain (Walton, Delius, Britten, Elgar),

IN THE KNOW
BEHIND THE SCENES

For a glimpse behind the scenes at Expo 2015, book a walking tour with **Milan Expo Tours** (mobile 335 120 5065, www.milanexpotours.com), a private travel company run by architectural tourism expert Mikaela Bandini and her team of multilingual architect, designer or journalist guides. The company's walking tours provide an insider's eye on the pavilions, explaining design considerations, budgets, the subtexts behind the exhibits, in-the-know information and curious facts. Expo Tours also leads quirkily themed walks around the city, exploring subjects such as hotel and food design.

Palazzo Italia. *See p27.*

France (Saint-Saëns, Debussy), Hungary (Liszt, Brahms, Kodaly) and Austria (Mozart, Strauss). A specially commissioned work by Italian composer Nicola Campogrande, entitled *24 Expo Variations*, will be played in fragments at concerts from May to December 2015, alongside better-known works by the likes of Mozart and Mahler. Each of the 24 is based on the national anthem of one of the Expo's participating countries. For a full programme of concerts, see www.laverdi.org.

Exhibition calendar

Food Civico Museo di Storia Naturale, Nov 2014-July 2015
Leonardo da Vinci Palazzo Reale, Apr-July 2015
Giotto Palazzo Reale, July-Sept 2015

AFTER THE SHOW IS OVER

At the time of writing, the fate of the Expo Milan site after November 2015 was still largely up in the air. Palazzo Italia – the Italian pavilion – will remain, and is intended, somewhat nebulously, to become a 'centre of technological innovation for the city'. The renovated farm building at Cascina Triulza will also be left standing, and will be handed to Milan City Council, which will utilise it for 'social' purposes. Most likely, it will be assigned to non-profit associations. The Lake Arena and Open Air Theatre are also likely to stay. The vast majority of the structures will, however, be demolished, with the exception of individual pavilions such as the United Arab Emirates edifice, which will be moved piece by piece to the UAE. At the end of 2014, the land will be offered to bidders. Among those showing an interest is the AC Milan football team, headed by Silvio Berlusconi's daughter, Barbara Berlusconi, which is considering building a stadium on the site.

Expo organisers are keen to stress the event's 'intangible legacy' – that of stimulating debate and possible answers to urgent questions facing the planet around nutrition and food. The Italian government has also promised to create a body to be called the International Food and Environment Security Centre, aiming to make a worldwide contribution to food safety long after Expo Milan closes its gates.

It remains to be seen whether Milan's high aims, ideals and ambitions outweigh the expense, corruption scandals and tardiness that have dogged the project so far. But whatever the final outcome, a visit to Expo 2015 will be a thought-provoking experience.

Visit

TICKETS

Prices will average €22, rising to a maximum of €32, free to under-4s. Single, multi-day and evening tickets will be available. They can be bought from **Expo Gate** (via Beltrami, North, open 10am-8pm daily), from www.expo215.org, or the free Expo 2015 official app. Also available from the Triennale (*see p77*), branches of Intesa Sanpaolo bank and other certified resellers.

GETTING THERE

By metro & train Milan's metro Line 1 (red) takes passengers directly from the city to the Rho FieraMilan metro stop, at the site's south-west. An extra-urban ticket (*biglietto extra-urbana*) is required, costing €2.55 one way or €5 return. A 500m-long walkway will link the FieraMilan trade-fair exhibition space, not far from the metro, to the Expo Milan 2015 site.
The S5 and S6 Passante (suburban railway lines) also stop at Rho FieraMilan, north-west of the site. The line links directly to various stops in the city, including Garibaldi station, as well as to the nearby towns of Novara, Gallarate and Varese. The station is a short walk from the fairground.
By car Three main roads connect to the Expo: the A4 Turin–Milan–Venice, the A8/A9 Milan–Como–Chiasso and the Milan–Varese. In addition, the Milan ring-road (Tangenziale Ovest) joins the A1 motorway connecting Milan to Rome and Naples. Car parks are located close to the Pero and Molino Dorino (Line 1) metro stops for park-and-ride access. Other confirmed car parks, connected to a free shuttle bus, are in Arese (13 kilometres away) and Via Novara in Milan (ten kilometres away). Keep an eye on the official Expo website for news of car parks closer to the Expo ground.

For general transport information, *see pp255-260* **Getting Around**.

ACCOMMODATION

While there are several hotels close to the Expo Milan 2015 site, your best bet is to stay in the centre of Milan, to make the most of events going on around town. Be warned, however, that prices will be subject to considerable hikes during the Expo period. It's probably best to book well ahead – or to be flexible about grabbing last-minute deals. For our Hotels chapter, *see pp246-254*.

Itineraries

Make the most of Milanese culture, shopping and food.

Day 1

10AM Gird yourself for a day of art, shopping and food in Milan's centre with a cappuccino and brioche at **Giacomo Caffé** (*p51*), at the entrance to **Palazzo Reale** (*p50*). Afterwards, head across piazza del Duomo to the northern flank of the **Duomo** (*p47*) to climb the 150 steps to the roof. Once on top, peer through the gargoyles to check out the lay of the land. Don't miss the spiked **Unicredit building** (*p80*), which some say is the new symbol of Milan.

11.30AM Make your way through the **Galleria Vittorio Emanuele II** shopping arcade (*p50*), admiring the domed glass ceiling and 19th-century mosaics. Dive into the subterranean **Feltrinelli** bookshop, then visit the world's first-ever **Prada** store. Don't forget to spin your heel on the bull's testicles – in the mosaic floor at the arcade's centre – as it's said to bring a year's worth of good luck.

12.30PM Walk through piazza della Scala and up via Manzoni to grab an early lunch overlooking a garden

Left: **Unicredit building.** Top: **Prada at Galleria Vittorio Emanuele II.** Middle: **Gallerie d'Italia.** Bottom: **Quadrilatero della Moda.** Right: **Eataly**

at **Corsia del Giardino** (*p65*). Alternatively, join the hordes of youngsters queuing for takeaway *panzerotti* at **Luini** (*p54*). After all, this greasy but moreish snack is practically Milan's most recognisable dish.

3PM If you're up for another dose of culture, take your pick of the museums in the vicinity: peek inside the Teatro alla Scala from **Museo Teatrale alla Scala** (*p56*); see art (for free) by artists from Canova to Guttuso at **Gallerie d'Italia** (*p55*); or visit quirky house-museums filled with curious objets at **Museo Bagatti Valsecchi** (*p64*) or **Museo Poldi Pezzoli** (*p64*). Or you could backtrack to piazza del Duomo and head to the **Museo del Novecento** (*p50*), Milan's 20th-century art museum.

5.30PM Time for a little window shopping in the **Quadrilatero della Moda** (*p63*) – the famed Golden Shopping Rectangle. If your budget is an issue, pop into **Dmagazine Outlet** (*p67*) for discounted fashion items; otherwise, simply observe the stylish people frequenting some of the world's most fabulous fashion shops.

7.30PM Catch the metro from San Babila (changing at Cadorna) or Montenapoleone (changing at Centrale) to Moscova (line 2, green; 10 mins) in the Brera area, and stop for happy hour *aperitivi* at **Princi** (*p84*) or **Radetzsky** (*p84*). Be careful not to over-indulge in the free buffet – the night is still young. Walk five minutes north to **Eataly** (*p87*), a multi-storey foodie emporium where you can choose from a variety of restaurants, including pasta, pizza and fry-up joints. Afterwards, take a postprandial stroll to **piazza Gae Aulenti** (*p80*), to mingle with the locals playing outdoor table football, or admiring the Unicredit skyscraper up close.

Day 2

9.30AM Explore a little further afield today, beginning with a stand-up breakfast of coffee, tea and cakes at the counter of **Pasticceria Marchesi** (*p141*), now owned by Prada, in one of the most elegant buildings in Milan.

10AM If you're prescient enough to have scored tickets months beforehand, now would be the ideal time to visit Leonardo's **The Last Supper** (*p138*). If not, make do with a visit to the cloister at the adjacent **Church of Santa Maria delle Grazie** (*p138*), with elements by Bramante, then head to the **Church of San Maurizio al Monastero Maggiore** (*p138*) to see fabulous frescoes by Bernardino Luini, a colleague of Leonardo's, who some claim surpassed the master here.

11AM Squeeze in a spot of shopping in the cobbled streets close to corso Magenta. Pick up herbal soaps, potions and lotions from the Milan outpost of

Florence's **Officina Profumo Farmaceutica Santa Maria Novella** (*p142*) and funky fashions and accessories from **Wait & See** (*p142*).

12.30PM All that culture and shopping will no doubt have induced a desperate need for a plate of pasta – so stop for lunch at **Buongusto** (*p137*), a fresh-pasta shop with restaurant. Alternatively, queue for takeaway pizza at hole-in-the-wall **Pizzeria Meucci** (*p141*).

2PM Take the metro three stops (line 1, red; 5mins) from Cordusio to Palestro. From here, walk five minutes to **Villa Necchi Campiglio** (*p101*), the fabulous 1930s house that featured in Tilda Swinton's 2009 film, *I Am Love*. After taking a tour of the property (book one day ahead for English), order tea in the garden café, beside the outdoor swimming pool.

3.30PM It's time to hop back on the metro, this time to piazza del Duomo (5mins). From here, catch tram 2 or 14 down via Torino to the start of **corso di Porta Ticinese** (10-15mins). Amble down this bohemian shopping street, stopping at vintage and second-hand shops such as **Bivio** (*p124*). For a spot of contemporary culture, cross piazza XXIV Maggio at the street's end and head alongside the Naviglio Pavese to photography gallery **Forma Galleria** (*p124*). You may have to hurry: it closes at 5pm.

6.30-7PM It's definitely time to relax with a drink now in one of the cafés and bars that line the canals. Tapas and cocktails at **Rebelot del Pont** (*p128*) on the Naviglio Grande will doubtless hit the spot. Still hungry? For a blow-out, slip next door to the Michelin-starred **Al Pont de Ferr** (*p126*), or head back to the Naviglio Pavese to the more down-to-earth **Trattoria Madonnina** (*p128*). Afterwards, stroll beside the banks enjoying the magical orange lights reflected in the gently rippling waters of the canals.

Clockwise from top left: **Wait & See**; **Rebelot del Pont**; **Church of Santa Maria delle Grazie**.

IN THE KNOW WHEN NOT TO VISIT

Monday is traditionally Milan's half-closing day, and many museums take the whole day off, so check before visiting. And it's best to avoid coming to the city at all during August, when just about everything shuts down.

DISCOUNT MILAN

These two tourist discount cards may help you save money on transport and museums. Check them out, then calculate carefully. For more tourist card discounts, *see pp266-267*.

MUSEO CARD

From July 2014, most of Milan's civic museums began charging a standard entry fee of €3-€5 per visitor. To save cash, ask for a cumulative three-day ticket (*abbonamento tre giorni*) at the first civic museum you visit. You can then visit all nine admission-charging museums in the circuit for €12 (the remaining three museums are, in any case, free).

For longer stays, invest in a Museo Card for €35, allowing you to visit all nine museums as many times as you wish in a single year. Discounts to exhibitions at Palazzo Reale, Palazzo della Ragione, PAC and to the Planetario will also be granted if you flash the card.

To buy the tickets online, and consult a complete list of civic museums, see www.turismo.milano.it.

MILANOCARD

Set up by a private company – but endorsed on the Provincia di Milano's tourism site – the MilanoCard includes free public transport all over the city, as well as discounts at museums, selected restaurants and on airport buses. A 24-hour pass costs €6.50, while a three-day pass is €13.

Buy the card online at www.milanocard.it, and then pick it up from the (hard-to-locate) offices at Stazione Centrale, airports or other pre-arranged spots.

Diary

A year-round guide to the best celebrations and events.

Top: **Mercato dei Fiori**.
Bottom: **Piano City**.
See p36.

Many of Milan's biggest annual events centre on the four Fs: fashion, furniture, food and film – though art, architecture, artisanship and music put in appearances too. The biggest event of the year is undoubtedly April's Salone Internazionale del Mobile (International Furniture Fair) and its popular Fuori Salone fringe event – attracting nearly 360,000 visitors in 2014. Spring is also the time to peek into *palazzi*, and there are several dedicated open-house events between March and May. The PianoCity festival blasts through Milan in May too, with concerts in parks, *piazze* and packed concert halls. Touring bands and DJs frequently visit Milan before Rome or Naples, with outdoor revelry at a number of key summer festivals. Come the winter, there's Christmas shopping around the Castello Sforzesco during the feast of Sant'Ambrogio, Milan's patron saint: it's the biggest street party of the year.

INFORMATION

It's worth finding out what's going on before arriving in Milan: the buzz generated by international events can be exciting, but hotels and taxis are harder to find. The best guide is the online magazine *Milano Mese*, a monthly listing of events throughout the city, available on the Provincia di Milano's tourist information site (www.visitamilano.it). For film festivals, *see p157*.

Spring

★ Stramilano

www.stramilano.it. **Date** Mar.

Locals and athletes from around the world take to the streets and race over two distances: the Stramilano (10km) or the half-marathon (21km). There's also a kids' event (5km). The Stramilano starts at piazza Castello or piazza del Duomo and finishes at the Arena Civica in Parco Sempione. Corso Sempione is a good place from which to watch.

★ Giornata FAI di Primavera

02 467 6151, www.fondoambiente.it. **Date** late Mar/early Apr.

On the last weekend in March or the first weekend in April, many of Milan's historic *palazzi* and monuments, which are usually closed to the public, open – thanks to the sponsorship of the Fondo Ambiente Italiano, Italy's version of the National Trust.

MiArt

FieraMilanoCity, via Scarampo, West (02 4997 6582, www.miart.it). Metro Lotto-Fieramilanocity, or bus 78. **Date** Mar-Apr.

One of Europe's biggest contemporary and modern art shows, bringing together critics, collectors, artists and dealers. There are associated cultural and fringe events all over the city.

Mercato dei Fiori

Naviglio Grande, South (02 8940 9971, www.navigliogrande.mi.it). Metro Porta Genova, or bus 47, 74, 79 ,or tram 3, 9. **Date** Apr.

This flower fair creates a spectacular splash of colour along the canal. Over 200 nurseries and horticultural schools from all around Italy take part.

★ Milan Marathon

www.milanocitymarathon.gazzetta.it. **Date** Apr.

More than 14,000 competitors participate in Milan's marathon, starting on a Sunday at around 9.20am. The race begins in Rho and finishes in piazza Castello.

★ Salone Internazionale del Mobile (Milan International Furniture Fair)

FieraMilano, Rho (02 725 941, www.fieramilano.it, www.cosmit.it). Metro Rho. **Date** mid Apr.

Milan goes into party mode for the world's largest exhibitions of furniture and fittings from top global designers (*see p235* **Furniture Frenzy**). The event's main base is in Rho, but the fringe fair – Fuori Salone – of exhibitions, events and parties back in town is what really makes it. Many galleries and smaller designers install themselves in *palazzi*, workshops and even open-air swimming pools. On Saturday and Sunday, the event is open to the public.

Orticola
Giardini Pubblici Indro Montanelli, North (02 776 544, www.orticola.org). Metro Palestro, Porta Venezia or Turati, or bus 61, 94. **Date** mid May.
It's not quite the Chelsea Flower Show, but this exhibition/market, attracting 30,000 visitors, does take over entire swathes of the park. It's organised by the Associazione Orticola di Lombardia.

★ Piano City
366 977 1338, reservations mobile 331 977 7766, www.pianocitymilano.it. **Date** May.
With 300 piano concerts over three days, the city's courtyards, stations, boats, museums, parks and markets thrum to the sound of African and classical music and jazz. Tickets can be hard to come by, so it's best to book early. *Photo p34.*

★ Cortili Aperti
02 7631 8634, reservations mobile 347 366 1174, www.adsi.it. **Date** late May.
Some ten private residences open their splendid courtyards for guided visits and classical concerts on one Sunday each year. In 2014, the event took place in the Brera district. Booking essential.

Break in Jazz
Piazza Mercanti, Centre (02 545 5428, www.associazionemusicaoggi.it). Metro Cordusio or Duomo, or bus 61, or tram 1, 2, 12, 14.
Date May-June.
Hundreds of pupils and their teachers from Milan's Civica Scuola di Musica offer free lunchtime jazz concerts in Milan's medieval marketplace.

Summer

Idroscalo in Festa
Idroscalo, Circonvallazione Idroscalo Est 51, Segrate (02 7740 2768, http://idroscalo.provincia.mi.it). Bus 73 to Linate, then bus 183 or 930. **Date** late May-Sept.
The summer season of sporting events, concerts, nightlife and picnics gets under way at the Idroscalo Park on the eastern outskirts of town.

Milano Moda Uomo Primavera/Estate
www.cameramoda.it. **Date** late June.
Men's Fashion Week (of the next spring and summer collections) isn't the most important event in Milan's fashion calendar, but it does bring some of the world's best-looking men to the city. Shows, events and special presentations take place all over town; most are by invitation only.

Milano Moda Donna Autonno/Inverno.

City Sound
Ippodromo di Milano, via Diomede 1, West (02 6379 3389, www.citysoundmilano.com). Metro Lotto. **Date** June-July.
Held in Milan's art deco Hippodrome, this popular music fest showcases international artists alongside eccentric home-grown performers such as Elio e Le Storie Tese and Alessandro Mannarino.

Estate al Castello
Castello Sforzesco, North (www.milanocastello.it). Metro Cadorna, Cairoli or Lanza, or bus 50, 57, 61, 94, or tram 1, 2, 4, 12, 14. **Date** June-Aug.
Open-air concerts, theatrical performances, outdoor film screenings and markets are organised to entertain those unfortunate *milanesi* who can't leave the city in the heat of summer. The action takes place in and around the grounds of the Castello Sforzesco.

Notturni
Castello Sforzesco, North (02 8912 2383, www.amicidellamusicamilano.it). Metro Cadorna, Cairoli or Lanza, or bus 50, 57, 61, 94, or tram 1, 2, 4, 12, 14. **Date** July.
A series of jazz and classical music concerts at the Castello Sforzesco. Performances start at 9.30pm.

Festival Latino Americando
Mediolanum Forum, via D Vittorio 6, Assago (02 47679, www.latinoamericando.it). Metro Assago Milanofiori Forum. **Date** mid June-mid Aug.
This festival on the outskirts of the city celebrates Latin music, arts, dance, food, crafts and cinema with more than 60 concerts, events and exhibitions.

Autumn

Milano Moda Donna Primavera/Estate
www.cameramoda.it. **Date** late Sept.
Yet another fashion week. On this occasion, leading Italian designers present their women's collections for the following spring and summer. Events are held at shops, theatres and galleries; most are by invitation only.

Bookcity

02 5811 2940, www.bookcitymilano.it. **Date** Nov.
This lively four-day literary festival promotes readings, book-related exhibitions and fairs in locations ranging from *pasticcerie* to *palazzi* and even prisons. Some events are in English. Salman Rushdie is among past participants.

Winter

★ Oh Bej! Oh Bej!

Piazza Castello, North. Metro Cadorna, Cairoli or Lanza, or bus 50, 57, 61, 94, or tram 1, 2, 4, 12, 14. **Date** around 5-8 Dec.
This annual street market is one of Milan's top celebrations, held on the feast day of the city's patron saint, Ambrogio. The streets around Castello Sforzesco throng with crowds sampling traditional food and drink such as pancakes, roast meat, chestnuts and mulled wine. Stalls sell crafts and antiques. Goldsmiths made a gift to the city of a silver statue of the saint, exhibited on this day in the Duomo; there's also a special morning service in the Sant'Ambrogio basilica.

La Scala opening night

Piazza della Scala, Centre (02 7200 3744, www.teatroallascala.org). Metro Duomo, or bus 61 or tram 1, 2. **Date** 7 Dec.
Piazza della Scala fills with feather boas and black ties as the great and good assemble for the first night of the season at La Scala (*see p56*).

Epiphany

Date 6 Jan.
Epiphany is also known as La Befana, after a kind-hearted witch who is said to bring presents to well-behaved children and coal to naughty ones. Crowds turn out for the morning procession of the Three Wise Men from the Duomo to the church of Sant'Eustorgio, where relics (said to be those of the Magi) are kept.

Milano Moda Uomo Autonno/Inverno

www.cameramoda.it. **Date** mid Jan.
Men's fashion week (for the next autumn and winter collections) is a bit of a sideshow to the women's event, but still attracts some first-rate talent.

Identità Golose/ Milano Food & Wine Festival

MICO Milano Congressi, via Gattamelata 5, Gate 14, West (02 4851 3258, www.identitagolose.it). Metro Amendola Fiera or Domodossola, or bus 57, 78, 94, or tram 1, 19, 33. **Date** Feb.
Famous chefs gather at the three-day Identità Golose food conference to give cookery lessons, present their latest culinary tomes and give their views on culinary issues of the day. There's also a small side event, where artisan food producers promote their wares. Non-pros are welcome, on payment of a hefty admission fee. Held on overlapping dates, the Milano Food & Wine Festival is aimed at dilettantes, offering plentiful opportunities to sample gourmet dishes and swig a vast selection of wines.

Milano Moda Donna Autonno/Inverno

www.cameramoda.it. **Date** late Feb.
Milan's moment in the global fashion spotlight, when 80 or so designers unveil their autumn and winter collections. Entry to the shows is by invitation only.

Carnevale

Date Feb/early Mar.
Milan's Carnevale takes place in the days after Shrove Tuesday, later than in the rest of Italy. The celebrations are largely for children, who roam the streets in costumes spraying confetti and foam. There's a fancy-dress parade on the first Saturday of Lent.

PUBLIC HOLIDAYS

New Year's Day (Capodanno)
1 January

Epiphany (Epifania)
6 January

Easter Monday (Pasquetta)
varies

Liberation Day (Festa della Liberazione)
25 April

Labour Day (Festa del Lavoro)
1 May

Republic Day (Festa della Repubblica)
2 June

Feast of the Assumption (Ferragosto)
15 August

All Saints' Day (Ognissanti)
1 November

Feast of Sant'Ambrogio (Festa di Sant'Ambrogio)
(Milan only) 7 December

Immaculate Conception (Festa dell'Immacolata)
8 December

Christmas Day (Natale)
25 December

Boxing Day (Santo Stefano)
26 December

Milan's Best

There's something for everyone with our hand-picked highlights.

Sightseeing

VIEWS

Brian & Barry p66
Check out the lay of the land from the 12th floor of this department store.

Duomo (roof) p46
See Milan's skyscraper-studded skyline outlined against the Alps.

Palazzo Lombardia p89
Dizzying vistas (Sunday only) from the 39th floor of the Lombard government's HQ.

Torre Branca p79
Gio Ponti's (scaled-down) answer to the Eiffel Tower, surrounded by greenery.

CLASSIC SIGHTS

Castello Sforzesco p73
Once home to the Viscontis and Sforzas, this Renaissance castle now houses Michelangelo's magnificent *Pietà Rondanini*.

Duomo (interior) p46
Milan's Gothic cathedral par excellence.

Galleria Vittorio Emanuele II p50
Possibly the world's most glamorous shopping arcade.

The Last Supper p138
Leonardo's famous fresco.

HOUSE MUSEUMS

Casa-Museo di Stefano-Boschi p101
A collector couple's apartment, hung from floor to ceiling with 20th-century works of art.

Museo Bagatti-Valsecchi p64
Gloom, doom and glamour at this faux-Renaissance palazzo – furnished by two brothers in the 19th century.

Top: **view from Torre Diamante**. Bottom: **Pinacoteca Ambrosiana**.

Museo Poldi Pezzoli p64
Quirky collections, plus art by Botticelli and others.
Studio Achille Castiglioni p79
Visit the legendary designer's workshop – accompanied by his family.
Villa Necchi Campiglio p101
Piero Portaluppi's 1930s villa, complete with poolside café.

STARCHITECTURE
CityLife p143
Towers by Zaha Hadid, Daniel Libeskind and Arata Isozaki will be completed on the former Milanofiera site between 2015 and 2017.
Expo 2015 (pavilions) p24
Pavilions by Rem Koolhaas and Sir Norman Foster are among the star attractions at the Universal Exposition (May-Oct 2015).
Fondazione Prada p113
Rem Koolhaas's contemporary art stronghold for the fashion hothouse promises to be the biggest opening of 2015.
Museo delle Culture p126
David Chipperfield's new ethnographic Museum of Cultures opened in the canal zone in autumn 2014.
Torre Diamante p81
Kohn Pedersen Fox designed this diamond-shaped skyscraper clad in glinting glass.
Torre Velasca p112
This top-heavy edifice by BBPR is among Milan's most iconic sights.
Unicredit p80
Erected in 2011, Cesar Pelli's bank building with a spire is now Milan's tallest edifice.

ART
Gallerie d'Italia p55
Canova, conceptual art and a chic café are three reasons to visit this shiny new gallery.
Museo del Novecento p50
A gleaming new museum housing modern masters from Morandi to Modigliani.
Pinacoteca Ambrosiana p59
A small but perfectly formed collection, containing a little-known Leonardo.
Pinacoteca di Brera p81
Milan's most famous art museum – with seminal works by Piero della Francesca, Mantegna and Caravaggio.

CHURCHES
San Bernardino alle Ossa p117
Bone-chilling beauty (of a kind) in a macabre ossuary.
San Maurizio p138
Fabulous frescoes by Bernardino Luini festoon this surprisingly obscure church.
Sant'Ambrogio p134
Better than the Duomo – according to the Milanese.
Santa Maria presso San Satiro p61
How deep is that apse? Will Bramante's false perspective fool you too?

Eating & drinking

CLASSIC MILANESE
L'Altra Isola p89
The local owner and his Chinese chefs make *ossobuco alla milanese* like no one else.
Antica Trattoria della Pesa p83
The best *riso al salto* (crunchy fried risotto) in town.
Trattoria Milanese p141
Here since forever – with good reason, say locals.

CLASSIC REGIONAL
Alla Collina Pistoiese p117
Enjoy a *bistecca alla fiorentina* – and save the train fare to Tuscany.

Delicatessen p98
Order rib-tickling tastes of the mountains at this Alto-Adige restaurant.
Giulio Pane e Ojo p119
Eat as the Romans eat.
Lucca p98
More Tuscan classics in a charming 1920s trattoria.
Pasta Madre p119
Fish dishes and home-baked cakes in a small but sensational Sicilian eaterie.

COOL CROWD, GOOD FOOD
Dry p83
Tasty gourmet pizzas in a fashionable restaurant.
Pisacco p83
Style and substance attract Milan's coolest crowd to this quirky dining room.
The Small p103
A fashion designer and a Sicilian chef run this OTT establishment.

RESTAURANTS WITH VIEWS
Alice (Eataly) p87
Gourmet fish and rooftop views on the top floor of Milan's Eataly.
Asola (Brian & Barry) p66
'Tailored cuisine' with a view from the ninth floor.
Ceresio 7 p83
Fashion brand Dsquared2's rooftop restaurant-with-pools.
Giacomo all'Arengario p51
Upmarket museum canteen – with a privileged perspective on the Duomo roof.

BLOWOUTS
Ristorante Berton p84
The top Milan-based chef struts his stuff at his new, own-name establishment.
Cracco p61
Carlo Cracco takes time off from TV to oversee culinary wonders at his original eaterie.

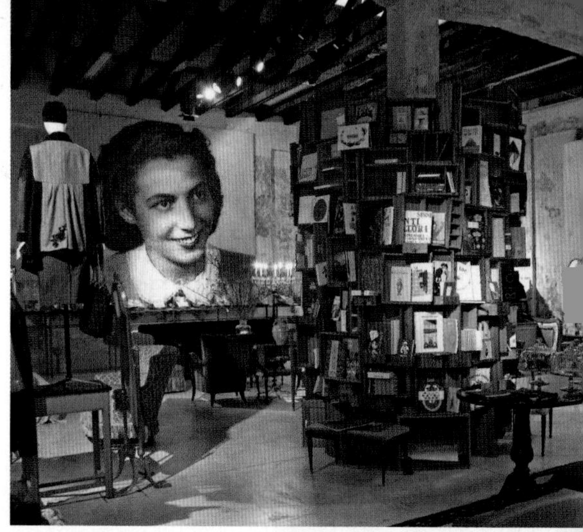

Da Noi In p126
Milan's most exciting new hotel restaurant.
Joia p98
Vegetarian food at its gourmet best – by one of the most respected chefs in Italy.
Al Pont de Ferr p126
Michelin-starred miracles on the waterfront.

BEST BARS & BAKERIES
Deseo p80
High design and cocktails with a view of Napoleon's triumphal arch.
HClub, Diana Garden p104
Cocktails amid the camellias.
Mint Garden Café p99
Sip aperitifs in this florist-cum-café.
Pandenus p99
House-baked bread is the backbone of this bakery/bar.
Princi p84
This multi-tasking bakery and eaterie is open all day.

Shopping

CONCEPT
10 Corso Como p88
The *non plus ultra* of Italian concept stores.

Nonostante Marras p129
Stunning designer shop, from Sardinia's fashion king.

FOOD & DRINK
Eataly p87
The artisanal food emporium taking the world by storm.
Miracolo a Milano p129
Miraculous mozzarella – made before your eyes.
N'Ombra de Vin p87
Vino amid the vaults in a former monks' refectory.
Peck p63
Milan's famous gourmet shop.
Mercato Comunale p147
Get down with the locals at this well-stocked market in western Milan.
SignorVino p55
Entrepreneur Sandro Veronesi does for wine what he previously did for lingerie.

Clockwise from top left: **Nonostante Marras**; **Auditorium di Milano**; **Da Noi In**.

BOOKS & MUSIC

American Bookstore p80
The only English-language bookshop in central Milan.

La Feltrinelli p54
Italy's equivalent of Barnes & Noble or Waterstones.

Open p121
New generation indie bookshop, selling both print and digital wares.

DESIGNER DISCOUNTS

Bivio p124
The new kid on the discounted fashion block.

Dmagazine p67
Packed to the rafters with cut-price designer styles.

Il Salvagente p109
A lifesaver for those on a budget, with up to 60% off last season's looks.

HISTORIC SHOPS

Antica Barbieria Colla p66
Est. 1904, this is the oldest barbering business in town.

Cappelleria Mutinelli p104
A gloriously old-fashioned hat shop.

Giovanni Galli Pasticceria p120
Milan's best address for marrons glacés.

Prada Milano Galleria (womenswear) p50
Founded in 1913, this is the world's first Prada shop.

INTERIOR DESIGN & GIFTS

Alessi p66
All the designer homewares you've ever dreamed of, from toothpick holders to toilet brushes.

Amoeba p86
One-of-a-kind lamps and home furnishings.

Jannelli & Volpi p105
Truly wondrous wallpapers – and much, much more.

Raw p87
Paperweights, candles and ashtrays at this *Wunderkammer* of a shop.

Rossana Orlandi p142
Milan's most stylish furniture and furnishings emporium.

INDIE FASHION BOUTIQUES

Crochette p152
Smart Milan-designed children's clothes.

Nir Lagziel p90
Colourful, retro, socially conscious designs.

Sara Rotta Loria p152
Cheerful kiddie apparel, featuring butterflies, fish and flowers.

Stephan Jansen p109
Memorable women's fashions; worth the splurge.

Wait & See p142
The place to head for that off-beat Milanese look.

Nightlife

CLUBS & LATE BARS

Blanco p164
Good-looking early morning/ late night bar, adored by the fashion flock.

Club Haus 80s p165
A temple to all things '80s – with a themed dress code.

Sala Venezia p164
Learn from the pros at this ballroom-dancing hall.

ROCK & JAZZ

Blue Note p170
Milan's best known jazz venue.

Mediolanum Forum p169
Madonna, Lady Gaga and U2 have all performed here.

Le Scimmie p170
Intimate canalside jazz club – with a boat.

Arts

OPERA, CLASSICAL MUSIC & BALLET

Auditorium di Milano p171
Home to internationally renowned Orchestra La Verdi under dynamic female conductor Xian Zhang.

Teatro alla Scala p172
The world's most famous opera house.

Explore

The Duomo & Central Milan

EXPLORE

Over the past few years, Milan's historic centre has undergone a quiet revolution that has spiced up the old and brought in the new. The Gothic Duomo is still the area's focus, along with La Scala opera house and the glass-roofed Vittorio Emanuele II shopping arcade. But in recent years, these grandes dames have been joined by worthy upstarts, including swanky new art museums Museo del Novecento and Gallerie d'Italia. The Galleria Vittorio Emanuele II itself has also undergone a major spruce-up, with home-grown designer brands grabbing top spots; and the Quadrilatero d'Oro ('Golden Rectangle') is in a state of perpetual ferment, with large fashion labels jostling for the best locations on these hotly contested streets.

Quadrilatero d'Oro.

Don't Miss

1 The Duomo roof Gargoyles, skylines and skyscrapers (p46).

2 Museo del Novecento 20th-century Italian art in all its glory (p50).

3 Teatro alla Scala Iconic opera house (p56).

4 Quadrilatero d'Oro The city's snootiest shopping streets (p63).

5 Galleria Vittorio Emanuele II Lucky bull's testicles – and Prada's original store (p50).

Duomo.

AROUND THE DUOMO

Positioned at the centre of this concentric city, **piazza del Duomo** – around the impossible-to-miss cathedral – has long functioned as Milan's social core. But over the past few years, the area's somewhat staid image has received a burst of new energy as new museums, shops, cafés and restaurants have opened. The long-awaited **Museo del Novecento** arrived in 2010, in the Palazzo dell'Arengario, a few steps from the Duomo's front door, with works by major 20th-century artists (from Italy and elsewhere). Just opposite, in part of the Palazzo Reale, the **Museo del Duomo** opened in 2013 following a seven-year restoration, allowing everything from a once-lost Tintoretto to a Lego model of the Duomo to be fittingly displayed. Between the two new kids on the block, the **Palazzo Reale** continues to challenge the modern-art dominance of Paris, London and New York with retrospectives of Klimt, Warhol and other crowd-pleasing exhibitions. The popular **Giacomo Caffé** at the palazzo's entrance attracts local *vigili* (traffic police) and office workers as well as museumgoers, creating a much-needed meeting point in this sometimes anonymous zone.

The glass-roofed **Galleria Vittorio Emanuele II** rivals the Duomo as Milan's most recognisable icon and draws shoppers and day-trippers, who troop up and down its magnificent marble floors. Once a fusty shadow of its former glorious self, the Galleria is now lined with fancy fashion stores and designer cafés, owned by the likes of Gucci and (from 2015) Prada, though locals prefer to take their espresso shots at venerable classics such as **Camparino in Galleria**, which still oozes the glamour of bygone days.

Sights & Museums

★ Duomo

Piazza del Duomo (02 7202 2656, www.duomo dimilano.it). Metro Duomo, or bus 54, or tram 1, 2, 3, 12, 14, 24. **Open** *Church & Baptistery (Santo Stefano)* 7am-7pm daily. *Baptistery (San Giovanni alle Fonti)* 10am-6pm (last entry 5pm) Tue-Sun. *Roof* May-Sept 9am-7pm (last entry 6.10pm) Mon-Thur, Sun; 9am-10pm Fri, Sat. Oct-Apr 9am-7pm (last entry 6.10pm) daily. **Admission** *Church & Baptistery (Santo Stefano)* free. *Baptistery (San Giovanni alle Fonti)* €6. *Roof* By lift €12; €6 reductions. On foot €7; €3.50 reductions. **Map** p49 E5 ❶

Milan's Duomo, which is the third-largest church in Christendom (outdone only by St Peter's in Rome and Seville's cathedral), is truly a joy to behold. Although the key elements were in place by 1391, the Duomo took the best part of 500 years to complete – and, indeed, work continues today. A five-year clean-up of the exterior was finished in 2008, and a major revamp of the interior should be completed by May 2015 (the cathedral remains open during the project).

The Duomo was begun in brick, but upgraded to marble as its architects understood the grandeur of the project. Over time, it was adorned with Gothic spires and an astonishing wealth of statues, and has been adored by a huge number of art and architecture aficionados. As generations of Lombard builders and architects argued with French and German master stone-cutters about the best way to tackle their mammoth task, an enormous array of styles was employed.

Construction began in 1386 by order of Bishop Antonio da Saluzzo, on a site that had been associated with places of worship since the third century: a Roman temple to the goddess Minerva once stood here. On the orders of Gian Galeazzo Visconti, then ruler of Milan, local stone was eschewed in favour of Candoglia marble shipped from Lake Maggiore on the Ticino river, and then along the Navigli, a network of canals, built in part for the purpose.

The cathedral was consecrated in 1418, but remained incomplete for centuries. Politics, physical setbacks (a pink granite column sank, in transit, in Lake Maggiore), a lack of money and downright indifference kept the project on permanent standby. Finally, early in the 19th century, the façade was put on the church by order of none other than Napoleon; he kick-started the final stages of construction, before crowning himself king of Italy here in 1805.

Exterior

A staggering 3,600 statues adorn the Duomo, about two-thirds of them on the exterior. The oldest are at the apse end (1386-1447); those along the sides were added as the building work progressed, between the late 15th and early 18th centuries. The façade is Baroque up to the first order of windows, and neo-Gothic above. Each of the five bronze doors was sculpted by a different artist between 1840 and 1965, along particular themes.

To appreciate the statues and 135 spires fully, take the lift or climb the 150 stairs (both are near the back of the Duomo, on the left-hand side) to the roof, from where, on clear days, you also get breathtaking views of the Alps. A roof visit brings you closer to an icon dear to the hearts of the Milanese: the *Madonnina* (1774), the gilded copper figure of Mary on the church's tallest spire, which was the city's highest point until it was pipped by the Pirelli skyscraper in 1958. (Both have now been superseded by the Unicredit building, visible from the rooftop, erected in 2012.)

Interior

The 52 pillars of the five-aisled Duomo correspond to the weeks of the year. On their capitals, imposing statues of saints stretch up into the cross-vaults of the ceiling, to vertiginous effect. On the floor near the main entrance is a sundial installed in 1768 by astronomers from the Osservatorio di Brera, placed so that it's struck by a ray of sunlight breaking through a hole in the opposite wall. On the summer solstice (21 June), the ray strikes the tongue of bronze set in the floor; on the winter solstice (21 December), it stretches out to reach the meridian. The sundial is so precise that it was once used to regulate clocks throughout the city.

In the first chapel on the right is the 11th-century sarcophagus of Bishop Ariberto d'Intimiano, and a 17th-century plaque commemorating the founding of the Duomo. The oldest of the stained-glass windows in the next three chapels was made in 1470-75 and is in the fifth bay on the right; it shows scenes from the life of Christ.

In the crossing of the transept, the presbytery floor has been worn by the passage of the many millions of pilgrims who have visited the Duomo over the centuries; Cardinal (later St) Carlo Borromeo wanted the Duomo to serve as his model Counter-Reformation church. Flanking the 15th-century high altar are two 16th-century gilded copper pulpits. The organ is here too, its wooden shutters painted with biblical scenes by Giovanni Ambrogio Figino, Camillo Procaccini and Giuseppe Meda.

A nail allegedly from the Cross hangs at the apex of the apse's vaulted roof. Once a year, on the Saturday closest to 14 September (prior to the beginning of vespers), the archbishop ascends to the apex to retrieve the nail, moving slowly and solemnly through the air in the Duomo's decorated wooden *nivola* – an angel-studded basket constructed in 1577 under Borromeo's orders, and significantly renovated and redecorated in 1701 (when the putti, or angels, were added). The nail is exhibited at the altar until the following Monday after vespers, when it's lifted back up to the church ceiling.

In the right transept you'll find a funerary monument to Gian Giacomo Medici, long attributed to Michelangelo but now recognised as the work of sculptor and collector Leone Leoni (1560-63).

On a pedestal in the wall opposite the Medici monument stands an arresting and remarkably lifelike statue of a flayed St Bartholomew. This incredibly accurate study of human anatomy was carved in 1562 by Marco d'Agrate, a student of Leonardo da Vinci. Above and to the right, the splendid stained glass showing St Catherine of Alexandria – who died on the original catherine wheel – is the work of the Arcimboldo brothers (1556).

Completed in 1614, the sculpture that closes the choir – designed by Pellegrino Tibaldi and carved by Paolo de' Gazzi, Virgilio del Conte and the Taurini brothers – is a masterpiece of its time. The three tiers of the sculpture represent (above) the life of St Ambrose, (centre) the martyred saints venerated by the Milanese church, and (below) the Milanese bishops Anatalone and Galdino.

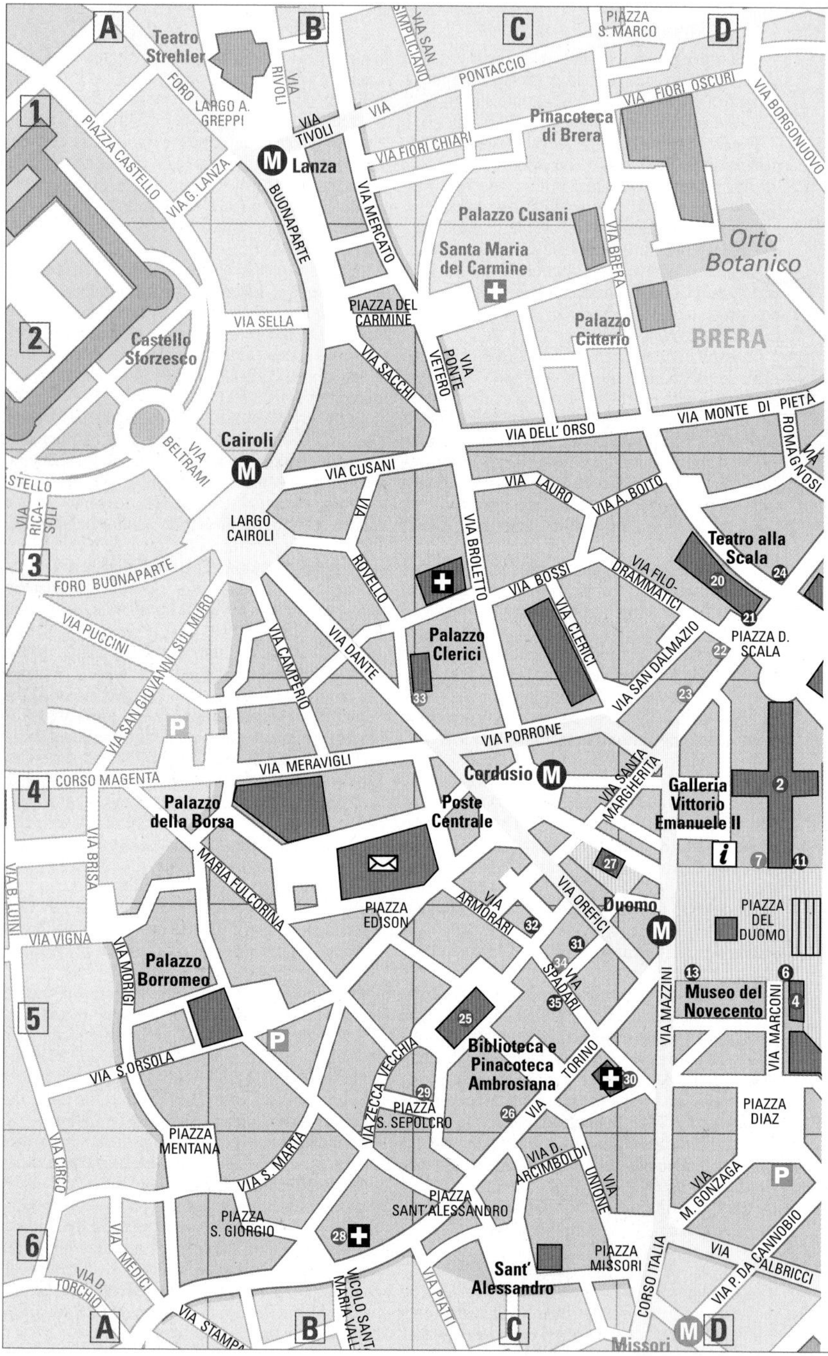

A
B
C
D
1
2
3
4
5
6
Teatro Strehler
FORO
LARGO A. GREPPI
VIA RIVOLI
VIA SAN SIMPLICIANO
VIA PONTACCIO
PIAZZA S. MARCO
VIA FIORI OSCURI
VIA BORGONUOVO
VIA TIVOLI
VIA FIORI CHIARI
Pinacoteca di Brera
PIAZZA CASTELLO
VIA G. LANZA
Lanza
BUONAPARTE
VIA MERCATO
Palazzo Cusani
VIA BRERA
Orto Botanico
Santa Maria del Carmine
PIAZZA DEL CARMINE
VIA SELLA
Castello Sforzesco
VIA SACCHI
VIA PONTE VETERO
Palazzo Citterio
BRERA
VIA MONTE DI PIETÀ
VIA DELL' ORSO
ROMAGNOSI
VIA BELTRAMI
Cairoli
VIA CUSANI
STELLO
VIA RICASOLI
LARGO CAIROLI
VIA ROVELLO
VIA BROLETTO
VIA LAURO
VIA A. BOITO
Teatro alla Scala
FORO BUONAPARTE
VIA BOSSI
VIA FILODRAMMATICI
VIA PUCCINI
VIA SAN GIOVANNI SUL MURO
VIA CAMPERIO
VIA DANTE
Palazzo Clerici
VIA CLERICI
VIA SAN DALMAZIO
PIAZZA D. SCALA
VIA PORRONE
VIA MERAVIGLI
Cordusio
VIA SANTA MARGHERITA
CORSO MAGENTA
Palazzo della Borsa
Poste Centrale
Galleria Vittorio Emanuele II
VIA BRISA
MARIA FULCORINA
VIA B. LUINI
PIAZZA EDISON
VIA ARMORARI
VIA OREFICI
Duomo
PIAZZA DEL DUOMO
VIA VIGNA
VIA MORIGI
Palazzo Borromeo
VIA SPADARI
VIA MAZZINI
Museo del Novecento
VIA MARCONI
VIA S. ORSOLA
VIA ZECCA VECCHIA
Biblioteca e Pinacoteca Ambrosiana
VIA TORINO
PIAZZA S. SEPOLCRO
PIAZZA DIAZ
PIAZZA MENTANA
VIA CIRCO
VIA S. MARTA
VIA D. ARCIMBOLDI
VIA UNIONE
VIA M. GONZAGA
PIAZZA SANT'ALESSANDRO
PIAZZA S. GIORGIO
VIA MEDICI
VIA D. TORCHIO
VICOLO SANTA MARIA VALLE
VIA PIATTI
Sant' Alessandro
PIAZZA MISSORI
CORSO ITALIA
VIA ALBRICCI
VIA P. DA CANNOBIO
VIA STAMPA
Missori
2 4 6 7 11 13 20 21 22 23 24 25 26 27 28 29 30 31 32 33 34 35

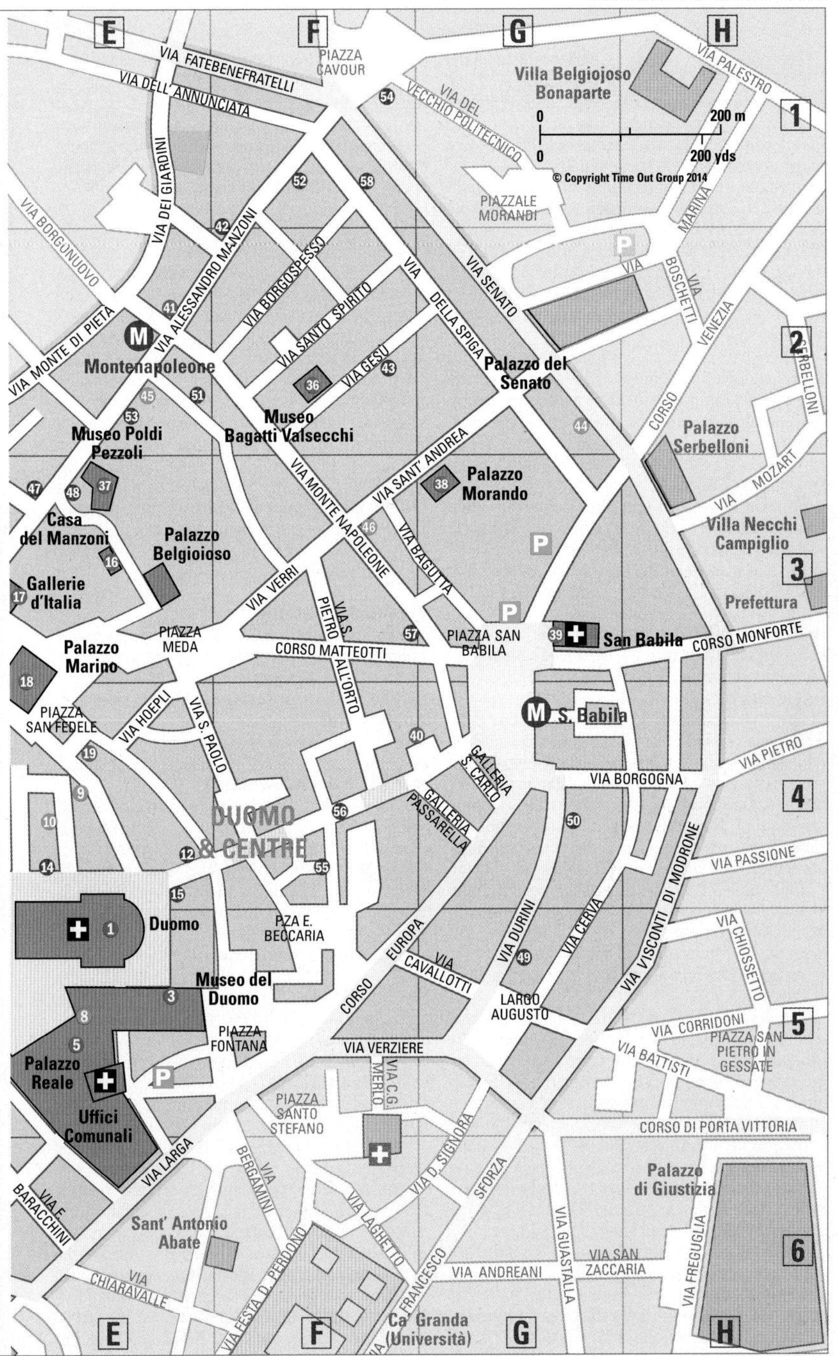

Villa Belgiojoso Bonaparte
0 200 m
0 200 yds
© Copyright Time Out Group 2014
Piazza Cavour
Via Fatebenefratelli
Via dell'Annunciata
Via del Vecchio Politecnico
Via Palestro
Piazzale Morandi
Via Marina
Via Borgonuovo
Via dei Giardini
Via Alessandro Manzoni
Via Borgospesso
Via Santo Spirito
Via della Spiga
Via Senato
Via Boschetti
Corso Venezia
Via Serbelloni
Via Monte di Pietà
Montenapoleone
Via Gesù
Museo Bagatti Valsecchi
Palazzo del Senato
Museo Poldi Pezzoli
Via Sant' Andrea
Palazzo Morando
Palazzo Serbelloni
Via Mozart
Villa Necchi Campiglio
Casa del Manzoni
Palazzo Belgioioso
Via Monte Napoleone
Via Bagutta
Gallerie d'Italia
Via Verri
Via S. Pietro all'Orto
Prefettura
Piazza Meda
Palazzo Marino
Corso Matteotti
Piazza San Babila
San Babila
Corso Monforte
Piazza San Fedele
Via Hoepli
Via S. Paolo
S. Babila
Galleria S. Carlo
Via Borgogna
Via Pietro
Galleria Passarella
Duomo & Centre
Corso Europa
Via Durini
Via Cerva
Via Visconti di Modrone
Via Passione
Duomo
Pza E. Beccaria
Via Cavallotti
Via Chiossetto
Museo del Duomo
Largo Augusto
Piazza Fontana
Via Corridoni
Piazza San Pietro in Gessate
Via Verziere
Via Battisti
Palazzo Reale
Via C.G. Merlo
Piazza Santo Stefano
Uffici Comunali
Via D. Signora
Corso di Porta Vittoria
Via Larga
Via Bergamini
Sforza
Palazzo di Giustizia
Via F. Baracchini
Via Laghetto
Sant' Antonio Abate
Via Guastalla
Via Freguglia
Via San Zaccaria
Via Andreani
Via Chiaravalle
Via Festa d. Perdono
Via Francesco
Ca' Granda (Università)

The ambulatory windows blaze with fabulous 19th-century stained glass by the Bertini brothers, and depict scenes from both Testaments. From the ambulatory, stairs lead down to the crypt, where Carlo Borromeo is buried. Entrances to the treasury and the choir are also in the ambulatory.

In the left transept, the fantastic monsters on the bronze Trivulzio Candelabra – an impressive example of medieval goldsmithing – represent the arts, professions and virtues, and were created by the great 12th-century goldsmith Nicolas of Verdun. In the left aisle, the Cappella del Crocifisso (third past the transept) has stunning 16th-century stained glass.

The remains of the earlier churches of Santa Tecla and the baptistery (where St Ambrose baptised St Augustine in 387) can be reached by descending the stairs just to the left of the main entrance. The stairs to the right lead to a set of early Christian excavations, two storeys below the Duomo's main door.

From 4 November until Epiphany, the great *Quadroni di San Carlo*, a devotional pictorial cycle with scenes from the life of the saint, are displayed in the naves between the pillars. The works are a compendium of 17th-century Lombard painting.

★ Galleria Vittorio Emanuele II

Between piazza del Duomo & piazza della Scala. Metro Duomo, or bus 54, or tram 1, 2, 3, 12, 14, 24. **Open** 24hrs daily. **Map** p48 D4 ❷

Connecting piazza del Duomo with piazza della Scala, the magnificent Galleria Vittorio Emanuele II is known as *il salotto di Milano* ('Milan's living room') – and functions as a glamorous shopping arcade. Designer Giuseppe Mengoni pioneered its complex marriage of iron and glass 20 years before the Eiffel Tower was built. The Galleria was officially opened in 1867 by Vittorio Emanuele II, king of a newly united Italy; but, in a sour twist of fate, Mengoni wasn't present, having fallen to his death from his own creation a few days earlier. Some say he committed suicide, afraid that his imposing new structure wouldn't live up to the exacting standards of the day.

The ceiling vaults are decorated with mosaics representing Asia, Africa, Europe and America. At ground level are mosaics of more local concerns: the coats of arms of Vittorio Emanuele's Savoia family, and the symbols of Milan (a red cross on a white field), Rome (a she-wolf), Florence (an iris) and Turin (a bull). If you can't see Turin's symbol, look out for the tourists spinning on their heels on the bull's nether regions – it's said to guarantee good luck. A cleaning and restoration operation should be finished by May 2015, ready for Expo 2015.

Shopping is, and always has been, the Galleria's main activity, along with sipping coffee and aperitifs at the (mostly) elegant cafés. In recent years, the once-fusty image has been upgraded as fashion powerhouses, from Gucci to Armani, Louis Vuitton and, most recently, Versace, have opened glitzy new boutiques. Prada is a long-time resident, having opened its first-ever shop here in 1913; complete with varnished wood fittings and chessboard tiled floors, it's still in its original space. Prada's second Galleria shop (selling menswear) opened in 2013 and will soon include a café and art gallery too.

The arcade's shiny new look has been aided by the presence of two luxury hotels in the vicinity, the Park Hyatt and the Seven Stars Galleria (for both, *see p248*). Other highlights include a Gucci Café, mostly frequented by Chinese and Arab tourists, and Camparino in Galleria (*see p51*), where it's worth splurging a few euros to sample Campari-laden cocktails while admiring the colourful art nouveau mosaics. Locals complain that the arcade's once-genteel character is being eroded by fashion blandness – in 2013, its historic Libreria Bocca (founded in 1775) launched a 'Save the Bookshop' campaign, while in 2014, silverware company Bernasconi, here since the 1940s, was forced to close its doors. But for the moment, you'll still find shops selling hats, fans, pipes and collector's coins between the bolder brand boutiques.

Museo del Duomo

Piazza del Duomo 12 (02 7202 2656, www.museo.duomomilano.it). Metro Duomo, or bus 54, or tram 1, 2, 3, 12, 14, 24. **Open** 10am-6pm (last entry 4.50pm) Tue-Sun. **Admission** €6; €4 reductions. **Map** p49 E5 ❸

See p52 **Milan's New Museums**.

★ Museo del Novecento

Palazzo dell'Arengario, piazza del Duomo (02 8844 4061, www.museodelnovecento.org). Metro Duomo, or bus 54, or tram 1, 2, 3, 12, 14, 24. **Open** 2.30-7.30pm Mon; 9.30am-7.30pm Tue, Wed, Fri, Sun; 9.30am-10.30pm Thur, Sat. **Admission** €5; free-€3 reductions. Free to all last hr of the day; Tue afternoon. **Map** p48 D5 ❹

See p52 **Milan's New Museums**.

Palazzo Reale

Piazza del Duomo 12 (02 8846 5230, www.comune.milano.it). Metro Duomo, or bus 54, or tram 1, 2, 3, 12, 14, 24. **Open & admission** varies. **Map** p49 E5 ❺

This once-opulent palace now hosts world-class art shows, including recent retrospectives of Arcimboldo (a Milanese native), Rodin, Warhol and Klimt. Built in the 1300s, the Palazzo Reale was ordered by the Visconti family, then updated in the 16th century as part of the series of architectural reforms under the Sforzas. Giuseppe Piermarini, architect of the Teatro alla Scala, gave the palazzo its neoclassical look when he was commissioned to design a residence for Archduke Ferdinand of Austria in the 1770s. Only a fraction of his stucco works and frescoes survived Allied bombing, but the Sala delle Cariatidi (now an exhibition space) remains in an interesting state of semi-dereliction. The mirrored Sala dei Matrimoni is used for civil wedding ceremonies.

In a separate part of the building is the Museo del Duomo (*see p50*), which reopened in 2013; and a walkway connects to the Museo del Novecento (*see p50*), which opened in 2010. *Photo p54.*

Restaurants

Wine shop and bar **Signor Vino** (*see p55*) also contains a regional restaurant.

Giacomo Arengario

Via Marconi 1 (02 7209 3814, www.giacomo arengario.com). Metro Duomo, or bus 54, or tram 1, 2, 3, 12, 14, 24. **Meals served** noon-midnight daily. **Average** €65. **Map** p48 D5 ❻
Traditional Mediterranean
Located on the top floor of the Museo del Novecento (*see p50*), this swanky eatery is a new outpost of Da Giacomo (*see p107*), one of Milan's most fashionable restaurants. The menu continues Giacomo's long-running tradition of fresh fish platters – such as spaghetti and mussels – with the addition of lighter options for art-loving lunchers, who drop in before or after trudging round the museum. But the restaurant's key asset is the magnificent bird's-eye view of piazza del Duomo. Be sure to bag a table in the 'Dehors' – a covered steel and glass terrace offering one of the most spectacular panoramas in Milan. The associated Giacomo Caffè (*see right*) is in Palazzo Reale, nearby.

Cafés, Bars & Gelaterie

Camparino in Galleria

Galleria Vittorio Emanuele II (02 8646 4435, www.camparino.it). Metro Duomo, or bus 54, or tram 1, 2, 3, 12, 14, 24. **Open** 7.15am-8.40pm Tue-Sun. **Map** p48 D4 ❼
Most bars in the Galleria are tourist traps, but this place is an institution. Once frequented by Verdi and Toscanini, it's been in the arcade since it opened in 1867 (and has had numerous name-changes over the years). The interior is spectacular, with art nouveau mosaics of colourful parrots and flowers by Angiolo d'Andrea. At *aperitivo* time, order a Campari-based cocktail (such as a negroni), the bar's speciality. You might want to stand and drink at the counter: prices rise sharply once you sit down and have a waiter come to your table.

★ Giacomo Caffè

Palazzo Reale, piazza del Duomo 12 (02 8909 6698, www.giacomomilano.com). Metro Duomo, or bus 54, or tram 1, 2, 3, 12, 14, 24. **Open** 7.30am-9.30pm Mon-Wed, Fri, Sun; 7.30am-10.30pm Thur, Sat. **Map** p49 E5 ❽
Bursting with locals, this old-fashioned café in a vaulted salon at the entrance to Palazzo Reale keeps up appearances with solid silver-hued cutlery, starched white napkins and branded tablecloths. The food is of a higher standard than at your average bar. At lunchtime, try light bites such as swordfish carpaccio scattered with pomegranate seeds. It's an offshoot of the fashionable Da Giacomo restaurant (*see p107*) and of Giacomo Arengario (*see left*).

EXPLORE

Galleria Vittorio Emanuele II.

MILAN'S NEW MUSEUMS

Art-lovers have four new venues to explore.

Museo del Novecento.

Over the past few years, a multitude of new museums has mushroomed around Milan. The most impressive of the new crop, just a few strides from the Duomo, is the **Museo del Novecento** (*see p50*), which houses a vast collection of predominantly 20th-century Italian and European art. It's located in the Arengario, a 1936 palazzo renovated by Italo Rota, with access to the main galleries via a narrow spiral staircase. Many locals linger halfway up to admire Giuseppe Pellizza da Volpedo's 1901 *Quarto Stato* (*The Fourth Estate*), an iconic painting of striking workers, another version of which is displayed at the Pinacoteca di Brera. The painting has a special status among Milanese left-wingers and you may hear some of them muttering about the rather cramped quarters their favourite painting now finds itself in.

In rooms 3 and 4 are paintings by Italy's Futurists, celebrating speed, movement and multiple points of view. Pause to consider Umberto Boccioni's remarkable triptych *Quelli che restano* (*Those who stay*), *Gli addii* (*The Farewells*) and *Quelli che vanno* (*Those who leave*), interpreting states of mind at a railway station. In the next room, Giacomo Balla's *Girl Running on a Balcony*, from 1912, shows the repeated, Seurat-like figure of a young girl in a blue dress with black boots in blurred motion. The picture was apparently inspired by the newfangled art of cinema.

Other highlights include Giorgio Morandi's quiet, contemplative still-lifes in room 5 and, in the very last room, a tin of Piero Manzoni's 1961 *Merda d'Artista* (*Artist's Shit*). Don't miss Lucio Fontana's extraordinary squiggle of fluorescent light – *Luce Spaziale: Struttura al Neon* (1951) – suspended from the ceiling in room 11. From here, you can enjoy a magnificent bird's-eye view of the Duomo – among the museum's most spectacular offerings. Refreshments are available at **Giacomo Arengario** restaurant (*see p51*) and the more affordable **Giacomo Caffè** (*see p51*) at the entrance to the next door Palazzo Reale.

More or less opposite La Scala are the (free) **Gallerie d'Italia** dedicated to mostly 18th- to 20th-century art, housed in three magnificently frescoed and stuccoed *palazzi*. The collection (owned by the San Paolo bank) kicks off with 197 works of late 18th- and 19th-century art, displayed in 13 sections across Palazzo Anguissola and Palazzo Brentani. In section 1 (rooms 1-4), three late 18th-century bas-reliefs by Antonio Canova portray the tragedy of

Socrates' enforced suicide. Despite being devoid of colour, the panel showing Crito closing the dead philosopher's eyes brings the story painfully to life.

In room 5 hangs one of the gallery's best-known artworks: Francesco Hayez's *I due Foscari*. This Romantic masterpiece depicts the Venetian Doge, Francesco Foscari, in the act of banishing his son from the republic for treason, or possibly homicide; note the cynical expression on the face of the Doge's sworn enemy, Pietro Loredan, indicating the boat the son is to sail upon. Rooms 10-14 contain a fascinating series of 19th-century paintings of the Duomo, the Navigli and views of Milan, showing how the street scene has and hasn't changed over the centuries.

The adjoining palazzo of the former Banca Commerciale Italiana is home to 189 works from the 20th century. Look out for slashed canvasses by Lucio Fontana and a striking picture of prickly pears by Sicilian artist Renato Guttuso (who painted the cover art for Elizabeth David's seminal 1954 Italian cookery book).

The gallery's pleasant café and buffet restaurant is a good place for lunch, or coffee and cake. On late-opening Thursday nights, classical music echoes through the relatively empty rooms.

Back in piazza del Duomo, the **Museo del Duomo** (*see p50*) is in a labyrinthine, vaulted wing of Palazzo Reale. Here since 2013, it houses treasures originally positioned in, or on, the Duomo. Highlights include a 16th-century Mexican archbishop's mitre made from hummingbird feathers (room 3), and a huge Tintoretto oil painting, depicting Jesus among the doctors, discovered in the Duomo's sacristy shortly after World War II.

On the way out, room 13 holds an eye-bogglingly detailed 16th-century wooden model of the Duomo, down to the last gargoyle. In the final room, another model – in 100,000 white Lego bricks – almost rivals it, ending the visit on an unexpectedly modern note.

Offering something completely different, **Il Mondo di Leonardo** (piazza della Scala, entrance in Galleria Vittorio Emanuele II, 02 8723 9773, www.leonardo3.net) has brought 200 interactive reconstructions of Leonardo's drawings and inventions from New York to Milan. Visitors can admire a mechanical walking lion that delivered lilies to the King of France and see a mock-up of Leonardo's famous helicopter – which turns out to be an aerial screw. Interactive digital screens show secrets of *The Last Supper* and *Mona Lisa*: click to see how Leonardo painted her eyes or her smile. The exhibition is above the Galleria in rooms belonging to the City Council and will be in place until at least November 2015 – when it may well be given a permanent home.

EXPLORE

Gallerie d'Italia.

Palazzo Reale. *See p50.*

★ € Luini

Via Santa Radegonda 16 (02 8646 1917, www.luini.it). Metro Duomo or San Babila, or bus 54, 60, 73, or tram 1, 2, 3, 12, 14, 24. **Open** 10am-3pm Mon; 10am-8pm Tue-Sat. No credit cards. **Map** p49 E4 ⑨

A Milan institution since 1949, Luini is famed for its *panzerotti*: rounds of dough stuffed with tomato and mozzarella, then folded into neat triangles and fried. The queue at lunchtime goes down the street so visit outside main mealtimes – or be prepared to wait.

STRAF

Via San Raffaele 3 (02 8050 8715, www.straf.it). Metro Duomo or San Babila, or bus 54, 60, 73, or tram 1, 2, 3, 12, 14, 24. **Open** 11am-midnight daily. **Map** p49 E4 ⑩

It's a seriously dressy crowd that gathers at the bar of the STRAF hotel (*see p248*). Wheels of parmesan and trays of *crostini* are brought out for happy hour (6-9pm daily). Try a Pina Picantera: pineapple juice mixed with lime, mint, gin and a hint of chilli pepper.

Shops & Services

For **Galleria Vittorio Emanuele II**, *see p50.*

La Feltrinelli/Ricordi Media Store

Piazza del Duomo 24 or via Ugo Foscolo 1-3 (02 8699 6897, www.lafeltrinelli.it). Metro Duomo, or bus 54, or tram 1, 2, 3, 12, 14, 24. **Open** 9.30am-9.30pm Mon-Thur; 9.30am-10pm Fri, Sat; 10am-8pm Sun. **Map** p48 D4 ⑪ **Books & music**

This vast, subterranean bookshop can be entered from the stairs at the back of the insalubrious, fast-food Autogrill restaurant in piazza del Duomo. The winding maze of bookshelves includes several shelves of English-language books and a well-stocked travel section. The complex leads directly into the Ricordi Media Store, which sells CDs, DVDs, vinyl, computer games and theatre tickets below the Galleria shopping arcade.

Furla

Piazza del Duomo 31 (02 8909 6794, www.furla.com). Metro Duomo, or bus 54, or tram 1, 2, 3, 12, 14, 24. **Open** 10.30am-7.30pm daily. **Map** p49 E4 ⑫ **Accessories**

Mid-range leather bags, soft sacks, wallets and luggage by the famous Bologna-based leather-goods company. Furla also stocks a good selection of affordable trinkets, including scarves and umbrellas.

Other locations corso Buenos Aires, at via Omboni 1, East (02 204 3319); corso Vercelli 11, West (02 4801 4189).

Mondadori Multicenter

Piazza del Duomo 1 (02 4544 1113, www.inmondadori.it). Metro Duomo, or bus 54, or tram 1, 2, 3, 12, 14, 24. **Open** 9am-11pm daily. **Map** p48 D5 ⑬ **Books & music/Cookery school**

This massive shopping complex sells everything from stationery to DVDs, computer games and books – including a selection in English. There's also a small cookery school on the premises (www.corso-di-cucina.it), which offers afternoon and evening classes for adults and children. Most are in Italian – but the teachers can be flexible.

Other location corso Vittorio Emanuele, at Galleria del Corso 4, Centre (02 760 551).

La Rinascente

Piazza del Duomo 3 (02 88 521, www.rinascente.it). Metro Duomo, or bus 54, or tram 1, 2, 3, 12, 14, 24. **Open** 9.30am-10pm daily (but check website

as times can vary). *Food hall & restaurants* 8.30am-midnight Mon-Sat; 10am-midnight Sun. **Map** p49 E4 ⓮ **Department store**
This eight-floor colossus (part of a nationwide chain) sells nearly everything you can think of, from lingerie to colourful ceramics. The sixth floor has a tax-free refund office, while the top floor hosts a branch of chic hairdresser Aldo Coppola (02 8905 9712, www.aldocoppola.it), an outpost of mozzarella bar Obika, and a 'lounge bar' where you can sip hot chocolate while admiring the gargoyles on the Duomo's roof. There's a 'Design Supermarket' selling Made in Italy housewares in the basement – but most of the the store is dedicated to fashion; brands range from affordable to top-of-the-line.

★ SignorVino

Piazza del Duomo, at corso Vittorio Emanuele (02 8909 2539, www.signorvino.it). Metro Duomo, or bus 54, or tram 1, 2, 3, 12, 14, 24. **Open** 8am-midnight Mon-Fri; 9am-midnight Sat, Sun. **Map** p49 E4 ⓯ **Food & drink**
Founded by Sandro Veronesi, the brains behind the Calzedonia and Intimissimi high-street chains, this shop and restaurant aims to do for Italian wines what the company has already succeeded in doing for beachwear and lingerie. The two floors are stacked with over 1,000 Italian labels – and expert staff are on hand to supply all the info you need. For tastings, head for the ground-floor bar, or order lunch in the reasonably priced first-floor restaurant. The menu features specialities from all the regions of Italy – paired with the appropriate wines. Arrive early (at dinner too) if you want to grab one of the few tables overlooking the Duomo (the others face on to corso Vittorio Emanuele – not a bad consolation prize).

AROUND PIAZZA DELLA SCALA

The shop-free **piazza della Scala** starts as you surface from the stores at the northern exit of Galleria Vittorio Emanuele II. One of the world's most celebrated opera houses, the **Teatro alla Scala** stands on the square's northern edge. Even if you can't experience one of the performances (listed outside), the neighbouring **Museo Teatrale alla Scala** offers an ample glimpse of La Scala's majesty.

Though it may not be immediately apparent, the winds of change blowing through Milan of late have transformed even this most venerable of corners. In 2004, world-renowned Swiss architect Mario Botta added an elliptical tower and rhomboid-shaped edifice – housing dressing rooms, rehearsal rooms and a deeper orchestral pit – to the back of the theatre, inevitably causing controversy, though the additions are only just visible behind the façade. Almost opposite, on the corner of the piazza and via Manzoni, the Intesa San Paolo bank opened **Gallerie d'Italia** in a series of historic *palazzi* in 2011-12 to display its impressive collection of mainly 19th- and 20th-century Italian art. The adjacent café, frequent cultural activities – and free admission – have made this one of the best-loved new attractions in Milan.

A 19th-century statue of Leonardo da Vinci by Pietro Magni separates La Scala theatre from Palazzo Marino on the other side of the square. Formerly a Genoese banker's private mansion, it's now the municipal hall. Nearby, in its eponymous piazza, the Jesuits' Baroque church of **San Fedele** faces a statue of Alessandro Manzoni, one of Italy's greatest writers. **Casa del Manzoni**, the novelist's perfectly preserved house, is just around the corner. En route, you'll pass the curious **Casa degli Omenoni** (via Omenoni 3), with its eight stone sentries of Atlas, sculpted in 1565 by Antonio Abbondio; and **Palazzo Belgioioso** (piazza Belgioioso 2), designed by Giuseppe Piermarini in 1777-81 for Alberico XIII di Belgioioso d'Este – his family's heraldic symbols figure large in the façade's decoration. West of piazza della Scala, the 18th-century **Palazzo Clerici** (via Clerici 5, 02 863 3131) has marvellous rococo interiors, and frescoes by Giambattista Tiepolo. It's open to visitors by appointment only.

EXPLORE

Sights & Museums

FREE Casa del Manzoni

Via Morone 1 (02 8646 0403, www.casadelmanzoni.mi.it). Metro Duomo or Montenapoleone, or bus 61, or tram 1. **Open** 9am-noon, 2-4pm Tue-Fri. **Admission** free. **Map** p49 E3 ⓰
A friendly curator will lead you around the wonderfully ornate former home of author and poet Alessandro Manzoni (1785-1873), second in Italian literature only to Dante and author of *Il Promessi Sposi* (*The Betrothed*). Several of the parquet-floored rooms are stocked with Manzoni's personal effects and early editions of his work, overlook what must be an estate agent's dream: The fire alarm is the only addition to the perfectly preserved room where Manzoni died, after falling on the steps of nearby San Fedele.

★ FREE Gallerie d'Italia

Piazza della Scala 6 (800 167 619 toll-free, www.gallerieditalia.com). Metro Duomo or Montenapoleone, or bus 61, or tram 1. **Open** 9.30am-7.30pm (last entry 6.30pm) Tue-Wed, Fri-Sun; 9.30am-10.30pm (last entry 9.30pm) Thur. **Admission** free. **Map** p49 E3 ⓱
See p52 **Milan's New Museums**.

Palazzo Marino

Piazza della Scala 2 (no phone, www.comune.milano.it). Metro Duomo or Montenapoleone, or bus 61, or tram 1. **Map** p49 E4 ⓲
Although you can't usually enter the Palazzo Marino (it's been the city government HQ since 1861), you

can enjoy its interesting history from all four sides. The architect, Galeazzo Alessi, was commissioned in 1558 by Tommaso Marino, a Genoese banker who collected taxes in Milan. Marino wanted to impress a noble Venetian lady, and Alessi was told, 'When finished, it should be the finest palazzo in Christendom.' The plan seems to have worked, as Marino married her. However, his financial ostentation irritated the locals, who predicted the palazzo, 'built by stealing, would either burn, fall into disrepair, or be stolen by another thief.' Marino died in financial ruin, and the Austrian army took over the palazzo in 1814 – but the building stands unburned for now.

▶ *Occasional guided tours (in Italian) are held on weekdays; for details, call 02 8845 6617.*

FREE San Fedele

Piazza San Fedele (02 863 521, www.centrosanfedele.net). Metro Duomo or Montenapoleone, or bus 61, or tram 1. **Open** 7.30am-4.30pm Mon-Fri; 6-7.30pm Sat; 10am-noon, 3.30-8pm Sun. **Admission** free. **Map** p49 E4 ⑲

This imposing Baroque church is the Milanese headquarters of the Jesuit order. It was designed by Pellegrino Tibaldi in 1569 as an exemplary Counter-Reformation church: note the single nave, an invention that let the priest keep his eye on the whole congregation. The cupola, crypt and choir were added by Francesco Maria Ricchini between 1633 and 1652, while the carved wooden choir stalls in the apse were lifted from Santa Maria della Scala, the church demolished to make way for the Teatro alla Scala.

San Fedele is a veritable hit parade of Milanese Baroque and Mannerist painting. In the first chapel on the right is Il Cerano's *Vision of St Ignatius* (1622); in a room leading to the sacristy beyond the second chapel on the right are a *Transfiguration* and *Virgin and Child* by Bernardino Campi (1565). The exuberant carvings on the wooden confessionals and the sacristy (designed by Ricchini and executed by Daniele Ferrari in 1569) help liven up the edifice's Counter-Reformation sobriety.

★ Teatro alla Scala & Museo Teatrale alla Scala

Piazza della Scala/largo Ghiringhelli 1 (02 8879 2473, www.teatroallascala.org). Metro Duomo, or bus 61, or tram 1. **Open** *Museum* 9am-12.30pm (last entry noon), 1.30-5.30pm daily (last entry 5pm). **Admission** *Museum* €6; €4 reductions. **Map** p48 D3 ⑳

If you can get hold of a ticket to La Scala (for booking information, see the website and *p173* **Scoring Tickets for La Scala**), you'll be the envy of opera-lovers worldwide. When the new season begins, on 7 December (the feast of Sant'Ambrogio, Milan's much-loved patron saint), paparazzi and TV crews descend to catch shots of the glamorously attired ladies and their suave male companions.

The opera house takes its name from Santa Maria della Scala, the 1381 church that once stood on the same site. Later, the Royal Ducal Theatre was built on the spot occupied by the church, but was destroyed by fire in 1776, leaving the city with no principal theatre. Under the auspices of Empress Maria Theresa of Austria, Giuseppe Piermarini was given the task of building a replacement – and what a fine job he did: La Scala has a massive stage, 2,015 seats and some of the best acoustics in the world; and it draws some of the very finest performers. Its musical directors are, naturally, always of the highest calibre too. When world-renowned musician Daniel Barenboim ends his remit in 2015, he'll be replaced by eminent conductor Riccardo Chailly (*see p174* **Backstage Drama**).

The *teatro* was inaugurated in 1778 with an opera by Salieri; many of the best-known works of Puccini, Verdi, Bellini and others premiered here. La Scala is also a significant symbol of national pride. Destroyed by heavy bombing during World War II, it was swiftly rebuilt after the war's close and re-inaugurated in 1946 with an opera conducted by one of Milan's favourites, Arturo Toscanini. A three-year refurbishment and additions by Swiss architect Mario Botta, completed in 2004,

San Fedele.

EXPLORE

Teatro alla Scala.

were controversial, but the benefits of bringing its beloved opera house up to date seem to have outweighed any perceived aesthetic slight in the public's mind.

The museum, created in 1913, gives a taste of La Scala's splendour. You'll have fun spotting music-related (if poorly labelled) memorabilia, including Puccini's watch, Rossini's glasses, a cast of Chopin's hand, Verdi's spinet – and his death mask. Then step inside a box for a peek at the splendid theatre itself.

Restaurants

Il Marchesino

Piazza della Scala 2 (02 7209 4338, www.gualtiero marchesi.it). Metro Duomo, or bus 61, or tram 1. **Meals served** *Caffè* 8am-8pm Mon-Sat. *Restaurant* 12.30-2.30pm, 8-10.30pm Mon-Fri; 8-10.30pm Sat. **Average** *Caffè* €30. *Restaurant* €110. **Map** p48 D3 ㉑ **Contemporary Italian**

Local superchef Gualtiero Marchesi (Knight of the Italian Republic, and the first non-Frenchman to win three Michelin stars) opened this chic little diner next door to La Scala in 2008. The bar area, serving breakfast and pre-performance snacks, is sexy in a 1980s NASA HQ kind of way; the restaurant is more refined, with deep red upholstery. Now in his eighties, Marchesi has handed the reins to head chef Riccardo Ferrero. The sometimes OTT (and somewhat overpriced) menu includes lobster in lobster sauce and saffron rice with real gold leaf – but you'll also find simpler fare, such as wholesome pumpkin soup. For more affordable options, head to the *caffè*.

Cafés, Bars & Gelaterie

Café Trussardi

Piazza della Scala 5 (02 8068 8295, www.cafe trussardi.com). Metro Duomo, or bus 61, or tram 1. **Open** noon-10pm Mon-Sat. **Map** p48 D3 ㉒

Half of this very upmarket café in the vast Trussardi store consists of a huge glass cube jutting into via San Dalmazio, making it a great place to be 'seen'. Not surprisingly, it's popular with the area's young banking and fashion sets. Salads and Aberdeen Angus burgers grace the short lunch menu. Upstairs, the Trussardi alla Scala restaurant, under recently appointed chef Luigi Taglienti, is among the most lauded gourmet restaurants in town. It's also one of the most expensive, with tasting menus starting at €140.

★ Grom

Via Santa Margherita 16 (02 8058 1041, www.grom.it). Metro Duomo, or bus 61, or tram 1. **Open** 11.30am-11.30pm daily. **Map** p48 D4 ㉓

Ice-cream goes boutique a stone's throw from La Scala. The strictly additive-free flavours include caramel and almonds, and coconut and chocolate. An ingredients list specifies which flavours are gluten-free, and which are suitable for vegans. It's part of a nationwide chain, with seven other branches in Milan. **Other locations** throughout the city.

Piazza dei Mercanti.

Shops & Services

Milano Libri
Via Verdi 2 (02 875 871). Metro Duomo or Montenapoleone, or bus 61, or tram 1. **Open** 11am-7.30pm Mon; 10am-7.30pm Tue-Sat. **Map** p48 D3 ㉔ **Books & music**
Here since 1962, this is one of Milan's most venerable bookshops, with a fine selection of fashion, design and textile tomes. There's also an extensive range of photography and fine art catalogues.

PIAZZA DEI MERCANTI, VIA TORINO AND AROUND

West of the Duomo, **piazza dei Mercanti** was once the centre of the city's medieval market, and has some of Milan's oldest buildings. This fact is also reflected in the various street names alluding to activities that took place in the surrounding lanes: via Spadari (sword-makers), via Cappellari (milliners) and via Armorari (armourers), to name three. Appropriately, the area around via Orefici (goldsmiths) still has a few jewellery stores.

The square is flanked by **Palazzo Affari ai Giureconsulti**, a magnificent building that was once the headquarters of the Collegio dei Nobili Dottori, which trained Milan's highest-ranking civil servants, and **Palazzo della Ragione**, built 1228-33 by Oldrado da Tresseno (then *podestà*, or mayor) to symbolise the independence Milan had won from its Germanic rulers in the 12th century. It's home to a museum of photography.

The coats of arms of patrician families who lived around the piazza are much in evidence (see, for example, the **Loggia degli Osii**, on the south-west side of the square, with Matteo Visconti's shield from 1316), as are portraits of classical scholars and church fathers (for instance, the 1645 **Palazzo delle Scuole Palatine**, with statues of St Augustine and the Latin poet Ausonius).

Piazza Cordusio links to via Dante and the Castello Sforzesco, but if you follow via Meravigli westwards, then take a southerly turn, you'll find yourself in 'Milan's Wall Street' – **piazza Affari**, built between 1928 and 1940. Here, the commanding grandeur of the **Palazzo della Borsa**, home to Milan's *borsa* (stock exchange), will remind you that many locals think of their city, the country's financial heavyweight, as the real capital of Italy. The Borsa was founded in 1808, but only settled in this, its permanent home, in 1931. The Palazzo della Borsa was designed by local boy Paolo Mezzanotte, and typifies the rationalist style of the late 1920s and '30s. These days, however, sightseers are more likely to head to piazza Affari to view Maurizio Cattelan's provocative sculpture depicting a hand with an obscenely raised middle finger (*see p61* **In the Know**). Placed here temporarily in 2010, the sculpture is now on permanent display.

Further south is the neoclassical **Banca d'Italia** (piazza Edison), built 1907-12, a vast structure that takes up the best part of an entire block. Nearby is **San Sepolcro** and

IN THE KNOW SOUNDING OFF

Walk beneath the colonnaded arches of the medieval **piazza dei Mercanti** and you may notice someone standing in the corner muttering, their face turned towards a pillar. This isn't some strange Milanese ritual: in fact, the one-time medieval marketplace is the site of a peculiar acoustic trick. For some reason, voices and other sounds travel along the arches and can be perfectly heard by a friend (or passer-by) positioned at the far end.

the unmissable **Biblioteca & Pinacoteca Ambrosiana**, which holds a beautiful collection of art and artefacts. The latter is also notable because it was from a balcony on the piazza San Sepolcro side of the Ambrosiana that Mussolini first explained the wonders of Fascism to an attentive crowd.

East of piazza San Sepolcro is **piazza Borromeo**, featuring a Baroque statue by Dionigi Bussola of the saint who gave the square its name, and the **Palazzo Borromeo**, with its 15th-century terracotta arches and internal frescoes. Another statue of Borromeo – by Costantino Corti – stands in piazza San Sepolcro. Further south is via Torino, a shopping street that runs from the south-west corner of piazza del Duomo to largo Carrobbio (a name derived from the Latin *quadrivium*, a place where four roads meet), providing the intrepid pedestrian with a wealth of bargain shops and inviting side streets. Towards its top end are the churches of **San Sebastiano** and the remarkable, Bramante-designed **Santa Maria presso San Satiro**.

Close by, at piazza Sant'Alessandro 1, is the often overlooked church of **Sant'Alessandro in Zebedia** (02 722 171, open 7.30am-6.30pm Mon-Sat, 10.30am-6pm Sun). Begun in 1601 and worked on by various architects including Francesco Maria Richini, it was given a rococo façade in the 18th century and is considered one of the earliest examples of Milanese Baroque. Inside are many interesting works, including Daniele Crespi's *Beheading of John the Baptist*.

Returning to via Torino and heading south-west again, you'll pass piazza San Giorgio and the church of **San Giorgio al Palazzo** on your right. Further along via Torino, via Soncino runs off left to the **Palazzo Stampa**, a beautiful building that was the scene of some major Renaissance shenanigans. At the beginning of the 16th century, owner Massimiliano Stampa was the right-hand man of Milan's rulers, the Sforza family. When the last ruling Sforza, Francesco II, died, he became the city's governor. Seen as a traitor by some, Stampa subsequently handed Milan over to Charles V, the Holy Roman Emperor, perhaps because he believed it was in the city's best interests. In return, he obtained the title of Count of the Soncino, plus a very large wodge of Emperor-funded cash.

However, Stampa's time in the limelight was relatively brief, and the palazzo passed to the Casati family. They made various changes to the building, opening, for example, a new entrance on to via Soncino – but they kept the count's 15th-century tower, crowned with the golden globe, eagle, crown and cross escutcheon (look straight up and you can still see it today), used by Charles V to express royal ownership.

Sights & Museums

★ Biblioteca & Pinacoteca Ambrosiana

Piazza Pio XI 2 (02 806 921, www.ambrosiana.it). Metro Cordusio or Duomo, or tram 2, 3, 14. **Open** *Pinacoteca* 10am-6pm Tue-Sun. *Library* 9am-5pm Mon-Fri. **Admission** €15; €10 reductions. **Map** p48 C5 ㉕

Founded in 1609 by Cardinal Federico Borromeo, this 400-year-old project began life as one of the first ever public libraries. The world-class paintings on

Pinacoteca Ambrosiana.

Cracco.

display, the palazzo setting and the scores of untitled statues dotted around reinforce the impression that Milan has more fine art in one city than most other countries have in their national collections.

Borromeo's private art collection of 172 paintings was put on display in 1618. There's Titian's *Adoration of the Magi* in room 1; Raphael's cartoon for *The School of Athens* and Caravaggio's *Basket of Fruit* in rooms 5 and 6; and works by Flemish masters, including Jan Brueghel and Paul Bril, in room 7. Renaissance works from outside the Cardinal's original donation are in rooms 2 and 3, including Sandro Botticelli's *Madonna del Padiglione* and Leonardo da Vinci's *Musician*. The rest of the Pinacoteca contains later works. A lachrymose *Penitent Magdalene* by Guido Reni – darling of the Victorians – is in room 13 on the upper floor. There are two works by Giandomenico Tiepolo in room 17. The De Pecis' donation of 19th-century works, including a self-portrait by sculptor Antonio Canova, can be found in room 18. The Galbiati wing also houses objects such as a lock of Lucrezia Borgia's hair (room 8) and the gloves Napoleon wore at Waterloo (room 9).

The Biblioteca's collection includes Leonardo's original *Codex Atlanticus*, a copy of Virgil with marginalia by Petrarch, an Aristotle with a commentary by Boccaccio, and autograph texts by Aquinas, Machiavelli and Galileo, among others. Pages from da Vinci's ancient work, especially those showing his inventions, are revolved every few months in glass cabinets in the recently restored Sala Federiciana (10am-6pm Tue-Sun). Other pages are on display in Bramante's sacristy at the church of Santa Maria delle Grazie (*see p138*).

The library is open to anyone over 18, in possession of an identity document. A formal request must be made at the entrance, involving some form-filling. Cotton gloves are obligatory when consulting manuscripts, which must be reserved 24 hours before. You can also peek into the library from a glass window inside the museum.

FREE Civico Tempio di San Sebastiano

Via Torino 28 (02 874 263). Metro Duomo or tram 2, 3, 14. **Open** 8am-noon, 3-6.30pm Mon-Sat; 10am-noon, 3.30-6.30pm Sun. **Admission** free. **Map** p48 C5 26

When Milan emerged from a bout of the plague in 1576, its residents heaved a sigh of relief and, to express their gratitude to God for their deliverance, built this church on the site where the 14th-century church of San Quilino had stood. They dedicated it to the patron saint of those with contagious diseases. Pellegrino Tibaldi designed the building, though he originally planned a much higher dome; if the heavenly vision of Agostino Comerio's *Evangelists and Church Fathers* (1832) inside the cupola makes your head spin, just imagine the effect Tibaldi was originally aiming for.

Palazzo della Ragione Fotografia

Piazza Mercanti (02 4335 3535, www.palazzodellaragionefotografia.it). Metro Cordusio or Duomo, or tram 1, 2, 3, 12, 16, 27. **Open** 9.30am-8.30pm Tue-Wed, Fri, Sun; 9.30am-10.30pm Thur, Sat. **Admission** €10; €5-€8.50 reductions; free under-6s. **Map** p48 C4 27

The courtyard of the Palazzo della Ragione – also known as Broletto Nuovo (from *brolo*, an old word denoting a place where justice was administered) – used to be one of the few quiet, sheltered corners of central Milan. But recently, things have livened up a bit, following the opening of a photography 'museum' in the building in June 2014. Retrospectives of William Klein, James Nachtwey and others have been programmed for 2014-2016.

The palazzo is one of the few remaining medieval buildings in Milan: restoration work in 1988 uncovered 13th-century frescoes. It was erected in 1233 by order of Oldrado da Tresseno, then *podestà* (mayor), to serve as law courts. Oldrado's portrait can be seen in relief on the façade facing piazza del Broletto Nuovo, and he is also the subject of an equestrian statue inside the arches of the *broletto*. Markets and public meetings were once held in the ground-floor porticoes; people also flocked here to witness hangings. In 1771, the Holy Roman Empress Maria Theresa decreed the building should become an archive for deeds, and had it enlarged.

FREE San Giorgio al Palazzo

Piazza San Giorgio 2 (02 860 831). Metro Duomo or tram 2, 3, 14. **Open** 7am-5.45pm Mon-Fri; 2.30-5pm Sat; 8.30-11am, 3-6pm Sun. **Admission** free. **Map** p48 B6 ㉘

Founded in 750, San Giorgio was rebuilt in 1129 and heavily reworked in the 17th and early 19th centuries. Among the neoclassical trappings are a baptismal font fashioned out of a Romanesque capital and a couple of pilasters from the original church at the far end of the nave. Don't miss the vivid *Scenes from the Passion of Christ* cycle by Bernardino Luini (1516), in the third chapel on the right. Commissioned to decorate the whole church with frescoes, it's said he fled Milan after being accused of killing a clergyman who was critical of his work.

IN THE KNOW THE FINGER

In 2010, a sculpture by Maurizio Cattelan, one of Italy's most famous living artists, was placed in **piazza Affari** outside the Borsa – Milan's Fascist-era stock exchange. Made from white Carrara marble, the four-metre (13-foot) artwork is of a mutilated hand with the middle finger raised. Cattelan has named his piece *L.O.V.E* – an acronym for 'Libertà, Odio, Vendetta, Eternità' (Liberty, Hatred, Vendetta, Eternity). But everyone knows its true message roughly translates as 'Up yours'. At a time when people love to hate bankers, the piece has been well received. Though initially intended to remain in its current position for a few weeks, the artist subsequently donated it to the local government, on condition that it would remain in situ for 40 years. The last laugh may be at the expense of the public, however. As commentators have noted, the offending finger faces away from the Borsa and towards the city. Could it be that the artist is suggesting shared culpability?

FREE San Sepolcro

Piazza San Sepolcro (no phone). Metro Cordusio or Duomo, or tram 2, 3, 14. **Open** noon-2.30pm Mon-Fri. **Admission** free. **Map** p48 C5 ㉙

The forum of Roman Mediolanum occupied the area between piazza San Sepolcro and piazza Pio XI. It was here that a church dedicated to the Holy Trinity was built in 1030, only to be rebuilt in 1100 and rededicated to the Holy Sepulchre. The church underwent the usual Counter-Reformation treatment in the early 1600s, and an 18th-century façade was replaced by a neo-Romanesque one in 1894-97. The crypt, which runs the whole length of the church, is all that remains of the original Romanesque structure. A forest of slim columns divides its five aisles, and by the apse is a 14th-century sarcophagus with reliefs of the Resurrection.

★ FREE Santa Maria presso San Satiro

Via Torino 19 (02 874 683). Metro Duomo or tram 2, 3, 14. **Open** 9.30am-5.30pm Tue-Sat; 2-5.30pm Sun. **Admission** free. **Map** p48 C5 ㉚

Satiro (or Satirus) was St Ambrose's brother. It was to this lesser-known sibling (who also became a saint) that a certain Archbishop Anspert wanted a church dedicated, and he left funds for the task when he died in 876. All that remains of the early basilica is the Greek-cross Cappella della Pietà. In 1478, Renaissance genius Donato Bramante was called in to remodel the whole church to provide a fitting home for a 13th-century image of the Virgin – said to have bled when attacked by a knife-wielding maniac in 1242 – and to accommodate the pilgrims flocking to see it. The fresco concerned is still visible on the high altar. Bramante's gift for creating a sense of power and mass – even in a space as limited as the one occupied by this church – emerges in the powerful, barrel-vaulted central nave that ends in a trompe l'oeil niche that simulates the perspective of a deep apse in the space of a mere 97cm (38in). The octagonal baptistery to the right was made by Agostino de' Fondutis in 1483 to Bramante's designs.

Restaurants

Cracco

Via Victor Hugo 4 (02 876 774, www.ristorantecracco.it). Metro Cordusio or Duomo, or tram 2, 3, 14. **Meals served** 7.30pm-12.30am Mon, Sat; 12.30-2.30pm, 7.30pm-12.30am Tue-Fri. **Average** €155. **Map** p48 C5 ㉛ **Contemporary Italian**

Thanks to Sky's *MasterChef Italia*, Carlo Cracco has become a celebrity, his cool, 'Clint Eastwood of the Kitchen' demeanour making him a favourite on TV chat shows. But this restaurant, where he's still to be found between other commitments, is where it all began. The two Michelin stars and consistently high ratings in the Italian *Gambero Rosso* and *Veronelli* dining guides show how seriously food is taken here (although Cracco's recent TV ad for a brand of potato crisp has undermined the high-minded principles of the early years). While he is loved and hated for his controversial ingredients, Cracco's best dishes are often the ones that seem most bizarre. For a palate-teaser, try the rice with lemon, anchovies and cacao, or opt for one of the tasting menus.

▶ *Cracco's latest enterprise is the lower-priced cocktail bar/restaurant Carlo e Camilla in Segheria (via Giuseppe Meda 24, South, 02 837 3963), housed in a former sawmill in the Navigli area.*

Peck Italian Bar

Via Cesare Cantù 3 (02 869 3017, www.peck.it). Metro Cordusio or Duomo, or tram 2, 3, 14. **Open** 7.30am-10pm, **meals served** 11.30am-9.30pm Mon-Sat. **Average** €45. **Map** p48 C5 ㉜
Traditional Italian

In addition to its gourmet food hall and restaurant (see *p63*), the Peck empire also includes a casual café, just down the road. The mood is one of upmarket bustle, with stockbrokers from the nearby Borsa rubbing elbows with Milanese *signore* out for a morning's shopping. The menu offers a seasonal selection of *primi* and *secondi*, along with a variety of pastries. There's also a panini bar. In a land where it's hard to sit down for a meal outside fixed meal times, Peck Italian Bar is unusual: it serves food all day.

Cafés, Bars & Gelaterie

★ Caffè Letterario

Piccolo Teatro Grassi, via Rovello 2 (02 7233 3505, www.sotisevents.com). Metro Cordusio, or bus 58, or tram 1, 27. **Open** 9am-11pm daily. **Map** p48 C4 ㉝

EAT, DRINK AND ADMIRE THE FLOWERS

Gardens, florists and bakeries give a stylish twist to Milan's happy hour.

Pre-dinner drinks – along with a serious buffet – are a rite of passage in Milan. Anyone who is serious about getting to know local culture should head for one of the many 'happy hours' available across the city, and join the natives as they battle over generous plates of food. Almost as important is the backdrop, which these days ranges from gorgeous gardens to chic florists and heavenly-smelling bakeries.

Most happy hours run from around 6pm to 9pm, and include platters of prosciutto, mozzarella and pasta salads, and occasionally even sushi and oysters, laid out for all to consume. But beware: with cocktails usually costing €8 to €15, the feeling that you're getting a free dinner can be illusory, especially if you indulge in more than one drink.

In Porta Venezia, the verdant garden at **HClub (Diana Garden)** (see *p104*) has been a stalwart of the fashion crowd's summer drinking scene for a number of years now – and deservedly so. The lush garden, with magnolias, cyclamens and centuries-old trees, is replanted seasonally, and is a great place in which to sample the vegetarian sushi.

Nearby, **Mint Garden Café** (see *p99*)provides mini pizzas, dried fruit and *bruschette*, served at your table, inside a florist's shop, amid cacti, orchids and bunches of cut flowers, while **Pandenus** (see *p99*) offers generous slabs of home-baked foccacia straight from the oven; this is, after all, a bakery.

HClub.

Near via Manzoni, **Hotel Bulgari** (see *p247*) serves aperitifs and finger food in another lush garden backing on to the Botanical Garden, forming one of the largest green areas in central Milan. Cocktails cost €20 a shot – so this isn't a cheap option, but it's a fabulous setting for a treat.

Though best known as a café and restaurant, **Fioraio Bianchi** (see *p83*), also in a florist's shop, provides what is surely one of the loveliest settings for aperitifs in Milan. Admire huge arrangements of irises or lilies against the artfully scraped-down walls while grazing on tabouleh or pasta dishes.

EXPLORE

Tucked away in a street close to busy piazza Cordusio is one of the most delightful lunch and *aperitivo* spots in all Milan. In the historic cloister of the Piccolo Teatro Grassi theatre, this atmospheric bar is open all day, from breakfast to dinner. The lunchtime menu – from salads to meat dishes – runs from noon until 6pm. In the evening, try the *apericena* – an amalgam of *aperitivo* and *cena* (dinner) – for €14, you get a drink and a platter from the generous buffet. If it's food for thought you require, step into the adjoining bookshop. Most offerings are to do with theatre, but you might find some gifts among the Piccolo Teatro merchandise, including bags and stationery.

★ € Ottimo Massimo

Corner of via Spadari & via Victor Hugo (02 4945 7661, www.ottimomassimogourmet.it). Metro Cordusio or Duomo, or tram 2, 3, 14. **Open** 7am-7.30pm Mon-Fri; 10am-7pm Sat. **Map** p48 C5 34

This minimal eaterie is a hit with locals, who queue out of the door at lunchtime in order to gorge on gourmet panini (try the salt cod, olive and orange), freshly made salads and more exotic platters – such as pumpkin soup with amaretti biscuits – all at a reasonable price. Grab a paper menu at the door, pay for your choices, then wander over to the appropriate counter to claim your selected dish. You can take away, or sit at one of the wooden tables around a bare-branched tree that looms over the centre of the room.

Other location Open bookshop, 1st floor, viale Montenero 6, Porta Romana (02 8342 5610).

Shops & Services

Peck

Via Spadari 9 (02 802 3161, www.peck.it). Metro Cordusio or Duomo, or tram 2, 3, 14. **Open** 3.30-7.30pm Mon; 9.30am-7.30pm Tue-Fri; 9am-7.30pm Sat. **Map** p48 C5 35 **Food & drink**

A temple of fine food and wine for more than a century, Peck was founded in 1883 by a humble pork butcher from Prague. This three-floor flagship has a butcher, bakery and delicatessen; a vast selection of wines from all over the world; prepared foods, oils and bottled sauces; an in-house restaurant; and a wine tasting bar in the basement. Its sit-down café, Peck Italian Bar (*see p62*), is nearby.

VIA MANZONI, QUADRILATERO MODA, CORSO VITTORIO EMANUELE & SAN BABILA

Via Manzoni is named after the 19th-century author, Alessandro Manzoni, whose house stands just off the Scala end of the street. Before his death in 1873, the thoroughfare was known as corsia del Giardino because it was lined with villas with lush gardens, and because it led to the district's public green space, the **Giardini Pubblici**. The park remains, but the road's elite status means that the private gardens have gradually been replaced by private banks and expensive property. On the right-hand side of the street, leading off from piazza della Scala, is the entrance to the **Museo Poldi Pezzoli**. This late 19th-century aristocratic residence holds one of Milan's most prestigious collections of European art, furniture and objets.

Heading north-east, via Manzoni culminates at the **Archi di Porta Nuova**, a gate that was once part of the fortifications built to protect the city from the attacks of Frederick Barbarossa. Erected in 1171, the gate was heavily restored in 1861, using white and black marble and the more friable sandstone. The arches were then decorated with Roman funerary stones found in the area. Beyond the gate is **piazza Cavour**. The style and wealth of Milan's fashion quarter, the **Quadrilatero della Moda**, is awe-inspiring; little wonder it's also known as the Quadrilatero d'Oro ('Golden Rectangle'). This designer heaven is delineated by via Montenapoleone, via Sant'Andrea, via Manzoni and pedestrianised via della Spiga. If you think €750 is a reasonable price for a pair of shoes, or your dog just won't go out without its Christian Dior coat, then this is the place for you (*see p68* **Big Brand Bonanza**). But you won't find much other than fashion round these parts, sadly: in 2014, via Montenapoleone's oldest shop, G Lorenzi – purveyor of everything from mother-of-pearl handled caviar spoons to badger-bristle shaving brushes – shut, and other such gems are long gone. A couple of places ply their wares for less outrageous prices, however – *see p67* **In the Know** for some hints.

Alternatively, a mooch round these streets makes for an eye-opening anthropological and cultural expedition. The people-watching is unparalleled, and the area is also home to two eccentric but rewarding museums – the **Museo Bagatti Valsecchi** and the **Palazzo Morando Costume Moda Immagine** – and to one of Milan's prettiest (and least-visited) churches, **San Francesco di Paola**.

At its southern end, via Montenapoleone leads into **piazza San Babila**, a heavily trafficked thoroughfare, surrounded by post-war edifices. The faux-Romanesque brick façade of the church of San Babila stands meekly in the north-east corner of the square, cowed by the surrounding abundance of steel and stone and the racing traffic.

From piazza San Babila, it's a shortish stroll down corso Vittorio Emanuele II, one of Milan's main commercial streets, back to piazza del Duomo. For people who can't afford designer prices, the porticoes of this wide pedestrian avenue are filled with mass-market Italian and international brands – from Max & Co and H&M to the ubiquitous Zara. Halfway down is the late neoclassical church of **San Carlo al Corso**, its light-filled cupola an inspired, ethereal addition. What with the fashion feeding frenzy nearby, you may well have it all to yourself.

Sights & Museums

★ Museo Bagatti Valsecchi

Via Gesù 5 (02 7600 6132, www.museobagatti valsecchi.org). Metro Montenapoleone or San Babila, or bus 61, 94, or tram 1. **Open** 1-5.45pm Tue-Sun. **Admission** €9; €6 Wed. **Map** p49 F2 36

This late 19th-century neo-Renaissance palazzo opened as a museum in 1994, and is a tribute to the extraordinary tastes of the two Bagatti Valsecchi brothers, Fausto and Giuseppe, who once lived here. When not messing around on penny-farthings and early hot-air balloons, the brothers shared a taste for all things Renaissance, and strove to reproduce 15th-century palazzo life in their own home. Inside are numerous works of Renaissance art, Murano glass, Flemish tapestries and objets d'art dating up to the 19th century. Look out for 19th-century mod cons disguised with Renaissance trappings – such as the shower hidden in a shell-capped marble niche. Artefacts are not labelled, in order to preserve the feel of a private home; instead, information sheets in English are available in each room, and free English-language audio guides can be borrowed from the ticket desk.

★ Museo Poldi Pezzoli

Via Manzoni 12 (02 796 334, www.museopoldi pezzoli.it). Metro Montenapoleone, or bus 61, or tram 1. **Open** 10am-6pm daily (last entry 5.30pm). **Admission** €9; €6 reductions. **Map** p49 E3 37

It's the curious touches that make this place so memorable. The room after room of tasteful collections amassed by notable art enthusiasts Giuseppe and Rosa Poldi Pezzoli, and later expanded by their son, Gian Giacomo, opened to the public in 1881. One room upstairs contains a selection of early timepieces, while downstairs there are more than 100 suits of flamboyant armour worn by Europe's poseur princes. The paintings are widely admired, and include Pollaiuolo's *Portrait of a Young Woman*, Vincenzo Foppa's *Portrait of Francesco Brivio* and Botticelli's *Virgin with Child*. The attractively displayed jewellery, tapestries, glasswork, porcelain, lacework and books can occupy further hours.

Palazzo Morando Costume Moda Immagine

Via Sant'Andrea 6 (02 8846 5735, www.costume modaimmagine.mi.it). Metro Montenapoleone or San Babila, or bus 61, 94, or tram 1. **Open** *Museum* 9am-1pm, 2-5.30pm Tue-Sun. *Temporary exhibitions* varies. **Admission** €5; free-€3 reductions. Free to all last hr of the day; Tue afternoon. **Map** p49 G3 38

Donated by Countess Attendolo Bolognini in 1945, the 18th-century Palazzo Morando Attendolo Bolognini now plays host to the grandly monikered Palazzo Morando Costume, Fashion & Image Museum. The first floor is divided into two zones: the rooms overlooking via Sant'Andrea house furniture and objects formerly belonging to the countess, including porcelain, sculptures and Egyptian artefacts, while a second area contains a permanent exhibition of artworks, donated by collector Luigi Beretta in 1935. This collection of Milan scenics has helped historians create a thorough picture of the city as it was during the Napoleonic era and under Austrian rule, and chart its urban development over the years. Look out for a painting showing the first stone being laid for the building of Galleria Vittorio Emanuele II. Items of historic clothing, accessories and uniforms, previously on show at the castle, are also on display on the first floor. A new space, restored a few years ago, displays temporary exhibitions, often with a fashion or costume theme. The ground floor has also been remodelled as a space for visiting exhibitions; recent shows have included the hat collection of British fashion eccentric Isabella Blow.

FREE San Babila

Corso Monforte 1 (02 7600 2877, www.sanbabila. org). Metro San Babila or bus 54, 60, 61, 94. **Open** 7.30am-noon, 3.30-7pm daily. **Admission** free. **Map** p49 F3 39

Standing out like a sore thumb in the midst of the post-war architecture of piazza San Babila is the church that gives the square its name. The original fourth-century basilica was rebuilt in the 11th century and further modified in the 16th, only to have its Romanesque façade badly 'restored' in 1906 by Paolo Cesa Bianchi, who also did the main altar. It's not the most inspiring church in Milan, but remains notable if only because famous Italian writer Alessandro Manzoni was christened here in March 1785.

FREE San Carlo al Corso

Piazza San Carlo, off corso Vittorio Emanuele II (02 773 302). Metro Duomo or San Babila, or bus 54, 61, 73, 94. **Open** 7.30am-noon, 4-8pm daily. **Admission** free. **Map** p49 G4 40

Considered to be the final work of the neoclassical movement in Italy, this church was begun in 1839 and completed in 1847. It stands on the site of Santa Maria de' Servi, built in 1317, which was demolished in order to create corso Vittorio Emanuele II. The present structure, essentially a cylinder covered by a voluminous dome, recalls the pantheons in Rome and Paris. The sunlight shimmering through the cupola in the centre is an enchanting sight.

EXPLORE

San Babila.

FREE San Francesco di Paola

Via Manzoni 30 (02 7600 2634). Metro Montenapoleone, or bus 61, or tram 1. **Open** 9am-noon, 3.30-7.30pm daily. **Admission** free. **Map** p49 E2 41

Displaying an almost divine sense of irony, this charming Baroque church constructed by the Minimi fathers (a particularly ascetic Franciscan order founded in 1506) lies right in the heart of the wealthiest and most ostentatious part of Milan. Its attractive Baroque façade (completed in 1891) plays with concave and convex forms; inside, in addition to the classic marble altars, gilded woodwork and detailed stucco, you'll find a painting in the vault by Carlo Maria Giudici showing the glory of San Francesco di Paola, the church's patron saint.

Restaurants

Armani/Nobu

Via Pisoni 1 (02 6231 2645, www.noburestaurants.com). Metro Montenapoleone, or bus 61, 94, or tram 1. **Meals served** 12.30-2pm, 7.30-11.30pm daily. **Average** €120. **Map** p49 F1 42 **Peruvian/Japanese**

Raw fish just doesn't get more fashionable than the sushi at the Milan outpost of Nobuyuki Matsuhisa's restaurant empire, housed in Giorgio Armani's megastore. Ceviche (Latin-style marinated sushi) and avocado or asparagus tempura are on the menu at lunch and dinner.

La Veranda

Four Seasons Hotel, via Gesù 6-8 (02 77 088, www.fourseasons.com/milan). Metro Montenapoleone or San Babila, or bus 61, 94, or tram 1. **Meals served** 7am-11pm daily. **Average** €90. **Map** p49 F2 43 **Milanese**

The flagship restaurant of one of Milan's leading hotels doesn't disappoint. La Veranda's atmosphere varies throughout the day (informal at breakfast and lunchtime; more formal in the evening) and it looks on to a beautiful cloistered garden – which you can now sit in (the nine outdoor tables can be booked in the warmer months). But Sergio Mei's award-winning food is the real star of the show. The recipes vary from innovative to traditionally Milanese – osso buco, beef *tagliata* and veal *cotoletta* – but there's a real touch of class in each dish. More playful are the desserts: the 100-calorie strawberry cup comes with a wild-fennel wafer, and the ginger and pepper ice-cream has a spicy edge.

Cafés, Bars & Gelaterie

Baglioni Caffè

Hotel Baglioni, via Senato 5, or via della Spiga 8 (02 77 077, www.baglionihotels.com). Metro Montenapoleone or San Babila, or bus 61, 94, or tram 1. **Open** 7am-1am daily. **Map** p49 G2 44

Among the best features of this elegant café inside the Hotel Baglioni is its private entrance/exit, which brings you directly on to via della Spiga. The place is laid out in drawing-room style, and has a small but attractive garden, facing via Senato. Food is supplied by Il Barretto, the hotel's historic restaurant, and ranges from tomato and buffalo mozzarella caprese salad to fillet steak with green peppercorns. The well-stocked bar has generous selections of whisky and cognac for late night sojourns – and there's also a designated indoor smoking zone.

★ Corsia del Giardino

Via Manzoni 16 (02 7628 0726; www.corsiadelgiardino.it). Metro Montenapoleone, or bus 61, or tram 1. **Open** 7.30am-8.30pm Mon-Fri; 8am-8.30pm Sat; 9am-8.30pm Sun. **Map** p49 E2 45

This minimally furnished café-cum-restaurant takes its name from the old appellation for via Manzoni, in the days when this busy street was flanked by verdant gardens and tall trees. Tucked into an inner courtyard, its huge plate-glass windows and few outside tables overlook one of the few surviving gardens, which belongs to a nearby private villa and is filled with leafy shrubs, camellias and Japanese maples. Food is freshly prepared and service speedy – making this a popular lunchtime haunt for local office workers and visitors to nearby museums. Try refined but

reasonably priced platters such as salad with piave cheese, pears and cashew nuts, perhaps followed by pineapple marinated in ginger.
► *On Sundays, there's brunch (11.30am-3.30pm) and a discount for kids.*

Cova

Via Montenapoleone 8 (02 7600 5599, www.pasticceriacova.it). Metro Montenapoleone or San Babila, or bus 61, 94, or tram 1. **Open** 7.45am-8.30pm Mon-Sat. **Map** p49 F3 46
See p143 **Let Them Eat Cake.**

Shops & Services

Alessi

Via Manzoni 14-16 (02 795 726, www.alessi.com). Metro Montenapoleone, or bus 61, or tram 1. **Open** 10am-2pm, 3-7pm Mon; 10am-7pm Tue-Sat. **Map** p49 E3 47 **Homewares**
Recently moved to this address, Alessi's flagship store has just about everything the company has ever done in bright plastic and polished steel, from rabbit-shaped toothpick-holders to the Merdolino loo brush. For the outlet store on Lago d'Orta, *see p187* **Alessi's Cave**.

★ Antica Barbieria Colla

Via Gerolamo Morone 3 (02 874 312). Metro Montenapoleone, or bus 61, or tram 1. **Open** 8.30am-12.30pm, 2.30-7pm Tue-Sat. **No credit cards. Map** p49 E3 48 **Health & beauty**
This barber's shop more than lives up to its name: it's been in business since Dino Colla opened up in 1904, and proudly displays the brush that was used on Puccini. The current owner, Franco Bompieri, began working here in 1960. A totally traditional shave starts with pore-opening hot towels and closes with splashes of soothing aftershave.

B&B Italia Store

Via Durini 14 (02 764 441, www.milano.bebitalia.com). Metro San Babila or bus 60, 94. **Open** 3-7pm Mon; 10.30am-7pm Tue-Sat. **Map** p49 G4 49 **Homewares**
The list of designers who've worked for minimalist kings B&B Italia is like a hit parade of international design, from geometric vases by Ettore Sottsass to salad bowls by Arne Jacobsen. Recent pieces include seating by Milan-based design stars Antonio Citterio and Patricia Urquiola. Additional B&B designs by Italian heroes are also on show at the Triennale (*see p77*).

Brian & Barry

Via Durini 28 (02 9285 3304, www.brianebarry.it). Metro San Babila or bus 54, 60, 61, 73, 94. **Open** 10am-10pm daily. *Food floors* 10am-11pm daily. **Map** p49 G4 50 **Department store**
Opened in 2014, this tall, skinny department store has 12 floors, mostly dedicated to food, fashion, beauty, high-tech goods and accessories. Owned by a Milan-based company, its main raison d'être is mid-priced fashion from labels such as Save the Duck and Jucca (you won't find Prada, Pucci or Gucci here). Four and a half floors are dedicated to food (partly run by Eataly, the artisan food emporium), where you can shop for Italian products or dine at the (often crowded) pizza, pasta or hamburger eateries. On the top floor is the Asola restaurant, serving *cucina sartoriale* ('tailored cuisine') by chef Matteo Torretta, with light portions of saffron-flavoured *risotto alla milanese* starting at €10. It also has one of the most panoramic views in the city, best admired from the outdoor terrace. There are no escalators, so take the lift or be prepared to climb a lot of stairs.
Other location corso Vercelli 23, West (02 8646 3562).

Brian & Barry.

Coccinelle

Via Bigli 28 (02 7602 8161, www.coccinelle.com). Metro Montenapoleone, or bus 61, or tram 1. **Open** 10am-7pm Mon-Sat; 11am-1pm, 2-7pm Sun. **Map** p49 E2 51 **Accessories**
This outpost of the Parma-based leather goods chain is one of the best stocked in Milan. Dive in for everything from classic wallets in pretty pastels to handbags with fringes, studs and whatever bits and

bobs the fashion crowd demands this season – all at prices that won't make you blanch.
Other locations corso Buenos Aires 42, East (02 2940 7717); corso Genova 6, South (02 8942 1347).

Dmagazine Outlet

Via Manzoni 44 (02 3651 4365, www.dmagazine.it). Metro Montenapoleone, or bus 61, 94, or tram 1.
Open 10am-7.30pm daily. **Map** p49 F1 ㊷ **Fashion**
See right **In the Know**; *p107* **Chic at Half the Price.**
Other locations via Bigli 4, Centre (02 3664 3888); via Forcella 13, South (02 8739 2443).

Donatella Pellini s

Via Manzoni 20 (02 7600 8084). Metro Montenapoleone, or bus 61, or tram 1. **Open** 3.30-7.30pm Mon; 9.30am-7.30pm Tue-Sat.
Map p49 E2 ㊸ **Accessories**
Granddaughter of Emma Pellini, the famous costume-jewellery designer, Donatella augments her signature glass and synthetic resin pieces with striking baubles and bangles that she's collected on her travels. She also designs hats, scarves and bags.
Other locations via Morigi 9, West (02 7201 0231); corso Magenta 11, West (02 7201 0569).

Downtown Palestre

Piazza Cavour 2 (02 7601 7122, www.downtown palestre.it). Metro Turati, or bus 61, 94, or tram 1.
Open 7am-11pm Mon-Fri; 10am-9pm Sat, Sun.
Map p49 F1 ㊹ **Health & beauty**
Downtown's clientele consists of the rich, the famous and the very beautiful (though ordinary mortals are occasionally spotted too). As well as a variety of fitness classes, there are two floors of equipment, including treadmills and stairclimbers; a spa and beauty centre offers all kinds of pampering.
Other location piazza Diaz 6, Centre (02 863 1181).

Excelsior

Corso Vittorio Emanuele, at Galleria del Corso 4 (02 7630 7301, www.excelsiormilano.com). Metro Duomo or San Babila, or bus 54, 60, 61, 73, 94.
Open 10am-8.30pm daily. *Food hall* 10am-9pm daily. **Map** p49 F4 ㊺ **Department store**
Designed by French architect Jean Nouvel and opened in 2011 in the former Excelsior cinema, this rather perplexing department store shows where the Milanese are putting their money at the moment. The ground and three upper floors, brimming with expensive designer clothes by the usual suspects,

IN THE KNOW DRESS SENSE

The price tags in the big-brand boutiques in the Golden Rectangle will leave mere mortals gasping. But there are ways to hunt down purchases that won't necessitate you taking out a second mortgage, even here. **Dmagazine** (*see left*), long a fixture on via della Spiga, has shifted around the corner to via Manzoni, where it continues to sell last season's looks – from Miu Miu to Marni – at decidedly more affordable prices.

EXPLORE

RETAIL KNOWLEDGE

Key facts to improve your shopping experience.

OPENING HOURS Traditionally, shops are open 9.30am-12.30pm, 3.30-7.30pm Tuesday to Saturday, with a half-day on Monday (3.30-7.30pm). Most shops still close on Sundays, though fashion stores stay open at weekends during the major trade fairs and, in these cash-starved times, at other times throughout the year. Few shops in central Milan still close for lunch.
HOLIDAYS Don't plan your shopping spree for August. Like the rest of the city, most shops shut down.
SALES These take place in January and July.
TAX REFUNDS Non-EU residents can claim back the value-added tax (IVA) on purchases totalling over €154.94 from a single store that displays a Tax-Free Shopping sign. To do so, ask for a 'VAT back' form at the moment of purchase, keep your receipts, have your passport handy, and pack your unworn new goods at the top of your suitcase (you may have to show them). Have the receipts stamped at airport customs when you leave Italy, and hand over your 'VAT back' paperwork. Next, head for a refund centre (those at Malpensa and Linate airports are open 7am-10.30pm and 6am-10pm daily, respectively) – or post the paperwork when you get back home.

There's also a tax-free centre on the basement level of La Rinascente department store (*see p54*), in the Coin department store (*see p109*) and the Bank of China (via Santa Margherita 14-16), where you can get your cash back before leaving the country (all are open on weekdays only), once customs have stamped your documents. Note that some centres have maximum refund caps, varying from €500 to €3,000. For more details, go to www.globalblue.com.

BIG BRAND BONANZA

Where to find the biggest names in fashion.

Milan is a couture powerhouse, where clothes jump rapidly from catwalk to clothes rail. Its designer stores fit into a (somewhat irregular) rectangle of via della Spiga, via Manzoni, via Sant'Andrea, via Montenapoleone – the **Quadrilatero d'Oro** (Golden Rectangle).

Listed below are the crème de la crème of Milan's shops. Most are open 3-7pm Monday, and 10am-7pm Tuesday to Saturday – some stay open later. They're best reached from Metro Montenapoleone or San Babila, by bus 61 or 94, or by tram 1.

Via della Spiga
Dolce & Gabbana (accessories), no.2
Brunello Cucinelli, no.5
Prada (accessories), no.18
Tod's, no.22
Dolce & Gabbana (womenswear), no.26
Frette, no.31
Byblos, no.33
Serapian, no.42
Sermoneta Gloves, no.46
Marni, no.50

Via Sant'Andrea
Missoni, no.2
Trussardi, no.5
Armani Casa, no.9
Chanel, no.10
Costume National, no.12
Moschino, no.12
Miu Miu, no.21
Prada (accessories), no.23

Via Montenapoleone
La Perla, no.1
Louis Vuitton, no.2
Giorgio Armani, no.2
Salvatore Ferragamo (womenswear), no.3
Fendi, no.3
Ralph Lauren, no.4
Bottega Veneta, no.5
Etro, no.5
Camper, no.6
Gucci, no.7
Prada (womenswear), no.8
Gianni Versace, no.11
Alberta Ferretti, no.18
Valentino, no.20
Salvatore Ferragamo (menswear), no.20
Christian Dior, no.21
Loro Piana, no.27

Via Manzoni
Paul Smith, no.30
Armani Superstore, no.31
Dmagazine, no.44

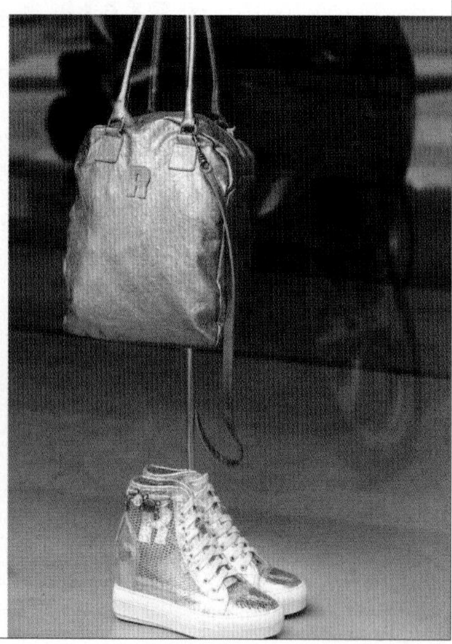

EXPLORE

are deserted. For the action, make your way to the section entitled 'Eats' on floors minus one and two. The food hall (on minus two) is packed with busy office workers, popping in to buy pre-packed gourmet lunches or to top up on edibles. At minus one, you'll find the White Sushi Italo-Japanese restaurant, serving a choice of pasta or sushi.

A word of warning: getting into and around the store is something of a puzzle. Once you've located the entrance, follow signs to the well-hidden *tapis roulant* (conveyor belts) to reach the upper floors.

★ Kiko

Corso Vittorio Emanuele 15 (02 7602 3330, www.kikocosmetics.it). Metro Duomo or San Babila, or bus 54, 60, 61, 73, 94. **Open** 9am-9.30pm Mon-Sat; 10am-9.30pm Sun. **Map** p49 F4 56 **Health & beauty**

Founded in nearby Bergamo, the Kiko chain stocks more than 1,500 affordable, safety-tested (but not on animals) nail varnishes, lipsticks, eye shadows and other products in an unparalleled range of colours. Today, the brand has more than 600 shops in eight countries, including Italy, the UK, France, Germany and Spain. Shopping at Kiko is always an experience – and this branch is no exception: the displays are surrounded by excited youngsters fighting over their favourite colours, while sales assistants double as cosmetic artists, pouncing on undecided customers and offering to make them up.

Other locations throughout the city.

La Perla

Via Montenapoleone 1 (02 7600 0460, www.laperla.com). Metro San Babila, or bus 61, 94, or tram 1. **Open** 10am-7pm Mon-Sat; 11am-7pm Sun. **Map** p49 G3 57 **Fashion**

La Perla's sophisticated lingerie, manufactured in Bologna, is pricey but flattering and of outstanding quality. The label also makes swimming costumes and glamorous nightwear.

Other locations corso Vercelli 35, West (02 498 7770); via Manzoni 17, Centre (02 805 3092).

Serapian

Via della Spiga 42 (02 7602 4451, www.serapian.com). Metro Montenapoleone or San Babila, or bus 61, 94, or tram 1. **Open** 10am-7pm daily. **Map** p49 F1 58 **Accessories**

If you want to splash out on a genuine, Italian-made leather handbag and price isn't a worry, ignore better-known brands and head to Serapian. Established in 1923, the company still has a small artisanal factory in the city's outskirts that creates elegant, swanky pieces that could only be 'Made in Italy'. Iconic designs include the capacious Doctor's Bag, and the Meliné, which has a craftily compartmentalised interior and locks swathed in mother-of-pearl. There's also a factory store, where prices are a little more accessible.

Other location via Jommelli 35, North-East (02 280 121).

Quadrilatero d'Oro.

EXPLORE

Castello Sforzesco, Brera & North

Milan's vast northern area stretches from the early Renaissance Castello Sforzesco in the north-west to the monolithic Fascist-era Stazione Centrale in the north-east, with the city's tallest skyscraper, the 21st-century Unicredit building, in between. Each building aimed to emphasise the city's status and power. The area is a hotchpotch of very different neighbourhoods. The select district of Brera is home to the Pinacoteca & Accademia di Brera, the city's main gallery and art school, while the recent Porta Nuova development, with its clutch of skyscrapers close to Garibaldi station, has become a showpiece for the new Milan. A pedestrian walkway now links Porta Nuova to the buzzing Isola area.

Unicredit building.

Don't Miss

1 Castello Sforzesco From Egyptian mummies to Michelangelo (p73).

2 Pinacoteca di Brera Mantegna, Caravaggio and more (p81).

3 Eataly The artisanal food emporium (p87).

4 Unicredit building The city's tallest edifice (p80).

5 10 Corso Como The original Milan concept store (p88).

CASTELLO SFORZESCO, PARCO SEMPIONE & THE CIMITERO

The imposing **Castello Sforzesco** is one of Milan's most recognisable monuments. Its successive roles as a Visconti stronghold, ducal residence and barracks for troops belonging to the city's Spanish, French and Austrian governors have produced a host of different architectural touches, ranging from the ostentatious to the menacing. Today it houses a clutch of mini-museums, containing everything from Egyptian mummies to sculptures by Michelangelo.

Behind the castle, the **Parco Sempione** is a legacy of Francesco Sforza's predilection for hunting: the park, and the areas extending beyond its current 47 hectares, once teemed with deer, hare and pheasants imported from nearby Varese and Como. These days, however, you're much more likely to spot some of the thousands of Milanese canines that have been crammed into a city where having a dog is, too often, little more than a fashion statement.

In the north-east corner of the park sit the Arena and the **Acquario** (the city's aquarium). Built in the distinctive art nouveau style known in Italian as Liberty (after the famous London shop), the latter structure was erected for the 1906 Milan International Exposition; indeed, it's all that remains of the original 225 buildings constructed for the occasion. The **Arena Civica** (via Byron 2), on the other hand, is a mini Colosseum designed in 1806 by Luigi Canonica, and is an addition from the city's Napoleonic period. Taking their cue from the Roman empire, the city's French rulers used it for open-air entertainment, including chariot races and mock naval battles (when it was flooded with water from the nearby canals, long since covered over). Since 2010, the Arena has been the home ground of the Amatori Rugby Milano, a rugby union club founded in 1927. In the western part of the park is the **Palazzo d'Arte**, built in 1933 to house the decorative arts exhibition held every three years – which explains why it's commonly known as the Triennale. The space is now home to the city's design museum, and is also a venue for architecture and design exhibitions of various kinds. Look out for the **iron bridge**, with mermaids at either end, over the water feature in the centre of the park. It used to span the canal at the junction of corso di Porta Romana and via Santa Sofia/via Francesco Sforza, and was moved here when the canals were covered over in the late 1920s.

At the far end of the park stands the **Arco della Pace**, an unmistakably neoclassical arch. From here, the broad avenue of corso Sempione, with its many bars and restaurants, heads north-west. North-east of corso Sempione are via Bramante and via Paolo Sarpi, the axes of Milan's **Chinatown**, containing shops both retail and wholesale, and restaurants – Chinese and otherwise – including a great Sicilian place, **Trattoria da Ottimofiore**. One block north is the **Cimitero Monumentale**, Milan's impressive cemetery and one of the city's most-visited monuments.

At the front of the castle, the main entrance overlooks one end of a long pedestrianised corridor that runs down via Dante, through piazza del Duomo, and all the way along corso Vittorio Emanuele II to piazza San Babila.

Via Dante is notable for several *palazzi*, all built in the mid to late 18th century. All, that is, except **Palazzo Carmagnola** (no.2 – not open to the public), which, despite its neoclassical façade, dates from the 14th century and retains its original courtyard. The Duke of Milan, Ludovico 'il Moro' Sforza, used this building to house his most illustrious guests, from Leonardo da Vinci and artist/architect Donato Bramante to his mistress Cecilia Galleriani (who is portrayed, aged 17, in Leonardo's *Portrait of a Woman with an Ermine*). Since 1947, the ground floor of the building has been the headquarters of the **Piccolo Teatro** (now called the Piccolo Teatro Grassi, *see p175*).

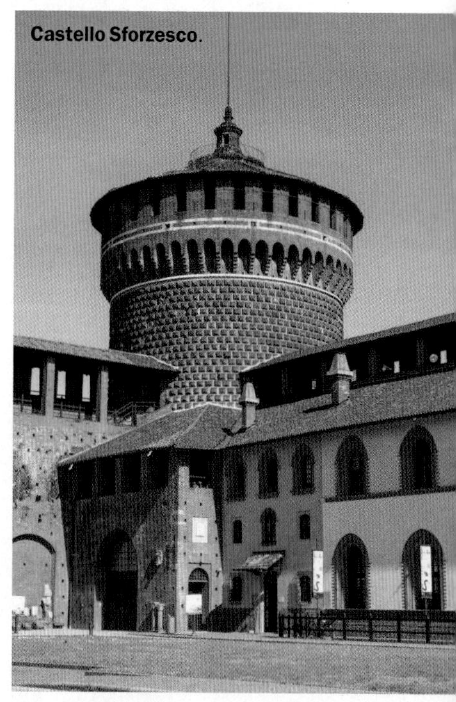
Castello Sforzesco.

EXPLORE

IN THE KNOW DINE ON A TRAM

For a quintessential Milanese experience, book for dinner aboard a 1928 vintage tram. Organised by ATM, Milan's transport authority, the **ATMosfera trams** leave from piazza Castello, at the corner of via Beltrami, each evening at 8pm, with occasional second sittings at 11pm. Diners can choose from meat, fish or vegetarian platters, all with a Milanese bent. The route goes past the new skyscrapers on the fringes of the lively Isola district, as well as the main sights in the centre (including the Duomo and La Scala opera house) and the southern Navigli zone. Booking (€65 a head) is essential: call 02 4860 7607 or visit www.atm.it.

Piazza Castello, surrounding the castle, has a central fountain facing the castle entrance. The piazza is cupped by the curved foro Buonaparte, which was pedestrianised in 2014. In front of the castle entrance is **largo Cairoli**, in the centre of which stands the 1895 bronze equestrian statue of Giuseppe Garibaldi by Ettore Ximenes, dedicated to Garibaldi's involvement in the Italian unification movement.

The controversial ExpoGate pavilions, by architect Alessandro Scandurra, were erected nearby in 2014. These transparent, pyramidal structures will serve as an information point from 1 May 2015 until the end of the Universal Exposition in 31 October 2015, after which their fate is currently unknown.

Walk westwards, and you'll come to Cadorna metro station and **Stazione Ferrovie Nord**, redesigned by Gae Aulenti in 1999. Its most striking feature is an 18-metre (60-foot) sculpture in the station piazza by Claes Oldenburg, entitled *Needle, Thread and Knot*. Clad in bright red, yellow and green polyester and polyurethane enamel, the artwork was intended as a tribute to Milan's role in the fashion trade. It was universally hated on its erection, but is now an inescapable part of the city scene.

Sights & Museums

Acquario

Viale Gadio 2, Parco Sempione (02 8846 5750, www.acquariocivico.mi.it). Metro Lanza or tram 2, 12, 14. **Open** 9am-1pm, 2-5.30pm Tue-Sun. **Admission** €5; €3 reductions; free under-18s. Free to all 2-5.30pm Tue; 4.30-5.30pm Wed-Fri. **Map** p75 F2 ❶

Designed by Sebastiano Locati, with decorations by sculptor Oreste Labò, for the 1906 World's Fair to celebrate the opening of the Simplon railway tunnel, the Milan aquarium is considered to be one of the city's best examples of the art nouveau (or Liberty) style. A huge Neptune, trident in hand, presides over the entrance, while fish, crustaceans, turtles and aquatic flora decorate the exterior. It takes less than half an hour to view the interior. There are several floor-to-ceiling tanks, with a special focus on fish and acquatic plants from seas, rivers and lakes around Italy. An added bonus: there are comfy sofas in the lobby area, and free Wi-Fi.

★ Castello Sforzesco/Civici Musei del Castello

Piazza Castello (02 8846 3700, www.milanocastello.it). Metro Cadorna, Cairoli or Lanza, or bus 43, 57, 61, 70, 94, or tram 1, 3, 4, 12, 14, 18, 19, 27. **Open** *Grounds* 8am-6pm daily. *Museums* 9.30am-5.30pm Tue-Sun. **Admission** *Grounds* free. *Museums* €5; €3 reductions; free under-18s. Free to all 2-5.30pm Tue; 4.30-5.30pm Wed-Fri. **Map** p75 G2 ❷

Along with the Duomo and the Galleria Vittorio Emanuele II, Castello Sforzesco is perhaps the best-known landmark in Milan. It was built by the Visconti family, the founders of the Duchy of Milan, who made it their home in 1368. From 1450, the castle was remodelled by Francesco Sforza, who wrested power from the Viscontis to become the fourth Duke of Milan. The court that gathered at the Castello Sforzesco between 1480 and 1499, rallied by Francesco's second son, Ludovico, was regarded as one of Europe's most refined. Known as 'il Moro' for his dark complexion, Ludovico wooed top-class local painters and lured both Bramante and Leonardo da Vinci to Milan. The former worked mainly as an architect, while the latter was initially employed for his musical and engineering skills (among his many talents, Leonardo was, apparently, a whizz on the lute). Disaster struck Ludovico when the new king of France, Louis XII, claimed his right to the Duchy of Milan in 1498. Unable to find allies, Ludovico was defeated in battle and ended up in prison in France, where he died in 1508.

Over the years, the castle changed its role and much of its original appearance. While Milan was bristling under French rule in the early 19th century, the castle's star-shaped bulwarks were demolished. In the late 1800s there was much talk of doing away with the rest, but, luckily for the city, architect Luca Beltrami came up with the idea of saving it. Between 1893 and 1904, he oversaw the work, rearranging and rebuilding unashamedly – including the reconstruction, in an early 20th-century fashion, of the original spindly-pointed, 15th-century tower.

Access to the castle is via the enormous piazza d'Armi; gates lead into the Rocchetta (the oldest part of the castle, on the left), and the Cortile (courtyard), and Palazzo della Corte Ducale (on the right), in Renaissance style.

The castle has been home to a number of mini museums since the start of the 20th century. The

EXPLORE

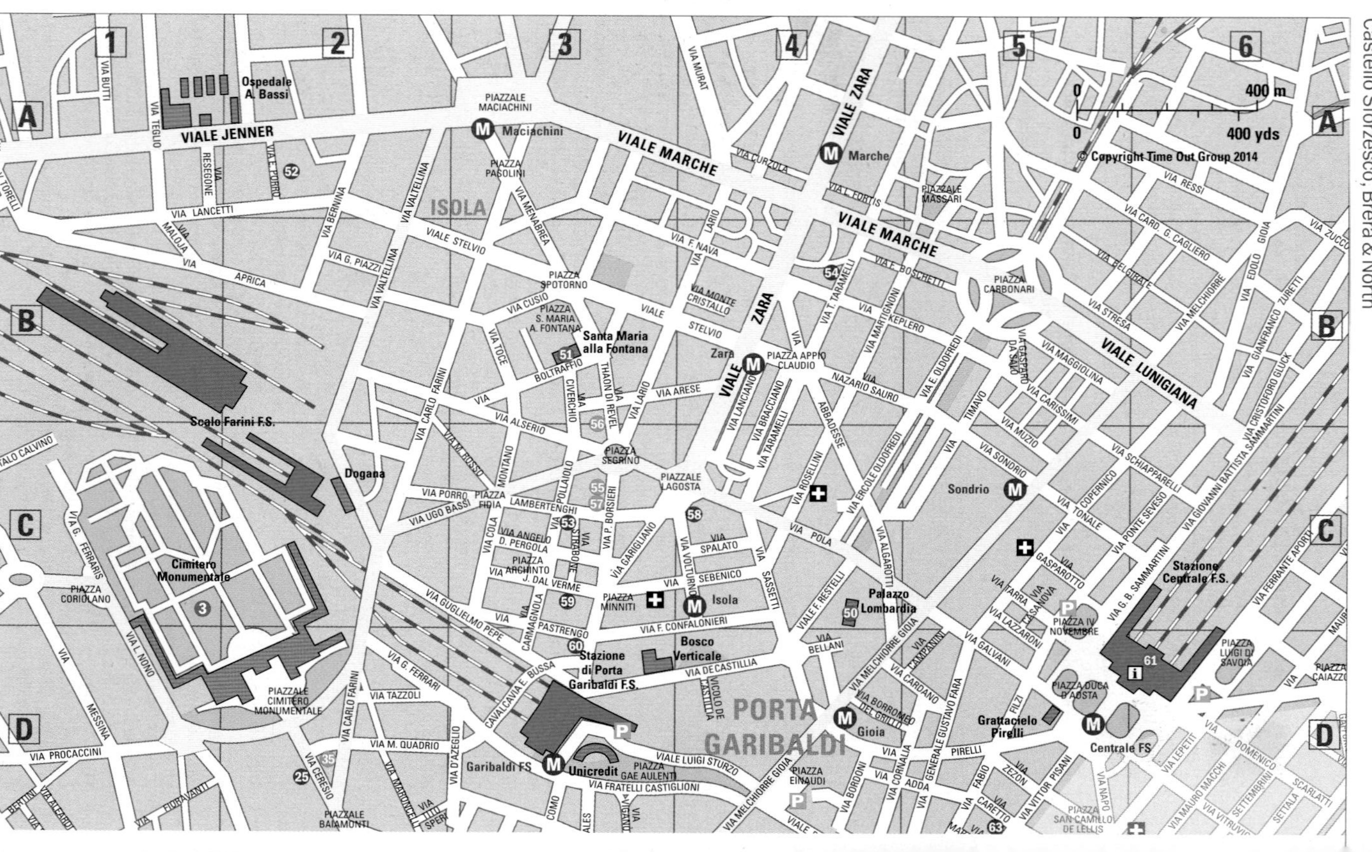

A
B
C
D
1
2
3
4
5
6
0
400 m
0
400 yds
© Copyright Time Out Group 2014
VIALE JENNER
VIALE MARCHE
VIALE ZARA
VIALE LUNIGIANA
VIA MURAT
VIA CURZOLA
VIA RESSI
VIA CARD. G. CAGLIERO
VIA BELGIRATE
VIA STRESA
VIA MELCHIORRE GIOIA
VIA EDOLO
VIA GIANFRANCO ZURETTI
VIA CRISTOFORO GLUCK
VIA GIOVANNI BATTISTA SAMMARTINI
VIA G. B. SAMMARTINI
VIA FERRANTE APORTI
VIA SCHIAPPARELLI
VIA PONTE SEVESO
COPERNICO
VIA TONALE
VIA GASPAROTTO
VIA CASANOVA
VIA TARRA
VIA LAZZARONI
VIA GALVANI
VIA FILZI
VIA SONDRIO
VIA MUZIO
VIA CARISSIMI
VIA MAGGIOLINA
VIA GASPARO DA SALÒ
PIAZZA CARBONARI
VIA TIMAVO
VIA E. OLDOFREDI
VIA ERCOLE OLDOFREDI
VIA ALGAROTTI
VIA F. BOSCHETTI
VIA KEPLERO
VIA MARTIGNONI
VIA T. TARAMELLI
VIA NAZARIO SAURO
PIAZZALE MASSARI
VIA L. PORTIS
PIAZZA APPIO CLAUDIO
VIA ABBADESSE
VIA ROSELLINI
VIA POLA
VIA TARAMELLI
VIA BRACCIANO
VIA LANCIANO
VIA MONTE CRISTALLO
VIALE STELVIO
VIA F. NAVA
VIA LARIO
VIA ARESE
PIAZZALE LAGOSTA
VIA SASSETTI
VIA SPALATO
VIA SEBENICO
VIA VOLTURNO
VIA F. CONFALONIERI
VIA GARIGLIANO
PIAZZA MINNITI
VIA P. BORSIERI
PIAZZA SEGRINO
VIA THAON DI REVEL
VIA CIVERCHIO
BOLTRAFFIO
POLLAIUOLO
VIA STRABONE
LAMBERTENGHI
VIA ANGELO D. PERGOLA
PIAZZA ARCHINTO
VIA J. DAL VERME
PASTRENGO
VIA CARMAGNOLA
VIA COLA
MONTANO
VIA ALSERIO
VIA TOCE
VIA CUSIO
PIAZZA S. MARIA A. FONTANA
PIAZZA SPOTORNO
VIA MENABREA
PIAZZA PASOLINI
PIAZZALE MACIACHINI
Maciachini
ISOLA
VIA M. ROSSO
PIAZZA FIDIA
VIA PORRO
VIA UGO BASSI
VIA CARLO FARINI
VIA GUGLIELMO PEPE
CAVALCAVIA E. BUSSA
VIA VALTELLINA
VIA G. PIAZZI
VIA BERNINA
VIA E. PORRO
VIA RESEGONE
VIA LANCETTI
VIA MALOJA
VIA APRICA
VIA TEGLIO
VIA BUTTI
V. TORELLI
Ospedale A. Bassi
Scalo Farini F.S.
Dogana
Cimitero Monumentale
PIAZZALE CIMITERO MONUMENTALE
VIA L. NONO
VIA G. FERRARIS
PIAZZA CORIOLANO
VIA MESSINA
VIA PROCACCINI
ITALO CALVINO
VIA CERESIO
PIAZZALE BAIAMONTI
VIA MARONCELLI
VIA M. QUADRIO
VIA TAZZOLI
VIA G. FERRARI
VIA D'AZEGLIO
Garibaldi FS
Stazione di Porta Garibaldi F.S.
Bosco Verticale
VIA DE CASTILLIA
VICOLO DE CASTILLIA
Isola
Zara
Marche
Sondrio
Unicredit
PIAZZA GAE AULENTI
VIA FRATELLI CASTIGLIONI
VIALE LUIGI STURZO
VIA VIGANÒ
COMO
PORTA GARIBALDI
PIAZZA EINAUDI
VIA MELCHIORRE GIOIA
VIA BORDONI
VIA CORNALIA
VIA ADDA
VIA FABIO
VIA GENERALE GUSTAVO FARA
PIRELLI
VIA CARETTO
VIA ZEZON
VIA VITTOR PISANI
Grattacielo Pirelli
PIAZZA DUCA D'AOSTA
PIAZZA IV NOVEMBRE
Centrale FS
Stazione Centrale F.S.
PIAZZA LUIGI DI SAVOIA
VIA NAPO
PIAZZA SAN CAMILLO DE LELLIS
VIA LEPETIT
VIA MAURO MACCHI
VIA VITRUVIO
VIA DOMENICO SCARLATTI
SETTEMBRINI
SETTALA
PIAZZA CAIAZZO
VIA ZUCCO
Palazzo Lombardia
VIALE F. RESTELLI
VIA BELLANI
VIA CARDANO
VIA CAMPANINI
VIA BORROMEO DEL GRILLO
Gioia
Santa Maria alla Fontana

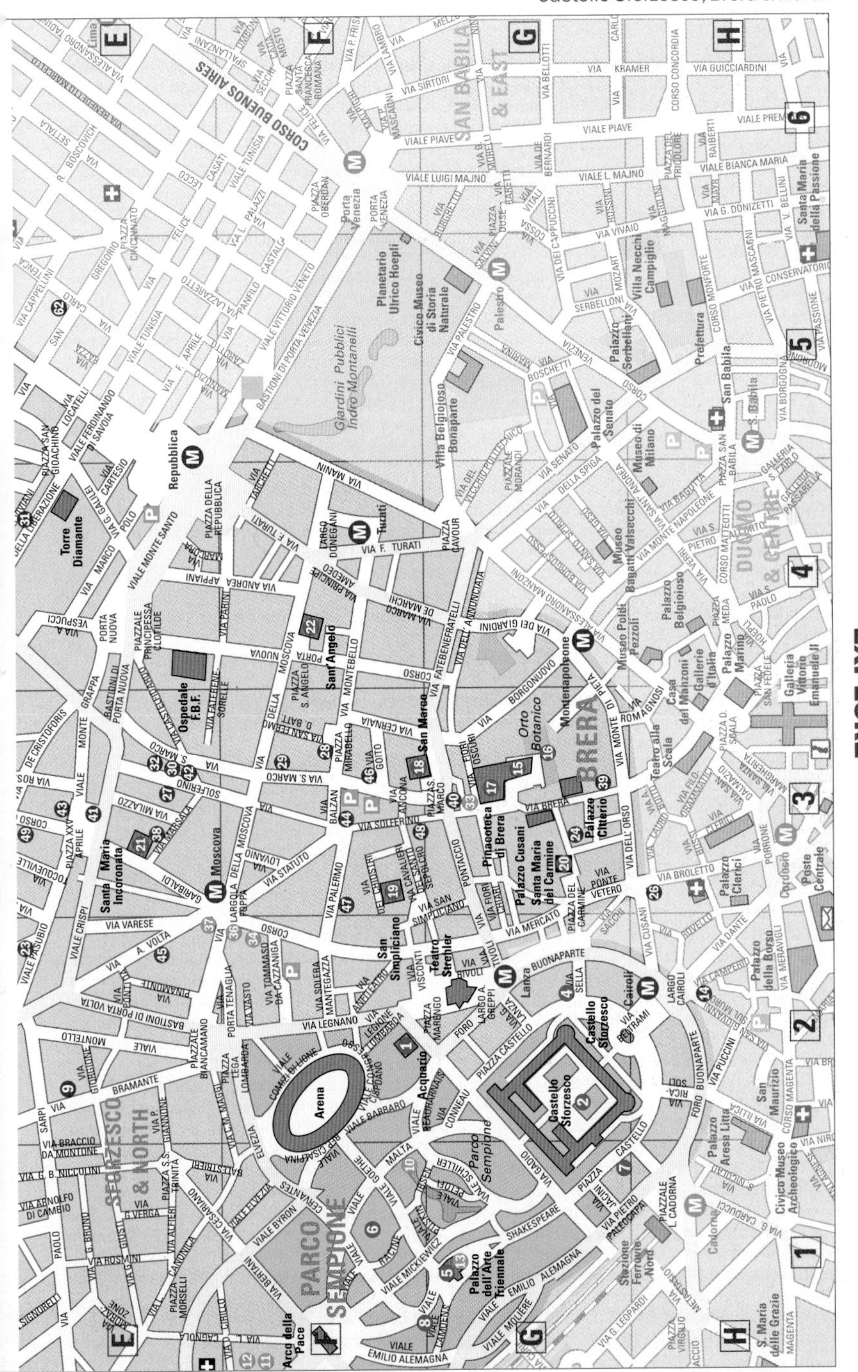
Castello Sforzesco
Arena
Acquario
Parco Sempione
Palazzo dell'Arte Triennale
Arco della Pace
Stazione Ferrovie Nord
Cadorna
Civico Museo Archeologico
Palazzo Arese Litta
San Maurizio
S. Maria delle Grazie
Palazzo della Borsa
Cordusio
Poste Centrale
Palazzo Clerici
Cairoli
Lanza
Teatro Strehler
San Simpliciano
Palazzo Cusani
Santa Maria del Carmine
Palazzo Citterio
Pinacoteca di Brera
Orto Botanico
BRERA
Montenapoleone
Teatro alla Scala
Casa del Manzoni
Gallerie d'Italia
Palazzo Marino
Galleria Vittorio Emanuele II
Museo Poldi Pezzoli
Palazzo Belgioioso
Museo Bagatti Valsecchi
Museo di Milano
Palazzo del Senato
San Babila
Palazzo Serbelloni
Prefettura
Villa Necchi Campiglio
Santa Maria della Passione
DUOMO & CENTRE
SAN BABILA & EAST
Villa Belgiojoso Bonaparte
Palestro
Civico Museo di Storia Naturale
Planetario Ulrico Hoepli
Giardini Pubblici Indro Montanelli
Porta Venezia
Turati
Repubblica
Torre Diamante
Ospedale F.B.F.
Sant'Angelo
San Marco
Moscova
Santa Maria Incoronata
SFORZESCO & NORTH
PARCO SEMPIONE
CORSO BUENOS AIRES
EXPLORE

seven currently open to the public cover everything from Renaissance masterpieces, musical instruments and furniture to Egyptian mummies. The principal must-see, however, is Michelangelo's *Rondanini Pietà* in the Civiche Raccolte d'Arte Antica, near the entrance on the ground floor. Located in the final room (room 15), the *Pietà* is the half-finished sculpture to which Michelangelo returned in the last year of his life and on which he was still working when he died, in 1564. Bought by the Milan City Council in 1952 (Michelangelo never came to Milan), the sculpture takes its name from the last owners, the Rome-based Rondanini family. By May 2015, the Pietà is due to be moved to a new purpose-built museum in the Ospedale Spagnolo, a part of the castle near Cadorna. Designed by Michele de Lucchi, the museum may have a separate entrance and new charges may come into play.

Until then, however, the same ticket will also take you to the Sala delle Asse (room 8), with heavily restored frescoes of trompe l'oeil exotic botanical scenes attributed to Leonardo da Vinci (1498). Ilex branches and leaves are used in a complicated structure on the octagonal ceiling, while fragments of a monochrome tempera decoration depict trees with branches and roots growing out of cracks in rock formations. Currently under restoration, the Sala delle Asse will be open again from May 2015.

The Civiche Raccolte d'Arte Antica are dedicated to ancient art, and contain sculptures from the early Christian periods as well as the Middle Ages. Highlights include a marble head of the Byzantine Empress Theodora, and a 12th-century bas-relief from Porta Romana, depicting the Milanese exiles returning to the city in 1171 after the Holy Roman Emperor, Frederick Barbarossa (or Red Beard), devastated the city in 1167. Other items worthy of note include the Lombard-Tuscan portal from the Milan branch of the Medici bank (1455), by Michelozzo, in room 14, which also houses a small collection of arms and armour.

Another important collection is the Pinacoteca, or art gallery (entrance via Corte Ducale, first floor, rooms 20 to 26). One of Milan's largest galleries, it starts with an impressive overview of 15th-century Italian painting, including Mantegna's majestic masterpiece *Madonna and Child with Saints and Angels in Glory* (1497) and Antonello da Messina's *St Benedict* (1470). The Veneto is represented by Giovanni Bellini's *Madonna con Bambino* (1470s) and there are several works by the Florentines, including the *Madonna dell'Umiltà* (1430s) by Filippo Lippi. There's also an extravaganza of Lombard painting, from the early to late Renaissance, including Vincenzo Foppa's stoic *St Sebastian* (before 1490) and a *Noli Me Tangere* (c1508) by Bramantino. The 16th-century schools are represented by the languorous male nudes in Cesare da Sesto's San Rocco polyptych (1520s), Correggio's *Madonna and Child with the Infant St John* (1517) and Moretto da Brescia's *St John the Baptist* (c1520). The Pinacoteca closes with 17th- to 18th-century works: Bernardo Strozzi's fleshy *Berenice* (1630) and photo-realistic views of Venice by Canaletto and Guardi.

Also worth popping into, especially if you have children, is the Museo Egizio, or Egyptian museum, located in the basement beneath the Cortile della Rocchetta. This pocket-sized collection consists of objects from the Old Kingdom to the age of Ptolemy, and includes sarcophaghi, mummies and books of the dead, as well as personal and household objects.

The remainder of the museums can be skipped around pretty fast. The City Museum of the Applied Arts (Civiche Raccolte d'Arte Applicata) includes ceramics of the world from the 15th to the 20th centuries (don't miss pieces by Gio Ponti), liturgical objects, ivories and scientific instruments.

The Museum of Prehistorical and Protohistory (Museo della Preistoria e Protostoria) recounts the story of Milan's earliest colonisers, from the Neolithic sixth to fourth millenia BC to the era of the Celts and Gauls, and highlights an early level of globalisation on the Lombardy plains via a helmet from Slovenia, a short-sword from Switzerland and shin guards from Greece.

Finally, the Museum of Musical Instruments (Museo degli Strumenti Musicali) consists of 640 instruments, which are arranged in five sections: string, plucked, keyboard, wind and exotic, and includes a spinet played by Mozart.

The Castello also houses historical and photo archives, a print collection and archaeological and art history libraries – all closed to the public.

★ FREE Cimitero Monumentale

Piazzale Cimitero Monumentale (02 8846 5600). Metro Garibaldi, or bus 37, or tram 2, 12, 14.
Open 8am-6pm Tue-Sun. **Admission** free.
Map p74 C1 ❸

Egypt had its pyramids; Milan has its Cimitero Monumentale (Monumental Cemetery), final resting place of everyone who was anyone in this town. Begun in 1866 by Carlo Maciachini, the cemetery has evolved into a macabre open-air museum: more than 25 hectares (62 acres) of pure eclecticism and funerary fashion, with monumental tombs, mausoleums, chapels and shrines in a variety of styles. Angels, putti, sphinxes, pyramids and poems adorn many of the memorials.

Those buried here include members of Milan's most illustrious families, including the Camparis and the Pirellis, and numerous artists, among them Arturo Martini, Gio Ponti, Lucio Fontana and Giò Pomodoro.

Worthy of note is the memorial to the 800-plus people from Milan who died in Nazi concentration camps, erected in 1946 and located in the centre of the cemetery. This is the work of the leading Italian architectural practice BBPR (Gianluigi Banfi, Lodovico Belgiojoso, Enrico Peressutti and Ernesto Nathan Rogers), which was also responsible for the loved-and-hated Torre Velasca (*see p112* **In the Know**). Both structures double as a kind of memorial to

Parco Sempione.

Banfi himself, who died in the Mauthausen concentration camp in 1945.

The whole complex is centred on the Temple of Fame (Famedio), where celebrated *milanesi* and other well-known individuals found their final homes. Illustrious occupants include Luca Beltrami (the architect who restored the Castello Sforzesco; died 1933), conductor Arturo Toscanini (1867-1957), poet Salvatore Quasimodo (1901-68), artist and designer Bruno Munari (1907-98) and singer-songwriter Giorgio Gaber (1939-2003). The most famous resident, though, is novelist Alessandro Manzoni (1785-1873), author of *I Promessi Sposi (The Betrothed)*, whose sepulchre is centre-stage within the circular Famedio under its splendid lapis lazuli blue dome.

Museo d'Arte e Scienza

Via Quintino Sella 4 (02 7202 2488, www.museoartescienza.com). Metro Cairoli or Lanza, or bus 57, 61, or tram 1, 2, 12, 14. **Open** 10am-6pm Mon-Fri. **Admission** €8; €4 reductions. **Map** p75 G2 ❹

An intriguing private museum focusing on art hoaxes – and the scientific techniques involved in exposing them. With explanations in English, the underground rooms line up fake weapons, icons, paintings and more. There are also permanent exhibitions devoted to Leonardo da Vinci's life and work. Don't miss a glimpse of the tunnel that offered a secret escape route for the Sforza family from their home, the Castello Sforzesco, across the street. Upstairs, you're invited into the working research labs that were established in 1993 to authenticate international art.

★ Palazzo d'Arte (Triennale)

Viale Alemagna 6 (02 724 341, www.triennale.it). Metro Cadorna or bus 61. **Open** 10.30am-8.30pm Tue-Sun. **Admission** varies. **Map** p75 G1 ❺

This superb building was the masterwork of rationalist architect Giovanni Muzio (also responsible for the Università Cattolica – *see p135*) and was built in 1933 to house the triennial decorative arts exhibition. Usually called the Triennale, the space has, since 2007, been home to Italy's first Design Museum, whose vast holdings include objects from all of Italy's top-name designers, including Achille Castiglioni, Gio Ponti and Vico Magistretti. An outstanding collection of rationalist furniture from the 1930s is rotated annually. The Triennale is also a venue for high-quality design and architectural shows of various kinds.

Non-design fans can browse the excellent bookshop or order coffee and cake in the Triennale's Design Café (*see p80*). The café's huge picture windows look on to the garden, one highlight of which is an unusual painted sculptural composition by the metaphysical artist Giorgio De Chirico called *The Mysterious Baths (i Bagni misteriosi)*. Created for the 15th Triennale Exhibition in 1973, the installation is incomplete; part of the work – two bathers and a fish – is exhibited at the Museo del Novecento (*see p50*).

FREE Parco Sempione

Metro Cairoli or Lanza, or bus 43, 57, 61, 94, or tram 1, 2, 12, 14, 19. **Open** *June-Sept* 6.30am-11.30pm daily. *May* 6.30am-10pm daily. *Mar-Apr, Oct* 6.30am-9pm daily. *Nov-Feb* 6.30am-8pm daily. **Admission** free. **Map** p75 F1 ❻

Parks are rare in Milan, and this 47-hectare (116-acre) expanse behind Castello Sforzesco is the city's biggest. Milan's French rulers began carving the orchards, vegetable gardens and a hunting reserve out of the remains of the ducal gardens in the early 1800s. It was only in 1893 that it was landscaped, by Emilio Alemagna. He opted for the then-popular 'English garden' look, with winding paths, lawns, copses and a lake. It's a firm favourite with everyone

ARTY FACTS

Uncover the contemporary art scene in northern Milan.

Aside from a scattering of galleries in the Porta Venezia area (*see p100* **Art Beat**), the best place to check out Milan's burgeoning contemporary art scene is in the north.

The Brera neighbourhood has long been frequented by artists, so it's no surprise that it's home to some of the most interesting galleries in the city. Close to a clutch of gourmet restaurants, **Antonio Colombo Arte Contemporanea** (via Solferino 44, 02 2906 0171, www.colomboarte.com) focuses on upcoming Italian and North American figurative artists, as well as emerging genres, including street art and pop surrealism. San Franciscan artist Zio Ziegler did a stint here in 2014, leaving one of his rich, street-art inspired murals on a wall.

Nearby, **Dilmos** (piazza San Marco 1, 02 2900 2437, www.dilmos.com) has been a stalwart of Milan's art and design scene since 1980. Crossing the line between furniture design and visual art, the gallery is a key player in the annual Fuori Salone section of the Milan Furniture Fair. Colourful artist-designer Alessandro Mendini was an early associate, while recent exhibitions have featured Brazilian brothers Fernando and Humberto Campana.

Heading north, **Galleria Post Design** (via della Moscova 27, 02 655 4731, www.memphis-milano.it) also explores the boundaries between design and art. Here since 1997, it's dedicated to the Memphis design movement, whose main proponent was the late Ettore Sottsass. A regular programme of exhibitions is held throughout the year, the main one coinciding with the Milan Furniture Fair.

Continuing in the direction of Stazione Garibaldi, **Galleria Carla Sozzani** (corso Como 10, 02 653 531, www.galleriacarlasozzani.org) is part of the fashion/culture/food/hospitality complex **10 Corso Como** (*see p88*). International names predominate, as does black and white photography; past exhibitors have included Annie Leibovitz, Bruce Weber, Bert Stern, Sarah Moon, David Bailey, Herb Ritts and Mary Ellen Mark.

Swinging past the station and the Cimitero Monumentale, you'll come to **C/O (Care Of)**, inside the Fabbrica del Vapore (via Procaccini 4, 02 331 5800, www.careof.org). Formerly a factory making tram and railway carriages, the Fabbrica is now a city-run arts centre, providing a venue for Italian and international contemporary artists to create site-specific installations. This pure white space hosts some of the best shows in Milan.

A few minutes' walk north of the cemetery, **Peep-Hole** (via Stilicone 10, 02 8706 7410, www.peep-hole.org) specialises in conceptual art. It's run by four partners, including Vincenzo De Bellis, curator of Milan's annual contemporary art fair **MiArt** (*see p35*). For 18 consecutive months, the gallery hosts non-profit exhibitions in collaboration with different institutions, galleries and artists. It then holds one commercial exhibition to finance the following non-profit period. Definitely worth a visit.

Antonio Colombo Arte Contemporanea.

from mums and toddlers to canoodling teenagers to summertime drinkers.

The park is home to the Arena Civica as well as a handful of museums and galleries, including the Palazzo d'Arte (*see p77*); near this palazzo are several abstract sculptures from the 1970s. Be sure to ascend Torre Branca (*see below*) for panoramic views of the city. At its base is designer drinking spot Just Cavalli. Other bars-in-the-park include Bar Bianco, a laid-back summer kiosk (*see right*).

Construction of the Arco della Pace, at the park's northern end, began in 1807 to a design by Luigi Cagnola, to celebrate Napoleon's victories. Work proceeded too slowly, however, and came to an abrupt halt in 1814 when Napoleon fell from power. Construction resumed in 1826 – with a few changes to the faces in the reliefs – and the arch was eventually inaugurated on 10 September 1838 by Austrian Emperor Ferdinand I, as a monument to peace. Among its decorative sculptures are the *Chariot of Peace* by Abbondio Sangiorgio, and *Four Victories* by Giovanni Putti.

★ Studio Museum Achille Castiglioni

Piazza Castello 27 (02 805 3606, www.achillecastiglioni.it). Metro Cadorna or Cairoli, or bus 50, 58, 61, 94. **Guided tours** 10am, 11am, noon Tue, Wed, Fri; 10am, 11am, noon, 6.30pm, 7.30pm, 8.30pm Thur. **Admission** €10; €7 reductions. **Map** p75 H1 ❼

The studio-museum of legendary furniture and industrial designer Achille Castiglioni is one of Milan's greatest treasures. The place is much as he left it on his death in 2002. Visitors are led through the four rooms by a guide, who unlocks secret drawers and cupboards, and explains the gadgets, models and inventions that crowd the shelves. Discoveries include a prototype of a reading light designed for his wife Irma, so that she could read in comfort in bed; and a miniature model of Castiglioni's iconic Arco lamp for Flos. If you're lucky, the guide may be a member of the family: Castiglioni's daughter, Giovanna. Reservations are requird for guided tours; these can me made online via the website.

Torre Branca

Via Camoens (02 331 4120). Metro Cardona or Conciliazione. **Open** *mid May-mid Sept* 3-7pm, 8.30pm-midnight Tue, Thur, Fri; 10.30am-12.30pm, 3-7pm, 8.30pm-midnight Wed; 10.30am-2pm, 2.30-7.30pm, 8.30pm-midnight Sat, Sun. *Mid Sept-mid May* 10.30am-12.30pm, 4-6.30pm Wed; 10.30am-1pm, 3-6.30pm, 8.30pm-midnight Sat; 10.30am-2pm, 2.30-7pm Sun. **Admission** €5. **Map** p75 G1 ❽

A short walk north of the Triennale is the Torre Branca, Milan's miniature answer to the Eiffel Tower, offering a 360° view of the entire city from a height of 108.6 metres (356 feet). On a clear day, you can see as far as the Alps. Designed by Gio Ponti for the Triennale's Exhibition of Decorative Arts in 1933, it was originally called the Torre Littoria but was renamed in 2002, when the Branca company (makers of the Fernet Branca digestive liqueur) sponsored its restoration, adding a glass-walled lift. The tower is constructed from steel tubes, in hexagonal sections tapering to a point, forming a more minimal version of Paris's famous monument.

Restaurants

Innocenti Evasioni

Via Privata della Bindellina (02 3300 1882, www.innocentievasioni.com). Bus 48, 57, 90, 91 or tram 1, 14, 19. **Meals served** 8-10.30pm Mon-Sat. **Average** €50. **Contemporary Italian**

This delightful restaurant is in an unlikely location: tucked away down a narrow private road (*via privata*) near piazzale Accursio. The two softly lit dining rooms with a strong Zen aesthetic overlook a pretty Japanese garden. The food is inventive, with nice little details that make it feel special: a basket of freshly baked breads; complimentary nibbles before the antipasto. You can check out the monthly menu on the website.

Trattoria da Ottimofiore

Via Bramante 26 (02 3310 1224). Metro Moscova or tram 4, 33. **Meals served** 7.30-11pm Mon; noon- 2.30pm, 7.30-11pm Tue-Sat. **Average** €35. **Map** p75 E2 ❾ **Traditional Sicilian**

Any doubt about the authenticity of this prime Sicilian joint is banished by one look at the menu. For starters, Ottimofiore's buffet (self-service, but you pay per item) includes Sicily's finest: deep-fried baby sardines, *caponata di verdure* (roasted peppers, aubergines and courgettes) and *frittelle alla salvia* (sage and vegetable fritters). The concise menu includes *pasta alla norma* (with aubergine and seasoned ricotta), *pasta alle sarde* (rigatoni with a sardine-based ragù) and pasta with pesto Trapani-style (basil, tomato and almonds).

Cafés, Bars & Gelaterie

Bar Bianco

Viale Enrico Ibsen 4, Parco Sempione (02 8699 2026, www.bar-bianco.com). Bus 57, 61, or tram 1, 14, 19. **Open** *May-Sept* 10am-1am Mon-Thur, Sun; 10am-2am Fri, Sat. *Oct-Apr* 10am-6pm daily (closed in bad weather). **Map** p75 F1 ❿

Located bang in the middle of Parco Sempione, Bar Bianco was originally a milk bar run by the local dairy, serving coffee and cappuccino to hassled mums and ice-cream to the kids – a role it still fulfils admirably. As the families head home after a fun day at the park, this designer kiosk and umbrella-studded terrace turns up the volume, and a hip, clubby crowd moves in. Drinks are served between 6.30pm and 2am, with DJ sets on Saturday night. There's also free Wi-Fi available.

EXPLORE

Bhangrabar

Corso Sempione 1 (02 3493 4469, www. bhangrabar.it). Bus 37, 43, 57 or tram 1, 19, 27. **Open** 6pm-2am daily. **Map** p75 F1 ⑪

Despite its name, this buzzing bar doesn't have much to do with either bhangra music or India. The generous happy-hour spread (6-10pm Mon-Sat, €10) features a handful of international/Indian specialities, but the focus is on *pizzette*, *focacce* and the usual Italian treats. Sunday brunch (noon-3pm, reservations preferred) is also popular.

Deseo

Corso Sempione 2 (02 315 164). Bus 57 or tram 1, 14, 19. **Open** 6pm-2am daily. **Map** p75 F1 ⑫

'Design' is the byword at this cocktail bar: white pouffes and sofas, dark furniture, mirrors and big columns all feature in the sophisticated interior. It's popular with an older, more discerning set, who head here for happy hour. The attractive outdoor terrace overlooks the Arco della Pace.

Triennale Design Café

Viale Alemagna 6 (02 8909 3899, www.triennale. it). Metro Cadorna or bus 61. **Open** 10.30am-5pm Tue-Sun. **Map** p75 G1 ⑬

The pleasant café at Milan's Design Museum is a great place for a quick lunch or a coffee break. It's also an ideal venue to check out which designer chairs to purchase for your living room. The café doubles as an archive of the greatest design hits of the 20th century, featuring 65 chairs by modern masters from Frank Lloyd Wright to Tom Dixon. Order your cappuccino – then chair-hop for as long as you like.

► *An outdoor version of the café, the Triennale Design Café all'Aperto, is open in the adjacent garden from mid April (to coincide with the start of the annual Milan Furniture Fair) to the end of September.*

Shops & Services

American Bookstore

Via Camperio 16, largo Cairoli (02 878 920, www.americanbookstore.it). Metro Cairoli, or bus 57, or tram 1, 2, 12, 14. **Open** 1.30-7pm Mon; 10.30am-7pm Tue-Sat. **Map** p75 H2 ⑭ **Books & music**

This delightful little shop is the only surviving English-language independent bookshop in central Milan. It has a good stock of popular and literary novels, as well as coffee table tomes and second-hand books, with volumes starting at €2.90.

Via Fauché

Via Fauché & via Losana (no phone). Bus 37, 57, 94 or tram 1, 12, 14, 19. **Open** 7.30am-1pm Tue; 7.30am-5pm Sat. **Map** p280 A3. **Market**

This twice-weekly general street market has long been one of the fashionistas' favourites. If you strike lucky, you may uncover discounted footwear samples by the biggest brands. Want to know which are the top stalls? Head for the huddles of well-dressed women fighting over the top finds.

BRERA, GARIBALDI & PORTA NUOVA

Once a working-class area frequented by artists, Brera is now one of Milan's chicest neighbourhoods. It's still home to Milan's most important public gallery, **Pinacoteca di Brera**, and an art school; these days the artists rub shoulders with the many well-dressed professionals and hipsters who haunt the antique shops, off-beat fashion boutiques and bars.

The Pinacoteca is part of the **Palazzo di Brera**, on via Brera, built by Francesco Maria Ricchini in 1651 on the site of a 14th-century convent that later became a Jesuit school. Aside from visiting the Pinacoteca itself, you can wander around the courtyard's porticoes and statues; you're also free to push on inside through the statue-filled corridors that line the Accademia di Belle Arti (Academy of Fine Arts). The palazzo also contains the Biblioteca Braidense, a library with richly decorated interiors and an intriguing collection of books. There's also an **observatory** and **botanical garden**.

Via del Carmine links to via Mercato, which segues into corso Garibaldi as it heads north. An interesting array of one-off shops and bars lines the road as it leads into largo La Foppa, and on past the church of **Santa Maria Incoronata** – a rare example of a double-fronted temple. The corso continues through the neoclassical arch of Porta Garibaldi, built in 1826 and renamed in Giuseppe Garibaldi's honour in 1860. Previously known as the Porta Comasina, it led to Como and the outlying Brianza district. Those looking for work entered the city via this arch, and then fanned out to seek their fortune, giving it a certain notoriety. Today, the surrounding piazza is home to Milan's newly opened branch of **Eataly**, the artisan food emporium-cum-eaterie (*see p86* **Calling All Foodies**).

From here, corso Garibaldi links to corso Como, a short pedestrianised street with several restaurants, clubs and shops – the fulcrum of independent upscale shopping and clubbing in Milan. The best-known venue is Carla Sozzani's **10 Corso Como**, a whimsical, one-of-a-kind shop, café, restaurant, gallery and B&B.

A short walkway (via Vincenzo Capelli) was recently built to connect the corso to piazza Gae Aulenti, the hub of the new **Porta Nuova** skyscraper zone. Looming overhead is Milan's latest symbol, erected in 2011: the **Torre Garibaldi**, aka the Unicredit skyscraper, by Argentine star architect Cesar Pelli. The 231-metre (758-foot) building – the city's tallest – is topped with an illuminated spire, echoing

Torre Diamante.

the spiked Duomo. During the day, locals come here for a spot of sightseeing and shopping: minimalist Milan fashion brand **Costume National** (02 8425 4310, www.costumenational.com) has opened on via Vincenzo Capelli, while piazza Gae Aulenti is home to a branch of bookshop-cum-café **Fetrinelli Red** (02 655 801, www.lafeltrinelli.it). At night, visitors can enjoy views of the spectacularly lit edifice, or play games of outdoor table football in the surrounding square.

The Porta Nuova development contains other new skyscrapers, some of which are worth taking a short detour to see. These include the **Torre Diamante** (Diamond Tower), a glass-covered, prism-shaped structure by Kohn Pederson Fox on viale della Liberazione, east of piazza Gae Aulenti. Other significant edifices lie slightly to the north, across the pedestrian walkway that connects to the villagey Isola zone (*see p88*).

Sights & Museums

FREE Museo Astronomico

Palazzo Brera, via Brera 28 (02 5031 4680, www.brera.unimi.it). Metro Montenapoleone, or bus 61, or tram 2, 12, 14. **Open** 9am-4.30pm Mon-Fri. **Admission** free. **Map** p75 G3 ⓯

Part of the State University of Milan, this small museum consists of scientific instruments used by the Astronomical Observatory that was established in 1764 by the Jesuits and which passed into government hands in 1773. Among the observatory's most notorious discoveries was that scientific concepts can be lost in translation. Around 1877, astronomer Giovanni Schiaparelli's observations of Mars led him to posit the presence, on the planet's surface, of what he called *canali*, which, in Italian, means channels – naturally occurring grooves in the ground. (His observations may have been influenced by the fact that he was colour-blind; the 'grooves' were probably mountain ridges, in reality.) By the time Schiaparelli's 'discovery' reached English-speaking scientists, the word had been translated as 'canals', in other words, man-made objects. The belief that Mars was inhabited led to a slew of sci-fi books and films on the subject, and endless speculation by pseudo-scientists for years to come. The telescope used by Schiaparelli is still housed in the museum.

★ FREE Orto Botanico di Brera

Via Fiori Oscuri 4 & via Fratelli Gabba 10 (02 5031 4680, www.brera.unimi.it). Metro Montenapoleone, or bus 61, or tram 2, 12, 14. **Open** *Feb-June, Sept, Oct* 9am-noon, 2-5pm Mon-Fri; 10am-5pm Sat. *July, Aug, Nov-Jan* 9am-noon Mon-Fri; 10am-4pm Sat. **Admission** free. **Map** p75 G3 ⓰

Accessed either from via Palazzo di Brera, or through the new entrance on via Fratelli Gabba (off via Monte di Pietà), the Botanical Garden is a relaxing spot, with aromatic herbs, climbers and vegetable gardens (for research, not the cooking pot). In the south-west corner stand two of Europe's oldest ginkgo biloba trees, brought from China in the early 18th century and now 30m (98ft) tall.

★ Pinacoteca di Brera

Palazzo Brera, via Brera 28 (02 722 631, reservations 02 8942 1146, www.brera.beniculturali.it). Metro Montenapoleone, or bus 61, or tram 2, 12, 14. **Open** 8.30am-7.15pm Tue-Sun (last entry 6.40pm). **Admission** €6; €3 reductions; free under-18s. **No credit cards**. **Map** p75 G3 ⓱

Considered the finest collection of northern Italian painting from the 13th to the 20th centuries, the Pinacoteca di Brera was created by the neighbouring Accademia di Belle Arti di Brera for its students. Both institutions are housed in a palazzo that was begun in 1651 by Francesco Maria Richini (also spelled Ricchini) for the Jesuits, who wanted to establish a college, astronomical observatory and botanical garden. The original collection of plaster casts and drawings was considerably enhanced with artworks from the churches and monasteries suppressed in the late 1700s, around the time when the school was established. Bequests and purchases added more; today, the gallery's 38 rooms contain some of the world's most important works of art.

Seminal pieces are Andrea Mantegna's exquisite exercise in foreshortening, the *Dead Christ*, Giovanni Bellini's *Madonna Greca*, Piero della Francesca's *Virgin and Child with Saints*, the disturbingly realistic *Christ at the Column* by Donato Bramante, and Caravaggio's atmospheric *Supper at Emmaus*. Other highlights include *Baptism and Temptation of Christ* by Paolo Veronese, *Finding the Body of Saint Mark in Alexandria* by Tintoretto, *Marriage of the Virgin*

Ceresio 7.

(Lo Sposaliazio) by Raphael, *Virgin and Child with Saints* (aka the *Brera Madonna*) by Piero della Francesca, and *The Fourth Estate* by Giuseppe Pellizza da Volpedo. On the 20th-century checklist are works by Giorgio Morandi, Umberto Boccioni, Mario Sironi, Giacomo Balla, Gino Severini and Carlo Carrà.

FREE San Marco

Piazza San Marco 2 (02 2900 2598). Metro Turati or Lanza, or bus 61, 94. **Open** 7am-noon, 4-7pm Mon-Sat; 8am-noon, 4-7pm Sun. **Admission** free. **Map** p75 F3 ⑱

San Marco was built in 1254 by the Augustinian Lanfranco Settala on the site of an earlier church that the Milanese had dedicated to Venice's patron, St Mark. This gesture was to express their thanks to the Venetians for their intervention in the battle against the Holy Roman Emperor Frederick I. The church's neo-Gothic façade was redone by Carlo Maciachini in 1872-73. Inside, nine chapels provide an overview of 16th- and 17th-century Lombard painting. The main organ, built in 1564, was played by Mozart, who stayed in the adjacent monastery during his Milan sojourn in 1770. The church has excellent acoustics and has been the venue for many concerts over the centuries. Giuseppe Verdi's *Requiem*, conducted by the maestro himself, premiered here on 22 May 1874.

FREE San Simpliciano

Piazza San Simpliciano 7 (02 862 274, www.sansimpliciano.it). Metro Lanza, or bus 43, 61, 94, or tram 1, 2, 12, 14. **Open** 9.30-11.30am, 3-6pm. **Admission** free. **Map** p75 F3 ⑲

One of the oldest churches in the city, San Simpliciano was probably founded in the fourth century by St Ambrose himself (and dedicated to his successor), and completed in 401. The present façade was added in 1870 by Carlo Maciachini in the neo-Gothic style he favoured, and the central entrance was reconstructed in the 11th and 12th centuries.

FREE Santa Maria del Carmine

Piazza del Carmine 2 (02 8646 3365, www.chiesadelcarmine.it). Metro Lanza, or bus 50, 57, 61, or tram 1, 2, 12, 14. Open 7.15am-noon, 4-7.15pm daily. **Admission** free. **Map** p75 G3 ⑳

Little remains of the original Romanesque church built in 1250 and rebuilt in 1400; the current façade (1880) is the work of Carlo Maciachini, who was very active in this part of Milan. Only ten of the original 16 chapels (which became 22 in the 16th century) survive, testifying to the decorative styles of the 16th and 17th centuries. The tomb (1472) of ducal councillor Angelo Simonetta can be seen in the right transept; and the body of finance minister Giuseppe Prina was brought to the sacristy after he had been lynched by a mob for raising the tax on salt in 1814. The sculptures on the wooden choir (1579-85) are the original plaster models used by the artists working on the spires of the Duomo in the 19th century. In the piazza in front of the church stands a bronze sculpture, *Il Grande Toscano*, by contemporary Polish artist Igor Mitoraj.

FREE Santa Maria Incoronata

Corso Garibaldi 116 (02 654 855, www.santamariaincoronata.it). Metro Garibaldi, or bus 43, 94 , or tram 2, 4. **Open** 7.30am-2.30pm, 3.30-7pm daily. **Admission** free. **Map** p75 E3 ㉑

This essentially Romanesque church is, in fact, two buildings erected by Guiniforte Solari and united in 1468. The one on the left went up in 1451, coinciding with the arrival in Milan of Duke Francesco Sforza; the Augustinian fathers dedicated it to the new duke. Nine years later, Francesco's wife, Bianca Maria Visconti, decided that another church should be erected, adjoining the first. Frescoes in the first chapel of the left nave are attributed to Ambrogio Borgognone, who also goes by the names of Ambrogio da Fossano, Ambrogio di Stefano da Fossano, Ambrogio Stefani da Fossano or, quite simply, il Bergognone.

FREE Sant'Angelo

Piazza Sant'Angelo 2 (02 632 481). Metro Turati or bus 43, 61, 94. **Open** 6.30am-8pm daily. **Admission** free. **Map** p75 F4 ㉒

Built in 1552 to a design by Domenico Giunti, this church replaced the original, which had been demolished to make way for the new set of city walls constructed by order of Milan's governor, Ferrante I Gonzaga. Sant'Angelo is a fine example of 16th-century Milanese ecclesiastical architecture. The interior has many paintings by noteworthy Milanese and Lombard artists of the 16th and 17th centuries, including Antonio Campi, Pier Francesco Mazzucchelli (il Morazzone), and Camillo Procaccini. Visitors to Milan on Easter Monday (Lunedì dell'Angelo, or *pasquetta*, in Italian) can visit the traditional flower market (9am-7pm) in the square in front of the church. In addition to plants and seedlings, you'll find clothing, regional food specialities and handicrafts.

Restaurants

★ Antica Trattoria della Pesa

Viale Pasubio 10 (02 655 5741, www.anticatrattoriadellapesa.com). Metro Garibaldi, or bus 94, or tram 2, 4, 33. **Meals served** 12.30-2pm, 7.30-11pm Mon-Sat. **Average** €40. **Map** p75 E2 ㉓ **Traditional Milanese**

Located in a 19th-century weigh station (*pesa*), from which it takes its name, this traditional restaurant features classic Lombard dishes, including a generous *cotoletta alla milanese* (breaded veal) that barely fits on to its plate. It also serves some of the finest pasta with *funghi porcini* in the city – when in season, of course. The original weighing scales, from the time when goods were weighed by customs officers on entry into Milan, can be seen by the entrance.

Carminio

Via del Carmine 3 (02 7202 2992, www.carminiocucina.com). Bus 61 or tram 1, 2, 12, 14. **Meals served** 12.30-2.30pm, 7.30-10.30pm Mon-Fri; 7.30-10.30pm Sat. **Average** €40. **Map** p75 G3 ㉔ **Contemporary Italian**

On a quiet, cobbled street behind the church of Santa Maria del Carmine, this health-conscious restaurant, run by an artist, serves innovative dishes such as goat's cheese quiche, and fig and frangipani tart to an artsy clientele. The decor is suitably boho, with a bright red bar and ethnic drapes adding colourful splashes to the pared-down, historic dining room.

Ceresio 7

Viale Ceresio 7 (02 3103 9221, www.ceresio7.com). Metro Garibaldi, or bus 37, 94, or tram 2, 4, 12, 14. **Meals served** *Bar* 12.30pm-1am daily. *Restaurant* 12.30-3pm, 7.30-11pm daily. **Average** €80. **Map** p74 D2 ㉕ **Contemporary Italian**

Canadian twins Dan and Dean Caten, the inventors of fashion label Dsquared2, are the brains behind this spectacular new eaterie, frequented by Milan's coolest crowd. It's located on the rooftop of the former Enel (electricity company) building, and the interior has a 1930s feel (the building dates from 1929). A twin theme runs throughout; the long, narrow restaurant is flanked at either end by a matching swimming pool with bar, open all day for lunch and drinks. Under former Hotel Bulgari chef Elio Sironi, the restaurant menu features spins on Mediterranean classics, such as lamb with capers, lemon and aubergine. In summer, you can book for an afternoon or full day at the rooftop pools (from €80 per head).

Da Claudio

Via Cusani 1 (02 8691 5741, www.pescheriadaclaudio.it). Metro Lanza, or bus 57, 61, or tram 1, 2, 12, 14. **Meals served** 12.30-2.30pm, 7.30-10.30pm Tue-Sat. **Average** €60. **Map** p75 H3 ㉖ **Seafood**

Da Claudio is Milan's best-known fishmonger, with a major sideline in quick, stand-up lunches or *aperitivi*. Choose from lovingly prepared platters of tuna tartare, diced swordfish with spring onions, or octopus carpaccio presented on crushed ice. There are also sauced-up half lobsters on the shell, all complemented with sparkling white wine on draught. Order and pay upfront at the cashier, then collect your dishes from the servers. There's a sit-down restaurant upstairs, but the buzz is at street level.

★ Dry

Via Solferino 33 (02 6379 3414, www.drymilano.it). Metro Moscova, or bus 37, 94, or tram 4, 33. **Meals served** 7pm-midnight daily. **Average** €25. **Map** p75 E3 ㉗ **Pizzeria**

See p85 **Milan's New Gourmet Street**.

★ Fioraio Bianchi

Via Montebello 7 (02 2901 4390, www.fioraiobianchicaffe.it). Metro Turati or Moscova, or bus 43, 61, 94, or tram 1, 2. **Meals served** 12.30-2.30pm, 8.30-11pm Mon-Sat. **Average** €65. **Map** p75 F3 ㉘ **Contemporary Italian**

With its artfully scraped-down walls and massive bunches of arum lilies or irises, this café and restaurant in a former florist's is one of the most attractive in Milan. Each dish is lovingly conceived, although you pay handsomely for that devotion. Alternatively, try the happy hour with buffet (6-8pm; €10).

La Latteria

Via San Marco 24 (02 659 7653). Metro Moscova or bus 43, 94. **Meals served** 12.30-2.30pm, 7.30-10pm Mon-Fri. **Average** €45. **No credit cards. Map** p75 F3 ㉙ **Traditional Italian**

This seven-table establishment has been serving simple Italian fare since 1965. The menu changes daily, but *maccheroni al pomodoro e burro* (pasta with butter and tomatoes) is a typical offering, and they also do a mean *bollito* (mixed boiled meats). Bookings aren't taken, so line up outside like everybody else.

★ Pisacco

Via Solferino 48 (02 9176 5472, www.pisacco.it). Metro Moscova, or bus 43, 94, or tram 4, 33.

Myke.

Meals served noon-3pm, 7pm-midnight Tue-Sun. **Average** €35. **Map** p75 E3 ㉚
Contemporary Italian
See p85 **Milan's New Gourmet Street**.

Ristorante Berton

Viale della Liberazione 13 (02 6707 5801, www.ristoranteberton.com). Metro Gioia or Garibaldi, or bus 37, 43, or tram, 4, 9, 33. **Meals served** 8-10.30pm Mon, Sat; noon-2.30pm, 8-10.30pm Tue-Fri. **Average** €90. **Map** p75 E4 ㉛
Contemporary Italian
Andrea Berton – previously the chef at Ristorante Trussardi alla Scala, where he gained two Michelin stars – opened his own eponymous restaurant at the end of 2013. On the ground floor of one of the skyscrapers flanking the Torre Diamante, the uncompromisingly modern interior features brushed metal, elm wood and concrete. The food is as good as you'd expect at these prices: try surprising combinations such as eel and passionfruit.

★ Zazà Ramen

Via Solferino 48 (02 3679 9000, www.zazaramen.it). Metro Moscova, or bus 37, 43, or tram 4, 9, 33. **Meals served** noon-3pm, 7pm-midnight Mon, Wed-Sun. **Average** €30. **Map** p75 E3 ㉜ **Japanese**
See p85 **Milan's New Gourmet Street**.

Cafés, Bars & Gelaterie

Bar Jamaica

Via Brera 32 (02 876 723, www.jamaicabar.it). Metro Lanza or Montenapoleone, or tram 2, 12, 14. **Open** 9am-2am daily. **Map** p75 G3 ㉝
Named for the Daphne du Maurier novel (and Hitchcock movie), not the Caribbean island, Bar Jamaica became a favoured hangout of journalists and artists (Giacometti included) in the 1950s, and started holding art and photography shows long before anybody else thought of combining arts and alcohol in this way. A Milan institution through and through, with tables out on bustling via Brera from spring to autumn.

Bottiglieria Moscatelli

Corso Garibaldi 93 (02 655 4602). Metro Moscova or bus 43, 94. **Open** 7am-2am Mon-Sat; 9am-10pm Sun. **Map** p75 F2 ㉞
Originally a 'bottle shop', Bottiglieria Moscatelli preserves an aura of authenticity, and its happy hour (6-9pm, with ample buffet for €8) is very popular. Inside, it gets very 'cosy' very quickly, so sit outside (there are heaters in winter) if you want more space.

Myke

Via Quadrio 25 (02 3674 1567, www.mykitchenexperience.it). Tram 2, 4, 12, 14, 33. **Meals served** noon-3pm Mon; noon-3pm, 7-10pm Tue-Fri; 7-10pm Sat. **Map** p74 D2 ㉟
Community and conviviality are the watchwords at Myke ('My Kitchen Experience'), a popular new eaterie, where the creative crowd gathers round communal tables to munch on healthy platefuls – perhaps burrito with chicken cooked at a low temperature for extra flavour, or huge salads with eggs, ham, potatoes and walnuts. The carefully selected suppliers of pasta, meat, coffee, beer and wine are listed on the website, if you feel like checking it out.

★ Princi

Largo La Foppa 2 (02 659 9013, www.princi.it). Metro Moscova or bus 43, 57, 94. **Open** 7am-midnight daily. **Map** p75 F2 ㊱
Princi is renowned for its industrial-strength cocktails and stylish, minimal interiors. There's no table service, so drinkers walk up to the barman and order whatever they fancy (having paid at the till first). Princi also has its own busy bakery, so expect the freebies dished out to the after-work crowd to include foccacia, cheesy breadsticks and olive bread.
Other locations via Speronari 6, Centre (02 874 797); piazza XXV Aprile 5, North (02 2906 0832); via Ponte Vetero 10, North (02 7201 6067).

Radetzky

Largo La Foppa 5 (02 657 2645, www.radetzky.it). Metro Moscova or bus 43, 57, 94. **Open** 8am-1.30am Mon-Wed; 8am-2am Thur-Sat; 10am-1.30am Sun. **Map** p75 E2 ㊲

MILAN'S NEW GOURMET STREET

A trio of exciting restaurants awaits on via Solferino.

The city's newest destination foodie street is via Solferino in the artsy Brera neighbourhood. It all began back in 2012, when Michelin-starred chef Andrea Berton (the force behind the acclaimed Ristorante Berton – *see p84*) and his partners opened **Pisacco** (*see p83*), a quirkily frescoed restaurant serving creative Italian fare to a crowd of fashionable professionals. The highly affordable food and buzzing ambience soon made this one of the city's most popular restaurants. The creative dishes, cooked to a consistently high standard, include the signature steamed eggs and spinach on toast, sprinkled with grated mullet roe.

Spurred on by the restaurant's success, Berton and squad then opened **Dry** (*see p83*), a gourmet pizzeria and cocktail bar, opposite Pisacco in 2013. Here, you can try cocktails such as a Gin Gin Mule (gin, mint and ginger beer) followed by pizza topped with pine nuts, raisins, ricotta and chicory. A few steps away, **Zazà Ramen** (*see p84*), owned by a Dutch chef and a Japanese entrepreneur, offers something completely different: Japanese noodles with unusual Italo-Japanese condiments, such as aubergine with miso. You'll need to book ahead at all three places.

Pisacco.

Dry.

Zazà Ramen.

City governor in the 19th century, Josef Radetzky was thoroughly despised in Milan for the fact that he stood between the Italians and their independence from Austria – so it's an odd name for a bar in this neck of the woods. No matter; this place has been here since 1988 and remains popular with fashion and advertising types. It gets extremely crowded of an evening, but is quiet enough to enjoy a leisurely breakfast most mornings.

Shops & Services

Amoeba

Via Marsala 11 (02 657 2810, www.joannalyle.com). Metro Moscova or bus 43, 94. **Open** 11am-7pm Tue-Sat. **Map** p75 E3 ㊳ **Homewares**

Run by British designer Joanna Lyle and Italian artisan Luca Gallotti, this small, colourful shop is a great place to pick up some memorable soft furnishings and souvenirs. Among the principal offerings featuring Lyle's intricate but classy designs are fabric table lamps with chunky wooden bases, and embroidered bags and cushions. They can quickly knock up pieces to your personal specifications, and will also organise delivery around the globe.

Cavalli e Nastri

Via Brera 2 (02 7200 0449, www.cavallienastri.com). Metro Moscova or tram 1, 3, 27. **Open** 3.30-7.30pm Mon; 10.30am-7.30pm Tue-Sat. **Map** p75 G3 ㊴ **Fashion**

Each piece stocked at this vintage clothes store is presented in mint condition and has been selected with a razor-sharp eye: this is the crème de la crème of second-hand chic. *Photo p88.*

Other locations via Giacomo Mora 3 & 12, South (02 8940 9452).

Centro Botanico

Piazza San Marco 1 (02 2901 3254, www.centrobotanico.it). Metro Moscova or bus 43, 61. **Open** 10am-7.45pm Mon-Sat; 3-7.30pm Sun. **Map** p75 G3 ㊵ **Health & beauty**

This centre for health and natural products stocks a wide range of organically grown produce, groceries and baked goods, along with vitamins, natural-fibre clothing and more. There's also a fresh juice bar and lunchtime café.

Other locations via Vincenzo Monti 32, West (02 463 807); via Cesare Correnti 10, West (02 7202 3525).

CALLING ALL FOODIES

Eataly offers gourmet gelato, perfect pasta and much, much more.

If you haven't heard of it yet, you soon will: **Eataly** (*see p87*) is one of the greatest Italian success stories of the past decade, a chain that brings artisanal food shops and eateries together under one roof. It all began in Turin in 2007 when visionary foodie Oscar Farinetti persuaded a group of high-quality producers to set up shop in a former vermouth factory. The group now has 11 emporia in Italy and a handful in cities elsewhere, including Dubai, Istanbul, New York and Tokyo. In spring 2014, the first stand-alone branch in Milan opened in the Teatro Smeraldo, a much-loved former theatre; Eataly already had smaller outposts within the Coin (*see p109*) and Brian & Barry (*see p66*) department stores.

Stand-out stalls include a booth where you can watch chefs preparing fresh pasta, plus branches of mozzarella-maker Miracolo a Milano (*see p129*) and Làit, the *gelato* specialist that uses milk from Bianca Piemontese cattle. There's also a cookery school. The top floor hosts gourmet restaurant **Alice** (02 4949 7340, www.aliceristorante.it), where lauded female chef Viviana Varese cooks up colourful fish dishes, and guests enjoy a spectacular rooftop view over central Milan.

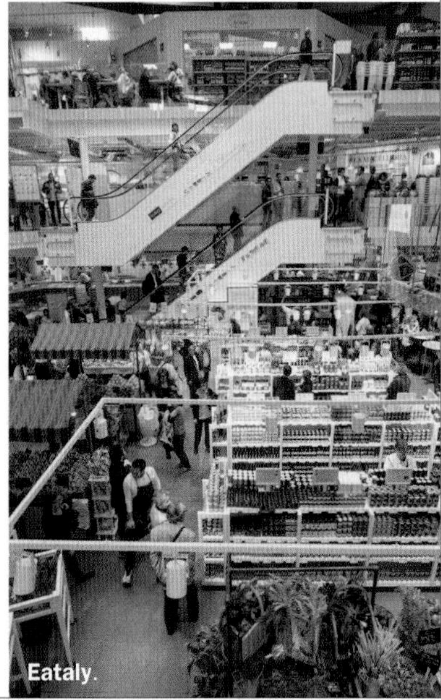

Eataly.

★ Eataly

Piazza XXV Aprile 10 (02 4949 7301, www.eataly.it). Metro Garibaldi, or bus 43, 94, or tram 4, 33. **Open** *Shop* 10am-midnight daily. *Eateries* noon-3pm, 7-11pm daily. **Map** p75 E3 ⓿ **Food & drink** *See p86* **Calling All Foodies**.

Enoteca Cotti

Via Solferino 42 (02 2900 1096, www.enotecacotti.it). Metro Moscova or bus 37, 94. **Open** 9am-1pm, 3-8pm Tue-Sat. **Map** p75 E3 ❹❷ **Food & drink**

The groaning shelves of Milan's oldest enoteca hold more than 1,000 wines plus grappas, whiskies, rums, cognacs and gourmet foodstuffs. Gift baskets are as ornate as their contents are delicious.

High-Tech

Piazza XXV Aprile 12 (02 624 1101, www.cargomilano.it). Metro Garibaldi, or bus 43, 94, or tram 4, 33. **Open** 1.30-7.30pm Mon; 10.30am-7.30pm Tue-Sun. **Map** p75 E3 ❹❸ **Homewares**

A labyrinth packed with everything for the design-conscious home, from kitchenware to office accessories and incense. Time evaporates as you wander from room to room – or simply try to locate the exit. Its offshoot, Cargo High-Tech, located in what was once an Ovaltine factory, sells cutting-edge design furniture, bathroom fixtures and fittings, and bedding. The discount corner offers bargains for the company's end-of-line products, from wardrobes to dishes. There's also a bar and restaurant.

Other locations Cargo High-Tech, via Meucci 39, East (02 272 2131); Coin, corso Vercelli 32, West (02 4399 0001).

Kristina Ti

Via Solferino 18 (02 653 379, www.kristinati.com). Metro Moscova or bus 43, 61. **Open** 3-7pm Mon; 10am-7pm Tue-Sat. **Map** p75 F3 ❹❹ **Fashion**

Kristina Ti began as a lingerie designer, but now has a super-feminine clothing line that's delicate, discreet and delightful. Worth checking out if you're looking for something very special.

Mediolanum

Via Volta 7 (02 657 2882, www.erboristeria mediolanum.it). Metro Moscova or bus 43, 57, 94. **Open** 3.30-7.30pm Mon; 9.30am-1pm, 3.30-7.30pm Tue-Sat. **Map** p75 E2 ❹❺ **Health & beauty**

Gabriella Fiumani presides over this intriguing shop, mixing tisanes, cosmetics and medicinal concoctions from more than 400 herbs stored in drawers and cupboards at the back. Other products include organic herbal cosmetics, as well as spices and seasonings – from myrrh granules to blue poppy seeds – displayed in huge glass jars.

★ N'Ombra de Vin

Via San Marco 2 (02 659 9650, www.nombradevin.it). Metro Moscova or bus 61, 94. **Open** 10am-2am Mon-Sat. **Map** p75 F3 ❹❻ **Food & drink**

Amoeba.

Owner and wine expert Cristian Corà can help you choose from among the 2,500-plus bottles in the atmospheric vaulted cellars of this 15th-century monastic refectory. A small wine bar at the entrance serves soups, cold cuts, cheese and pan-fried risotto (*riso al salto*), as well as wines by the glass. It's especially popular for *aperitivi*, with a sophisticated crowd of wine aficionados spilling into the street.

Raw

Via Palermo 1 (02 8494 7990, www.raw milano.it). Metro Moscova, or bus 43, 57, 61, 94, or tram 2, 12, 14. **Open** 3.30-7.30pm Mon; 10am-2pm, 3.30-7.30pm Tue-Sat. **Map** p75 F3 ❹❼ **Homewares**

Edginess and unusualness are the distinguishing features of Raw, which describes itself as a 'cabinet of curiosities'. Most of the objets have been hand-picked by interior designer Paolo Badesco and architect Constantino Affuso in markets in Paris, Amsterdam, Berlin and beyond, and include everything from ashtrays stamped with prints of insects to quirky notebooks. Prices run the gamut from affordable to the opposite.

Other location Corso Magenta 96, West (02 8494 7990).

IN THE KNOW SUMMER BREAK

Thinking of planning a shopping trip to Milan in August? In a word: don't. Most shops, as well as restaurants, clubs, bars and offices, take a two- to four-week break over the hottest month – and the shopping streets resemble a ghost town. So do as Milan's shop assistants do, and head elsewhere in August. There's plenty of time for shopping during the other 11 months of the year.

Cavalli e Nastri. *See p86.*

Le Solferine

Via Solferino 2 (02 655 5352, www.lesolferine.com). Metro Moscova or bus 43, 61. **Open** 11am-7.30pm Mon; 10am-7.30pm Tue-Sat; 11am-2pm, 3-7pm Sun. **Map** p75 F3 ㊽ Accessories

Boasting an outstanding selection of unusual designer women's footwear, including the owner's own Silvia Bertolaja range, Le Solferine is worth stepping inside, if only to check out the latest trends. Accessories, costume jewellery and a capsule collection of apparel are also sold.

★ 10 Corso Como

Corso Como 10 (02 2900 2674, www.10corsocomo.com). Metro Garibaldi or tram 2, 4, 33. **Open** 3.30-7.30pm Mon; 10.30am-7.30pm Tue, Fri-Sun; 10.30am-9pm Wed, Thur. **Map** p75 E3 ㊾ Concept store

Former *Vogue* editor Carla Sozzani's multifunctional emporium, which occupies an old *casa di ringhiera* (working-class apartment building), includes a fashion store for both men and women, a bookshop, an art gallery, a café/restaurant and a three-room B&B called, appropriately enough, 3Rooms (*see p249*). Prices are not for the faint-hearted, but this favourite with fashion folk and celebrities certainly oozes style. Visit if only to admire the highly original, whimsical decor by Sozzani's partner, Kris Ruhs. Shoppers on a budget, take note: the nearby outlet store sells the previous season's stock at reduced prices – *see p107* **Chic at Half the Price**.

Other location 10 Corso Como Outlet, via Tazzoli 3, North (02 2901 5130).

ISOLA

The *quartiere* of the Isola ('Island') may have been so named because it was on the 'wrong side of the tracks': to get there you had to cross the railway lines around Garibaldi station, which isolate it from the northern Brera and Garibaldi zones. Until recently, the only route was by crossing the via Farini bridge, close to Garibaldi, or a narrow flyover, but now a pedestrian walkway links the Isola to Porta Nuova, via piazza Gae Aulenti and the Unicredit tower.

During the 19th century, the Isola became the main housing area for workers at Garibaldi station, and the district still has numerous *case di ringhiera* (traditional low-cost housing blocks, which once had communal bathrooms and shared balconies). Subsequently, carpenters, blacksmiths, artists and the like started to move in, and the neighbourhood filled with the sound of industry.

More recently, boho residents, tired of the city-centre glitz and ever-rising property prices, have colonised the area: designers, architects and other young professionals have set up home and studios here, and it's become a hub for countercultural shopping and nightlife. This isn't really a neighbourhood where visitors come to sightsee; it's a place to hunt down indie designer fashions, go to the market, eat a pizza or perhaps take in some jazz at the Milan branch of the famous New York club, Blue Note. It's also great for exploring real-life Milan and soaking up the atmosphere.

There are a couple of sights worth noting, however. From piazza Segrino in the heart of the area, via Thaon di Revel leads to the cloistered church of **Santa Maria alla Fontana**, once thought to be designed by Leonardo da Vinci. On a more contemporary note, heading north from piazza Gae Aulenti, it's worth pausing in via Confalonieri to admire the **Bosco Verticale** ('Vertical Woodland'), designed by Milan-based Studio Boeri; the façades of these two residential skyscrapers are covered in luxuriant greenery, consisting of more than 1,000 trees and plants. The project was ongoing in 2014.

Further east, on the fringes of the district, is the recently erected **Palazzo Lombardia**, the headquarters of regional government, which rises up from piazza Città di Lombardia. The views from the 39th floor are among the most spectacular in the city.

Sights & Museums

FREE Palazzo Lombardia

Piazza Città di Lombardia 1, at via Restelli (02 67 651, www.regione.lombardia.it). Metro Gioia or bus 43. **Open** 10am-6pm Sun. **Admission** free. **Map** p74 C4 50

Built in 2010, the 161.3m (529ft) Palazzo Lombardia was – briefly – the tallest building in Milan. It was superseded in 2011 by the Unicredit building (*see p80*), but still adds a monumental new dimension in glinting glass and steel to this side of town. Designed by New York's Pei Cobb Freed & Partners, it's the Lombardy regional government's HQ. On Sundays, until the end of Expo 2015 (31 October 2015) – and possibly beyond, the main tower is open to visitors (no reservation necessary) who wish to view Milan and its surroundings from the 39th floor.

FREE Santa Maria alla Fontana

Piazza Santa Maria alla Fontana 11 (02 688 7059). Metro Garibaldi or Zara, or bus 60, 90, 91, or tram 4. Open *Church* 8am-noon, 3-7pm daily. *Sanctuary* 9am-noon, 3-5.30pm daily. **Admission** free. **Map** p74 B3 51

This attractive, cloistered church is essentially a modern structure in the neo-Renaissance style, with various additions. The presbytery, however, rests on a much older sanctuary, open for viewing. For many years, the spring here was considered a source of healing, and a plaque commemorates the fact that Charles d'Amboise, the French governor of Milan at the start of the 16th century, and Leonardo da Vinci's new patron, was miraculously cured here, and so had a church built on the spot in 1506. The design for the building was attributed to Leonardo da Vinci and Donato Bramante, but more rigorous scholarship has identified it as the work of Giovanni Antonio Amedeo.

Restaurants

L'Altra Isola

Via Porro 8 (02 6083 0205). Metro Maciachini or bus 82, 90, 91. **Meals served** 12.30-2pm, 7.30-10.30pm Mon-Fri; 7.30-10.30pm Sat. **Average** €45. **Map** p74 A2 52 **Traditional Milanese**

Just beyond the northern edge of the Isola district, this simple, homely restaurant serves some of the best Milanese cuisine in town. The place is run by local old-timer Gianni Borrelli, who has trained his Chinese chef to create the likes of *risotto al salto* – crunchy, refried risotto, a Lombard speciality. When the main rush is over, you might see Chinese and Italian staff playing cards around the table, adding to the general conviviality.

Il Bue e la Patata

Via Porro Lambertenghi 24 (02 3982 0524, www.ilbuelapatata.com). Metro Garibaldi, or bus 60, or tram 4, 7, 33. **Meals served** 12.30-2.30pm, 7.30-11pm daily. **Average** €40. **Map** p74 C3 53 **Steakhouse**

'Beef and potatoes' says the sign, and that's what you get – Italian-style, of course. Order your steak the way you prefer it – and don't underestimate what can be done with the spuds: try the hand-made potato crisps or the deep-fried potato skins. They also do pizza, if you're not into meat 'n' mash.

Vietnamonamour

Via Torquato Taramelli 67 (02 7063 4614, www.vietnamonamour.com). Metro Zara, or bus 60, or tram 7, 31, 33. **Meals served** 12.45-2.30pm, 7.30pm-midnight Tue-Sat; 7.30pm-midnight Sun. **Average** €35. **Map** p74 B4 54 **Vietnamese**

In a bright pink villa on the northern border of the Isola, Vietnamonamour delivers sophisticated variants on Vietnamese cuisine, in a colourful, ethno-chic space. Much appreciated by the creative crowd, dishes include delicate coconut curry and house-made mango or ginger cake; a lower-priced menu is offered at lunch. The Parisian-Vietnamese-Italian owners run a B&B (*see p251*) above the restaurant and a sister establishment (restaurant plus B&B) near piazza Piola, on the other side of town. **Other location** via Pestalozza 7, East (02 7063 4614).

Cafés, Bars & Gelaterie

★ Blue Note

Via Borsieri 37 (02 6901 6888, www.bluenotemilano.com). Metro Garibaldi, Isola or Zara, or bus 37, 60 or tram 4, 7, 31, 33. **Open** Sept-June 7.30pm-midnight Tue-Sun. *Brunch* Oct-Mar noon Sun (followed by afternoon concert). Closed June-Aug. **Map** p74 C3 55

This popular venue (opened 2003) is the only European outpost of New York's Blue Note jazz club. With over 250 performances a year by Italian and international musicians whose style can (sometimes loosely) be called jazz, it's one of the few places in Milan for this kind of music. See the website for the schedule, to book tickets or to make restaurant reservations.

► *For more on the club's music, see p170.*

Deus Ex Machina

Via Thaon di Revel 3 (02 8343 9230, www.deuscustoms.com). Metro Garibaldi or Zara, or bus 37, or tram 1, 4, 5, 9. **Open** 9.30am-1am Mon-Thur, Sun; 9.30am-2am Fri, Sat. **Map** p74 C3 56

'Wheels and waves' is the motto of this Australian bicycle, motorcycle and surfboard brand – though the waves have got a bit lost in landlocked Milan. But custom-made vehicles are prominently on display at this laid-back shop-cum-café, where bikers and non-bikers congregate for breakfast, lunch and happy hour.

Nordest Caffè

Via Borsieri 35 (02 6900 1910, www.nordestcaffe.it). Metro Garibaldi, Isola or Zara, or bus 37, 60,

or tram 4, 7, 31, 33. **Open** 8am-9pm Mon; 8am-11.30pm Tue-Sat; 8.30am-9pm Sun. **Map** p74 C3 57
This Isola hotspot is one of the longest-established in the area. It has a compact and stylish interior, plus a few pavement tables outside. Folk aged seven to 70 come here for cappuccino and brioche at breakfast or for Sunday brunch (€25); at *aperitivo* time (6-9pm; €7.50 per drink, including buffet), a more serious drinking crowd moves in. Outside summer, the busiest nights are Thursdays and Sundays, when the place thrums to the sounds of live jazz. Nordest is also a great place to get into the mood before heading to the Blue Note (*see p89*) jazz club next door.

Shops & Services

Mercato Isola

Via Garigliano, via Sebenico & via Volturno (no phone). Metro Garibaldi or Zara, or bus 43, 82, or tram 2, 7, 11. **Open** 8.30am-1pm Tue; 8.30am-5pm Sat. **Map** p74 C4 58 **Market**
If you like the bustle of street shopping, then head for this lively local market on Tuesdays or Saturdays. As well as the usual fruit and veg, there's clothing, footwear, hosiery and the occasional stall selling fabric offcuts. There are some real bargains, if you're prepared to rummage.

EXPLORE

Nir Lagziel

Via Jacopo dal Verme 12 (02 8645 4166, www.nirlagziel.com). Metro Garibaldi or bus 37, 60 or tram 4, 7, 33. **Open** 2.30-7.30pm Mon; 10am-7.30pm Tue-Sat. **Map** p74 C3 59 **Fashion**
Clothing with a conscience is the raison d'être at this colourful, intimate boutique, where each year Milan-based Israeli designer Nir Lagziel develops a line of T-shirts, the profits from which are used to buy much-needed items for orphanages in developing countries. Designs tend to be colourful, youthful and feminine, hovering between streetwear and flirty evening chic.

Rapa Design

Via Pastrengo 5A (02 2316 7868, www.rapadesign.com). Metro Garibaldi, or bus 37, or tram 4, 33. **Open** 3.30-7.30pm Mon; 10.30am-2.30pm, 3.30-7.30pm Tue-Fri; 11am-7pm Sat. **Map** p74 D3 60 **Fashion**
Extra-wide trousers in wild floral fabrics, and bright hooded tops are among the street-smart looks at this indie fashion shop, selling designs by Sara Rotta Loria and Paola Pezza. Loria also creates colourful children's clothes, which she sells in a designated section of the boutique.

STAZIONE CENTRALE & BICOCCA

To the east of Porta Garibaldi, on a site once occupied by the Pirelli tyre factory, rises the Grattacielo Pirelli, or **Pirellone** ('Big Pirelli'), as the locals call it. Erected between 1955 and 1960, this is an exemplar of post-war reconstruction, designed by a team of architects that included Gio Ponti, Pier Luigi Nervi and Arturo Danusso. The sides of the building are tapered, to breathtaking effect. More controversially, it was the first building in Milan to dare to rise higher than the golden Madonnina (Virgin Mary) statue on top of the Duomo; a mini replica of the Madonnina was soon placed upon the building's roof to defuse the situation. On 18 April 2002, the Pirelli building made headlines again when a light aircraft collided with it, killing the pilot as well as two people in the building.

Near the Pirellone is the massive bulk of Ulisse Stacchini's **Stazione Centrale**, begun in 1906, and completed under the Mussolini regime. The front is entirely covered in Aurisina stone from the Trieste area, while the roof is composed of five glass and iron vaults, the central one spanning the station's 24 platforms, with two others, of decreasing size, on either side.

The building and adjacent *piazze* have been renewed recently. New arrivals include a three-floor branch of **La Feltrinelli** (*see p54*) selling books, magazines, newspapers, snacks and music; and **Bistrot Milano Centrale** (02 6748 1995, entrance at platform level), an attractive faux-rustic eaterie specialising in local produce, such as panini that use naturally leavened bread made with Lombard flour.

The area around the station isn't the most salubrious, and is a haven for pickpockets and scammers. It's advisable to keep your wits and luggage about you, take only the official white taxis from the designated ranks, and ignore offers of help with suitcases or at the ticket machines.

That said, the neighbouring streets do contain some worthwhile eateries, such as **Osteria del Treno**, a representative of the Slow Food movement. And due south, the main artery, via Vittor Pisani, links piazza Duca d'Aosta, outside the station, to piazza Repubblica, home to the luxurious **Hotel Principe di Savoia** and **Westin Palace** (for both, *see p250*).

North of the station is the post-industrial district of Bicocca, home to the University of Milano-Bicocca, an offshoot of Milan's public university. Once home to the Pirelli industrial zone, it was redeveloped by Milan-based architect Vittorio Gregotti and opened in 1998. The main reason to visit this area, however, is the **Teatro degli Arcimboldi** (*see p172*), another Gregotti-designed edifice, which opened in 2002, and was used briefly by Teatro la Scala during its restoration work. These days, it hosts mostly orchestral and Italian pop concerts, and dance shows. Also in the Bicocca is the **Museo Interattivo del Cinema** (*see p156* **Movie Museums**), a cinema museum whose exhibits include magic lanterns and animation clips.

Stazione Centrale

Sights & Museums

Stazione Centrale

Piazza Duca d'Aosta 1 (02 6673 511, www.milanocentrale.it). Metro Centrale FS. **Map** p74 D6 61

Just as the Universal Exposition of 2015 has prompted major innovation in the city, so did the one held in 1906. On 29 April of that year, King Vittore Emanuele III laid the first stone for the new Milan Central Station (previously, the main station had been in what is now piazza Repubblica). Despite the king's contribution, construction took some time, not least because the railway company changed its mind several times. In 1912, Florentine architect Ulisse Stacchini won the public competition with his ambitious design, which took its cue from Union Station in Washington, DC. Work began, but World War I slowed progress, and it wasn't until 1925 that building started again. Spurred on by Mussolini's desire for a station that would reflect the might of his Fascist regime, the outcome was an exuberant combination of styles. Colossal golem-head fountains flank the imposing façade, which is 207m (679ft) long. Two magnificent winged horses – 8m (26ft) long from nose to tail – stand guard on either side of the entrance; these are the work of Armando Violi and represent 'progress, guided by determination and intelligence'. The entrance is also graced with the date 'Anno IX', meaning 1931, the ninth year of Mussolini's Fascist regime, which was when the station opened. Look out for the signs of the zodiac, embellished in low-relief, in the huge ticket hall.

The Central Station has played a central role in Milan's history: the marble, ebony and onyx in the royal waiting room are a reminder of Italy's pre-1948 days as a monarchy; platform 21, in 1944, was the departure point for a one-way journey – to Auschwitz.

The station has also been the scene of mass arrivals. From the mid 1950s to the mid '70s, workers moved from the south to find work in factories in Milan and throughout Lombardy. From the station, the new migrants fanned out to catch trams and buses to addresses written on scraps of paper, where a relative or friend waited to help them make their first moves in the 'big city'. More recently, it's been an arrival point for immigrants from north Africa and the Middle East, including an influx of refugees from Syria.

The station has been extensively refurbished to show off its handsome architectural detailing. Some complain that it now resembles a shopping mall, but many of the changes have simply brought it into the 21st century, making it a fitting home for the high-speed trains that now travel daily to and from Bologna, Florence, Rome, Naples and beyond.

Restaurants

★ Osteria del Treno

Via San Gregorio 46 (02 670 0479, www.osteriadeltreno.it). Metro Centrale, or bus 37, or tram 1, 4, 5, 9. **Meals served** *Sept-June* 12.30-2.30pm Mon-Fri; 8-10.30pm daily. *July, Aug* 12.30-2.30pm, 8-10.30pm Mon-Fri. **Average** €35. **Map** p75 E5 62 **Traditional Italian**

This superb eaterie is one of a select few in Milan linked to the Slow Food movement – which comes as no surprise to anyone who's eaten here. The ambience is just as you'd imagine the perfect *osteria* to be, with bottle-stacked walls and wooden tables draped in cloths. There's a buffet lunch on weekedays. In the evenings, the place becomes more formal, and the menu bristles with Slow Food-protected ingredients, and a fabulous selection of rare cheeses. Try to peek inside the adjacent Sala Liberty – a spacious art nouveau function room, where weddings and tango nights are held.

Tomoyoshi Endo

Via Vittor Pisani 13 or via Fabio Filzi 8 (02 6698 6117, www.tomoyoshi-endo.com). Metro Centrale or Repubblica, or tram 2, 9. **Meals served** noon-2.30pm, 7-10.30pm Mon-Sat. **Average** €50. **Map** p74 D5 63 **Japanese**

If you have a yen for Japanese food while in Milan, this is probably the place to start. Italy's oldest Japanese restaurant is tucked away on the ground floor of a nondescript office block. As well as the usual selection of sushi and sashimi, specialities include *tonno scottato* (pan-seared tuna, with crisp edges and a deep red centre) and *guancia di tonno* (tuna cheeks baked in a salt crust). Service can be offhand, but the food makes it a must-visit.

EXPLORE

San Babila & East

Judging by the high concentration of *palazzi*, the elegant zone around San Babila has long been the district of choice for the wealthy. A handful of these exquisite residences are now open to the public: among them are Milan's 1930s house-museum, the stylish Villa Necchi Campiglio; and Casa Museo Boschi-di Stefano, a relatively small apartment hung floor to ceiling with a phenomenal stash of modern art. These days, meanwhile, the area around Porta Venezia, flanking the verdant Giardini Pubblici Indro Montanelli, is the neighbourhood of choice for the creative crowd and the gay community. In the evening, bars, cafés and bakeries throng with young, hip professionals. Follow the roads east, and you'll come to Linate airport and the Idroscalo, a popular summer spot for clubbers and families. And to the north-east, corso Buenos Aires, the shopping strip, leads to Loreto, and on to the post-industrial zone of Lambrate, an emerging hub for food and design.

HClub (Diana Garden)

Don't Miss

1 Villa Necchi Campiglio Milan's chicest house-museum (p101).

2 HClub (Diana Garden) Cocktails amid the camellias (p104).

3 Joia Vegetarian food at its most gourmet (p98).

4 Via Malpighi Milan's finest examples of art nouveau (p102).

5 Jannelli & Volpi Wondrous wallpapers and souvenirs (p105).

PIAZZA CAVOUR TO GIARDINI PUBBLICI

A short stroll from the Quadrilatero d'Oro is **piazza Cavour**. The statue of the Conte di Cavour, the 19th-century statesman credited with bringing about the unification of Italy, is on the north-east corner of this busy square. Close by is the grey neoclassical **Palazzo dell'Informazione** (no.2), designed in 1942 as the headquarters for the Fascist newspaper *Il Popolo d'Italia*. Mussolini's daily only survived until July 1943, but thanks to its relative proximity to the most newsworthy area of the city (the finance capital of piazza Affari), the building was once the Milanese headquarters for many Italian and international news organisations, most of whom have moved elsewhere in recent years.

The **Giardini Pubblici** leading off piazza Cavour is the best place to relax with a book or newspaper. Cool and shaded in summer, it contains a couple of rambling museums, including the **Civico Museo di Storia Naturale** and the **Planetario Ulrico Hoepli**. Over in via Palestro is the opulent **Galleria d'Arte Moderna**, in the Villa Reale, once the home of Napoleon. The attached **PAC** gallery has some interesting contemporary art and photography exhibitions.

Sights & Museums

Civico Museo di Storia Naturale

Corso Venezia 55 (02 8846 3337, www.comune.milano.it/museostorianaturale). Metro Palestro or Turati, or bus 94, or tram 9. **Open** 9am-5.30pm Tue-Sun. **Admission** €5; free-€3 reductions. Free to all last hr of the day; Tue afternoon. **Map** p97 E3 ❶

Giovanni Ceruti's neoclassical building was put up in 1838 to house the natural history collections left to the city by aristocrat Giuseppe de Cristoforis. It's a decent rainy-day distraction: the displays cover botany, mineralogy, geology and palaeontology, with a life-size triceratops the highlight of the last department. At times, it feels like a museum of taxidermy, with diorama after diorama of jungle, prairie and arctic scenes populated with a stuffed cast. English explanations are scattered seemingly at random throughout the museum.

Civico Planetario Ulrico Hoepli

Corso Venezia 57 (02 8846 3340, www.comune.milano.it/planetario). Metro Palestro or Porta Venezia (passante), or tram 9. **Open** *Shows* 9pm Tue, Thur; 3pm, 4.30pm Sat, Sun. **Admission** €5; free-€3 reductions. Free to all last hr of the day; Tue afternoon. **Map** p97 E3 ❷

A gift to the city from publisher Ulrico Hoepli, the planetarium was built in 1930 by Pietro Portaluppi (who also designed Villa Necchi Campiglio – *see p101*) in faux-classical style. Projections take place in a great domed room, whose octagonal shape ensures all-round visibility. Explanations are in Italian.

Galleria d'Arte Moderna (GAM)

Villa Belgiojoso Bonaparte, via Palestro 16 (02 8844 5947, www.gam-milano.com). Metro Palestro or bus 61, 94. **Open** 9am-1pm, 2-5.30pm Tue-Sun. **Admission** €5; free-€3 reductions. Free to all last hr of the day; Tue afternoon. **Map** p97 E2 ❸

It's little wonder that Napoleon chose to live here in 1802, followed by the Austrian field marshal Count Joseph Radetzky. This recently restored neoclassical villa, formerly known as the Villa Reale, is one big conspicuous display of wealth. The English-style grounds, complete with pond and footpaths, simply add to the majesty. The building's marble columns were erected in 1790 by Austrian architect Leopold Pollack, who designed the mansion for Count Ludovico Barbiano di Belgiojoso. After unification, ownership passed to the Italian royal family, who gave it to the city of Milan in 1921. Today, it's the home to the Galleria d'Arte Moderna.

The collection is splendid. Made up of bequests from leading Milanese families, it occupies over 40 rooms in the central building, and the first and second floors of the west wing of this U-shaped complex. The ground floor is given over to 19th-century neoclassical paintings, sculpture and bas-reliefs, including works by Antonio Canova and Francesco Hayez. Spread across the ballroom and former living areas on the first floor are paintings from the Romantic period, among them several works by Giovanni Segantini, known for his brilliant use of light and shade. The second floor showcases the Grassi and Vismara collections, the latter including works by modern Italian and international masters such as Giorgio Morandi, Modigliani, Renoir, Matisse and Picasso.

FREE Giardini Pubblici Indro Montanelli

Metro Palestro, Porta Venezia, Repubblica or Turati, or bus 94, or tram 1, 9, 33. **Open** *Mar, Apr, Oct* 6.30am-9pm daily. *May* 6.30am-10pm daily. *June-Sept* 6.30am-11.30pm daily. *Nov-Feb* 6.30am-8pm daily. **Admission** free. **Map** p96 D2 ❹

As corso Venezia takes you away from the built-up areas of the city centre towards the built-up areas of the outskirts, you'll notice the green expanse of the recently renamed Giardini Pubblici Indro Montanelli on your left. The gardens were designed in the English style by La Scala architect Giuseppe Piermarini in 1786, and enlarged in 1857 to include the Villa Reale (now renamed Villa Belgiojoso Bonaparte – home to the Galleria d'Arte Moderna) and the Palazzo Dugnani. The park's present arrangement, complete with natural elements such as waterfalls and rocky outcrops, was the work of Emilio Alemagna in the 1890s. In addition to the galleries and museums on its outer edges, the park contains a small children's train, the Bar Bianco with outdoor tables (open 8am-8.30pm daily) and the popular Tropical Island kiosk (*see*

THE WISE MAN OF GIARDINI PUBBLICI

The park is named after famed giornalista *Indro Montanelli.*

In 2002, Milan City Council gave the public gardens around Porta Venezia a new name: **Giardini Pubblici Indro Montanelli** (*see p94*). But who was Montanelli? And why does he have a public park named after him?

A clue comes from a bronze sculpture by Italian artist Vito Tongiani at the park's entrance in via Palestro. It depicts a thin, balding man, sitting on a stack of newspapers as he hammers away on a Lettera 22 typewriter (an iconic model by Olivetti). Below, a label reads: 'Indro Montanelli, journalist'. But Montanelli was more than a simple journalist. He was a living legend, a figure whose intellect and experience hovered over the nation's public life for decades.

His career began in the early 1930s. Initially a supporter of Mussolini, he returned to Italy after the disastrous Abyssinian campaign with radically altered opinions. The public devoured his articles, which were highly critical of the Axis during the Spanish Civil War and the invasions of Norway, Poland, Estonia and Lithuania. In 1943, he joined a partisan resistance group, but was arrested and sentenced to death.

He managed to escape and made a dash for Switzerland, where he stayed until the end of the war, writing for the *Corriere della Sera*, the most prestigious Italian daily paper. He defined himself as an 'anarcoconservative', and his reporting during the Soviet occupation of Hungary was instrumental in de-romanticising the USSR in post-war Italy.

A champion of journalistic integrity, he left the *Corriere* when it took a swing towards radical chic in 1973. Montanelli then founded a successful new daily, *Il Giornale*, aimed at the liberal-conservative middle classes. In 1977, as he walked along via Manin past the Giardini Pubblici (close to the spot where his statue now presides), members of the Red Brigades, a communist terrorist group, shot him in the legs. Having been sentenced to death by fascists for being anti-fascist, he was now shot at by communists for being anti-communist.

That year, *Il Giornale* was bought by a young Silvio Berlusconi, who agreed that Montanelli could control the paper's editorial line. However, once '*il Cavaliere*' entered the political arena and imposed his views, Montanelli quit and founded *La Voce*. But that soon folded, and he spent the last eight years of his life as letters editor for the *Corriere*. It's said that he gauged public opinion by talking to old-timers on the benches of the Giardini Pubblici – where he would stop for a few minutes every day on his way to work.

Montanelli died on 22 July 2001, and was promptly celebrated as Italy's greatest journalist. The next day, the *Corriere* published a full front-page letter of farewell to his readers. The visitors who paid their respects at his wake found no coffin; only a folded copy of the *Corriere* on a chair.

EXPLORE

EXPLORE

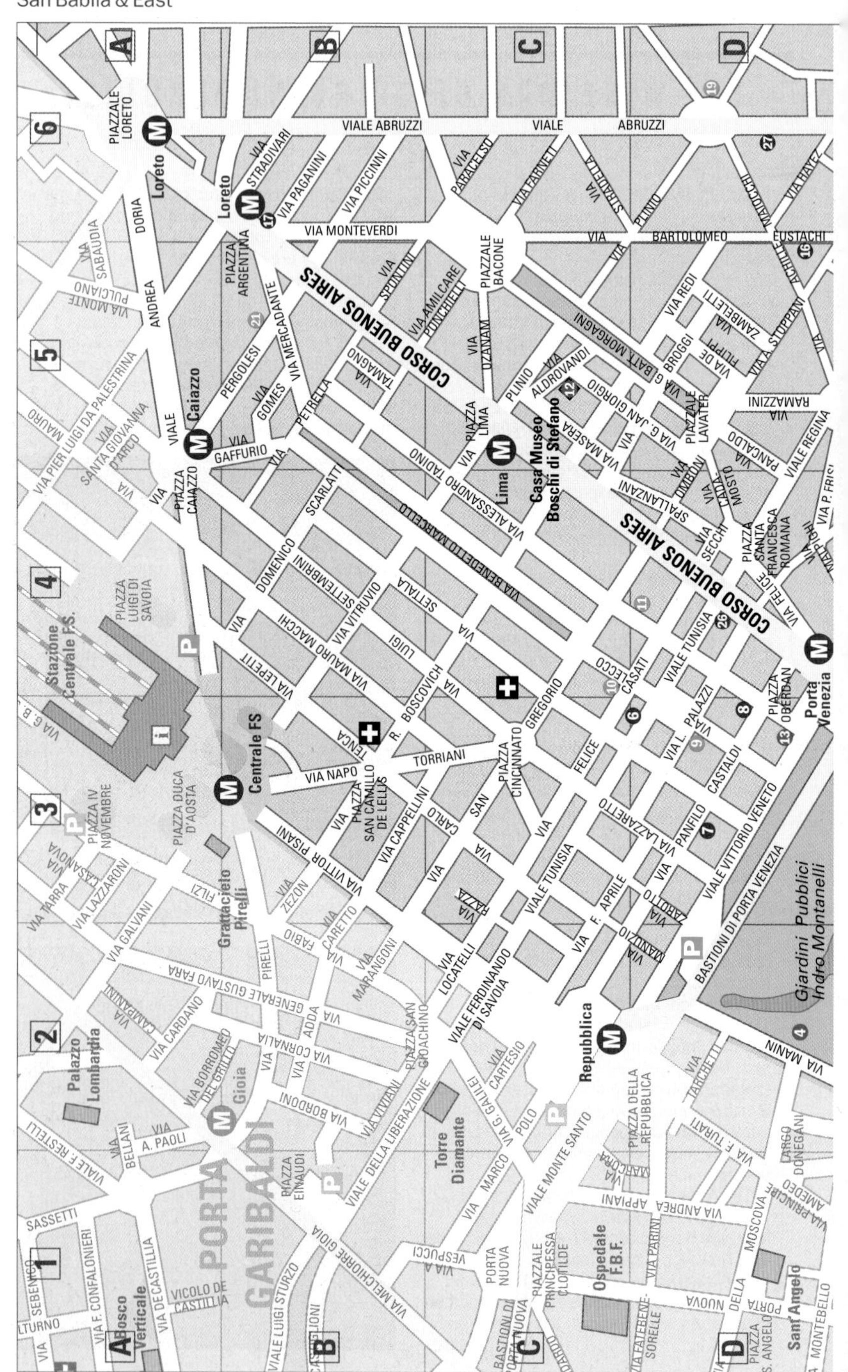
Piazzale Loreto
Loreto
Viale Abruzzi
Via Stradivari
Via Paganini
Via Piccinni
Via Paracelso
Via Farneti
Via Stradella
Via Plinio
Via Morgagni
Via Hayez
Via Monteverdi
Via Bartolomeo Eustachi
Piazza Argentina
Corso Buenos Aires
Via Spontini
Via Amilcare Ponchielli
Piazzale Bacone
Via Ozanam
Via Redi
Via Zambeletti
Via Broggi
Via G. Batt. Morgagni
Via Aldrovandi
Via Pergolesi
Via Mercadante
Via Gomes
Via Petrella
Via Tamagno
Piazza Lima
Lima
Casa Museo Boschi di Stefano
Via Jan
Via Giorgio
Piazzale Lavater
Via Ramazzini
Via Pancaldo
Viale Regina
Caiazzo
Piazza Caiazzo
Via Gaffurio
Via Scarlatti
Via Alessandro Tadino
Via Benedetto Marcello
Via Spallanzani
Via Settembrini
Via Vitruvio
Via Settala
Via Lecco
Via Casati
Viale Tunisia
Piazza Santa Francesca Romana
Via Felice
Porta Venezia
Piazza Oberdan
Piazza Luigi di Savoia
Stazione Centrale F.S.
Centrale FS
Via Lepetit
Via Mauro Macchi
Via Luigi
Via Boscovich
Via Napo Torriani
Piazza San Camillo De Lellis
Via Cappellini
Piazza Cincinnato
Via Gregorio
Via Lazzaretto
Via Panfilo Castaldi
Viale Vittorio Veneto
Piazza Duca d'Aosta
Piazza IV Novembre
Grattacielo Pirelli
Via Vittor Pisani
Via Carlo
Via San
Via Fabio Filzi
Via Lazzaroni
Via Galvani
Via Tarra
Via Casanova
Via Zezon
Via Caretto
Via Pirelli
Via Marangoni
Via Locatelli
Viale Ferdinando di Savoia
Via F. Aprile
Via Manunzio
Bastioni di Porta Venezia
Giardini Pubblici Indro Montanelli
Via Manin
Repubblica
Piazza della Repubblica
Via Tarchetti
Via F. Turati
Largo Donegani
Via Gustavo Fara
Via Generale
Via Cardano
Via Campanini
Palazzo Lombardia
Via Borromei del Grillo
Gioia
Via Cornalia
Via Adda
Piazza San Gioachino
Via Bordoni
Via Viviani
Viale della Liberazione
Torre Diamante
Via G. Galilei
Via Cartesio
Via Polo
Via Marco
Viale Monte Santo
Via Andrea Appiani
Via Principe Amedeo
Via A. Paoli
Via Bellani
Viale F. Restelli
Porta Garibaldi
Piazza Einaudi
Via Melchiorre Gioia
Via Vespucci
Porta Nuova
Piazzale Principessa Clotilde
Ospedale F.B.F.
Via Parini
Via Moscova
Sant'Angelo
Via Sassetti
Via F. Confalonieri
Via de Castillia
Vicolo de Castillia
Via Luigi Sturzo
Bosco Verticale
Via Fatebenesorelle
Piazza S. Angelo
Via Montebello

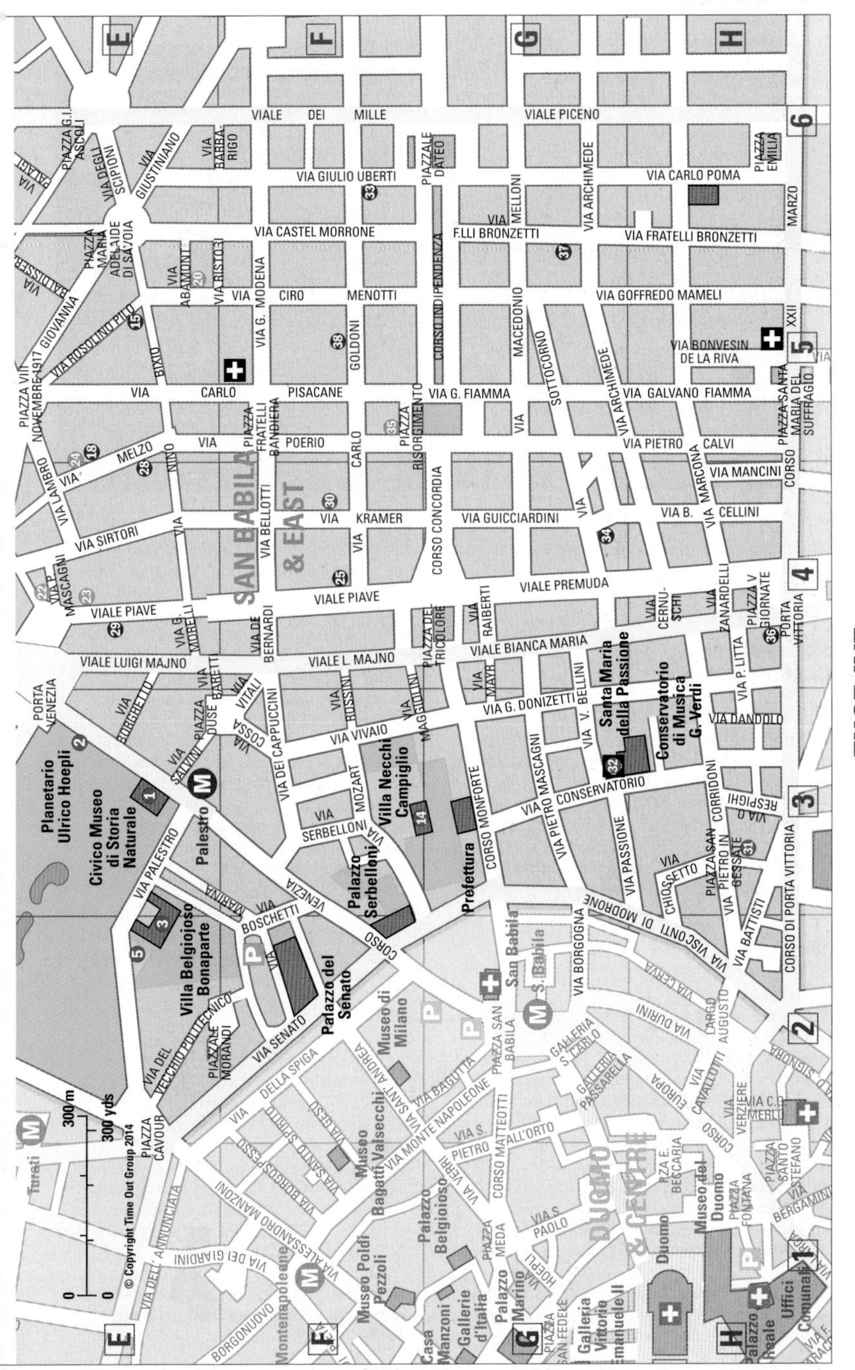

San Babila & East
Planetario Ulrico Hoepli
Civico Museo di Storia Naturale
Villa Belgiojoso Bonaparte
Palazzo del Senato
Palazzo Serbelloni
Villa Necchi Campiglio
Prefettura
Santa Maria della Passione
Conservatorio di Musica G. Verdi
San Babila
Palestro
Museo di Milano
Museo Bagatti Valsecchi
Museo Poldi Pezzoli
Palazzo Belgioioso
Casa Manzoni
Gallerie d'Italia
Palazzo Marino
Galleria Vittorio Emanuele II
Duomo
Museo del Duomo
Palazzo Reale
Uffici Comunali
Duomo & Centre
Montenapoleone
Turati
Viale dei Mille
Viale Piceno
Via Giulio Uberti
Via Castel Morrone
Via Ciro Menotti
Via Carlo Pisacane
Via G. Fiamma
Via Galvano Fiamma
Via Carlo Poma
Via Fratelli Bronzetti
Via Goffredo Mameli
Via Bonvesin de la Riva
Via Pietro Calvi
Via Mancini
Via Poerio
Via Kramer
Via Guicciardini
Via B. Cellini
Viale Premuda
Viale Piave
Viale L. Majno
Viale Luigi Majno
Viale Bianca Maria
Via G. Donizetti
Via Vivaio
Via Conservatorio
Corso Monforte
Corso Concordia
Corso Indipendenza
Corso Venezia
Corso di Porta Vittoria
Via Borgogna
Via Visconti di Modrone
Via Dandolo
Via Palestro
Via Senato
Via della Spiga
Via Monte Napoleone
Via Sant'Andrea
Via Alessandro Manzoni
Via dei Giardini
Corso Matteotti
Corso Europa
Piazza San Babila
Piazza Cavour
Piazza Fontana
Piazza Santo Stefano
Piazza V Giornate
Piazza Risorgimento
Piazzale Dateo
Porta Venezia
Porta Vittoria
0 300m
0 300 yds
© Copyright Time Out Group 2014

EXPLORE

Delicatessen.

p159 Ciringay), an oasis of cool for the hip crowd in the summer. There are also more dogs than you could throw a stick at.

► *For more on Indro Montanelli, see p95 The Wise Man of Giardini Pubblici.*

PAC (Padiglione d'Arte Contemporanea)

Via Palestro 14 (02 8844 6359, www.pacmilano.it). Metro Palestro or Turati, or bus 61, 94, or tram 1. **Open** 9.30am-7.30pm Tue, Wed, Fri-Sun; 9.30am-10.30pm Thur. **Admission** €8; €4-€6.50 reductions; free under-6s. **Map** p97 E2 ❺

The PAC organises exhibitions of international contemporary art and photography, and generally features a wide range of well-established artists. It was designed in the 1950s by Ignazio Gardella (1905-99), who rebuilt it after it was nearly destroyed by a deadly Mafia bomb in 1993.

Restaurants

★ Delicatessen

Viale Tunisia 14 (02 2952 9555, www.delicatessen.eu). Metro Repubblica, Porta Venezia or Porta Venezia (passante), or tram 1, 5, 33. **Meals served** noon-2.45pm, 7-11pm daily. **Average** €45 dinner. **Map** p96 D3 ❻ **Traditional Alto-Adige**

This oak-clad restaurant brings a taste of the mountains to Milan. Specialising in dishes from the Alpine region of Alto-Adige, its cosy interior features deer antlers and a ceiling made from real hay, yet miraculously manages to stay on the right side of kitsch. Whet your appetite with a glass of Hugo – a refreshing mix of prosecco, elderflower cordial and mint – then follow with rib-warming dishes such as *canederli* (giant dumplings with cheese and speck) and *kaiserschmarrn*, a sweet omelette with raisins, topped with apple mousse and cranberry jam.

★ Joia

Via Panfilo Castaldi 18 (02 2952 2124, www.joia.it). Metro Repubblica, Porta Venezia or Porta Venezia (passante), or tram 1, 9, 33. **Meals served** *Restaurant* 12.20-2.30pm, 7.30-11pm Mon-Fri; 7.30-11pm Sat. *Joia Kitchen* 7.30-11pm Mon-Fri. **Average** *Restaurant* €80. *Joia Kitchen* €40. **Map** p96 D3 ❼ **Vegetarian**

This calm, minimalist but wood-warm space near the Giardini Pubblici is the domain of Swiss chef Pietro Leemann, whose often inspired and always creative cooking has earned him a Michelin star – a rare achievement for a vegetarian restaurant. Half the fun is finding out what lies behind the names of the dishes, such as 'Serendipity in the garden of my dreams' and 'Every day is spring'. The tasting menus include a €75 *scoperta* ('discovery') menu and an €85 *enfasi della natura* ('natural emphases') menu, a whimsical array of the chef's finest creations; or you can eat à la carte. The bistro-like Joia Kitchen, an informal space close to the kitchen, is more affordable.

Lucca

Via Panfilo Castaldi 33 (02 2952 6668, www.ristorantelucca.it). Metro Repubblica, Porta Venezia or Porta Venezia (passante), or tram 1, 9, 33. **Meals served** 12.30-2.30pm, 7-11.30pm Mon-Fri; 7-11.30pm Sat. **Average** €40. **Map** p96 D3 ❽ **Tuscan**

A Tuscan gem, here since 1922, with traditional trattoria decor, chilled-out tunes and friendly staff. The menu oscillates between traditional and borderline experimental, with the occasional vegan dish tossed in; the risotto with red radicchio leaves and Chianti is refreshingly different; the focaccia with white or wholemeal Kamut flour is made in-house. Watch the chefs at work in the glass-fronted kitchen next to the smokers' room at the rear.

Cafés, Bars & Gelaterie

Frank

Via Lecco 1 (02 2953 2587). Metro Repubblica, Porta Venezia or Porta Venezia (passante), or tram 1, 9, 33. **Open** 7am-2am Mon-Sat; 6pm-2am Sun. **Map** p96 D3 ⑨

A clubby outpost with tons of outdoor seating, and a kitchen that stays open all day. It's a seafood specialist: oysters, amberjack carpaccio with almonds, and king crab feature on the light lunchtime menu.

Mint Garden Café

Via Felice Casati 12 (02 8341 7806, www.mintgardencafe.it). Metro Lima, Repubblica, Porta Venezia or Porta Venezia (passante), or tram 5, 9, 33. **Open** 8am-11pm Mon; 8am-midnight Tue; 8am-1am Wed, Thur; 8am-1.30am Fri; 8.30am-1.30am Sat; 8.30am-midnight Sun. **Map** p96 C4 ⑩

Doubling as a florist's shop, this green and airy bar is popular with the thirtysomething *aperitivo* crowd, who come here to sip prosecco amid the cacti, orchids and cut flowers (for sale). During the day, try the sumptuous chocolate cake.

★ Pandenus

Via Tadino 12 (02 2952 8018, www.pandenus.it). Metro Lima or tram 9. **Open** 7am-10.30pm daily. **Map** p96 D4 ⑪

This recently opened bakery-cum-bar chain has become something of a phenomenon among *aperitivo*-goers in Milan. The lavish buffet in via Tadino (the original outpost) is usually packed with after-work revellers fighting over the courgette *frittate*, house-baked *foccace* with melted cheese and tomatoes, and colourful sticks of raw veg. An added bonus: those who've forgotten to nip to the supermarket can snap up a loaf of Pandenus's freshly baked bread.

Other locations Corso Concordia 11, West (02 9176 0875); Largo La Foppa 2, North (02 6556 0824); Via Melzi d'Eril 3, North (02 3361 1071).

PIAZZA SAN BABILA TO PORTA VENEZIA

Shooting straight out of **piazza San Babila**, the elegant corso Venezia leads north-east to Porta Venezia. The street is notable for a string of classy noble residences, including the late 15th-century **Casa Fontana Silvestri** (no.10) on the right. It's one of the few remaining examples of a Renaissance residence in the city; the terracotta decoration on the façade is typically Lombard. Across the street, at no.11, is the **Seminario Arcivescovile**, commissioned by Carlo Borromeo in 1564 to implement the Council of Trent's regulations concerning the education of the clergy. The monumental doorway, decorated with

CLOSE TO THE VEG

Once a rarity, vegan and vegetarian cuisine is now on the menu.

Not so very long ago, vegetarian restaurants were almost impossible to find in Milan. Were you to say the word 'vegan', most natives would have looked blank – but over the past few years, that's begun to change.

Joia (*see p98*), a temple to veggie haute cuisine in the streets behind the Giardini Pubblici, was previously one of few exceptions to the meaty norm. A more recent addition is nearby **Radice Tonda** (via Spallanzani 16, 02 3673 7924, www.radicetonda.it), which specialises in organic vegan dishes including lasagne, salads with creamy vegan mayo, and spectacular chocolate cake.

In the northern Isola area, **Capra e Cavoli** (via Pastrengo 8, 02 8706 6093, www.capraecavolimilano.it) serves a 'quasi-vegetarian' buffet or à la carte menu, in a light-infused, plant-filled conservatory. Amid the abundant platters of couscous, steaming pasta and home-made cakes without egg, milk or butter, you may find occasional dishes featuring shrimp or chicken – so watch out.

Erba Brusca

Non-specialist eateries, too, have woken up and smelt the scent of vegetables in recent years. Back near the Giardini Pubblici, Tuscan trattoria **Lucca** (*see p98*) now has a couple of vegan dishes on the menu, while, in the Porta Romana area, **Cascina Cuccagna** (*see p119*) whips up a generous selection of mostly organic veggie platters, and canalside **Erba Brusca** (*see p126*) has delicious dishes inspired by its very own veg patch. **Juice Bar** (02 885 2458, www.juicebar.it), located on the seventh floor of department store La Rinascente (*see p54*), serves vegetarian salads, sandwiches, smoothies and other fast foods.

allegorical representations of Hope and Charity, was added in 1652.

The neoclassical **Palazzo Serbelloni** (no.16), at the intersection with via San Damiano, was finished in 1793; Napoleon and Josephine stayed here in 1796, Metternich in 1838 and Vittorio Emanuele II and Napoleon III in 1859. It now hosts conferences and fashion events, and can be visited by appointment (02 7600 7687). Across the road is via Senato, which leads to **Palazzo del Senato** (built 1608-30). The palace has housed the state archives since 1872, but was used as government offices under Austro-Hungarian Emperor Joseph II and, later, Napoleon. The courtyards were designed by Fabio Mangone and the concave façade by Francesco Maria Richini. The aforementioned via San Damiano in turn leads to the **Villa Necchi Campiglio** museum, managed by the FAI, Italy's equivalent of the National Trust. It's a little piece of the 1930s, preserved inside and out.

Back on corso Venezia, **Palazzo Rocca Saporiti** (no.40) was built to a plan by La Scala's stage designer Giovanni Perego in 1812; its imposing Ionic columns and cornice surmounted by statues of gods make it a perfect example of neo-Palladian architectural precepts. The façade is decorated with a frieze displaying scenes from the history of Milan. At no.47 is Giuseppe Sommaruga's art nouveau **Palazzo Castiglioni** (1900-03), once known to the Milanese as the Ca' di Ciapp (House of Buttocks), because of the two provocative, semi-nude female statues formerly positioned on the façade.

Corso Venezia ends in **piazza Oberdan**, where deafening, lung-testing traffic screams across Porta Venezia. Originally known as Porta Orientale, this was one of the eight main entrances in the 16th-century Spanish fortifications. It was the first to be redesigned by Giuseppe Piermarini (architect of La Scala) in 1782. In 1828, Piermarini's original neoclassical gate, which he left unfinished, was replaced by the two triumphal arches still standing today; bas-reliefs of Milanese history decorate the two buildings. The one on the left is the **Casa del Pane**, which is used for occasional art and design exhibitions. Run by the Milan bakers' association, the buildings also house a new permanent display of bread-related utensils and machinery (opening in autumn 2014) and a 6,000-volume bread-themed library (02 775 0322; open 2.30-5.30pm Mon, Wed, Thur). To the north-west of the piazza is **Spazio Oberdan**, a minimalist exhibition space and cinema.

ART BEAT

Tracking down contemporary art in eastern Milan.

Increasingly the zone of choice for Milan's arty crowd, the Porta Venezia area is home to some of the most exciting commercial contemporary art galleries in town.

A five-minute walk from the Porta Venezia metro station, **Giò Marconi** (via Tadino 15, 02 2940 4373, www.giomarconi.com) specialises in avant-garde pieces by European and international artists, often with a political, economic or scientific theme. The white and yellow space hosts exhibitions on everything from Chinese medicine to factory lunch breaks, in all manner of media from paintings and sculptures to video installations and photo-montages.

Giò Marconi.

Five minutes from Marconi, across the busy corso Buenos Aires, **Studio Guenzani** (via Eustachi 10, 02 2940 9251, www.studio guenzani.it) represents leading lights from the home-grown art scene, including influential Milan-based artist Stefano Arienti, and Como-born abstract photographer Luisa Lambri. Also on the books are international hotshots such as Cindy Sherman and Hiroshi Sugimoto, both of whom have exhibited here.

From here, it's ten minutes by tram (no.23) to **Galleria ZERO...** (viale Premuda 46, 02 8723 4577, www.galleriazero.it), which opened here in 2014. Founder Paolo Zani is an authority on contemporary art in Europe; works are an eclectic mix of paintings, drawings, videos and installations, and might include anything from modern takes on stained-glass windows to provocative prints of washing machines.

For more contemporary art addresses, in northern Milan, *see p78* **Arty Facts**.

Villa Necchi Campiglio.

Continuing north-east from Porta Venezia, corso Buenos Aires extends all the way to **piazzale Loreto**. The historically minded visitor might be tempted to visit this square, as it's where Mussolini and his lover Clara Petacci were publicly displayed, hanged by their feet, after their execution in 1945; but gory memories aside, it's a basically a traffic hub. Along the way, the highly commercial corso Buenos Aires contains a mix of high-street chain stores and the occasional survivor of a more genteel age, such as olde-worlde hat shop **Cappelleria Mutinelli**. Art admirers will find a visit to the small but interesting **Casa Museo Boschi-di Stefano** is well worth the slight detour. From Loreto, it's two metro stops east to **Lambrate**, a frontier zone that is becoming increasingly fashionable (*see p108* **On the Edge**).

Sights & Museums

★ FREE Casa Museo Boschi-di Stefano

2nd floor, Via Giorgio Jan 15 (02 2024 0568, www.fondazioneboschidistefano.it). Metro Lima, or bus 60, 81, or tram 1, 5, 33. **Open** 10am-6pm Tue-Sun. **Admission** free. **Map** p96 C5 ⑫

Husband and wife Antonio Boschi and Marieda di Stefano took their modern art collection seriously: they once sold their car to buy more paintings, and even hid part of their collection behind a false wall in their country home during World War II. So it's no surprise that they left their life's work to the people of Milan. Opened in 2003, the museum contains 300 pieces of 20th-century art dating up to the end of the 1960s, hung floor to ceiling in 11 crammed rooms (including the bathroom). Works include serene landscapes and flowers by Giorgio Morandi and the nightmarish *Dream of Anne Boleyn II* and *Battle of the Insects* by 1950s artists Roberto Crippa and Cesare Peverelli, respectively.

Spazio Oberdan

Viale Vittorio Veneto 2 (02 7740 6316, http://oberdan.cinetecamilano.it). Metro Repubblica, Porta Venezia or Porta Venezia (passante), or tram 1, 5, 9, 33. **Open & admission** varies. **Map** p96 D3 ⑬

This outpost of Cineteca di Milano designed by Gae Aulenti and Carlo Lamperti hosts sporadic art and design shows. Its in-house movie theatre, Cineteca di Milano (*see p154*), shows golden oldies, Italian classics and foreign films.

★ Villa Necchi Campiglio

Via Mozart 14 (house 02 7634 0121, cafeteria 02 7602 0873, www.fondoambiente.it). Metro Palestro or bus 54, 61, 94. **Open** *House* 10am-6pm Wed-Sun. *Cafeteria* 10am-6pm daily. **Admission** €9; €4 reductions. *Tours* For tours in English, book one day ahead. **Map** p97 G3 ⑭

Built between 1932 and 1935 to a design by rationalist architect Piero Portaluppi, Villa Necchi Campiglio was the dream home of sisters Nedda and Gigina Necchi, the daughters of a wealthy Lombard industrialist whose fortune came from cast iron and sewing machines. Gigina's husband, Angelo Campiglio, lived with them until his death in 1984. The state-of-the-art facilities included an intercom system, a tennis court and a heated swimming pool (now home to a popular outdoor/indoor garden café) – while the interiors set the standard for stylish 1930s Milanese taste. The family's circle included members of the Spanish and Savoy royal families.

The Small.

The Necchi-Campiglio's idyll was interrupted by World War II, when the mansion became HQ for the Fascists and the family were forced to move to the countryside. On their return, they engaged architect Tomaso Buzzi to add some reassuring, less rational, touches, including wood panelling, marble fireplaces and antique furniture. Gigina, who died in 2001, donated the property to the Fondo per l'Ambiente Italiano (FAI), Italy's equivalent of the National Trust. After a €6 million renovation, it reopened to the public a few years back.

IN THE KNOW
ART NOUVEAU STREET

Wedged between the Sheraton Diana Majestic hotel on viale Piave and the bustling corso Buenos Aires, the very short **via Malpighi** is one of Milan's best-kept secrets. Its sumptuously decorated *palazzi* are the best examples of art nouveau in Milan. Treasures include the Casa Guazzoni (no.12, 1904-05) with its ornate wrought-iron balconies held up by plaster cherubs, and Casa Galimberti (no.3), whose façade features cement flowers, more wrought-iron railings and gleaming ceramic tiles depicting Klimt-like women, trees and plants. Both were designed by Giovan Battista Bossi.

At the end of the street, on the corner of via Frisi, the low-rise former Cinema Dumont (1910) by architects Tettamanzi and Mainetti is now the Biblioteca Venezia, a public library. Once used as a garage, part of the building was demolished in the 1980s. The surviving arched portal is festooned with abundant fruit and flowers, and has a massive head sitting on the rooftop, its downcast eyes scrutinising all who enter.

The obligatory tours take in the conservatory with its huge windows overlooking the tree-filled garden, entrance hall with a 1930s walnut staircase, kitchens, gaming room and library. Upstairs, the sisters' wardrobes still brim with pieces from Chanel and Dior, and an array of hats; framed family photos grace the tables. The house is also home to an important collection of art, including works by Canaletto, Sironi, Martini and Magritte – some donated to the FAI by other collectors over the years. In 2009, the house became a movie set, when *I Am Love* – starring Tilda Swinton – was filmed in its picture-perfect interior, bringing its glamorous past briefly back to life.

Restaurants

Da Giannino L'Angolo d'Abruzzo

Via Rosolino Pilo 20 (02 2940 6526, www.dagianninolangolodabruzzo.it). Metro Porta Venezia or Porta Venezia (passante), or tram 5, 23, 33. **Meals served** noon-2.30pm, 7.30-11pm daily. **Average** €30. **Map** p97 E5 ⓯
Traditional Italian

Barely changed since 1963, this restaurant, as its name suggests, is a typical Abruzzese diner: hot, busy and redolent of grilled meat. Dishes from the central Italian region are thrown down on the checked red tablecloths with abandon. The *grigliata mista* (mixed grill) is a popular choice: a platter of lamb, *arrosticini* (kebabs), scamorza cheese, sausages and *lonza* (pressed pork). Meals start with grilled bruschetta, and may finish with a homemade *digestivo*.

Poporoya Shiro

Via Eustachi 17 (02 2940 6797, www.poporoyamilano.com). Metro Lima, Porta Venezia or Porta Venezia (passante), or bus 60, or tram 5, 23, 33. **Meals served** 6-9.30pm Mon; 11.30am-2pm, 6-9.30pm Tue-Sat. **Average** €20. **Map** p96 D5 ⓰
Japanese

This sushi bar is set in the back of a minuscule Japanese supermarket. Check out the menu as you queue among the seaweed and soy sauce – you'll need to place your initial order before you sit down. You'll be squeezed in at one of nine tables, or at the bar. No reservations are taken. The owners also run a slightly more formal restaurant, Shiro, just down the street at no.20.

★ The Small

Via Paganini, at piazza Argentina (02 2024 0943, www.thesmall.it). Metro Lima or Loreto, or bus 39, 55, 56, 90, 92. **Meals served** 11.30am-3.30pm, 6.30pm-1am Mon-Sat. **Average** €35. **Map** p96 B6
⑰ **Contemporary Sicilian**
Managed by Alessandro Lo Piccolo and his partner Giancarlo Petriglia – a former designer for Trussardi and the creative director for PQuadro – this bizarre bistro-cum-bazaar is a one-of-a-kind experience. Cluttered with 18th-century mirrors, French dishes, crystal bottles, Limoges forks and Herman Miller chairs, the eaterie doubles as a showroom: every item is for sale. Dishes are mostly creative twists on Italian classics, such as the luscious aubergine-based caponata from Lo Piccolo's native Sicily. Regulars reckon they serve the very best burrata (a creamy version of mozzarella, with organic tomatoes, basil, mint and olives) in Milan.

Warsa

Via Melzo 16 (02 201 673, www.ristorantewarsa.it). Metro Porta Venezia or Porta Venezia

IN THE SWIM

Fancy a dip? Then dive in!

Milan's first purpose-built outdoor swimming pool was **Piscina Argelati**, built in 1962 and located in the Navigli district. These days, it's ringed by unattractive tower blocks but the three pools (including one for kids only) are lively and spacious. Also outdoors is **Piscina Romano** (1929), the work of Luigi Secchi. It's located near Città Studi, one of Milan's university zones, so is popular with students. Both are unheated and open only in summer.

Piscina Cozzi is the most central of Milan's public indoor pools. Again the work of Secchi, it was built in 1934 with a grandiose Fascist exterior and a Soviet-style interior. It's Olympic-sized, but often crowded. Opening hours are extended during the summer.

When going swimming, remember your bathing cap, as well as flip-flops or similar footwear – you won't be allowed in without them. A padlock for the lockers is also a good idea. For details of all the pools, see www.milanosport.it.

Piscina Argelati
Via Segantini 6, South (02 5810 0012). Bus 47, or tram 2. **Open** *Early June-mid Aug* 10am-7pm daily. *Mid Aug-early Sept* 10am-7pm Mon, Wed-Sun. **Rates** €5 Mon-Fri; €5.50 Sat, Sun. **No credit cards**. **Map** p282 B9.

Piscina Cozzi
Viale Tunisia 35, at via Antonio Zarotto, Porta Garibaldi (02 659 9703). Metro Porta Venezia or Repubblica, or tram 1, 5, 9, 33. **Open** 7am-3pm, 6.30-10.30pm Mon; 7am-3pm, 9-11pm Tue, Thur; 7am-3pm, 6-9pm Wed; 7am-3pm, 9-10.30pm Fri; 11am-7pm Sat; 10am-7pm Sun. **Rates** €4 Mon-Fri; €5.50 Sat, Sun. **Map** p96 C3.

Piscina Romano
Via Ampère 20, South (02 7060 0224). Metro Piola, or bus 9, 62, 90, 91, or tram 11, 23, 33. **Open** *Early June-mid Aug* 10am-7pm daily. *Mid Aug-early Sept* 10am-7pm Mon, Tue, Thur-Sun. **Rates** €5 Mon-Fri; €5.50 Sat, Sun; €40 11 sessions. **No credit cards**. **Map** p145 B2.

Piscina Cozzi.

(passante), or tram 23. **Meals served** noon-3pm, 7-11.30pm Mon, Tue, Thur-Sun. **Average** €25. **Map** p97 E5 ⓲ **Eritrean**
Thanks to Italy's colonial history, Eritrean cooking was one of the first ethnic cuisines to establish itself in Milan, with many such restaurants opening in the Porta Venezia area, home to much of Milan's large African community. Warsa is a tad more sophisticated than the norm, with a safari-chic interior and a menu of seafood and meat platters, plus plenty of vegetarian options – all eaten with your fingers. Don't forget to try the *miès*, an aromatic wine made from fermented honey.

Cafés, Bars & Gelaterie

Bar Basso

Via Plinio 39 (02 2940 0580, www.barbasso.com). Metro Lima or Piola, or bus 60, 81. **Open** 9am-1.15am Mon, Wed-Sun. **Map** p96 D6 ⓳
Mirko Stocchetto, Bar Basso's owner since 1967, is credited with introducing luxury hotel-lounge cocktails to bars in Milan. Stocchetto and his son Maurizio still enjoy coming up with interesting concoctions. The menu lists more than 500 drinks; the house special is the negroni sbagliato ('bungled'), made with prosecco instead of gin.

★ La Belle Aurore

Via Abamonti 1, at via Castel Morrone (mobile 349 633 7809). Bus 60, 62, 92, or tram 5, 23, 33. **Open** 11.30am-4pm, 6pm-2am Mon-Sat. **Map** p97 E5 ⓴
This Parisian-style joint has been a favourite haunt of local writers and artists for over 25 years. Students and intellectuals come to sip coffee, order one of chef Adele's splendid soups, read the newspapers or add to their oeuvre. A gem of a bar.

La Bottega del Gelato

Via Giovan Battista Pergolesi 3 (02 2940 0076, www.labottegadelgelato.it). Metro Caiazzo or Loreto, or bus 91, 92, 93. **Open** 10am-10pm Mon, Tue, Thur-Sun. No credit cards. **Map** p96 B5 ㉑
With ice-cream shops in Milan having gone corporate, thanks to Grom and others, it's worth remembering the traditional one-off, family-run gelateria of yesteryear: slightly scruffy but serving some of the city's tastiest ice-cream. The 48 rotating flavours include pink grapefruit, avocado, creamy pine nut and cape gooseberry.

Ca'puccino

Via Malpighi 1 (02 2953 3923, www.ca-puccino.com). Metro Porta Venezia or Porta Venezia (passante), or bus 54, 61, or tram 9, 23. **Open** 8am-8pm daily. **Map** p97 E4 ㉒
Opened in 2013, this chic coffee house is the 11th in an Italian chain, which has spread across Italy and into the UK. Inside, studded cream leather armchairs, metal tables and bookshelves create an intellectual, though not intimidating, atmosphere. For breakfast, choose from various types of brioche or indulge in *pasticcini* from Piedmont. The coffee specials resemble desserts, and include a super-sweet *caffè* flavoured with tiramisu.

★ HClub (Diana Garden)

Sheraton Diana Majestic, viale Piave 42 (02 2058 2081, www.sheraton.com/dianamajestic). Metro Porta Venezia or Porta Venezia (passante), or bus 54, 61, or tram 9, 23. **Open** 7am-1am daily. **Map** p97 E4 ㉓
The Sheraton Diana Majestic hotel (*see p251*) is something of a hotspot for Milan's fashion elite, who come here to sip aperitifs in the stylish lounge bar and verdant garden, which features magnolia, wisteria, plane trees and a statue of Diana the Huntress by a leafy pool. Cocktails cost upwards of €10, but the generous accompanying nibbles include such delights as robiola cheese and courgette 'sushi', and mozzarella and tomato tartare.

Lelephant

Via Melzo 22 (02 2951 8768). Metro Porta Venezia or Porta Venezia (passante), or tram 9, 23. **Open** 6.30pm-2am Tue, Sun; 6.30pm-3am Wed-Sat. **Map** p97 E5 ㉔
Although first and foremost a gay and lesbian bar (*see p160*), this establishment caters to all. The scruffy chairs and peeling paint are worn as a badge of maturity and longevity. Cocktail prices drop to cheap and cheerful during happy hour (6.30-9.30pm).

Shops & Services

L'Altro Vino

Viale Piave 9 (02 780 147). Metro Porta Venezia or Porta Venezia (passante), or bus 54, 61, or tram 9, 23. **Open** 11.30am-7.45pm Tue-Sat. **Map** p97 F4 ㉕ **Food & drink**
Thanks to the knowledgeable and approachable proprietors, you can wander around this well-stocked wine shop without feeling intimidated. It has a vast selection of Italian and international vintages, and holds regular tastings on the first and third Thursdays of the month.

★ Cappelleria Mutinelli

Corso Buenos Aires 5 (02 869 3314, www.mutinellicappelli.com). Metro Porta Venezia or Porta Venezia (passante), or tram 5, 9, 33. **Open** 3-7.30pm Mon; 10am-1pm, 3-7.30pm Tue-Sat. **Map** p96 D4 ㉖ **Accessories**
It's hard to believe that anything more than five years old has survived on brash corso Buenos Aires, where run-of-the-mill high-street chains are the order of the day. But stepping into Cappelleria Mutinelli is like climbing into a time machine. The chequerboard marble floor, polished wood fittings and shelves stacked with hats transport you back at least a century, to an era when personal service was the order of the day. Perhaps that's why this place is

EXPLORE

always packed with customers of all ages, trying on everything from felt trilbies and tweed deerstalkers to knitted skiing caps.

Hammam della Rosa

Viale Abruzzi 15 (02 2941 1653, www.hammam dellarosa.com). Metro Lima or Piola, or bus 92, or tram 5, 23, 33. **Open** varies. **Rates** €40-€180, plus €10 1yr membership. **Map** p96 D6 ㉗ **Health & beauty**

At these upmarket Turkish baths, you follow a circuit of varying temperatures, rooms and plunge pools. Start off by relaxing in the warm, mosaic-panelled tepidarium, before hitting the moist 45°C heat of the caldarium. Stretch out on a bed to be vigorously scrubbed from head to toe. After a dip in the frigidarium, you'll be plied with sweets, tea and an (optional) ten-minute massage. Heaven? Awfully close. Opening times – for women only, men only and couples – varies; call for details. Reservations are required.

★ Jannelli & Volpi

Via Melzo 7 (02 205 231, www.jannellievolpi.it). Metro Porta Venezia or Porta Venezia (passante), or tram 9, 23. **Open** 10am-7pm Mon-Sat. **Map** p97 E4 ㉘ **Homewares**

For anyone interested in home interiors, this spacious three-floor store is a rare treat. Founded in 1952, family-run Jannelli & Volpi is best known for its graphic, witty wallpapers (it still has two factories in Milan), but the shop also stocks a whole range of goodies from other producers – many with a similar, colourfully patterned style. Look out for flower-powered clothes by Marimekko, Spanish folding fans made from J&V's own wallpapers, and notebooks with graphic covers by Milan's top architects and designers – all of which make excellent souvenirs.

Piave 37

Viale Piave 37 (02 2951 1408). Metro Porta Venezia or Porta Venezia (passante), or bus 54, 61 or tram 9, 23. **Open** 3.30-7.30pm Mon; 10am-2pm, 3.30-7.30pm Tue-Sat. **Map** p97 E4 ㉙ **Fashion**

This bright pink shop opposite the Sheraton Diana Majestic hotel is where Milan-based fashion designers Domenico Dolce and Stefano Gabbana promote upcoming Italian and international designers who they feel worthy of an extra boost. Stock changes regularly, but outré outfits might include girly frocks by Christian Pellizzari, fruit-printed T-shirts by Nhivuru, or Sicilian fabric hats. Prices are mostly in the €90-€500 range.

CORSO MONFORTE & SOUTH

Corso Monforte connects piazza San Babila to bustling **piazza del Tricolore**, a block away from the **Museo dei Beni Culturali Cappuccini**, a religious art museum. From corso Monforte, via Conservatorio leads south to the **Porta Vittoria** zone. Just past the political science department of the Università di Milano, located in the late baroque **Palazzo Resta-Pallavicino** (no.7), is a little piazza whose south-east corner is framed by **Santa Maria della Passione**, Milan's second largest church, famed for its twin organs. Directly opposite is via della Passione, opened up in 1540 to create an unobstructed view of the church and allow access to the canals that once ran through the area.

Continue south on via del Conservatorio past the **Conservatorio di Musica Giuseppe Verdi** (a former monastery) to corso di Porta Vittoria. Once on this thoroughfare, head west to reach the church of **San Pietro in Gessate**, or east for **piazza V Giornate**, with its 1895

EXPLORE

HClub (Diana Garden).

IN THE KNOW
ANTIQUES SHOPPING

Though the antiques trade is hardly booming in these tricky economic times, **via Pisacane** (metro Porta Venezia) and the surrounding streets have long been home to more than 30 antiques shops. Spend an afternoon hopping between high-end art specialists and junk shops, and you'll find everything from exquisite examples of 17th-century furniture to quaint timepieces and vintage hats. For a complete list of shops in the neighbourhood, see www.milanomia.com/aapisacane/pisacane-eng.htm.

monument by Giuseppe Grandi in honour of five days in March 1848, when the Milanese ended 33 years of Austrian rule.

Crossing corso di Porta Vittoria brings you to a heavy, travertine-clad building, the **Palazzo di Giustizia** (law courts). This monstrous monument to justice was built between 1932 and 1940 by Marcello Piacentini in the Fascist style as a replacement for the old Palazzo dei Tribunali in piazza Beccaria. It has well over 1,000 rooms, and covers a vast area. Hopefully, you won't have any reason to see the building's interior (though its enormous atrium, decorated with mosaics, would be worth a look), but a long walk around the outside will give you an idea of its colossal proportions. The Tribunale was the centre of the original Tangentopoli ('Bribesville') scandal back in the 1990s; more recently, it's been the scene of some of Silvio Berlusconi's trials. Just to the west, at corso di Porta Vittoria 6, one of the city's biggest libraries is housed in the splendid 17th-century **Palazzo Sormani**.

Eight kilometres (five miles) east of corso di Porta Vittoria is **Linate airport** (*see p255*). The **Idroscalo** (*see p152*), Milan's artificial lake, popular with clubbers and families, is just beyond the airport on the same road. Milan's most famous discount shopping outlet, **Il Salvagente**, and **Wow!**, the new cartoon and animation museum, are also worth a visit.

Sights & Museums

FREE Museo dei Beni Culturali Cappuccini

Via Antonio Kramer 5 (02 7712 2580, www.museodeicappuccini.it). Metro Palestro or Porta Venezia, or bus 54, 61, or tram 9, 23. **Open** 10am-6.30pm Tue; 1.30-6pm Wed-Sat. **Admission** free. **Map** p97 F4 30

A collection of religious artworks from the Cappuccini order of monks. Talks on iconography, religious art and other subjects take place regularly.

FREE San Pietro in Gessate

Piazza San Pietro in Gessate, at corso di Porta Vittoria (02 5410 7424). Bus 60, 73, 77, 84 or tram 12, 23, 27. **Open** 7.30am-6pm Mon-Fri; 8am-noon, 5-6.30pm Sat; 10.30-11.30am, 5.30-6.45pm Sun. **Admission** free. **Map** p97 H3 31

Commissioned by Florentine banker Pigello Portinari, this church was built between 1447 and 1475 to a design by Pietro Antonio and Guiniforte Solari. In 1862, frescoes were discovered under a layer of plaster. In the 16th and 17th centuries, even art was affected by plague paranoia: these frescoes had been covered with lime-based plaster in order to disinfect them. The church's eight-stall choir is a reconstruction based on what was left of the one built in 1640 by Carlo Garavagli: the orginal was used as firewood during World War II. The façade was put up in 1912 by Diego Brioschi, but the 17th-century entrance has been preserved.

FREE Santa Maria della Passione

Via Conservatorio 14 (02 7602 1370). Metro San Babila, or bus 54, 61, or tram 9, 23. **Open** 7.45am-noon, 3.30-6pm Mon-Fri; 9.30am-12.30pm, 3.30-6.30pm Sat, Sun. **Admission** free. **Map** p97 H3 32

Construction here began in 1486, to a design by Giovanni Battagio. It was originally a Greek-cross church, but one arm was lengthened to form a nave and six semicircular side chapels were added in 1573, making it the second-largest church in Milan after the Duomo. The barrel vault has frescoes by Giuseppe Galbesio da Brescia (1583) of the Evangelists, St Ambrose, St Augustine, angels and allegories of the virtues. More intriguing are the paintings lower down in the church's three-aisled interior, a veritable gallery of works by many of the leading 16th- and 17th-century Lombard artists, including Crespi, Procaccini and Bramantino; Crespi's masterpiece *San Carlo Borromeo Fasting* is perhaps the most impressive. The church has two magnificent 16th- to 17th-century organs, on which double concerts are often played.

Wow! Museo del Fumetto

Viale Campania 12 (02 4952 4744, www.museowow.it). Porta Vittoria (passante), or bus 73, 90, 91, 93, or tram 27. **Open** 3-7pm Tue-Fri; 3-8pm Sat, Sun. **Admission** *Ground floor* free. *Exhibitions* usually €5; €3 reductions.

Opened in 2011, Wow! is dedicated to the art of Italian and international cartoon making, with exhibits covering everything from illustrated comic strips to film animations. Themes vary: past shows have focused on local publishers and the World Cup. There's also a library with 9,000 books, a café, and a shop selling comic books, T-shirts and other memorabilia.

Restaurants

13 Giugno

Via Goldoni 44 (02 719 654, www.ristorante13giugno.it). Bus 54, 61, X73, or tram 9, 23.

EXPLORE

Meals served noon-2pm, 7.30-11pm daily. **Average** €65. **Map** p97 F6 33 **Seafood**
This Sicilian seafood specialist feels like a gentlemen's club. Past the golden doorbell and leather chesterfields lies an extremely elegant dining room, with background music provided by a pianist. Sicilian specials include pillowy ravioli stuffed with sheep's milk ricotta and plump red shrimp; the *gran misto alla griglia* (platter of grilled lobster, tuna, scallops and squid) is pricey but sublime.
► *The restaurant recently opened a cheaper bistro at the same address, with a separate entrance, and a plant-filled winter garden.*

Da Giacomo

Via P Sottocorno 6 (02 7602 4305, www.giacomo milano.com). Tram 9, 23. **Meals served** 12.30-2.30pm, 7.30pm-midnight daily. **Average** €60. **Map** p97 G4 34 **Mediterranean**
It looks unremarkable on the outside: an anonymous trattoria in an anonymous street. But this is one of Milan's most exclusive (though by no means most expensive) restaurants. In a series of mint-green rooms decorated by the late Renzo Mongiardino, major players from Milan's fashion and business worlds jostle for elbow room. The competent Mediterranean cuisine, with the emphasis on fish, might not win any prizes. But this is just what the city's movers and shakers want: colour and comfort food, while rubbing shoulders with the great and good.
► *Other outlets include Giacomo Arengario (see p51) and Giacomo Caffè (see p51), both near the Duomo.*

Cafés, Bars & Gelaterie

Gold

Piazza Risorgimento (02 757 7771, www.dolce gabbana.com/gold). Bus 54, 61, X73, or tram 9, 23. **Open** 8am-1am Mon-Wed; 8am-2am Thur-Sat. **Map** p97 F5 35
Dolce & Gabbana's flamboyant Gold café, bistro and restaurant lives up to its name with a vengeance. Mirrored and metallic surfaces dominate the whole place – take a trip to the loos if you've ever

CHIC AT HALF THE PRICE

Discounted designer fashions in and out of town.

When in Milan, do as many of the chicest Milanese do – and seek out cut-price designer looks at the city's many discount stores. These treasure troves are packed full of end-of-season shop and warehouse returns, stock from boutiques that have closed down, and some factory seconds. There's one drawback: even at discounts of 50-70 per cent, the price tags can still provoke the occasional 'Ouch!' Also, bear in mind that refunds are pretty much unheard of, so try before you buy.

Among Milan's best-known and longest-established outlets is **Il Salvagente** ('the lifesaver'; *see p109*), which has three floors of top stuff for men and women, all carefully arranged by size and colour, with discounts of up to 60 per cent off most of the top brands. A short bus ride away, **Salvagente Bimbi** (*see p109*) deals in discounted clothing for children, though it's no longer connected to the main store.

Equally worthwhile bargains can be found at more convenient, centrally located discount shops – such as **Dmagazine Outlet** (*see p67*). Be prepared to dig deep to find pricey women's lines for as little as 20 per cent of their original cost (men – look elsewhere). A third branch opened recently in the Navigli zone.

Vogue readers on a budget should visit the **10 Corso Como Outlet** (*see p88*), a slightly shabbier version of the super-cool original store (*see p88*) with endless racks of mostly black clothes by Helmut Lang, Chloé, Comme des Garçons et al. But even with prices slashed by half, it's still expensive.

Many hotels have flyers for the big out-of-town outlets, which are popular with visitors to Milan. These have many more discounted brand shops under one roof: one example is the 250-store **Fox Town** (+41 (0)848 828 888, www.foxtown.ch) in Mendrisio, just across the Swiss border from Lago di Como, though local fashionistas swear by **Serravalle Designer Outlet** (0143 600 000, www.mcarthurglen.com), equidistant from Milan, Turin and Genoa. See the website for details of a daily shuttle bus.

ON THE EDGE

Welcome to the vibrant, upcoming neighbourhood of Lambrate.

Upcycle.

Until a few years ago, the outlying north-eastern district of Lambrate was an area most Milanese only ever ventured into because they had to: perhaps to visit the Istituto Nazione dei Tumori, a cancer hospital, or the Politecnico, the architecture, design and engineering university. But then a Dutch design group fell in love with the wide streets and abandoned factories in the ex-industrial area east of Lambrate station, and set up a series of temporary exhibitions during the 2010 Milan Furniture Fair. By 2014, the event – in the streets around **via Ventura** (www.venturaprojects.com) – attracted 80,000 visitors, making it the focus of fringe-y new design in Milan. But the area is also home to an innovative mix of B&Bs, bars and restaurants, providing an antidote to the fashion-centric slickness of much of Milan.

Galleria Massimo De Carlo (via Ventura 5, 02 7000 3987, www.massimodecarlo.com) 39 is a dazzling white space presenting global contemporary art from the likes of Maurizio Cattelan (*see p61* **In the Know**) and Yan Pei-Ming. Professional kitchenware emporium **Medagliani** (via Privata Oslavia 17, 02 4548 5571, www.medagliani.com) 40, is where top chefs come to pick up everything from sauce sieves to copper pans.

To the west of Lambrate station, the long-established **Birrificio Lambrate** (via Adelchi 5, 02 7060 6746, www.birrificio lambrate.com) 41 is a microbrewery with attached pub; try the appropriately named Lambrate, a strong German-style beer. Newcomer **Upcycle** (via Ampère 59, 02 8342 8268, www.upcyclecafe.it) 42 is a bike café in a former garage. Customers order beers or house-made cakes in the Scandi-style café while watching cycling events such as the annual Giro d'Italia on a communal TV, or attend bicycle repair workshops.

If you're in need of sustenance, **Al'Less** (viale Lombardia 28, 02 7063 5097, www.alless.it) 43 serves traditional Milanese and Piedmontese dishes, such as boiled meats or horsemeat stew with polenta, in a former greenhouse that's decorated in a studiously old-fashioned style. The restaurant also sells herbs and other plants, and there are vintage magazines and books to browse or buy. Slightly to the north, award-winning Slow Food restaurant **Trattoria Mirta** (piazza San Materno 12, 02 9118 0496, www.trattoria mirta.it) 44 serves innovative, regularly changing dishes by Uruguayan chef Juan, in a friendly and unpretentious atmosphere.

Finally, if you'd like to stay in the neighbourhood, check out **RossoSegnale** B&B (*see p251*). In keeping with the zone's arty vibe, it doubles as an art gallery.

wondered what gold-plated bamboo looks like. Breakfast (excellent tea, coffee and surprisingly good *pasticcini*) is astonishingly low-key: you may find models mingling with local ladies clutching plastic shopping bags. Things get decidedly more upbeat in the evening, when a glamorous crowd swoops in. The gold theme even creeps into the menu; be sure to leave room for the chocolate bar wrapped in edible gold leaf.

Shops & Services

Coin

Piazza V Giornate 1A (02 5519 2083, www.coin.it). Bus 60, 73, or tram 9, 12, 23, 27. **Open** 10am-8pm Mon-Fri, Sun; 10am-8.30pm Sat. **Map** p97 H4 ㊱ **Department store**

This eight-storey department store caters to the refined Milanese taste for reasonable quality, good value, classic clothing and accessories for men, women and children, with most of the big-name brands represented. It also has a food hall (run by artisan food promoters Eataly – *see p86*), cosmetics and shoes. Globe restaurant, serving Italian cuisine, is on the panoramic top floor, should you start to flag.

Other locations corso Vercelli 30-32, West (02 4399 0001); piazza Cantore 12, West (02 5810 4385); viale Monza 1, East (02 2611 6131); via Panicale 7, North (02 3300 2316).

Il Salvagente

Via Fratelli Bronzetti 16 (02 7611 0328, www.salvagentemilano.it). Metro Dateo (passante), or bus 54, 60, 61, 62, 73, 92, or tram 12, 27. **Open** 3-7pm Mon; 10am-7pm Tue-Sat. **Map** p97 G5 ㊲ **Fashion**

See p107 **Chic at Half the Price**.

Il Salvagente Bimbi

Via Balzaretti 15 (02 2668 0764, www.salvagentebimbi.com). Metro Piola or bus 62, 90, 91 or tram 23, 33. **Open** 3-7pm Mon; 10am-7pm Tue-Sat. **Children**

See p107 **Chic at Half the Price**.

Other location via Arona 4, North (02 8905 4321).

Stephan Janson

Via Goldoni 21 (02 752 6171, www.stephanjanson.com). Bus 54, 61, X73, or tram 9, 23. **Open** 10am-6.30pm Mon-Fri. **Map** p97 F5 ㊳ **Fashion**

A French designer based in Milan for over 20 years, Janson sells his flowing day and evening dresses, shirts, coats and trousers at this out-of-the-way shop in a 19th-century palazzo draped with an antique butterfly collection. If you're looking to bring back a memorable piece of Milanese fashion, it's worth the hike. Prices from €600 to €1,300.

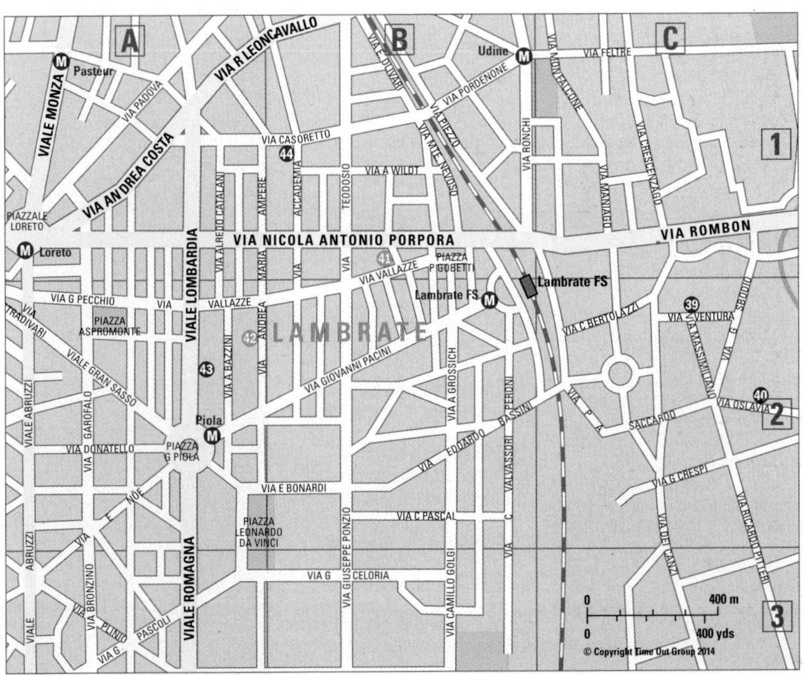

Porta Romana & the Navigli

In recent years, the 16th-century gateway of Porta Romana has become the hub of a vibrant district known for its design studios,fashion houses, trendy bars and restaurants.

A short tram ride to the west, the Navigli (canals) area is known for a more boho brand of fashion and design. The canal network's centre was once the Darsena (port), currently undergoing a major revamp, scheduled for completion by spring 2015.

North of the Darsena, the bohemian shopping thoroughfare known as corso di Porta Ticinese leads to the Colonne di San Lorenzo, a row of ancient Roman columns in a piazza; its neighbouring hotchpotch of bars is a favourite hangout of the young. South of the port, the two main canals are lined with alternative one-off shops, restaurants, bars and a clutch of new hotels. At night, the illuminated, orange-flecked waterways are among the most memorable scenes in all of Milan.

Torre Velasca.

Don't Miss

1 Museo delle Culture New museum by starchitect David Chipperfield (p126).

2 Torre Velasca Milan's ugliest edifice (p112)?

3 Miracolo a Milano Miraculous mozzarella made in front of you (p129).

4 Nonostante Marras Stunning Sardinian concept store (p129).

5 Al Pont de Ferr Michelin-starred meals on the waterfront (p126).

Ca' Granda. *See p116.*

PIAZZA FONTANA TO PORTA ROMANA

Just south-east of the Duomo, **Piazza Fontana** initially appears to be notable only for its small fountain – an unusual sight in Milan – decked out with hanging foliage and two kneeling nymphs. Behind it, you'll see the **Palazzo del Capitano di Giustizia**, the headquarters of the Milan judiciary between 1578 and the early 19th century. On the west side of the square is the **Palazzo Arcivescovile** (no.2). This archbishop's palace dates from 1170, when a previous structure was rebuilt after Barbarossa sacked the city. Much of what we see today, though, including the rectory courtyard, was the work of Pellegrino Tibaldi from 1565 onwards.

Since 12 December 1969, the piazza has been most closely associated with a terrorist blast that killed 17 people; a plaque on the Banca Nazionale dell'Agricoltura commemorates the bomb that went off inside. On the Palazzo del Capitano's lawn opposite the bank, two smaller plaques recall 'Giuseppe Pinelli, anarchist railwayman. An innocent man tragically killed at police headquarters, 16.12.1969.' Pinelli was reported by local police to have jumped from a window while being questioned about the bombing, thus confirming his guilt. Several commissions of enquiry have cast this claim into serious doubt. Most people now believe that he was already dead and was thrown out. The event was dramatised by Nobel prize-winning author, and local boy, Dario Fo in his 1970 play *Accidental Death of an Anarchist*.

Across via Larga, in piazza Santo Stefano you'll find the church of **San Bernardino alle Ossa**. The church itself, dedicated to St Bernard of Siena, is not particularly special, but the attraction lies in the *ossa*, or bones. The bones in question came from corpses disinterred from the nearby hospital cemetery, which didn't have enough space to keep every dead body in the ground in perpetuity. An ossuary was built in 1210 to store these remains. In 1269, the church was added. In 1679, the edifice was restored by Giovanni Andrea Biffi, who decorated the walls of the ossuary using the very human skulls and tibiae that had previously been stored there. Arranged in geometric patterns all the way up the walls, to a height of about four metres, the bones soon became a major attraction.

Piazza Santo Stefano leads into via Festa del Perdono, where the university zone begins. Indeed, you can't miss what is now the magnificent arts faculty of the Università degli Studi di Milano, which was originally built in the late 15th century as the **Ca' Granda** ('Big House') in order to bring the city's 30-plus minor hospitals under one roof.

Cross the gardens between largo Richini and via Festa del Perdono, and take a sharp right into via Sant'Antonio. Halfway down, the church of Sant'Antonio Abate is worth a quick look. Built between the 14th and 18th centuries, it has a cloistered courtyard and several interesting paintings, including works by Camillo and Giulio Cesare Procaccini and Marazzone (Pier Francesco Mazzucchelli), plus a St Cajetan by Cerano (Giovan Battista Crespi).

Returning to via Larga, you can't help but notice the 106-metre (345-foot) **Torre Velasca** (*see below* **In the Know**) looming over central Milan. The skyscraper's top-heavy structure was the architects' response to the need for more office space than the ground area allowed, although many believe the unusual structure recalls the

IN THE KNOW LOVE IT OR LOATHE IT

The jury is out on whether **Torre Velasca** (*see above*) is Milan's ugliest or most iconic modern building. Many architects love it; many visitors hate it. The *Daily Telegraph* recently dubbed it one of the '30 ugliest buildings' in the world. The 26-storey skyscraper has a protruding, cantilevered upper section, which some find ungainly. It's reminiscent of a medieval tower – although the building's architects, Studio BBPR, claimed this wasn't their main influence.

forms of medieval towers. Opened in 1958, the building takes its name from the square on which it stands, which was named after Juan Fernandez de Velasco, Spanish governor of the Duchy of Milan from 1592 to 1600 and 1610-12. It's home to shops, offices and private apartments and is not open to visitors.

At the southern end of via Sant'Antonio, via Richini leads to largo Richini. From here, the tiny vicolo Santa Caterina in the right-hand corner pops you into piazza San Nazaro and corso di Porta Romana.

Heading left, this wide thoroughfare leads south-east down to **Porta Romana** (Roman Gateway), a 1598 monumental gate, designed by Aurelio Trezzi, which acted as a customs point for visitors to and from the south. Standing proud in the centre of piazza Medaglie d'Oro, it was one of the six main entrances into the city in the Spanish Walls (Mura Spagnole). The walls – to which the gateway was once attached – were built between 1548 and 1562, to encompass the suburban sprawl that had grown up in the shadow of the city's previous set of *mura*. Still forming a disjointed 11-kilometre (six-mile) girdle around the city, the Spanish encirclement could be seen from the Alps, as described by Stendhal in his memoir, *Rome, Naples et Florence*. (Constructed in 1171, the former, medieval walls are the site of the current ring road, inside the Spanish walls, plied by the 94 bus. The road is also known as the Cerchia dei Navigli, because the canals that later encircled the city also followed its design.)

One of the most vibrant areas of contemporary Milan, the Porta Romana district can be roughly divided into two rectangles, with the Porta Romana gateway (piazza Medaglie d'Oro) at its centre and corso Lodi (to piazzale Lodi) creating a common boundary. To the east, corso XXII Marzo marks the limits of the territory; via Ripamonti forms the western edge. Over the last 15 years, fashion houses have snapped up abandoned industrial buildings throughout the area, while contemporary art galleries, design

PRADA'S TEMPLE TO ART

The fashion brand's new arts centre opens in spring 2015.

Fondazione Prada's spectacular new headquarters and arts centre – designed by superstar Dutch architect Rem Koolhaas and his Office of Metropolitan Architecture – is scheduled to open in spring 2015 in largo Isarco, a ten-minute walk from the Piazzale Lodi metro stop. Koolhaas plans to add three striking new buildings to the seven existing edifices of the late 19th- and early 20th-century complex, which was originally the Società Distillerie Italiane (the city's primary distillery). The new buildings will include temporary exhibition areas, an auditorium and a nine-storey tower, housing works from the permanent art collection that the Milan-based fashion company has built up over the years.

The non-profit foundation – Prada's cultural wing – began with a small collection of sculpture in 1993. Between then and 2010, it organised 24 solo contemporary art shows in Milan. As well as buying most of the exhibits, the foundation also commissioned specific installations and the collection multiplied – it now includes pieces by Anish Kapoor, Carsten Höller, Steve McQueen, Laurie Anderson, Tom Friedman, Tobias Rehberger, Tom Sachs, Nathalie Djurberg and John Baldessari. A lack of exhibition space has meant that most of the pieces have remained in storage – but largo Isarco will change all that.

Contemporary art isn't the foundation's only interest: the new complex will host film screenings, performances and other events. Plans are also afoot for exhibition spaces in one of the two Prada stores in the Galleria Vittorio Emanuele II (*see p50*).

EXPLORE

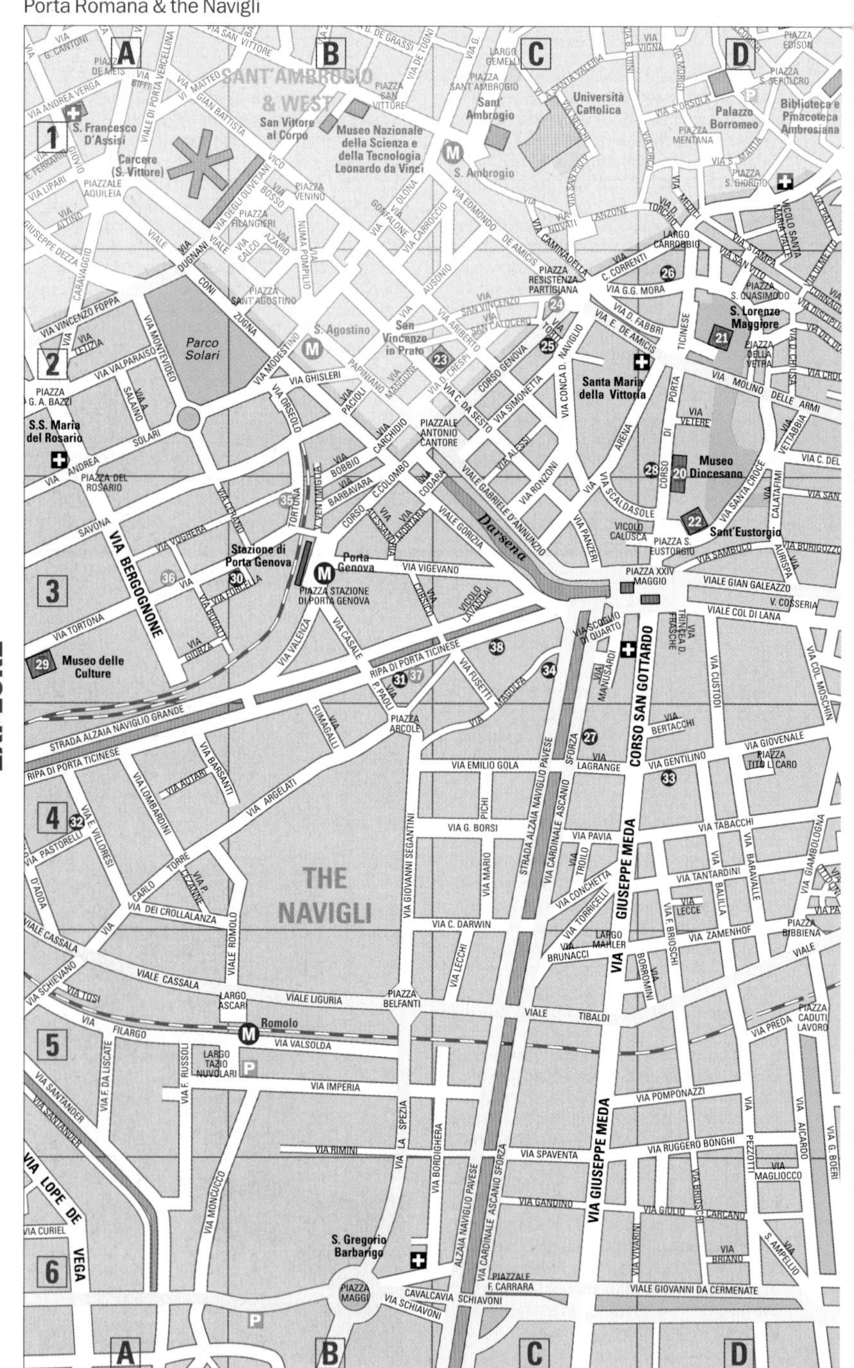
SANT'AMBROGIO & WEST
THE NAVIGLI
S. Francesco D'Assisi
Carcere (S. Vittore)
San Vittore al Corpo
Museo Nazionale della Scienza e della Tecnologia Leonardo da Vinci
Sant' Ambrogio
S. Ambrogio
Università Cattolica
Palazzo Borromeo
Biblioteca e Pinacoteca Ambrosiana
Parco Solari
S. Agostino
San Vincenzo in Prato
S. Lorenzo Maggiore
Santa Maria della Vittoria
Museo Diocesano
Sant'Eustorgio
Darsena
S.S. Maria del Rosario
Stazione di Porta Genova
Porta Genova
Museo delle Culture
Romolo
S. Gregorio Barbarigo
PIAZZA SANT'AMBROGIO
LARGO GEMELLI
PIAZZA EDISON
PIAZZA S. SEPOLCRO
PIAZZA MENTANA
PIAZZA S. GIORGIO
PIAZZALE AQUILEIA
PIAZZA VENINO
PIAZZA FILANGIERI
PIAZZA SANT'AGOSTINO
PIAZZA RESISTENZA PARTIGIANA
LARGO CARROBBIO
PIAZZA S. QUASIMODO
PIAZZA DELLA VETRA
PIAZZA G. A. BAZZI
PIAZZA DEL ROSARIO
PIAZZALE ANTONIO CANTORE
PIAZZA S. EUSTORGIO
PIAZZA XXIV MAGGIO
PIAZZA STAZIONE DI PORTA GENOVA
PIAZZA ARCOLE
PIAZZA TITO L. CARO
PIAZZA BIBBIENA
LARGO MAHLER
LARGO ASCARI
PIAZZA BELFANTI
PIAZZA CADUTI LAVORO
LARGO TAZIO NUVOLARI
PIAZZA MAGGI
PIAZZALE F. CARRARA
VIALE DI PORTA VERCELLINA
VIA SAN VITTORE
VIA DEGLI OLIVETANI
VIA CARROCCIO
VIA EDMONDO DE AMICIS
VIA CAMINADELLA
VIA S. VINCENZO
VIA ARIBERTO
CORSO GENOVA
VIA CONCA D. NAVIGLIO
VIA VINCENZO FOPPA
VIA MONTEVIDEO
VIA VALPARAISO
VIA SOLARI
VIA CORIO CONI ZUGNA
VIA MODESTINO
VIA GHISLERI
VIA ORSEOLO
VIA TORTONA
VIA BERGOGNONE
VIA SAVONA
VIA VIGEVANO
VIA CASALE
VIA VALENZA
RIPA DI PORTA TICINESE
STRADA ALZAIA NAVIGLIO GRANDE
VIALE GABRIELE D'ANNUNZIO
VIALE GORIZIA
VIA SCALDASOLE
CORSO DI PORTA TICINESE
VIA SANTA CROCE
VIALE GIAN GALEAZZO
VIALE COL DI LANA
CORSO SAN GOTTARDO
VIA GIUSEPPE MEDA
STRADA ALZAIA NAVIGLIO PAVESE
VIA CARDINALE ASCANIO SFORZA
VIA EMILIO GOLA
VIA G. BORSI
VIA C. DARWIN
VIA GIOVANNI SEGANTINI
VIA ARGELATI
VIA LOMBARDINI
VIALE CASSALA
VIALE LIGURIA
VIALE TIBALDI
VIA VALSOLDA
VIA IMPERIA
VIA LA SPEZIA
VIA RIMINI
VIA BORDIGHERA
VIA MONCUCCO
VIA LOPE DE VEGA
VIA SANTANDER
VIA SPAVENTA
VIA GANDINO
VIA POMPONAZZI
VIA RUGGERO BONGHI
VIA AICARDO
VIA G. BOERI
VIALE GIOVANNI DA CERMENATE
CAVALCAVIA SCHIAVONI
VIA SCHIAVONI
VIA COL. MOSCHIN
VIA CUSTODI
VIA TABACCHI
VIA ZAMENHOF
VIA BRUNACCI
VIA BORROMINI
VIA PREDA

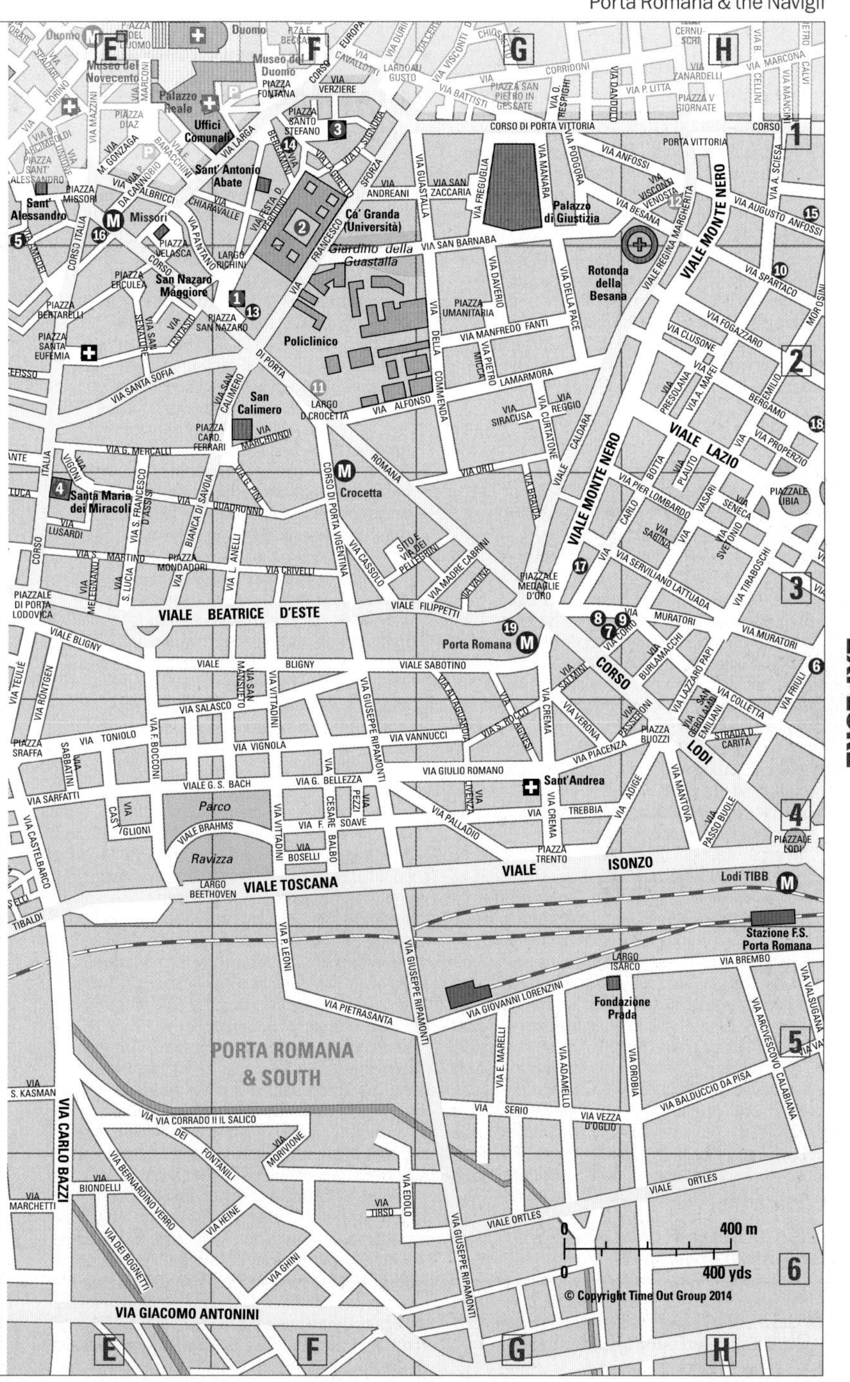
E
F
G
H
1
2
3
4
5
6
Duomo
Museo del Novecento
Museo del Duomo
Palazzo Reale
Uffici Comunali
Sant' Antonio Abate
Ca' Granda (Università)
Giardino della Guastalla
Sant' Alessandro
Missori
San Nazaro Maggiore
Policlinico
San Calimero
Palazzo di Giustizia
Rotonda della Besana
Crocetta
Santa Maria dei Miracoli
Porta Romana
Sant'Andrea
Lodi TIBB
Stazione F.S. Porta Romana
Fondazione Prada
Parco Ravizza
PORTA ROMANA & SOUTH
CORSO DI PORTA VITTORIA
VIALE MONTE NERO
VIALE LAZIO
VIALE BEATRICE D'ESTE
CORSO LODI
VIALE ISONZO
VIALE TOSCANA
VIA CARLO BAZZI
VIA GIACOMO ANTONINI
CORSO DI PORTA VIGENTINA
VIA GIUSEPPE RIPAMONTI
VIALE ORTLES
PIAZZALE LIBIA
PIAZZALE MEDAGLIE D'ORO
PIAZZALE DI PORTA LODOVICA
PIAZZALE LODI
0
400 m
0
400 yds
© Copyright Time Out Group 2014

EXPLORE

shops and fashion boutiques vie for the attention of passers-by. A 15-minute walk north-east of Porta Romana, along viale Montenero, lies the elegant **Rotonda di via Besana** (via Besana 12, open daylight hours), This circular, porticoed structure, built at the end of the 17th century as a graveyard for the Ca' Granda hospital, now houses a children's museum, **MUBA** (*see p151*).

South-east from Porta Romana, corso Lodi leads eventually to the old Porta Romana railway station (close to piazzale Lodi), with its vast railway yards. Prada, ever the pioneer, is now pushing back the neighbourhood's frontiers: its new Rem Koolhaas-designed HQ and art gallery, due to open on nearby largo Isarco in 2015, will bring new life to 'the wrong side of the tracks'.

Sights & Museums

FREE Basilica dei Santi Apostoli e Nazaro Maggiore

Piazza San Nazaro 5 (02 5830 7719). Metro Crocetta or Missori, or bus 94, or tram 16, 24. **Open** 7.30am-noon, 3.30-6.30pm Mon-Sat; 8am-12.30pm, 3.30-7pm Sun. *Sacristy* 3.30-5.30pm Mon-Fri. **Admission** free. **Map** p115 F2 ❶

San Nazaro was one of the four basilicas built during St Ambrose's evangelising drive between 382 and 386. Constructed to accommodate the remains of the apostles Andrew, John and Thomas, the church was given the name Basilica Apostolorum. When Ambrose brought along the remains of local martyr St Nazarus (who died in 396), the church was rededicated. You can see the saintly remains in the two altars of the choir, but their silver container is a copy; the one St Ambrose commissioned is in the treasury of the Duomo.

When it was built, the basilica stood outside the city walls in a Christian burial area established by Ambrose while still a bishop. This explains the sarcophagi you can see behind the church, which can be reached through the sacristy. Destroyed by fire in 1075, the church was rebuilt using material from the original structure, including the pilasters supporting the central dome. The *basilichetta* of San Lino, to the right of the altar, dates from the tenth century. The octagonal Cappella Trivulzio, designed by Bramantino – his only known architectural work – was added to the church in 1512. Reworked in the late 16th century and given a neoclassical interior in the 1830s, the basilica suffered considerable damage during World War II. Between 1946 and 1963, it was stripped of many of its post-fourth-century trappings to restore a sense of its early Christian austerity.

FREE Ca' Granda (Università degli Studi di Milano)

Via Festa del Perdono 5 (02 503 111, www.unimi.it). Metro Duomo or Missori, or bus 54, 60, or tram 12, 23, 24, 27. **Open** 8am-6pm Mon-Fri; 8am-12.30pm Sat. **Admission** free. **Map** p115 F1 ❷

Now home to the arts, history and law faculties of Milan University, the Ca' Granda began life as a hospital and hospice. It was Francesco Sforza who set out, in 1456, to consolidate Milan's 30 hospitals into one Casa Granda, or Ospedale Maggiore ('main hospital'). It was also a place providing succour to the poor and sick (thus ensuring the salvation of its sponsors in the life beyond); its less worthy function was to keep beggars, lunatics and other social embarrassments out of the public eye.

Francesco's favourite architect, Antonio 'il Filarete' Averlino, saw this as an opportunity to boost his grand plan to transform Milan into an ideal Renaissance city. The building had one wing for men and another for women, each subdivided into four inner courts and separated by the Cortile Maggiore ('great court'). The façade, with its typically Lombard terracotta decoration, is one of few in the city to survive from the 1400s. The courtyards, also from the 15th century, contained the women's baths. Work continued on the project after Filarete's death (around 1469), but ground to a halt with the fall of Ludovico 'il Moro', picking up again from time to time during the 17th and 18th centuries. In 1942, the hospital was moved

A FARMHOUSE IN MILAN

Rural peace in the heart of the city.

A farmhouse dating from 1695, **Cascina Cuccagna: Un Posto A Milano** (*see p119*) is located in the midst of a remarkable green space just 200 metres from viale Umbria, one of Milan's busiest thoroughfares, with trams trundling and cars racing along at all hours of the day and night. Inside, all this is forgotten: the place is now a bar and restaurant, and also provides community services including legal and tax advice, and regular courses.

It's popular with families, especially in summertime, and is also a hotspot for aperitifs, though you may need to come armed with patience: the receipt, drinks and accompanying snacks all require different queues. Still, the superb surrounds make the wait worthwhile.

Things calm down considerably at dinner, when the restaurant serves delicacies ranging from home-made *rigatoni* with organic broad beans and pecorino, to sweet 'n' crunchy chocolate, ricotta and orange cones. It's particularly good for vegetarians and vegans, uses lots of organic ingredients and has a kids' menu – including choices for babies still being weaned.

out to its new headquarters at Niguarda, in the northern suburbs. The university took up residence here in 1958.

The Cortile Maggiore, with its Renaissance portico and Baroque loggia, is decorated with busts sculpted in the yellow, rose and grey stone from Angera on Lake Maggiore. It was reconstructed after sustaining heavy damage in World War II. *Photo p112.*

FREE San Bernardino alle Ossa

Piazza Santo Stefano (02 7602 3735). Metro Duomo, or bus 54, 77, or tram 12, 15, 23, 27. **Open** 7.30am-noon, 1-6pm Mon-Fri; 7.30am-12.30pm Sat; 9.30am-12.30pm Sun. **Admission** free. **Map** p115 F1 ❸

One of Milan's most bizarre attractions, San Bernardino alle Ossa's ossuary chapel manages to create a freakish sort of beauty from a bone-chilling template. The chapel (marked '*ossario*'; to the right as you enter) is decorated in delightfully disturbing fashion, with symbols and patterns picked out in human bones supplied by the nearby Ospedale del Brolo. And there were plenty, from the hospital and other cemeteries – adding up to more than 3,000 skulls, tibias and femurs. The interior gloom is enlivened by the bright colours of the vault painting by Sebastiano Ricci (1659-1734), *Triumph of the Soul Among the Angels.*

FREE Santa Maria dei Miracoli presso San Celso

Corso Italia 37 (02 5831 3187, www.santamaria deimiracoliesancelso.it). Bus 94 or tram 15. **Open** 7am-noon, 4-6pm Mon-Sat; 8.30am-12.30pm, 4-7pm Sun. **Admission** free. **Map** p115 E3 ❹

Two little chapels once stood on this site, where, according to legend, St Ambrose was led by a vision to the bodies of martyrs Nazaro and Celso. The chapel of San Nazaro fell down long ago, but so great was the flow of pilgrims to the remaining chapel of San Celso – where, earlier in the 15th century, the Blessed Virgin Mary was said to be hard at work performing miracles galore – that in 1493 construction began on something bigger: Santa Maria dei Miracoli (St Mary of Miracles). Preceded by a beautiful early 16th-century quadriportico, the lively façade is from the same era, animated by sculptures by Stoldo Lorenzi and Annibale Fontana. The interior of the church was decorated by the usual cast of Lombard Renaissance, Mannerist and Baroque artists, with Ambrogio Bergognone's particularly impressive *Madonna tra i santi* in the first chapel on the left. It's referred to locally as the *chiesa degli sposi* (newlyweds' church), and it's the custom for newly married couples to drop in with a bouquet of flowers – an offering to the Virgin in hope of a long and happy life together.

Through a gate and across the garden, San Celso was founded in the ninth century and rebuilt in the 11th, and is decorated with frescoes that date from the 11th to 15th centuries. The building is usually closed to the public but if you wish to view it, ask at the sacristy.

Restaurants

Alla Collina Pistoiese

Via Amedei 1 (02 8645 1085, www.lecolline pistoiesi.it). Metro Missori ,or bus 54, or tram 12, 15. **Meals served** 12.30-2.30pm, 7.30-10.30pm Mon-Thur, Sun; 7.30-10.30pm Sat. **Average** €40. **Map** p115 E1 ❺ **Traditional Tuscan**

EXPLORE

San Bernardino alle Ossa.

A perennial favourite of the Milanese, this classy restaurant serves traditional Florentine platters beneath wood-panelled ceilings on tables clad in creamy tablecloths. Save yourself the train ride to Tuscany by trying specialities such as cavolo nero (kale) soup or *bistecca alla fiorentina* (Tuscan T-bone steak).

★ Cascina Cuccagna: Un Posto a Milano

Via Cuccagna 2, corner of via Ludovico Muratori (02 545 7785, www.unpostoamilano.it). Metro Porta Romana, or bus 90, 91, 92, or tram 9. **Open** *Bar* 10am-1am Tue-Sun. *Meals served* 12.30-2.30pm, 7.30-10.30pm Tue-Sun. **Average** €45. **Map** p115 H3 ❻ **Traditional Italian**

See p116 **A Farmhouse in Milan.**

Dongiò

Via Corio 3 (02 551 1372). Metro Porta Romana or tram 9. **Meals served** 12.30-2.30pm, 7.30-10.30pm Mon-Fri; 7.30-10.30pm Sat. **Average** €30. **Map** p115 G3 ❼ **Traditional Calabrian**

The fragrance of slowly simmering pasta sauces, often flavoured with spicy 'nduja sausage, awaits at this popular Calabrian trattoria, which has been here for years and years. It serves some of the finest steaks in town, grilled *al rosmarino* (with rosemary) or *al finocchio selvatico* (with wild fennel). If you have room for dessert, try the *brusetti freddi* – dark chocolate with pistachio nuts and crème pâtissière.

Giulio Pane e Ojo

Via Ludovico Muratori 10 (02 545 6189, www.giuliopaneojo.com). Metro Porta Romana or tram 9. **Meals served** 12.30-2.30pm, 8pm-12.30am Mon-Sat. **Average** €35. **Map** p115 G3 ❽ **Traditional Roman**

A rare find in Milan, this typically Roman *osteria* is one of the city's liveliest eateries. The very affordable lunch menu (€10) is justly popular; get there early to avoid the queue. In the evenings, reservations (for two sittings, at 8.30pm or 10.30pm) are essential – and once dinner is over, you'll be expected to leave to make way for other guests. The menu is tempting but short, ensuring fresh seasonal ingredients: favourite dishes include classic *spaghetti cacio e pepe* (with crumbled, seasoned sheep's cheese and black pepper) and *abbacchio* (tender spring lamb).

Masuelli San Marco

Viale Umbria 80 (02 5518 4138, www.masuelli trattoria.com). Bus 84, 90, 91, 92. **Meals served** 8-10.30pm Mon; 12.30-2.30pm, 8-10.30pm Tue-Sat. **Average** €40. **Map** p283 H9. **Traditional Lombard & Piemontese**

Doing brisk business on these premises since 1921, this Milanese institution lives up to its fine local reputation, with attentive service and a warm atmosphere. It's not a place for vegetarians, especially in winter, when the menu includes intense meaty dishes such as tripe, lard and calf's tongue. The summertime Friday special, fried cod with onions, is a daily main course the rest of the year. Order the *risotto alla Milanese* and you'll get a Masuelli souvenir plate to take home.

► *Traditional it may be, but Masuelli is also bang up-to-date technology-wise. See the summer and winter menus online, or download the app to make a booking.*

★ Pastamadre

Via Corio 8 (02 5519 0020). Metro Porta Romana or tram 9. **Meals served** noon-3pm, 7-11pm Mon; 8am-3pm, 7.30-11pm Tue-Sat. **Average** €35. **Map** p115 H3 ❾ **Contemporary Sicilian**

With its simple wooden tables and sunny yellow lampshades, this hole-in-the-wall eatery is perhaps the best Sicilian restaurant in Milan. Well known as a *pasticceria* (Sicilian delicacies stuffed with ricotta and chocolate are on display in a glass-fronted counter), the action starts early, with locals flooding in for abundant breakfasts of home-made brioche and cappuccino, frothed up with almond milk. At lunch and dinner, fish is among the many specialities, from shrimp with rhubarb to pasta with octopus ragù.

Trattoria La Rondine

Via Spartaco 11 (02 5518 4533). Metro Porta Romana. **Meals served** noon-3pm, 7.30-11pm Mon-Sat. **Average** €35. **Map** p115 H2 ❿ **Traditional Milanese**

This small, unassuming restaurant is one of the area's most popular *trattorie*. Classically Milanese standouts on the epically long menu include *ravioli al burro tartufato* (plump ravioli stuffed with ricotta and spinach, doused with truffle-scented butter) or polenta with slow-cooked beef stew. The dessert menu is quirky but tasty: witness the lip-smacking fluorescent mint mousse. Some say it's not as good since 2011, when the former chef, Giorgio, and his crew moved on, but it's still worth checking out.

Cafés, Bars & Gelaterie

There's also a branch of fancy ice-cream chain **Grom** (corso XXII Marzo 5, 02 5519 9175, www.grom.it).

£ Bar della Crocetta

Corso di Porta Romana 67 (02 545 0228, www.crocetta.com). Metro Crocetta or tram 16, 24. **Open** 8am-1am daily. **Map** p115 F2 ⓫

This panini specialist is the perfect place to grab a quick lunch.

Umberto

Piazza Cinque Giornate (02 545 8113). Bus 60, 73, 77, or tram 9, 12, 23, 27. **Open** varies. **No credit cards.** **Map** p115 H1 ⓬

EXPLORE

NEW GENERATION BOOKSHOP

Digital and print get equal-billing in this innovative new space.

'More than books' is the motto at **Open** (*see p121*), a groundbreaking new bookshop that opened in 2013 close to the Porta Romana metro station. Founded by digital expert Giorgio Fipaldini, it's co-owned by 20 partners, many found via crowdsourcing.

As in a conventional bookshop, Open has shelves of books for sale, ranging from novels to travel, art, design, sport, kids and cookery. Most are in Italian, though English-language publications feature too, especially among the artier tomes. The store's digital agenda is what sets it apart: a section is devoted to games and apps, and 50 tablets are available for customers to borrow (in store), each containing around 100 apps and 30 newspapers and magazines. A 'digital bookseller' is on hand to dish out advice and technical support.

Inside the light, airy space, customers read books or browse laptops on sofas by Lago, the design company for whom the shop doubles as a showroom. Others sip coffee, chat or surf the net at a long communal table that also acts as an informal meeting point.

The coffee – along with smoothies, cakes, salads and other goodies – comes from the in-house branch of **Ottimo Massimo** (*see p63*). Other facilities include a separate, 40-seat co-working area (from €12 per half day) with dedicated Wi-Fi, printers and three meeting rooms. Among the regular events are book, ebook and app launches, and digital workshops for older people and kids. There is also a Friday night cultural babysitting service (*see p151* **In the Know**) and Sunday brunch.

EXPLORE

This place is a Milanese institution: despite its (seriously) unpredictable opening hours and (seriously) grumpy staff, locals reckon its ice-cream is among the city's best. Unchanged for decades – the wood and leather decor has been carefully preserved – Umberto serves a maximum of seven traditional flavours, including a sumptuous dark chocolate.

Shops & Services

Abside

Vicolo Santa Caterina 1 (02 5831 5234, www.ab-side.it). Metro Crocetta, or bus 94, or tram 16, 24. **Open** 10am-7pm Mon-Sat. **Map** p115 F2 ⓭ **Fashion & accessories**

Tucked around the corner from piazza San Nazaro in Brolo, off corso di Porta Romana, Abside stocks a cool mix of own-brand clothes and jewellery, as well as unique pieces by other Italian and European designers. Pick up patchwork belts, felt bags and funky earrings made from old French francs; prices are very reasonable.

Anaconda

Via Bergamini 7 (02 5830 3668, www.anacondamilano.com). Bus 54, 60, or tram 12, 15, 23, 27. **Open** 11am-7pm Tue-Sat. **Map** p115 F1 ⓮ **Accessories**

Want to wow? Follow those in the know to the city's jewellery show-stopper. Designer Monica Rossi mixes antique gems and modern techniques, with extraordinary results.

L'Antica Arte del Dolce

Via Anfossi 10 (02 5519 4448, www.ernstknam.eu). Bus 62, 73, 84, or tram 9. **Open** 10am-1pm, 4-8pm Tue-Sat; 10am-1pm Sun. **Map** p115 H1. ⓯ **Food & drink**

Gourmet cakes, chocolates, biscuits, jams and desserts are whizzed up in the kitchens by pastry chef Ernst Knam (who trained under renowned Milanese restaurateur Gualtiero Marchesi) and his able team. Among the more daring concoctions are apple and rosemary tart, as well as aubergine and chocolate mousse.

★ Giovanni Galli Pasticceria

Corso di Porta Romana 2 (02 8645 3112, www.giovannigalli.com). Metro Missori, or bus 54, or tram 16, 24. **Open** 8.30am-1pm, 2-8pm Mon-Sat; 8.30am-1pm Sun. **Map** p115 E1 ⓰ **Food & drink**

This is undoubtedly Milan's best address for marrons glacés, made daily with fresh chestnuts in Galli's own kitchens, according to its own 1898 recipe. The *alchechengi* (cape gooseberries

dipped in chocolate), and the pralines filled with mint, nougat or orange are just as good.
Other locations via Victor Hugo 2, Centre (02 8646 4833).

★ Open

Viale Monte Nero 6 (02 8342 5610, www.openmilano.com). Metro Porta Romana, or bus 62, 77, or tram 9. **Open** *Bookshop* 10am-9pm Mon, Tue, Sun; 10am-10pm Wed-Sat. *Co-working* 9am-9pm daily. **Map** p115 G3 ⑰ **Books & music**
See p120 **New Generation Bookshop**.

Pastificio Pellegrini

Via Cadore 48 (02 5518 4207, www.pastificio pellegrini.it). Bus 62, or tram 12, 16, 27. **Open** 3.30-7.30pm Mon; 10.30am-12.30pm, 3.30-7.30pm Tue-Sat. **Map** p115 H2 ⑱ **Food & drink**
This family-run shop has been making delectable pasta for more than 50 years. The ravioli fillings are seasonal – comprising anything from artichokes to porcini mushrooms.

★ Terme Milano

Piazza Medaglie d'Oro 2 (02 5519 9367, www.termemilano.com). Metro Porta Romana, or bus 62, 77, or tram 9. **Open** 10am-10pm daily. **Rates** €35-€45 Mon-Fri; €42-€50 Sat, Sun. **Map** p115 G3 ⑲ **Spa**
Housed in a gorgeous palazzo built in 1908, the recently renovated Terme Milano has had various uses, having been a leisure centre for tram drivers and a rock disco bar. Now, the building has been restored to its former art deco glory and kitted out with steam baths, open-air pools – and even a sauna in a tram car. A day pass provides access to all areas; there are also special rates after 5.30pm, and after 7.30pm. No under-14s. Terme Milano is part of a chain that includes the Bagni Vecchi and Bagni Nuovi in Bormio (0342 910 131, www.bagnidibormio.it), in the Valtellina region of Lombardy.
▶ *A special babysitting arrangement at Open bookshop offers discounted Terme Milano tickets, see p120* **New Generation Bookshop**.

PORTA TICINESE

Porta Ticinese is where Milan's wilder kids hang out; consequently, the pavements, bars and trendy shops are packed during evenings and on Saturday afternoons.

Corso di Porta Ticinese shoots south out of largo Carrobbio, passing by via Gian Giacomo Mora on the right; the name of this street commemorates a man falsely accused of spreading the plague, and tortured, in 1636. His house was demolished, and a pillar was put up on the site. A plaque and a small sculpture by Ruggero Menegon, by the main entrance of a brand-new apartment building, have replaced the pillar. Further down corso di Porta Ticinese, on the left, is the church of **San Lorenzo Maggiore**. Opposite are 16 massive Roman columns, recovered some time after the third century – most likely from a Roman spa or temple – and erected here in commemoration of St Lawrence, who was martyred in 258.

At the junction of corso di Porta Ticinese with via de Amicis and via Molino delle Armi is the **Antica Porta Ticinese**, which dates from the 12th century. It marks what, in ancient times, was the entry point into the city for travellers coming from Ticinum (modern-day Pavia, south of Milan), before the city walls were demolished and rebuilt further out to encompass the city's growing population.

Via de Amicis leads west from here to the site of the **Roman Amphitheatre** (no.17, 02 8940 0555, www.comune.milano.it, closed Sat afternoon & all Sun). First discovered in 1936 but only brought fully to light in the 1970s, the structure has suffered not so much the ravages of time as those of church-builders: much of it was dismantled and used to build San Lorenzo Maggiore, a common recycling practice in past centuries. The **Antiquarium Alda Levi**, a small museum of coins, tools, shards and other antiquities, is open 9am-2pm Wed, Fri, Sat.

Across corso Genova, the little church of **San Vincenzo in Prato** stands in what was a pre-Christian necropolis. Behind San Lorenzo is **piazza della Vetra**, a name that probably derives from *castra vetera* (old barracks), an allusion to the fact that Roman soldiers defending the imperial palace camped here, or that there was a newer one somewhere in the vicinity. During the Middle Ages, the piazza was often used as a point from which to defend the city; the Seveso and Nirone rivers converged here and were redirected to feed defensive waterworks around the city walls. All these military associations may have prepared piazza della Vetra for an even bloodier use as an execution ground. For a period of nearly 800 years, from 1045 to 1840, the square was the place where commoners condemned to death were beheaded. (The nobility met their gruesome end in the more central, slightly more attractive, piazza Broletto.)

From here you can strike south across via Molino delle Armi to the **Parco delle Basiliche** and along corso di Porta Ticinese to the **Museo Diocesano**, a vast collection of religious art and artefacts. Just behind the museum is the church of **Sant'Eustorgio**, set on the spot where Milan's first Christians are said to have been baptised by the apostle Barnabus. If you head east along via Banfi, and take via Cosimo del Fante to corso Italia, you'll find the church of **Santa Maria dei Miracoli**.

San Lorenzo Maggiore.

Sights & Museums

Museo Diocesano

Corso di Porta Ticinese 95 (02 8942 4714, www.museodiocesano.it). Bus 94. **Open** *Mid Sept-June* 10am-6pm Tue-Sun. *Mid June-Aug* 7pm-midnight Tue-Sat. **Admission** €4 Tue; €8 Wed-Sun; €5 reductions; €12 combined ticket with Cappella Portinari at Sant'Eustorgio & Cappella di Sant' Aquilino at San Lorenzo Maggiore. Free to all mid June-Aug. **No credit cards. Map** p114 D2 ⑳

The Museo Diocesano (opened 2001) occupies three floors of the former Dominican convent of Sant'Eustorgio and houses a large collection of religious art treasures taken from churches and private acquisitions throughout Lombardy.

On the ground floor are works from the former Basilica di Sant'Ambrogio museum, including the olive-wood frame of St Ambrose's letterpress. The first floor houses the collections of several archbishops: that of Federico Visconti (1617-93) includes two notable drawings – portraits of Raphael and Titian – and a painting of San Carlo Borromeo by Cerano (Giovanni Battista Crespi). The collection of Giuseppe Pozzobonelli (1696-1783) contains 17th-century Italian landscapes; that of Cesare Monti (1593-1650) has Lombard and Venetian works of the 16th and 17th centuries (including Tintoretto's *Christ and the Adulteress*, 1545-47).

The museum recently gained a collection of 15th- to 20th-century drawings by artists including Van Gogh, Lucio Fontana and Jean Cocteau. The 105 artefacts were donated by banker Antonio Sozzani.

FREE San Lorenzo Maggiore

Corso di Porta Ticinese 39 (02 8940 4129). Bus 94, or tram 2, 3, 14. **Open** *Church* 7.30am-12.30pm, 2.30-6.45pm Mon-Sat; 9.30am-12.30pm, 2.30-6.45pm Sun. *Cappella di Sant'Aquilino* 9.30am-12.30pm, 2.30-6.30pm daily. **Admission** *Church* free. *Cappella* €2; €1 reductions; €12 combined ticket with Museo Diocesano & Cappella Portinari at Sant'Eustorgio. **No credit cards. Map** p114 D2 ㉑

At the time of its construction in the fourth century, San Lorenzo was the largest church built on a central plan in the western world. Fire all but destroyed it in 1071, but it was swiftly rebuilt. When the cupola collapsed in 1573, the new dome – the tallest in Milan and in a distinctly Renaissance style – outraged the locals, so different was it from the original Romanesque model, a 15th-century reproduction of which can be seen inside the church.

On the right-hand side of the interior, the octagonal fourth-century Cappella di Sant'Aquilino may have been an imperial mausoleum. Legend has it that a group of porters discovered St Aquiline's corpse in a ditch; taking it to the Duomo, they got lost in the fog and ended up in San Lorenzo. Thus his remains are still here, in a glass coffin on top of the altar; he also became the patron saint of porters. On the walls of the chapel are fragments of late fourth-century mosaics. Behind the altar, stairs descend to a passage under the church, where stones from pre-existing Roman structures used in the construction of San Lorenzo can be seen.

Outside the church stand 16 Corinthian columns from the second and third centuries. They were moved here from an unidentified pagan temple some time in the fourth century and topped with pieces of architrave, only some of which date from the same period. The 17th-century wings flanking San Lorenzo's entrance were designed to link the columns to the church in a sort of pseudo-ancient atrium. In the centre, a bronze statue of Emperor Constantine is a copy of one in Rome – a reminder of his Edict of Milan (313), which put an end to the state persecution of Christians.

FREE Sant'Eustorgio

Piazza Sant'Eustorgio 1-3 (02 5810 1583, Cappella Portinari 02 8940 2671). Bus 5, or tram 3, 9, 15. **Open** *Church* 7.30am-noon, 3.30-6.30pm daily. *Cappella Portinari* 10am-6pm Tue-Sun. **Admission** *Church* free. *Cappella Portinari* €6; €4 photography fee; €12 combined ticket with Museo Diocesano & Cappella di Sant'Aquilino at San Lorenzo. **No credit cards. Map** p114 D3 ㉒

Eustorgio (later, St Eustorgio), the ninth bishop of Milan, had this church built in the fourth century to house the relics of the Three Kings. The specific site was chosen when animals pulling the relic-laden cart reached this spot and refused to budge. In 1164, Frederick Barbarossa absconded with said relics but they were returned (in part) in 1903 and are venerated on 6 January (Epiphany). Each year, on that morning, a procession led by the 'Three Kings' (a trio of Milanesi) proceeds from the Duomo to Sant'Eustorgio.

The church is filled with works by Milanese and Lombard artists from the 13th to the 15th centuries, including Bernardino Luini and the *maestri campionesi*. Notable works include Giovanni di Balduccio's Gothic funerary monument to Stefano Visconti (1327), on the left wall of the fifth chapel on the right. The fourth chapel on the right contains a 14th-century painted wooden crucifix that was supposed to cure pregnant women of fever.

The main attraction, however, is the Cappella Portinari next door, built between 1462 and 1466 by Florentine banker Pigello Portinari for his own tomb and as a repository for the remains of St Peter Martyr, murdered when heretics stuck a knife into his skull 200 years earlier. Perhaps the earliest example of Renaissance architecture in the city, the chapel unites the classical forms championed by Brunelleschi in Tuscany with typical Lombard fresco decoration by Vincenzo Foppa. Foppa's scenes of the life of the Virgin and of St Peter Martyr's miracles (1466-68) are perhaps the painter's masterpieces. In the centre of the chapel, the intricate, carved Ark of St Peter Martyr, containing most of the saint's remains, is by Giovanni da Balduccio (1336-39); Peter's skull, meanwhile, is in a silver urn in a little chapel to the left of the Cappella Portinari.

The chapel's admission fee includes access to an oppressive but interesting palaeo-Christian cemetery, located under the Sant'Eustorgio Basilica.

FREE San Vincenzo in Prato

Via Daniele Crespi 6 (02 837 3107, www.sanvincenzoinprato.it). Metro Sant'Agostino, or bus 94, or tram 2, 14. **Open** 7.45-noon, 3.30-7pm daily. **Admission** free. **Map** p114 C2 ㉓

The only church in Milan to have maintained its original palaeo-Christian appearance, its name, 'in Prato', derives from its location in the *pratum* (field) area owned by bishop Odelpertus.

In 1797, by order of Napoleon (Lombardy having become part of the Cisalpine Republic, a French client republic in northern Italy that lasted until 1802), the church was deconsecrated and was turned into a storehouse and then into a barracks. By 1810, it was a chemicals factory, belching fumes that earned it the nickname 'la Casa del Mago' ('the magician's house'). It was restored and reconsecrated in the 1880s.

EXPLORE

Cucchi. *See p124.*

Cafés, Bars & Gelaterie

Cucchi

Corso Genova 1 (02 8940 9793, www.pasticceria cucchi.it). Metro Sant'Ambrogio, or bus 94, or tram 2, 14. **Open** 7am-10pm Tue-Sun. **Map** p114 C2 ㉔

Cucchi has been family-run since 1936, and its bow-tie-clad waiters serve elegant fruit-filled tartlets, *cannoncini* (cream horns) and savoury snippets such as *pizzette* (tiny pizzas). A favourite stop for Milanese, especially after Sunday mass, it's a lovely spot – grab a table in the shade and watch the world go by. *Photo p123*.

Shops & Services

★ Biffi

Corso Genova 6 (02 8311 6052, ww.biffi.com). Metro Sant'Ambrogio, or bus 94, or tram 2, 14. **Open** 3-7.30pm Mon; 9.30am-1.30pm, 3-7.30pm Tue-Fri; 9.30am-7.30pm Sat. **Map** p114 C2 ㉕ **Fashion & accessories**

A Milanese institution for men's and women's classic designer labels, Biffi also carries the mildly wild trend pieces of the season. Among the designers represented are Fendi, Gucci, Marc Jacobs, Marni, Moncler, Roger Vivier and Junya Watanabe. Across the street (and with the same opening hours) is Biffi's sportswear store. There's also a branch in Bergamo (*see p185*).

Other locations Banner, via Sant'Andrea 8, Centre (02 7600 4609, www.biffi.com).

£ Bivio

Via Gian Giacomo Mora 4 (02 5810 8691, www.bivio.it). Bus 94, or tram 2, 14. **Open** 11am-7.30pm Tue-Sun. **Map** p114 D2 ㉖ **Fashion & accessories**

See below **Handbags & Gladrags**.

Forma Galleria

Via Ascanio Sforza 29 (02 8907 5420, www.formagalleria.com). Bus 47, or tram 3, 9. **Open** 11am-5pm Tue-Fri. **Map** p114 C4 ㉗ **Gallery**

The commercial Forma Galleria opened in June 2014 alongside the Pavese canal; like its predecessor, the Spazio Forma, it's one of Milan's few serious photography venues. It represents some of the world's top lensmen (and women) – from Elliott Erwit to William Klein – and aims to attract both collectors and first-time buyers. One of its strengths is its mix of vintage and contemporary; another is Italian photographers of all stripes. Interesting finds include 1950s photographer Piergiorgio Branzi, one of the first to experiment with deep black, and contemporary female photographer Giorgia Fiorio, who specialises in closed male communities.

► *Fondazione Forma's founder, Roberto Koch, worked with the city council on the new photography museum at Palazzo della Ragione (see p60).*

Mauro Leone

Corso di Porta Ticinese 103 (02 5810 5041, www.mauroleone.com). Bus 94, or tram 2, 9, 15.

HANDBAGS & GLADRAGS

Welcome to Milan's first fashion swap shop.

Launched in 2013, **Bivio**'s (*see above*) concept of fashion 'resale' is new to Milan. It sells barely used fashions and accessories, from Alaia to Zara, at a fraction of the original price, and has been a hit with the city's style-seekers. The shop was founded by San Francisco native and Milan resident Hilary Belle Walker, who imported the idea from the US. So where do these coveted items come from? The wardrobes of local fashionistas, who often use the proceeds of what they've sold to buy something else. (Unlike traditional consignment stores, Bivio buys outright, either for one-third of the retail value, or in exchange for a credit voucher for 50 per cent of the final price). Walker's discerning eye ensures that the merchandise is bang on trend; she even displays a seasonal wish list, to tell potential traders what she, and her customers, are looking for. This includes colours, styles and key pieces (boat shoes or metallic accents, anyone?).

Biffi.

Open 3-7.30pm Mon; 10am-7.30pm Tue-Sat; 2.30-7pm Sun. **Map** p114 D2 ㉘ **Accessories**
From basic black knee-high boots (in store from September) to ballerinas in myriad hues (from March/April), this colourful shop is popular with Milanese fashionistas fighting over the latest footwear styles. In all, there are a dozen branches throughout Italy.
Other locations corso di Porta Ticinese 60, South (02 8942 9167); via San Pietro all'Orto, Centre (02 7602 2573).

THE NAVIGLI

North-west of piazza Sant'Eustorgio, the two canals that connect Milan with the Ticino and Po rivers flow into the **Darsena**, Milan's main port, a hotbed of commercial activity from 1603 until the middle of the 20th century. Today, the Darsena is once more the focus of attention, thanks to a controversial revamp of the waterways – 'a revitalised landscape… with walking tours, bike paths, conservation works, new gardens and areas dedicated to socialising and entertainment,' according to a billboard at the construction site – with costs estimated (in July 2013) at €42 million. Renderings show wooden walkways floating above the port's waters, surrounded by lilies and reeds. The Darsena is to be paved along its edges and lined with trees, benches and seats, and piazza XXIV Maggio is to be transformed into a large pedestrian zone. Work is scheduled for completion in time for the opening of the Universal Expo in May 2015.

The two main *navigli* (canals), which extend south and west from the Darsena between Porta Ticinese and Porta Genova, are all that remain of a once vital network that criss-crossed much of the city, though most have been filled in. (The relics of other canals include the Tombon di San Marco in the northern Brera district.) Today, they're a popular destination on Sundays and weekends, when the Milanesi head here to shop, drink and dine – but the district is also a potent reminder of an important part of the city's illustrious past and bold thinking.

Excavations for the **Naviglio Grande** (perhaps Europe's first canal) began in 1177, to carry the waters of the diverted Ticino river from Lake Maggiore to the Darsena. Barges arrived with coal and lumber and departed bearing iron, grain, fabric and other manufactured goods.

In 1359, a scheme was launched to build the **Naviglio Pavese**. The waterway was designed to irrigate Gian Galeazzo Visconti's hunting reserve near Pavia, but in the 15th century, Ludovico il Moro called in Leonardo da Vinci to improve the system and create a canal network that extended into the heart of the city. Partly as a result of Da Vinci's engineering gifts, Milan gained a reputation as a thriving port. Funding issues hampered a 1597 plan to extend the *navigli* still further, which stalled at the Conca Fallato ('failed lock') in the southern suburbs until Napoleon applied himself to the task in the early 19th century. Not long after the extension's inauguration in 1819, its traffic rates were outstripping those on the Naviglio Grande.

Although by the 1930s much of the historic network had been filled in, following World War II, materials for reconstructing the badly bombed city were transported by water. The last working boat moored up on 30 March 1979. These days, boutiques, antiques restorers, restaurants, a clutch of new hotels and plenty of nightspots line the canal banks and side streets. A popular canalside antiques market (*see p129* **In the Know**) is also held here on the last Sunday of every month, except for July, and canal cruises are available from **Navigli Lombardi** (*see p267*).

Sights & Museums

★ Museo delle Culture

Via Tortona 56 (02 8846 3724, http://museodelle culture.it). Metro Porta Genova or bus 68, 74 or tram 14. **Open & admission** call for details. **Map** p114 A3 ㉙

See p127 **Culture Club**.

Restaurants

Da Noi In

Via Forcella 6 (02 837 8111, www.magnapars-suitesmilano.it). Metro Porta Genova, or bus 68, 74, or tram 2, 19. **Meals served** 12.30-2.30pm, 7.30-10.30pm Mon-Sat. **Average** €60. **Map** p114 B3 ㉚ **Contemporary Italian**

In the basement of the swanky Magna Pars hotel (*see p252*), overlooking a sunken botanical garden (where you can dine in summer), this new restaurant in the Tortona district is making a name for itself as an innovative gourmet stop. As you enter, you'll see the team of chefs hard at work in the glass-fronted kitchen, fashioning everything from ice-cream to bread. Chef Fulvio Siccardi loves to experiment, and his signature platters include an egg, steam-cooked at a low temperature for 60 minutes, and served with cream, parmesan and truffle flakes.

▶ *Unusually for Milan, the restaurant offers free valet parking.*

Da Noi In.

IN THE KNOW
ANYONE FOR GOLF?

The countryside around Milan, especially Lake Como, has some of the loveliest golf courses in Italy. Closer to home, less then eight kilometres (five miles) south of the Navigli is Golf Le Rovedine South (02 5760 6420, www.rovedine.com), the only public club in Lombardy. Getting a reservation to play at the 18-hole, par-72 course is tricky – only Tuesday, Wednesday and Friday mornings are free from competitions, and weekends are often booked by locals – but it's worth a shot. Allow a few days' advance notice.

★ Erba Brusca

Alzaia Naviglio Pavese 286 (02 8738 0711, www.erbabrusca.it). Metro Piazza Abbiategrasso then 15min walk. **Meals served** 12.30-2.30pm, 8-11pm Wed-Sun. **Average** €50. **Contemporary Italian**

A canalside green oasis just beyond the outer ring road, this veggie-based restaurant is well worth the trek. Erba Brusca's French-American-British chef Alice Delcourt uses herbs and vegetables from the restaurant's garden to put together creative, seasonal platters. These might be asparagus with goat's ricotta, mint and honey, or risotto with bacon, lemon and bergamot. On summer Sundays, the à la carte brunch beneath the pergola (served noon-3pm) is especially popular; in the cooler seasons, book lunch or dinner in the relaxed and airy restaurant. There's entertainment from jazz musicians on Wednesday evenings. *Photo p128.*

Al Pont de Ferr

Ripa di Porta Ticinese 55 (02 8940 6277, www.pontdeferr.it). Metro Porta Genova, or bus 47, 74, or tram 2, 19. **Meals served** 12.30pm-2.30pm, 8-11pm daily. **Average** €60. **Map** p114 B3 ㉛ **Contemporary Italian**

You never quite know what you'll find on your plate at this innovative, Michelin-starred restaurant – but you can be certain it will be memorable. Uruguayan chef Matias Perdomo delights in teasing his customers' palates with dishes such as crispy red sugar balls blown to resemble an onion, and stuffed with goat's cheese mousse and onion jam. The ambience is surprisingly informal, with brick walls, shelves of bottles, and tables strewn with paper mats.

CULTURE CLUB

The long-awaited Museum of Cultures finally opens.

Designed by British architect David Chipperfield, Milan's **Museo delle Culture** is scheduled to open in October 2014. In the pipeline since 1999 and with a final cost of over €60m, the museum is in a revamped 19th-century industrial building (once the home of Ansaldo, one of Italy's oldest and most important engineering companies). It was purchased by the city council during the 1990s boom – but there have long been fears that it might turn into a white elephant.

Chipperfield's design is spectacular. The factory courtyard is enclosed by curved, translucent glass walls, rising to a four-lobed glass lantern that suffuses the building with light. The ground-floor atrium is covered with mirrors and yet more glass. Still the architect himself has been reported as saying: 'The city has paid for a vast, empty museum in a well-constructed building, whose decline starts now.'

In the event, the focus will be on temporary exhibitions, though the museum will also house a permanent (and relatively low-cost) display of some 7,000 objects from the city's holdings, including pre-Columbian works and anthropological curiosities, as well as modern and contemporary art, fashion and design. The exhibits are mainly from non-European cultures – hence the name – and come from the Castello Sforzesco (*see p73*), the Pinacoteca Ambrosiana (*see p59*) and the Museo di Storia Naturale (*see p94*).

Among the most interesting is a wunderkammer once belonging to Manfredo Settala (1600-80), who's credited as a pioneer of ethnography in Milan. Inspired by the 'cabinet of curiosities' that he'd seen at the court of Gonzaga in Mantua while in his teens, he joined the craze for eclectic collecting that was then popular in Europe – creating an antecedent for our modern museums. At its peak, Settala's collection contained more than 3,000 pieces, taking in stuffed animals, vases, clocks, jewellery, crockery, precious stones, crystals and the instruments that Settala himself constructed. About 60 of these treasures will be on display.

The museum's architecture may well outclass its contents, but it's certain to be well worth perusing – not least to check out the Chipperfield-designed bookshop and coffee bar.

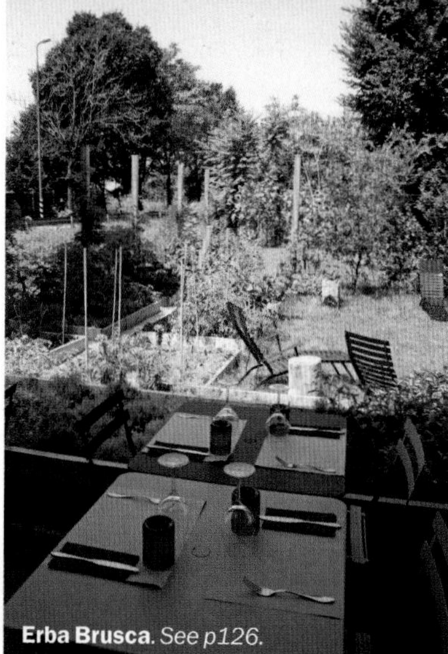
Erba Brusca. *See p126.*

Tano Passami l'Olio

Via Villoresi 16 (02 839 4139, www.tanopassami lolio.it). Metro Romolo, or bus 74, or tram 2. **Meals served** 8-11.30pm Mon-Sat. **Average** €60. **Map** p114 A4 ㉜ **Contemporary Italian**

Although quite a hike from the centre of *navigli* action, this small, dinner-only restaurant has much to tempt, especially if you like olive oil. Eminently contemporary dishes, such as caramelised quail eggs served on tuna mousse, or duck ravioli perfumed with sage, are enhanced with the flavour of one of 40 Italian olive oils, ranging in provenance from Lake Garda and Lake Como to Calabria and Sicily. The atmosphere is formal, with prices to match. At night, this area can feel a little remote; budget for a taxi to take you home.

► *For more on local olive oils, see p194 Liquid Gold.*

Trattoria Madonnina

Via Gentilino 6 (02 8940 9089, www.trattoria-lamadonnina.it). Tram 3, 9. **Meals served** noon-2.30pm Mon-Wed; noon-2.30pm, 8-10.30pm Thur-Sat. **Average** *Lunch* €40. *Dinner* €20. **Map** p114 D4 ㉝ **Traditional Italian**

A down-to-earth place with an appealingly rustic vibe, thanks to the wooden tables, red and white checked tablecloths, and old road signs and posters. The food couldn't be more traditional: four daily *primi*, pasta with tomato or meat sauce, and four *secondi*, often meat cutlets with potatoes or veg, and all at reasonable prices. In spring, you can eat in the courtyard, framed by a jasmine-covered pergola.

Turbigo

Alzaia Naviglio Grande 8 (02 8940 0407, www.turbigomilano.it). Bus 167, or tram 2, 3, 14, 19. **Meals served** noon-3pm; 7-11pm daily. **Average** €50. **Map** p114 C3 ㉞ **Contemporary Italian**

Opened in 2014, Turbigo is attached to the intimate Maison Borella hotel (*see p252*), and part of the same group as the popular Pisacco (*see p83*) and Dry (*see p83*) restaurants in the Brera area. With antique wooden rafters, neon installations and designer trappings, the interior segues from traditional to contemporary – just like the food. The Neapolitan chef's signature dishes include risotto with tomato and smoked scamorza cheese, and raw shrimps with earl grey tea and snow peas. An affordable set menu (from €11) is offered at lunch; in the evening, bills can be quite steep.

Cafés, Bars & Gelaterie

Ese House

Via Tortona 7 (mobile 340 970 1020, www.esehouse.it). Metro Porta Genova, or bus 47, or tram 2, 14, 19. **Open** 7.30am-10pm Mon-Fri; 8pm-3am Sat; 10am-5pm Sun. **Map** p114 B3 ㉟

This super-cool bar is a great place for a mid-morning stop, a quick lunch or aperitifs. Close to Superstudio, where many fashion shoots take place, it's frequented by a mix of models, students from the nearby private European School of Economics and *signore* out for a spot of shopping. The staff are never too cool to be friendly, however, and will happily rustle up some satisfying snacks – perhaps a hot dog with grated carrot, or house-made brownies – even in the middle of the afternoon.

God Save the Food

Via Tortona 34 (02 8942 3806, www.godsave thefood.it). Bus 68, 74, or tram 14. **Open** 7.30pm-midnight Mon-Sat; 8am-6pm Sun. **Map** p114 A3 ㊱

Here since 2011, this stylish, spacious bistro in a former supermarket serves wholesome snacks such as home-made houmous, and salmon club sandwiches with wholemeal bread. Most of the food, from the wood-oven baked loaves to the tempting cakes, is made daily specially for the eaterie. Most items on the menu can also be ordered to go – and there's a 20% discount on pre-packed takeaway dishes from 5pm.

Rebelot del Pont

Ripa di Porta Ticinese 55 (02 8419 4720, www.pontdeferr.it). Metro Porta Genova, or bus 47, 74, or tram 2, 19. **Open** 5.30pm-1am Mon-Sat; noon-3pm, 6pm-midnight Sun. **Map** p114 B3 ㊲

Tapas and cocktails are the thing at this rustic-chic canalside bar, with bare brick walls, wooden tables and paper tablecloths. Taster plates of three to eight tapas (€18-€48) may include delicacies such as oysters with quince or duck with *caffè*. It's in the same building as the Michelin-starred Al Pont de Ferr restaurant (*see p126*), and run by the same team, so quality is guaranteed.

IN THE KNOW ANTIQUES HUNT

On the last Sunday of each month (except July), around 400 antiques dealers display their wares at the **Mercatone dell' Antiquariato sul Naviglio Grande** (02 8940 9971, www.navigliogrande.mi.it). Running for two kilometres alongside the city's oldest canal, the market sells everything from furniture to vintage watches and pulls in close to 150,000 people. Nearby bars and restaurants stay open all day. Enjoy the atmosphere, but don't expect to strike the bargain of the century.

Shops & Services

Fashion shop **DMagazine** (*see p67*) has a branch here, at via Forcella 13 (02 8739 2443).

★ Miracolo a Milano

Via Stendhal 47 (02 4229 3325). Metro Sant'A gostino, or bus 50, or tram 14. **Open** 9am-1.30pm, 4-8pm Mon-Sat. **Food & drink**

Named after the famous magical-realist film by Vittorio de Sica, this tiny dairy really has performed what amounts to a 'Miracle in Milan'. Every day, milk is brought in from a farm just outside the city, near Lodi, and mozzarella is made in vast steel vats at the back of the shop, right before your eyes. It's stored underwater in tanks, and fished out with a ladle for the constant queue of customers. Fresh bread, milk and an exquisite blue cheese are also on sale.

Other locations Eataly, piazza XXV Aprile 10, North (02 4949 7301).

★ Nonostante Marras

Via Cola di Rienzo 8 (02 7628 0991, www.nonostante marras.it). Bus 50, 68, or tram 14. **Open** 10am-7pm Tue-Sat. **Map** p282 A11. **Concept store**

In a city filled with stylish shops, this new concept store, from Sardinian fashion designer Antonio Marras, outdoes most of the competition in a space that manages to be retro, futuristic and bang up to date – all at the same time. The atmospheric former workshop, with its criss-crossing rafters and peeling walls, features racks of Marras's eccentrically cut clothes, a haphazardly shaped bookcase stuffed with quirky books, and artworks, contemporary jewellery and plants. It's worth the trip to this out-of-the-way street, even if just to browse.

Pourquoi Moi?

Ripa di Porta Ticinese 27 (mobile 339 579 2838). Metro Porta Genova. **Open** *Sept-May* 3-7.30pm Mon; noon-7.30pm Tue-Sat; 3-7pm Sun. *June-Aug* 3-10.30pm Mon; noon-10.30pm Tue-Sat; 3-7pm Sun. **Map** p114 C3 (38) **Fashion & accessories**

Formerly known as Superfly, Pourquoi Moi? still carries vintage clothing and accessories, but now covers the period from the 1950s through to the '80s, specialising in retro Scandinavian fashion. The quirky selection comes courtesy of British couple Giuliana Osei (who leads a double life as Kleopatra, the DJ) and her boyfriend, Keith Livingstone. On the last Sunday of the month, the shop moves to the adjacent canal bank to participate in the Mercatone dell' Antiquariato (11am-7pm).

Turbigo.

Sant'Ambrogio & West

Sant'Ambrogio is home to one of the city's leading tourist attractions, Leonardo's *The Last Supper*, but it's also the site of what many Milanese consider their most important church: Sant'Ambrogio, named after the city's patron saint. In the surrounding streets are occasional Roman relics, Renaissance bas-reliefs and magnificent rococo façades.

The district was once the heart of Mediolanum, Roman-era Milan – but it's far from stuck in its ways. Students at the nearby Università Cattolica bring a youthful vibe and there are dozens of chic bars, shops and restaurants to offset the ancient history.

Further west is corso Vercelli, a buzzing shopping strip. Slightly to the north is the San Siro district, dominated by the famous football stadium. It's also the location of a striking new development in the former city fairground, with soon to be erected skyscrapers by Daniel Libeskind, Arata Isozaki and Zaha Hadid.

San Maurizio.

Don't Miss

1 Leonardo da Vinci's The Last Supper Flaky but fabulous (p138).

2 Sant'Ambrogio The locals' favourite church (p134).

3 San Maurizio Better than *The Last Supper* – according to some (p138).

4 Wait & See Funky fashions for Milan's creative crowd (p142).

5 Pasticceria Marchesi *Pasticcini* by Prada (p141).

Sant'Ambrogio. See p134.

SANT'AMBROGIO & AROUND

The Duomo may be more famous and more beautiful to look at, but **Sant'Ambrogio** is more important to the Milanese. Named after the city's patron saint, it dates from Roman times and has the stronger claim to be the city's 'true' church. Sant'Ambrogio was built outside the Roman city walls in an area of early Christian cemeteries and imperial buildings. Nine Italian kings were crowned at its altar between the ninth and 15th centuries (four of whom are buried here). Napoleon and Ferdinand of Austria paid a visit to Sant'Ambrogio immediately after their coronations in the Duomo (1805 and 1838), as Kings of Italy.

The square out front is often filled with students from the nearby **Università Cattolica del Sacro Cuore**, a former monastic complex that has housed Milan's private Catholic university since 1921. The original building, on which Bramante worked at the behest of Ludovico 'il Moro' Sforza in the late 1400s, has extensive 1930s and '40s additions by Giovanni Muzio, who also designed the Milan Triennale (*see p77*).

South-west across the square, the **Pusterla di Sant'Ambrogio** is a 1939 imitation of the medieval gate that once stood here, part of the 1171 defences built after Barbarossa's attacks. Some older materials, including a 14th-century relief showing saints Ambrose, Gervasius and Protasius, have been incorporated. Just to the west of the basilica's main entrance is the Roman *colonna del diavolo*, a column marked by two holes, allegedly made by the Devil's horns: the evil one is said to have suffered a fit of pique at Ambrose's purity and incorruptibility.

North-west, beyond the Pusterla, the **Museo Nazionale della Scienza e della Tecnologia Leonardo da Vinci** is full of technological wonders. Next door, the church of **San Vittore al Corpo** backs on to via degli Olivetani, where San Vittore jail has loomed threateningly since its construction in the 1870s.

Sights & Museums

Museo Nazionale della Scienza e della Tecnologia Leonardo da Vinci

Via San Vittore 21 (02 485 551, www.museo scienza.org). Metro Sant'Ambrogio or bus 50, 58, 94. **Open** 9.30am-5pm Tue-Fri; 9.30am-6.30pm Sat, Sun. **Admission** €10; €4.50-€7 reductions; free under-3s. **Map** p133 C3 ❶

This enormous science and technology museum is a fitting tribute to Milan's revered former resident. Offering over 23,000sq m (248,000sq ft) of exhibition space, and more than 10,000 artefacts, it's essential that you plan your visit here. One of the most fascinating halls displays modern models based on Leonardo da Vinci's sketches, in the fields of military theory, ballistics and aeronautics.

Originally a 16th-century monastery, the buildings have had various incarnations – military hospital (Napoleon), barracks (Italian army) and rubble (World War II Allied bombs). Established just after the war, the current museum was finally inaugurated in 1953, and is now the largest of its kind in Italy. Wandering through, it's hard to think of any aspect of industry or technology that isn't covered: displays deal with metallurgy, printing, bell-casting, minting, engines and horology, as well as the sciences of physics, optics, acoustics and astronomy.

A big draw is the *Enrico Toti*, Italy's first post-war submarine. It was launched on 12 March 1967 as an SSK (hunter-killer submarine), primarily as a deterrent against Soviet nuclear-propelled torpedo-launchers. Decomissioned in 1999, the vessel was donated by the navy to the museum the following year. Its journey from Cremona to the museum involved a 93km (58-mile) road trip aboard a 240-wheel flatbed truck; thousands turned out late one August night to

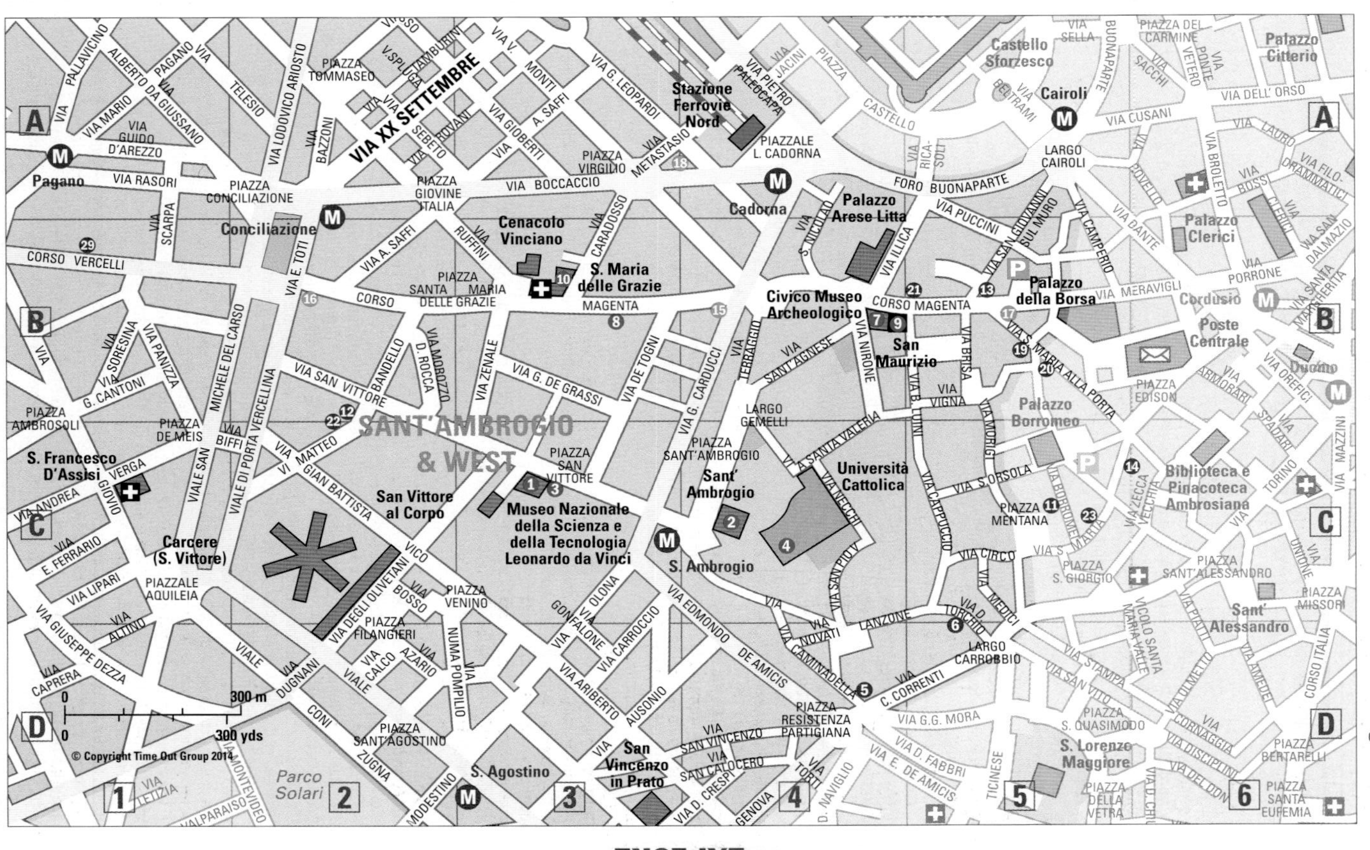

SANT'AMBROGIO & WEST
Palazzo Citterio
Castello Sforzesco
Cairoli
Palazzo Clerici
Cordusio
Poste Centrale
Duomo
Palazzo della Borsa
Biblioteca e Pinacoteca Ambrosiana
Sant' Alessandro
Palazzo Borromeo
S. Lorenzo Maggiore
San Maurizio
Università Cattolica
Palazzo Arese Litta
Civico Museo Archeologico
Stazione Ferrovie Nord
Cadorna
Sant' Ambrogio
S. Ambrogio
S. Maria delle Grazie
Cenacolo Vinciano
Museo Nazionale della Scienza e della Tecnologia Leonardo da Vinci
San Vincenzo in Prato
S. Agostino
San Vittore al Corpo
Conciliazione
Pagano
Carcere (S. Vittore)
S. Francesco D'Assisi
Parco Solari
VIA XX SETTEMBRE
CORSO MAGENTA
FORO BUONAPARTE
VIA DANTE
CORSO VERCELLI
VIA G. CARDUCCI
VIALE DI PORTA VERCELLINA
VIA GIUSEPPE DEZZA
VIA EDMONDO DE AMICIS
CORSO ITALIA
PIAZZALE L. CADORNA
PIAZZA SANT'AMBROGIO
PIAZZA CONCILIAZIONE
PIAZZA RESISTENZA PARTIGIANA
PIAZZALE AQUILEIA
300 m
300 yds
© Copyright Time Out Group 2014

EXPLORE

COFFEE CULTURE

The low-down on caffeine highs.

Milanese coffee culture is complex and often confusing. Just remember never to order a cappuccino after midday, if you want to avoid patronising smiles from the barman (most Milanese think post-morning cappuccino is indigestible). Choose from this list of the city's most frequently ordered caffeine-packed tipples – and you can't go far wrong.

Americano: an espresso served with a miniature jug of hot water, in case you can't drink it neat like the locals.

Cappuccino: a froth-topped blend of milk and espresso, known locally as a *cappuccio*. Can be ordered *decaffeinato*, *scuro* (with less milk) or *senza schiuma* (without foam). It's typically a breakfast drink, but it can also be ordered (exceptionally) as a late-afternoon pick-me-up.

Caffè macchiato: an espresso with a splash of *latte caldo* or *freddo* (hot or cold milk).

Corretto: a 'corrected' espresso – in other words, given a dash of grappa, or other high-octane liqueur. A popular breakfast boost with older men in neighbourhood bars.

Decaffeinato: decaffeinated espresso without the kick.

Espresso: or more simply, *un caffè*. A steamed round of ground coffee. Can be ordered as a *doppio* (double) or *lungo* (with extra water). In the latter case, also known as an americano (*see left*).

Latte: a glass of milk. Order a *latte macchiato* if what you'd like is what is called a 'latte' in English-speaking countries.

Marocchino: a petite glass of espresso, cocoa powder and milk froth, increasingly popular with Milanese.

Orzo: a popular coffee substitute made with barley, for those who want a natural substitute for a *decaffeinato*.

Ristretto: a concentrated espresso, if you can imagine such a thing.

Shakerato: a refreshing summer option; a chilled *caffè lungo*, shaken over ice.

EXPLORE

watch its progress as it rumbled through the streets of Milan. It finally opened to the public in December 2005. Viewing regulations are strict: there's a maximum of six helmeted visitors at any one time, led by a museum guide. Tickets (€8-€10) can be booked in advance or on the day, and paid for at the museum's reception area.

★ FREE Sant'Ambrogio

Piazza Sant'Ambrogio 15 (02 8645 0895, www.basilicasantambrogio.it). Metro Sant'Ambrogio or bus 50, 58, 94. **Open** *Church & San Vittore chapel* 10am-noon, 2.30-6pm Mon-Sat; 3-5pm Sun. **Admission** free. **Map** p133 C4 ❷

The charismatic Bishop Ambrose (Ambrogio) – who defended orthodox Christianity against Arianism and later became Milan's patron saint – had this 'Basilica Martyrum' built between 379 and 386. His remains lie here in the crypt, alongside those of local martyr-saints Gervasius and Protasius.

The church was enlarged in the eighth century, when the Benedictines erected the Campanile dei Monaci (monks' bell tower) to the right of the façade. In the ninth century, under Archbishop Anspert, the atrium preceding the façade was added; it was here that the populace sought sanctuary in times of trouble, of which there was plenty. The church's Romanesque appearance stems from ninth- and tenth-century redesigns. Anspert's atrium was remodelled in the 11th century, when a reconstruction of the church got under way. Its capitals feature biblical scenes and mythical beasts symbolising the struggle between Good and Evil. The Torre dei Canonici (the Tower of the Canons, rather than 'cannons'), to the left of the façade, was built between 1128 and 1144. Further changes to the interior of the church were made in 1196 after the dome collapsed.

In 1492, Ludovico 'il Moro' Sforza called on Donato Bramante to remodel the eighth-century Benedictine monastery. The fall of il Moro in 1499 put an end to Bramante's makeover, which as a result was limited to one side of the old cloister (the Portico della Canonica, accessible from the left of the nave). The church underwent a fairly conservative remodelling job in the 17th century, but suffered severe air-raid damage in 1943; the bombing destroyed Bramante's work, which was subsequently rebuilt using salvaged original materials.

The interior has the sober proportions of the austere Lombard Romanesque style, its three aisles covered with ribbed cross-vaults and false galleries holding up the huge walls. Beneath the pre-Romanesque pulpit, reconstructed from the original pieces after the dome collapsed on it in 1196, lies what is known as the

Stilicone Sarcophagus. This fourth-century masterpiece was traditionally believed to have been the burial place of the Roman general Stilicone, who served the Emperor Honorius and died in 408; later research disproved this legend, however.

The 12th-century golden altar, illustrated with scenes from the life of Christ on the front and of St Ambrose on the back, once covered the porphyry casket commissioned to house the remains of Ambrose, Protasius and Gervasius when they were exhumed in the ninth century. (They were moved from the casket to their current location in the crypt in the 19th century.)

To the right of the main altar, a series of chapels leads to the Sacello di San Vittore in Ciel d'Oro. Part of the church's original fourth-century structure, this chapel was reworked in the 1930s, so that only its glowing, golden fifth-century mosaics in the dome remain to remind us of its antique glory. These portray St Ambrose standing between saints Gervasius and Protasius, with a number of other minor local martyrs looking on. This section of the church has been converted into a small museum (access is through the 18th-century Cappella di Sant'Ambrogio Morente) consisting of the mosaics and precious church furnishings. The Antico Oratorio della Passione (piazza Sant'Ambrogio 23A) is used as an occasional exhibition space.

FREE San Vittore al Corpo

Via San Vittore 25 (02 4800 5351, www.basilica sanvittore.it). Metro Sant'Ambrogio or bus 50, 58, 94. **Open** *Sept-June* 7.30am-12.30pm, 3.30-6.30pm Mon, Tue, Thur; 7.30am-12.30pm Wed; 7.30am-6.30pm Fri, Sat; 8am-1pm Sun. Closed July, Aug (except for mass). **Admission** free. **Map** p133 C3 ❸

The neglected exterior of this complex provides no hint of the magnificence that lies within. The church and former monastery of San Vittore al Corpo grew up around the mausoleum of Emperor Valentinian II, who died in 392; parts of this ancient structure are beneath what has since become the Museo Nazionale della Scienza e della Tecnologia Leonardo da Vinci (*see p132*). The structure was taken over in 1010 by Benedictine monks, who got down to some serious rebuilding. It was given another overhaul in 1560, when it became one of Milan's most sumptuously decorated churches. Works by many local names of the late 16th and 17th centuries – Girolamo Quadrio, Camillo Procaccini, Giovanni Ambrogio Figino, Carlo Francesco Nuvolone and Daniele Crespi – are still here. The choir stalls with wood-inlay intarsia work from the 1580s are worth a close look.

FREE Università Cattolica del Sacro Cuore

Largo Gemelli 1 (02 72 341, www.unicatt.it). Metro Sant'Ambrogio or bus 50, 58, 94 or tram 16, 27. **Open** 7.45am-6.30pm Mon-Fri; 8am-2.30pm Sat. **Admission** free. **Map** p133 C4 ❹

In 1497, Ludovico 'il Moro' Sforza called upon Donato Bramante to expand what had been – before it was turned over to the Cistercian order in the late 15th century – the most powerful and influential Benedictine monastery in northern Italy. Although Bramante was hired to add four grand cloisters, only two were completed (an Ionic one in 1513 and a Doric one in 1630). In 1921, as a result of an agreement between the Catholic Church and the Fascist government, the ex-monastery became home to this private Catholic university. Throughout the 1930s and '40s, architect Giovanni Muzio overhauled the complex in his characteristic dry, straightforward style. The student life has occasionally proved more colourful than the architecture: the 1968 protests kicked off here, after a hike in tuition fees.

EXPLORE

Università Cattolica del Sacro Cuore.

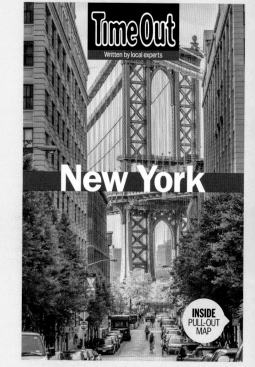

Restaurants

★ Buongusto

Via Caminadella 2 (02 8645 2479, www.buongusto.eu). Bus 94 or tram 2, 14. **Meals served** noon-3pm, 6.30pm-midnight Tue-Sat. **Average** €40. **Map** p133 D4 ❺ **Contemporary Italian**

This tiny fresh-pasta shop and 30-seat restaurant is definitely one to try if you want to see how far traditional Italian ingredients can be pushed. Ravioli may be stuffed with unusual ingredients such as broad beans, or cacio cheese, pepper, saffron and coffee; tagliolini may come with leeks, caper powder and candied lemon peel. For something really different, try the Surprise Menu (€70): you might be able to guess the ingredients, but the chef works her magic on them in her own special way. As a bonus: buy some of the *bottega*'s fresh pasta to take home.

€ Il Fontanino

Via del Torchio 8 (mobile 338 372 8084). Tram 2, 3, 14. **Open** *Sept-June* 9am-7.30pm Mon-Fri. *July* 9am-3pm Mon-Fri. **Average** €4-€5. **No credit cards. Map** p133 D5 ❻ **Pizzeria**

Il Fontanino's pizzas, *foccaccie*, savoury tarts and desserts are all made daily in these hole-in-the-wall premises, which mostly function as a takeaway. If you want to sit in, there are a few stools, but competition is fierce. Try the signature tomato and leek pizza; desserts include chocolate and pear cake. Note that the choice of sweet stuff is wider in the winter – Italian guys and gals begin watching their weight as soon as the sun comes out and they start thinking of cutting a fine figure at the beach.

SANTA MARIA DELLE GRAZIE & AROUND

Running south from the Castello, stylish corso Magenta is the continuation of via Meravigli, segueing, eventually, into the more commercial corso Vercelli. At the beginning of the corso, the historic **Pasticceria Marchesi** has just been bought by Prada. Pop in for a quick pick-me-up in the form of coffee and cake, before you attempt the area's many major monuments.

With its dazzling wall-to-wall, floor-to-ceiling frescoes by Bernardino Luini, among others, the 16th-century church of **San Maurizio** is just one of these. Be sure to duck through the small doorway to the left of the altar and visit the massive frescoed Convent Hall.

Next door is the **Civico Museo Archeologico**, a less colourful though no less interesting sight. The two both formed part of the **Monastero Maggiore**, a Benedictine convent that housed the city's most influential order of nuns.

Across the street at no.24, the **Palazzo Arese Litta**, home to Milan's oldest theatre – **Teatro Litta** (*see p176*) – as well as the HQ of the Italian state railways, has a rococo façade with two colossal telamones flanking the entrance. It was designed between 1642 and 1648 by Francesco Maria Ricchini (or Richini), and the rococo façade by Bartolomeo Bolli was added in the mid 18th century.

This stretch of corso Magenta is home to two additional buildings of note. Back at no.12, you'll find the **Casa Rossi**, designed by Giuseppe Pestagalli around 1860, simulating the superimposed loggias of the Venetian Renaissance style. The building has a pretty little octagonal courtyard that's worth a look, as well as the organic herbalist **Officinali di Montauto** (02 8905 0915).

At no.29, set back from the road and thus not visible, is what remains of a palazzo given to Lorenzo de' Medici in 1486 by the Sforzas, for when he came from Florence to visit them in Milan: it's just a short walking distance from the castle, where the Sforzas lived. You can catch a glimpse of this sadly neglected building from the little park round the corner in via Terraggio, the entrance to which is just past the Nuova Orchidea cinema.

Continuing westwards along corso Magenta, you'll come to **Santa Maria delle Grazie** and the refectory housing Milan's most precious work of art, *The Last Supper*. While you're here, pay a visit to the church itself, a welcome break from the rather intense atmosphere surrounding Leonardo's masterpiece.

Across the street from Santa Maria delle Grazie, the Palazzo delle Stelline houses a charitable foundation, the **Fondazione Stelline**, which works to promote the cultural, social and economic development of the city. Many conferences are held here throughout the year, as well as the occasional art show.

On nearby via Carducci, stop for a drink in the buzzing **Bar Magenta**, a Milan mainstay.

Sights & Museums

Civico Museo Archeologico

Corso Magenta 15 (02 8844 5208, www.comune.milano.it). Metro Cadorna, or bus 50, 58, 94, or tram 16, 27. **Open** 9am-5.30pm Tue-Sun. **Admission** €5; free-€3 reductions. Free for all last hr of the day; Tue afternoon. **No credit cards. Map** p133 B4 ❼

The buildings of the archaeological museum are as interesting as the collections within. The initial courtyard was once the entrance to the Monastero Maggiore; and a detailed model, just past the museum's reception, shows what Milan looked like in Roman times. Indeed, almost the entire ground floor is dedicated to artefacts from the important Roman settlement known as Mediolanum, including the unique Coppa Trivulzio Diatreta from the late fourth century, a cup created from a single piece of glass, and the outstanding stone head of Zeus from the first or second century. The impressive

Santa Maria delle Grazie.

prehistoric section covers the Milan area from the Neolithic period to Roman times. Downstairs, you'll find a stretch of Roman city walls (built by Emperor Maximian in the third century) and an area containing a small selection of Greek artefacts. There's also a surprisingly extensive collection of Buddhist art from the ancient kingdom of Gandhara (now northern Pakistan and eastern Afghanistan), acquired by the museum in the 1980s.

In the garden at the rear is a polygonal tower, originally part of the city's defence system under the Romans (Mediolanum ended here; on the other side of the wall was the countryside). This was later transformed into a chapel for the monastery. The circular interior bears traces of 13th-century frescoes, including a vivid image of St Francis of Assisi receiving his stigmata from Jesus himself.

FREE Fondazione Stelline

Palazzo delle Stelline, corso Magenta 61 (02 4546 2411, www.stelline.it). Metro Cadorna or tram 16, 27. **Open** *Fondazione Stelline* 9am-6pm Tue-Sun. *Sala del Collezionista* 10am-6pm Tue-Sun. **Admission** *Fondazione Stelline* free. *Sala del Collezionista* varies. **Map** p133 B3 8

Built on the site of the original Santa Maria della Stella convent after it burned to the ground, Palazzo delle Stelline was designated an orphanage in 1578 by the archbishop, later saint, Carlo Borromeo, and continued to function as such until the 1970s. The building is now a conference centre, and also houses the offices of the European Union, the French Cultural Centre and the Hotel Palazzo delle Stelline (*see p254*). To the right of the pretty, cloistered courtyard is a small exhibition space, the Sala del Collezionista, sheltered from the road noise of corso Magenta. Shows have ranged from 18th-century works by Lombard painter Cesare Ligari to sculptures by contemporary light artist Massimo Uberti.

★ FREE San Maurizio al Monastero Maggiore

Corso Magenta 15 (02 85 561). Metro Cadorna, or bus 50, 58, 94, or tram 16, 27. **Open** 9.30am-5.30pm Tue-Sat. **Admission** free. **Map** p133 B4 9

Located on the corner of corso Magenta and via Luini, the Monastero Maggiore was once home to the city's most important female Benedictine convent. Today, most of what's left of the original building is given over to the Archaeological Museum (*see p137*), while the 16th-century church of San Maurizio survives pretty much intact, and is a definite must-see. Inconspicuous on the outside, its interior boasts some of the most beautiful frescoes to be found in Milan.

The most famous of these are by Lombard artist Bernardino Luini, who worked with Leonardo da Vinci, and who some claim surpassed his master here (though they may just be beating the local boy's drum). Luini was responsible for painting the Cappella Santa Caterina (third on the right) in the public hall, and for frescoes on the partition wall that separated the main church from the smaller church, reserved for the cloistered nuns. Among his most notable frescoes is *Christ at the Column*, depicting a moribund Christ being removed from an imposing marble pillar, in place of the usual cross. Other artists who contributed to the church's interior included his brother Aurelio, as well as the Piazza family, Ambrogio Bergognone – another of Luini's maestros, and the Venetian artist Simone Peterzano, who taught Caravaggio.

★ Santa Maria delle Grazie & The Last Supper

Church *02 4676 1123, www.grazieop.it.* **Open** 7am-noon, 3-7pm Mon-Sat; 7.30am-12.15pm, 3.30-9pm Sun. **Admission** free. **The Last Supper (Il Cenacolo)** *02 9280 0360, www.cenacolovinciano.net.* **Open**

(reservations compulsory) 8.15am-6.45pm Tue-Sun. *English Guided tours* 9.30am, 3.30pm Tue-Sun. **Admission** €8; free-€4.75 reductions.
Both *Piazza Santa Maria delle Grazie. Metro Cadorna or Conciliazione or tram 16, 18.*
Map p133 B3 ⑩

The church of Santa Maria delle Grazie was begun in 1465 to a plan by Guiniforte Solari. Just two years after it was finished, in the 1480s, Ludovico 'il Moro' Sforza commissioned architect Donato Bramante to turn the church into a family mausoleum in the new Renaissance style; this work was never completed – but down came Solari's apse and up went a Renaissance tribune, usually attributed to Bramante, in its place. At the same time, the adjoining Dominican monastery was given the *chiostrino* (small cloister) and a new sacristy. The monks ran an active branch of the Inquisition from 1553 to 1778, and continued to endow their church with decorative elements. After Napoleon's suppression of religious congregations in 1810, the complex was turned into barracks and a military warehouse. Control of the church was returned to the Dominican monks in 1905. In 1943, bombing destroyed the great cloister of the monastery, but fortuitously spared the three walls of the refectory, including the one bearing Leonardo's *The Last Supper* (*see below* **Leonardo's Last Supper**), and the *chiostrino*.

The terracotta façade of the church is in the best Lombard tradition; again, the portal is attributed

LEONARDO'S LAST SUPPER

Probably the world's most famous fresco.

A wealth of art can be seen in Milan's many galleries and churches, but Leonardo da Vinci's *Il Cenacolo* (1495-97), known in English as *The Last Supper*, remains the biggest art draw of them all.

The work is arguably the greatest painting of the Renaissance. It depicts the dramatic moment immediately after Jesus has revealed that one of his disciples will betray him. Da Vinci portrays their expressions of shock, amazement and hostility with acute psychological acuity.

The painting is in a seriously deteriorated condition. Da Vinci experimented with a new technique, painting on to dried-out plaster, rather than the traditional method of applying colour to wet plaster. The objective was to retain control over tone and nuance, and to make amendments as he went along, but the downside was that the paint was prevented from impregnating the plaster base.

The work has a history of dereliction. Paint began to peel off even within Leonardo's lifetime. In the early 19th century, invading French soldiers used the monastery refectory as a stable, and the Renaissance masterpiece was, allegedly, used for target practice. World War II air raids destroyed parts of the church, including the great cloister, but *The Last Supper* was unscathed. Despite surviving all this, the work still suffers from a wound inflicted early in its life: the door that was cut into the bottom centre, cutting off Christ's feet. Though the mural has been more or less under restoration since it was first painted, the most radical restoration started in 1977. Layers of paint and detritus accumulated over the centuries were removed to allow some of the original luminous colours to re-emerge; the fresco was unveiled once again in 1999.

To preserve the integrity of the work, visitors are allowed a 15-minute time slot to see the painting (*see p140* **Ticket Tricks**). Visitor numbers shot up after the publication of Dan Brown's novel *The Da Vinci Code*, followed by the movie of the book. The novel claims that da Vinci hid secret messages in the painting, and that the disciple to Jesus's right ('with flowing red hair, delicate folded hands, and the hint of a bosom') is actually Mary Magdalene. The book has fired the imagination of millions, but for all that is a work of fiction. The figure on Christ's immediate right is – as Cenacolo staff will point out – clearly identified in da Vinci's sketchbooks as John the Apostle; and art historians know that it was common practice to paint John with a feminine aspect in da Vinci's time.

Also worth noting is the work at the other end of the room: the *Crucifixion* fresco (1495) by Giovanni Donato da Montorfano. Da Vinci added the portraits of Ludovico il Moro, his wife Beatrice d'Este and their children, but they have faded beyond recognition.

EXPLORE

to Bramante. Inside, Solari's Gothic tendencies in the three-aisled nave clash with the fresco-covered arches and Bramante's more muscular style. Standing out among works by leading local artists from the 15th to 17th centuries is an altarpiece (in the sixth chapel on the left) showing the Holy Family with St Catherine, by 16th-century Venetian painter and student of Titian, Paris Bordone. The carved wooden choir stalls in the apse date from 1470.

The garden provides a welcome break from the bustle in the piazza outside the church. During mass, the cloisters can be reached through a door in via Caradosso 1 (same opening times as the church).

Restaurants

Hostaria Borromei

Via Borromei 4 (02 8645 3760, www.hostaria borromei.com). Bus 50, 58 or tram 16, 19. **Meals served** 12.30-2.45pm, 7.30-10.45pm daily. **Average** €50. **Map** p133 C5 ⓫ **Traditional Italian**

With its deep-yellow courtyard hidden within a 15th-century palazzo, flowers and hanging baskets, Hostaria Borromei is made for summer nights. However, if you're a non-smoker, you may prefer to book a table in the cosy interior. The menu varies according to the seasons, and might contain such delights as whitebait omelette and the excellent house-made hot apple tarte tatin; check the website for updates.

Pane e Acqua

Via Bandello 14 (02 4819 8622, www.paneacqua.com). Bus 50, 58 or tram 16. **Open** phone for details. **Map** p133 B2 ⓬ **Contemporary Italian**

One of this place's main attractions has always been the very funky decor by home-grown designer Paola Navone, featuring mismatched chairs by Dutch designers Piet Hein Eek and Maarten Baas, vintage pieces, napkins hanging from the ceiling, and blow-up printouts of cutlery on the walls. A change of chef and management was scheduled as this guide went to press, so the jury is still out on what modifications will be made to the fine Mediterranean menu.

TICKET TRICKS

How to bag tickets for The Last Supper.

Along with La Scala (*see p172*), Leonardo da Vinci's world-famous masterwork is Milan's hot ticket. In both cases, getting hold of said tickets is something of an enterprise.

The official way to score tickets to view *The Last Supper* is to book directly, either by phone or online – but concierges at top hotels say they're almost impossible to get their hands on, as many seem to be allocated to tour operators automatically. However, with a little patience, you might be in luck.

Tickets for each month become available on a set date a few months before, revealed at **www.cenacolovinciano.net** (a service provided by online ticketing agency www.vivaticket.com). For the start of Expo in May 2015, for instance, bookings open in early February; for June 2015, they begin in early March. Be ready to go for it, immediately. To protect the fragile artwork, admission is in groups of 25-30 people. You have 15 minutes to view the painting. Time-slots run throughout the day from 8.15am to 6.45pm. To enjoy the services of an English-speaking guide, opt for the 9.30am or 3.30pm session; for an Italian-speaking guide, go for 10am or 4pm (a guide costs €3.50 extra). The other slots are without a guide.

To book online, you'll need to register. Much patience will be required. Alternatively, you can call **Vivaticket** on 02 9280 0360. An automatic answering service will ask you to choose your language, and you will then, with any luck, be put through to an operator.

Tickets cost €6.50, plus a handling fee of €1.50. Arrive 30 minutes ahead of the appointed time to collect your tickets from the office outside, especially if you've booked an audio-guide (€3.50), as this lasts 20 minutes, including a five-minute introduction before you enter the hallowed refectory.

For those who like to live dangerously, there is another way: show up at the ticket office at 8am, and say, very politely, that you want to buy tickets from 'cancelled reservations' (*prenotazioni annullate*) for today. If they say they have none, try hanging around for about 15 minutes and, as they get organised and cancellations from the tour companies come up on their screens, they may turn up a couple. At this point, you pay the standard €6.50. You may end up as part of a 'tour' that speaks an incomprehensible language, but you can say that you got in to see *The Last Supper* without booking ahead.

There's a final option. You can always resort to tagging along with a tour company: the half-day tour of Milan with **Zani Viaggi** (*see p267*), for instance, includes tickets to *The Last Supper*. It costs €50-€60, but you are guaranteed a ticket. Even so, be sure to book a few days in advance.

€ Pizzeria Meucci

Via Meravigli 18, entrance on via San Giovanni sul Muro (02 8645 0526). Bus 50, 58 or tram 16, 19. **Meals served** 11.30am-3.30pm, 7-11pm Mon-Sat; 7-11pm Sun. **Average** €20. **No credit cards. Map** p133 B5 ⓭ **Pizza**

You'll spot the lunchtime queue before you reach Meucci's minuscule entrance. It has just six tables, so you're encouraged to order while you wait. Unlike anywhere else in the city, Meucci's pizzas are small and deep, perfect for a light meal. They also do takeaway.

Trattoria Milanese

Via Santa Marta 11 (02 8645 1991). Metro Cordusio or tram 2, 3, 14. **Meals served** noon-2.30pm, 7.15-10.30pm Mon-Sat. **Average** €45. **Map** p133 C5 ⓮ **Milanese**

Seemingly unchanged in 50 years, this trattoria is refined yet inviting. Its fine, traditional Milanese cuisine is well known, and you'll share dining space with locals and guidebook-wielding foodies. Saffron-infused risotto (*risotto alla Milanese*) is the house speciality, along with *osso buco* and *cotoletta alla Milanese* (breaded veal chop).

Cafés, Bars & Gelaterie

Bar Magenta

Via Carducci 13 (02 4229 2194, www.barmagenta.it). Metro Cadorna, or bus 58, 94, or tram 16, 19, 27. **Open** 8am-2am Mon-Fri; 9am-2am Sat, Sun. **Map** p133 B4 ⓯

Bar Magenta's wooden interior is more Edwardian London than modern Milan. Despite this, or perhaps because of it, the place is an institution and one much loved by young Milanese as well as the expat community. There's beer on tap; some lunchtime specials (pasta, salads) and panini are served throughout the day and into the evening. It's often more packed than the proverbial sardine can.

Biffi

Corso Magenta 87, at piazza Baracca (02 4800 6702, www.biffipasticceria.it). Metro Conciliazione or bus 67, 68 or tram 16, 18. **Open** 6.30am-8.30pm daily. **Map** p133 B2 ⓰

One of Milan's historic cafés and cake shops, Biffi is set in the Magenta/Vercelli neighbourhood. The counter is cosy but never overcrowded and the tearoom has a handful of tables for chatting and resting; the place reeks of refined elegance. It's particularly famed for its *panettone*, the Milanese Christmas cake it has been producing since 1847.

► *If you don't make it to the café, the panettone can be bought online.*

★ Pasticceria Marchesi

Via Santa Maria alla Porta 11A (02 876 730, www.pasticceriamarchesi.it). Bus 50, 58 or tram 16, 19, 27. **Open** 8am-8pm Tue-Sat; 8am-1pm Sun. **Map** p133 B5 ⓱

Bar Magenta.

In one of Milan's most beautiful buildings – with gorgeous, early 20th-century sgraffito ornamentation and original interiors – this historic *pasticceria* and bar serves coffee and wonderful old-fashioned cakes. It was recently acquired by Prada, who, for the moment, very sensibly haven't changed a thing. Marchesi also sells prettily packaged own-brand chocolates (a sign in the window apologises in advance for keeping customers waiting as confections are hand-wrapped). In the run-up to Christmas, its sought-after panettone should be ordered weeks in advance; at Easter, its dove-shaped colomba cakes are equally in demand. *See also p143* **Let Them Eat Cake**.

★ Shockolat

Via Boccaccio 9 (02 4810 0597, www.shockolat.it). Metro Cadorna, or bus 94, or tram 1, 27. **Open** 7.30am-1am daily. **Map** p133 A3 ⓲

This gorgeous café excels in all things chocolate. From huge, sensual mounds of ice-cream in flavours such as chilli chocolate, ginger chocolate, orange chocolate and amaretto chocolate, to tarts, brownies and slabs of chocolate flavoured with figs or hazelnuts, everything is utterly irresistible.

Shops & Services

Calé Fragranze d'Autore

Via Santa Maria alla Porta 5 (02 8050 9449, www.cale.it). Bus 50, 58 or tram 16, 19, 27. **Open** 3-7pm Mon; 10am-7pm Tue-Fri; 10am-7.30pm Sat. **Map** p133 B5 ⓳ **Health & beauty**

Silvio Levi, grandson of the founder of this family-run firm, sniffs out rare, artisanal perfumes for both men and women, as well as shaving creams and hair products. Finds include the company's own Calé Fragranze d'Autore, produced by Levi in association

EXPLORE

with famous 'noses' Maurizio Cerizza and Mark Buxton. The wood-beamed room upstairs houses a collection of historic bottles and packaging – not to be missed.

E Marinella

Via Santa Maria alla Porta 5 (02 8646 7036, www.marinellanapoli.it). Bus 50, 58 or tram 16, 19, 27. **Open** 10am-7pm Mon-Sat. **Map** p133 B5 ⑳ **Accessories**

Until a few years ago, fans of made-to-measure tie-maker E Marinella had to head to Naples. Now, there's an outpost in Milan, tucked away in a 17th-century palazzo in the city's financial district. To those in the know, the company's silk neckpieces (made to order from €130), with tiny daisy or flower motifs, act like an old school tie. Select your own fabric, wait one month for delivery – and join the club.

► *E Marinella also has a generous selection of ready-to-wear ties – they cost slightly less too.*

Other location via Manzoni 23, Centre (opens late 2014).

Wait & See.

EXPLORE

Officina Profumo Farmaceutica di Santa Maria Novella

Corso Magenta 22 (02 805 3695, www.smnovella.it). Bus 50, 58 or tram 16, 19. **Open** 3-7pm Mon; 10am-7pm Tue-Sat. **Map** p133 B5 ㉑ **Health & beauty**

This small outpost of the famous Tuscan herbalist and apothecary may not have the cachet of the original 17th-century store in Via della Scala, Florence – but it does have most of the products, from hand creams and body lotions to hand-moulded mint and olive oil soaps. All make fabulous gifts in their traditional packaging.

Other location via Madonnina 11, North (02 3651 9630).

★ Rossana Orlandi

Via Bandello 14 (02 4674 47224, www.rossanaorlandi.com). Bus 50, 58, 68. **Open** 3-7pm Mon; 10am-7pm Tue-Sat. **Map** p133 B2 ㉒ **Homewares**

Those anxious to understand all the fuss over Milanese design should head directly to this shop. Design guru Rossana Orlandi conjured this magical gallery/concept store from a small, early 1900s industrial space. You'll find exquisitely edited pieces by big-name furniture and product designers, as well as items by up-and-coming international names – all reflecting Orlandi's impeccable, but never pretentious, taste. There's no street-front: ring the bell to gain access, cross the courtyard and the entrance is on the left. Inside, the goodies stretch over two floors: the gallery, established in 2008, exhibits limited editions and one-off pieces; head upstairs for fabrics and kitchen accessories.

★ Wait & See

Via Santa Marta 14 (02 7208 0195, www.waitandsee.it). Metro Cordusio or tram 1, 2, 27. **Open** 3.30-7.30pm Mon; 10.30am-7.30pm Tue-Sat. **Map** p133 C5 ㉓ **Fashion**

If you're curious about tracking down the latest alternative Milanese fashion looks, this funkily furnished former convent down a narrow alleyway is the place to come. You'll learn almost as much about what's hot around town from the clients as you will from the carefully edited racks of clothes from Italy, Europe and the US. Customers in transparent overdresses, or hats, full skirts, socks and ankle boots, search the colour-coded rails for gems such as long striped T-shirts from Italian company Happy Ship, or un-hemmed chiffon evening frocks by Semi-Couture. Other brands to look out for: Happy Sheep and Dove nuotono gli squali (Where the sharks swim). Dresses are mostly in the €150-€300 range.

LET THEM EAT CAKE

Pasticcini by Prada and Louis Vuitton.

Hungry for more than just fashion, big brands in Milan have been gobbling up the city's top cafés and bakeries – and even fighting over who gets to have first bite. The Battle of the Cakes began in summer 2013, when Milan-based Prada and French fashion giant Louis Vuitton Moët Hennessy (LVMH) raced to acquire a majority stake in the **Cova** café (www.pasticceriacova.it), on the corner of via Montenapoleone and via Sant'Andrea, right in the heart of Milan's Golden Rectangle. In the end, the French conglomerate grabbed the biggest slice, buying an 80 per cent share for a reported €35 million. The coveted café hasn't changed much since the purchase, its chichi interior remaining a hangout for well-off tourists, shoppers and ladies-who-lunch – though LVMH has said it wants to expand Cova's operations overseas. As it is, Cova already has franchises in cities such as Hong Kong, Shanghai and Tokyo – as well as on cruise ships run by Celebrity Cruises Inc.

Not to be outdone, Prada cast its greedy eye over **Pasticceria Marchesi** (*see p141*), housed since 1824 in one of Milan's most gorgeous *palazzi*, in the elegant corso

Magenta zone. In spring 2014, the company snaffled an 80 per cent stake in the café and bakery. For now, nothing much has altered here either: Milanese *signori*, models and bankers rub shoulders at the elegant wooden bar with discerning tourists, consuming cappuccino and old-fashioned cakes (such as the exquisite confections filled with chocolate and custard cream). Prada has murmured about developing the brand, and will be serving Marchesi's goodies at its new café, opening in 2015 in its newly refurbished Galleria Vittorio Emanuele menswear store. But for now, if you fancy a taste of the *dolce vita*, it's best to head to the original cafés.

SAN SIRO & THE FIERE

Although fashion always makes for attention-grabbing headlines, Milan is a major European player in many other areas. Two of the biggest have important outposts in this north-westerly zone. One of them is football – at the famous **San Siro Stadium**. The other is trade fairs, where thousands of businesses meet and buy; between them, **FieraMilanoCity**, and **FieraMilano** out in the northerly satellite town of Rho, receive five million visitors a year. Smaller trade shows are held in the city-centre location, while the really important events take place at the vastly bigger Rho site, which opened in 2005. For some of the largest fairs, such as the Milan International Furniture Fair (Salone Internazionale del Mobile, *see p35*) in April, hotel rooms are booked months in advance and finding a taxi becomes almost impossible.

In 2008, to a mixed local response, demolition engineers blasted FieraMilanoCity's vast Pavilion 20 to smithereens. The area is now home to **CityLife**, a district that includes low-rise residential complexes designed by starchitects Daniel Libeskind and Zaha Hadid. The duo, along with Japanese architect Arata Isozaki, are also responsible for three skyscrapers that will form the development's focal points. Isozaki's building is scheduled for completion by May 2015; the other two should be finished by 2017. A shopping district is also in the offing, along with a transport system involving underground access roads and parking, and a new metro stop on the no.5 (lilac) line. The result will be a ten-hectare (24 acre), car-free zone of green parkland, dotted with water features, where pedestrians and cyclists will reign.

If you're not in town for a trade event, or a football match, it's unlikely you'll be drawn to this eminently residential, tree-lined neighbourhood, unless it's to visit the **Casa di Riposo per Musicisti** – the retirement home for musicians established by Giuseppe Verdi, and also his final resting place. It's just a short walk down leafy via Buonarroti from the piazzale Giulio Cesare side of the Fiera. Further south, the commercial corso Vercelli shopping strip heads east from piazza Piemonte, and is worth a quick browse, if only to dive into department store Coin.

West of the Fiera is the San Siro district, another upmarket residential district, which is also home to the city's world-famous San Siro football stadium (or, to give it its proper name, Stadio Giuseppe Meazza), where both

STEPPING OUT

For handcrafted men's shoes, visit via Belfiore.

Walking down the bustling corso Vercelli, it's easy to miss the turn-off for via Belfiore, one of Milan's most discreet shopping streets. This little-known thoroughfare hides a secret: it's home to two of the classiest men's shoe shops in Milan, **Belfiore** and **Cardinale** (for both, *see p147*). The boutiques are situated side by side and share an address, and both are family-run – but by different families and they're very keen to ensure that everyone knows the difference. Each specialises in what might be termed the 'English' look: not scruffy trainers long past their use-by dates, but tasselled loafers and impeccably artisan-made Oxfords, all in high-quality materials, with a distinctively Italian touch. Though not crafted on the premises, shoes for both shops are rigorously made in Italy. Each specialises in ready-to-wear, rather than made-to-measure, though Belfiore will stamp the client's initials on the sole or uppers, upon request (Cardinale eschews such fripperies.) Prices are surprisingly accessible: Belfiore's shoes start at €179; Cardinale's cost €159-€230.

FC Inter(nazionale) and AC Milan play. There's also a joint must-see museum for football followers, while a new, standalone museum for AC fans recently opened close by. While in the area, don't miss Leonardo da Vinci's enormous bronze *Giant Horse* (Cavallo di Leonardo), created in 1999 from the master's drawings.

EXPLORE

Sights & Museums

FREE Casa di Riposo per Musicisti – Fondazione Giuseppe Verdi

Piazza Buonarroti 29 (02 499 6009, www.casaverdi.org). Metro Buonarroti, or bus 67, or tram 16. **Open** *Crypt* 8.30am-6pm daily. **Admission** free (donations welcome). **Map** p145 C3 ㉔

A statue of composer Giuseppe Verdi presides over piazza Buonarroti, where a neo-Romanesque palazzo, designed in 1899 by architect Camillo Boito (the top floor is a post-war addition), houses a retirement home for musicians. Across the courtyard – often filled with the sounds of tenors or sopranos running through a few scales – stairs lead down to the crypt where Verdi and his wife Giuseppina Strepponi are buried. Concerts are also held here (check the website for details).

Casa Milan

Via Aldo Rossi 8 (02 62 281, http://casamilan.acmilan.com). Metro Lotto, or bus 90, or tram 14. **Open** *Museum* 10am-7pm Mon-Wed, Fri-Sun; 10am-9.30pm Thur. *Shop* 10am-8pm Mon-Wed, Fri-Sun; 10am-10.30pm Thur. *Restaurant* 8am-8.30pm Mon-Wed; 8am-11pm Thur; 8am-10pm Fri-Sun. **Admission** varies, see website for details. **Map** p145 C1 ㉕

Since May 2014, Silvio Berlusconi's football club has had its very own museum, in the formerly industrial Portello district close to the FieraMilanoCity – much to the excitement, no doubt, of AC Milan fans across the globe. Designed by local architect Fabio Novembre, the museum has exhibits including holograms of Barbara Berlusconi (AC's vice-president and daughter of Silvio) and footballers Andriy Shevchenko and Kakà, among others; and a trophies room built around a 3m (10ft) high model of the European Cup. There's also a shop (of course), carrying personalised jerseys, professional G500 foosball tables, giant Milan teddies and other such essentials, as well as a restaurant, Cucina Milanello, decorated in the club's red and black colours.

FREE Cavallo di Leonardo

Piazza dello Sport 16 (02 482 161, www.ippodromimilano.it). Metro Lotto, or bus 78, or tram 16. **Open** 9am-5.30pm Tue-Sun. **Admission** free. **Map** p145 A2 ㉖

Commissioned by Ludovico 'il Moro' Sforza in 1482 in honour of his father Francesco, this enormous bronze horse took over 500 years to complete. Leonardo da Vinci made drawings and a colossal clay model, and sketched out a new method for casting bronze on such a large scale. But Charles VIII's 1494 attempt to invade the city meant that the 70 tonnes of bronze went, in short order, from potential art to working weapons. In 1999, American Charles Dent supplied the funds necessary to make the vision a reality, and da Vinci's 7.2m (23.6ft) horse is now the largest equestrian statue in the world. The 'Gran Cavallo' stands inside the grounds of Milan's Racetrack (*ippodromo*). Large photos show the making of the sculpture, but there's little in the way of additional information.

FieraMilano

Strada Statale del Sempione 28 (02 49 971, www.fieramilano.it). Metro Rho Fiera; shuttle buses from Linate, Malpensa and Orio al Serio airports for major trade events.

Visitors coming by train to Expo 2015 will be able to admire Milan's steel and glass commercial trade fair hub by architect Massimiliano Fuksas, which lies opposite the Expo exhibition site, 12km (seven miles) north of Milan. Opened in 2005, FieraMilano is among the largest trade fair complexes in Europe. Milan's most important trade events, including the Salone Internazionale del Mobile and the annual MiArt contemporary art show – both of which are open to the public, take place here.

FieraMilanoCity

Piazzale Carlo Magno 1 (02 499 71, www.fieramilano.it). Metro Lotto or bus 78. **Map** p145 C2 ㉗

Milan's original trade fair was set up near Porta Venezia in 1920 in an effort to kickstart an economy that was slow to recover from World War I. As events grew, the structure was moved to its current address, expanding as permanent pavilions were added over the years. Of the original buildings, only a portion of the Palazzo dello Sport (1925) and a few art nouveau edifices near the corner of via Domodossola still survive. *Photo p147.*

★ Museo & Tour San Siro

Stadio Giuseppe Meazza, piazzale dello Sport 1, Gate 14 (02 404 2432, www.sansirotour.com). Metro Lotto then bus 49. **Open** 9.30am-6pm daily. **Admission** *Museum & tour* €17; €12 reductions. *Museum only* €7; €5 reductions. Free under-6s. **Map** p145 A2 ㉘

An essential place of pilgrimage for any football fan, small but chock-full of AC Milan and FC Inter paraphernalia. Highlights include a pair of 1928 Inter cufflinks, documentation on Berlusconi's purchase of AC Milan in 1986, and white ceramic busts of AC Milan stars Marco van Basten, Ruud Gullit and Frank Rijkaard. There are also plenty of other items of historical interest, including old table-football sets, photos from the stadium's first Milan-Inter match and a display of football boots showing how they've developed over the past century. The experience continues with a tour of the stadium and the highlight – a visit to the changing rooms.

Here, the very different characters of the teams, and their managers, come to the fore. Silvio Berlusconi's Milan players each have their own designated spot, with stars getting special treatment; under former president Massimo Moratti, Inter's changing-room places were democratically interchangeable, though the new Indonesian-born president Erick Thohir (incumbent since 2013) may

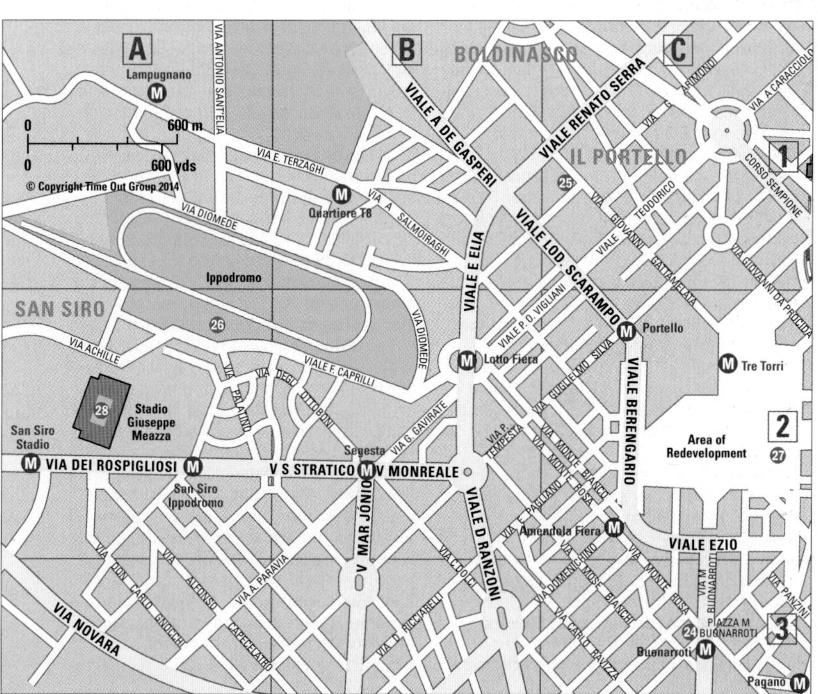

FORZA INTER! FORZA MILAN!

Sixty years of shared history at San Siro may be coming to an end.

Stadio Giuseppe Meazza, aka **San Siro**, is home to two of Italy's top teams, AC Milan and FC Inter(nazionale) Milan. It's one of the most illustrious grounds in Europe, and even on non-match days its museum and tour (*see p145*) can bring the 85,000-seat stadium to life.

AC Milan was established in 1899 by a group of British expats, who found themselves with few outlets for English sports in a cycling-mad city. So successful was the club that, in 1908, the Italian Football Federation decided to exclude foreign players from the championship. The internationals on AC's roster formed their own club and called it Football Club Internazionale Milano, or simply Inter. Eventually, they won the right to compete in the championship and kicked off a rivalry that stands to this day.

From 1925, AC Milan played at the newly built San Siro stadium, while Inter's home ground was the Arena Civica. It wasn't until 1947, following World War II, that Inter moved, as tenants, on to AC's turf.

Once upon a time, team affiliations were split fairly neatly along political lines. From the 1950s until Silvio Berlusconi bought the nearly bankrupt AC in 1986, its supporters were known as *cacciaviti* (screwdrivers), a reference to their blue-collar professions. During the tumultuous 1970s, the club represented the hard left, and the red of their red and black strip signalled their communist leanings. Inter, on the other hand – with regal blue and black stripes – has always been associated with the bourgeoisie; the Moratti family of oil barons presided over the club for most of the 20th century, until, in 2013, Indonesian businessman and media mogul Erick Thohir bought a 70 per cent stake in the club from Massimo Moratti, and became president.

The not-always-friendly rivalry over their home ground may soon come to an end, however. Guided by Barbara Berlusconi (Silvio Berlusconi's daughter and AC Milan's vice-president), AC has expressed interest in building its own stadium on the Expo 2015 site, near the suburb of Rho, with opening kick-off planned for 2017. If all goes according to plan, a 60-year-long era will come to a close.

The two teams face off against each other in the San Siro stadium twice a year. Tickets can be bought on the clubs' websites (www.acmilan.com, www.inter.it). For Inter home games, you can also try any branch of Banca Popolare di Milano (a central one is situated at via Meravigli 2, Centre, 02 8646 0598, www.bpm.it, closed Sat, Sun). Ticket prices start at €20; thereafter, the sky's the limit. If you're lucky enough to get a ticket (matches generally sell out well in advance), turn up a good hour ahead of kick-off to secure your spot. Each team's *curva*, or end zone, is extremely raucous; the safest places are away from the police, as they're the most popular target for missiles.

have introduced a new philosophy. The distance between the two teams is increasing, however: Milan recently opened its own independent museum, Casa Milan (*see p144*), and may build its own stadium on the Expo 2015 site, to be opened in 2017. Note that visits to the stadium may be curtailed between mid May and mid July, when various sporting fixtures and the occasional rock concert take place.

▶ *For more information on the stadium and buying tickets for matches, see p146* **Forza Inter! Forza Milan!**

Restaurants

Da Leo

Via Trivulzio 26 (02 4007 1445, www.ristorante leomilano.com). Metro Gambara or bus 72, 80. **Open** 12.30-2.30pm, 7.30-10.30pm Tue-Sat; 12.30-2.30pm Sun. **Average** €50. **Fish & seafood**

Giuseppe Leo has been going to Milan's fish market at the crack of dawn for the past 30 years to select the freshest produce for his fish-only restaurant. The dishes are simple and wholesome: *spaghetti in bianco* (without tomatoes) with tuna, clams, king prawns or calamari, and a range of main-course fish dishes. The interior is unpretentious and the service, though sometimes slow, is usually friendly.

Cafés, Bars & Gelaterie

Gelateria Marghera

Via Marghera 33 (02 468 641). Metro De Angeli or tram 16. **Open** 10am-1am daily. **No credit cards.**

One of Milan's longest-established ice-cream parlours, Marghera offers a mind-boggling array of flavours, with six chocolate options that include a yummy rum chocolate. The high quality of the product means you can expect queues, and staff who are occasionally a little harassed.

Shops & Services

Belfiore

Via Belfiore 9 (02 468 042, www.calzaturebelfiore.com). Metro Wagner, or bus 61, or tram 16. **Open** 2.30-7.30pm Mon; 9.45am-7.30pm Tue-Fri; 9.45am-7pm Sat. **Accessories**

See p144 **Stepping Out**.

Cardinale

Via Belfiore 9 (02 498 1857, www.cardinale scarpe.it). Metro Wagner, or bus 61, or tram 16. **Open** 3-7.30pm Mon; 10am-7.30pm Tue-Sat. **Accessories**

See p144 **Stepping Out**.

Coin

Corso Vercelli 30-32 (02 4399 0001, www.coin.it). Metro Pagano, or bus 61, or tram 16. **Open** 10am-7.30pm Mon-Fri; 10am-8pm Sat; 10am-1pm, 3-7.30pm Sun. **Map** p133 B1 ㉙ **Department store**

This seven-floor department store is known for stylish, good-value clothing and accessories. The fifth floor features merchandise from Milan-based shops High-Tech (*see p87*) and Cargo – reckoned to be among the city's top venues for affordable, quality design. Department store Excelsior (*see p67*) is also operated by the Coin group.

Other locations piazza V Giornate 1A, East (02 5519 2083); piazza Cantore 12, West (02 5810 4385); viale Monza 1, East (02 2611 6131); via Panicale 7, North (02 3300 2316).

★ € Mercato Comunale

Piazza Wagner (no phone, www.milanomia.com). Metro Wagner or bus 67, 199. **Open** 8.30am-1pm Mon; 8.30am-1pm, 4-7.30pm Tue-Sat. **Market**

In existence since 1929, this covered market is one of the city's best outlets for gourmet food, including fruit, fish, meat, cheese and dried porcini mushrooms.

EXPLORE

FieraMilano. *See p145.*

Arts & Entertainment

Children

Although Milan has few activities aimed directly at children, you can take kids almost anywhere: most restaurants and museums will welcome your *bambino* with a friendly smile. As of 2014, there's a dedicated children's museum, MUBA (Museo dei Bambini Milano), where youngsters can participate in interactive exhibitions and workshops, or enjoy a snack in the indoor/outdoor café. Much of the city centre – from the Duomo to the Castello Sforzesco – is pedestrianised, filled with cafés, museums and child-friendly shops, and is easy to get around. The two main parks, Parco Sempione and the Giardini Pubblici, are great for letting off steam, with numerous play areas, and a children's train in the Giardini Pubblici. Milan can be a polluted and hectic at rush hour; but with a *gelato* in hand, kids will find this fascinating city great fun.

GETTING AROUND

Although public transport is one of the many things that the Milanese complain about, it can actually be enjoyable if you're in no great hurry. Tickets are relatively cheap: €1.50 per person (valid for 75 minutes) and €4.50 for a 24-hour pass. Children aged up to five travel free; and two children up to ten years old can travel free with each adult (if challenged, children must be in possession of ID). The metro is quick but crowded (for a map, *see p288*), buses are slow and crowded, and trams are a great way to hop around. There are various types, including small, yellow ones dating from the 1920s, which have period interiors with wooden benches and glass lampshades; larger, orange 1970s ones; and even larger futuristic green ones, known locally as 'caterpillars'. The **City Sightseeing Milano** hop-on, hop-off bus tour (*see p267*) is also a good way to see the city.

Some words of caution: in Italy, people park anywhere and everywhere, so it can be hard to negotiate pavements with a buggy. Also, the two older metro lines, 1 (red) and 2 (green), do not have lifts in every station, so you may have to lug your pushchair down the stairs or escalators – although locals will often offer to help. Lines 3 (yellow), 5 (lilac) and the *passante* (blue) are fitted with somewhat unreliable lifts.

INFORMATION

Children's events are listed in Wednesday's *ViviMilano* supplement of the *Corriere della Sera* and on the website, in Italian (http://vivimilano.corriere.it/bambini); and also in Thursday's *Tuttomilano* supplement of *La Repubblica*.

SIGHTSEEING

Around the Duomo

One of the advantages of Milan's compact, Duomo-centric layout is that many of the must-see attractions are within walking distance of one another. A good bet is to start at the **Duomo** (*see p46*). It's on most tram routes (take the metro if you're pressed for time), and is in the middle of a large, mainly pedestrianised zone from piazza San Babila to the Castello Sforzesco. Piazza del Duomo and the nearby **Galleria Vittorio**

Emanuele II (*see p50*) are good places for watching the world go by (and chasing the occasional pigeon), but the best attraction for families is the cathedral roof. Climb 150 steps or take the lift to the top; once on the well-barricaded roof, kids can clamber along little parapets, pick out the weirdest of the 3,600 sculptures or simply pretend that they're drifting around on a pink marble wedding cake. You'll get a great view of the city and, in good weather, even the Alps.

Back on terra firma, look for the shiny leg on the Duomo's early 20th-century brass door: superstitious Milanese say that touching it brings good luck. Next, nip inside the Duomo to check out the sundial (on the floor behind the entrance). Children can spot the hole in the roof through which a beam of light shines on sunny days, hitting the metal timeline at noon.

Past the street performers pretending to be sculptures in piazza del Duomo, accumulate more good luck by emulating the Milanese practice of spinning your heels on the nether regions of the mosaic bull on the floor beneath the central dome of the Galleria Vittorio Emanuele. There's usually a crowd of tourists – and families – doing just that.

Less well known are the peculiar acoustics of the colonnades in nearby piazza dei Mercanti (*see p59* **In the Know**) next to via dei Mercanti, a medieval street that occasionally hosts buskers, clowns and other interesting characters, especially at weekends.

Museums & Attractions

These days, the leader of the pack of Milan's child-friendly museums is **MUBA**. Also worth a visit is the **Museo Nazionale della Scienza e della Tecnologia Leonardo da Vinci** (*see p132*), which is not too far from **The Last Supper** (*see p138*). The museum's large collection of fossils and models of Da Vinci's inventions might not be every child's idea of fun, but its 'railway pavilion' (*padiglione ferroviario*) is outstanding. This large shed contains real trains and trams dating from the 19th century, which can be clambered on. However, the museum's star is its submarine, the *Enrico Toti*, although guided tours cost an additional €8-€10 per person, children included.

A trip to the **Civico Museo di Storia Naturale** (*see p94*) can also be entertaining for young visitors, thanks to its model dinosaurs and other exhibits, though the displays are on the fusty side. The museum is in the **Giardini Pubblici** (*see p94*), Milan's best park for kids, which also contains the **Civico Planetario Ulrico Hoepli** (*see p94*) planetarium, a children's play park and a mini train.

Another enjoyable place is the **Castello Sforzesco** (*see p73*), a short walk from the Duomo. Of particular interest is the armoury hall (room 14), which features a knight on horseback and some vicious-looking swords. There's also a small collection of mummies and other Egyptian artefacts tucked away in the castle's Egyptian Museum. On designated days, you can also pre-book guided tours (through Ad Artem – 02 659 6937, www.adartem.it) around the castle's underground passageways. For safety reasons, they are open only to adults and children aged over eight. Participants are asked to bring a torch. Be warned: there's quite a lot of Italian chat. The expanse of **Parco Sempione** (*see p77*) beyond the Castello is kiddie heaven, with cafés and poolside walkways aplenty. There's also the small but pleasant **Acquario** (*see p73*), with its indoor fish tanks.

If all this culture is more than your juniors can stand, take football enthusiasts for a tour of the **San Siro Stadium** (*see p145*), including the dressing rooms of the Inter and Milan squads. Otherwise, on Sundays, think about taking older children and teens to an actual match. Be sure to avoid the *curva* (area behind the goals), which is where the hardcore fans congregate.

★ MUBA (Museo dei Bambini Milano)

Rotonda della Besana, via Besana 12, East (02 4398 0402, www.muba.it). Metro Crocetta or Porta Romana, or bus 77, 84, or tram 9. **Open** 9.30am-3.30pm Mon; 9.30am-6.30pm Tue-Fri; 10am-7pm Sat, Sun. **Admission** *Exhibitions & workshops* €8 children; €6 adults. *Play area, bistro & bookshop* free. **Map** p283 G7.

Opened in 2014, MUBA is housed in a Baroque edifice, with a courtyard and lots of greenery – it's impossible to imagine that it was once a hospital and cemetery. Today, the building rings with the excited shouts and laughter of kids aged two to 11, who come here to enjoy the many activities the space provides. Access to the play area – with magnet and chalk boards, and a toy bartering zone – is free. Families can also enjoy breakfast, lunch, afternoon snacks or an early supper at the Rotonda Bistrot, or head to the bookshop to pick up colourful classics (mostly in Italian), such as the fabulously illustrated works of design genius

IN THE KNOW
CULTURE KIDS

Innovative bookshop **Open** (*see p121*) has a babysitting service for culture-starved parents of kids aged five to ten, usually on selected Friday nights. From 7pm to 11pm, children are entertained with reading, art workshops and digital activities, plus pizza. Meanwhile, parents can head to the local Teatro Franco Parenti (*see p176*) or Terme Milano (*see p121*), where they enjoy discounted admission fees.

Original-language Films

★ Anteo spazioCinema

Via Milazzo 9, North (02 659 7732, www.spaziocinema.info). Metro Moscova, or bus 43, 94, or tram 33. **Tickets** €4.50-€8. **Map** p280 D4.

With a restaurant, bookshop, exhibition space and film courses – not to mention three screens – the Anteo is one of Milan's best cinemas. English-language films are shown on Mondays as part of the Sound & Motion initiative.

Apollo spazioCinema

Galleria de Cristoforis 3, Centre (02 780 390, www.spaziocinema.info). Metro Duomo, or bus 54, 60, or tram 1, 2, 3, 12, 14, 27. **Tickets** €8.90. **Map** p284 E6.

Working in collaboration with the Anteo (*see above*), this multi-screen cinema, just off the Corso Vittorio Emanuele, occasionally offers original-language versions (with Italian subtitles) of one of the more popular movies they're currently showing in Italian.

Arcobaleno Film Center

Viale Tunisia 11, East (02 2940 6054, information 02 2953 7621, www.cinenauta.it). Metro Porta Venezia or tram 1, 5. **Tickets** €5-€6; 10-film pass €30. **Map** p281 G4.

This mainstream cinema (with three screens) participates in the popular Sound & Motion scheme, which brings the best foreign-language titles to the city. If you're staying in Milan for a month or more, the ten-film card is a bargain, and is valid at the other cinemas in the circuit.

Cinema Mexico

Via Savona 57, South (02 4895 1802, www.cinemamexico.it). Metro Porta Genova or Sant'Agostino, or bus 68, 90, 91, or tram 14. **Tickets** €6-€7. **No credit cards. Map** p282 A8.

English-language films are shown here on Thursdays as part of the Sound & Motion initiative. The Mexico also gives space to some Italian productions that have struggled to get distribution elsewhere. The weekly screening – in English – of *The Rocky Horror Picture Show*, which has been shown here every Friday night for more than 30 years, is legendary in Milan.

Cineteca di Milano

Spazio Oberdan, viale Vittorio Veneto 2, East (02 7740 6300, www.cinetecamilano.it). Metro Porta Venezia or tram 5, 9. **Tickets** €6 plus €3 annual membership. **No credit cards. Map** p281 F5.

Four screenings a day of international independent movies, most in the original language, from Korean to Finnish, with Italian subtitles.

First-run Films in Italian

Odeon

Via Santa Radegonda 8, Centre (02 875 283, www.medusacinema.it). Metro Duomo, or bus 54, 60, or tram 1, 2, 3, 12, 14, 27. **Tickets** €8.90. **Map** p284 E6.

Located right in the centre of town, just steps from the Duomo and adjacent to the Rinascente department store, this grand old theatre was Milan's first multi-screen cinema (1986). Sadly, the days when English-language films were screened here are long gone.

Anteo spazioCinema.

ESSENTIAL MILAN FILMS

Discover the city on screen.

I Am Love.

BAGNI DIANA/PIAZZA DEL DUOMO LUMIÈRE BROTHERS (1896)
Footage of Milan shot by the early-film pioneers includes *Piazza del Duomo* (43 seconds), of the piazza del Duomo, complete with trams, horse-drawn trolley buses, and women in ornate hats; and *Bagni Diana* (27 seconds), of high divers bouncing off boards into the city's newly opened swimming pool (now the gardens of the Sheraton Diana Majestic).

MIRACOLO A MILANO VITTORIO DE SICA (1951)
A magic-realist fable filmed in Milan using professional and non-professional actors, *Miracle in Milan* centres on a Christ-like orphan, Totò, whose magic dove grants the wishes of the impoverished inhabitants of post-war Lambrate. In the uplifting finale, the shanty town's residents fly away on broomsticks, circle the Duomo and soar into the sky – the supposed inspiration for the famous flying bicycles in *E.T.*

ROCCO E I SUOI FRATELLI LUCHINO VISCONTI (1960)
Dealing with a tragic feud between two brothers, and the disintegration of a southern Italian peasant family after emigrating to Milan, Visconti's three-hour masterpiece (starring a young and beautiful Alain Delon as Rocco) begins with majestically framed shots of Stazione Centrale, then follows the family's tram journey to Lambrate. Other locations include the Duomo roof and the Navigli.

LA VITA AGRA CARLO LIZZANI (1964)
Based on Luciano Bianciardi's best-selling novel of the same name, *It's a Hard Life* is a satirical black comedy telling the story of a left-wing radical (played by Ugo Toniazzi) who is seduced by the glitter and glamour of city life. Losing his principles – and eventually his lover – he becomes part of the Milanese bourgeoisie he originally despised.

TEOREMA PIER PAOLO PASOLINI (1968)
A beautiful young man (Terence Stamp) enters the life of an upper-middle-class Italian family. After engaging in cataclysmic sex with everyone from the maid to the industrialist father, he leaves, having shaken them all to the core. The virtually wordless film left many viewers speechless too, but the shots of Milan are indisputably riveting.

I AM LOVE LUCA GUADAGNINO (2010)
Shot mostly in Milan's glamorous Villa Necchi-Campiglio, this determinedly stylish film stars Tilda Swinton as the Russian wife (with an impeccable wardrobe, supplied by Jil Sander and Fendi) of a wealthy industrial magnate. Her passionate attraction to a younger chef leads her to place desire above duty and rationality. The memorable scene on the Duomo roof was apparently inspired by Alain Delon and Anne Giradot in *Rocco and his Brothers*.

MOVIE MUSEUMS

Explore Milan's filmmaking past.

Museo Interattivo del Cinema.

Opened in 2011 in a 1930s former tobacco factory in the northern Bicocca zone, the **Museo Interattivo del Cinema** (Interactive Cinema Musem), or MIC, focuses on the origins of cinema and Milan's involvement in the world of film. Exhibits include magic lanterns from the 1700s, animations from the 1950s to '80s – when the legendary *Carosello* television programme was produced in the city for RAI TV – and an exploration of Milan as a centre of filmmaking in Italy. The list of directors who've chosen Milan as a backdrop is impressive: from Federico Fellini to Luchino Visconti and Luca Guadagnini, whose *I Am Love* starred (and was co-produced) by Tilda Swinton. The museum's film programme runs throughout the year (except August) and includes a smattering of vintage Italian classics.

A delight for both film fans and graphic designers, the **Fermo Immagine, Museo del Manifesto Cinematografico di Milano** (Milan Film Poster Museum) houses a collection of vintage Italian movie posters, lobby cards and other ephemera. Changing exhibitions draw upon their 50,000-strong poster archive. Head to the shop to pick up some vintage posters of your own.

Fermo Immagine, Museo del Manifesto Cinematografico di Milano

Via Gluck 45, North (02 3650 5760, www.museofermoimmagine.it). Metro Stazione Centrale, or bus 87, 90, 91, or tram 2, 5. **Open** 2-7pm Tue-Sun. **Admission** €5. **Map** p281 G1.

★ Museo Interattivo del Cinema

Manifattura Tabacchi, viale Fulvio Testi 121, North (02 8724 2114, www.cinetecamilano.it). Metro Bicocca, or bus 31, or tram 7. **Open** 3-6pm Mon-Fri, Sun. **Admission** €5.50.

Fermo Immagine, Museo del Manifesto Cinematografico di Milano.

Milano Film Festival.

FESTIVALS

Festival of African, Asian & Latin American Cinema

02 6671 2077, 02 669 6258, www.festivalcinemaafricano.org. **No credit cards. Date** May.

Celebrating its 25th edition in 2015, this is one of the longest-running independent film festivals in Milan. The week-long event, held at various locations, is the only festival on this theme in Italy – and one of only three in Europe.

★ FestivalMix

Piccolo Teatro Strehler di Milano, largo Greppi 1, Centre (www.cinemagaylesbico.com). Metro Lanza or tram 2, 4, 12, 14. **Date** mid June.

Founded in 1985, this five-day gay film festival has become an institution in Milan. The line-up offers international previews of major films with gay topics; shorts, documentaries and TV programmes also get a look-in. Live music, special guest appearances and DJ sessions happen before and after the screenings, and the delightful square in front of the theatre is packed with LGBT film fans from *aperitivo* time until late.

★ Film Festival Internazionale di Milano (MIFF)

02 9287 1578, www.miff.it. **Date** Sept.

Launched in 2000, this ten-day festival showcases the most outstanding independent cinema from across Italy and the world. The Cavallo di Leonardo (Leonardo's Horse) is awarded to the best film in various categories, from short films to documentaries.

Milano Film Festival (MFF)

02 7233 3222, www.milanofilmfestival.it.
Date mid Sept.

The Milano Film Festival was inaugurated in 1995 as a showcase for shorts by young local filmmakers, then opened out to international contributors and feature films in 2000. A ten-day interdisciplinary affair, it also covers art exhibitions, performances and workshops in various locations throughout the city, including open-air screenings in Piazza del Canone in Parco Sempione (*see p77*).

Invideo

Spazio Oberdan, viale Vittorio Veneto 2, East (02 7740 6300, www.mostrainvideo.com). Metro Porta Venezia or tram 5, 9. **Date** early Nov. **Map** p281 F5.

Established in 1990, this international festival of 'outsider' video art and cinema focuses on experimental documentary works, and is Italy's most important festival for electronic arts and new technologies. So, if your interest is non-mainstream cinema, video documentaries, or art and animation, this is the festival for you.

Sport Movies & TV International Festival

Palazzo Giuresconsulti, piazza Mercato, Centre (02 8940 9076, www.sportmoviestv.com). Metro Duomo or Cordusio, or tram 1, 2, 3, 12, 16, 27.
Date Dec. **Map** p284 D6.

Dedicated to sports films, documentaries and TV programmes, this six-day festival is held just two minutes' walk from the Duomo. Featuring more than 150 films and videos, it's been going for over 30 years.

IN THE KNOW WATCH IT AT HOME

Arthouse cinema is pretty much a thing of the past here, as it is elsewhere in Italy. If you want to see a classic Antonioni or Fellini on the big screen, opportunities are few – though you can always try the new **Museo Interattivo del Cinema** (*see p156* **Movie Museums**). But you can still buy DVDs of celluloid gems, past and present. Try the shop attached to the **Anteo spazioCinema** (open 3-10.30pm Mon-Fri; 2.30-10.30pm Sat, Sun – *see p154*). In the Porta Venezia area, **Bloodbuster** (via Panfilo Castaldi 21, 02 2940 4304, www.bloodbuster.com) specialises in Italian horror and *poliziesco* (detective) B-movies.

Gay & Lesbian

Welcome to the most glamorous and gay-friendly of all Italian cities: style and fun are not options here, they're guaranteed. Gay-friendly fashionistas visiting from all over the world add a cosmopolitan sparkle to a community of attractive Italians. The Milanese are cool but reserved, and sometimes unadventurous with new venues – so finding the latest hot address can be tricky, even for them. *Pride* and *Lui* (free magazines found in many of Milan's bars, clubs and shops) will help you find the highlights of the month. Keep 'em peeled and, as they say here: *Divertiti!* – Enjoy!

THE SCENE

Milan is about fashion, and Milanese gays love drama and posing – but the city is not merely fashion-oriented. There are underground venues aplenty, and there's also scope for visitors who crave harder action, or have a penchant for leather and dark rooms.

To get into many gay clubs, bars and saunas, you'll need a membership card issued by Arcigay (Italy's gay and lesbian organisation; *see below*). The card (valid for a year) costs €15, and can be bought at most venues that require it. If you're in Milan for a short visit, you can opt for the one-month visitor's card (€8).

A focal point of the year is June's Milano Pride week (www.milanopride.it), now sponsored by the Comune (Municipality) with events mostly in the Porta Venezia area, the destination of the traditional parade. The site also gives links to a somewhat controversial official Gay Life app, which can be downloaded for free.

INFORMATION & RESOURCES

Arcigay

Via Bezzecca 3, East (02 5412 2225, helpline 02 5412 2227, www.arcigaymilano.org). Bus 45, 60, 73, or tram 12, 23, 27. **Open** *3.30-8pm Mon-Fri; 3.30-7.30pm Sun. Closed 1wk Aug, 1wk Dec.* **Map** p283 G7.

Arcigay has a website and helpline, and issues the Arcigay card, which is often needed to get into Milan's gay venues. The office opens on Sundays to welcome new members and answer questions, and on Wednesday evenings (9-11pm) for cultural events. It also has a small library stocked with gay-related books, magazines and videos. ArciLesbica (*see below*) is in the same building.

ArciLesbica Zami

Via Bezzecca 4, East (mobile 328 409 7115, www.arcilesbica.it/milano). Bus 45, 60, 73, or tram 12, 23, 27. **Open** *9pm Tue (meetings); other times vary.* **Map** p283 G7.

Although less active than Arcigay, this is Italy's main political organisation for lesbians, with a centre in the same building as Arcigay (*see left*). Its website has a calendar of events, from workshops to screenings.

Collettivi Donne Milanesi

Corso Garibaldi 91, North (no phone, www.cidiemme.org). Metro Moscova, or bus 41, 43, 94, or tram 2, 4, 12, 14. **Map** p280 D4.

A lesbian group that organises events, political evenings and film screenings (listed on the website), with a welcoming open night every Tuesday from 8.30pm.

GAY MILAN

Bars, clubs & discos

Afterline

Via Sammartini 25, North (02 3651 9232, www.afterline.eu). Metro Centrale, or bus 90, 91, or tram 5. **Open** 9pm-2am Fri, Sat. **Admission** free. **Map** p281 G2.

This kitsch, baroque disco pub was one of Milan's first gay meeting points, and is located in via Sammartini, one of the city's oldest 'gay streets'. It offers themed evenings and performances by go-go boys on Fridays; there's no planned programme on Saturdays – but it's a friendly place to relax and drink before heading into the night.

★ Ciringay

Tropical Island, Bastioni di Porta Venezia, Giardini Pubblici Indro Montanelli, East (02 2951 1599). Metro Porta Venezia or Repubblica, or tram 1, 9, 33. **Open** *May-Sept* 7pm-2am Wed-Sat. **Admission** free. **Map** p281 F5.

Adjacent to the Giardini Pubblici Indro Montanelli, this 'cirinquito' is a refreshing outdoor oasis in the centre of the city open only during the summer months. It draws a huge crowd, which heads here for the happy music, good snacks and drinks, and chilled atmosphere. Located next to the second entrance to the park from Piazza Oberdan, it's the perfect urban 'getaway' for when the weather gets sticky and hot.

Company

Via Benadir 14, North (02 287 0295, www.companyclub.org). Metro Cimiano, or bus 56. **Open** 9.30pm-2am Tue-Thur, Sun; 9.30pm-5am Fri, Sat. **Admission** Arcigay card or Company card (€5).

Bears and bear-lovers, welcome to paradise. Always busy during the week, with themed nights inspired by the leather and bear worlds, this eclectic space also features regular art shows. You can dance in the newly opened club room, or chat in the crowded little garden. The club is run by Arcigay (*see p158*).

Executive G

Eleven Club, via di Tocqueville 11, Centre (mobile 339 334 2610). Metro Garibaldi, or bus 37, or tram 2, 4, 7. **Open** 8pm-3am Tue. **Admission** €12 (incl drink). **Map** p280 D4.

This colourful night at the Eleven Club kicks off every Tuesday with a gay *aperitivo* (buffet). You won't be short of food or drink, and the fun disco starts after 10pm. The drag queens' performances, between the *aperitivo* and dancefloor opening, are well worth a look.

Farm

Magazzini Generali, via Pietrasanta 16, South (02 539 3948, www.thefarmmilano.com). Metro Lodi, or bus 38, or tram 24. **Open** noon-5am Sat. **Admission** €16-€20 (incl drink). **Map** p283 E10.

Frequented by dance addicts and muscle-lovers, the Farm hosts events with international DJs, and wild outdoor parties in summer. For up-to-date info on what's on, see www.upmilano.com. Note that MaGAYzzini (*see p161*) is held on the same night in the same venue – but in a separate space with a separate entrance fee.

Milano Pride.

Vogue Ambition

Amnesia, via Gatto, East (no phone, www.amnesia milano.com/vogue-ambition). Bus 45, 73, or tram 27. **Open** 11.30pm-5am Fri, Sat. **Admission** €15 (incl drink).

This glam night is for fashion-forward people who love to dance to Italian and international pop hits from the last three decades. Don't dress to impress – dress to kill.

Cruising bars

Cruising bars are a popular underground phenomenon in Milan. Often housed in anonymous blocks (sometimes the only clue is a tiny plaque at the entrance), these establishments offer total discretion, where you can relax in the knowledge that you're among like-minded people.

Bangalov

Via Calabria 5, North (02 3322 0193, www. bangalov.com). Metro Machiachini, or bus 92, or tram 2. **Open** 10pm-3am Tue-Thur; 10pm-5am Fri, Sat. **Admission** Arcigay card. **Map** p280 B1.

The newest cruising bar in town offers a varied platter of themed nights, including leather, fetish, gym, naked and mask. The weekly 'open night' party welcomes men and women, bisexual and trans.

Depot

Via dei Valtorta 19, North (02 2897 0999, www.depotmilano.com). Metro Turro, or bus 56. **Open** 10pm-3am Mon-Wed, Fri, Sat; 3-10pm Sun. **Admission** €10.30.

This dark, cosy cruising/fetish bar on three floors is for people looking for hard and raw encounters – from leather to sportswear fetishes. The Fog Party is the event of the season, while the Naked Party (no clothes, shoes only) at weekends is extremely popular. Note that the Arcigay card is not accepted here, and you'll need ID to get the Depot's own membership card.

Flexo

Via Oropa 3, North (02 2682 6709, www. fenixsauna.it). Metro Cimiano, or bus 56. **Open** 9pm-3am Thur-Sat. **Admission** Arcigay card.

A two-floor cruising bar in the north-east suburbs, with cubicles, glory holes, a chill-out area, a labyrinth and a mirror room. There's a large bar area in which to meet friends and mingle, and a leather tower upstairs for harder action. There are naked parties on Thursdays, and other themed nights during the weekend. As you'd expect, it gets particularly busy on Friday and Saturday.

Saunas

Fenix

Via Oropa 3, North (02 2851 0528, www. fenixsauna.it). Metro Cimiano, or bus 56. **Open** 1-9pm Wed-Sat; noon-midnight Sun. **Admission** Arcigay card.

This sauna has a bar, Turkish bath, Finnish sauna, Jacuzzi and massage room – all on the first floor. The second floor hosts chill-out and cruising fun. It's in the same building as Flexo (*see left*).

Metro Centrale

Via Schiapparelli 1, North (02 667 1089, www.metroclubmilano.it). Metro Centrale, or bus 42, 53, 90, 91, or tram 2, 5, 9, 33. **Open** noon-1.30am daily. **Admission** €17; €13 reductions. **Map** p281 G2.

Metro Centrale occupies three floors, with Jacuzzis, a steam bath, a massage room, a Finnish sauna and a gym area. For your private viewing pleasure, there are videos in the chill-out rooms, as well as an internet terminal. It's frequented by a young crowd taking advantage of discounts for under-25s. A buffet is served on the first and third Sundays of the month.

Festivals

FestivalMix

For listings, *see p157.*

Held each June, this annual gay and lesbian film festival has become one of the most-anticipated events of the calendar.

LESBIAN MILAN

Gay Milan stands proud, but facilities for lesbians, whether residents or visitors, are fewer and further between. That said, the **Gaia360** website (www.gaia360.com) is a good starting point. There's also **Kick-Off** (www.kickoff.biz), which coordinates events and parties at a variety of bars and clubs.

★ Cicip & Ciciap

Via Col di Lana 8, Centre (02 8699 5410, www. cicipeciciap.org). Metro Porta Genova, or bus 59, 79, or tram 9. **Open** 7pm-1am Wed-Sun. **No credit cards. Map** p284 C7.

This centre for the politically and non-politically minded has recently reopened in a new venue. Cicip & Ciciap hosts discussion groups for women of all ages, and there's a bar and a reasonably priced restaurant too.

Rhabar

Alzaia Naviglio Grande 150, South (mobile 393 971 9561, www.rhabar.it). Metro Porta Genova, or tram 2. **Open** 7pm-2am Wed-Sat. **Admission** free.

This recently renovated bar/disco on the canal offers live music, DJ sets and themed nights in a cosy atmosphere. It appeals to younger, style-conscious women. Check out the singles' party, normally on Wednesdays.

Nightlife & Music

Add a 'work hard, party hard' ethic to a young, upwardly mobile city population, and what do you get? An incessant demand for places in which to party like there's no alarm clock. Much of Milan's nightlife is concentrated in three areas: the post-industrial north, the swanky corso Como area, and hipsterish Navigli in the south. In the summer season, most clubs either close or move their operations to outdoor venues: some of the best are in the eastern suburbs at Idroscalo, the man-made lake beside Linate airport. Although it can't match the range of London or New York, Milan is also home to Italy's liveliest music scene. Most major Italian rock, pop and jazz artists perform in Milan at some point, and the city is on the concert circuit for the biggest international acts. So slip on your glad rags and head into the Milanese night. A good time is pretty much guaranteed.

Nightlife

As trends shift, classic clubs such as **Hollywood** (*see p165*), in the corso Como area, have undergone radical transformations. Once a home from home to the champagne-swilling pinstriped crowd, the club is now embracing the artsy and hip communities with enthusiasm. Other clubs of note, such as the ever-popular **Rocket** (*see p167*), are also gay-friendly. Many of the more chichi clubs, looking to get the punters in early, also serve dinner before the night begins in earnest: the food is unlikely to be great, but it will definitely be more than palatable.

Reserving a table in advance usually ensures access to the 'privé' (VIP area) and a bottle of champagne. Although most clubs are legally bound to close the bar at 2am, many have secured a semi-legal special licence, and will continue to stay open, and serve alcohol, as they see fit. And if you crave one last 4am nightcap, Milan is rich in *baracchini*, open-air mobile bars that serve drinks and panini until dawn; they're often set up conveniently close to Milan's nightlife hotspots. If you're out until the early hours in the corso Como area, don't miss **Princi** bakery and café (*see p84*), which is open late. Note that the admission price to clubs usually includes a drink.

INFORMATION

Zerodue (www.zero.eu) is a small, free, fortnightly magazine that's indispensable for finding out what's on – in terms of both club nights and concerts. You'll find it at venues around town. Other useful websites are www.2night.it and www.milano.tonight.eu. As most Milanese clubs operate on a six-month season, opening dates and admission details may vary, so check

> **IN THE KNOW TAXI!**
>
> Some venues are in out-of-the-way districts, and chances are that public transport will have stopped running by the time the concert ends. Make sure you've got a cab number (*see p257*) in your pocket just in case; in smaller venues, staff will be happy to book one for you.

Armani Privé.

before setting out. Many of the regular clubs close from May/June to August/September, when the summer venues come into their own. You can safely assume that most of the non-summer clubs are closed in August, as is much of Milan.

CLUBS & BARS

Duomo & Centre

Armani Privé

Via Pisoni 1 (02 6231 2655, www.armani ristorante.com). Metro Montenapoleone, or tram 1. **Open** 11pm-2.30am Wed-Sat. **Admission** free (1st drink €20). **Map** p281 E5.

Giorgio Armani knows how to accessorise. Right below his Nobu restaurant, Armani created one of the most elegant clubs in Milan. All drinks cost €20 and it's difficult to get in; but if you manage to swing it, your efforts will be rewarded. Models abound and the older guests ooze class. If you aren't catwalk material, get there early or try to blag your way past the bouncers. The best crowd comes on Thursday and Saturday. Smart dress required.

Punks Wear Prada

Santa Tecla, via Santa Tecla 3 (02 8310 5114, www.natashaslater.com). Metro Duomo or Missori, or tram 12, 15, 16, 23, 24, 27. **Open** 11.30pm-4am Fri. **Admission** €15 (incl drink). **Map** p284 E7.

This wittily named club night takes place at the Santa Tecla discotheque every Friday night. It's a fashion-forward party for style junkies, models, hipsters and cool hunters. Dress to impress.

San Babila & East

★ Blanco

Via Morgagni 2 (02 2940 5284, www.blanco milano.it). Metro Lima or Porta Venezia, or bus 60, or tram 5, 33. **Open** 7pm-2am Mon-Sat; 6pm-1am Sun. **Admission** free.

This good-looking breakfast and lunch bar turns into a super-cool place from *aperitivo* time until the small hours. The fashion crowd (PRs, stylists, designers) invades en masse from Thursday to Sunday for the DJ sessions and the impressive cocktails. It's gay-friendly on Thursday night.

★ Sala Venezia

Via Alvise Cadamosto 2 (02 204 3765). Metro Porta Venezia, or tram 5, 33. **Open** 10pm-1am Sat, Sun. **Admission** membership card available at door €10/yr. **No credit cards. Map** p281 G4.

Sala Venezia is one of Milan's secret venues. The *balera* (the northern Italian name for a ballroom dancing venue) has a classic 1940s dancefloor – you'll feel like you're heading into a time warp as you step down the stairs. There's no try-hard glamour, no fanciness: everything seems genuine. In the past couple of years, the place has become incredibly popular, drawing a younger crowd who want to dance boogie-woogie and rock 'n' roll among older, seemingly professional dancers. Dinner (fixed price €20) can be reserved in advance. Or just have a beer for €2 at the old-fashioned counter, where the serving style is another throwback to the '40s.

Castello Sforzesco, Brera & North

★ Alcatraz

Via Valtellina 25 (02 6901 6352, www.alcatraz milano.it). Metro Maciachini, or bus 70, 90, 91, 92, or tram 3, 4. **Open** 10pm-4am Fri, Sat. **Admission** €12-€18 (incl drink). **Map** p280 D1.

During the week, this large ex-industrial building hosts gigs (*see p169*); at weekends, it turns into a dance club. Visit on Fridays for Notorious with house, Latino and 'revival' music, while Saturdays bring classic rock 'n' roll, funk and swing.

The Club

Corso Garibaldi 97 (02 655 5318, www.theclub milano.it). Metro Moscova, or bus 43, or tram 2, 14. **Open** 11.30pm-5am Tue-Sat. **Admission** €18 (incl drink). **Map** p280 D4.

The black walls and iron decorations give the Club a very 'Berlin techno' feel. Tuesday's Fidelio is a must for house fans; Wednesday is for hip hop; Thursday is student night, with free entrance for those with student ID, and Saturday is the extravagant 'fashion night', when Milan's yuppies, VIPs and football players can be spotted in droves.

Club Haus 80s

Via Valtellina 21 (mobile 335 694 9981, www. clubhaus80s.com). Metro Maciachini, or bus 90, 91, 92, 70, or tram 3, 4. **Open** 11.30pm-5am Fri, Sat. **Admission** €20-€25 (incl drink). **Map** p280 D1.

Lovers of the 1980s – welcome! Are you missing the wild music, the clothes, the overall mood? This is your party. Music shifts from late '70s disco to early electronic and pop; Boy George, Depeche Mode, Grace Jones and other immortal music icons of the decade all put in an appearance. Each night has a dress code, so be inspired.

Dude

Via Plezzo 16 (02 4547 3602, www.dude-club.net). Metro Lambrate or Udine. **Open** 11.30pm-5am Fri, Sat. **Admission** €15-€20.

Launched in a one-time industrial factory in 2012, this underground club quickly became a point of reference for the electronic music scene in Milan. The website has updates on upcoming DJs and international guests.

Hollywood

Corso Como 15 (mobile 328 437 8169, www. discotecahollywood.it). Metro Garibaldi, or tram 2, 4, 7, 8, 33. **Open** 10.30pm-4am Wed-Sun. Closed June-Aug. **Admission** €18-€25 (incl drink). **Map** p280 D3.

There's always been a high model-to-mortal ratio in this place, but recently the club has been pitching for a trendier, more artsy crowd. Sunday is the glam night – and hard to get in – when football players, models and TV celebrities show up.

Loolapaloosa

Corso Como 15 (02 655 5693, www.loolapaloosa. com). Metro Garibaldi, or tram 2, 4, 7, 8, 33. **Open** *Lunch* 11.30am-5pm Mon-Sat. *Aperitivo & club* 7pm-5am Mon-Sat. **Admission** free before 10pm; €10 (incl drink) after 10pm. **Map** p280 D3.

Famous for its late nights and the wild dancing on the bar and tables (watch out or the bartenders will scoop you up), Loolapaloosa is now just as popular for its evening *aperitivo*; it turns into a club after 10pm. Tuesday is international night. The tunes tend to be commercial. It's in the same building as Hollywood (*see above*). *Photo p166.*

Punks Wear Prada.

Loolapalooza. See p165.

Tocqueville Club
Via Tocqueville 13 (mobile 342 810 2013, www.tocqueville13milano.com). Metro Garibaldi, or tram 2, 4, 7, 8, 33. **Open** 11pm-5am Tue-Sat. **Admission** €15-€20 (incl drink). **Map** p280 D4.
Tocqueville attracts footballers, models and local VIPs, though they're likely to be hidden away in the privé, a small private room on the first floor. Tuesday goes back to the 1990s, with special guests. Dinner is served on Sunday evening from 10pm; if you dine, you can ask for a pass to the privé (free with a table booking if requested in advance).

Parco Sempione

Just Cavalli
Via Camoens, next to Torre Bianca (02 311 817, http://milano.cavallidub.com). Metro Cadorna, or bus 61, or tram 1, 27. **Open** *Restaurant* 7pm-1am daily. *Club* 11pm-5am daily. **Admission** €15-€20 (incl drink). **Map** p280 B5.
In the middle of Parco Sempione, under the iconic Torre Branca (*see p79*), designer Roberto Cavalli's signature spot is still a place to see and be seen. Models and modish Milanese shimmy in for an early dinner, then dance the night away. The restaurant and club are open daily; the liveliest nights are Thursdays and Saturdays. It's worth a visit in summer to enjoy the outdoor garden, though it's not quite as 'hot' as it used to be.

★ Old Fashion Club
Viale Alemagna 6 (02 805 6231, www.oldfashion.it). Metro Cadorna, or bus 61, or tram 1, 27. **Open** 8pm-5am daily. **Admission** varies. **Map** p280 C5.
In the Palazzo d'Arte (Triennale building, *see p77*) the Old Fashion Club draws crowds throughout the week, especially during the hot summer months, when its open-air bars and heaving dancefloor spill out into the vast green garden flanking Parco Sempione. If beautiful people are what you're after, Mondays and Saturdays are best; Wednesday is student night. Thursday offers Popstarz, a gay-friendly glam night starting with an *aperitivo* and ending with a perfect blend of electro, pop, rap and hip hop sounds.

Porta Romana & South

Lime Light
Via Castelbarco 11 (342 091 9739, www.limelightmilano.it). Bus 79, 90, 91, or tram 15.
Open 11pm-5am Fri, Sat. **Admission** €10-€15 (incl drink). **Map** p282 D9.
Suffering from a mild personality disorder, Lime Light seems to offer anything and everything. Not only is it a venue for live music and international parties, it also opens its doors to students on Fridays, and takes bookings for private gatherings. For cutting-edge music, you may want to head elsewhere, but for sweaty, lively crowds, it's a good bet.

★ Magazzini Generali
Via Pietrasanta 16 (02 539 3948). Metro Lodi, or bus 38, or tram 24. **Open** 11.30pm- 4am Wed-Sat. Closed June-Aug. **Admission** €15-€20 (incl drink). **Map** p283 F10.
With a capacity of around 1,000, Magazzini is a favoured venues for all genres of live music, and also hosts popular club nights. Thursdays and Fridays brings a mix of house and techno upstairs, and 'dirty electro' in the room below, which is a meeting point for Milan's hipster intelligentsia. Saturday is a gay night with a double helping of events: the Farm (*see p159*) and MaGAYzzini (*see p161*).

★ Plastic Palace
Viale Gargano 15 (no phone). Metro Brenta or Corvetto, or bus 24, 95. **Open** 11.30pm-5am Fri-Sun. Closed mid June-Aug. **Admission** €25 (incl drink) Fri, Sat; free Sun.
Now in a new location, this club is the Studio 54 of Milan: it's been a den for fashionistas, electro-music gurus and an arty-glam cool crowd for more than 30 years. Saturday night is House of Bordello, when the worlds of fashion, design and art get together and dance to DJ Sergio Tavelli's music. On Sundays, the Match features electro music, sexy people and free admission.

★ Rocket
Alzaia Naviglio Grande 98 (mobile 333 331 3817, www.therocket.it). Metro Porta Genova, or tram 2, 14. **Open** 11.30pm-5am Tue-Sat. **Admission** €10-€13. **Map** p282 D11.

Just Cavalli.

Alcatraz.

Although it's been around for a while now, the small but ultra-cool Rocket is still explosive. The tunes are excellent (rock, electro, classic) and the bartender mixes great cocktails – though these days the club charges admission. Friday night brings Alphabet, a young, gay-friendly party.

Summer venues

Most of the action on summer nights takes place at the **Idroscalo** (*see p152*), a huge man-made lake near Linate airport. It's not the easiest place to get to by public transport, so make sure you keep enough cash for the taxi home. Right on the lake (as its name suggests), **Le Jardin au Bord du Lac** is popular for summer parties, while just down the road, the **Beach** has several indoor and outdoor dancefloors, around a lush garden.

Back in the city, **Papaya Infinity** – the former Borgo del Tempo Perso – is another hopping club, with DJs, drinks and dancing both inside and out in its two garden areas; it gets so crowded it's sometimes hard to move at weekends. A new and growing trend is for public swimming pools, such as **Piscina Saini** at via Corelli 126 (02 756 2741), to turn into nightclubs.

In summer, the Navigli area is often closed to traffic after 8.30pm, and canalside bars and cafés stay open until late. Bars in Brera, corso Como, corso Garibaldi and Porta Ticinese also spill out on to the pavement, making these areas lively places in which to grab a cocktail, chat or just people-watch.

Beach

Via Corelli 62, East (02 9455 7554, www.thebeachmilano.com). Bus 38, 54. **Open** 11pm-5am Thur, Fri; 8.30pm-5am Sat, Sun. **Admission** €10-€15.
The indoor dancefloors are open year-round, the gardens from June to September.

Le Jardin au Bord du Lac

Circonvallazione Idroscalo 51, West (mobile 340 980 5101, www.lejardinaubordduIac.com). Bus 73, then 10min walk. **Open** *May-Sept* 9pm-4am Fri, Sat. Closed Oct-Apr. **Admission** €10-€20 (incl drink).

★ Papaya Infinity

Via Fabio Massimo 36, South (02 569 4755, www.papayabeachclub.it). Metro Corvetto or Porto di Mare then 15min walk. **Open** *May-Sept* 1pm-4am Fri, Sat; 8pm-2am Sun. Closed Oct-Apr. **Admission** €10-€20 (incl drink).

Music

ROCK, POP & JAZZ

If you'd rather catch a concert than hit a club, you're in luck: there will generally be something musical going on that suits you, whatever your taste. Aside from instantly recognisable global names, Milan offers the chance to take in home-grown music, from huge-voiced, easy-listening performers such as Laura Pausini, to the poetic lyrics and clever musicality of singer-songwriters. Look out for Cristiano De André, son of the late Genoese legend Fabrizio de André, and folksy Monza-born singer Davide van de Sfroos, as well as smaller, Milan-based names.

Italian jazz generally enjoys an enthusiastic local reception. In addition to old-timers such as Paolo Conte and Enrico Rava, there's an exciting new generation that includes trumpeter Paolo Fresu, and pianists Stefano Bollani and Giovanni Allevi.

The best places to get tickets for rock and pop concerts are often booking agencies such as **Ticketone** (www.ticketone.it). You can also buy tickets in large bookshops and music stores, such as **Mondadori** and **La Feltrinelli** (for both, *see p54*).

Note that the main act may not kick off until an hour or two after the performance is billed to start. Most concerts start at around 9pm (though some begin earlier – so always check), with tickets costing €25-€45.

Rock & Pop

Alcatraz

Via Valtellina 25, North (02 6901 6352, www.alcatrazmilano.it). Metro Maciachini, or bus 70, 90, 91, 92, or tram 3, 4. **Open** 10pm-4am Fri, Sat. **Admission** €12-€18 (incl drink).

This largeish site doubles as a disco (*see p164*) and concert venue. It's in a converted industrial space just beyond the Isola district, but is still reasonably accessible. Alcatraz hosts Italian and international acts, including Gloria Gaynor and Belgian singer-songwriter Stromae.

Mediolanum Forum

Via G di Vittorio 6, Assago, South (02 488 571, www.mediolanumforum.it). Metro Assago Milanofiori Forum. **No credit cards.**

This sports and music venue was built for the 1990 World Cup, and is one of the most love-it-or-hate-it concrete structures in the city. The Forum can now be reached via a direct metro line (a vast improvement on the previous adventurous travel arrangements), but the acoustics aren't the best, and the auditorium is huge – it's the sort of place where acts that favour bombast over sound quality can be expected to gig. Still, the biggest names in the business have all put in an appearance here, from U2 and Madonna to Lady Gaga and Elton John. Seats aren't always numbered, so it's a good idea to arrive as early as possible. Next door (part of the same complex) is the cosier Teatro della Luna, where you can see Italian singers and some touring bands, such as Yes. Since 2009, the smaller Live Forum venue (within the main complex, opposite the Teatro della Luna) has hosted slightly more intimate music shows.

Stadio Meazza (San Siro)

Viale Piccolomini 5, West (02 4879 8201, www.sansiro.net). Metro Lotto then bus 49. **No credit cards.**

Mediolanum Forum.

This iconic city-owned football stadium (known as San Siro throughout the football world) is shared by the city's two fiercely competitive clubs, Milan and Inter. During the summer months, however, it takes time off from the serious business of *il calcio* to host the occasional mega concert. Past performers have included world-renowned acts such as Bruce Springsteen, Robbie Williams and Kasabian, as well as Italian stars Jovanotti, Laura Pausini and Vasco Rossi.

Jazz

★ Blue Note

Via Borsieri 37, North (02 6901 6888, www.bluenotemilano.com). Metro Garibaldi, Isola or Zara, or bus 37, 60 or tram 4, 7, 31, 33. **Open** *Box office* 2-10pm Tue-Sat. **Meals served** *Sept-June* 7.30pm-midnight Tue-Sun. **Brunch** *Oct-Mar* noon (followed by afternoon concert) Sun. **Performances** *Sept-June* 9pm, 11pm Tue-Fri; 9pm, 11.30pm Sat; 1pm, 9pm Sun. **Admission** approx €20-€45. Closed June-Aug.

The Blue Note club, restaurant and bar is the largest and most prestigious of the Milan jazz venues, and part of a venerable international franchise. The range of music is broad, although it focuses mostly on jazz, soul, world music and blues. Recent guests have included jazz trumpeter Paolo Fresu, upcoming Italian singer Renzo Rubino and US jazz veteran Dee Dee Bridgewater. Most spectators opt for the music-and-dinner formula.

Nordest Caffè

Via Borsieri 35, North (02 6900 1910, www.nordestcaffe.it). Metro Garibaldi or Isola or Zara, or bus 37, 60 or tram 4, 7, 31, 33. **Open** 8am-9pm Mon; 8am-11.30pm Tue-Sat; 8.30am-9pm Sun.

Located in the same street as Blue Note, this buzzing bar hosts local and international jazz artists on Thursday and Sunday nights.

La Salumeria della Musica

Via Pasinetti 4, South (02 5680 7350, www.lasalumeriadellamusica.com). Tram 24. **Open** 9pm-2am Mon-Sat. **Admission** free-€10.

This venue, whose name means 'the delicatessen of music', serves an eclectic mix of jazz, funk, rock, pop, soul and cabaret. Shows start at 9.30pm or 10.30pm, but you might want to get there early to grab a platter of cheese or cold cuts and a glass of wine.

★ Le Scimmie

Via Ascanio Sforza 49, South (02 3981 1039, www.scimmie.it). Metro Porta Genova then bus 59, or tram 3. **Open** 7pm-5am Tue-Sun. **Admission** €10-€30.

This cosy club and restaurant in the Navigli area rightfully describes itself as 'the temple of Milan jazz', although, in a generous ecumenical gesture, it now hosts other types of music as well – mostly rock, funk and blues. It also has a boat moored on the canal, which makes a perfect location for wooing that new date.

Nordest Caffè.

Performing Arts

Say 'Milan' and 'music', and the next word rolling off your tongue is likely to be 'opera' – or maybe even 'La Scala'. Milan's original importance in the music world can be attributed largely to its famed opera (and ballet) house – but there are plenty of other opportunities to see and hear some excellent music here. At the Auditorium di Milano, the dynamic female conductor Xian Zhang leads world-class performances that leave audiences gasping; while the venerable Conservatorio provides an opportunity to listen to some superb music.

Milan's theatrical scene is thriving too, but plays performed in English are infrequent.

OPERA, CLASSICAL MUSIC & BALLET

In addition to the venues listed below, look out for concerts in churches, such as the series of free organ concerts by **Cantantibus Organis** (www.sites.google.com/site/cantantibus organismilano) – including performances on the twin organs at the Basilica of Santa Maria della Passione, a thunderous evening that you won't easily forget.

Venues

★ Auditorium di Milano

Largo Gustav Mahler 1, South (02 8338 9401, www.laverdi.org). Bus 55, 71 or tram 3, 15. **Tickets** €13-€50. **Map** p282 C9.

This 1,400-seat auditorium is the home of the city's Orchestra La Verdi (which performed at London's Proms in 2013). Known for its innovative musical programme, the orchestra has an energetic female conductor in Xian Zhang, who at the time of her appointment in 2009 was the first – and still remains the only – woman to be music director of an Italian symphony orchestra. Exceptionally, the Orchestra La Verdi will not be taking a summer break in 2015, but will present a special series of events to coincide with Expo, from May to October 2015 (*see p28*). *Photo p172.*

Conservatorio di Musica Giuseppe Verdi

Via Conservatorio 12, East (02 762 110, www.consmilano.it). Metro San Babila, or bus 61, 94. **Season** Oct-June. **Tickets** vary. **Map** p284 F6.

Founded in 1808, this prestigious institution now bears the name of Giuseppe Verdi (who, ironically, was refused admission to the place). It offers post-graduate courses, as well as running an acclaimed music high school, Liceo Musicale. There are two concert halls: the Sala Verdi for symphonic and choral music and the smaller Sala Puccini for

> **IN THE KNOW**
> **MAKING SENSE OF OPERA**
>
> Bagged tickets for an opera at La Scala – but worried you won't understand a word of the performance? Fret no more! Once inside, get hold of one of the voluminous programmes (€12); the key sections, including an outline of the plot, are in English, French, German, Russian and Japanese, as well as Italian. Failing that, each box/seat has a mini screen showing the subtitles – you can choose Italian, English, French or German.

chamber music. Concerts are organised by three musical associations, depending on the day of the week the concert is held: Serate Musicali (02 2940 9724, www.seratemusicali.it, Mon); Società del Quartetto (02 795 393, www.quartettomilano.it, Tue); and Società dei Concerti (02 6698 4134, www.soconcerti.it, Wed). You can buy tickets online, or at the Conservatorio (cash only) one hour before the start of the concert.

There's also a library – the official repository for music in Lombardy – containing over 35,000 volumes and 460,000 musical works, including original manuscripts by Mozart, Donizetti, Bellini and Verdi. It's open to academics only, by appointment.

★ Teatro alla Scala

Piazza della Scala, Centre (02 860 775, www.teatroallascala.org). Metro Duomo, or bus 61, or tram 1. **Season** 7 Dec-Nov. **Tickets** vary. **Map** p284 E6.

Teatro alla Scala was commissioned in 1774 by Empress Maria Theresa of Austria and inaugurated in 1776. Its opening night (*see p37*), on 7 December, is a major event in the city's calendar. While a privileged few get to attend the glittering gala in person, many more watch on big screens in Galleria Vittorio Emanuele and at screenings across Lombardy. If you've managed to bag a ticket for one of the other performances, and are wondering what to wear, bear in mind that the opening night is when the jewellery comes out of the bank vault. Clean and tidy is probably the best way of describing the dress code for the rest of the year.

► *For more on the theatre itself, see p56; for ticket protocol, see p173 Scoring Tickets for La Scala; for political goings-on, see p174 Backstage Drama.*

Teatro dal Verme

Via Giovanni sul Muro 2, North (02 87 905, www.dalverme.org). Metro Cairoli, or bus 50, 58, or tram 1, 4, 16, 18, 19. **Season** mid Oct-mid July. **Concerts** usually 9pm Thur, 5pm Sat. **Tickets** prices vary. **Map** p284 D6.

Built in 1872, the Dal Verme was one of Italy's leading opera houses in the late 19th century; Leoncavallo's *Pagliacci* had its debut here in 1892. Later converted into a cinema, the theatre reopened as a classical music venue in 2001. Concerts are usually at 9pm on a Thursday and 5pm on a Saturday.

Teatro degli Arcimboldi

Viale dell'Innovazione 20, North (02 641 142 200, box office 02 641 142 212, www.teatroarcimboldi.it). Metro Zara then tram 7, or Stazione Centrale then bus 87. **Season** Oct-July. **Tickets** vary.

The Arcimboldi was built to be the temporary home of La Scala (while the real thing was undergoing renovation from 2002-2004). These days, it hosts dance, Italian pop and orchestral events, as well as the occasional musical (in Italian).

THEATRE

Despite some recent high-profile closures – most notably the much-loved Teatro Smeraldo (now occupied by Eataly, *see p87*) – Milan's theatrical scene is rich, varied and sometimes outlandish, with a mix of larger and smaller venues and productions to match. Plays in English are infrequent – but non-Italian speakers can always take in a performance of dance, musicals, jazz or mime. Fortunately, there are still plenty of classy options in Milan.

Auditorium di Milano. *See p171.*

SCORING TICKETS FOR LA SCALA

Getting a seat for a show is a performance in itself.

Getting tickets for the world's most famous opera house is not impossible using **La Scala**'s (*see p172*) automated telephone booking or internet reservation systems. The process is somewhat counter-intuitive, however, so you may need to make several trial runs before bagging the tickets you want. You need to be online, or on the phone, exactly at the time when booking opens (usually 9am local time – see the website for dates); keep trying if the line is busy or the online tool doesn't respond.

The ticketing system may be (almost) 21st-century, but the seating arrangements are definitely late 18th. As Stendhal confirms in his memoir *Rome, Florence et Naples* (1817), La Scala was where you came to be seen (or not, as the case might be, which explains the depth of the boxes), and to train your eye-glass upon the audience. Getting great sightlines of whatever was happening on the stage was merely an incidental benefit.

Times have changed. Today, people want to see the action on stage – which means military-style scrutiny of the seating plan. The La Scala website helpfully includes images of what sightlines to expect. There are two main options: seats on the main floor (*platea*) or in a box (*palco*). If you opt for the latter, be sure to pick the front seats (numbers 1 and 2) in a box facing the stage. The unfortunate holders of tickets for seats 3 and 4 will be perched on stools. Or they'll be standing, either because the stools are uncomfortable, or because they're trying to get a decent view.

A third option is to go for the best seats in the galleries. These are rather less elegant, and access is via a separate entrance, to ensure that the hoi polloi doesn't rub shoulders with the great and good. You may still get an obstructed view – but at least you won't be sweating over the amount you've parted with.

If you decide to wait until you get to Milan, there are various possibilities. On the day of each performance, 140 gallery tickets go on sale. To get one, you need to be in the queue outside La Scala's Evening Box Office (in via Filodrammatici – to the left of the opera house as you face it), though it's tricky to know when to turn up: 7am may be too early, 10am too late. At 1pm, a member of the L'Accordo music association, wearing an official badge, will take the names of the first 140 lucky punters in the queue. At exactly 5pm, the official will call the roll (again at the Evening Box Office), handing out a voucher to each of the listed people who turn up. This entitles you to buy one gallery ticket (€10).La Scala explains the procedure on its website.

In the hour before each performance, any available tickets will be sold at an average 25 to 50 per cent discount. These might include seats allocated to season ticket holders who are unable to attend. Chances are slim for the top-name opera performances, but you might find tickets for a concert or ballet.

Alternatively, turn up on the night in the hope that you can pick up tickets from unfortunates who find they can't make it. You'll need your wits about you, though. While some people may genuinely be trying to sell their tickets at face-price, beware. Some may be asking for a considerable mark-up. The tickets themselves may be fake, to boot.

The final option is to find a friend of a friend who has a season ticket and cannot attend. For that, you're on your own.

BACKSTAGE DRAMA

Revamps, rows and resignations.

La Scala.

To those close to the action, it sometimes seems like there's more drama behind the scenes than on the stage at **La Scala** (*p172*). The last few years have been eventful, to say the least.

In 2002, the company left the theatre it had called home since 1778, taking up temporary residence at the modern **Teatro degli Arcimboldi** (*see p172*), so that vital restoration work (costing €61 million) could be done. The company made a triumphant return to La Scala on the opening night of the 2004-05 season, presided over by Giorgio Armani and Sophia Loren.

In purely practical terms, the revamp (by Swiss architect Mario Botta) left a considerable legacy. The theatre now has much more storage space, thanks to a controversial new concrete 'fly tower', visible from piazza della Scala. Scene changes are easier: the tower allows a stage set to slide up and down as well as sideways. And airline-style seat-back screens offer an instant translation of the lyrics, much appreciated by audiences. Though, when it comes to the traditional complaint that you get a pretty poor view of the stage from many of the seats, not much appears to have altered.

But what planners couldn't have foreseen was the dramatic upheaval that would take place after the restoration, in 2005, when the company's music director and chief conductor for 20 years, Riccardo Muti, resigned. Muti's official reason for leaving was 'the vulgar show of hostility' by his colleagues. Opponents of Muti criticised him for being dictatorial. Defenders of Muti saw him as a misunderstood genius and a victim of La Scala's highly unionised, 800-strong workforce. Recently, all seems to have been forgiven. In 2013, there was even talk of a triumphant return to La Scala – at least for a concert or two – but the conductor's denial on Facebook seems to have put paid to that – for now.

From 2006 to 2014, things were less turbulent, thanks to the appointment of Israeli-Argentine conductor Daniel Barenboim. He presided over eight years of relative tranquillity and world-class music – but is stepping down, two years before his contract ends, in 2015, to be replaced by Riccardo Chailly.

Unfortunately, at time of writing, the backstage shenanigans appear to have flared up again. The newly appointed general director Alexander Pereira (who had signed on for five seasons, replacing Stéphane Lissner) has taken up his post, but has been asked to sign an official letter of resignation, which will terminate his contract when the 2014-15 season ends. The accusation, it seems, is that Pereira bought four operas for La Scala from the Salzburg Festival, where he was still director, in an alleged conflict of interest. Pereira has stated that he would be willing to continue his original five-year contract, should La Scala's directors have a change of heart.

A solution will, no doubt, be forthcoming – but for now, the offstage drama continues.

To find out what's playing, see the Italian-language websites www.teatripermilano.it or www.lombardiaspettacolo.com (key words: Cartellone and Programmazione Milano Teatro). If you only have time to visit one venue, however, make it La Scala (*see p172*) – to see an orchestral concert, opera or ballet.

TICKETS & INFORMATION

The theatre season runs from roughly September/October to May/June. Theatres are 'dark' on a Monday; Sundays usually feature afternoon matinées and, in a couple of cases, morning shows. Performances start between 8.30pm and 9pm (Tue-Sat), and between 3pm and 4pm (Sun). In London's West End or on Broadway, a show will run as long as it draws an audience; in Milan, it tends to run for a maximum of a week. Therefore, if you hear about a show that sounds appealing, you need to book pretty much immediately or you'll miss it.

You can book tickets for most shows on the phone using a credit card. The larger theatres also offer online booking, often through a ticket agency, such as **TicketOne** (892 101, www.ticketone.it) and **Ticketweb** (892 424, www.vivaticket.it) – expect to pay a commission.

Venues & companies

CRT

Teatro dell'Arte, via Alemagna 6, West (02 7243 4258, www.crtmilano.it). Metro Cadorna, or bus 61, or tram 1, 2. **Tickets** prices vary. **Map** p280 B5.

The CRT – or Centro di Ricerca per il Teatro (Centre for Theatre Research), to give it its full name – was founded in the 1970s, and is based at the Palazzo dell'Arte, adjacent to the Triennale, on the edge of Parco Sempione. Its programme combines contemporary theatre, music and dance.

★ Piccolo Theatre Group

Piccolo Teatro Strehler *largo Greppi, North. Metro Lanza, or bus 57, or tram 4, 12, 14.* **Map** p280 D5.
Piccolo Teatro Grassi *via Rovello 2, Centre. Metro Cordusio, or bus 58, or tram 1, 27.* **Map** p284 D6.
Both *02 4241 1889, www.piccoloteatro.org.*
Season Sept-May. **Tickets** €25-€40.

Named in honour of the late Giorgio Strehler, the Piccolo Teatro Strehler is generally acknowledged as the city's top venue. Its director, Luca Ronconi, is highly respected, and the fact that the theatre is publicly owned means that it's one of the very few to receive adequate funding. Probably best known for its productions of Goldoni's *A Servant to Two Masters (Il servitore di due padroni)*, the Piccolo also plays host to visiting companies from other countries in Europe and beyond.

There are actually two spaces in regular use at the main site: the Teatro Strehler and the Teatro Studio. The Piccolo Teatro Grassi is on via Rovello, on the corner of via Dante, a stone's throw from the Duomo. The cloistered courtyard is the perfect place for an early morning coffee, since the theatre bar opens at 9am.

► *For more on Caffè Letterario, the lovely bar at Piccolo Teatro Grassi, see p62.*

Teatro Arsenale

Via Correnti 11, South (02 832 1999, www.teatroarsenale.it). Metro Sant'Ambrogio, or bus 50, 58 or 94, or tram 2, 14. **Season** Oct-June. **Tickets** €30. **Map** p284 C7.

Housed in a deconsecrated 13th-century church at the far end of via Torino, Teatro Arsenale offers a sporadic programme. The company, directed by Annig Raimondi, tends to specialise in modern work, such as Beckett and Sartre, or older material

Piccolo Teatro Grassi.

by authors not generally known for theatre (such as Copi and Céline). An Italian adaptation of TS Eliot's *The Waste Land* (*La terra desolata*) has been playing to enthralled audiences for the last 20 years.

Teatro Carcano

Corso di Porta Romana 63, South (02 5518 1377, www.teatrocarcano.com). Metro Crocetta or bus 77, 94 or tram 16, 24. **Tickets** €25-€34. **No credit cards. Map** p283 E8.

Opened in 1803, this theatre used for the premières of operas by Bellini and Donizetti. Not surprisingly, it tends to concentrate on theatrical classics (Molière, Sophocles, Shakespeare, Pirandello).

Teatro Elfo Puccini

Corso Buenos Aires 33, East (02 0066 0606, www.elfo.org). Metro Lima or Porta Venezia, or bus 60, 81, or tram 5, 33. **Season** Oct-June. **Tickets** €30 (€20 Tue). **Map** p281 G4.

This group was founded in 1973 by, among others, Gabriele Salvatores, who went on to direct movies such as the Oscar-winning *Mediterraneo* (1991). Elfo has a reputation for non-traditional theatre, with the odd Chekhov or Shakespeare play thrown into the mix.

Teatro Franco Parenti

Via Pier Lombardo 14, South (02 5999 5206, www.teatrofrancoparenti.com). Metro Porta Romana, or bus 62, 77, or tram 9, 16. **Season** Oct-May. **Tickets** €32-€40. **Map** p283 G8.

IN THE KNOW WHO'S WHO IN MILANESE THEATRE

Milan's home-grown stars include Nobel prize-winner Dario Fo, now in his eighties and best known internationally for his 1970 smash hit *The Accidental Death of an Anarchist*, based on real events in the city. Look out for his works at the smaller theatres. Fo's wife, Franca Rame, who died in 2013, was also his professional partner and a mainstay of Italy's feminist movement. Her most famous pieces include the provocative *Tutta Casa, Letto e Chiesa* (*It's All Bed, Board and Church*). The city's other theatre legend is the late, great Giorgio Strehler (1921-97), who is justly honoured with a theatre in his own name – now Milan's most prestigious theatrical venue (*see p175*). Highly influential in Italy, he is credited with, among other things, reviving interest in the work of the Venetian playwright Carlo Goldoni, whose 1743 play *A Servant to two Masters* inspired the West End and Broadway smash *One Man, Two Guv'nors*, by Richard Bean.

Director Andrée Ruth Shammah is renowned for tireless fundraising and for producing a varied programme, complemented by lectures, book launches and some cinema.

Teatro Leonardo da Vinci

Via Ampère 1, at piazza Leonardo da Vinci, East (02 2668 1166, www.teatroleonardo.it). Metro Piola, or bus 62, 90, 91, or tram 23. **Season** Oct-June. **Tickets** €22 (€10 Tue). **No credit cards. Map** p109 B2.

The home of Quelli di Grock, an experimental theatre company established in 1976 and named after the famous Swiss clown Grock (Charles Adrien Wettach, 1880-1959). Originally taking its inspiration from mime, clown techniques and dance, the company reinterprets the classics, especially Shakespeare, Molière and Beckett, but also Carlo Goldoni. The company also runs a theatre school (at another location).

Teatro Litta

Corso Magenta 24, West (02 8645 4545, www.teatrolitta.it). Metro Cadorna, or bus 50, 58, or tram 16. **Season** mid Oct-June. **Tickets** €19. **Map** p284 C6.

This is a splendid baroque building in an elegant part of Milan. The company, though, is young, and presents work by contemporary authors as well more traditional names (including Dario Fo, Pirandello, Goldoni and Thackeray). Young people's theatre is shown regularly.

Teatro Manzoni

Via Manzoni 42, Centre (02 763 6901, www.teatromanzoni.it). Metro Montenapoleone or San Babila, or bus 61, 94, or tram 1. **Season** Oct-May. **Tickets** €30. **Map** p281 E5.

This spectacular theatre is part of Silvio Berlusconi's vast media empire. The programme has more than a sprinkling of celebrities for an audience that is sometimes described as 'the bourgeoisie in fur coats'.

Teatro Nuovo

Piazza San Babila, Centre (02 794 026, www.teatronuovo.it). Metro San Babila, or bus 54, 60, 73. **Season** Oct-Apr. **Tickets** vary. **Map** p284 F6.

In spite of its central address, this theatre is hard to find, located downstairs among the shopping arcade colonnades at San Babila. The programme tends towards comedies and musicals that are often vehicles for TV starlets, as well as dance and acrobatics.

Teatro Out Off

Via Mac Mahon 16, South (02 3453 2140, www.teatrooutoff.it). Bus 78 or tram 12, 14. **Season** Oct-early July. **Tickets** €18. **No credit cards. Map** p280 A2.

This company, set up 1976, works out of a converted cinema. Recent productions have included works by Pier Paolo Pasolini, Harold Pinter and Sarah Kane; there's also contemporary dance.

ESSENTIAL MILAN MUSIC

Sounds of the city.

EXSULTATE, JUBILATE WOLFGANG AMADEUS MOZART (1773)

Mozart first came to Milan just before his 14th birthday, in January 1770.This catchy religious motet, composed and premiered in Milan in January 1773, is a vocally ostentatious work. It was written for Venanzio Rauzzini, the leading castrato of Mozart's third opera, *Lucio Silla*, but is now performed by sopranos.

O MIA BELA MADUNINA GIOVANNI D'ANZI (1934)

Written in dialect by the Milanese singer-songwriter Giovanni D'Anzi, 'Oh my beautiful little Madonna' soon became the city's unofficial anthem. Euologising the golden statue of the Virgin Mary atop the Duomo's tallest spire, its mildly xenophobic lyrics are a response to the nostalgia-filled melodies of immigrants from southern Italy.

PANINARO PET SHOP BOYS (1986)

In Milan to promote their debut album, *Please*, the British synthpop duo became obsessed with the *paninari*, Milanese design-junkies who hung around sandwich (panini) bars. Penned as an admiring tribute, the single was initially released as a limited edition of 5,000, in Italy only. The original video features a number of recognisable Milan locations.

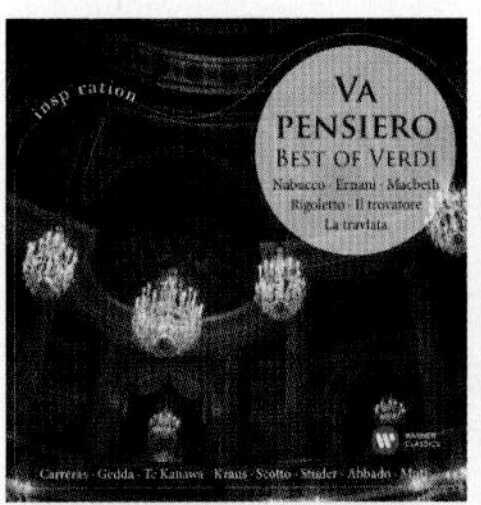

VA' PENSIERO GIUSEPPE VERDI (1842)

When Verdi's opera *Nabucco* was first rehearsed at La Scala, this glorious hymn to a land lost caused the stagehands to stop working and bash their tools appreciatively on the floor. 'Va' pensiero' ('Fly, thought...') remains to this day one of Italy's most popular and instantly recognisable tunes.

LA LUNA È UNA LAMPADINA ENZO JANNACCI (1964)

This Milanese singer-songwriter offers a surreal vision of his native city, often in dialect. His songs tell of everyday misadventures: tramps hoping to reach the Idroscalo, trams missed, girls ditto – and this one ('The Moon is a Lamp'), with lyrics by Nobel Literature Laureate Dario Fo, is the classic example.

I'M TOO SEXY RIGHT SAID FRED (1992)

'I'm too sexy for Milan,' brags Richard Fairbrass, lead singer of this British pop group, with more than a hint of irony. Riffing on the idea of a narcissistic model who is far 'too sexy' for his shirt, hat or car, this moderate satire on the fashion-victim culture of 1980s London was just as relevant to Milan of the same period – and, indeed, of the present day.

Escapes & Excursions

Escapes & Excursions

Milan is blessed with one of Europe's biggest attractions right on its doorstep. Or five of the biggest, to be exact: its lakes. Each of the region's great lakes has its own distinct character. West of Milan, Lago di Orta is a tranquil getaway; in the east, Lago di Garda's family-friendly expanse is ideal for both sports fanatics and lovers of luxury; Lago di Como, 40 minutes to the north, is hip and historic. Lago Maggiore is arguably the region's most majestic lake; while Lago d'Iseo is a little tourist spot with an island in the middle that is, in fact, a mountain.

Lombardy also boasts several towns that make ideal day-trip destinations. Bergamo, built high on a hill, prides itself as a world apart. Monza has a beautiful park, and one of the oldest and fastest motor-racing circuits in the world, site of Formula 1's Italian Grand Prix since the sport's beginning.

Monza

While the towns on the edge of Milan might appear to be nothing more than a desolate strip of (often abandoned) low-rise factories and isolated residential complexes, the area north of the city provides a welcome exception: here lies the hilly, temperate Brianza area, with its charming regional capital, Monza.

Once the jewel in the crown of the Lombard empire (we're talking seventh century here), Monza is nowadays a quaint and affluent town, drawing visitors principally for beautiful *palazzi*, gastronomic delights, a staggeringly huge park and the world-famous Formula 1 racing track, the **Autodromo Nazionale Monza** (*see p181* **Fast Track**).

The magnificent **Duomo** (piazza Duomo, 039 389 420) and its stunning basilica offer a glimpse of the town's historic past. With a Romanesque façade that was later decorated with Gothic motifs, it includes two star attractions: the **Cappella di Teodolinda**, which contains a cycle of frescoes depicting the life of the seventh-century Lombard queen; and the historic Iron Crown of Lombardy, one of the most ancient European royal insignia, which was allegedly built around an iron nail from the crucifixion. The crown was used in the coronation ceremony of Charlemagne in 774, of Otto I the Great in 962, of Frederick Barbarossa in 1154 and of Napoleon in 1805.

IN THE KNOW
JOURNEY PLANNING

The Lombardy regional council's website has a journey planner (www.trasporti.regione-lombardia.it; in Italian), which works a treat. It has listings and timetables for all forms of public transport in the area.

When you're ready for a break, hit the hip **Tearose Café** (piazza Duomo, 039 2356 0203, www.tearosecafe.it) for a quick (if pricey) bite as well as a great view of the cathedral.

The 13th-century town hall, known as the **Arengario**, lends its medieval charm to the city, and some of the lesser churches, such as **Santa Maria in Strada** and **San Pietro Martire**, are also worth a peek. In nearby via de Amicis, the charming **Mulino a Vino** wine bar (no.21, 039 384 180, www.enotecailmulino.it) is a short distance from a pretty medieval bridge over the Lambro river.

No visit to Monza would be complete without a walk through the enormous **Parco di Monza**, one of the largest parks in Europe. Its many attractions include the immense **Villa Reale** (viale Regina Margherita 2, 039 322 086), which reopened after a lengthy restoration in September 2014. Formerly the Archduke of Austria's hunting lodge, the villa became the summer retreat of Italy's ruling family, the Savoys, in 1859. King Umberto I's assassination in Monza, in 1900, led to a change of plan: the villa was abandoned and subsequently donated to the town.

AROUND MONZA

East of Monza, in **Arcore**, the beautiful grounds of the 18th-century **Villa Borromeo d'Adda** (039 60 171, www.villadarcore.com) are open to the public. But the town is mostly famous – or infamous – for its links with former prime minister Silvio Berlusconi, whose primary residence is here.

Despite being a thriving manufacturing centre, **Vimercate**, adjacent to Arcore, has preserved much of its original charm. Its new museum, covering the city's history from Roman times to the present, and tantalisingly named the **MUST** (Museo del Territorio Vimercatese), begs a visit. It's in Palazzo Sotto Casa (via Vittorio Emanuele II 53, 039 665 9488, www.museo must.it, closed Mon, Tue & Aug). Also worth seeing is the **basilica of Santo Stefano**, built between the tenth and 11th centuries on earlier foundations. Along via Cavour, off the central piazza Roma, are several 15th-century *palazzi* and the little Romanesque Oratorio di Sant'Antonio, with frescoes dating from 1450. At the end of the street, the **Ponte di San Rocco**, built from recycled Roman remains, was part of the town's medieval fortifications.

North of Monza is **Biassono**. Its town hall, Villa Verri, is a perfect example of early 18th-century *barocchetto* architecture, while the **Museo Civico** (via San Martino 1, 039 220 1077, www. museobiassono.it) offers good archaeological and ethnographic reconstructions of Brianza farm life through the ages.

FAST TRACK

Calling all petrolheads.

The **Autodromo Nazionale Monza** (Parco di Monza, 039 24 821, www.monzanet.it) is one of the world's most famous Grand Prix circuits. The long straights, the sweeping Curva Parabolica and the infamous chicane make for a compelling race, for both drivers and spectators. Like many Italian institutions, its birth was linked to the constant rivalry with its neighbours across the Alps. If France's Automobile Club had a Grand Prix at Le Mans, why shouldn't the Italians have one too? And so, in 1922, a group of Italian speed freaks decided to mark the 25th anniversary of the Milan Automobile Club by setting up a circuit at Monza.

Since then, the Autodromo has had more makeovers than a Hollywood star. Most frequent have been the safety improvements to limit the death toll. Between 1922 and 2000, 18 drivers and 41 spectators died in crashes; the most dramatic accident came in 1961, when Count Wolfgang von Trips' Ferrari collided with a Lotus driven by Jim Clark, bounced into the crowd and killed 15 spectators. Safety regulations are much stricter than they were in the past, and the track's record has improved.

But the Autodromo is so much more than just a celebration of speed and progress. It's now a year-round attraction offering, within its verdant grounds, a campsite, an Olympic-size pool and a car museum. If you fancy driving on the track that's the spiritual home of Team Ferrari, you can – one circuit of the six-kilometre (3.7 mile) track in a Ferrari F430 or a Lamborghini Gallardo costs from €239. Book online at www. puresport.it or call 039 606 6098. There are also cheaper self-drive days during December, January and February, when you can roll up in your own vehicle and book a 30-minute session (www.monzanet.it).

IN THE KNOW DRIVING

Once you've exited Milan's *tangenziale* (ring road) at the relevant junction, the *autostrade* (motorways) will lead you efficiently from A to B. You can pay for these toll roads with cash or at an automated credit-card machine. Alternatively, there's a far-reaching and, on the whole, well-maintained network of *strade statali* (SS: state highways). *Strade provinciali* (SP: provincial roads) will provide slower, more picturesque journeys.

Getting There

By bus Buses operated by Brianza Trasporti (www.brianzatrasporti.it) serve Monza from the termini of both Lines 1 (red) and 2 (green) of the Milan metro. From Sesto San Giovanni (Line 1), catch bus Z221 or Z222; from Cologno Monzese (Line 2), it's bus Z203 that you need.

By car For Monza, take viale Zara out of Milan, which becomes viale Fulvio Testi (journey time 15mins-1hr, depending on traffic). From Monza, local roads lead to Biassono, Carate Brianza, Arcore, Oreno and Vimercate. Vimercate can also be reached by taking the Tangenziale Est (A51) *autostrada*.

By train Trains for Monza leave Milan's Stazione Centrale or Porta Garibaldi every 15mins or so, and take 15mins. Trains also leave hourly (every 30mins at rush hour) from both stations for Arcore (23mins).

Monza. *See p180.*

Bergamo

The Venetians fortified this enchanting hilltop town, and its wealth, culture and unique cuisine have remained constant to this day. Bergamo's numerous treasures are divided between the **Upper City** (Città Alta) and the **Lower City** (Città Bassa). Just 30 minutes from Milan, it's the perfect antidote to the Lombard capital's stress and air pollution, though it also pulls in plenty of visitors in its own right, not least from the international airport ten minutes away.

CITTA ALTA

A ride on Bergamo's wedge-shaped funicular (035 364 211, www.atb.bergamo.it) from viale Vittorio Emanuele II (15 minutes on foot from the railway station) brings you up to the bustling **piazza Mercato delle Scarpe**. Follow the restaurant-lined via Gombito into the heart of Bergamo's enchanting old city, and turn up via Rocca to the **Rocca** itself (piazzale Brigata Legnano, 035 226 332), a defensive bastion dating from the time when Bergamo was under the rule of the Venetian Republic. The Rocca now houses a museum of the city's history, and boasts superb views of the valley from its grounds. Look out for Garibaldi's pistols and a striking bust of Napoleon.

At the intersection with via Lupo stands the **Torre Gombito** (035 399 111, visits by appt), a defensive turret recalling the Guelph-Ghibelline struggles of the Middle Ages. Beyond the tower, via Gombito opens out into the lovely, spacious **piazza Vecchia**, which shows off Bergamo at its finest. The beautiful bone-white buildings on the square's eastern side house the offices of the local university. On the south-western side of the square sits the magnificent **Palazzo della Ragione**, which houses Donato Bramante's *Tre Filosofi* frescoes (1477), but is only open for exhibitions.

The neoclassical **Palazzo Nuovo** on the north-east of piazza Vecchia is home to the municipal archives and library. Another feature of the piazza is the 53-metre (173-foot) **Torre Civica** (035 247 116), dating from the 12th century, also known as the Campanone; go up to the top on foot or using the glass-walled lift for great views.

Piazza Duomo houses some of Bergamo's most captivating buildings: the **Duomo** (officially known as the Cattedrale di Sant'Alessandro; 035 210 223, www.cattedraledibergamo.it), the basilica of Santa Maria Maggiore and the Cappella Colleoni. Standing on a spot previously occupied by an early Christian church, the Duomo was constructed to a design by Antonio 'il Filarete' Averlino, with work starting in 1459. The project passed through the hands of several architects, and was not completed until 1886. Among the mostly 18th-century works surrounding the main altar is Giambattista Tiepolo's *Martyrdom of St John the Bishop*. The statue of Pope John XXIII at the Duomo's entrance is a reminder of the city's esteem for 'their' pope, who was born in a village close to Bergamo in 1881.

Next door is the equally impressive **Santa Maria Maggiore** (035 223 327). Construction, again atop the remains of an earlier church, began in 1157, and did not end until 1521. Each period of building added something of beauty, from the presbytery (1187), to the baptistery (1350), to the new sacristy (late 15th century). The most stunning element, however, is the series of wooden inlay works on the presbytery stalls. These exquisite 16th-century carvings, most designed by the Venetian artist Lorenzo Lotto, portray Old Testament stories, as well as references to alchemy.

The **Cappella Colleoni** (035 210 061), to the south-west of piazza Vecchia, was built by the Venetian general Bartolomeo Colleoni. He had the old sacristy of Santa Maria Maggiore demolished to make way for his mausoleum, which was finished in 1475, a year after his death. Colleoni's tomb and that of his daughter Medea grace the chapel, as do frescoes (1733) by Giambattista Tiepolo. On the gate outside the chapel, visitors looking for luck have rubbed the Colleoni coat of arms to a bright sheen. The coat of arms, it should be noted, bears three testicles – as, allegedly, did Colleoni. Leading off the piazza is via Arena, home of the **Museo Donizettiano** (via Arena 9, 035 399 269, 035 428 4769), a treat for fans of the Bergamo-born composer Gaetano Donizetti (1797-1848). Tucked away on the first floor of an evocative palazzo, it contains a fascinating collection of handwritten letters, harpsichords and opera posters highlighting the composer's life.

Beyond piazza Vecchia, via Gombito becomes via Bartolomeo Colleoni and leads to piazza Mascheroni, home to **La Cittadella**, built in the 14th century to defend the Città Alta from attacks

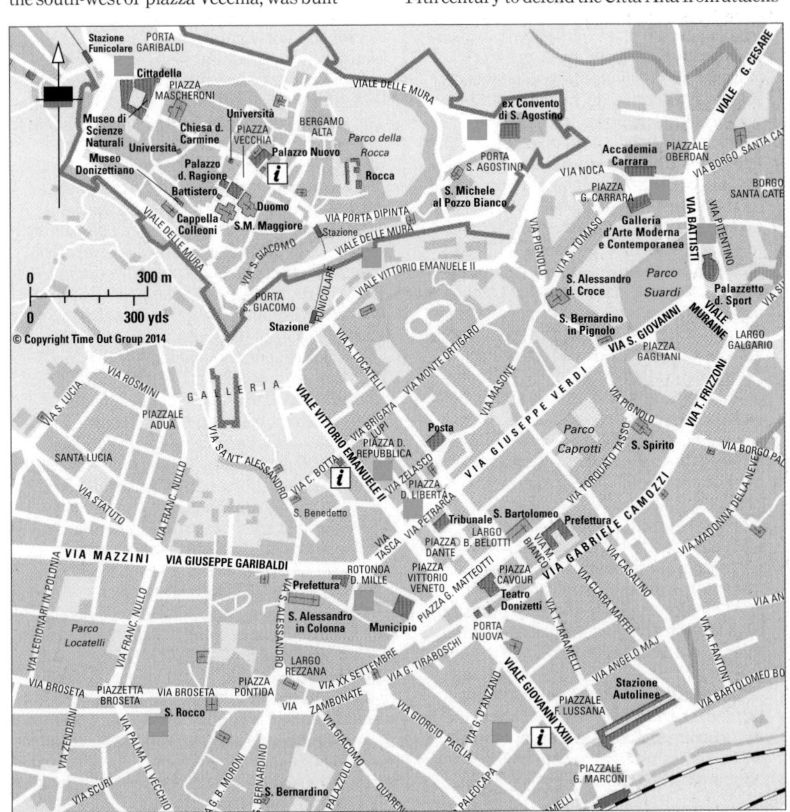

'D' FOR DELICIOUS

The power of polenta, good and bad.

Look in the window of any *pasticceria* in Bergamo, and you'll see a round yellow cake studded with chocolate bits. Called *polenta e osei* ('polenta and little birds'), it's made neither of polenta nor, thankfully, birds. Instead, these little sponge cakes rolled in fondant icing are a tribute to the traditional dish of the same name – which was exactly what its name suggests.

Now a dish of choice in fashionable restaurants worldwide, polenta was a staple of the poor in northern Italy for centuries, with dire consequences, especially in the areas where it was the only option seven days a week. Cornmeal, from which polenta is made, lacks niacin (aka vitamin B3) – and a chronic lack of niacin leads to a disease called pellagra. Although pellagra was first diagnosed in Spain, it takes its name from the Lombard dialect term *pelle agra*, which means 'dark skin'. This 'dermatological' problem was just one of the five Ds that distinguish pellagra, the last being 'death'. As for the others, if you're so inclined, you can look them up for yourself.

Now this dread disease is, thankfully, a thing of the past, polenta has become a popular foodstuff. It is, in fact, rather healthful when supplemented with protein: these days, succulent meats and sausages, and cheeses such as gorgonzola or branzi (a local speciality from the town of the same name some 30 kilometres/20 miles north of Bergamo), have replaced the wild songbirds, such as thrush, that were once used.

Grilled, fried, boiled or baked, polenta is, undeniably, the most humble of foods. But like those circular yellow cakes in the *pasticceria*'s windows, when served well and wisely, it is a treat to sate the stomach and comfort the soul.

from the west. Rising above the square is the **Torre della Campanella**; built in 1355, this bell tower wasn't finished until the 19th century, hence the relatively modern-looking clock face.

Cross piazza Cittadella and walk through the Porta Sant'Alessandro to Colle Aperto, an open space overlooking the foothills of the Alps. However pleasant, these views are nothing compared to the breathtaking sights to be had by taking Bergamo's funicular line from Porta Sant'Alessandro to the castle of San Vigilio, a former Venetian stronghold high above town. A three-minute ride and you're there. The fare is €2.50 – or use the one-day ticket for transport in Bergamo (*see p186*). It's a pleasant 15-minute amble back down, with picture-postcard views of the Città Bassa and Lombard plains far below.

Near Bergamo's other funicular at piazza Mercato delle Scarpe, the **Enoteca Al Donizetti** wine bar (via Gombito 17A, 035 242 661, average €25) serves platters of prosciutto, *lardo* and *salame*, plus local cheeses accompanied by walnuts and honey. The historic **Antica Trattoria la Colombina** (via Borgo Canale 12, 035 261 402, www.trattorialacolombina.it, closed Mon & 2-3wks June-July, average €40), just outside the Città Alta walls, dishes up seriously traditional cuisine in its sun-dappled dining room. The *stinco al forno con polenta* (baked pork shank with polenta) is just one example. There's a weekday lunchtime tasting menu for €15.

La Marianna (colle Aperto 2, 035 237 027, www.lamarianna.it, closed Mon & 2wks Jan, average €15) is both a restaurant and bar/pastry shop. Enjoy a bellini sorbet, rose-petal ice-cream or warm *torta al cioccolato* (chocolate tart) while sitting on the terrace overlooking the valley. If you're flying out of Bergamo Orio al Serio airport, check out the Marianna bar there too, for one last cappuccino. Open since 1956, **Da Mimmo** (via Colleoni 17, 035 218 535, www.ristorantemimmo.com, closed lunch Tue, average €45) is a pizzeria/restaurant. The lunchtime *antipasto* buffet is great value, and there's a €60 dinner *menu degustazione* for serious foodies. Cheap and cheerful, **Da Ornella** (via Gombito 15, 035 232 736, closed Thur, average €30) is popular with the locals. The decor may be 30 years out of date, but dishes such as *casoncelli alla Bergamasca* (meat pasta pockets served with melted butter) are timeless.

Bergamo is blessed with an array of hotels to suit all budgets. In the Città Alta, the **Agnello d'Oro** (via Gombito 22, 035 249 883, www.agnellodoro.it, double €85) offers great value for money. The building dates from the 16th century and is laden with antiques; some of the 20 rooms face on to the pretty square below, although street noise at night may be a problem.

Adjacent to the medieval Torre del Gombito, the **GombitHotel** (via Mario Lupo 6, 035 247 009,

Città Alta, Bergamo. See p182.

www.gombithotel.it, double €160-€250), prides itself on being the first design hotel in Bergamo Alta, juxtaposing original features from the 13th-century building with contemporary design and modern art. One caveat: the nearby church bells start ringing at 7am.

Across from the Cittadella, the upmarket **Hotel San Lorenzo** (piazza Mascheroni 9A, 035 237 383, www.relaisanlorenzo.com, double €240-€750) has recently been refurbished to a high standard, with sleek modern furnishings. The restaurant preserves the carefully restored ruins of Roman and medieval walls. The cuisine is especially suited to those with hearty appetites. Starters focus on cold cuts, particularly own-made *salame* and *lardo* (creamy white slices of pork fat, which tastes better than it might sound), while main courses tend towards roasts and braised dishes, often served with polenta (*see p184* **'D' for Delicious**).

CITTA BASSA

Bergamo's lower city offers all the perks of modern living that the far more attractive historic zone lacks – plus a couple of key museums. Buses, cars and people throng busy streets, edged with chain stores, bars, pizza joints and restaurants. The main shopping drag, via XX Settembre, is lined with low- to mid-priced boutiques, from Zara to Benetton to Kiko, while some swankier stores, such as multi-brand fashion shop Biffi, can be found on nearby via Tiraboschi. Piazza Vittorio Veneto leads off from here and forms the Città Bassa's centrepoint, alongside **Porta Nuova**, the city's main entrance from 1837 onwards. Further east is the church of **Santo Bartolomeo e Stefano**, which contains Lorenzo Lotto's *Madonna col Bambino e Santi* (1516), also known as the Martinengo Altarpiece.

The **Galleria d'Arte Moderna e Contemporanea** (GAMeC; via San Tomaso 53, 035 270 272, www.gamec.it, closed Mon) has been home to groundbreaking exhibitions, including regular expositions of artists' films. Its permanent collection includes works by Balla, Boccioni, de Chirico, Kandinsky and Morandi, as well as more contemporary names such as Vanessa Beecroft and Jan Fabre.

Scheduled to reopen in 2015, after several years of restoration, is the prestigious **Accademia Carrara** (035 270 413, www.accademiacarrara.bg.it) with its 2,000 magnificent masterpieces by the likes of Raphael, Bellini and Tiepolo, donated by local benefactor Count Giacomo Carrara, who died in 1796.

While Bergamo's most appealing dining spots are located in the Città Alta, **Le Iris** (viale Vittorio Emanuele II 12, 035 217 037, www.leiris.it, closed Sun, average €35) in the Città Bassa offers tempting treats of its own; try carpaccio of swordfish with pink pepper, and grilled *branzino* (sea bass) with local vegetables.

North of Bergamo, in Bracca, **Trattoria Dentella** (*see p209* **Dining Slow**) serves traditionally based gourmet food.

Getting There

By air For information about Bergamo's Orio al Serio airport, 5km (3 miles) from Bergamo, and about 45km (28 miles) from Milan, *see p255*.

By car Take the A4 *autostrada* from Milan eastbound, direction Venice; exit at Bergamo (55km/33 miles).

By train Services run from Milan's Stazione Centrale (53mins) and Stazione Porta Garibaldi (60mins). The latter option, which also stops at Monza and Arcore, has the added sightseeing advantage of crossing the Adda river over the dramatic Ponte di Paderno.

Getting Around

By public transport Bergamo's buses are operated by ATB (035 364 211, www.atb.bergamo.it), as are its two funiculars. Tickets (€1.25 for Zone 1) must be bought before boarding; they're sold at tobacconists and some newsstands around town, including the *edicola* in Bergamo train station. A one-day (*giornaliero*) ticket (€3.50) provides unlimited transport in the city centre, including the funiculars and one journey to Orio al Serio airport.

Lago d'Orta

Just west of Lago Maggiore, this small stretch of water (measuring just 18 square kilometres, or six square miles) has a lazy, magical air. Stroll along the shoreline paths, check the views from a mountain summit, or just sip a sundowner in one of the picturesque squares. The lake's one must-do is a boat trip to the mystical island of **Isola San Giulio**, dominated by an ancient abbey. Fans of Italian design icon Alessi can visit the town of **Omegna** and pick up the latest kitchen lines direct from the factory (*see p187* **Alessi's Cave**).

ORTA SAN GIULIO

Visitors to this medieval lakeside town could be forgiven for thinking they've somehow stumbled on to a vintage movie set. Stone buildings adorned with the odd peeling hotel sign make up the main lakeside square of piazza Motta, seemingly unchanged for 80 years. Villas in various states of repair, from the crumbling to the impeccably restored, most with lovely gardens, skirt the shoreline, and can be seen from the footpath (via 11 Settembre 2001) that extends from the end of via Motta to the car parks at via Panoramica.

Back in the café-lined main square, piazza Motta, photo shoots occasionally take place beneath the frescoes and loggia stilts of the 16th-century **Palazzo della Comunità** (the former town hall). Another photographic tradition, on Saturday afternoons between April and June, is for newlyweds to have their pictures taken on the lakeside, with the island of San Giulio in the background. Lovers of local crafts shouldn't miss **Penelope** (piazza Motta 26, 0322 905 600, www.penelope-orta.it), which specialises in hand-woven kitchen linens traditionally printed with antique wooden stamps and natural dyes – perfect as authentic, reasonably priced souvenirs.

Winding uphill from piazza Motta, through the gateway on the right of the yellow-stained church of **Santa Maria Assunta** (1485), is a pleasant pilgrims' path that leads to the 17th-century church of San Nicolao. The latter is within the wooded **Sacro Monte nature reserve** (0322 911 960, www.orta.net/sacromonte), which is punctuated with 20 small late Renaissance, Baroque and rococo chapels (1590-1785) containing 376 remarkably life-like terracotta sculptures in tableaux depicting events from the life of St Francis of Assisi.

Perched on the hill above Orta San Giulio, Vacciago di Ameno houses the **Collezione Calderara di Arte Contemporanea** (via

Orta San Giulio.

ALESSI'S CAVE

One of the most famous names in Italian design.

Away from its mystical monasteries and alleyways, Lago d'Orta is home to a doyen of international design. It's a long story. Giovanni Alessi set up shop near sleepy Omegna in 1921, harnessing local materials and talent to make tableware. In the 1950s, the company started contracting out its product design; in the 1970s, it began to work with the leading figures of the Italian design phenomenon, including Achille Castiglioni, Richard Sapper, Alessandro Mendini and Ettore Sottsass. In more recent years, the company has employed designers from as far afield as Australia and Japan. In all, Alessi has been responsible for more than 22,000 items of inventive homeware, from brightly coloured bathroom accessories to Philippe Starck's iconic leggy lemon juicer. Examples of Alessi products now reside in design museums worldwide, including MoMA in New York and the V&A in London.

Industry specialists can apply to peek into Alessi's historical collection, but mere mortals can revel in the company's huge factory shop. The entire Alessi range is on sale, from steel and leather champagne buckets to transparent plastic egg cups, with special offers on seconds and end-of-line articles.

Alessi Outlet Store *Via Privata Alessi, Crusinallo di Omegna (0323 868 648, www.alessi.com).*

Bardelli 9, 0322 998 192, www.fondazione calderara.it, closed mid Oct-mid May except by appt). This museum was converted from a late 17th-century home by Antonio Calderara (1903-78), and of its 327 paintings and sculptures, 56 are by him. The impressive collection documents the international avant-garde from the 1950s and '60s, with an emphasis on kinetic art, geometric abstraction and visual poetry.

Back in town, on its oldest street, **Al Boeuc** (via Bersani 28, 339 584 0039 mobile, closed Tue Apr-Dec & Mon-Wed Jan-Mar, average €15) is a cosy little wine bar housed in a 500-year-old building, serving bruschette, local cheese and cold cuts, along with more than 350 wines.

Just off the main drag, **La Campana** (via Giovanetti 43, 0322 90 211, closed Wed, average €20) is long established as an affordable pizza place. It's resolutely no-frills, but has plenty of atmosphere and the food is decent. Ask for an outdoor table in summer. One caveat: be sure to double-check your bill.

The luxurious **Villa Crespi** (via Fava 18, 0322 911 902, www.hotelvillacrespi.it, closed early Jan-mid Mar, €200-€400 double) is an over-the-top, ornate Moorish villa on the road to the station, about a ten-minute walk from town. It's at its most spectacular in winter, when the surrounding mountains are covered in snow. Chef Antonino Cannavacciuolo, from Naples, oversees the villa's two Michelin-starred restaurant (closed Mon & lunch Tue, average €130).

In a former 17th-century convent, the four-star **Hotel San Rocco** (via Gippini 11, 0322 911 977, www.hotelsanrocco.it, €211-€450 double), offers elegant rooms, fine dining (average €60) and a convenient location, close to the lakeshore.

In a red-stained, 18th-century palazzo located on the lakefront just below the Sacro Monte, the recently opened **Al Dom** (via Giovanetti 57, 335 249 613 mobile, www.aldom57.com, €140-€170 double) has three tastefully appointed rooms. Breakfast is abundant and the owners are always willing to give advice.

ISOLA SAN GIULIO

According to legend, St Julius (San Giulio) sailed to this island by floating on his cloak, then got down to banishing its multitude of snakes and dragons. Next, he established his 100th church, where he was eventually laid to rest. These days, you can reach the enchanting island and its basilica (founded in 392) by ferry (every 40 minutes, €4.50 return) or taxi boat (333 605 0288 mobile, www.motoscafisti.com) from piazza Motta at Orta San Giulio. You can also book a 30-minute tour of the lake including a stop on the island (€10).

Inside the basilica, a black marble pulpit has rare Saxon-influenced carvings, while frescoes from many centuries battle for space around its walls. A pathway (via alla Basilica) encircles the island, past the cloistered Benedictine abbey

Isola San Giulio. *See p187*.

and the many other handsome buildings. If you're here for St Julius's feast day, 31 January, you can apparently rap on the convent door to get a bag of *pane San Giulio* (dried fruit, nut and chocolate bread) for a small donation (this treat can be found at the bakeries in Orta San Giulio all year round).

There's no hotel on the island, but it's occasionally possible to stay at the **Mater Ecclesiae abbey** (via Basilica 5, 0322 905 010), which belongs to a closed order of Benedictine nuns. You'll be expected to follow the monastic way of life, rising for dawn prayers at 4.50am. The island also has a not especially recommendable restaurant.

AROUND THE LAKE

Pettenasco stands on the shore north of Orta. Drive or get there on the bus to Omegna (www.comazzibus.com). Its Romanesque church tower started life attached to the church of Sant'Audenzio, Audenzio being a pal of San Giulio as well as Pettenasco's town prefect in 300. The intricate woodwork for which the town was once famous is commemorated at the **Museo dell'Arte della Tornitura del Legno** (via Vittorio Veneto, 0323 89 622, closed mid Sept-mid June), which features tools, wooden items and machines from the town's old factories.

At the lake's northernmost point, **Omegna** is said to be named after the battle cry *Heu moenia!* ('Woe to you, walls!'), uttered by Julius Caesar before he ploughed through its defences. Today, it's the largest town on Lago d'Orta and is still well known for its metal kitchenware; brands such as Alessi (*see p187* **Alessi's Cave**), Bialetti and Lagostina are based here.

Pella is the village that's visible on the far shore when you look straight across the lake from Orta San Giulio. Quite some way above it, you can see a church. Drive around the lake, then take the signposted road that climbs uphill for ten kilometres (six miles) to get some stunning views. En route, the hamlet of **Artò** has an old *lavatoio*, where the women went to do their laundry until the advent of indoor plumbing. Look out for the sundials and the building adorned with a 16th-century fresco. **Boleto** is even smaller, and is picture-perfect, with its cobbled lanes and church. Finally, at the top, you'll reach the church: the **Madonna del Sasso** (1730-48), sitting 638 metres (2,093 feet) above the lake on a granite outcrop. Most of its frescoes are the work of local artist Lorenzo Peracino, and the painting above the pink, grey and black marble altar is a *Pietà* (1547) by Fermo Stella da Caravaggio.

Located about 14 kilometres (8.5 miles) south of Lago d'Orta and fringed by woodlands and vineyards, **La Capuccina** (via Novara 19B, 0322 839 930, www.lacapuccina.it, €90-€130 double), is a family-run, environmentally conscious farmhouse hotel and restaurant. Enjoy the farm's own produce in dishes prepared by the owner-chef in the 40-seat restaurant (dinner for two from €60).

Getting There

By car From Milan, take the A8 motorway for the lakes (Autolaghi). Approaching Gallarate, take direction Malpensa/Varese/Sesto Calende, then join the A26/E62 in the direction of Gravellona Toce. Exit at Borgomanero, then follow the signs to Gozzano and Lago d'Orta.

By train Mainline service from Milan's Stazione Centrale or Porta Garibaldi to Novara, then local service stopping at Orta/Miasino, then Omegna–Arona bus service. Alternatively, from Orta/Miasino station, you can walk 15mins to Orta San Giulio or call a taxi (346 211 1587 mobile, www.taxilagodorta.it).

Getting Around

By boat From Easter to September, Navigazione Lago d'Orta (0322 905 163, www.navigazionelagodorta.it) operates a daily boat service around the lake, stopping at Orta, Isola San Giulio, Omegna, Pella, Pettenasco and elsewhere. A day-rover ticket (€4.90) includes stops at Isola San Giulio and Pella; a Libera Circolazione ticket (€8.90) also includes Omegna. You can buy tickets on board; no credit cards. Alternatively, book a tour in a water taxi from the Servizio Pubblico Motoscafi (333 605 0288 mobile, www.motoscafisti.com) at Orta San Giulio.

By car A car is essential for visiting all the towns around the lakeshore. Orta San Giulio's town centre is closed to traffic. Various car parks are available, but have change handy for the ticket machines.

Lago Maggiore

For many people touring the Italian lakes, Lago Maggiore is the number-one choice. It's a perfect blend of rich history and sublime topography, a necklace of all too beautiful towns framed by verdant shorelines on one side and dramatic mountain landscapes on the other, with a balmy microclimate to boot. Emerging from the mist in the early morning, the lake's three lush islands are about as close as you'll come to an earthly paradise.

Part of the majesty stems from the Visconti era (1277-1447): the family built several castles in the area, joined later by the beautiful homes of the Borromeo dynasty, which succeeded theirs. There are also the fine establishments that accommodated the participants of the Grand Tour, as well as the travellers of the belle époque.

Maggiore is actually three lakeland regions in one. The top fifth is Switzerland's sunniest corner, a setting for fun activities and great summer festivals. The Lombard (eastern) side of the lake is impressive in its own right, with plenty of attractive villages, walks, churches and quiet corners waiting to be discovered – though it's often ignored in favour of the outstanding wealth

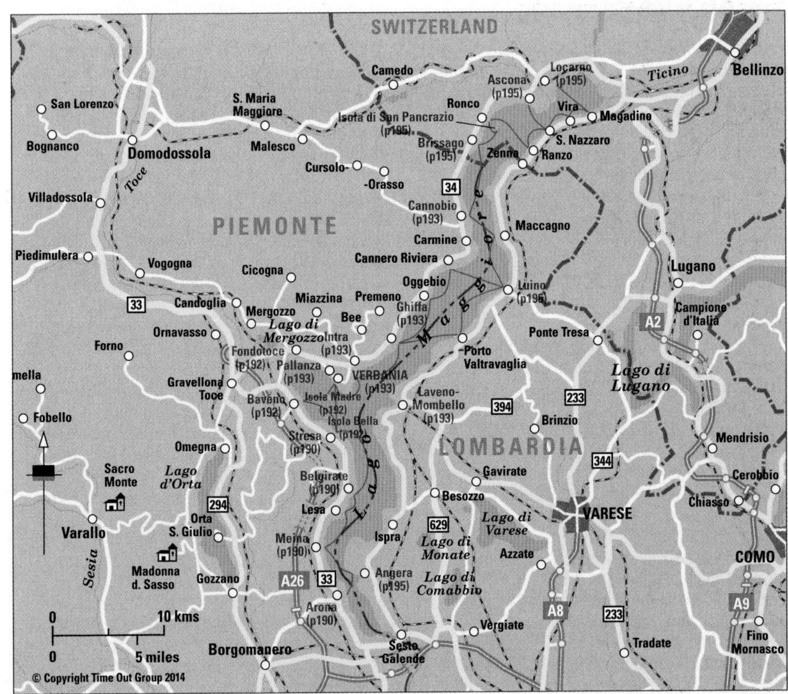

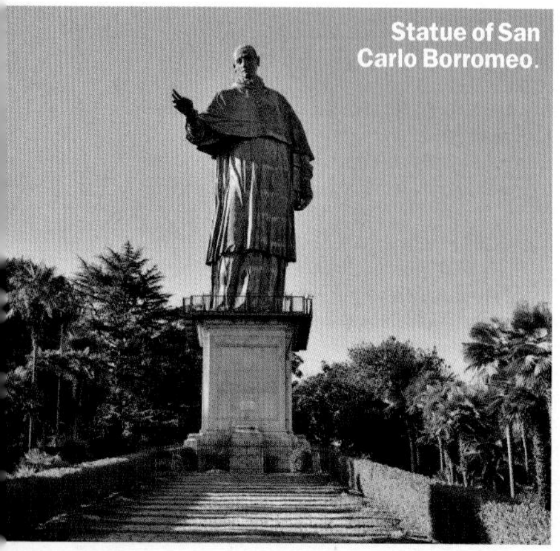
Statue of San Carlo Borromeo.

of beauty on the Piedmont shore opposite. This long, western stretch takes in the picturesque town of Stresa, the three Borromeo islands (Isola Bella, Isola Madre and Isola dei Pescatori), graceful hotels, lakeside promenades and gardens of unrivalled elegance.

THE PIEDMONT SHORE

A trip along the Piedmont shore by ferry or train provides an unparalleled experience, offering privileged glimpses of beauty untold. By road – whether you're travelling by bicycle or car – the thrill is still there though the views aren't quite as good. At every turn, there's a villa, a handsome hotel or another red-roofed old town to admire.

Inevitably, such a lovely natural setting draws visitors from all over the world, but also from other parts of Italy. The only drawback is the summer throng around the main attractions. To avoid the crowds, come off-season, but be aware that many of the major sites close from October to March.

At the southern tip of Lago Maggiore is **Arona**, a lively commercial town with a pretty, historic centre. San Carlo Borromeo was born here in 1538, and a 35-metre (115-foot) copper **statue** (piazzale San Carlo 9, 0322 249 669, closed Mon-Fri Mar, Oct & Nov, Mon-Sat Dec & all Jan & Feb) of this local hero stands high on a hill a couple of kilometres from town. It was constructed in the 17th century using the technique later employed on the Statue of Liberty; those with steely nerves can climb a narrow internal spiral staircase and ten-metre (32-foot) vertical ladder to the statue's head, and peer out at the lake through the saint's eyes.

Arona's fine selection of places to eat includes **Osteria del Triass** (via Marconi 59, 0322 243 378, closed Tue & 2wks Nov-Dec, average €35) and **Café de La Sera** (lungolago Marconi 85, 0322 241 567, closed Mon & 2wks Jan-Feb, average €30), both with outdoor terraces.

A few kilometres north, the smaller town of **Meina** has some attractive private residences. A dark event mars the serene town's history: in September 1943, Nazi troops executed 16 Jewish guests at a local hotel.

Above **Belgirate**'s tiny historic centre is the church of Santa Maria del Suffragio (closed Mon-Sat), lavishly adorned with frescoes by the school of Bernardino Luini, the 16th-century artist who was born in Dumenza, near Luino, on the Lombardy side of the lake.

Stresa stands magnificently on the Golfo Borromeo, which, with the three islands, forms the heart of the lake. The town became famous with English-speaking tourists after Byron and Dickens, among others, gave it rave reviews; Hemingway also set part of *A Farewell to Arms* here, in the Grand Hotel des Iles Borromées (*see p191* **Hemingway's Haunts**). At the turn of the 20th century, Stresa's palatial hotels, refined attractions and casino rivalled those of Monte Carlo and the Venice Lido. **Villa Pallavicino** (via Sempione Sud, 0323 30 501, www.parcozoo pallavicino.it, closed Nov-Feb) has a vast garden with broad lawns set off by cedars, magnolias and palms, as well as a zoo. The town is also known for its classical music festival (www. stresafestival.eu) between July and September.

Dining choices are plentiful in Stresa and most of the restaurants in the town's centre are good. Particularly tasty pizzas and grilled lake fish come out of the wood-fired oven at **Taverna del Pappagallo** (via Principessa Margherita 46, 0323 30 411, www.tavernapappagallo.com, closed Wed & mid Dec-Jan, average €40). Stresa has a collection of sumptuous belle époque hotels, including the **Grand Hotel des Iles Borromées** (corso Umberto I 67, 0323 938 938, www.borromees.it, closed 3wks Dec-mid Jan, double €265-€410), a landmark for stylish travellers since 1861. Guests have access to two swimming pools, a sauna, Turkish bath and gym. **The Hotel Regina Palace** (corso Umberto I 33, 0323 936 936, closed 2wks Dec-Jan, double €128-€365) is another grand lakeside hotel.

Standing above Stresa is the 1,491-metre (4,892-foot) **Mottarone**, also known as the 'Mountain Between Two Lakes', since it gives marvellous views of both Lago Maggiore and Lago d'Orta. On a clear day you can enjoy a stunning view of the Alps, and on really exceptional days you can see as far as Milan and Turin. The Mottarone can be reached by **cable car** (0323 30 295, www.stresa-mottarone.it, closed Dec-Feb) or via a five-hour hike from Stresa. A recent addition is **Alpyland** (0323 30 295, www.alpyland.com), an amusement park that includes the Alpine Coaster, a 750-metre (820-yard) bobsled-based downhill

HEMINGWAY'S HAUNTS

Lago Maggiore was a key place in the author's life and work.

American author and journalist Ernest Hemingway was a thrill-seeker from an early age. In the last year of World War I, he volunteered, aged 18, for service as an ambulance driver with the Red Cross. Just a few weeks after he took up his post on the Austrian front in Italy, he was wounded by sniper fire. A semi-autobiographical narrative of these events appeared in 1929 as *A Farewell to Arms*, a passionate, often funny, anti-war novel.

The story's wounded American volunteer, Lieutenant Frederic Henry, is sent to convalesce in Milan. This situation echoes the novelist's own experience: he spent time at the Red Cross Hospital in via Armorari in central Milan (you can see the plaque, near the corner with via Cantù, when you are in the Cordusio area of the city). While recuperating, Hemingway fell in love with an American nurse, Agnes von Kurowsky. Although she eventually spurned him, her character was fictionalised as British nurse Catherine Barkley, whom he meets on the battlefront. She and Frederic spend time in Milan, and then he joins her in Stresa, on Lake Maggiore, as he flees from the Italian military police.

Hemingway was probably just fleeing boredom when, in September 1918, he checked into the **Grand Hotel des Iles Borromées** (*see p190*), then, as now, Stresa's leading hotel. This was the start of an enduring association with the hotel: he stayed there on and off until the 1950s, whenever possible in his favourite suite, no.106, overlooking Isola Bella. In the novel, the Italian military police come close to arresting Lt Henry at the hotel. Tipped off by the barman, the couple flee, and the penultimate chapter has them rowing, all night, across Lago Maggiore to Switzerland.

Although there are few actual Hemingway sights in Stresa, even non-residents can have a dry martini in the Grand Hotel's bar. The stately hotel has welcomed many famous names in its 150 years; guests before World War I included the King of Italy, the Queen of Romania, the Prince of Prussia, the Duchess of Genoa and King Alfonso XIII of Spain. Later signatories to the guest book ranged from Princess Margaret to the Vanderbilts.

Read *A Farewell to Arms*, if you haven't already – and see if you don't agree that the sight of Isola Bella on Lago Maggiore 'beats paradise all to hell'.

Grand Hotel des Iles Borromées.

ride. In winter, a chairlift from the cable-car station takes skiers up to 21 kilometres (13 miles) of pistes. The cable car stops at the **Giardino Alpinia** (0323 20 163, closed Nov-Mar), which features hundreds of alpine plant species; it also offers a picture-perfect view over the three **Isole Borromee** – Isola Bella, Isola Madre and Isola dei Pescatori – set a few hundred metres off Stresa's shore, and all owned by the aristocratic Borromeo family.

Isola Bella was named in honour of Isabella d'Adda, whose husband Carlo Borromeo III began transforming the island in 1632 (previously it had been inhabited by fishermen and their families). The island's baroque **Palazzo Borromeo** (0323 30 556, www.isoleborromee.it, closed mid Oct-mid Mar), where Napoleon and Josephine slept after Napoleon's conquest of northern Italy, provides an awe-inspiring display of (very) old money. Its stately Italian-style gardens descend to the lakeshore via ten terraces; roaming the grounds are albino peacocks.

The largest of the three islands, **Isola Madre** (0323 30 556, www.isoleborromee.it, closed mid Oct-mid Mar) is a vast and magnificent botanical garden with yet more peacocks. Its 16th-century mansion, also called **Palazzo Borromeo**, can be visited – and includes an 18th-century puppet theatre.

Isola dei Pescatori (Fishermen's Island) is the most down-to-earth of the trio. It's a strip of narrow lanes, stray cats and whitewashed houses, ending in a park with benches and shady trees. It's also home to a picturesque hotel.

The best-known restaurant on Isola dei Pescatori is **Ristorante Casabella** (1 via del Marinaio, 0323 33 471, average €45). In cooler weather, eat fish or local meat dishes in the cosy, wood-panelled dining room; on sunny days, head for the rooftop terrace for views of the neighbouring Isola Bella. The blissfully romantic **Hotel Verbano** (0323 30 408, www.hotelverbano.it, closed Nov-Feb, double €150-€185) is the only hotel on Isola Pescatori. The cosy rooms have floral fabrics and wooden floors.

Beyond Stresa, **Baveno** is home to the notable tenth-century church of the saints Gervasio and Protasio; the octagonal baptistery dates from the fifth century. The local pink granite is exported worldwide – you can see the evidence of centuries of quarrying in the surrounding hills: not necessarily a pretty sight. The marble used in Milan's Duomo was quarried at nearby **Candoglia**, which plays host to a popular music festival (www.festivalgiordano.it) in July.

Further north, at **Fondotoce**, the reed thickets in the **Riserva Naturale** (0323 496 596, www.lagomaggiore.net) at the mouth of the Toce river are home to 130 species of birds (including European storks and snipe), wild pond turtles and 240 plant species, among them a rare water chestnut, only found here. Some of the reserve's hiking and bike trails lead to the **Lago di Mergozzo**, a mirror-like alpine lake to the west of Lago Maggiore and north of Lago d'Orta, at the mouth of the Val d'Ossola, which can also be reached by road. Its verdant shores hide **Piccolo Lago** (via Filippo Turati 87, 0323 586 792, average €100), the proud owner of two Michelin stars and home of some of the area's most innovative cuisine, courtesy of chef Marco Sacco. The menu zigzags between fish specialities and alpine traditions, sometimes combining the two; try the pasta with nettle-flavoured goat's

Isola dei Pescatori.

cheese, shrimps and coconut. In Mergozzo itself, the central **Ristorante Vecchio Olmo** (piazza Cavour 2, 0323 80 335, closed Thur Oct-Apr & 2wks Feb, average €30) serves pizza and also has a good-value set menu.

The rather confusing provincial capital of **Verbania** may sound like it's an actual place, but in fact it's an administrative construct, created in 1939 and linking the small towns of **Intra** and **Pallanza**. Peaceful Pallanza is renowned for its gardens, and has an attractive lakeside promenade. Just 30 metres offshore, the islet of San Giovanni Battista is tantalisingly close, yet strictly off-limits. Acquired in 1632 by the Borromeo family, who built the lovely palazzo, this delightful spot was where conductor Arturo Toscanini spent his summers from 1927 to 1952.

The garden at **Villa Taranto** (via Vittorio Veneto 111, 0323 556 667, www.villataranto.it, closed Nov-mid Mar), between Pallanza and Intra, was laid out by Captain Neil McEacharn, who bought the property in 1931. It contains more than 20,000 plant varieties, including giant Amazonian lilies and Japanese maples.

The pick of Pallanza's restaurants is the elegant **Milano** (corso Zanitello 2, 0323 556 816, www.ristorantemilanolagomaggiore.it, closed Tue & Jan-Mar, average €60), which serves classic Italian cuisine in its lake-facing dining room and terrace. The busiest place on the main square is **Bolongaro** (piazza Garibaldi 9, 0323 503 254, average €25), with pizza being the order of the day. Pallanza's **Grand Hotel Majestic** (via Vittorio Veneto 32, 0323 509 711, www.grandhotelmajestic.it, closed Oct, double €190-€360) is a delightful belle époque hotel offering breathtaking views of the three islands. It also has a spa, gardens and an elegant 1920s vibe.

The San Bernardino river marks the boundary between Pallanza and Intra (indeed, the latter takes its name from the fact that it lies between – *intra* in Latin – the San Bernardino and the San Giovanni rivers). For tourists today, Intra is what lies between them and the Lombardy shore of Lake Maggiore: the **car ferry** (800 551 801 toll-free, www.navigazionelaghi.it), which crosses the lake to Laveno (every 20mins, 6am-11.30pm daily) departs from here.

In Intra, on piazza Castello, **La Bottiglieria** (0323 516 579, closed Sun) is the place for hunks of cheese and local wine, while, next door, **Osteria del Castello** (0323 516 579, www.osteriacastello.com, closed Sun, average €35) offers heartier fare. In summer, they take over the whole piazza.

One of Europe's largest wilderness areas, the **Parco Nazionale della Val Grande** stretches behind Verbania. Dozens of hiking and bike trails lead to meadows, gorges and peaks, where chamois outnumber hikers. Wonderful as it looks, the area is to be approached with reverence.

Villa Taranto.

Find an expert guide/ranger at www.parcovalgrande.it. For more information, go to the tourist information office (IAT) in Pallanza.

Heading towards Switzerland, the 23-kilometre (14-mile) drive from Intra to Cannobio takes in some of the lake's loveliest views. If you don't have access to a car, you can take the bus from Intra, destination Brissago (www.vcoinbus.it).

Bordered by weathered stone walls, the road skirts the shoreline, passing through quiet little towns and offering great views of the lake. Across the water, you can see the mountains rising precipitously from the sparsely inhabited Lombard shore.

North of Intra is **Ghiffa**, one of the western shore's most peaceful villages. Here, the **Museo dell'Arte del Cappello** (corso Belvedere 279, 0323 59 209, www.comune.ghiffa.vb.it, closed Mon-Fri Apr-Oct & all Nov-Mar) commemorates the local felt hat-making tradition. **The Riserva Naturale Sacro Monte della Santa Trinità** (information office at via Santissima Trinità 48, 0323 59 870, www.sacromonteghiffa.it, closed Sat & Sun), extending behind Ghiffa, offers several hiking trails, as well as spectacular views across the lake to the Lombard pre-Alps, from the summit of the **Sacro Monte** (Sacred Mount). This devotional complex, which was supposed to portray episodes from the Old and New Testaments, was never completed. Similar in conception to the one at **Orta** (*see p186*), it's one of the nine Sacri Monti of Piedmont and Lombardy on the UNESCO World Heritage list.

Emerging from the waters not far from the Cannobio shoreline are the evocative ruins of the Malpaga castles, known as the **Castelli del Cannero**, built on two rocky islets between the 13th and 14th centuries. The property of the Borromeo family, who also own the **Rocca di Angera**, the castles are not open to the public, but plans are afoot for a museum to be built here over the coming years.

The last stop before reaching the Swiss border is **Cannobio**, one of Lake Maggiore's best-preserved villages. Its palm trees are testament to the lake's balmy microclimate, although visitors in winter might notice that the sun disappears earlier than in other places, as the mountain blocks its path. A leisurely hour's walk leads to the **Orrido di Sant'Anna** (www.lagomaggiore.net), a dramatic gorge that plunges into dark depths, at the bottom of which one can see the river that wrought this wonder. Experience the thrill from one of the two stone bridges spanning the gorge. The 17th-century church of **Sant'Anna** (open August afternoons) sits perilously on one edge.

Cannobio's **Lo Scalo** (piazza Vittorio Emanuele 32, 0323 71 480, www.loscalo.com,

LIQUID GOLD

Olive oil production is increasing in the northern lakes.

Travelling beside the northern lakes, you may spot the distinctive silvery-green of olive groves among the luxuriant vegetation. Though more usually associated with the warmer south, olive oil production has been linked with these shores since Roman times – and the region's small-production, niche products are once again gaining cachet. While Lago di Garda's oils are undoubtedly the best known, Lago di Como and Lago d'Iseo also boast some fine results – and Lago Maggiore is fast catching up.

Lake Garda's economy has long been tied up with olive oil. Indeed, much of the terracing in the surrounding hills was planted with olives for many centuries, providing sustenance for the local community, while the oil served as bartering currency in the nearby Austro-Hungarian empire.

Enjoying DOP (Denominazione Origine Protetta, or Protected Designation of Origin) status since 1997, the extra-virgin olive oil produced around Lake Garda needs little introduction to the cognoscenti. With some 665 hectares (1,640 acres) of olive groves planted mainly with Casaliva, Frantoio and Leccino cultivars, the local oil producers' consortium has 474 members across all three of the regions bordering the lake: Lombardy, Veneto and Trento.

In Puegnago del Garda, the **Comincioli** olive oil press (via Roma 10, Frazione Castello, 0365 651 141, www.comincioli.it) produces one of Italy's few pitted olive oils. Tangy with a spicy back-kick, the oil is a wonderful greenish-gold. Comincioli also makes grappa and wine.

On Lago di Como, olive oil was traditionally made in the area known appropriately enough as the 'Zoca de l'Oli' or Olive Bay, on the western shore. These days, however, olives come increasingly from the centre and northerly (Altolago) area.

On the western shore, at Lenno, **Osvaldo Vanini** (via Silvio Pellico 10, 0344 551 27, www.oliovanini.it), creates fruity, full-flavoured oils using traditional methods. On the eastern shore near Bellano, adventurous types can drive up the winding road to the high-tech **Azienda Agricolo Poppo** (Frazione Biosio, 335 260 989, www.biosio.it) for the press's prestigious bottles of pungent, grassy oil.

Following in the footsteps of Lakes Garda, Como and Iseo (which shares the DOP with Como), Lake Maggiore recently established an olive growers' association. With just seven founder members (and another ten applying for membership), 1,500 trees and about 500 litres of oil produced annually, it's still early days. Nonetheless, there are plenty of precedents: in the tenth century, olives were to be found in the Montorfano and Ossola areas, while olive groves existed on Isola Madre and around Lago d'Orta until the 1400s. Located in a variety of terroirs, the Lake Maggiore olive producers are using the Frantoio, Leccino and Pendolino cultivars, the objective being to achieve DOP status for Lake Maggiore olive oil in the near future – rivalling the other lakes.

closed dinner Sun, all Mon & 4wks Jan-Feb, average €45) serves creative Italian dishes and has a tempting tasting menu. The family-run **Hotel Pironi** (via Marconi 35, 0323 70 624, www.pironihotel.it, closed mid Nov-mid Mar, double €140-€165) offers contemporary comfort in a 16th-century townhouse with frescoes complementing the original 1970s patterned bathroom tiles, and a zesty colour scheme.

THE SWISS SHORE

A faintly perceptible change occurs as you cross over into Switzerland. The towns appear more orderly and the hills more Alpine. As the country's warmest spot, Switzerland's Lake Maggiore zone features many activities, from scenic railways to speedboat hire, and a number of summer festivals.

Brissago's reputation rests on its production of fine cigars. During the summer months, boats operated by Navigazione Lago Maggiore serve the two **Isole di Brissago**. The larger island, **Isola di San Pancrazio**, has a botanical garden (0041 91 791 4361, closed Nov-late Mar) containing some 1,500 species from the Mediterranean, subtropical Asia, South Africa, the Americas and Oceania; the smaller island, **Isola di Sant'Apollinare**, is given over to spontaneous vegetation.

North-east of Brissago is the ancient fishing village of **Ascona**, which hosts an important one-week jazz festival (www.jazz.ascona.ch, June/July) and a classical music festival (www.settimane-musicali.ch, late Aug-Oct).

Locarno, at the lake's northern tip, hosts a prestigious film festival (www.pardo.ch) in August. Most visitors, though, are content to wander along the town's well-manicured lakeside promenade or rent a speedboat (SF50 per hour). For a more exhilarating experience, there's a **cable car** (0041 91 735 3030, www.cardada.ch, closed Dec-Feb) running 1,000 metres (3,280 feet) up to a choice of viewing platforms suspended in mid-air. One provides a 180-degree window over the unforgettable views of Lake Maggiore, the Centovalli and part of the Maggia Valley; the other, on the highest point of Cimetta, offers a 360-degree panorama of the whole region and surrounding mountains. To reach the loftily perched **Madonna del Sasso church** (not to be confused with the Madonna del Sasso near Lake Orta – *see p188*), with its highly ornate interior, take the funicular or walk up the steep hill flanked by the Stations of the Cross.

Located in the Muralto section of Locarno's waterfront promenade, **Ristorante DiVino** (viale Verbano 13, 0041 91 759 1122, www.divino-ti.ch, average SF60) has heartier, meatier cuisine than that served over the border, plus a great selection of local cured meats, cheeses and wines. There's also a special afternoon menu, offering salads, soups, pasta and pizza. Also on the waterfront, the elegant **Centenario** (lungolago Motta 17, 0041 91 743 8822, closed Mon, Sun & Feb, average SF90) specialises in nouvelle cuisine.

In Locarno, **La Rinascente** (via al Tazzino 3, www.larinascente.ch, double SF180-SF320) is a 15-room boutique hotel in a restored 16th-century building, just off piazza Grande. North-facing rooms look on to the mountains; the glass-walled bathrooms may cause privacy concerns.

THE LOMBARDY SHORE

For all its great rail and boat links, and a string of pretty villages, Lago Maggiore's eastern shore attracts fewer visitors than it deserves. Those who do visit are in for a treat, as there's a lot to explore, bags of afternoon sunshine – and a complete dearth of souvenir shops.

Starting from the south, **Rocca Borromeo** (via alla Rocca, 0331 931 300, www.isoleborromee.it, closed late Oct-mid Mar), a fortress built in the 11th century and expanded and fortified up until the 17th, dominates the lake from its clifftop location in Angera. In Visconti hands from

Cannobio.

the 13th century, it became Borromeo property in 1449. One wing contains a rare cycle of 14th-century frescoes by local Lombard artists; another houses a collection of dolls, children's playthings and fully functional, 19th-century wind-up toys. The Borromeo wing features frescoes taken from the family's palazzo in Milan, along with details about this famous family, who were related to both a pope (Pius IV) and his brother (Gian Giacomo Medici), who was a pirate and mercenary. The latter's tomb can be seen in Milan's Duomo. Outside, walk around the ramparts, admire the vineyards and visit the recently planted Medieval Vegetable Garden.

The attractive **Hotel dei Tigli** (via Paletta 20, 0331 930 836, www.hoteldeitigli.com, closed 3wks Dec-Jan, double €120-€150) is in a red-walled palazzo in a side street just a few minutes' walk from the lake.

Laveno is a pleasant transport hub with two train stations as well as passenger and car ferries to Intra (Pallanza/Verbania). Its clutch of churches and quiet streets warrant a mooch. At weekends, from March to October, a **cable car** (0332 668 018, www.funiviedellagomaggiore.it) with bucket-like cabins runs daily up Sasso del Ferro, a panoramic plateau and hang-gliding launch point above town. It's a 12-kilometre (seven-mile) drive from here to tiny Lago di Varese, a birdwatcher's paradise beside the lake town of Azzate.

It's possible to walk the six kilometres (four miles) from Laveno to **Eremo di Santa Caterina del Sasso Ballaro** (0332 647 172, www.santacaterinadelsasso.com, closed Mon-Fri Nov-Feb). This exquisite 12th-century church is perched on the rock face 18 metres (60 feet) above the water near Leggiuno. Home to Benedictine monks and lavishly adorned with 16th-century frescoes, the sanctuary offers heart-stopping views across the lake. If you arrive by road, you can take the lift from the car park, or brave the 250-odd steep steps. The best approach, however, is by boat from Stresa (*see p190*): from the water, you get the full impact of this beautiful church. There are usually ten crossings a day (10mins), but check the website (0322 233 200, www.navigazionelaghi.it).

North along the shore from here is the pleasant harbour town of **Caldé**, with a pretty beach. Beyond it lies **Luino**, a tranquil old town sprawling up (and down) the hill. At the top is the church of San Pietro in Campagna, which has a Romanesque bell tower, and frescoes attributed to Bernardino Luini, who was from nearby Dumenza. The town's **Camin Hotel Luino** (viale Dante 35, 0332 530 118, www.caminhotelluino.com, closed 5wks Dec-Jan, €180-€210 double) occupies a 19th-century villa with a garden. Some of the 13 rooms overlook the garden; the others have a lake view.

In the village of **Maccagno**, the last town before the Swiss-Lombard border, the yellow **Santuario della Madonna delle Punta** protrudes into the lake to the south; there's also a beach here.

Getting There & Around

By boat Navigazione Lago Maggiore (Italian side 0322 233 200, Swiss side 0041 91 751 6140, www.navigazionelaghi.it) operates boats and hydrofoils to many of the towns around the lake, including the Swiss side. Private water taxis can be hired at most ports.

By bus VCO Trasporti (0323 518 711, www.vcoinbus.it) operates between Verbania (Intra/Pallanza) and Brissago, Switzerland, via Ghiffa, Oggebbio, Cannero and Cannobio. On the Swiss side, FART (Ferrovie Autolinee Regionali Ticinesi) runs both a bus and a ferry service between Locarno and Brissago (0041 91 756 0400, www.centovalli.ch).

By car The A8 motorway gets you from Milan to Sesto Calende. For towns on the lake's western (Piedmont) shores, cross the bridge over the River Ticino, and take the A26 towards Gravellona Toce. The S33 skirts the lake to Fondotoce, where it becomes the S34 to Cannobio. For the eastern shore, take the S629 to Laveno, then the S394, which skirts the lake, via Caldé, to Luino and beyond. For Locarno, on the lake's Swiss side, take the A9 motorway from Milan to Como, switch to the A2 motorway (direction Bellinzona), and follow the signs. The road that runs along the lake is via Cantonale 13.

By train For the Piedmont (western) shore, take the Domodossola service from Milan's Garibaldi station. This stops at Sesto Calende, Arona (journey time 1hr), Meina, Lesa, Belgirate, Stresa (1hr 30mins), Baveno, Verbania/Pallanza (1hr 40mins), Mergozzo and Candoglia. Express trains from Stazione Centrale serve Arona (45mins) and Stresa (1hr). For Laveno, take the Trenord service from Cadorna station (1hr 30mins). Change there for Caldé and Luino, 15mins to the north.

For the Swiss shore, take the train to Domodossola from Milan's Stazione Centrale (1hr). Travelling by train from Domodossola (Italy) to Locarno (Switzerland) involves taking one of the finest mountain railway journeys anywhere in Europe: the **Centovalli** (0041 91 756 0400, www.centovalli.ch), or 'hundred valleys' railway. This ride (1hr 40mins) involves crossing some 86 bridges over exquisitely rugged Alpine landscapes, and offers spectacular views of mountains, rockfaces, waterfalls and tiny villages, providing some idea of how life is, even in the 21st century, in these small communities.

Lago di Como

The deepest of the Italian lakes, at more than 400 metres (1,300 feet), Lake Como is also the most accessible from Milan. The train journey to Como takes just 40 minutes, and you can be in the delightful, old stone village of Varenna within an hour. From there, it's a 15-minute ferry ride to Bellagio, whose panoramic position on a promontory in the middle of the lake has earned it its reputation as the 'pearl of the lake'. When you've had your fill of these postcard-perfect (though sometime bustling) villages, head back, maybe stopping off at one of the other lakeside towns on the way.

But why rush back? Book a hotel and spend a little longer touring the sweeping shorelines, and you may find yourself reluctant to leave. You'll be part of a long tradition, beginning with Como-born Pliny the Younger (AD 62-112), who wrote ecstatically of the 'several villas' he possessed on the lake, explaining of one that 'you can quite simply cast your line out of the window without getting out of bed.' In 569, the Lombards decided they wanted a piece of the action and promptly took up residence within the walls of Como town itself. In the 19th century, Stendhal, Rossini and Shelley all lodged at the Villa Pliniana at Torno, while Verdi apparently wrote much of *La Traviata* at Villa Margherita Ricordi at Cadenabbia di Griante, near Tremezzo. More recent part-time residents famously include George Clooney, who drops by occasionally to enjoy the quiet life at his lakeshore villa in Laglio.

Lake Como, or the Lario as it's been known since Roman times, extends in an inverted Y shape from the Alps in the north to the cities of Como and Lecco, some 50 kilometres (30 miles) away, in the south-west and south-east, respectively. The two southern 'arms' come together to form the promontory of Bellagio. Although the lake has a 178-kilometre (110-mile) perimeter, it is never more than 4.5 kilometres (three miles) wide, creating a pleasing sense of intimacy. Moreover, each of the lake's three

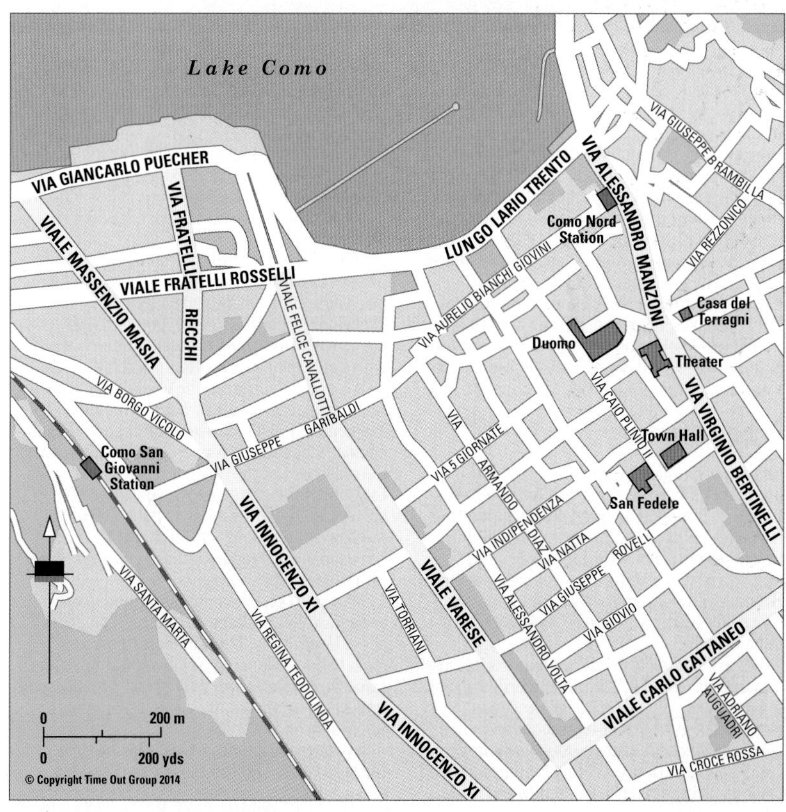

Lake Como.

'arms' is different. The Como section is relatively narrow; the mountains behind are somewhat uniform, with plenty of little towns and grand villas along the shoreline. The Lecco branch is more rugged, the jagged edges of the Grigne range providing a strong contrast. The northern part features deep valleys and tall mountains, and is the most dramatic. The scenery is probably at its most beautiful in the central section of the lake, around the triangle formed by Bellagio, Menaggio and Varenna.

The best time to come? It's a common belief in Italy that lakes in general, not just Como, are *tristi* (sad) from October to March. Make up your own mind, but it's worth noting that some hotels and restaurants are closed during the winter months.

COMO

Busy, industrialised and traffic-ridden: first impressions as you enter Como, the unofficial capital of the lake, can be rather disappointing. If you're arriving from Milan and this is your first experience of Italy's lakes, you might even suspect the whole thing's an elaborate wind-up. But once you reach the old town and sip your first coffee by the water, the pieces will start to fall into place.

Como's architectural showstopper is its Duomo (piazza del Duomo, 031 265 244), a brilliant fusion of Romanesque, Gothic, Renaissance and Baroque. Begun in 1396, it is unique as well as spectacularly beautiful. Its late-Gothic façade (1455-86) is even more striking for the fact that pride of place is given to two renowned pagans – the Plinys, Elder and Younger. A short walk away, along viale Battisti, the remaining stretches of Como's 12th-century walls run to the imposing **Porta Torre** gate (1192). For those interested in silk and the silk industry, in which Como used to be a world leader, walk or take the 7 city bus to the **Museo Didattico della Seta** (via Castelnuovo 1, 031 303 180, www.museosetacomo.com, closed Mon, Sat, Sun).

On the lakeside by the ferry jetty (*imbarcadero*), **piazza Cavour** is one of Como's most popular meeting points. Traffic and recent concrete 'embellishments' mean it's not much to look at, but on a warm evening the place will be buzzing with locals taking their evening stroll.

West of the square in the **Giardini Pubblici**, the neoclassical **Tempio Voltiano** (viale Marconi, 031 574 705, www.cultura.provincia.como.it, closed Mon) was erected in 1927 to mark the centenary of the death of Alessandro Volta, the Como-born physicist who invented the battery and gave his name to the volt – not to mention scores of streets all over Italy. The museum in the temple's interior contains some of his original instruments.

No trip to Como is complete without a visit to **Brunate**, the village 720 metres (2,360 feet) above Como town. The **funicular railway** (next to Como Nord Lago railway station, www.funicolarecomo.it), will whizz you up there in just under seven minutes, saving you a 90-minute uphill slog on foot.

By general consensus, **Le Colonne** (piazza Mazzini 12, 031 266 166, closed Tue Oct-Mar, average €25), on a quiet piazza set back from the

lake, serves the best pizza in Como – and their tagliatelle with lake fish (*al profumo del lago*) must be tried.

Walk through the *salumeria* (delicatessen) at **Castliglioni** (via Cesare Cantù 9, 031 263 388, www.castiglionistore.com, closed Sun, average €40) for a lunchtime treat in the small courtyard at the back – it's also a wine bar serving salami and cheese platters throughout the day. For *bresaola* from nearby Valtellina and other regional specialities, stop for lunch at the rustic **Osteria Del Gallo** (via Vitani 16, 031 272 591, average €30), where you'll be served by owners Rosanna and Giuseppe.

The top dinner option is the **Ristorante Sociale** (via Rodari 6, 031 264 042, www.ristorantesociale.it, closed Tue, average €40) in an attractive location near the lake. Dishes include stunning risottos, a popular steak tartare and the spicy house creation, penne Satanik. On weekends, there's a set-lunch menu for €13. Reservations are essential. Housed in a former convent, **La Colombetta** (via Diaz 40, 031 262 703, www.colombetta.it, average €90) provides a touch of flair. If you're just after a takeaway snack, you could do a lot worse than nearby **Peach Pit** (via Diaz 41): take your pick of more than a dozen focaccia sandwiches at €4 a throw.

Around 16 kilometres (ten miles) east of Como, Slow Food-recommended **Trattoria Inarca** (*see p209* **Dining Slow**) serves local delights in a former 13th-century chapel.

Set among the main cluster of lakefront hotels, the four-star **Albergo Terminus** (lungo Lario Trieste 14, 031 329 111, www.hotelterminus-como.it, €155-€270 double) tends to attract a relatively mature crowd. Its 16-room annexe and two stunning apartments have an elegant boutique feel, with lake views.

Reopened in 2013 after a two-year closure, **Borgo Antico** (via Borgovico 47, 031 338 0150, www.borgoanticohotelcomo.it, €100-€180 double) is a five-minute walk from Como San Giovanni railway station and ten minutes from the lake. Its 24 rooms have wrought-iron bedheads and pretty colour schemes.

Next to the base of the Brunate Funicular, **Hotel Marco's** (via Coloniola 43, 031 303 628, www.hotelmarcos.it, double from €150) is a clean, no-frills three-star outfit, with an attractive breakfast patio overlooking the water.

Opened in summer 2014 in the untouristy village of **Lezzeno**, halfway between Como and Bellagio, the **Hotel Palazzo del Vice Re** (Località Pescaù 51, 031 952 059, www.palazzodelvicere.com, €272 double, closed Nov-Feb), promises to be one of the most sought-after addresses on the lake. Its five rooms blend artisan furnishings and original features in this noble palazzo, once home to the Spanish viceroys of Italy.

THE WESTERN SHORE

Pretty and compact, **Cernobbio** is the first major stop on the boat service from Como. This town of magnificent villas and private boat jetties is dominated by the **Villa d'Este** (*see below*), which is often described as one of the world's great hotels. Regular guests included Alfred Hitchcock, who used the setting for some scenes in his debut movie, *The Pleasure Garden* (1924). The lakeside promenade has a lively market on Wednesday morning.

Trattoria del Glicine (Vittorio Veneto 1, 031 511 332, closed 2wks Jan, average €45), on the corner of via Paolo Carcano, serves typical Mediterranean cuisine under a wisteria-covered pergola with a splendid view of the lake in summer, switching indoors, and to a more Alpine menu, come winter. For unbeatable hotel luxury and a chance to show off your latest designer threads, head to the exclusive **Villa d'Este** (viale Regina 40, 031 3481, www.villadeste.it, closed mid Nov-Feb, from €800 double). If you're on a budget, you can still have a drink in the bar and visit the hotel's magnificent gardens, which include a water staircase and much statuary.

From Cernobbio, you can hop on the boat and head north for **Moltrasio**. In spring, as the snow on the hills above melts, the gorge that splits this small town in two fills with a rapidly flowing torrent. Moltrasio is home to many notable villas, including **Villa Le Rose**, Winston Churchill's destination of choice for some R&R after World War II, and also the 18th-century **Villa Passalacqua** (www.thevillapassalacqua.com),

VERDANT VILLAS

The best gardens and villas on the lake.

Villa del Balbianello.

The balmy microclimate of Lake Como has provided splendid opportunities to gardeners and garden-lovers over the centuries. One of the best gardens is at **Villa del Balbianello** (via Comoedia 5, 0344 56 110, www.visitfai.it/dimore/villadelbalbianello, closed Mon, Wed & mid Nov-mid Mar), located just south of Lenno. Built on a headland, the garden interacts with the lake and shoreline rather than following any set design or concept. Approaching by water (from Lenno) adds to the impact: you get an idea of what it would have been like to arrive as a guest of the various owners – among them Cardinal Durini, the Porro Lambertenghi and Arconati Visconti families, and the explorer Count Guido Monzino. The latter bequeathed Balbianello to the FAI (Fondo Ambiente Italiano), Italy's equivalent of Britain's National Trust. The garden follows a steep slope, where statues alternate with wisteria, while azaleas and rhododendrons provide exhilarating bursts of colour though spring and into early summer; look out for the plane trees pruned into the shape of candelabra. The villa, built in the 16th century and extended in the 18th, is also open to visitors.

Rhododendrons are also much in evidence among the 500-plus plant varieties in the huge garden at **Villa Carlotta** (via Regina 2, 0344 40 405, www.villacarlotta.it, closed Nov-mid Mar) in Tremezzo. The villa was built in neoclassical style in the early 1700s for the Marquis Giorgio Clerici, but is named after a Prussian princess, Charlotte, who received it in 1843 as a wedding present from her mother, Princess Marianna of Nassau. Leading to the villa are five terraces, with steps on either side; the geometric lines are softened by vines, roses and geraniums. The house contains many sculptures, including Antonio Canova's *Cupid and Psyche*.

Villa Melzi and Villa Serbelloni, in Bellagio, are not open to the public, but their gardens are well worth seeing. **Villa Melzi** (lungolario Manzoni, 031 950 204, www.giardinidivillamelzi.it, closed Nov-Mar) has a pretty Japanese garden and splendid water lilies. **Villa Serbelloni** (piazza della Chiesa, 031 951 555, www.bellagiolakecomo.com, closed Mon & Nov-Mar) sits on the end of the promontory that divides Lake Como into its two branches. The gardens are open for 90-minute guided tours daily (11am, 3.30pm). The walk up to the belvedere takes half an hour, but the views are worth it. The trees, added in the 19th century, are worth noting. Magnolias, oleanders, palms and cedars are now common in Italy, but the ones here were among the first planted in the country.

Villa Carlotta.

where Vincenzo Bellini wrote his opera *La Sonnambula* between 1829 and 1833. The property can be rented by the week, for holidays, weddings and other gatherings – at a price. For more affordable rest stops, the **Albergo Posta Ristorante** (piazza San Rocco 5, 031 290 444, www.hotel-posta.it, closed Jan & Feb, €120-€160 double) is a popular and reliable bet, while Lenno's **San Giorgio** (via Regina 81, 0344 40 415, www.sangiorgiolenno.com, closed Oct-Mar, €125-€165 double) is modest but pleasant, in a modern building with a garden.

For many years, the tiny village of **Laglio**, just north of Moltrasio, was mostly ignored. Then George Clooney bought **Villa Oleandra** here, and the place became world-famous. The actor himself is rarely in residence, but you can see his house when you cruise past on the boat. Laglio is also home to one of Lake Como's most delightful boutique hotels, the **Relais Villa Vittoria** (via Regina 6, 031 400 859, www.relaisvillavittoria.com, double €160-€550) whose 13 chic rooms feature washed wood floors and white and ecru colour schemes. Best of all is the location, with a magically lit garden stretching down to the lake.

The next town up is the little resort of **Argegno**. From here, a daily cable-car service (every 30 minutes) makes the journey to **Pigra**, a hamlet with superb views across the lake to **Isola Comacina** (the only island on the lake) and the Bellagio promontory. One man and his **water taxi** (031 821 955, 335 707 4122 mobile, www.boatservices.it, closed Nov-Feb) spend the day making the five-minute trip to and from the minuscule port on Isola Comacina. There's a 50:50 chance you'll have to stand on the end of the pier to hail the boat from the other side to the island, which is just 600 metres long and 200 metres wide, and houses a handful of ancient ruined churches and an eccentric restaurant, **Locanda dell'Isola Comacina** (0344 55 083, www.comacina.it, closed Tue in Mar-June & Sept-Oct, all Nov-Feb, average €68). This lively spot has earned renown and a good income by serving the same five-course menu, for lunch and dinner, ever since it opened in 1947. Every meal ends with the owner telling the story of the island and leading a toast of ceremonial local *liqueur flambé*, in order to combat an alleged curse.

LA TREMEZZINA

Awash with azaleas and dotted with luxurious villas, **La Tremezzina** is a gorgeous stretch of coast from **Lenno** to Menaggio. Lenno may have been the site of Commedia, one of Pliny the Younger's villas; now, its jetty is the departure point for boats to the picture-perfect **Villa del Balbianello** (*see p200* **Verdant Villas**). Once home to an eccentric explorer, the mansion was used in the Star Wars prequel *Attack of the Clones*, and was also where Daniel Craig's James Bond recuperated in *Casino Royale*. In Lenno, you can buy olive oils direct from the press at **Osvaldo Vanini** (*see p194* **Liquid Gold**). In nearby **Tremezzo**, the neoclassical **Villa Carlotta** (*see p200* **Verdant Villas**) boasts sculptures by Antonio Canova and a spectacular garden. You'll need to book a couple of days ahead in high season if you want to snag a lakeside table at the town's top spot, the **Hotel Restaurant La Darsena** (via Regina 3, 0344 43 166, www.hotelladarsena.it, closed Jan & 1wk Feb, €280-€320 double). The sumptuous creative Italian menu (average €50) features lake fish and much more; the hotel offers classical rooms with modern touches in a picturesque red house. The town's luxury option, offering spectacular views over the lake, is the splendid art nouveau **Grand Hotel Tremezzo Palace** (via Regina 8, 0344 42 491, www.grandhoteltremezzo.com, closed late Nov-late Feb, €570-€980 double).

Relais Villa Vittoria.

This western arm of the lake reaches one of its widest points at **Cadenabbia**. A foot and car ferry plies between here and Bellagio, and another car ferry goes to Varenna.

Pretty pink-and-ochre **Menaggio** lacks the in-your-face charm of its opposite numbers Bellagio and Varenna, but is certainly worth a peek. Once a bustling commercial town and now

Santa Maria del Tiglio.

an equally bustling resort, it has a ruined castle and lovely views across to the eastern shore. Menaggio is 12 kilometres (eight miles) from Lake Lugano, and keen walkers (with the emphasis on keen) might want to consider the hike up to **Monte Bregagno**, from where, on a very clear day, it's possible to see both lakes.

In a corner of the main piazza in Menaggio, the **Osteria Il Pozzo** (piazza Garibaldi, 0344 32 333, closed Wed, average €50) has a pretty courtyard and a menu that includes roast kid and rabbit with polenta. A good alternative is the unpretentious **Pizzeria Lugano** (via Como 26, 0344 31 664, average €30). For a place to stay, the **Grand Hotel Victoria** (lungolago Castelli 7, 0344 32 003, www.grandhotelvictoria.it, closed Nov-Feb, €140-€260 double) is set in its own extensive grounds overlooking the lake, with great views of Bellagio.

THE NORTHERN REACHES

Continuing north towards the peaks overlooking the Valchiavenna valley, you'll reach the Tre Pievi ('three parishes') of **Dongo**, **Gravedona** and **Sòrico**. Dongo, remembered as the place where Mussolini and his lover Clara Petacci were captured on 27 April 1945 as they fled to the Swiss border, was the scene of earlier violence in 1252, when St Peter Martyr was finished off with a hatchet by Cathar heretics.

A popular watersports centre these days, Gravedona was the most important of the Tre Pievi, and a key ally of medieval Milan – which is why it was razed by Como in the 12th century. The Romanesque church of **Santa Maria del Tiglio**, on via Roma, is simple, severe and stunning. **Palazzo Gallio** (also known as Palazzo del Pero) was the second of the three houses commissioned by Cardinal Tolomeo Gallio from 16th-century architect/painter/sculptor Pellegrino Tibaldi (another was Villa d'Este – *see p199*).

The fishing village of **Domaso** still produces a white wine that was mentioned by Pliny the Elder. It's also Lake Como's recognised windsurfing centre. In fortified Sòrico, tolls were extracted from travellers arriving on the lake's shores from the nearby Alpine valleys of Valchiavenna and Valtellina (*see p203* **Hitting the Slopes**).

THE EASTERN SHORE

Relatively few tourists sample the unhurried charms of Lake Como's mountainous eastern edge – which is all the more reason to explore this area by road, rail or boat. There's village after village to mooch around, with the alluring Varenna deserving a special mention.

From **Cólico**, an attractive, if average, port town at the far end of the lake's northern arm, a visit to the beautiful **Abbazia di Piona** (0341 940 331, www.abbaziadipiona.it), situated on a small promontory separating Lake Como proper from the strikingly green **Laghetto di Piona**, is a tantalising prospect. (But, unless you have your own transport, that's precisely what it will remain.) The complex has a 13th-century cloister whose columns are in a style between Romanesque and Gothic, as well as fragments of 12th-century frescoes and the abbey church of San Nicolao. There's also a tempting shop, selling beauty products such as propolis and beeswax soap and the Cistercian monks' abbey-made brews, including the bitter elixir of San Bernardo, limoncello and mandarin liqueur.

The Pioverna river thunders down the **Orrido di Bellano** (338 524 6716 mobile, www.comune.bellano.lc.it), near the appealing village of **Bellano** itself. This gorge provides the driving force for the hydroelectricity that once powered the area's (now-defunct) textile industry. You can appreciate its power for yourself by braving the walkway suspended above the torrent.

You could also take a detour to buy olive oil at one of the lake's few presses, **Azienda Agricolo Poppo**, at **Frazione Biosio** (*see p194* **Liquid Gold**). Go armed with a spirit of adventure (and be sure to call ahead for an appointment): it's not the easiest of places to find.

Clustered around the lake, the old stone buildings of **Varenna** make this one of the lake's most enchanting destinations. In the summer, it can get crowded; in the low season, you might be the only visitors here. The lakeside

HITTING THE SLOPES

Three of Lombardy's top ski resorts.

Continue up the eastern shore of Lago di Como on the SS36, and you'll come to a fork: head north and you'll reach the Alpine region of Valchiavenna; head east and you'll plunge straight into Valtellina, a 150-kilometre (93-mile) valley flanked by Alps on either side. Pizzo Bernina, at over 4,000 metres/13,000 feet), is the highest peak in the area, and both valleys are home to some decent ski resorts.

APRICA, VALTELLINA

Small, quiet and family-oriented, Aprica (www.apricaonline.com) is an ideal spot for beginners who will appreciate having the slopes pretty much to themselves during the week. The resort has 50km (31 miles) of pistes, with 4 black runs, 8 red runs, 13 blue runs, 3 cableways, 6 chairlifts, 5 draglifts, a cross-country track in the nearby Pian di Gembro nature reserve, and an ice-rink.
Ski & boot hire *Larino Sport, corso Roma 115 (0342 745 434, www.larinosport.it).*
Ski schools *Scuola Italiana Sci Aprica, piazza Palabione 46 (0342 745 108, www.apricasci.com).*

BORMIO, VALTELLINA

The Valtellina region's classiest ski resort, Bormio (www.bormio.eu, www.bormio.ski.it) has a historic town centre and one of the most scenic positions in the valley. Bursting with hotels and restaurants, it also has 50km (31 miles) of pistes, including one of the biggest vertical drops in Europe (Pista Stelvio) – from 3,012m (10,180ft) to 1,225m (4,020ft). In total, there are 2 black runs, 6 red and 5 blue, 5 chairlifts, 4 draglifts and 2 cableways, plus cross-country tracks and an outdoor ice-rink.
Ski & boot hire *Celso Sport, via Vallecetta 5 (0342 901 459, www.celsosport.it).*
Ski school *Scuola Sci Contea di Bormio, via Btg Morbegno 13 (0342 911 605, www.scuolascibormio.it).*

MADESIMO, VALCHIAVENNA

A family-friendly resort near pretty Chiavenna, Madesimo (www.madesimo.eu) has the notorious Canalone run, said to be one of Italy's most spectacular. There are 60km (37 miles) of pistes, with 3 black runs, 13 red runs, 14 blue runs, 9 chairlifts, 2 cableways and a funicular railway. There are also 70km (43 miles) of motor-sled pistes.
Ski & boot hire *Olympic Sport, via de Giacomi 3 (0343 54 330).*
Motor-sled hire *Team Extreme Team, via Emet 43 (0343 56 222, www.team extremeteam.com).*
Ski school *Scuola Italiana di Sci Madesimo, via alla Fonte 4 (0343 53 049, www.scuolascimadesimo.org).*

Bormio.

path leading from the boat terminal to the waterside **Villa Monastero** (0341 295 450, www.villamonastero.eu) is the stuff of fantasy.

A short distance away is another lakeside spot steeped in history. The **Villa Cipressi** (*see right*) houses a surprisingly affordable hotel and restaurant; its spectacular gardens are a must. Many a wedding reception has been held here.

Starting from via della Croce, close to Hotel Monte Codeno (no.2), a 40-minute walk leads to the ruined **Castello di Vezio** (0341 814 911, www.castellodivezio.it, closed Dec-Mar), surrounded by olive groves and boasting a splendid view of the lake.

Another path leads from Varenna to the **Fiumelatte** ('river of milk'). This is Italy's shortest, most mysterious and most predictable river. Its frothy, milk-white water rushes for all of 250 metres down the rockface and crashes into the lake, from the end of March to the end of October each year – and then stops. Leonardo da Vinci climbed down to find out what happened to it the rest of the year, but neither he nor anyone else has ever discovered the secret.

Passenger ferries connect Varenna with Menaggio (*see p201*), while a car ferry links it to Cadenabbia (*see p201*) and Bellagio (*see p206*).

Varenna's a good place for accommodation and eating options. **The Royal Victoria** (piazza San Giorgio 5, 0341 815 111, www.royalvictoria.com, double €130-€220) has period furniture in its public rooms and a lakeside swimming pool. Its Ristorante Gourmet (closed Mon except summer) serves upmarket Italian fare (average €40), while the Pizzeria Victoria Grill does what it says. **Vecchia Varenna** (contrada Scoscesa 14, 0341 830 793, www.vecchiavarenna.it, closed Mon & Jan, average €35) is a little more experimental than most restaurants in town, with an emphasis on quality over quantity; book early to get a table on the terrace overlooking the lake.

Hotel Villa Cipressi (via IV Novembre 22, 0341 830 113, www.hotelvillacipressi.it, closed Nov-Feb, €150-€200 double) combines relatively basic rooms with lakeside charm and 800 years of aristocratic history. The restaurant, with its outdoor terrace, is of a much higher quality. Rather more curated are the 16 rooms inside the restored 19th-century palazzo of **Hotel du Lac** (via del Prestino 4, 0341 830 238, www.albergodulac.com, closed mid Nov-mid Feb, €160-€250 double).

It's a 15-minute walk, plus funicular ride, from Varenna's centre to the **Eremo Gaudio** (0341 815 301, €126-€250 double) – but the spectacular location makes any inconvenience worthwhile. Perched high on a cliff face, this former hermitage affords incomparable views of Lake Como. If you have luggage, take a cab from the station (the road is steep) to the reception area, and then take the private panoramic funicular railway to your (no-frills) room. Make sure you book a room with a terrace, to get some of the very best views of the lake.

Varenna. *See p202*.

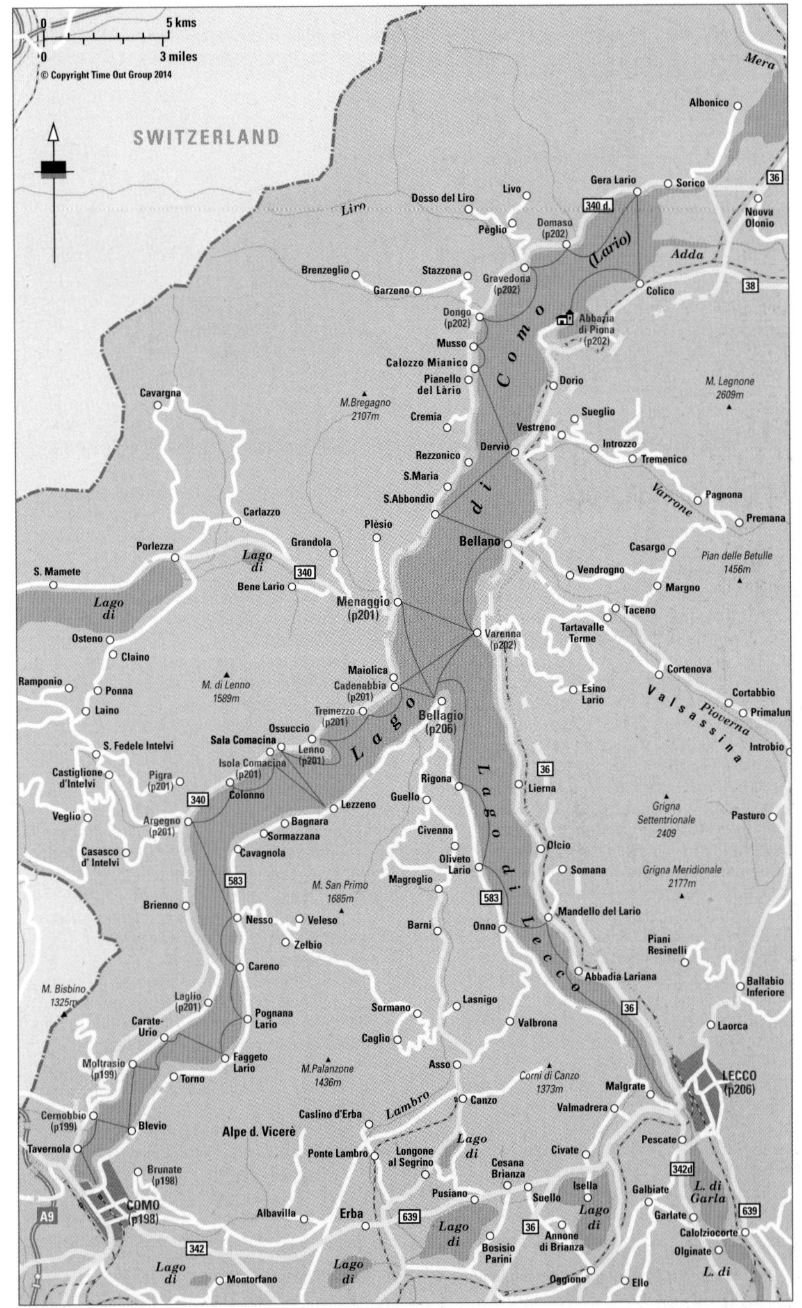

ESCAPES & EXCURSIONS

Lecco.

LECCO & BELLAGIO

With its peaceful lakeside promenade and large main squares lined with pavement cafés, **Lecco** is a quiet, elegant provincial town. Its past, though, has been fairly action-packed. A key location on trading routes since ancient times, the town was an important link in the defences of Visconti-era Milan; in 1336, Azzone Visconti built an eight-arch bridge over the River Adda – three more arches were added later – and the bridge is used to this day. Although it still bears its maker's name, it's usually referred to as the **Ponte Vecchio** (Old Bridge).

But to most Italian visitors, Lecco signifies just one thing: it's the birthplace of Alessandro Manzoni (1785-1873), the author of one of the most well-known novels in the Italian language: *I Promessi Sposi* ('The Betrothed'). Lakeside piazza Manzoni hosts a statue of the town's most famous son, while **Villa Manzoni** (via Don Guanella 1, 0341 481 247, www.museilecco.org, closed Mon) houses a collection of his memorabilia and manuscripts. A block to the north, in piazza Cermenati, stands the basilica of **San Niccolò**, the city's cathedral, with its early 20th-century, neo-Gothic bell tower.

Acquario (via Lungo Lario Cadorna 1, 0341 184 3456, closed Tue, average €25) is a popular pizzeria/restaurant serving crispy pizzas and abundant pasta dishes, such as *spaghetti al cartoccio*, with succulent seafood cooked in foil. For more first rate fish (at top prices) and a more refined atmosphere, try **Al Porticciolo 84** (via Valsecchi 5-7, 0341 498 103, www.porticciolo84.it, closed lunch Wed-Sat, all Mon & Tue, 2wks Jan & all Aug, average €80).

Perched at the tip of the southern promontory in a simply glorious setting, **Bellagio** has exercised its plentiful charms for many centuries. Among those who came and were enchanted were Liszt, Stendhal and Flaubert. Two villas stand out: **Villa Serbelloni** – crowning the hill where Pliny the Younger's Villa Tragedia may have stood – and **Villa Melzi**, a Napoleonic pile surrounded by lush gardens (for both, *see p200* **Verdant Villas**).

A dozen different trees cover the terrace of Bellagio's **Bilacus** (salita Serbelloni 32, 031 950 480, closed Mon, average €60), which can be found up a steep set of narrow steps; its risottos are top-notch. On the outskirts of Bellagio, towards Como, the family-run **Silvio** hotel and restaurant (via Carcano 12, 031 950 322, www.bellagiosilvio.com, closed mid Nov-mid Dec, 6wks Jan-Feb, average €35) cooks lake fish caught on the day by the owner and his son. The classy restaurant has huge windows overlooking the lake; there are also 21 simple, clean, inexpensive rooms (€70-€130 double). Silvio also rents a selection of upmarket apartments around the town (www.bellagioapartments.it).

The well-appointed **Hotel du Lac** (piazza Mazzini 32, 031 950 320, www.bellagiohoteldulac.com, closed Nov-Mar, €175-€280 double) has been welcoming travellers for 150 years. The same owners run the boutique **Hotel Bellagio** (salita Grande 6, 031 950 424, www.hotelbellagio.it, €80-€170 double), where some rooms have a lake view. Facilities at the refined **Grand Hotel Villa Serbelloni** (via Roma 1, 031 950 216, www.villaserbelloni.com, closed Nov-Mar, €400-€932 double) include indoor and outdoor pools, a sauna, Turkish bath and spectacular spa, and out-of-this-world lake views. Non-residents can stop in for a €10 cup of earl grey in the ornate lounge where Churchill and JFK have sat (not together, obviously).

Getting There

By car For Como, take the A8/E35 westbound, and exit at Como Centro. For Lecco, exit from Milan along via Viale Zara, and then follow the SS36.

By train Three Milan stations serve Como. There's an hourly service from Porta Garibaldi station to Como San Giovanni station (journey time 1hr). It takes half the time (but costs twice the price) from Stazione Centrale on the international Como–Chiasso–Lugano route to Como San Giovanni station. The Ferrovie Nord service departs every 30mins from Cadorna station for Como Nord Lago station (journey time 1hr), which is close to the Brunate cableway (*see p198*). For Lecco, there's an hourly service from Porta Garibaldi (75mins), and one train every hour or so from Stazione Centrale (45mins). Also from Stazione Centrale, services run every 90mins to Cólico, via Varenna and Bellano (journey time 90mins).

Getting Around

By boat Navigazione Lago di Como (via per Cernobbio 18, Como, 031 579 211, www.navigazione laghi.it) operates ferry and hydrofoil services all year round. The boats run frequently, and there are point-to-point commuter services to Tavernola, Cernobbio, Moltrasio, Torno, Urio and Argegno at the southern end of the lake; Cólico at the lake's northern tip; and to intermediate towns such as Bellagio, Varenna, Cadenabbia and Menaggio. There are also some car-ferry services. Special tourist cruises run in summer. A reduced timetable operates between October and Easter.

Bellagio.

By bus Buses operated by SPT (031 247 111, www.sptlinea.it), among others, depart from the bus station (Stazione Autolinee) in piazza Matteotti, next to the Como Nord railway station. Destinations include Argegno (40mins), Bellagio, Lecco and Menaggio (1hr), and Cólico (2hrs 20mins). Bear in mind that a 'frequent' service may be only once an hour. Note also that bus services are geared to schoolchildren, so will usually drop off after 8am, when school starts, peaking again around 1pm when schools close; services are also reduced in the school holidays, between June and early September. In any event, expect buses to stop running around 8pm, and reduced service on Sundays.

By car The SS340 (Regina) on the western shore from Como to Cólico, and the SP72 on the eastern shore from Lecco to Cólico are very scenic, but both roads are narrow and traffic is heavy, especially in summer and at weekends. On the eastern side, the SS36 is a quicker, albeit less picturesque alternative, from Lecco to Cólico. The minor roads into the hill villages can be challenging, especially as they're favoured by motorcyclists and cyclists.

Lago d'Iseo

Little known outside Italy, Lago d'Iseo is nestled amid the mountains between Bergamo to its west and Brescia to its east. Locals often refer to the lake by its Roman name, the Sebino, and the towns around it have a plentiful supply of towers, monasteries and castles that date from the past two millennia. It's the most tranquil of northern Italy's lakes: visitors are rewarded with uncrowded restaurants, clean Alpine air and little-used footpaths around the many sights. A recently built bypass means its eastern shore is now blissfully free of racing traffic; and a couple of chic new hotels and restaurants have begun to up the style quotient.

THE BERGAMO SHORE

Sarnico, at the south-western tip of the lake, has been inhabited since prehistoric times. It's a popular spot for waterskiers and windsurfers, and the original headquarters of Riva yachts – the Rolls-Royce of motor yachts. On summer weekends, the town packs out with campers visiting for supplies and gelato, but you can escape into the winding streets of the town's medieval centre. Just a couple of kilometres outside Sarnico, the surprisingly chic **Cocca Hotel Royal Thai** (via Predore 75, 035 426 1361, www.coccahotel.com, from €150 double) includes therapeutic showers, a Turkish bath, jacuzzi and use of the heated indoor pool in its rates. Book a room on one of the higher floors for panoramic views of the lake. Seven kilometres (four miles) from Sarnico, in Adro, Slow Food shop and restaurant **Dispensa Pani e Vini** (*see p209* **Dining Slow**) dishes up local gourmet specialities.

Towards the northern end of the lake, **Riva di Solto**, which has been an important harbour since Roman times, has maintained its medieval urban layout. The 17-kilometre (ten-mile) **Sebino Nature Walk** starts here, and the sheer gorge of the **Orrido di Zorzino** is a short distance north; black marble from the nearby quarry was used for some of the pillars of St Mark's Cathedral in Venice. **Castro** has a pretty lakeside terrace, its atmosphere enhanced by a weighty bronze 'book' featuring a description of the lake by contemporary Italian poet Raul Montanari.

Lovere, in the north-west corner, was historically important for its strategic position guarding the passage from the lake to the textile-producing heart of the Valcamonica area. Three medieval towers rise above the café-lined *piazze* and elegant *palazzi* along the shore, the latter a mark of the prosperity the small town has enjoyed over the centuries. The imposing **Accademia Tadini** (via Tadini 40, 035 962 780, www.accademiatadini.it, closed Nov-Mar) houses a fine selection of Lombard paintings from the 14th to the 18th centuries, as well as works by sculptor Antonio Canova (1757-1822).

THE BRESCIA SHORE

Across from Lovere sits **Pisogne**. Long known for its rich iron-ore deposits, its once busy via Valeriana was part of the Roman road linking Brescia with the Valcamonica. Since the advent of the bypass, the town has become a lot quieter, making it perfect for a tranquil stroll in the small medieval *borgo* behind the lakefront piazza del Mercato, with its 13th-century Torre del Vescovo. A short walk from the centre is the church of **Santa Maria della Neve**, which is decorated with frescoes by Romanino (1532-34).

From **Marone**, a narrow road (SP32) climbs through a series of hairpin turns to **Zone**, a hamlet surrounded by mountain peaks and offering glimpses of the lake. In Zone's small nature reserve, erosion has left bizarre boulders stranded on towering pinnacles; walking trails around them allow a closer look. At the entrance to the park, the isolated 15th-century church of San Giorgio is decorated with stunning frescoes.

Heading south, outside Sale Marasino, the family-run **Villa Kinzica** (via Provinciale 1, 030 982 0975, www.villakinzica.it, €100-€170 double) is delightfully distanced from the lake's summer bustle.

Further south, **Iseo** is the lake's principal town. Despite its focus on modern-day tourism, Iseo manages to retain a peculiar timelessness, thanks to its labyrinth of narrow alleys, the 12th-century Pieve di Sant'Andrea church and the 13th-century

Cocca Hotel Royal Thai.

Castello Oldofredi. There's also a former Jewish ghetto area at the south end of the town, which now houses artisan shops and cafés. Reservations are essential at **Il Volto** (via Mirolte 33, 030 981 462, closed Wed, Thur, 3wks July & 1wk Jan, average €60), which does a wonderful blend of haute cuisine and regional specialities; or you might want to try the excellent *antipasto al lago*, based on lake fish, at **Al Porto** (via Porto dei Pescatori 12, 030 989 014, www.alportoclusane.it, closed Wed in winter, average €40) in nearby Clusane. Here, you'll also find the 29-room **Romantik Relais Mirabella** (via Mirabella 34, 030 989 8051, www.relaismirabella.it, closed Nov-Mar, €134-€174 double), which has lovely lake views and a swimming pool.

MONTE ISOLA

The ferry from Sulzano to the gloriously car-free island of Monte Isola only takes a few minutes, but carries visitors to a very different world. The ferry lands at **Peschiera Maraglio**, well known for its handmade fishing nets; there are a number of other small, characterful villages.

A lakeshore path runs the full nine kilometres (six miles) around the island, from Peschiera to **Sensole** on the south-western corner, where the Mediterranean-style microclimate allows for olive cultivation (*see p194* **Liquid Gold**). The quaintly traditional villages of **Menzino**, **Sanchignano** and **Siviano** occupy the western coast, and two small islands – **Isola di Loreto** and **Isola di San Paolo**, both privately owned – stand off the northern and southern shores, respectively. The more adventurous can hike up to the 13th-century **Madonna della Ceriola sanctuary** at the top of the mountain (from Peschiera, follow the signs for Senzano, then Cure), which offers unparalleled views of the lake.

Getting There & Around

By boat Navigazione Lago d'Iseo (035 971 483, www.navigazionelagoiseo.it) runs point-to-point ferries (including stops at Monte Isola) every 1-2hrs, from around 8am to 6pm; some stops are less frequently served. To visit Monte Isola, ferries depart from Sulzano for Pescheria every 15mins or so; ferries between Sale Marasino and Carzano run approximately every 20-30mins. In summer, Navigazione Laghi also runs non-landing cruises of the lake.

By car From Milan, take the A4 towards Brescia; exit at Palazzolo sull'Oglio and follow signs for Lago d'Iseo. For Sarnico, Lovere and points in between, take the lake road (SP469) towards Sebina Occidentale. On the eastern shore, opt for the shore road, which goes through all the pretty villages, or take the recently built SP510 (direction Sebina

DINING SLOW

Lunch or dinner – take your time.

When a group of journalists in Piedmont learned in the mid 1980s that McDonald's was opening in Rome's historic heart, they mobilised – at their neighbourhood *osteria*. The result? A manifesto to promote local, seasonal ingredients and counter 'the degrading effects of fast food'. The **Slow Food** (www.slowfood.com) movement was born. The philosophy soon swept from one Italian region to another, and further afield. Slow Food now embraces close to 100,000 members worldwide. For a slow approach to eating in Italy, buy the annual Slow Food bible, *Osterie d'Italia*. The following are just three places that hold the Slow Food Snail award for excellence. They're a little out of the way, but what's an extra 20 minutes when a feast of gourmet delights awaits at the end of the detour?

Trattoria Dentella (via Dentella 25, 0345 97 105, www.trattoriadentella.com, closed dinner Mon, average €40) is in Bracca, 25 kilometres (15 miles) north of Bergamo, and has been a hostelry for more than 100 years. The current owners serve local platters with a twist, such as *gnocchi di zucca con fonduta di stracchino* (pumpkin dumplings with a cheese sauce) and *stracotto d'asina* (donkey stew). Look out for dishes featuring the local black truffle, when it's in season.

Located in the village of Prosperio, 16 kilometres (ten miles) east of Como, **Trattoria Inarca** (via Inarca 16, 031 620 424, www.ristoranteinarca.it, closed Mon, average €40) recently moved to new premises: a former 13th-century chapel with a panoramic terrace. The menu changes weekly, and might include risotto with taleggio, pigeon with pigeon pâté, or the more challenging *testina di vitello con cipolla rossa* (calf's head with red onions).

A shop, wine bar, modern *osteria* and restaurant, the **Dispensa Pani e Vini** (via Principe Umberto 23, Adro, 030 745 0757, www.dispensafranciacorta.com, closed Mon, average €40) is located in Franciacorta, an increasingly prestigious wine-producing area between Brescia and Lago d'Iseo. Try local fishy dishes such as *luccio mantecato e broccoletti* (creamy pike with broccoli) or *trippa in brodo* (trout in broth). And be sure to sample the Franciacorta wine, either sparkling or still.

Isola di Loreto. *See p209.*

Orientale), which whizzes through tunnels beneath the flanking mountains, bypassing all the settlements. Exits include Provaglio d'Iseo, Iseo, Sulzano, Zone, Marone, Vello and Pisogne.

By train From Milan, take a train to Brescia (www.trenitalia.it) and change for the enchanting single-track Brescia–Iseo–Edolo line, which offers splendid views of the lake and countryside. Stops include Iseo, Sulzano, Sale Marasino, Marone and Pisogne. It takes 2hrs to get to Edolo in the Alpine valley of Valcamonica.

Lago di Garda

Surrounded by mountains rising sharply from the water's edge, Lake Garda is the largest of the Italian lakes, stretching over 50 kilometres (31 miles) from north to south, and measuring nearly 17 kilometres (ten miles) at its widest point. Its depth (average 135 metres/443 feet), means it stays pleasantly cool even in the hottest months, making it popular with bathers anxious to escape the heat. Sandy and pebbly beaches are dotted around the lake, while exhilarating mountain breezes refresh the northern towns of Limone sul Garda and Riva del Garda, creating ideal conditions for wind- and kite-surfing. All this makes it an ideal spot for both campers (mostly German) and swankily-dressed A-listers – though each have their carefully delineated territories, ensuring that the two rarely mix.

If the thrills of the water don't float your boat, explore the small, picturesque towns that line the east and west shores. Many have medieval centres complete with fine Romanesque churches, and some also have ruined castles – a reminder of how hotly contested these lands once were. Villas, most from the 19th or early 20th centuries, abound, attesting to great wealth, either inherited or created by industrious local entrepreneurs. The vegetation benefits from the lake's microclimate: olives turn the eastern shore a silvery-green, while lemon groves are common on the western shore. Palms, oleanders, bougainvillea, mimosa and acacia grow everywhere, lending the lake a Mediterranean air. Vineyards also thrive in these balmy climes, ensuring a copious supply of top-notch wines, among them Bardolino, Custoza and Lugana, which can be tasted in the area's many delightful restaurants.

THE SOUTHERN SHORE

Nestled in Garda's south-western corner, **Desenzano del Garda** is the biggest of the lakeside towns. Behind the quaint old port is the arcaded piazza Malvezzi, with its statue of St Angela, and the cathedral of **Santa Maria Maddalena**. Inside the church is a striking *Last Supper* by Giambattista Tiepolo. To the west, along via Crocefisso, are the remains of the fourth-century **Villa Romana** (no.22, 030 914 3547, closed Mon). Discovered in 1921, it has some fine mosaics. The **Hotel Giardinetto** (viale Marconi 33, 030 914 1704, www.hotel-giardinetto.com, closed Mar, double €85-€110) is situated between the train station and the lake; ask for a room with balcony. A mother-and-daughter team runs the **Relais Il Giardino Segreto** (via Curiel 2, 030 917 2294, www.relaisilgiardinosegreto.it, €100-€150 double), also in Desenzano and a ten-minute walk from the lake. It has five rooms set in a large garden featuring oleanders, and olive and lemon trees.

Some ten kilometres (six miles) to the east, at the tip of a narrow promontory, lies the lake's main tourist magnet: **Sirmione**, crowned by the picturesque 13th-century castle of **Rocca Scaligera** (piazza Castello, 030 916 468, closed Mon). Also here is the first-century **Grotte di Catullo** (piazza Orti Manara, 030 916 157, closed Mon); set among olive groves at the tip of the headland, these ruins of a Roman villa bear the name of the poet Catullus, although it's more likely that such a colossal edifice actually belonged to his wealthy family, who lived in Verona. The **Osteria Al Torcol** (via San Salvatore 30, 030 990 4605, closed Wed & Jan, average €45) serves home-made pasta and local specialities.

Peschiera del Garda, at the south-eastern corner of Lake Garda, has been fortified since Roman times; in the 19th century, the Austrians rebuilt and strengthened its 16th-century Venetian defences, making Desenzano one of the four corners of their territory. The lake's south-eastern tip is a paradise for bored kids and their desperate families. Just to the north of Peschiera is **Gardaland** (045 644 9777,

Rocca Scaligera, Sirmione.

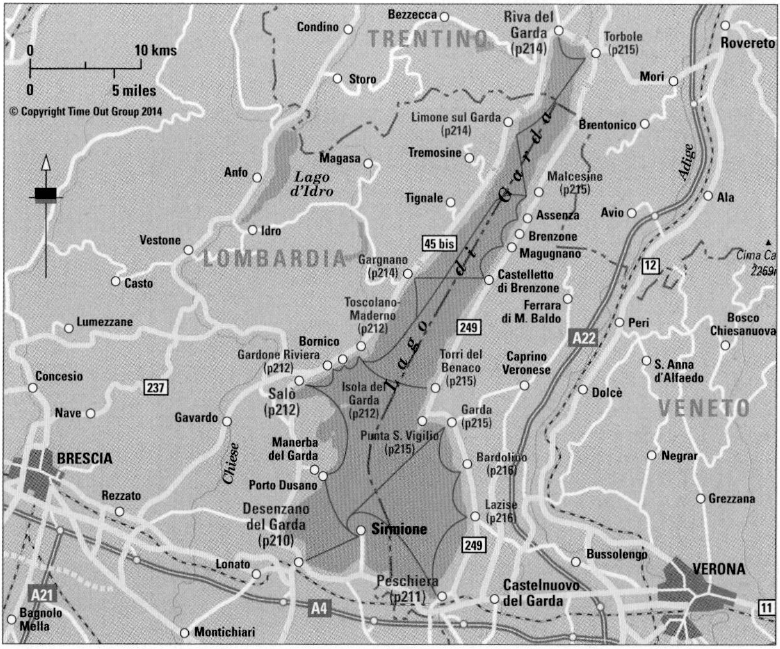

0 10 kms
0 5 miles
© Copyright Time Out Group 2014
TRENTINO
LOMBARDIA
VENETO
Lago di Garda
Lago d'Idro
Bezzecca
Condino
Riva del Garda (p214)
Torbole (p215)
Rovereto
Storo
Mori
Limone sul Garda (p214)
Brentonico
Magasa
Tremosine
Anfo
Malcesine (p215)
Tignale
Assenza
Avio
Ala
Adige
Brenzone
Magugnano
Idro
Vestone
Gargnano (p214)
Castelletto di Brenzone
Cima Carega 2259m
Casto
Toscolano-Maderno (p212)
Ferrara di M. Baldo
Peri
Bosco Chiesanuova
Lumezzane
Bornico
Gardone Riviera (p212)
Torri del Benaco (p215)
Caprino Veronese
S. Anna d'Alfaedo
Concesio
Salò (p212)
Isola del Garda (p212)
Dolcè
Nave
Gavardo
Garda (p215)
Punta S. Vigilio (p215)
Manerba del Garda
Chiese
BRESCIA
Bardolino (p216)
Negrar
Porto Dusano
Rezzato
Lazise (p216)
Grezzana
Desenzano del Garda (p210)
Sirmione
Bussolengo
Lonato
VERONA
Peschiera (p211)
Castelnuovo del Garda
Bagnolo Mella
Montichiari
45 bis
12
249
237
A22
A21
A4
11

www.gardaland.it, closed Nov-late Mar except school holidays), Italy's answer to Disneyland. Over three million people, mostly Italian, visit each year, to explore the 32 rides and attractions, enjoy the shows and visit the themed aquarium. Further to the north lies the **Canevaworld Resort**, containing **Aquaparadise** (www.aquaparadise.it), probably Europe's largest water park. All play a part in generating the traffic that strangles the road system in high season.

THE WESTERN SHORE

The tropical palms and 18th-century villas, including ones that belonged to Mussolini and the poet Gabriele d'Annunzio, make Garda's rugged western shore one of the lake's most stunning stretches. The lakeside road heads north, skirting the deep bay, from Desenzano to **Salò** (known in Roman times as Salodium). Salò would love to be remembered solely as the birthplace of Gasparo di Bertolotti, also known as Gasparo da Salò (1540-1609), who was one of the first great violin-makers. However, the town's name is notoriously linked with the puppet republic set up here by the Nazis for Mussolini in 1943. In piazza del Duomo, the **Cathedral of the Annunziata** has a Renaissance portal in its unfinished façade, and a splendid Venetian Gothic interior complete with gilded statues of saints, two paintings by Romanino and a polyptych by Paolo Veneziano.

On the hillside a mile from the lake at Salò, the chic, minimal **Villa Arcadio Hotel & Resort** (via Palazzina 2, 0365 4281, www.hotelvilla arcadio.it, €180-€360 double) occupies a former 13th-century convent, and has views over olive groves to Lake Garda's palm-studded shores.

South of Salò, at Puegnano del Garda, **Comincioli** (*see p194* **Liquid Gold**) turns out some pretty serious grappas, wines and olive oils – stop in for a tasting.

A few kilometres north of Salò is the popular holiday resort of **Gardone Riviera**. Its main cultural attraction is the magical **Giardino Botanico Hruska** (via Roma 2, 336 410 877 mobile, www.hellergarden.com, closed mid Oct-mid Mar), also known as the Heller Garden after the current owner, artist André Heller. Created in 1910 by Arturo Hruska, a dentist and naturalist, it has plants from every continent and climate, including magnolias, bamboo copses and orchids. The park is also dotted with sculptures, quirky paths and art installations, including works by Keith Haring and Roy Lichtenstein. Gardone is also one of several pick-up points for trips to the beautiful **Isola del Garda**, the lake's largest island (*see p217* **Private Island**).

On the hill above Gardone Riviera is the old town of **Gardone di Sopra**, notable mostly as the site of the grandiose **Vittoriale degli Italiani**, once home to poet and man of action Gabriele d'Annunzio (*see p213* **Poet or Pike?**)

Further north, **Toscolano-Maderno**, comprising the two adjacent towns of Toscolano and Maderno, separated by the river Toscolano, is a busy resort with a great beach. Roman and Byzantine vestiges can be found in Maderno's 12th-century Romanesque church of **Sant' Andrea** (piazza San Marco), particularly in the recently restored pillar capitals.

Salò.

POET OR PIKE?

Visit the remarkable museum dedicated to Gabriele D'Annunzio.

On the hill above Gardone Riviera is Gardone di Sopra, notable mostly for the **Vittoriale degli Italiani**. 'Vittoriale' is an adjective meaning related to victory, so you could call it a Shrine to Italian Victories. Whether or not the epithet appeals, this overstuffed house-museum is well worth a visit for the insights it offers into Gabriele D'Annunzio – poet, journalist, novelist, dramatist, a man of action and a grand poseur – who lived here from 1922 until his death in 1938.

Though his works are pored over in Italian schools, until recently, D'Annunzio hadn't impinged all that much upon the Anglo-Saxon consciousness. That changed in 2013, when Lucy Hughes-Hallett won the Samuel Johnson and Costa book awards for non-fiction and biography with her 704-page brick of a book, *The Pike* (Fourth Estate). Hughes-Hallett takes her enigmatic title from Romain Rolland, who called D'Annunzio a pike, a predator lurking 'afloat and still, waiting for ideas'. She describes her subject as 'a frightful gnome with red-rimmed eyes and no eyelashes, no hair, greenish teeth, bad breath, the manners of a mountebank and the reputation, nevertheless, for being a ladies' man.' A conundrum, in other words.

Essentially, the Vittoriale is an extravagant monument to its owner, and no aspect of his character or achievements is ignored. The interior, with its claustrophobia-inducing clutter, reveals D'Annunzio's numerous interests: music, literature, art, the Orient and – most of all – sex. Highlights include the spare bedroom, with the coffin in which D'Annunzio would meditate, and the dining room, which has an embalmed and bronzed pet tortoise that died from over-eating. The grounds celebrate some of his more extrovert passions, from theatre (his most famous love affair was with the actress Eleonora Duse) to politically dubious wartime heroics: D'Annunzio planted the prow of the battleship Puglia in his garden to commemorate his quixotic attempt to 'liberate' the city of Fiume (now Rijeka) from Yugoslav rule. The Museo della Guerra (War Museum; closed Wed), also in the grounds, celebrates D'Annunzio's more aggressive adventures. From the ceiling hangs the plane he flew to drop propaganda leaflets over Vienna in 1918, as World War I drew to a close. The house was, in effect, a 'gilded cage', funded by Mussolini to keep him as far from Rome as possible.

And his writing? There was an enormous amount of it. His *Opera Omnia* ran to 42 of the planned 46 volumes before, one assumes, the money, or the patience, ran out. Among his works published in English translation are The *Child Of Pleasure* (*Il Piacere*; Mondial, 2006), *Alcyone: a Selection* (St Martin's Press, 1978) and *The Triumph of Death* (*Il Trionfo della morte*; Buccaneer Books, 1999). Whether or not you plough through his opus, a visit to the D'Annunzio residence offers illuminating insights into this larger-than-life character and, indeed, into Italian history.

Il Vittoriale degli Italiani
Via Vittoriale 22 (036 529 6511, www.vittoriale.it). **Open** *Museum* Apr-Sept 8.30am-7pm Tue-Sun. Oct-Mar 9am-4pm Tue-Sun. *Gardens* Same hours, but daily.

TWO WHEELS GOOD

Explore Lake Garda by bicycle.

Lago di Garda's varied topography makes it a dream destination for pedallers at all levels – from beginners to experienced mountain cyclists. The tourist information website (www.visitgarda.com) lists dozens of routes, from an 18-kilometre (11-mile) tour of the olive groves on the eastern shore, to a strenuous six- to seven-hour climb 1,300 metres (4,265 feet) up Mount Tremelzo in the west.

Bus company **APAM** (0376 230 346, www.apam.it) runs a Bus & Bike service (Bicibus) from Peschiera del Garda to Mantova from March to October, with a trailer capable of carrying up to 40 bikes at a time, so that cyclists don't have to pedal both ways.

If you fancy a dedicated holiday, **Garda Bike Hotel** (via Venezia 26, Peschiera del Garda, 045 640 1050, www.gardabike hotel.it) has accommodation in 45 stylish but practical rooms. The hotel also provides bike hire (De Rosa and Eddy Merckx are the brands available, with carbon frames), special diets and guided rides for all levels of ability. Non-cycling friends and family are welcome to stay.

DH Lawrence completed *Sons and Lovers* in nearby **Gargnano**, where he lived in 1912-13. His collection of essays, *Twilight in Italy*, contains – amid reflections on Italian phallocentricity – some highly evocative descriptions of the lake. Along the Gardesana (the lakeside road), bare pillars that used to support protective greenhouse covers during the winter months now stand, as Lawrence fancifully put it, like 'ruined temples… forlorn in their colonnades and squares… as if they remained from some great race that had once worshipped here.'

By the lake is **Palazzo Feltrinelli**, built in 1898-99 for a wealthy industrialist family. It's now a conference centre for Milan University, but during the Republic of Salò period served as Mussolini's administrative HQ. Il Duce's private residence was in the larger **Villa Feltrinelli** (via Rimembranza 38-40, 0365 798 000, www.villafeltrinelli.com, closed Nov-Mar, €1,000-€2,800 suite), built in 1892 and set in a vast garden to the north of the town. It's now one of Italy's premier luxury hotels; all jazzed up to remove the taint of its Fascist associations, it's an exclusive getaway for those with the means.

Beyond Gargnano, the lake narrows and the mountains appear to rise from the water. The Gardesana continues as a series of tunnels. A good 15 kilometres (ten miles) further north, and lined by a beach, **Limone sul Garda** has a small port and a medieval centre with steep, narrow streets and staircases. It's unclear whether the town's name derives from the Latin *limen* (border) or from its lemon plantations, which date from the 13th century and are thought to have been the first in Europe.

Reached through yet more tunnels, **Riva del Garda** is the largest town on the northern half of the lake. It stands between Monte Brione to the east and the sheer cliffs of Monte Rocchetta to the west, which bring early dusk to the town. Riva was once a major port: from 1813 until 1918, it lay in Austrian territory, and saw fighting during World War I. The centre of the town is piazza 3 Novembre, home to the city's imposing symbol, the 13th-century **Torre Apponale** (piazza Catena, 0464 573 869, closed Nov-Feb). Climb the 165 steps to experience a fine view over the lake. The square is also home to the 14th-century **Palazzo Pretorio** (not open to the public) and picturesque medieval porticoes. An archway beneath the palace leads to piazza San Rocco, where the surviving apse of the church of San Rocco, destroyed by a bomb in World War I, has been converted into an open-air chapel; the location of the original walls are marked on the piazza's pavement. East of piazza 3 Novembre is the moat-encircled **Rocca** (fortress), containing the **Museo Civico** (piazza Battisti 3, 0464 573 869, closed Mon Mar-June & Sept-Nov, all Dec-Feb), with collections of archaeology and armour

Malcesine.

as well as occasional exhibitions by Italian artists. The more energetic can follow a zigzag path up to the **Bastione**, a cylindrical tower 212 metres (695 feet) high, built by the Venetians in 1508, which commands spectacular views over the town. Try the **Ristorante Al Volt** (via Fiume 73, 0464 552 570, www.ristorantealvolt.com, closed Mon & mid Feb-mid Mar, average €40) for specialities from the Trentino region.

The **Grand Hotel Riva** (piazza Garibaldi 10, 0464 521 800, www.gardaresort.it, double €114-€205) is a large and comfortable hotel by the Rocca; its top-floor dining room commands panoramic lake views. Nearby, in Arco, the sleekly designed **Vivere Suites & Rooms** (via Gobbi Epifanio, 0464 514 786, www.agrivivere.com, double €132-€170) offers a new take on the *agriturismo*, or farmhouse holiday, phenomenon. Its six suites have floor-to-ceiling windows and are set in a vineyard, with amazing views.

THE EASTERN SHORE

Medieval towns edge the northern half of the eastern shore, while campsites and amusement parks crowd much of its southern end. Poised on Garda's north-eastern corner is pretty **Torbole**, a historic town of quite considerable strategic importance. In 1439, it witnessed the launch of 26 Venetian ships that had been hauled over the mountains for a surprise (but unsuccessful) attack on the Milanese rulers, the Visconti.

Malcesine, 15 kilometres (9.5 miles) south, is arguably the eastern shore's most delightful stopover, especially notable for the **Castello Scaligero** (via Castello, 045 657 0499, closed Mon-Fri Feb-Mar, all Nov). The castle was built, like many in the region, by Verona's ruling Della Scala family (from which the name Scaligero derives). Situated on a craggy headland looming over the medieval quarter, the castle also has a small museum that holds sketches by Goethe. While drawing them in 1786, the poet was arrested for spying. For a blast of Alpine air, take a 15-minute cable-car ride from Malcesine to the top of **Monte Baldo** (www.funiviedelbaldo.it, closed 2wks Mar, mid Nov-mid Dec, €20 return), a popular ski resort in winter.

Further down the coast, in **Torri del Benaco**, are remnants of the ancient town walls and the 14th-century fortress also called **Castello Scaligero** (viale Fratelli Lavanda 2, 045 629 6111, www.museodelcastelloditorridelbenaco.it, closed Nov-Mar); its *limonaia*, an outdoor plantation for growing lemons, is one of the few on the lake still in operation. The church of the **Santissima Trinità** (in the eponymous square) contains 15th-century frescoes, including a splendid *Christ Pantocrator* in gleaming floral garb.

In a deep bay in the shadow of Monte Garda, the town of **Garda** is home to a wide lakefront promenade and several notable Renaissance *palazzi*. It was in a (now long-gone) castle in the area known as the Rocca di Garda, south of the town, in the tenth century that Queen Adelaide was imprisoned by Berengar II, after he'd murdered her husband and she had refused to marry him (or his son Adalbert – sources are divided). For a more cheerful time, take the sunny villa- and garden-lined path north along the curving shore towards **Punta San Vigilio**.

At the tip of the headland is a harbour with a tiny chapel dedicated to San Vigilio. From here, a pathway leads up to the 16th-century

Bardolino.

Villa Guarienti-Brenzone; it's privately owned, but a glimpse can be caught of its splendid formal gardens, much loved by Winston Churchill and Laurence Olivier, among others. The promontory is also home to an atmospheric hotel, the **Locanda San Vigilio** (045 725 6688, www.locanda-sanvigilio.it, closed mid Nov-Mar, double €270-€890). There are 12 luxurious rooms in an antiques-filled 15th-century building, which also has a private garden, right on the lake, and its own *limonaia*. On the far side of the promontory is the tiny **Baia delle Sirene**, which has a beach.

In Garda, away from the shore, **Stafolet** (via Poiano 9, 045 627 8939, www.stafolet.com, closed Tue in winter, average €30) specialises in steaks and pizza. Eat on the terraces if it's fine.

South of Garda is the pleasant town of **Bardolino**. Famed for its wine, it's flanked by gardens leading to the lake. Some of the gardens are the property of **Guerrieri Rizzardi** (via Verdi 4, 045 721 0028, www.guerrieri-rizzardi.com, visits by appt), a wine-producing company that is personally overseen by Countess Maria Cristina Rizzardi. Her family have owned the gardens – and accompanying lakeside villa – for over 560 years. Summer wine tastings (including Bardolino, a dry red, and Chiaretto, a translucent rosé) are held in the villa's kitchen garden.

The town also has two fascinating churches. The ninth-century **San Zeno** is reached by turning eastwards off the Gardesana along via San Zeno; this is one of very few extant churches from the Carolingian period in Italy. **San Severo**, a well-preserved 12th-century building with a campanile, has notable 12th- and 14th-century frescoes. In **Lazise** there's yet another **Castello Scaligero**, this one now incorporated into the garden of a privately owned villa. To the south lie the family-oriented delights of the Canevaworld Resort and Gardaland amusement park (*see p211*).

In the countryside near Costermano, six kilometres (four miles) from Garda, the classy, aristocratic **Locanda & Osteria San Verolo** (045 720 0930, www.sanverolo.it, from €195 double) has rooms overlooking the neighbouring vineyards. The menu at the *osteria* (average €35) features local, seasonal produce.

Getting There & Around

By car The Milan–Venice A4 motorway has exits at Desenzano, Sirmione and Peschiera del Garda.

By train Many trains on the Milan–Venice line from Stazione Centrale (www.trenitalia.it) stop at Desenzano (journey time 1hr 15mins). Some stop at Peschiera del Garda (1hr 30mins).

By boat Hydrofoil and steamer services are frequent in summer, connecting the most important points on the lake. All year round, a regular car-ferry service (roughly every 40mins, journey time 30mins) runs between Toscolano-Maderno and Torri del Benaco. All boat services are operated by Navigazione sul Lago di Garda (030 914 9511, www.navigazionelaghi.it).

By bus From Desenzano, bus LN027, run by SIA (030 44 061, 8406 2001 toll-free in Italy, www.trasportibrescia.it), travels to Riva del Garda along the western shore, stopping at Salò, Gardone Riviera, Fasano, Maderno, Toscolano and Limone. The LN026 bus between Brescia and Verona serves Desenzano, Sirmione and Peschiera del Garda on the southern shore. Verona's ATV (045 805 7922, www.atv.verona.it) runs the LN162 service along the eastern shore to Riva del Garda, via Peschiera, Lazise, Bardolino, Garda, San Vigilio, Torri del Benaco, Malcesine and Torbole.

By car The road that skirts the lake from Sirmione to Riva del Garda (70km/43 miles) on the western shore is called the Gardesana, and is the scenic route par excellence. In summer, expect heavy traffic, particularly around Gardaland amusement park.

PRIVATE ISLAND

Take a tour of Lake Garda's loveliest isola.

Now owned by seven siblings (four brothers and three sisters) from the aristocratic Cavazza family, **Isola del Garda** (328 384 9226 mobile, www.isoladelgarda.com) has been open for guided visits since 2002 – but remains a place of fascination and mystery.

It's the largest island on Lake Garda, though not big: about a kilometre long, and only 70 metres (230 feet) at its widest point. Its history is long and remarkably varied: inhabited during the Roman Empire, it later became a game reserve. In the ninth century, Charlemagne gave it to the monks of St Zeno of Verona and it was subsequently transformed into a centre for meditation by St Francis of Assisi in the 13th century. In 1797, Napoleon decided it was time for a shift of power and handed it over to the state, but 60 years later the island was given to the army, who promptly auctioned it. The new owners, Duke Gaetano de Ferrari of Genoa and his wife, the Russian archduchess, Maria Annenkoff (from whom the current proprietors are descended), were responsible for the construction of the extraordinary Venetian-Gothic-style villa, between 1890 and 1903. Designed by architect Luigi Rivelli, the ornate villa dominates the island and is among the largest private residences on the lake.

Between April and October, the Cavazza family organises tours to the island most days, departing from various locations around the lake. The ticket (€25-€30) covers the boat fare plus a two-hour guided tour of the island, often accompanied by a family member, with a visit to the gardens, park and parts of the villa, as well as a small *aperitivo*. It's a chance to take a closer look at the imposing villa, with its crenellated tower and neo-Gothic floral decorations. The tour also takes in the Italianate lakeside terraces, with persimmons, pomegranates and pears, and the wild park, part of which resembles Garda's answer to a mangrove swamp. In summer, look out for classical music concerts and family days with games and activities.

In Context

History

More ups and downs than the hemlines on its catwalks.

Italy's strategic gateway to the north has had 2,000 years of two-way traffic: trade out, and occupying armies in. At one stage or another, Celts, Goths, Romans, Spaniards, French and Austrians have ruled the city, and at times it seems that the Milanese have taken traits such as style, passion and a prodigious work ethic from each one. For the most part, its Italian overlords – including the Viscontis, the Sforzas and, later, Mussolini himself – bequeathed the grandest gifts on the city, although their rule was often as cruel as the rest. But when the going gets really tough, the locals look up from their balance sheets and firmly give their leaders the boot.

EARLY SETTLEMENTS

From prehistoric times up to the Roman conquest, Lombardy's earliest inhabitants, the Camun people, had settlements in the Valcamonica area in the province of Brescia. Down on the marshy plain of the Po river, other tribes, mostly from Liguria, dwelt in stilt-houses by the side of the region's many lakes. The rest of the Italian peninsula was populated by Italic peoples and Etruscans. Gallo-Celtic tribes moved across the Alps and into the fertile plains of the Po Valley some time between the fifth and fourth centuries BC, spreading into territory occupied by Ligurians and Etruscans, and pitching camp in the vicinity of what are now Milan, Brescia, Bergamo and Lombardy's other major cities.

These Celts – particularly the Insubre tribe, whose settlement where Milan now stands was large and dominant by this time – had their hearts set on further expansion towards the south. But it was not to be, as it was the Romans who pushed their borders northwards into what they termed Cisalpine Gaul ('Gaul this side of the Alps'). In the 280s BC, they began their slow drive across the Po Valley from the east, founding colonies as they went and conquering the town they renamed Mediolanum ('in the middle of the plain') in 222 BC.

ROMANS AND CHRISTIANS

It was not all plain sailing for the Roman conquerors: during the Second Punic War (218-201 BC), for example, northern Italy's Celts and Ligurians rallied to Hannibal, helping the great Carthaginian general's exhausted troops beat the Romans back across the Po.

It was a temporary hitch, however, and by 42 BC, Rome had exerted its hold over Cisalpine Gaul sufficiently to make it officially part of its Italian territories. In his reorganisation of Italy in 15 BC, Emperor Augustus made Mediolanum the capital of the Transpadania region, which included the towns of Como, Bergamo, Pavia and Lodi, and extended as far west as Turin. No longer a mere military garrison, and with its own municipal and judicial structures, Mediolanum began to take on the importance expected of a city placed so strategically between the Italian peninsula and the areas beyond the Alps where Roman interests were so strong.

During the relatively peaceful times that followed from the reign of Augustus, the placid agricultural zone of northern Italy flourished: roads were built and rivers made navigable, to the benefit of communications and trade. And though the area's elite still preferred their country villas to urban residences, towns were endowed with suitably imposing monuments.

When barbarian tribes began baying at the Roman empire's northern borders in the third century AD, Diocletian split the empire into two halves to streamline its military capacities. From AD 292, Mediolanum became the effective capital of the western emperor – Diocletian himself – whereas Byzantium was home to Maximian, his eastern counterpart, leaving Rome to languish.

As Mediolanum's political and military star rose, so did its importance as a centre of Christianity, which (according to local lore) was brought to the city by St Barnabas, a friend of St Paul. Under Diocletian and his persecuting successors, Milan chalked up nearly as many top-notch martyrs as Rome.

Charlemagne.

Constantine the Great (306-37), who reunified the two halves of the empire under his sole control and was strongly aware of Mediolanum's strategic importance, diplomatically issued the Edict of Milan (313), putting an end to the persecution of Christians and paving the way for Christianity to become the religion of state. St Ambrose was elected bishop of Mediolanum in 374, remaining in that office until his death in 397. His celebrated piety and charity conferred untold prestige on the local Church, giving his successors in the region unrivalled spiritual and temporal clout for centuries to come.

'By the time Attila the Hun had finished with the city in 452, it was a smouldering wreck.'

In 402, Emperor Honorius moved the seat of the empire to Ravenna, which meant that Mediolanum was now pretty much at the mercy of waves of attacking barbarian tribes. By the time Attila the Hun had finished with the city in 452, it was a smouldering wreck. It was partially rebuilt, only to be razed again by the Goths in 489 and 539. Most of the population had taken refuge in the countryside, and the clergy had fled to Genoa. However, by that time, the fate of the beleaguered city – now known as Milan – was of little interest to anyone.

After the death in 476 of the last western emperor, Romulus Augustulus, and the collapse of the empire, Odoacer – the Latinised Goth who wielded the greatest power on the peninsula – had himself crowned king in what had become northern Italy's most important town: not Milan, but Pavia, to the south.

GERMANIC INVASIONS

For decades, Goths and Byzantines alternately colluded and squabbled for control of the Italian peninsula, heedless of the threat mounting on the other side of the Alps, where the bloodthirsty King Alboin was forging antagonistic tribes of Germanic Lombard peoples into something like a unified front. In 568, the Lombards began their relatively challenge-free rampage through northern Italy, setting up their capital in Pavia, which had fallen to invaders after a siege in 572.

The region they overran was a shadow of its former self, its agriculture and infrastructure in tatters. This seemed to matter little to the Lombards, who taxed and oppressed with glee, only becoming slightly less hostile after wily Pope Gregory the Great (590-604) persuaded the Lombard Queen Theodolinda (*see p224* **Milan's Heroines**) to convert her people from Arianism – the heretical version of Christianity espoused by the Lombards, which taught that Christ was not one with the Father, but rather saw Jesus as a created being, even if pre-eminent – to Roman-style Christianity.

Later popes continued to clash with the ever-expanding Lombards, whose territory now extended from the myriad dukedoms of the Po Valley to the far south of mainland Italy. With the Normans of southern Italy also making life difficult for the occupant of the throne of St Peter's, outside help was sought, in the shape of the Franks.

In the second half of the eighth century, the head of this Germanic tribe was Charlemagne, a mighty warrior and impressive politician, who, although illiterate, had established a glittering court at Aachen, from where he had set out to conquer much of western Europe. In 774, Charlemagne turned his attention to Italy, where he crushed the Lombards – at the time under the leadership of King Desiderius, who was Charlemagne's own father-in-law – and added King of the Lombards to his long list of titles.

Pope Leo III awarded him yet another title – *imperator augustus*, later known as Holy Roman Emperor – in 800. In the short term, it was a sound move on the part of the pontiff, forcing Charlemagne to uphold papal rights against encroaching foes. But after Charlemagne's death in 814, no one could live up to his mighty reputation, and even before his direct family line died out, his empire fell into the hands of bickering minor lords.

Northern Italy was no exception. Already, under Lombard and Carolingian rule, religious orders had established control over large swathes of countryside, building monasteries in the midst of rich agricultural and pastoral holdings. With Magyar invaders harrying them

MILAN'S HEROINES

In praise of the city's leading female figures.

You may have noticed that streets in Milan (and, indeed, all over Italy) are often named after famous people. Perhaps inevitably, most of these are men, but there are also some women worth remembering.

Maria Gaetana Agnesi was one. Her street runs from via Giulio Romano to viale Sabotino, in the Porta Romana area (*see p113*). Born in Milan in 1718, Agnesi soon revealed her remarkable intellectual gifts, including a phenomenal aptitude for mathematics. She also wrote a discourse to show that liberal studies were not unsuited to her sex. And proved her point. Indeed, her *Instituzioni Analitiche* was published in 1748 – when she was 30. Such was her reputation that, in 1750, she was appointed to replace her father as professor of mathematics at the University of Bologna after he became ill.

Two years later, when he died, she withdrew from academic circles, shifting her attention to more local matters. She turned the family home in via Pantano (between the Duomo and the State University's city-centre location) into a hospice. Forced to move from there, she then opened a home for the mentally ill in nearby via della Signora. In 1771, she took over the women's section of the Trivulzio Hospice, which was run by the Blue Nuns. She held this post until her death in 1799, aged 81.

Luisa Battistotti Sassi is another woman who has a street named after her. It's on the east side of the city, on the way to Linate airport. Born just outside Pavia, Sassi came to Milan to marry an artisan. On the first day of the 1848 riots, when the uprising against the Austrians known as the *Cinque Giornate* (*see p230*) took place, she snatched one of the Austrian soldiers' pistols, and used it to force five other soldiers to surrender. She then changed into men's clothing and took to the first barricades, where she fought for the remaining five days.

Recognised as an undisputed heroine of the *Cinque Giornate*, she was given a state pension. Her stature grew so much in the minds and hearts of the people of Milan that her effigy was sold on the streets of the city. Luisa spent her later years in the US, where she died.

Queen Theodolinda.

Beatrice d'Este was the duchess of Milan and has a *viale* named after her, in the Porta Romana area. Born in Ferrara, Beatrice married Ludovico 'il Moro' (*see p228*) in 1491, when she was 16, and helped him fulfil his desire of bringing the best minds to the court in Milan, including Bramante and Leonardo da Vinci. She also acted as advisor to her husband, even if she didn't get involved directly with his political intrigues. Beatrice had two sons: Ercole, later called Massimiliano, and Francesco. She died in childbirth in 1497 and her funeral was held in the church of Santa Maria delle Grazie (*see p138*), which had been built by Ludovico, who wanted to be buried alongside her. Their funerary monument is now housed in the church of the Certosa di Pavia.

While all these women could be dubbed high-flyers, **Rosina Ferrario** really was one, literally. Born in Milan in 1888, she was the first Italian woman to get her pilot's licence – in 1913, when there were only about ten other female pilots in the entire world. In the same year, she was invited to fly with one of Italian aviation's legendary figures, Achille Landini, to commemorate the centenary of Giuseppe Verdi's birth. Ms Ferrario was praised for her achievement, but several commentators implied that motherhood would have been a nobler calling. Via Rosina Ferrario is tucked away in Villapizzone, in the northern suburbs of the city, almost as a reluctant tribute to this proto-feminist (who did, later, marry and have a family, in case you were wondering).

There is one last famous female figure in Milan's past worth mentioning, and although no street is named after her, there is a chapel dedicated to her in the city's Duomo (*see p46*).

IN CONTEXT

Theodolinda was a gorgeous blonde Lombard queen, whose beauty beguiled the inhabitants of the region in the late sixth and early seventh centuries AD. Daughter of Duke Garibaldo of Bavaria, she married Autari, king of the Lombards, in 589. Autari died the following year, but because Theodolinda was such a hit with the people they confirmed her as queen – contrary to usual practice – and invited her to take another husband. She chose Duke Agilulf of Turin, who dismayed many by allowing himself to be bought off by Pope Gregory the Great. Pope Gregory forged a friendship with Theodolinda; encouraged by him, she went on to convert her people from Arianism – the locally practised 'heretical' version of Christianity – and founded many churches and monasteries in the region.

Beatrice d'Este.

through the ninth and tenth centuries, the locals barricaded themselves into a series of fortified hamlets, each proclaiming its territorial rights over the surrounding countryside and laying the foundations of an extensive feudal system that would later come into conflict with the religious oligarchy.

With the end of the Carolingian line in 888, northern Italy passed into the control of a series of Frankish *reucci* ('little kings'), who sometimes found themselves in conflict with the questionable characters titled *imperator augustus* by popes kept under the thumbs of Roman nobles. It was the unwise attempt by kinglet Berengar II to force Adelaide, widow of his predecessor Lothar, to marry him (or possibly his son Adalbert; sources are divided) that upset this state of affairs. In 961, the eastern Frankish king Otto I responded to a plea for help from the beautiful Adelaide, who had been locked up in a tower overlooking Lake Garda by her would-be spouse (or, possibly, father-in-law). Otto invaded Italy, carried Adelaide off, and the following year was crowned Holy Roman Emperor in Rome.

Under Otto I, Otto II and, in particular, the devout Otto III, Lombardy's clergy had a field day. The Church was given precedence over the landed nobility, whose uppity behaviour irked the emperors and whose power was consequently reduced. In Milan, a building boom gave the city a succession of new Romanesque landmarks – including the basilica of Sant'Ambrogio (*see* p134). Allied with the *cives* – city-dwelling merchants or tradesmen – the clergy became the effective rulers of Lombardy's increasingly wealthy cities from some time around the start of the new millennium.

MERCHANT RANCOUR

By the end of the 11th century, the *cives* were demanding a greater degree of control: in Milan, a *consulatus civium* (town council meeting) was recorded in 1097. The towns of Bergamo, Brescia, Como, Cremona and Mantova followed suit in the second decade of the following century. The first of these meetings was held very much under the clergy's auspices, in the *brolo* (garden) of the bishop's palace – hence the abundance of later town halls around Lombardy called palazzo del Broletto.

Battle of Legnano.

But increasing civic feistiness also brought the various settlements of the Lombardy region into conflict with one other. Milan, the strongest and wealthiest, imposed its supremacy over Lodi, Cremona, Como and even Pavia, in spite of the latter's imperial connections. This was too much for the Holy Roman Emperor of the time, Frederick Barbarossa, who marched across the Alps to bring Milan to heel. At the end of a seven month siege in 1162, the emperor had the city's fortifications pulled down and the palaces of leading anti-imperial agitators destroyed.

Hated as Milan was by many of its neighbours, Barbarossa's heavy-handed treatment failed to endear him to any of the wary cities of Lombardy. In 1167, at a meeting of their representatives at Pontida, the *comuni* (towns run by the people) banded together in the Lega Lombarda (Lombard League). Its symbol was a large cart (*carroccio*) with the Lombard standard flying atop it; popular lore has it that the forces of the Lombard League were rallied around this cart when they engaged with and beat back the imperial troops at the Battle of Legnano in 1176. Sentimentalists of the Risorgimento (*see p230*) see this battle – the subject of the eponymous opera by Giuseppe Verdi – as the beginning of Italian resistance to foreign tyrants; but if truth be told, it was the emperor as tax-imposer, rather than as foreign power, they were fighting against. The moment the Holy Roman Empire ceased to be a threat, the *comuni* returned to their self-interested squabbling.

The Battle of Legnano was followed by further skirmishing against the emperor's forces, but in 1183 the Peace of Konstanz finally awarded Milan the privileges of independence and self-government it had long dreamed of. The city could now settle down to its own internal bickering. Most of the trouble arose from conflicts between the old aristocracy and the pushy ranks of merchants and tradesmen. The city's institutions were powerless to resolve these problems, so solutions were sought from outside, with the aristos lining up with the pro-empire Ghibelline party, and the parvenus joining the pro-papal Guelphs.

This was yet another indication of Milan's innate inability to free itself from outside interference. Admittedly, geography was against it: Lombardy was inevitably the doorway into Italy for a stream of northern invaders. But the city's habit of wavering between outside powers eventually sealed its fate. In 1266, Pope Clement IV summoned Charles d'Anjou from France to deal with Barbarossa's heirs in Sicily. Forced into a decision, Milan's dominant Guelph (that is, pro-papacy) faction, led by the Torriani family, opted to back the anti-empire movement.

But if there was one thing you could be sure of, it was that popes never backed winners forever: they were unwilling to let anyone get too strong. Charles conquered the south and became king of Sicily, but then the pope switched allegiance, championed a German candidate for the title of emperor, and even backed anti-papal Ghibelline forces in the north.

FAMILY RULE

Among these forces was one Ottone Visconti, an archbishop of Milan who had been ousted by the Torriani family. Ottone seized the initiative, scoring a major victory over the Torrianis in the Battle of Desio in 1277. One year later, he was declared *signore* (lord) of the city. The old *comune* system was over: Milan – like many other northern Italian cities – was going the way of one-family rule.

In 1294, on payment of 50,000 florins to Holy Roman Emperor Henry VII, Ottone's great-nephew and designated successor, Matteo, was given the title of *vicario imperiale* (imperial delegate), a rank that also gave him a claim to authority over Milan's neighbours. He was driven out of Milan in 1302 by the Torriani family, but with the emperor's support made a triumphant return in 1311. From then on, the Viscontis went from strength to strength. In 1330, Azzone Visconti was proclaimed *dominus generalis* (general ruler). Within the space of a generation, the surrounding cities all acknowledged Visconti rule.

The family's splendour reached its zenith with the rule of Gian Galeazzo Visconti (1378-1402), who obtained the title of Duke of Milan in 1395 from Emperor Wenceslas. Two years later, he was promoted to Duke of Lombardy: Gian Galeazzo ruled over the second-largest *signoria* in Italy (only the kingdom of Naples was bigger), which included Milan, Pavia, Bergamo, Brescia, Como, Lodi and Cremona, among other cities. Gian Galeazzo was a man of learning and culture, but there was nothing velvet-gloved about his command. Local feudal lords who refused to recognise his authority had their castles razed and were whisked off to prison. One chancellor, accused of treachery, was walled up alive.

It was under this intelligent but ruthless despot that Milan became the largest city in Italy, with a population of around 250,000 at the turn of the 15th century. Major building projects were embarked upon in the region, including the Certosa (charterhouse) in Pavia and the Duomo of Milan (*see p46*). When Visconti died of the plague in 1402, the great duchy was divided among his heirs, with his wife Caterina left as regent and tutoress.

Elsewhere in the duchy, Gian Galeazzo's death was the signal for other *signori* to raise their heads; Pandolfo III Malatesta declared himself *signore* of Bergamo and Brescia, and Facino Cane took over the territory in the west. In Milan, meanwhile, Caterina died – perhaps poisoned – just two years after her husband; and their eldest son, Giovanni Maria, was killed on his way to church. It fell to the younger son, Filippo Maria, to try to regain control of things. He had inherited his father's ambitious spirit and intelligence, along with his bookish habits and suspicious mind. But Milan's further-flung neighbours proved more resilient than they had been in his father's day: despite a number of wars against Florence and Venice, Filippo Maria ruled over a much-reduced duchy, with Bergamo and Brescia seceding, and joining Venice.

A CULTURAL COURT

When Filippo Maria died in 1447, leaving no male heirs, a group of noblemen attempted to re-establish republican life, setting up the Aurea Repubblica Ambrosiana (literally, Golden Ambrosian Republic). Never slow to take advantage of a neighbour's weakness, Venice attacked, grabbing Piacenza and Lodi. The new authorities of Milan foolishly entrusted their defence to Francesco Sforza, husband of Filippo Maria Visconti's illegitimate daughter, Bianca Maria, and the closest thing there was to a direct Visconti

Ottone Visconti at the Battle of Desio.

heir. Francesco won back the lost cities, but then did a secret deal with the Venetians, giving them Brescia and other territories in exchange for their recognition of him as the new duke of Lombardy.

After a brief siege, Milan's republican forces capitulated in 1450. Francesco's rule was even more magnificent than that of Gian Galeazzo Visconti. He transformed the city into a powerful metropolis, building among other things the Castello Sforzesco (*see p73*) and the Ospedale Maggiore, now Ca' Granda (*see p116*). On his death in 1466, he was succeeded by his pleasure-loving son Galeazzo Maria, whose determination to turn the court into a brothel-cum-circus did not endear him to all his subjects. This was made clear in 1476, when he was stabbed to death in church by three young patricians.

As his son was only seven at the time, Galeazzo Maria's wife gave the regency to a trusted minister and two of her husband's brothers. The younger, Ludovico Mauro, known as *il Moro* ('the Moor') because of his dark complexion, was clearly the dominant figure, and very soon he had the reins of power securely in his hands.

He proved a good ruler, encouraging agricultural development and the silk industry. Under him, the court became one of Italy's great centres of art and culture, with architects such as Donato Bramante and polymaths such as Leonardo da Vinci given free scope. Only the court of Mantova could compete for brilliance: there, Ludovico's sister-in-law, the urbane Isabella d'Este, had married into the Gonzaga family and reigned over a centre of high culture that included court painter Andrea Mantegna.

The life expectancy of these brilliant Renaissance courts was, however, short. On a military level, they hadn't a hope of vying with Europe's great powers. In a fatally flawed attempt to neutralise two birds with one cunningly thrown stone (Naples and France both had a claim on the Duchy of Milan through complicated inter-dynastic marriages), Ludovico suggested that King Charles VIII of France might wish to regain the throne of Naples, which had been seized from the French Anjous by the Spaniards. Charles, who had dreams of becoming a second Charlemagne, was just waiting to be persuaded, and in 1494 he

Top: Francesco Sforza. *See p227.*
Bottom: Castello Sforzsco.

IN CONTEXT

descended into Italy, with encouragement also from Florence and the Pope.

However, after a fairly easy victory in the south, Charles decided upon what was to become a French habit in Italy, and began looting the Kingdom of Naples. At this point he lost the approval of the Neapolitan population and also learned how short-lived papal support could be. Pope Alexander organised the Holy League Alliance to drive him out, getting the backing of Ludovico as well. In 1495, Charles was defeated at Fornovo, near Parma, and returned to France.

But four years later, France's new king, Louis XII, took his revenge. When he invaded Italy – determined, among other things, to claim his rights to Milan – Ludovico appealed to the Holy Roman Emperor Maximilian. The ragged army of Swiss and German mercenaries that the emperor drummed up could not match French firepower, and with the help of Mantova's Gonzaga family, the French took *il Moro* prisoner in 1499; he died in France in 1508.

In the same year, French-ruled Milan joined the League of Cambrai, which had been summoned by the great – if not exactly holy – warrior Pope Julius II to counter the threat posed by the expansion of Venice to the Italian mainland. The League scored a major victory against the Venetians at Agnadello (1509), after which the pope – surprise, surprise – switched sides and supported the Venetians. In 1513, the papal armies, Venice and Spain all turned on the French, who were expelled from Lombardy, and Ludovico's son Massimiliano was put in power.

By this time, though, Lombardy's role as rugby ball in the endless scrimmages between the great powers – France, Austria and Spain – was firmly established: for the next three and a half centuries, the region was trampled over by foreign armies and swapped among the great rulers. It was to become a pawn in the Thirty Years War (1618-48), which pitted Catholic leaders against Protestant, and the Habsburgs against just about everyone else in Europe.

SPANISH SUBORDINATION

The region enjoyed a 14-year semblance of autonomy after France's king, Francis I, was defeated at Pavia in 1525, his efforts to assert French hereditary rights over Lombardy stymied by imperial forces. Massimiliano Sforza's brother Francesco ruled under the tutelage of the Holy Roman Emperor Charles V (a Habsburg, and King Charles I of Spain); but when Francesco died in 1535, Charles assumed direct power. So began 170 years of Spanish domination. The once-proud independent Duchy of Milan became the neglected capital of a province: administered, guarded and taxed by foreigners.

Milan's population fell from 130,000 to 70,000; industry and agriculture wouldn't recover from the crisis until near the end of the 17th century. In 1627, the convoluted war of Mantuan succession broke out, bringing invaders, famine and disease to neighbouring territories, including Milan. In 1630, a plague epidemic devastated the city, killing thousands.

Towards the second half of the 17th century, Milan's religious life was given fresh vigour by the imposing Cardinal (later Saint) Carlo Borromeo. He was a leading figure of the Counter-Reformation – the movement that had arisen out of the Council of Trent (1545-63), which was convened to clean up a corrupt Catholic Church so it could hold its own against the spread of Protestantism.

The 18th century began with the impossibly complicated War of Spanish Succession (1701- 14), following attempts by the French king Louis XIV – who was married to a Habsburg – to grab for France all the various European possessions of Spain's last Habsburg monarch, Charles II. In 1706, in the course of this war, Milan was occupied by Eugenio von Savoy (whose Italian/German/French name indicates the complexity of his background) on behalf of Emperor Joseph I of Austria; the Peace of Utrecht (1713), and then the Treaty of Rastadt (1714), confirmed the new occupation.

AUSTRIAN ENLIGHTENMENT

Administratively, the Austrians were a step up from the Spaniards, who had made it their business to improve as little and tax as much as possible. The Austrians implemented various reforms, one of which was to draw up a land registry for tax purposes. Suddenly, aristocratic landowners faced an unprecedented need to make their land profitable, which helped get the economy moving.

The Austrians also did their best to alleviate some of the worst judicial abuses, abolishing ecclesiastic tribunals and the use of torture (to the dismay of some conservative Lombards). The intellectual climate brightened as well: a number of lively journals were published in Milan, and Enlightenment ideas began to trickle down through the educated classes. Numerous learned institutions were founded, including the Accademia di Brera, instituted by Empress Maria Teresa in 1776. The Teatro alla Scala (*see p56*) was opened in 1778.

'Mussolini and his mistress Clara Petacci were strung up for all to see in piazzale Loreto.'

Despite the Habsburg queen's best efforts, many Milanese resented foreign domination, and Napoleon, seen by optimists as embodying the spirit of democratic reform, was received enthusiastically when he marched into Milan in May 1796. Milan became the capital of Napoleon's Cisalpine Republic. It was perhaps with rather less enthusiasm, in 1805, that the Milanese watched the French emperor assume the throne of Italy in the Duomo – and the same iron crown that had once sat on the heads of the old Lombard kings.

After Napoleon's fall in 1814, the Congress of Vienna restored Lombardy to Austria. Although the region thrived culturally and economically during the 19th century, the Milanese remained largely hostile to Austrian rule. This hostility found a musical outlet in some of Verdi's early operas, but finally exploded in the heroic *Cinque Giornate* ('five days') of 1848, after an initial street protest led to the capture of the Austrian seat of power, the Palazzo del Governo (the building now known as the Palazzo Reale; *see p50*).

Inspired by the spirit of the Risorgimento – the Italy-wide movement to create a united country – the Milanese succeeded in throwing the Austrians out of the city after five days of street fighting. However, owing to the military incompetence of Carlo Emanuele of Piedmont, to whom the generally republican leaders of the insurrection had reluctantly turned for aid, the uprising eventually failed. Austrian forces re-entered the city, which, along with the whole of the Lombardy region, was placed under the iron-fisted control of their commander-in-chief, Count Joseph Radetzky.

UNIFICATION AND FASCISM

Liberation didn't come until the Second War of Independence in 1859. This time, under the pressure of combined military intervention by the French and the Piedmontese – and with the decisive action of Risorgimento hero Giuseppe Garibaldi and his guerrilla troops – the Austrians were forced to cede Lombardy to Vittorio Emanuele II of Savoy, the first king of a united Italy.

Though few doubted that the seat of government had to be Rome, Milan clearly considered itself the new country's cultural and financial capital. In the years immediately after unification, the city celebrated its free status by undertaking a number of grandiose building projects, including the construction of the great Galleria Vittorio Emanuele II (*see p50*).

On a more practical level, the opening of the San Gottardo tunnel through the Alps facilitated trade with northern Europe, and gave another boost, if one were needed, to Lombardy's industry. The flip side of this boom was suffering and unrest among the workers. Support for socialism grew; a general strike in 1898 was repressed with extreme brutality, leaving 81 'subversives' dead and 502 injured. Just after World War I, there were 445 strikes within the space of a single year; it was in this tumultuous climate that the Fascist Party began its thuggish activities, with some of its earliest attacks being launched in Milan against the socialist newspaper *Avanti* (previously edited, curiously enough, by Mussolini himself).

With Fascism established, demonstrations of proletarian discontent disappeared. It was not until 1943 that Milanese workers dared manifest their displeasure once again, bringing several factories in Milan and Turin to a halt; these protests contributed to the downfall of Mussolini's regime in July of the same year. In April 1945, the population of Milan rekindled the old 1848 spirit, rising up against the occupying Nazi forces and

Vittorio Emanuele II of Savoy.

liberating the city in just three days. If there's one thing that characterises the Milanese, it's their determination to improve on past records. And it was in Milan that the fallen Mussolini made his grisly final public appearance. Having been captured in Dongo on Lake Como and executed by partisans in 1945, Mussolini and his mistress Clara Petacci were strung up for all to see in piazzale Loreto.

POST-WAR PROSPERITY

At the end of World War II, Lombardy was instrumental in the boom that transformed Italy from an agricultural country to an industrial powerhouse. Over nine million Italians moved from one part of the country to another in search of work between 1955 and 1971, and many ended up in Milan and the larger cities of Lombardy, where work was plentiful.

Rich in heavy industry, such as steelworks, car manufacturing and railway construction, the area also provided good opportunities for anyone with a winning idea and plenty of energy to set up their own small concern. As they expanded to become players on the international stage, these small, often family-run companies found they needed help promoting their businesses. Milan soon developed into the capital of Italy's media industries, including PR and advertising. Long the home of most of the country's book and magazine publishers, the city also provided the base for the birth of commercial television. Silvio Berlusconi caught this wave in the early 1970s when he founded Telemilano.

Despite urban terrorism in the late 1970s and early '80s, Lombardy's new industries continued to gain momentum. In 1975, trying to secure his place in the country's burgeoning fashion industry, which was finding its focus in Milan, Piacenza-born Giorgio Armani sold his Volkswagen to finance his business. Having left his home in Reggio Calabria for Paris, Gianni Versace returned to Italy in 1978 and started plying his trade – in Milan.

By the 1980s, Lombardy – one of Italy's 20 regions – was generating 20 per cent of the country's GDP. The spectacular wealth that Milan had accumulated proved too tempting; in 1992, a scandal blew up: businesses were having to hand kickbacks (*tangenti*) to government officials if they wanted to win contracts. Led by judge Antonio di Pietro, a six-year investigation – dubbed *tangentopoli* – followed. Arrests were numerous, but convictions were few, the statute of limitations saving many from jail sentences.

Being nothing if not resilient, however, Lombardy as a whole, and Milan in particular, was able to absorb the blow to its reputation as the 'moral capital of Italy'. Economically, a new wave of immigration, the introduction of the euro and a global boom in design, finance and fashion helped the city to grow and prosper through the start of the new millennium. And in 2008, Milan won the role of host city of Expo 2015, allowing the city to affirm its position as Italy's economic and, perhaps, cultural capital. In the wake of its announcement, the city has undergone an intensive new building programme, erecting dozens of skyscrapers in the Porta Nuova and former Fiera zones, and opening a clutch of innovative new museums. Despite some wobbles along the way (the old ghost of *tangentopoli* reared its ugly head again in 2014), Expo 2015 has injected new zest into the city, building on centuries of resilience, entrepreneurship, hard graft and the irrepressible desire of the Milanese people to strive for improvement and change.

Design

Milan – where mass production meets artistic flair.

In the 1940s, Italy's industrial powerhouse rebuilt itself – not for the first time – with all the energy it could muster. Milan put the misery of World War II behind it, and by the early 1950s the world at large got a taste of what would become Milan's modernist yet utterly practical trademark: industrial design.

In and around Milan, design firms founded in the 1920s and '30s began to resurface. Alessi, creating kitchenware on Lago d'Orta, had been set up in 1921; brothers Cesare and Umberto Cassina had established Cassina in Meda, Brianza in 1927, making high-end furniture for cruise ships and restaurants; and Gio Ponti, Lucio Fontana and Pietro Chiesa had created FontanaArte in 1932 while they were still unknown young designers. After the war, these designers and manufacturers sprang back into action, and practical objects were deftly created with a now-familiar Italian flair.

The origins of industrial design as a movement are hard to pinpoint. The term defines a blend of function and aesthetics, and the concept was born of an attempt to achieve mass production with a modicum of artistic beauty – or perhaps, more accurately, a creative injection of cleverness and humour. Whether it was the Milanese curiosity or pure and simple passion, the city soon boasted a range of great individual designers and design manufacturers.

NEW YORK

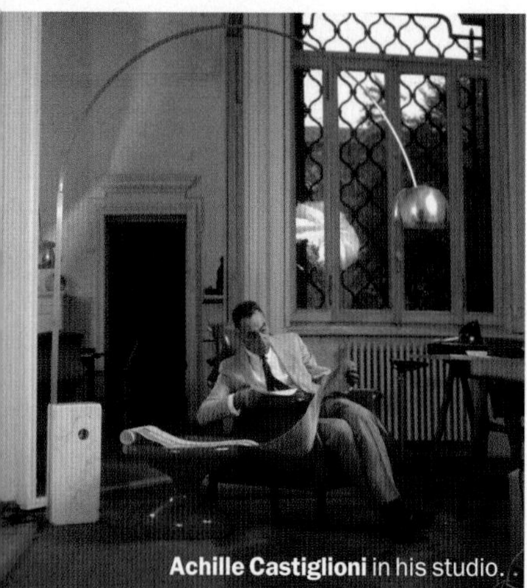
Achille Castiglioni in his studio.

THE DESIGNERS

Milan-born **Achille Castiglioni** (1918-2002, www.achillecastiglioni.it) became one of Italy's most renowned industrial designers. After studying architecture, he and his two brothers set up a studio in the city in 1944. Paring down the form of existing items to their very essence, Castiglioni shot to fame during the 1950s with his Mezzadro stool, made from the chair of a tractor, and the Sella stool, created from a bicycle seat. **Zanotta** (piazza Tricolore 2, 02 7601 6445, www.zanotta.it), established by manufacturer Aurelio Zanotta in 1954, produced both items.

Through the '50s – a decade of great post-war reconstruction for Italy – and the '60s, the Castiglioni brothers continued to create experimental home furnishings and lamps. They developed strong ties with Milan-based manufacturer **Flos** (corso Monforte 15, 02 798 457, www.flos.com). Castiglioni designed the company's showroom, and Flos produced Castiglioni's designs. Particularly popular was the Arco, a massive, arched lamp with a marble base that could be stood in a corner and still overhang the centre of a room.

A genius in his field, Castiglioni came up with the revolutionary 'principal design component' theory. Any good design, he believed, must be approached with a clear idea of what will make it work – this component could be its practical function, or the use of a newly developed technology – and not purely aesthetics. This theory helped to establish a more general understanding of what makes objects in industrial design successful.

In 1961, the Salone Internazionale del Mobile (*see p235* **Furniture Frenzy**) was launched, with 328 exhibitors and 12,000 visitors. This new annual event, paired with the city's thriving design activity, meant the creative world's attention was slowly beginning to focus on Milan. As most of the country's factories had been built shortly after the war, they contained the latest technology, and were able to draw on cheap labour; and from the outset, the fair was notable for its fine, innovative and high-quality products.

The charismatic **Ettore Sottsass** (1917-2014) – a fount of big, bold ideas – landed on the Milanese scene at around the same time as Castiglioni, establishing his own studio in the city in 1947. Experimenting in the fields of fine art, journalism and architecture, while curating exhibitions at the city's Triennale (Milan's craft and design headquarters since 1933; *see p77*), Sottsass rocketed to fame after his design for Olivetti's ELEA 9003 mainframe computer won the prestigious Compasso d'Oro industrial design award. He also designed the famously sexy red Valentine typewriter for Olivetti in 1970. Sottsass was a passionate amateur photographer. He was obsessed with the documentation of his own life and used the world around him – his memory often triggered by his thousands of photos – to inspire his imagination and object development. He designed pieces for most of the big Lombardy-based manufacturers, such as Alessi and FontanaArte – which produced a range of his glass table-top containers and vases.

In 1980, Sottsass founded the **Memphis group**, which took its name from the Bob Dylan song 'Stuck Inside of Mobile (With the Memphis Blues Again)' – the song was supposedly jammed on repeat during the group's first gathering. With a group of young designers that included such up-and-coming talents as **Michele De Lucchi** and **Marco Zanini**, the Memphis group exhibited their first collection of individually designed works at the Arc '74 showroom at the 1981 Salone Internazionale del Mobile. The exhibition rocked the design world,

FURNITURE FRENZY

Welcome to the world's biggest, and most important, design fair.

For anyone with even a passing interest in aesthetics, the world's biggest design fair, the **Salone Internazionale del Mobile** (*see p35*), is the place to be. A €20 day pass provides more enlightenment than a year's subscription to *Design Week*. For six days every April, makers of things as diverse as household robotics, airline cutlery and mood lighting ply their pioneering wares at Europe's largest trade ground, the FieraMilano near the northerly satellite town of Rho. The latest concepts from the 1,200-plus exhibitors range from the understated to the bizarre.

The 2014 fair attracted more than 357,000 visitors from 160 countries. The fillip to Milan's economy is immense: hotels are booked up three months in advance and anyone with a second language and a smile is drafted in to hand out flyers on the street or help visitors buy the right ticket on the metro. Since moving location to out-of-the-way Rho in 2006, the fair has become less of an attraction for many punters – though it's still the quickest means of picking up on the latest trends from the big hitters, from Artemide to Zanotta. To discover what's really up-and-coming, the **Salone Satellite** pavilion has the edge. It's a chance to mingle with 650 of the finest young designers from as far afield as Malaysia and Turkey, their projects frequently more fantastic than those at the main fair.

Yet the chief reason for joining the frenzy, for many visitors, is the fringe festival, or **Fuorisalone**, outside the official fair. Free shows take place in galleries, showrooms, former factories, exhibition spaces and other locations across Milan. For years, the prime centre of Fuorisalone action has been the zone around via Tortona, dominated by multi-brand exhibits at the vast Superstudio and ex-Ansaldo exhibition areas. But of late, the epicentre seems to be moving to the eastern district of via Ventura, Lambrate, which, in 2014, saw displays by Rem Koolhaas, numerous pop-up restaurants – and eccentric exhibits of everything from light bulb-shaped candles to wooden beards. Also in 2014, Brera's Botanic Garden (*see p81*) and design company Living Divani hosted one of the most talked-about events. The dedicated booklet produced by *Interni* magazine (www.internimagazine.it) is the best guide to the prime spots, but there's a profusion of mini magazines telling visitors what's on where.

Fuorisalone.

provoking responses that ranged from public incredulity to critical nausea. Their creations were brightly coloured, with a heavy pop-art influence; they defiantly took forms to minimalism's polar opposite.

Well established Milanese manufacturers, even those who had been previously firmly wedded to a strict template of design sophistication, found they simply couldn't resist the group's playful tug. Lighting giant **Artemide** (via Manzoni 12, 02 7787 12201, www.artemide.com) picked up Sottsass's Pausania table lamp (and later Michele De Lucchi's iconic Tolomeo table lamp), and Zanini managed the group's designs of office furniture for American company **Knoll** (piazza Bertarelli 2, 02 722 2291, www.knollint.com). Sottsass left Memphis on a high in 1985, when the group was still making waves. Although Memphis stopped showcasing as a group in 1988, their influence endures: current designers, including Philippe Starck, cite the movement as one of their primary inspirations.

'Milan's modernist yet utterly practical trademark: industrial design.'

The list of local design stars includes **Gio Ponti** (1891-1979), renowned for his architectural designs, such as Milan's Pirelli Tower (Italy's first skyscraper, 1958) and the Denver Art Museum (1971). He also created a range of furniture and lights for some of the city's biggest names, including the Mod Distex and Superleggera chairs for **Cassina** (via Durini 16, 02 7602 0745, www.cassina.com).

Italy's northern capital nurtured the visionaries listed above, as well as scores of other hugely influential designers: people such as **Vico Magistretti**, **Bruno Munari** and, later, **Antonio Citterio** and **Piero Lissoni**. MoMA's 1972 exhibition, 'Italy: the New Domestic Landscape', partially sponsored by Cassina and Pirelli, demonstrated Milanese

IN CONTEXT

ESSENTIAL ADDRESSES

Where to see – and buy – the best of Milanese design.

Apart from trawling around the major design showrooms, the best way to get a rapid insight into Milanese (and Italian) design is to visit the **Salone Internazionale del Mobile** (*see p235* **Furniture Frenzy**), held each April. The biggest industrial design-related event in the world, attracting 350,000 visitors from around the globe, the fair is a haven of futuristic designs, creativity, networking and inspiration.

At other times of the year, the **Triennale** (*see p77*) hosts design-related exhibitions, and also has a permanent collection of some of the city's finest design icons. In 2007, a portion of the museum became the dedicated Museo del Design (www.triennaledesignmuseum.it), its layout devised by Michele De Lucchi to chronicle the history of Italian industrial design. For a peek into the inner workings of Milanese design, visit the **Studio Museo Achille Castiglioni** (*see p79*), Achille Castiglioni's studio for his entire working career.

When it comes to quality souvenirs, there's no shortage of choices. **Galleria Post Design** (via della Moscova 27, 02 655 4731, www.memphis-milano.it) sells objects designed by 1980s superstars, the Memphis group. Close by, **Raw** (*see p87*) offers an edgy eye on contemporary Milanese taste, with an eclectic mix of souvenirs, from ashtrays to notebooks (although most are made in France and the UK, rather than Italy). Also in the area, **P8/Segno Italiano** (via Palermo 8, 02 5656 7833, www.segnoitaliano.it) saves artisanal icons from obscurity – including ultralight chairs from Chiavari, blown green glass from Empoli and ceramic fruit (sold by weight) from Padova. Across town, **Rossana Orlandi**'s courtyard (*see p141*) packs in historical pieces as well as new designs by young creative minds. In the Porta Venezia area, manufacturer **Jannelli e Volpi** (*see p105*) devotes part of its roomy store to upcoming designers of everything from costume jewellery to fans, in between its own colourful Made-in-Milano wallpaper designs.

Finally, if you're thinking of making a career out of design, Domus Academy (www.domusacademy.com) and the Istituto Europeo di Design (www.ied.it) offer undergraduate and masters courses based in Milan.

talent to an American audience. Curated by Emilio Ambasz, the exhibition focused on compact, modular housing: by that time, over 50 per cent of Italy's population lived in tight urban environments. Designs by **Marco Zanuso**, **Gaetano Pesce** and **Gae Aulenti** were typical of the brilliant, multifunctional concepts popular in Milan at the time.

THE MANUFACTURERS

It was not only the designers, but also the manufacturers who helped to solidify Milan's position as the design capital that it is today. Some partnerships, including **Paolo Chiesa** and **FontanaArte** (corso Monforte 13, 02 8721 3872, www.fontanaarte.it), had their origins in the 1930s, whereas other enduring relationships began more recently. Many of Milan's main manufacturers have continued to be prominent forces in the city and within the design world.

De Padova (corso Venezia 14, 02 777 201, www.depadova.it) has been producing furnishings since the 1950s, as well as household 'extras' such as candles and rugs, with an eye to the creation of a functional leisure space. Kitchen and bathroom specialist **Boffi** (via Solferino 11, 02 879 0991, www.boffi.com) is renowned for its natural stone bath tubs. And Zanotta produced the revolutionary beanbag Sacco in 1968, created by Franco Teodoro, Piero Gatti and Cesare Paolini, as well as manufacturing lines for 1970s Florence-based design group **Superstudio**.

The affluent 1980s saw Milanese designers make a slight shift in direction. The industry began to focus on businesses and the workplace, which led to an examination of previously overlooked office environments. Architects Riccardo Sarfatti, Sandra Severi and Paolo Rizzato set up **Luceplan** (corso Monforte 7, 02 7601 5760, www.luceplan.com) in 1978. Winning its first Compasso d'Oro design award in 1981 for the D7 lamp, Luceplan has remained a key exponent of streamlined lighting to this day.

Over the past 20 years, Milanese manufacturers have melded home and office designs, producing furnishings and objects that can be placed according to artistic taste. **Kartell** (via Turati, corner of via Porta, 02 659 7916, www.kartell.it) produces furniture by design greats such as Philippe Starck, Antonio Citterio, Piero Lissoni and Patricia Urquiola, as well as founder Anna Castelli Ferrieri. Although originally specialising in car parts, in 1963 it began to create furnishings primarily in plastic.

Top manfacturer **Cassina** retains the exclusive right to furniture designed by Le Corbusier; it also produces items by Frank Lloyd Wright. It's one of the city's most consistently prominent design companies, and a recent exhibition at Milan's Triennale was dedicated to Cassina's history, designers and products.

Alessi (*see p66*) continues to forge relationships with big-name designers, including Philippe Starck (he of the iconic long-legged Juicy Salif lemon squeezer) and, more recently, Zaha Hadid (designer of one of their Tea and Coffee Tower sets). **Danese** (piazza San Nazaro in Brolo 15, 02 5830 4150, www.danesemilano.com) has a showroom that's used for design-related events, and exhibits furnishings by Enzo Mari, James Irvine and Paolo Rizzato. Centrally located **B&B Italia** (*see p66*) is a capacious venue designed by Antonio Citterio & Partners. B&B produces everything from garden furniture to lighting and textiles, including Patricia Urquiola's Fat Sofa and Fat Fat-Lady Fat tables.

Juicy Salif lemon squeezer (Alessi).

Sacco beanbag (Zanotta).

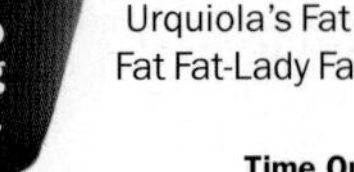

Fashion

Think of the world's fashion capitals, and you're likely to come up with: Paris, New York, London and Milan. Yet it wasn't until the late 20th century that the last burst on to the world's fashion stage. Parisian fashion began well over a century earlier, when English draper Charles Frederick Worth (the father of haute couture) opened his private atelier in Paris in 1858 and began showing his seasonal collections on live models for the first time; during that period, Italy had other preoccupations, such as the small matter of national unification. It wasn't until the 20th century that the innately stylish Italians began to elbow their way into the fashion spotlight – in Florence and Rome. It took until the late 1960s for Milan – the most dynamic and forward-looking of Italy's cities – to begin to impinge upon the fashion consciousness, and it wasn't until the 1980s that the city became a force to be reckoned with.

In the 1920s and '30s, **Salvatore Ferragamo** crafted dazzling handmade shoes for Hollywood stars from his Florentine atelier; in the 1940s the Rome-based Fontana sisters made couture creations, such as Linda Christie's wedding gown for her marriage to Tyrone Power. But Italian fashion as we know it today truly began to make a name for itself in the 1950s with the first fashion shows in the Sala Bianca at Florence's Palazzo Pitti, showcasing clothes from the likes of **Gattinoni** and **Roberto Capucci**. The late 1960s and '70s ushered in a whole new era as the country found itself in the midst of social change: terrorism was rife; students rebelled; divorce and abortion were legalised; mass-produced ready-to-wear began to definitively replace tailoring and couture.

ENTER MILAN

During these decades of change, psychedelic Emilio Pucci made a name for himself in Florence, while the pop art-influenced **Elio Fiorucci** opened his first ground-breaking shop in central Milan. Florence's Sala Bianca was still the main venue for catwalk shows, however, and it was there, in the early 1970s, that a southern-born, Milan-based designer named **Gianni Versace** showed his knitwear collection, 'Florentine Flowers'.

On train trips, while shuttling between Milan and his producer in Ancona, Versace would bump into **Gianfranco Ferré**, a Milanese architect whose beautifully constructed clothes were made in Bologna. And in the same years, a drop-out medical student and window dresser for La Rinascente named **Giorgio Armani** began designing his stylishly sober creations for Nino Cerruti. Between 1975 and 1978, all three set up their own businesses, based in Milan.

Other names were also emerging. Milan-based **Krizia** and **Missoni** (at Sumirago, on Lake Verese) had begun creating knitwear

– but now shifted into ready-to-wear. Bergamo-based **Trussardi**, a glove manufacturer, was expanding its product range, and Milanese textile manufacturer **Etro** also moved into fashion during these years.

By now, Florence's Sala Bianca had become so popular that the venue was bursting at the seams – and the city's airport could no longer cope with the influx of buyers, designers and producers flooding in and out. In 1975, the first Settimana della Moda was held in Milan – and the city took over Italy's number one fashion slot, encouraging a host of new names to start up in the city.

The 1980s saw the rise of Milan-based brands including **Dolce & Gabbana**, **Romeo Gigli** and **Moschino**, while the '90s saw the emergence of cult label **Marni**, and **Prada**, whose intellectual, often minimalist aesthetic was the epitome – as was Giorgio Armani – of unshowy Milanese style. Like Florentine leather bag producer Gucci, Prada was, in fact, a historic brand: Fratelli Prada was founded in 1913 as a maker of leather goods and seller of imported English luggage, and Miuccia's grandfather, Mario, set up the first Prada shop in the Galleria Vittorio Emanuele II (*see p50*) the same year. In 1978, Miuccia Prada took over the Milan company, morphing the label into a major international player. Starting with backpacks, nylon totes and shoes, she launched Prada's first prêt-à-porter line in 1989, to great acclaim. The less-pricey label **Miu Miu**, aimed at a younger clientele, arrived in 1992.

FROM CLOTHES TO HOTELS AND BEYOND

In the last three decades, most designers (Italian or otherwise), have pushed fashion's boundaries and tried their hand at some form of spin-off. Some have stayed within the strict realm of fashion, including accessories; others have expanded outwards, with forays into art, food or design – including hotels, home furnishings, bakeries, bars and spas. It has been partially based on the success or failure of these ventures, that fashion houses have opted (or been forced) to follow one of two trends: joining a conglomerate and succumbing to multinational pressure in the 1980s and '90s; or forging their own path, strengthening internal company creativity and independently blurring the boundaries between fashion, design and art.

Whether or not this is emblematic of an independent, go-it-alone mentality, the second route had been the one followed by Milan's big three fashion houses – Armani, Dolce & Gabbana and Prada – in marked contrast to the big French brands.

Miu Miu, Summer 2014.

THE BIG THREE

Giorgio Armani has long experimented with different creative outlets. In addition to his famous prêt-à-porter lines, Armani debuted his Giorgio Armani Privé haute couture collection in 2005. He's overseen the design of a number of non-fashion lines, such as Armani Casa (home furnishings), cosmetics, cafés and restaurants (in collaboration with Nobu). In 2001, the company purchased the former Nestlé factory just off via Tortona (a former industrial zone transformed into a hotbed of design); renovated by Japanese architect Tadao Ando, it's now a venue for fashion shows. In 2010, the first Armani hotel opened in the world's tallest building in Dubai. A second opened on the top floor of the designer's Milan megastore (*see p246*) in 2011, while a third hotel is slated to open in Marrakech in 2015. Despite celebrating his 80th birthday in July 2014, Armani still controls the entire company himself.

Domenico Dolce and Stefano Gabbana founded Dolce & Gabbana in Milan in 1986. The pair has produced men's and women's ready-to-wear lines, lingerie, accessories and perfumes, as well as a spa, old-fashioned barber, bar and restaurant (*see p107*). In 2014, they opened a second Milan restaurant, the Martini Bistrot, inside their corso Venezia store, consolidating their interests in the food sector. They also opened a boutique promoting young designers that they feel deserve an additional boost. Dolce and Gabbana were recently caught up in a tax scandal, from which they have now been absolved. As with Armani, the pair retain firm, hands-on control.

Through the late 1990s, Prada purchased shares in Gucci (sold a year later), Fendi (sold in 2001) and Helmut Lang and Jil Sander (both sold by 2006), but since then the company has pretty much turned its back on the conglomerate, though it still has stakes in two footwear brands (Church's and Car Shoes) and became a listed company in 2011. Seemingly rested and refreshed, Prada's efforts are now being poured into its non-profit art foundation, Fondazione Prada, with attention focused on the new office and exhibition space (*see p113* **Prada's Temple to Art**) designed by Rem Koolhaas, scheduled to open in 2015. The firm did, however, buy an 80 per cent stake in the historic *pasticceria*-cum-café Marchesi (*see p142* **Let Them Eat Cake**) in 2014.

Despite various mooted projects over the years, Milan still does not have a comprehensive fashion museum (although Armani has said he wants to open his archives to the public before Expo 2015). Yet, perhaps by going it alone, Milan's best-known brands have emerged as some of the world's greatest influences on fashion and style.

Dolce & Gabbana, Men's Fashion Summer 2015.

Food

A half-millennium of foreign invasion, conspicuous wealth and grinding poverty has left Lombardy with the most varied of all Italy's regional cuisines. Surprisingly, in what is the nation's most dynamic state, the cuisine is still intensely localised. Serious foodies may have to hunt down copper pan-cooked polenta in Bergamo, the elusive *lavarello* on Lake Como and luscious cream cheese in Lodi. Oh, the hardship!

That said, the Milanese are ever eager to absorb ideas from abroad: words such as sushi, couscous and curry are now common parlance. But in times of hardship – and in Lombardy there have been many – locals are quick to fall back on tasty staples. Think Italy, think pasta; but Lombardy is also justly proud of its rice paddies, dairies and herds. So take a deep breath, loosen your belt – and tuck in.

AMARETTI
These crisp biscuits made with bitter and sweet almonds, apricot kernels and egg whites become sticky as they melt in the mouth. The name derives from *amaro*, meaning bitter. The most famous amaretti are made by Lazzaroni and sold in a red tin box under the name Amaretti di Saronno – after the Lombard town where they were first made in the 1600s. The popular amaretto liqueur, Disaronno, has been made since 1525 from a secret recipe including burnt sugar, fruit and herb essences soaked in apricot kernel oil.

ARBORIO
One of the stubby-grain rice varieties grown in Lombardy. Introduced to the region in the 14th century by a wayward member of the ruling Visconti family, rice soon became a local staple. The flatlands of the Po valley easily flooded and were turned into rice paddies. Along with *carnaroli*, *arborio* is one of the best varieties for making the beloved risotto (a 19th-century invention).

BITTO
It's the name of a river, a valley, an annual fair and, most famously, a mountain cow's- and goat's-milk cheese from the Alpine region of Valtellina. Fragrant and slightly sour when young, and bold when aged for up to ten years, the best of *bitto* is a prestigious treat that has a DOP designation.

BOLLITO
This northern version of assorted boiled meats, potatoes, carrots and onions relies on good-quality beef (though other meats are often used as well). It's served as a simple dish of broth – normally the strained stock – with tortellini, followed by a platter of slowly cooked meats and vegetables. Condiments are either **mostarda** (*see p242*) or salsa verde, a mix of parsley, garlic, oil and anchovies.

IN CONTEXT

BRESAOLA DELLA VALTELLINA
Another delicacy from the mountains, this lean, dried beef is best when sliced thin and splashed with oil, black pepper and lemon.

CAMPARI
Milan is rightly proud of its cochineal-tinted aperitif made with mysterious, mostly herbal ingredients. Some call it alcoholic cough syrup; others sip it happily with a spritz of prosecco, soda, a splash of gin or orange juice.

CASSOEULA
Traditionally made to celebrate the slaughtering of a pig, this hearty winter stew features various porcine pieces, including ears and skin (*cotenna*), *salamini* (sausages) and cabbage leaves. Best consumed along with glassfuls of strong red wine.

COTOLETTA ALLA MILANESE
Popular lore has it that this fried, breaded chunk of veal is derived from Austria's wiener schnitzel. Not so. Originally taken from a different cut of meat and served on the bone, the *cotoletta* (or *costoletta*, in the boned version) is fried in butter and not lard. More to the point, Milan's breaded veal fillet dates from at least the 12th century.

FISH
Although many of Lombardy's waterways are polluted, they nonetheless teem with excellent freshwater fish. The Po has pike and perch, while the lakes have a range of small and larger varieties, including tiny *alborelle* (bleak) and the highly prized *lavarello* (lavaret) of lakes Como and Garda.

FRANCIACORTA
This is one of the few wine-making regions of note in Lombardy, its sparkling white made mostly from chardonnay grapes with a little pinot noir and pinot blanc (instead of the pinot meunier of Champagne). Produced in the hills of Lake Iseo, these wines were the first Italian bubbly to get a DOCG rating, thanks to the vision of producer Guido Berlucchi.

GORGONZOLA
You're on the Milan metro, looking for your stop on the map overhead, and you have a sudden craving for a nice piece of gorgonzola. No wonder: you're looking at the name on the map. Before it became a Milan suburb, this was the town where the creamy blue cheese originated – and it's still where some of the best is made.

KRAPFEN
These sweet little doughnuts of leavened pastry, fried and then filled with jam, were imported from Austria and are now made across northern Italy, where they're found in many bakeries.

MASCARPONE
The main ingredient in tiramisù and other rich desserts, this luscious cream cheese is good eaten plain or with a little cocoa and sugar on top. It originally came from Lodi, just south-west of Milan.

MINESTRONE ALLA MILANESE
Rice replaces the usual pasta in the standard Italian veggie soup. Other typical ingredients are greens, pancetta and onion.

MISSOLTINO
This tasty little shad (*agone*) from Lake Como is salted, sun-dried for ten days, then pressed with bay leaves in tins known as *tolle*. One of Slow Food's 224 protected *presidia*, they're excellent eaten with polenta on winter nights.

MOSTARDA
A spicy preserve from Cremona, made of candied fruit (normally peaches, cherries and pears), with an added kick of powdered mustard seeds. Nicer than it sounds, and great with cold cuts or *bollito* (*see p241*).

OSSOBUCO

Ossobuco, the definitive Lombardy dish, reflects the region's love of slowly stewed veal. Thick slices of shank – *ossobuchi* – from milk-fed calves are tied into bundles, browned in butter and then cooked with wine. Some people add tomatoes or peas, but purists disapprove of this. The marrow in the shank makes the dish rich and velvety.

PANETTONE

Literally, 'big bread'. Milan's own fragrant Christmas fruit cake, notable for its dome shape, is an oversized brioche scented with citrus peel, laced with eggs and butter, and flecked with plump raisins. *Colomba* ('dove') is the Easter edition, crowned with toasted almonds and moulded in the shape of a bird.

PIZZOCCHERI

Served with melted butter, potatoes and greens, this highly calorific dish, made with hand-rolled buckwheat tagliatelle from the Valtellina region, is an ideal pick-me-up after strenuous exercise.

POLENTA

In Italy, the pejorative term for Lombards is 'polenta eaters'. Once at the bottom of the food chain – you ate polenta if you couldn't afford bread – the pap was a kind of porridge originally made from spelt, millet and buckwheat and later from cornmeal (*see p184* **'D' for Delicious**). Polenta rose in status through literature, famously in Alessandro Manzoni's *I promessi sposi (The Betrothed)*, and even today most self-respecting Lombard households are in possession of a polenta copper pot. The instant variety is frowned upon.

SAFFRON

The yellow spice used in *risotto alla milanese*, one of the city's most famous dishes. The Spanish ruled Milan for nearly two centuries, starting in the 1500s, and left behind saffron (*zafferano*), which provides the risotto's deep golden hue.

SAN PELLEGRINO

The salty, mineral-saturated waters of this spa town north of Bergamo have been drawing thirsty travellers for their reputed health-giving properties for centuries. It's the source of the bottled sparkling water of the same name.

SOAVE

A subtle, crisp white from the balmy microclimate east of Lago di Garda, proudly possessing a DOCG rating. The region's name allegedly derives from the Suevians, a Germanic Lombard tribe that moved south in the sixth century.

STRACCHINO

This family of typically Lombard cheeses used to be made only in the autumn when tired *stracche* (cows) were milked after their long descent from the mountains. Gorgonzola is a member of the family, as is *crescenza*, a super-white, fresh *stracchino*.

TALEGGIO

Although farmhouse versions are still available in all their nutty glory, this rich cow's-milk cheese can also be found in its industrially produced form in supermarkets. In Bergamo, it's often served at the end of a meal with preserved fruit. Eating this makes you an honorary Lombard.

TRIPE

Bovine innards have been a traditional part of the Lombard diet for centuries. The Milanese version (*trippa alla milanese*) involves two kinds of tripe, tomatoes and white Spanish beans. There's also a soupier version, known as *busecca*, minus the beans.

VEAL

Milk-fed calf is central to the classic meat dishes ossobuco and *cotoletta alla milanese*.

ZUCCA

An alcoholic drink made with rhubarb and named after its creator, Ettore Zucca of Milan, former proprietor of Il Camparino (*see p51* – previously known as Zucca) in Galleria Vittorio Emanuele II.

Essential Information

Hotels

As you'd expect from Italy's most fashionable city, many of its hotels epitomise the chic, minimal – and sometimes quirky – style for which Milan is so well known. This is especially true of the most recent crop of establishments, across all categories, from budget to deluxe. At the top end, fashion and jewellery houses Armani, Bulgari and Moschino have moved into the hotel market, setting the bar for good-looking luxury. Some high-end guest rooms are so minimal, you might fear your suitcase will entirely ruin the look; others are more whimsical, playing to fashion-crowd fantasies. As Expo 2015 looms, the top hotels have been getting their houses in order: the Four Seasons has a new subterranean gym, while the TownHouse group is opening a whole series of swanky new suites. Luckily, the burgeoning selection of boutique hotels, B&Bs and even hostels means you can still afford good design, as long as you can forgo 24-hour room service, or white-gloved butlers catering to your every whim.

STAYING IN MILAN

Outside the slack summer period, booking in advance is absolutely essential. As well as a constant flow of business travellers, thousands from all over Italy and further afield descend on Milan to attend trade fairs, when prices rise. The key events are the fashion shows, held four times a year (late February and late September for the women's collections, mid January and late June for men's); and the annual furniture fair, Salone Internazionale del Mobile (mid April). Prices during Expo 2015 (1 May to 31 Oct 2015) are also likely to experience a considerable hike.

Milan suffers from a shortage of parking spaces. Some hotels have their own car park, although many have deals with local garages for overnight parking. The price of this service varies considerably, but can be as high as €50 or more per day. That said, a car is superfluous in compact Milan: there's an efficient public transport system, and your hotel can call you a taxi if you must arrive in style. Also, check out the possibility of bike sharing or hiring an electric car (*see p259*).

As a general rule of thumb, **Deluxe** in Milan means a double room will start at €500 and stop at nothing; **Expensive** means it will cost €300-€500 per night; **Moderate** means €150-€300 and **Budget** will come in below €150. However, it really does pay to check hotel websites – and booking sites – carefully, especially at peak times.Facilities for wheelchair users are slowly improving in Milan, and we've indicated those establishments with disabled access rooms.

DUOMO & CENTRE

Deluxe

Armani Hotel Milano

Via Manzoni 31 (02 8883 8888, http://milan.armanihotels.com). Metro Montenapoleone, or bus 61, or tram 1. **Rooms** 95. Disabled access. **Map** p284 E5.

Situated atop Italian designer Giorgio Armani's rationalist flagship space flanking the Golden Rectangle of shopping, Armani Hotel Milano is a shrine to luxurious simplicity. The hotel's 95 rooms and suites were personally designed by King Giorgio himself, and all are furnished with studiously minimal linens and fabrics, and custom furniture from his Armani Casa line. Upon arrival, each guest is assigned a Lifestyle Manager, who is dedicated to fulfilling the hotel's promise of a 'home away from home'. On the top floor is a tip-top restaurant, lounge bar and 1,000sq m (10,760sq ft) spa, all with floor-to-ceiling windows. Nothing at Armani is done by halves – naturally, the building provides one of the city's very best views.

Bulgari

Via Privata Fratelli Gabba 7B (02 805 8051, www.bulgarihotels.com). Metro Montenapoleone, or bus 61, or tram 1. **Rooms** 58. Disabled access. **Map** p284 E5.

At the end of a private road behind the Pinacoteca di Brera's botanic gardens, the Bulgari oozes the same exclusivity and class as the brand's fine jewellery, with due attention paid to precious materials, in interiors by home-grown archi-star Antonio Citterio. The neutral-toned bedrooms are understated yet luxurious with oak flooring, while the capacious bathrooms feature black marble and travertine. Floor-to-ceiling windows open on to teak balconies overlooking the huge private gardens surrounding the hotel. The spa is a study in contemporary calm, and the bar is a magnet for style-conscious locals as well as hotel guests; drinks are served in the garden in summer.

IN THE KNOW TOURIST TAX

In 2012, Milan's City Council decided to levy an *imposta di soggiorno* – or tourist tax. All non-residents staying in Milan are required to cough up, with rates costing €2-€5 per person, per day, for up to 14 nights, depending on hotel category and type. Come August, the tax is reduced by 50%, to encourage low-season stays.

Travellers at high-end establishments, in particular, may be in for a bit of a shock: the tax bill for two people in a five-star hotel adds up to an extra €70 per week. The tax is usually collected by the hotelier independently of the room rate, though under-18s do not have to pay. Hostel guests aged under 30 are also, thankfully, exempt.

In its first eight months, the *imposta di soggiorno* netted a reported €17 million, mostly from four-star hotels. The cash was originally 'destined to finance interventions in the area of tourism', including the restoration of *beni culturali* (cultural sites and monuments), but, at the time of writing, the exact nature of these 'interventions' remains unclear.

Armani Hotel Milano.

★ Four Seasons Hotel Milano

Via Gesù 6-8 (02 77 088, www.fourseasons.com/milan). Metro Montenapoleone or San Babila, or bus 61, 94, or tram 1. **Rooms** 118. Disabled access. **Map** p284 E6.

Discretion and luxury are the watchwords at this award-winning hotel, which continues to be a favourite with the fashion and film crowd. No doubt they appreciate its location – slap-bang in the middle of the famous Golden Rectangle. The hotel is housed in a 15th-century convent, although you'd never know it – apart from the idyllic, cloistered courtyard that many of the rooms face on to. Each of the spacious guest rooms is individually designed, with Fortuny fabrics, and pear and sycamore wood furniture. Some suites have parts of the original frescoes, as do the library bar and lobby. The opulent marble bathrooms, kept toasty with underfloor heating, are well stocked with huge towels and plush bathrobes. The recently opened luxury spa, designed by architect Patricia Urquiola, has a swimming pool, fitness centre and seven treatment rooms (including a deluxe suite for couples), all housed beneath 19th-century vaulted brick ceilings.

Grand Hotel et de Milan

Via Manzoni 29 (02 723 141, www.grandhotel etdemilan.it). Metro Montenapoleone, or bus 61, 94, or tram 1. **Rooms** 95. Disabled access. **Map** p284 E6.

In an elegant 19th-century palazzo, the five-star Grand is as sumptuous as it gets: all marble, rich draperies and antiques. The gorgeous suites are named after illustrious past guests, such as Luchino Visconti, Maria Callas and Giuseppe Verdi (the composer lived in the hotel on and off for 27 years, and died here in 1901). The efficient service is as discreet as it is friendly. The room prices may seem shocking at first glance, but it's worth asking about weekend rates: you may be pleasantly surprised.

Seven Stars Galleria.

The refurbished bar is a relaxed place for a drink (the waiters still wheel in a trolley), and the Don Carlos restaurant next door, run by chef Angelo Gangemi, is one of the finest in the city.

Park Hyatt Milan

Via Tommaso Grossi 1 (02 8821 1234, www.milan.park.hyatt.com). Metro Cordusio or Duomo, or tram 1, 2, 3, 12, 14, 15, 16, 23, 24, 27. **Rooms** 108. Disabled access. **Map** p284 E6.

Carved out of an old bank building, the Park Hyatt is an exercise in serenity and elegant simplicity. The courtyard was covered over with glass to create a splendid top-lit lounge; the warm, beige rooms are equipped with generously proportioned bathrooms (around the same size as the sleeping area) and modern luxuries such as flatscreen TVs and free internet access. Relaxing treatments are available in the small spa, which has separate steam rooms for men and women. The Michelin-starred Ristorante VUN seats just 52, providing diners with an intimate, understated experience, while the hotel bar is a favourite spot for the fashionable Milanese crowd.

Seven Stars Galleria/TownHouse 8/ Seven Stars Duomo

Via Silvio Pellico 8 (02 8905 8297, www.townhousegalleria.it). Metro Duomo, or tram 1, 2, 3, 12, 14, 15, 16, 23, 24, 27. **Rooms** 9/26/14. Disabled access. **Map** p284 E6.

Queen of the TownHouse chain, Seven Stars Galleria, named for its star rating, is located above the Prada shop in Galleria Vittorio Emanuele II, and offers some of the most unashamedly luxurious service in Milan. All nine suites have a duplex loft, which is kitted out according to the guest's advance requests: suggestions include private gym, personal office or children's play area. The two most popular rooms are crowned with ceiling frescoes. Each features a view of the Galleria and has private butler service. On the floors above, TownHouse 8 has 26 similar rooms (14 of which opened in 2014), but no personal butler service; prices are adjusted accordingly. Around the corner, at piazza del Duomo 21, Seven Stars Duomo will open a further 14 butler-serviced rooms with terraces facing the Duomo by the end of 2014. The TownHouse's other operations range in price from moderate to expensive; check the website for details.

Other locations TownHouse 12, Piazza Gerusalemme 12, North (02 8907 8511); TownHouse 31, Via Goldoni 31, East (02 70 156); TownHouse 33, Via Goldoni 33, East (02 9143 7635).

Expensive

Gray

Via San Raffaele 6 (02 720 8951, www.hotelthegray.com). Metro Duomo, or tram 1, 2, 3, 12, 14, 15, 16, 23, 24, 27. **Rooms** 21. Disabled access. **Map** p284 E6.

The Gray, together with the STRAF (*see below*), was one of Milan's first boutique hotels. Despite the name (chosen by architect Guido Ciompi), little is half-tone here: the dominant colour scheme backs neutral hues with splashes of electrifying vibrancy. The clean-lined rooms – three of which look out on to Galleria Vittorio Emanuele II – are sleek, contemporary and equipped with enormous TVs and jacuzzis. One room has its own Turkish bath, and two have private gyms. The hotel also has its own chic restaurant, Le Noir.

STRAF

Via San Raffaele 3 (02 805 081, www.straf.it). Metro Duomo, or tram 1, 2, 3, 12, 14, 15, 16, 23, 24, 27. **Rooms** 64. Disabled access. **Map** p284 E6.

The STRAF is an upmarket hotel run by the family that manages the Grand Hotel et de Milan (*see p247*). The ultra-modern, minimalist rooms – by fashion designer and architect Vincenzo De Cotiis – have metallic, industrial overtones, and are equipped with electronic and audio-visual amenities galore. Its central location makes it an ideal base for shopping, but the weight of the bags won't get you down: the hotel offers an energy boost in the form of in-room mini spas, Japanese massage chairs, chromotherapy and aromatherapy. Other attractions include the excellent breakfast buffet and cooler-than-thou hotel bar (*see p54*). And for all its high-design atmosphere, the STRAF is a remarkably good deal for its category.

Moderate

Alle Meraviglie

Via San Tomaso 6 (02 805 1023, www.allemeraviglie.it). Metro Cairoli or Cordusio, or bus 61, or tram 1, 2, 12, 14, 16, 27. **Rooms** 6. **Map** p284 D6.

The *meraviglie* – or wonders – that await at this lovely B&B, just off via Dante, are six inviting rooms with bright white beds, lavish silk curtains and fresh flowers. (The bathrooms, on the other hand, are run of the mill, with basic showers and large bottles of everyday products.) Despite being set in a converted townhouse, with plenty of olde-worlde character, it also has up-to-date touches such as free Wi-Fi in each room (though not all have a TV). If you're planning to stay in town for a while, you might consider the Milanosuites, also run by Paola Ora and her team. These mini apartments, complete with cooking facilities, are available by the week or the month. The proprietors also own the Antica Locanda dei Mercanti next door, a less expensive, slightly more twee, option.

★ Palazzo Segreti

Via San Tomaso 8 (02 4952 9250, www.palazzosegreti.com). Metro Cairoli or Cordusio, or bus 50, 57, 61, or tram 1, 2, 4, 12, 14, 16, 27. **Rooms** 18. Disabled access. **Map** p284 D6.

Blink and you might miss the entrance to Palazzo Segreti, which is located just off via Dante, one of Milan's main shopping strips, connecting Piazza del Duomo to Castello Sforzesco. As its name suggests (*segreti* means 'secrets'), this boutique hotel in a historic palazzo doesn't want to be noticed: its subtle colour scheme (neutral with splashes of plum, mustard or electric blue), chiaroscuro lighting and air of quiet mystery create a sanctuary from the chaotic city just beyond its walls. Each of the 18 rooms is individually decorated in a modernist key, with furnishings by Moroso and Fritz Hansen, and spacious bathrooms; the Junior and Unique suites both have large, inviting bathtubs directly in the room. The cosy bar is perfect for relaxing with a glass of wine after a long day of trudging around Milan's hectic streets.

Rosa Grand

Piazza Fontana 3 (02 88 311, http://rosagrand.starhotels.com). Metro Duomo, or bus 54, or tram 12, 15, 23, 27. **Rooms** 327. Disabled access. **Map** p284 E7.

A prime location and reasonable tariffs are the reasons why most guests choose the Rosa Grand – just a short walk from the Duomo and corso Vittorio Emanuele II, the city's main shopping promenade. Part of the Starhotels chain, it's the largest hotel in the centre, with an entirely new wing of rooms and suites, built while the existing structure was upgraded in 2009 with glitzy decor jazzed up with rose-themed works by Italian photographer Maurizio Galimberti. The Grand Lounge & Bar is a popular *aperitivo* spot for guests and locals; for a sit-down dinner, try the modernised, Milanese cuisine at the hotel's Roses restaurant.

SFORZESCO & NORTH

Expensive

3Rooms

Corso Como 10 (02 626 163, www.3rooms-10corsocomo.com). Metro Garibaldi, or bus 37, or tram 33. **Rooms** 3. **Map** p280 D3/4.

You've browsed the boutique, gazed in the gallery and posed at the bar – and now you can even spend the night at Milan's multi-purpose style emporium, 10 Corso Como (*see p88*). Describing itself as a 'bed and breakfast', 3Rooms is actually three apartments,

Palazzo Segreti.

ESSENTIAL INFORMATION

each consisting of three rooms: bedroom, bathroom and living room (plus lots of closet space). Each apartment occupies an entire floor, overlooking the internal courtyard and tea garden, and is individually decorated, with furnishings handpicked from the iconic designers of the last century – Arne Jacobsen, Eero Saarinen, Charles and Ray Eames, Marcel Breuer and Sebastian Matta, among others. Be warned: there's no lift, and the apartments are on the second, third and fourth floors of the building. Needless to say, you should book far ahead.

Hotel Principe di Savoia

Piazza della Repubblica 17 (02 62 301, www.hotelprincipedisavoia.com). Metro Repubblica, or bus 37, or tram 1, 9, 33. **Rooms** 301. Disabled access. **Map** p281 F4.

Now part of the Dorchester Collection, the Principe's over-the-top marble foyer and reams of polished oak provide a fine antidote to Milan's proliferation of modern design hotels. Most of the rooms are stately and traditional, complete with lavish marble bathrooms and Acqua di Parma toiletries. Frank Sinatra, Robert De Niro and Madonna have all stayed in the presidential suite, which has its own pool. Staff are efficient and down-to-earth, and the gym is one of the best in Milan, with panoramic views of the city. As for dining options, you can enjoy a Murano chandelier-lit dinner at Acanto or an afternoon tea at the opulent Il Salotto, which was designed by architect Thierry Despont.

Westin Palace, Milan

Piazza della Repubblica 20 (02 63 361, www.westinpalacemilan.com). Metro Repubblica, or bus 37, or tram 1, 9, 33. **Rooms** 227. Disabled access. **Map** p281 F4.

Owned by Italian hoteliers Starwood, the Westin Palace manages to combine contemporary touches with unbridled luxury. Around 90 rooms were renewed in 2012, while a second batch will be revamped in summer 2014: do try to snare the ones with the new look by designer Irene Pansadoro, featuring snowy white linens against no-nonsense silver-grey bedheads and walls. The vibe is clean-lined classic with a hint of 1950s-influenced masculinity. Fitness freaks should book one of the rooms kitted out with treadmills or spinning bikes, while ten suites have private steam rooms. The hotel's location, on piazza della Repubblica, isn't its greatest asset, though its relative proximity to Stazione Centrale makes it convenient for those who need to move around. Look out for deals in the off-season, when prices may be lower than you expect.

Moderate

Antica Locanda Solferino

Via Castelfidardo 2 (02 657 0129, www.anticalocandasolferino.it). Metro Moscova, or bus 43, 94. **Rooms** 11. **Map** p281 E4.

This lovely hotel is set in a Napoleonic-era palazzo in the heart of the arty Brera district and was a favourite of Italian film legends Marcello Mastroianni and Federico Fellini. Each of the rooms features floor-to-ceiling windows, antique furniture and Daumier lithographs on the walls, creating the illusion that you've stepped into a corner of 19th-century Milan. Reserve well in advance and ask for a room at the rear of the building if you're a light sleeper, or one of the five balcony rooms on the front.

Maison Moschino

Viale Monte Grappa 12 (02 2900 9858, www.maisonmoschino.com). Metro Porta Garibaldi, or bus 37, 43, or tram 33. **Rooms** 65. Disabled access. **Map** p281 E4.

Milan-based fashion house Moschino, which is famed for its quirky, often ironic sense of style, transformed this disused 19th-century neoclassical train station into a boutique hotel while keeping the impressive original facade. But it's the highly photogenic interiors that have made it popular with the fashion crowd. The 65 rooms follow one of 16 whimsical themes, and have names such as Alice's Room, the Forest, and Sleeping in a Ballgown. Furniture includes pastry-shaped pillows, trees as bedposts and tables shaped like giant teacups. Be warned, however, that some of the lower-priced rooms are a little cramped. The hotel restaurant is being revamped and should reopen in late 2014, or you can head just down the road to corso Como for an endless choice of trendy bars and restaurants.

Budget

★ LaFavia Four Rooms

Via Carlo Farini 4 (mobile 347 784 2212, www.lafavia4rooms.com). Bus 37, 94, or tram 2, 4, 12, 14, 33. **Rooms** 4. **Map** p280 D3.

Owners Fabio and Marco collected ideas and inspiration from their travels around the world and poured them wholeheartedly into this quaint little B&B. The four rooms, in a 19th-century palazzo, are

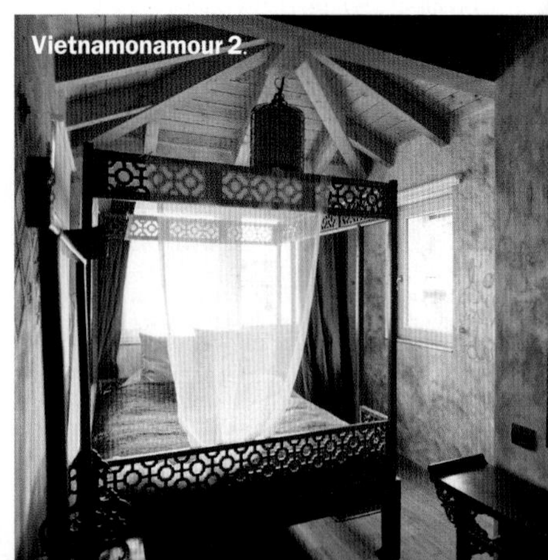
Vietnamonamour 2.

Magna Pars Suites. *See p252.*

decorated with impeccable taste, blending modern and multicultural elements to create distinctive, beautiful spaces alongside a veranda and spacious roof garden. Barceloneta and LaIndia mix 1970s lamps, retro sofas and hand-woven Indian rugs in mellow tones; Oaxaca and LaPalmera feature bold Manuel Canovas 1960s wallpapers in zesty orange and green. In an effort to offset emissions, the owners plant trees in Costa Rica and follow eco-friendly practices such as serving purified rather than bottled water and keeping two bicycles for guest use. Breakfast includes organic produce and, when in season, oranges from the owners' own citrus grove in Cimitale (in the province of Naples).

Vietnamonamour 2

Via Taramelli 67 (02 7063 4614, www. vietnamonamour.com). Metro Zara, or bus 60, or tram 7, 31, 33. **Rooms** 4. Disabled access. **Map** p281 E1.

French-Vietnamese fashion stylist Christiane Blanchet and her Italian husband, Dario Arlunno, opened their second B&B in October 2013, with four rooms above a Vietnamese restaurant. In an eye-popping pink villa on the fringe of the artsy Isola zone, the property feels decidedly more Asian than its sister structure, Vietnamonamour 1 (*see p252*), in the Piola/Loreto neighbourhood. Bright colours and quirky details – such as patchworks of Vietnamese printed papers and ribbons, or a collection of miniature oriental keys – bring a slice of the East to this fashionable, yet relatively tranquil, part of Milan.

SAN BABILA & EAST

Expensive

Sheraton Diana Majestic

Viale Piave 42 (02 20 581, www.sheraton.com/dianamajestic). Metro Porta Venezia, or tram 9, 23. **Rooms** 107. Disabled access. **Map** p281 G5.

This four-star art nouveau hotel is named after Milan's first public swimming pool, which opened on this site in 1842. The pool has since been replaced with a garden and the first of the city's many summertime outdoor cocktail bars, HClub (*see p104*). The homely 1920s feel, apparent as you push through the revolving door, is period luxury – not faded grandeur. The resolutely old-fashioned rooms feature deco-style curtains and original furniture. The best are on the third and fourth floors, with garden views.

Moderate

Foresteria Monforte

Piazza Tricolore 2 (mobile 340 237 0272, www. foresteriamonforte.it). Bus 54, 61, or tram 9, 23. **Rooms** 3. **Map** p281 G6.

Foresteria Monforte is a contemporary take on bed-and-breakfasting with three colour-coded guest rooms that combine high-end design pieces with the odd antique: the cream one is an upmarket suite; the antique-filled brown is more classic; the purple is stylishly modern. All overlook the tree-lined piazza below. Visitors can use the espresso pots and cheeseboards in the petite shared kitchen at any time, although the lack of space means that breakfast in bed is compulsory. The concierge/proprietor is the English-speaking pharmacist downstairs.

Budget

★ RossoSegnale

Via Sacchini 18 (02 2952 7453, www.rossosegnale. it). Metro Loreto, or bus 39, 55, 56, 62, 81, 90, 91. **Rooms** 3.

Named after the bright red elevator and stairwell that ascends through the centre of the building, RossoSegnale seamlessly blends art with hospitality. Every couple of months, the B&B's three rooms and public spaces – including a garden, a terrace and an art gallery – are hung with the works of a new artist from territories as diverse as Europe and the Far East. The three rooms cater to different tastes, so make sure you pick the one best suited to you: Bianconeve is a study in minimalist monochrome; Giallonovecento channels travel of yore; while Rosaconiglio features pink rabbits and hints of Japan. The changing atmosphere is as dynamic as the owners, Alberto and Raoul, whose passion for all things visual is only equalled by their desire to make your stay as enjoyable as possible. Tap them for their highly personalised suggestions on where to eat and what to do.

★ Vietnamonamour 1

Via Pestalozza 7 (02 7063 4614, www.vietnamonamour.com). Metro Piola, or bus 39, 55, 62, 81, 90, 91. **Rooms** 4.

An aura of complete calm pervades this Italian-Vietnamese concept B&B located within an early 1900s villa in one of Milan's quietest streets. Hardwood floors and heavy furniture imported from South-east Asia decorate the guest rooms, and the walls are covered in pink floral patterns, earthy colour washes or bare brick. Breakfast – orange juice, green tea, home-made mango or ginger cake – in the covered garden is a delight. The eponymous restaurant downstairs serves creative Vietnamese cuisine with Italian and French wines. The owners have recently opened a second B&B, Vietnamonamour 2 (*see p251*).

PORTA ROMANA & SOUTH

Expensive

★ Magna Pars Suites

Via Forcella 6 (02 833 8371, www.magnaparssuitesmilano.it). Metro Porta Genova, or tram 3, 9. **Rooms** 28. Disabled access. **Map** p282 B8.

Room-specific floral or wood aromas greet guests as they enter any of the 28 rooms at Magna Pars Suites, located in a former perfume factory in Milan's design-led Tortona zone. Owned by the Martone scent and cosmetics family, the suites are named after fragrant plants (gardenia, rosewood, vetiver) and feature white-and-wood decor, pillow menus and spectacular contemporary botanical paintings by students from the city's Brera Academy. The Martone's daughter, Giorgia, who passes by the hotel most days, designed the bespoke Aqua Adornationis bathroom products, featuring orange essence, sandalwood and musk. The family also provided the collection of 6,000 leather-bound antique volumes (from Dickens to Tolstoy), which guests can borrow from the ground-floor lounge/library. The olfactory experience continues at the Da Noi In restaurant (*see p126*), which overlooks a compact but intense botanical garden containing 1,500 scented plants.

Petit Palais Hotel de Charme

Via Molino delle Armi 1 (02 584 891, www.petitpalais.it). Bus 94, or tram 3, 15. **Rooms** 18. **Map** p282 D8.

Close to one of Milan's most important canals, this 17th-century palazzo opened as the Petit Palais in 2007, after more than five years of restoration. It's a luxurious property and no expense has been spared, from the Murano chandeliers to the crystal wine glasses. The exquisite top-floor suites have roof terraces for your own private view of the (somewhat distant) Duomo; the hotel is a 15-minute walk from the city centre, yet peacefully far from the crowds.

Moderate

★ Maison Borella

Alzaia Naviglio Grande 8 (02 5810 9114, www.hotelmaisonborella.com). Bus 167, or tram 3, 9. **Rooms** 25. Disabled access. **Map** p282 C9.

This canalside boutique hotel was created from the restoration of a *casa ringhiera*, an apartment building with shared balconies, typical of Milan. Old blends seamlessly with new in the interiors, which mix classic elements such as hardwood floors and visible ceiling beams with contemporary furniture. The intimate atmosphere is a welcome antidote to the bohemian bedlam along the canals – though several of the rooms have *naviglio*-facing balconies, offering picturesque views and the chance to people-watch. The hotel's restaurant, Turbigo (*see p128*), is open all day and serves typical Italian dishes with a modern twist.

NHOW

Via Tortona 35 (02 489 8861, www.nhow-hotels.com). Metro Porta Genova, or bus 74, 90, 91. **Rooms** 246. Disabled access. **Map** p282 A9.

On Milan's design-centric via Tortona, the highly contemporary NHOW sits in the shell of the city's former General Electrics factory. From the polished concrete lobby up to the fourth floor, the hotel is dotted with a rotating selection of artworks and limited-edition furniture. Rooms are decked out with Artemide lights and funky printed wallpaper, and showers are colourful. Exhibitionists should book the Presidential Suite, complete with a glass-bottomed bathtub that acts as part of the living room's ceiling.

★ Yard

Piazza XXIV Maggio 8 (02 8941 5901, www.theyardmilano.com). Metro Porta Genova, or tram 3, 9. **Rooms** 28. Disabled access. **Map** p282 C9.

Once a discotheque, this bright red, low-rise structure close to the Darsena (canal port) is now a 28-room hotel, with the feel of an eccentric gentlemen's club. The lobby is crammed with sports- and travel-related objets – from vintage Louis Vuitton trunks, to top hats and riding boots, to backgammon sets, all of it for sale. The rooms also have sporting themes, from hunting to polo to golf. Furnishings are mostly monochrome, though details vary: 'Lodge' has pictures of east African animals; 'Cambridge' has an oar above the bed. Not surprisingly, the place has been discovered by celebrities looking for a hideaway, though the management won't reveal exactly who. Try to book one of the rooms with terraces overlooking the quiet courtyard – surely among the most desirable accommodations in all of Milan.

SLEEP IN A SHOP

Stay in a converted shop or office – right in the heart of Milan.

TownHouse Street Milano Goldoni.

Milan-based TownHouse is usually associated with the unbounded luxury available at its private butler-serviced Seven Stars Galleria hotel (*see p248*), but the group also caters to less affluent visitors anxious to claim their quotient of Milanese style. The 'Street' project began in 2010, just east of Porta Venezia, with four independent short-stay apartments in former shops.

Guests at **Townhouse Street Milano Goldoni** check into the nearby TownHouse 31 hotel (at via Goldoni 31), where they're shown to their apartment and given a door code. Designed by Simone Micheli, each apartment has giant photographs of Milanese street scenes papered on the walls, and custom-designed furniture in eye-popping shades of red, yellow, orange or green. The effect is ultra-hip urban chic, of the sort only to be found in Milan. Curious passers-by might press their noses against the streetside, shop-sized windows – but the one-way filters prevent them from seeing anything. If you want breakfast, it's available (for a fee) at TownHouse 31 – but otherwise, guests don't need to pass back through reception until it's time to pay.

The second Street initiative opened in 2012. Named **TownHouse Street Milano Duomo**, it's close to the cathedral, in a former office block in via Radegonda – above the Luini *panzerotti* takeaway restaurant (*see p54*). The seven apartments are similar in style to those in via Goldoni, but with a sunny yellow colour scheme. Here, check-in, check-out and breakfast (for a fee) are at the nearby Seven Stars Galleria hotel. None of the rooms is at ground level, so you won't have window-shoppers gazing in; but since Luini attracts queues of youngsters, stretching round the block, it's not the place for those for whom silence is a priority.

Costing €250-€500 per apartment per night, both locations are great value for money – especially for small groups, or for families of up to four people. And you'll certainly feel like you've got your finger on the throbbing pulse of Milan.

★ TownHouse Street Milano Duomo
Via Santa Radegonda 14 (02 8905 8297, www.townhouse.it). Metro Duomo, or tram 1, 2, 3, 12, 14, 15, 16, 23, 24, 27. **Map** p284 E6.

★ TownHouse Street Milano Goldoni
Via Goldoni 33 (02 9143 7635, www.townhouse.it). Bus 54, 61, or tram 9, 23. **Map** p282 H6.

TownHouse Street Milano Duomo.

ESSENTIAL INFORMATION

Budget

★ Cocoon

Via Voghera (02 832 2769, www.cocoonbb.com). Metro Porta Genova, or tram 3, 9. **Rooms** 3. Disabled access. **Map** p282 B8.

A scarlet-hued former cement factory, on a street flanked by colourful workers' cottages, is home to this design-led B&B. The ground-floor rooms have muted colour schemes and Cole & Son floral wallpapers. The spacious Red room faces the grassy inner courtyard; White and Gray look on to the sleepy street. Mia Buzzi, the architect owner, lives across the courtyard and can offer great advice on restaurants and shops.

SANT'AMBROGIO & WEST

Moderate

Antica Locanda Leonardo

Corso Magenta 78 (02 4801 4197, www.antica locandaleonardo.com). Metro Conciliazione, or bus 58, 68, or tram 16. **Rooms** 16. **Map** p282 B6.

This immaculate little hotel is set in an internal courtyard off busy Corso Magenta. The property is in a late 19th-century palazzo, and the rooms are all tastefully decorated with modern or antique wooden furniture (some have a Japanese feel to them, as a nod to one of the owners). There's also a cosy breakfast/bar area where tea and cakes are served. The hotel has been managed by the same courteous family for more than 40 years, and it shows in the attention to detail. Five rooms overlook the flower-filled back garden.

Hotel Palazzo delle Stelline

Corso Magenta 61 (02 481 8431, www.hotel palazzostelline.it). Metro Cadorna or Conciliazione, or bus 50, 58, 94, or tram 1, 16, 27. **Rooms** 105. Disabled access. **Map** p282 B6.

This hotel and conference centre is housed in a beautiful 16th-century monastery that has maintained, to this day, the historical architecture that renders it one of the most important cultural sites of Milan. Arched cloisters overlooking a grass courtyard and a huge magnolia tree offer total privacy, cocooned from the hubbub of the city. Somewhat businessy, the rooms are functional and comfortable – though don't quite match the promise of the exceptional surrounds. Breakfast is served with a view of the internal garden and includes sugar- and gluten-free foods. Leonardo da Vinci is said to have grown vines on this site while painting *The Last Supper* at the Santa Maria delle Grazie monastery across the road.

Budget

★ Ostello Bello

Via Medici 4 (02 3658 2720, www.ostellobello.com). Tram 2, 14. **Rooms** 10. Disabled access. **Map** p282 C7.

Founded by three young entrepreneurs who'd done their fair share of budget travel, Ostello Bello is the living proof that staying in a hostel doesn't have to be synonymous with hardship and sacrifice. The 60 beds are spread across ten rooms filled with vintage furniture, each with its own bathroom. The list of amenities and services will get even the most hardened backpacker rubbing their hands in glee: expect free Wi-Fi, air-conditioning, a terrace with hammocks, musical instruments, free local SIM cards and a 24-hour reception, among many other thoughtful bonuses. A series of events – from open mic evenings to Pearl Jam tribute bands to a monthly vintage market – provide a great way to meet the natives without it all becoming a terrible strain.

Ostello Bello.

Getting Around

ARRIVING & LEAVING

By air

Aeroporto di Malpensa (MXP)
02 7485 2200, www.milano malpensa-airport.com.
Milan's intercontinental airport is about 50km (32 miles) from the centre of Milan. Terminal 1 is for intercontinental, international and domestic flights. Terminal 2 is for budget airlines.

Trenord's **Malpensa Express train** (800 500 005, www.malpensa express.it) runs at 23 and 53 minutes past the hour from 6.53am to 9.53pm daily between Malpensa (Terminal 1 only) and Milan Cadorna station (journey time 40mins), stopping at Busto Arsizio, Saronno and Bovisa/ Politecnico. Tickets (€12) can be bought from ticket booths or vending machines and must be stamped in the ticket machines on the platform before boarding.

The train is replaced by a non-stop bus service (50mins) in the early morning (4.20am and 5am from Cadorna, and 5.53am from Malpensa) and evening (9-10.30pm from Cadorna, and 10pm-1.30am from Malpensa). Terminals 1 and 2 are connected by a shuttle bus.

Two **bus** services link Malpensa to Milan. The **Malpensa Bus Express** (02 240 7954, www.caronte.eu) departs every 30mins (6am-12.30am from Malpensa, and 4am-11.30pm from Stazione Centrale) and takes 75 minutes. Tickets cost €10 and are available in the arrivals terminals or on the bus. The service also stops at Terminal 2. The **Malpensa Shuttle** (0331 258 411, www.malpensashuttle.it) departs every 20mins (5am-12.15am) from Terminal 1 (10mins later at Terminal 2), journey time 40mins; and 3.45am-12.30am from Stazione Centrale, journey time 50mins. Tickets (€7) can be bought in the airport arrivals halls or on the bus. Malpensa Shuttle also runs ten shuttle bus services a day each way between Malpensa Terminal 1 and Linate airport (journey time 70mins), with request stops at Terminal 2. Tickets (€10) can be bought on board.

Taxis from Malpensa to Milan operate on a fixed fee of €90. Mention this when getting into the cab. Journey time is 45mins, more in rush hour. Use only official white taxis at the ranks. Ignore anyone who asks if you need a cab as you head towards the line.

Aeroporto di Linate (LIN)
Flight information 02 7485 2200, switchboard 02 74 851, www.milano linate-airport.com.
Milan's city airport is just 7km (4.5 miles) from the city centre. Domestic and European flights arrive and depart from here.

The **ATM city bus** service 73 leaves every ten minutes for San Babila metro station. Travel time is around 25mins (40mins in rush hour). An ordinary €1.50 city bus ticket, available at the newstand in the arrivals hall, is valid.

Starfly buses (02 5858 7237, www.airportbusexpress.com, www.autostradale.it) depart every 30mins (15mins at peak times) from Linate airport for Stazione Centrale (7.45am-10.45pm from Linate, and 5.30am-10pm from Stazione Centrale). Tickets cost €5 and can be bought on board.

A city ordinance sets the minimum **taxi** fare, to or from Linate, at €13 – but expect to pay €20-€25.

Aeroporto di Orio al Serio (BGY)
035 326 323, www.orioaeroporto.it.
Bergamo's airport is in Orio al Serio, about 45km (28 miles) from Milan and 5km (3 miles) from Bergamo. It's Italy's fourth-busiest airport, handling national, international and budget airline flights. Its largest carrier is Ryanair (899 678 910, www.ryanair.com), serving 51 destinations year-round and another 22 seasonally.

From the airport, the **ATB bus** 1C (035 236 026, www.atb.bergamo.it) services Bergamo train station every 30mins, 5am-midnight (journey time 10mins), for €1.65. A **taxi** into Bergamo will cost about €20. **Trains** leave regularly from Bergamo station for Milan Stazione Centrale or Milan Garibaldi. Prices vary, starting at €5; journey time is about 1hr.

Autostradale buses (information 02 7200 1304, www.autostradale.it) run 7.45am-11.30pm daily from Orio al Serio to Milan's Stazione Centrale, and 2.45am-11.15pm in the other direction. Tickets can be bought on board and cost €8.90 (three tickets €17.80).

Orioshuttle buses (035 319 366, www.orioshuttle.com) run 3am-11.40am from Orio al Serio to Stazione Centrale; same times back. Journey time 1hr. Tickets cost €8 and can be bought on the bus, or from Orioshuttle staff at the airport. During trade fairs, Orioshuttle provides buses from the airport to Rho Fiera, the Milan fairgrounds complex, at the following times: 8.45am, 9.15am, 10.30am from Orio al Serio, and 3pm, 4.15pm, 5.45pm back.

With no special Milan city ordinances in place for Orio al Serio airport, which comes under the jurisdiction of the city of Bergamo, **taxi** fares are subject to negotiation and will not cost less than €100.

By rail

International and long-distance train services arrive at and depart from Milan's Stazione Centrale and Stazione Garibaldi. Railway stations, especially Centrale, are a pickpocket's paradise, so keep a careful eye on your possessions. Keep a close eye on your luggage to avoid being scammed. If you arrive late in the evening, it's advisable to take a taxi to your destination. Note that taxi ranks are now at the sides of the station. For more on train travel, *see p260*.

By coach

Long-distance buses use the central bus station, located close to Lampugnano metro stop (02 300 891, via Giulio Natta, line 1, red). Two companies operate from here: **Autostradale** (02 7200 1304, www.autostradale.it) runs a Milan–Turin service, while **Eurolines** (www.eurolines.it) serves a number of European cities.

PUBLIC TRANSPORT

For a transport map, *see p288*; for assistance for disabled travellers, *see p261*.

Milan's public transport company is the **Azienda Trasporti Milanesi** (ATM, 800 808 181, www.atm-mi.it). The city's extensive network includes four metropolitan railway lines (the metro), an urban railway (the *passante*), buses, trolley buses and Milan's famous trams. Transport maps are available on the ATM website, or you can download a

free app (iATM – iOS, ATM Mobile – Android), which includes a bus and metro map, bus and tram stops, timetables, routes and ticket information). It also provides locations of the citywide BikeMi bike-rental service (*see p260*).

Public transport in Milan is fairly safe, even at night. Watch out for pickpockets in packed buses and subways.

Metro & rail

Milan's **metro** and **urban railway** lines are numbered, but are also identified by colour (most people use the colours): **1 rossa** (red), **2 verde** (green), **3 gialla** (yellow), **4 passante** (blue) and **5 lilla** (lilac).

Stations are signposted with a red 'M', except for the *passante* (line 4) which is indicated by the letter 'R' above ground. As well as providing a link between metro stations inside the city, the *passante* serves as a suburban and regional railway, connecting Milan to the towns of Novara, Pavia, Varese, Lodi, Treviglio and Gallarate.

Metro trains run every 4-5mins, 6am-12.30am daily; after 9pm, services run every 10-12mins. Metro lines 1, 2, 3 and 5 operate until 12.30am Mon-Thur and Sun. On Fri and Sat, night buses replace 15 lines (including metros 1, 2 and 3) until normal service resumes at 6am.

Buses & trams

The city centre is circled by three concentric ring roads, two of which are served by public transport. **Buses** 50, 58, 61 and 94 cover portions of the inner ring, while **trolley buses** 90, 91 and 92 ply the outer ring. Many **trams** cut across the city, intersecting the ring roads and continuing into outlying or suburban areas. These include the 1, which runs from Stazione Centrale in the north to many tourist spots, such as via Manzoni, piazza della Scala, piazza Duomo, via Torino, corso Genova and ripa di Porta Ticinese in the southern Navigli zone.

Bus and tram services operate between 6am and midnight daily, departing every 5-20mins. Board the bus or tram via the doors marked *Entrata*; to alight, head for a door marked *Uscita*. All stops are by request. If you want to get off, and no other passenger has done so, press the red button by the exit doors.

Bus stops show routes, and timetables for weekdays (*feriali*), Saturdays (*sabato/pre-festivi*) as well as Sundays and holidays (*domenica e festivi*). Public transport operates a reduced service in summer, when schools close and many residents go on holiday.

Fares & tickets

Tickets must be bought before boarding your bus or tram. Get these from a *tabaccheria* (*see p265*), bar, or newsstand close to the stop. They can also be purchased at metro stations (ticket machines), or from the five ATM points, which are open 7.45am-7.15pm Mon-Sat, and are located at stations Duomo, Loreto, Stazione Centrale, Cadorna, Garibaldi and Romolo.

Each ticket is valid for 90mins on any tram or bus on the inner-city network (for map, *see p288*), plus one trip on the metro. If you're likely to use up to ten tickets, then buy a carnet – costing €13.80; this offers a small discount on the standard €1.50 ticket. The carnet is also worthwhile because finding somewhere that sells tickets after 8pm is an arduous task. Getting caught without a ticket means an on-the-spot fine.

When you board a tram or bus, stamp your ticket in one of the machines by the rear, middle or front doors. In the metro, swipe your ticket in the machine as you go both in and out.

If you're attending an event at the Milan Fairgrounds Complex and want to take the metro to get there (Rho Fiera, red line) you need a special 'extra-urban' ticket (*biglietto extra-urbana*). This costs €2.55 single, €5 return. If you don't have the right ticket, you may be fined. Note, inspectors may be in plain clothes.

TAXIS

Licensed taxis are white and meter-operated. If a driver approaches you at the airport, Stazione Centrale or any of the major tourist spots muttering 'Taxi?', always refuse: these are likely to be unlicensed cars.

The vast majority of Milan's taxi drivers are honest; if, however, you suspect you're being ripped off, make a note of the driver's name and number. Report misdemeanours to the drivers' co-operative (the number is on the outside of each car) or, in serious cases, the police.

Taxi ranks

There is no tradition of hailing cabs in Italy. You need to go to a taxi rank (or phone – *see right*). Ranks are indicated by a white sign with 'Taxi' in black. If a taxi is not present, you can phone for one. There are taxi ranks at railway stations, as well as piazza Duomo, via Manzoni/corner of via Pisoni, largo Augusto, largo Carrobbio, via Cordusio and piazza Fontana. For a more detailed list of taxi ranks, see www.taxitam.it.

Calling a taxi

The main taxi services in Milan are:

Radio Taxi *02 8585.*
Taxi Blu *02 4040.*
Yellow Taxi *02 6969.*

There is no guarantee that the operator will speak anything but the most basic English. Once you have stated your pick-up address, the operator will give you the taxi code (usually a location and a number – for example, Como 69). This is painted on the side of the taxi, and provides confirmation that this is the cab you ordered. You will also be told how long you will have to wait (*tre minuti* – three minutes, say). Note that the meter starts running from the time the taxi sets off to pick you up. Milan's taxi services are usually rapid and efficient, but if you are using a taxi at rush hour, during a major event or in bad weather, order well in advance.

Fares

When you pick up a taxi at a rank, the meter should read zero. As you set off, it will indicate the minimum fare – €5 at time of writing – for the first 200m, after which the charge increases according to time and distance. Minimum fare on Sundays, public holidays and at night (9pm-6am) is €6.50.

Only a few Milan taxis are equipped with credit-card facilities, so it's best to have cash ready, just in case. Most drivers prefer lower-denomination notes. A receipt is not automatically generated. If you need one, ask for '*la ricevuta, per cortesia*'. You are under no obligation to leave a tip. If the fare comes to €12.50, for example, round it up to €13.

DRIVING

Visitors should have no trouble driving with their home licences, although if they are in different scripts or less common languages, an international licence can be useful. Driving licences from other EU states are valid in Italy, and there is no legal obligation to convert them. Other licences must be converted after the owner has been resident in Italy for one year. Full details at Automobile Club d'Italia (*see p259*).

Italy's system of points (*punti*) brings the country's road legislation in line with the rest of Europe, albeit in the opposite fashion. In Italy, you have 20 points to start with. Traffic cops deduct a certain number of points for infringements such as speeding, jumping red lights and so on.

Short-term visitors should be aware that driving in Milan can be challenging. Parking is difficult, and the centre of the city is subject to a congestion charge. Local drivers are sharp-witted and unforgiving, and expect the same of everyone else on the road. Trams can also be a hazard for new drivers.

Restricted areas

A congestion charge operates within the area delimited by the inner ring road (Cerchia dei Navigli). This is known as 'Area C'. As you enter this section of town, your number plate will be photographed. You then have 24 hours to pay the daily €5 charge. When you park, find a machine (grey, with a white 'P' on a blue background), where you will be asked to punch in your licence-plate number. If you're driving to a hotel, call ahead and ask if the hotel staff can arrange for the payment to be made on your behalf. Alternatively, you can pay online, before or after you enter the area. For further details, see http://areac.atm-mi.it.

Large areas of the inner city (for example, via Dante to piazza Duomo) are pedestrianised and can only be accessed by taxi or on public transport.

As a measure to combat pollution and raise awareness of the benefits of not driving in Milan, some Sundays are no-car days – these are usually advertised well in advance online and in local media. However, for economic reasons, these are increasingly rare.

Breakdown services

National motoring organisations, such as the AA or RAC in Britain, or the AAA in the US, can arrange reciprocal agreements with the **Automobile Club d'Italia** (ACI, corso Venezia 43, 02 77 451, www.aci.it), or **Europ Assistance** (piazza Trento 8, 02 583 841, www.europassistance.it). Check the details with your own motoring organisation before you leave home.

If you're not a member of a national motoring association, Europ Assistance's emergency breakdown number (803 803) could prove useful.

Parking

Parking in Milan is a complete nightmare: it's best to leave your car in one of the 20 or so supervised car parks. For a list, visit www.tuttocitta.it/parcheggi/milano.

Alternatively, use the Sosta Milano parking system, which operates in most of the city. You can park for up to two hours in the spaces marked within blue lines (those within yellow lines are strictly 'residents only'). Buy tickets (€2 per hour) at newsstands, *tabaccherie* (*see p265*) or at the ATM points in Duomo and Cadorna metro stations, and scratch them to indicate the date and time. Leave the ticket visible on the dashboard.

Parking is generally free after 7pm except within the inner ring road area (Area C), where fees apply 24/7. Cars with disabled signs can park free within blue lines.

Watch out for signs by entrances saying '*passo carrabile*' (entrance)or '*sosta vietata*' (no parking), and road signs denoting spaces reserved for disabled drivers. The sign '*zona rimozione*' (tow-away area) means precisely what it says.

Weekly street cleaning provides another obstacle to overnight on-street parking. Signs will tell you when streets are to be cleaned – and this means from midnight onwards of that day. If your car is found parked on the road at that time, expect a €50 fine. Your car may also be towed away (*see below*).

In some areas, self-appointed *parcheggiatori* will look after your car for a small fee. The practice is illegal, but it's often worth coughing up to ensure your tyres remain intact.

Car pounds

If you can't find your car, chances are it's been towed away. There's an information office staffed by the *polizia locale* in via Beccaria 19. It's open 24hrs; call 02 7727 0280 quoting your number plate, car model and where the car was last seen and they'll tell you which car pound it has been taken to. It costs €140 to recover your car, on top of a fine of €80.

Fuel

Petrol stations (*distributori*) sell unleaded petrol (*senza piombo* or *verde*) and diesel (*gasolio*). Many stations offer full service on weekdays until 7pm; they may close for lunch. Self-service pumps accept €5, €10 or €20 notes in good condition. Most stations accept credit cards.

Car hire

You must be over 21 (in some cases, 23) to hire a car, and have held a licence for at least one year. It's advisable to take out collision damage waiver (CDW/*franchigia*) and personal accident insurance on top of basic third-party cover. Avoid car rental companies that do not offer CDW.

Please note when calling companies that, if the answering machine responds, it's unlikely that there's an English-language option.

Avis/Budget

National bookings 06 452 108 391, www.avisautonoleggio.it. **Open** 24hrs daily.
Linate airport 02 715 123. **Open** 7am-midnight daily.
Malpensa airport 02 585 8481. **Open** 8am-midnight daily.
Piazza Diaz 6, Centre 02 8901 0645. Metro Duomo or bus 54. **Open** 8am-7pm Mon-Fri; 8am-2pm Sat. **Map** p284 E7.
Via Gasparotto 4, North (02 6707 0884). Stazione Centrale. **Open** 8am-1pm, 2-7pm Mon-Fri; 8am-1pm Sat. **Map** p281 F2.

Hertz

National bookings 199 113 311, www.hertz.it. **Open** 8am-11pm daily.
Linate airport 02 7020 0256. **Open** 7.30am-12.30am daily.
Malpensa airport 02 5858 1081. **Open** 7.30am-midnight daily.
Via Cappellini 10, North (02 6698 5151). Stazione Centrale. **Open** 8am-8pm Mon-Fri; 8am-2pm Sat, Sun. **Map** p281 F3.

Car-sharing

Car-sharing has arrived in Milan in recent years. The service known as **E-vai** (www.e-vai.com) – operated by the Trenord railway company (www.trenord.it) and ENI (www.eni.it) – offers electric cars from Milan Cadorna (8am-5pm Mon-Fri; 9am-6pm Sat, Sun) and 50 other locations, including railway stations on the Trenord network and Linate and Malpensa airports (Terminal 1). Cars can be rented for a minimum of one hour and a maximum of seven days. There's no annual subscription and customers can sign up online from abroad. Costs start at €5 an hour; when the rental exceeds 12 hours, the cost is €60 a day. Cars can be returned to a destination that differs from the pick-up, for which there is an extra €15 charge.

Three other conventionally fuelled car-sharing services operate from

Cadorna. If you have a subscription to **Car2Go** (www.car2go.com) in your own country, then you can use it in Milan. As for the other two services, ATM's **GuidaMI** (www.atm.it/it/guidami) involves a €200 annual subscription, while ENI's **Enjoy** (www.enjoy.eni.com) service requires an Italian social-security number and is intended for residents.

BICYCLES & MOTORBIKES

Aggressive drivers, tram tracks and cobbled streets make Milan tough on cyclists, though increased pedestrianisation of the central areas has helped somewhat. Where they exist, cycle paths tend to end abruptly and you'll have to brave the traffic.

Bicycles are allowed on the metro after 8pm on weekdays, after 10am on Saturdays and all day Sundays, holidays and during August. There's an extra €1 charge and you have to use the second, fifth or last carriage of the train. Bikes can also be taken on all direct, regional and inter-regional trains for €3.50.

Bike & motorbike hire

To rent a scooter, moped (*motorino*) or motorbike, you'll need a credit card, ID and a cash deposit. Helmets are required. For bicycle hire, it's normally enough to leave ID; for mopeds up to 50cc, you need to be over 14; a driver's licence is needed for anything over 50cc.

AWS Bicimotor *Via Ponte Seveso 33, North (02 6707 2145, www.awsbici.com). Metro Centrale or Sondrio, or bus 90, 91, 92.* **Open** 9am-1pm, 3-7pm Tue-Sat. **Rates** €15/24hrs, minimum 3 days; then €2.60/additional day; €100 deposit. **Map** p281 G2.
City, mountain and electric bikes.

Biancoblu *Via Novara 131, West (02 308 2430, www.biancoblu.com). Metro Gambara then bus 80.* **Open** 9am-12.30pm, 2.30-7pm Mon-Fri; 8-9am, 6-8pm Sat; 8-10am, 6-8pm Sun. **Rates** €26/day; deposit 30% of total.
Scooters and motorcycles (including BMW).

Cicli Rossignoli *Corso Garibaldi 65-71, North (02 804 960, www.rossignoli.it). Metro Moscova, or bus 41, 43, 94, or tram 2, 4.* **Open** 2.30-7.30pm Mon; 9am-12.30pm, 2.30-7.30pm Tue-Sat. **Rates** €6/half day; €10/day; €18/wknd; deposit €50. **Map** p280 D5.
City bikes.

Mototouring *Via del Ricordo 31, East (02 2720 1556, www.mototouring.com). Metro Crescenzago then bus 53.* **Open** 9am-6pm Mon-Sat. **Rates** €63-€160/day; from €1,000 deposit.
Bicycles, motorbikes and scooters.

Bike-sharing

Milan's bicycle-sharing scheme is called **BikeMi** (www.bikemi.it). Register using your mobile phone and a credit card (no debit cards), and rent a bike for 50c an hour, first 30mins free (maximum two hours at a time). Exceed the limit and a €2 per hour penalty kicks in. Weekly and annual subscriptions also available. There are bike stations across the city centre – the website has a map.

REGIONAL RAIL

Train services

Mainline train services out of Milan are mostly operated by **Ferrovie dello Stato** (FS, aka Trenitalia), leaving from Stazione Centrale and Garibaldi.

Two other companies also run services from Milan. The privately run **Italo** operates a high-speed service out of Garibaldi and Milan Rogoredo to/from Rome, covering the 662km (411 miles) in just under 3hrs. Italo also serves Turin, Venice, Padua, Bologna, Florence, Naples and Salerno.

Trenord (previously known as Ferrovie Nord) uses Milan's Cadorna station as its base and runs local and regional services to 120 stations in Lombardy and Piedmont, including Como Nord and Varese Nord, as well as the Malpensa Express airport service (*see p255*). Trenord also operates the Brescia–Edolo service, which skirts Lake Iseo.

Ferrovie dello Stato *892 021, 06 6847 5475 (from outside Italy), www.trenitalia.it.* **Open** 7am-9pm daily.

Italo *06 0708, www.italotreno.it.* **Open** 6am-11pm daily.

Trenord *02 7249 4949, www.trenord.it.* **Open** 7am-9pm daily.

Fares & tickets

Tickets for both FS and Trenord trains can be bought at the relevant stations, at the ticket office or ticket machines. Expect long lines at the former, and temperamental technology at the latter. If you're approached by someone asking if they can help you purchase a ticket at the machine, refuse. This is often a scam. You can also buy train tickets at travel agents with an FS sticker in the window, and – via a rather complex process – from www.trenitalia.it.

Under-12s pay half the adult fare; under-4s travel free if they don't occupy a seat. There are also special deals for family bookings.

Train fares in Italy are cheaper than in the UK, and various tariffs may be available on one route. Be aware that the cheaper the fare, the longer the train takes. However, do check timetables carefully – for short distances, trains with obligatory reservations may be only slightly quicker than an inter-regionale, but will be more expensive.

Always stamp your train ticket – and any supplements – in one of the yellow machines by each platform before boarding the train. There's no need to stamp tickets that are dated and include a compulsory seat reservation, such as those for Freccia Argento and Freccia Rosso.

Should you have to board a train without a ticket, get on at the front and find the conductor (*capo treno*) immediately. This way, you may only have to pay a €5 penalty. If you wait for the ticket collector to come and find you, you'll be liable for a fine of €40.

Tickets for the privately run Italo service can be bought online (www.italotreno.it) or by phone (06 0708, open 5am-midnight daily). Alternatively, there are ticket machines on or near the platforms in the stations served by Italo. Some travel agencies can also issue Italo tickets, though there may be a service charge. For last-minute departures, tickets are on sale (with a 15 per cent surcharge) from Italo personnel on the platform up to three minutes before departure.

Stazione Centrale *Piazzale Duca D'Aosta, North.* **Map** p281 G3.
Connects with metro lines 2 (green) and 3 (yellow).

Stazione di Cadorna *Piazzale Cadorna, West.* **Map** p280 C6.
Connects with metro lines 1 (red) and 2 (green) and the Malpensa Express.

Stazione Lambrate *Piazza Bottini, North.*
Connects with metro line 2 (green).

Stazione Porta Garibaldi *Piazza Freud, North.* **Map** p280 D3.
Connects with metro line 2 (green), 5 (lilac) and the *passante ferroviario* (blue).

Resources A-Z

TRAVEL ADVICE

For up-to-date information on travel to a specific country – including the latest on safety and security, health issues, local laws and customs – contact your home country government's department of foreign affairs. Most have websites with useful advice for would-be travellers.

AUSTRALIA
www.smartraveller.gov.au

CANADA
www.voyage.gc.ca

NEW ZEALAND
www.safetravel.govt.nz

REPUBLIC OF IRELAND
foreignaffairs.gov.ie

UK
www.fco.gov.uk/travel

USA
www.state.gov/travel

AGE RESTRICTIONS

Buying/drinking alcohol 18
Sex (hetero- and homosexual) 14
Smoking 16
Driving 18
Renting a car 21

COURIERS & SHIPPERS

DHL *199 199 345, www.dhl.it*
FedEx *199 151 119, www.fedex.com*
TNT *199 803 868, www.tntitaly.it*
UPS *02 3030 3039, www.ups.com*

CUSTOMS

If you arrive from an EU country, you are not required to declare goods imported into or exported from Italy, as long as they're for personal use. For those arriving from a non-EU country, the following limits apply:

- 200 cigarettes or 100 cigarillos or 50 cigars or 250g (8.8oz) of tobacco
- 1 litre of spirits or 2 litres of wine
- 50g (1.76oz) of perfume
- Gift items not exceeding €430 (€150 for under-15s)

Visitors are also allowed to carry up to €10,000 in cash. Anything above these limits will be subject to taxation at the port of entry. For more information, see the Italian Customs website: www.agenziadoganemonopoli.gov.it.

If you're not an EU citizen, remember to keep your official receipts (*scontrini*) as you're entitled to a rebate when you leave on IVA (sales tax) on purchases over €155. Consult the tax refunds website www.globalblue.com, and *see p264*.

DISABLED

With its (often) cobbled streets, tramways, limited disabled access, and scarce facilities and information, visiting Milan in a wheelchair is challenging – though not impossible. Some museums and metro stations now have ramps, lifts and disabled toilets, as do a few of the more modern restaurants and bars.

The following websites may help you plan your trip.

AIAS *www.aiasnazionale.it.*
For enquiries, write to info@aiasnazionale.it. The website is in Italian only.
Milano Per Tutti
www.milanopertutti.it.
Contains itineraries and lists of museums, hotels, bars, restaurants, nightclubs and so on, with wheelchair access ratings, some in English. At the time of writing, however, the site was in need of a serious update.
Ufficio Informazione Turistica Provincia di Milano
www.visitamilano.it.
The provincial government's tourist information website provides up-to-date listings of museums, sites and monuments in English, each with an impaired-movement symbol, indicating whether access is free, limited or impossible.

Wheelchair hire

Contact the orthopaedic specialist store **Baldinelli** (corso XXII Marzo 5, 02 5518 3116, www.ortopediebaldinelli.it, open 9am-7pm Mon-Sat) if you need to rent a wheelchair (*carrozzina*). Rates start at €2.80 a day, with a minimum booking of 15 days. A €200 deposit is required.

Transport in Milan

While some city transport services are equipped for disabled travellers, restrictions are rife. Only one wheelchair-bound passenger is allowed to travel per train, for example. Responsibility for getting from the street to the platform is firmly in the hands of the passenger. All stations on the new metro line 5 (lilac) are accessible by lift, and some stations on line 3 (yellow) – but the older lines 1 (red) and 2 (green) still have considerable limitations. A number of stations have stairlifts, but you need staff assistance to use them.

For information on where lifts are working on the day you're due to travel, call 02 4860 7607 (7.30am-7.30pm) at least one hour before setting off. If you're travelling alone on the metro, call the same number at least 24 hours beforehand, since you will undoubtedly need assistance.

All the city's buses are fitted with a platform that can be lowered to hoist a wheelchair on board, but only 32 per cent of trams and 42 per cent of trolley buses offer the same facilities. The **Malpensa Express** train to Malpensa airport is wheelchair-friendly, as is the 73 bus (use the middle doors) to Linate airport – for both, *see p255*.

Book taxis in advance, specifying if you need a car large enough to cope with a wheelchair.

Rail travel

Long-distance trains are gradually being fitted with devices to permit access for wheelchairs – look for a wheelchair symbol on timetables. The **Sala Blu service** (199 303 060, www.rfi.it) offers assistance to wheelchair-bound passengers using Ferrovie dello Stato (FS) trains at 260 railway stations (out of a total of 2,150) across Italy. In Milan, the service is based at Garibaldi station, but also helps passengers at Stazione Centrale and Cadorna. Call (Italian only) to make arrangements at least 24 hours before you plan to travel, or one hour before from Garibaldi. The service is available 6.45am-9.30pm.

For international trains, a request must be made at least 48 hours in advance by calling 06 4730 8579 (Italian-language only, service available 6.45am-9.30pm).

Half of the 51 stations on the Trenord railway service (Lombardy and Piedmont) can be accessed autonomously by passengers in wheelchairs. For the rest, assistance is available with 48 hours' notice. See 'Assistenza' on www.trenord.it.

For passengers using the **Italo** service (www.italo.it) at Garibaldi station, 12 hours' notice is required if you need assistance; call 060 708. Note that assistance cannot be guaranteed at Milan Rogoredo station.

DRUGS

Anyone caught in possession of any quantity of drugs of any kind will be taken before a magistrate. There is no distinction between possession for personal use and intent to supply. All offenders are therefore subject to stiff penalties including lengthy prison sentences. Foreigners can expect to be swiftly deported. Couriering or dealing can land you in prison for up to 20 years.

ELECTRICITY

Italy's electrical system runs on 220/230V. To use British 240V appliances, you will need a two-pin adaptor plug (*riduttore*); these are best bought before leaving home, as they're hard to find in Italy. If you do need to buy one in Milan, try an electrical retailer such as **RFL** (viale Lazio 5, South, 02 5518 4356, www.wellcome.it) or **GBC** (via Tamagno 4/6, East, 02 2952 6680, www.gbcelettronicamilano.com). For US 110V appliances, you'll need to use a transformer.

EMBASSIES & CONSULATES

Australia *Via Borgogna 2, Centre (02 7767 4200, australian-consulate-general-milan@austrade.gov.au). Metro San Babila or bus 54, 60, 61, 73.* **Map** p284 F6.

South Africa *Vicolo San Giovanni sul Muro 4, Centre (02 885 8581, after-hours 348 715 5925 mobile, consular.milan@dirco.gov.za). Metro Cairoli or tram 1, 4, 19, 27.* **Map** p284 D6.

UK *Via San Paolo 7, Centre (02 723 001, info.consulate@fco.gov.uk). Metro Duomo or San Babila, or bus 15, 60, 73, or tram 1, 2.* **Map** p284 E6.

US *Via Principe Amedeo 2-10, North (02 290 351, general enquiries 02 2903 5333, uscitizensmilan@state.gov). Metro Turati or tram 1, 2, 94.* **Map** p281 E5.

EMERGENCIES

See also below **Health**; *p264* **Money**; *p265* **Police**; *p265* **Safety & Security**. Thefts or losses should be reported immediately at the nearest police station (either the Polizia di Stato or the Carabinieri). Report loss of your passport to your embassy or consulate (*see above*). Report loss of credit cards to your credit card supplier (*see p264*).

Ambulance 118
Infant emergency 114
Fire 115
Police *Carabinieri* 112; *Polizia di Stato*: 113.

GAY & LESBIAN

See pp158-162 **Gay & Lesbian**.

HEALTH

The *pronto soccorso* (casualty/accident and emergency/emergency room) of public hospitals provides free emergency treatment for travellers of any nationality. Before coming to Milan, EU citizens should obtain an EHIC (European Health Insurance Card). In the UK, this can be applied for online (www.dh.gov.uk) or by phone (0300 330 1350 from within the UK, 00 44 191 218 1999 from outside the UK). For minor treatments, take your EHIC card to any doctor for a free consultation. Drugs they prescribe can be bought at chemists at prices set by the health ministry. Tests or appointments with specialists in the public system (*Sistema sanità nazionale*, SSN) are charged at fixed rates (known as *il ticket*) and a receipt issued.

For a fee, all travellers can request an appointment with a doctor at one of Milan's long-established private international health clinics (*see p263*). Pharmacies (*see p263*) are often excellent sources of information for minor ailments.

Non-EU citizens should review their private health insurance policies to see if travel is covered. If not, some form of health insurance is advisable.

Accident & emergency

Should you need urgent medical care, head to the 24-hour emergency department (*pronto soccorso*) of one of the hospitals listed below. Children should be taken straight to the **Ospedale dei Bambini Vittore Buzzi**.

Ospedale dei Bambini Vittore Buzzi *Via Castelvetro 32, North (02 5799 5363, 02 57 991). Metro Garibaldi, or bus 78, or tram 12, 14, 19.* **Map** p280 A3.
Specialism: gynaecology, obstetrics, paediatrics.

Ospedale Fatebenefratelli *Piazza Principessa Clotilde 2, North (02 6363 2239). Metro Garibaldi, Repubblica or Turati, or bus 61, 94, or tram 1.* **Map** p281 E4.
Specialism: ophthalmology.

Ospedale Gaetano Pini *Via Quadronno 25, South (02 5829 6248). Metro Crocetta, or bus 94, or tram 24.* **Map** p283 E8.
Specialism: orthopaedics.

Ospedale Luigi Sacco *Via Giovanni Battista Grassi 74, North (02 3904 3051). Tram 12, 19.*

Ospedale Macedonio Melloni *Via Macedonio Melloni 52, East (02 6363 3220). Metro Piazzale Dateo or bus 54, 61, 92.*
Specialism: gynaecology, obstetrics.

Ospedale Mangiagalli *Via della Commenda 12, South (02 5503 2252, 02 55 031). Metro Crocetta, Missori or San Babila, or bus 60, 73, 77, 94, or tram 12, 27, 23.* **Map** p283 F8.
Specialism: gynaecology, obstetrics.

Ospedale Niguarda *Piazza Ospedale Maggiore 3, North (02 6610 1029, 02 64 441, www.ospedaleniguarda.it). Metro Maciachini then tram 4, or tram 4, 5.*
Specialism: poisons.

Ospedale San Giuseppe *Via San Vittore 12, Centre (02 8599 4532). Metro Cadorna, or bus 94, or tram 16, 27.* **Map** p282 B7.

Policlinico *Via Francesco Sforza 33-35, South (02 5503 6672). Metro Crocetta, Missori or San Babila, or bus 60, 73, 77, 94, or tram 12, 24.* **Map** p283 E7.

Dentists

Dentistry in Italy is mainly private and expensive; your insurance may not cover it. However, for dental emergencies, go to the hospital casualty departments listed above.

The private **International Health Centre** (*see p263*) has English-speaking dentists. Alternatively, contact Dr Susanne Horsving, a private, English-speaking Danish dentist with an established practice in Milan (corso Italia 50, 02 8645 0634).

International health clinics

Milan's long-established international health clinics have highly qualified medical staff, can do tests and also deal with some emergency situations.

American International Medical Center (AIMC) *Via Mercalli 11, South (02 5831 9808, www.aimdinic.it). Metro Crocetta or Missori, or bus 94, or tram 15.* **Open** 9am-6pm Mon-Fri. **Map** p283 E8.
International Health Centre *Galleria Strasburgo 3, Centre (02 7634 0720, www.ihc.it). Metro Duomo or San Babila, or bus 61.* **Open** 9am-7pm Mon-Thur; 9am-6pm Fri. **Map** p284 F6.

Opticians

Salmoiraghi & Viganò *Via Broletto 16, Centre (02 8646 0718, www.salmoiraghievigano.it). Metro San Babila or bus 54, 61.* **Open** 10am-7pm Mon-Sat. **Map** p284 D6.
Italy-wide chain, with other locations throughout the city.

Pharmacies

Pharmacies (*farmacie*) – marked by an illuminated green cross above the door – are run by qualified chemists who will dispense informal advice and assistance for common ailments, as well as filling prescriptions. If you need regular medication, bring adequate supplies. Also, make sure you know the generic name of any medicines you need, since brand names may differ.

Most chemists are open 9am-12.30pm, 3.30-7.30pm Mon-Sat. Night service typically runs 8pm-8.30am. A list outside the door of any pharmacy indicates the nearest one open. Below are two late-opening pharmacies:

Carlo Erba *Piazza del Duomo 21, Centre (02 8646 4832). Metro Duomo, or bus 54, or tram 1, 2, 3, 12, 14, 24.* **Open** 8am-11pm daily. **Map** p284 D6.
Farmacia Stazione Centrale *(platform level) Piazza Duca d'Aosta, North (02 669 0735). Metro Centrale FS.* **Open** 7.30am-8.30pm, 9.30-10.30pm daily. **Map** p281 G3.

Women's health

EHIC-card holders (*see p262*) can see a local doctor about gynaecological, contraceptive or other health issues. Anyone can book a consultation at the private international health clinics (*see left*), or at **GEPO** (via San Giovanni sul Muro 5, Centre, 02 805 7045, www.gepoconsultorio.com), a private gynaecological and paediatric health centre.

HELPLINES

ALA *800 861 061, www.alainrete.org.* **Open** *Free helpline* 1-6pm Mon-Fri. *English-speaking operator* 1-6pm Mon.
STD, HIV and AIDS helpline.
CADMI *02 5501 5519, www.cadmi.org.*
Sexual violence and rape helpline. Personal appointments available. An English-speaking volunteer may be available.
Ospedale Mangiagalli *Via della Commenda 12, South (02 5799 2489). Metro Crocetta, Missori or San Babila, or bus 60, 73, 77, 94, or tram 12, 27, 23.* **Open** *Hotline* 24hrs daily. *Drop-in centre* 9am-5pm Mon-Fri. **Map** p283 F8.
Sexual violence first-aid helpline.

ID

You are required by law to carry photo ID with you at all times. You will be asked to produce it if you are stopped by traffic police (who will also demand your driving licence, which you must carry when you're in charge of a motor vehicle). You will also need ID when checking into a hotel. Most take your details and return it to you immediately.

INTERNET

Milan City Council offers Free Wi-Fi Indoor – a service that provides free Wi-Fi access in public libraries and other public spaces. Complementing this, for use outdoors, is Open Wifi Milano. You're allowed 60 minutes and 300MB of traffic daily. To register for one or both services, go to: http://info.openwifimilano.it/en/howtoregister.aspx.

Most hotels in Milan have free wireless access, but the majority of cafés and bars are still, as far as customers are concerned, unwired.

LEFT LUGGAGE

Linate Airport *Arrivals hall (02 716 659, www.milanolinate-airport.com).* **Open** 6am-9.30pm daily. Look for *Banche e servizi*.
Malpensa airport *Terminal 1, ground floor, exit 7 (02 5858 0298, www.milanomalpensa-airport.com).* **Open** 6am-10pm daily. Look for *Banche e servizi*.
Stazione Centrale *Ground floor, on corridor leading to piazza Luigi di Savoia (393 015 0291 mobile, www.milanocentrale.it).* **Open** 6am-11pm daily. Look for *Deposito bagagli*.

LOST PROPERTY

Ufficio Oggetti Rinvenuti *Via Friuli 30, South (02 8845 3900, 02 8845 3908). Bus 90, 91, 92 or tram 12.* **Open** 8.30am-noon, 1-3.30pm Mon-Fri. **Map** p283 G9.
For objects lost in the city, including at Stazione Centrale.

MEDIA

National daily newspapers

Sometimes lengthy, turgid and featuring indigestible political stories with very little background explanation, traditional Italian newspapers can be a frustrating read. That said, they are also delightfully unsnobbish, and happily mix serious news, pieces by international commentators and well-written crime and human-interest stories.

Sports coverage is extensive, but die-hard fans can also try the sports papers *Corriere dello Sport*, *La Gazzetta dello Sport* and *Tuttosport*. For the business community, there are the financial dailies, *Il Sole 24 Ore*, *Italia Oggi* and *Milano Finanza*.

Corriere della Sera *www.corriere.it.*
To the centre of centre-left, this serious, Milan-based paper has a daily Milan section, which is useful for information on films and cultural events, roadworks, the inevitable transport strikes and so on. Its *ViviMilano* supplement (Wednesday) has listings.
Il Fatto Quotidiano *www.ilfattoquotidiano.it.*
Priding itself on not accepting public funding, *Il Fatto* is the most recent addition to Italy's daily papers, aiming to 'tell it like it is'. Slimmer than the rest, it provides a different and more digestible perspective on the national scenario. Recommended for those looking to improve their Italian-language skills.
Il Giornale *www.ilgiornale.it.*
Owned by Silvio Berlusconi's family, *Il Giornale* is understandably pro-Berlusconi – often to a nauseating (when not risible) extent.
La Repubblica *www.repubblica.it.*
This left-ish daily has a Milan section and, on Thursdays, a weekly listings magazine, *TuttoMilano*.
Il Sole 24 Ore *ww.ilsole24ore.com.*
This business, finance and economics daily has a great arts

ESSENTIAL INFORMATION

supplement on Sundays. The paper comes in an attractive shade of pink.

Freesheets

Metro *www.metronews.it.*
Leggo *www.leggo.it.*
Early risers will find these free dailies (by different publishers) at metro stations in Milan. Offering a brief overview of world and local news, as well as sports and a letters page, most have been snapped up by 9am.
Zero *http://milano.zero.eu.*
A5 in size, but packed with ideas for where to go and what to do, *Zero* magazine is a free monthly publication, featuring highly original cover art, which you can pick up throughout Milan. Rome, Turin, Bologna, Florence and Naples have their own editions.

Weekly news magazines

The centre-right *Panorama* (www.panorama.it) and centre-left *L'Espresso* (www.espresso.repubblica.it) provide a round-up of the week's news, while *Sette* and *Venerdi* – respectively the colour supplements of *Corriere della Sera* (Thursday) and *La Repubblica* (Friday) – have great photos and some lively articles. The leading papers' other weekly supplements, the *Corriere della Sera*'s *Io Donna* (Saturday) and *La Repubblica*'s *D-Donna* (Tuesday), are colourful, and often provide a good read – not just for women. *Internazionale* (www.internazionale.it) puts together an excellent digest of interesting bits and pieces gleaned from around the world the previous week.

For *Hello*-style scandal, try *Gente* and *Oggi*, with their peculiar mix of sex, glamour and religion, or the scandal sheets *Novella 2000* and *Cronaca Vera*, if you must.

English-language press

The *Financial Times*, *Guardian*, *International New York Times*, (previously *International Herald Tribune*), *Wall Street Journal* and other British and European dailies, along with weeklies such as *Newsweek*, *Time*, the *New Yorker* and the *Economist*, are all available; most can be found after 10am at central newsstands. Try the one in largo Augusto, Centre (02 7602 1898). For a selection of foreign-language monthlies, visit **Mondadori Multicenter** (*see p54*) or **La Feltrinelli** (*see p54*). At Stazione Centrale, your best bet is **Hudson News** (open 5.50am-9.15pm daily), which stocks one of the widest selections of English-language magazines in Milan. It's on the gallery floor, one flight down from the platforms. (It beats the English periodicals section of Stazione Centrale's branch of La Feltrinelli hands-down.)

Easy Milano *www.easymilano.it.*
Free fortnightly classified ads print (and online) mag for the English-speaking community, distributed at consulates and expat meeting places.
The Informer *www.informer.it.*
Based in Arese near Milan, this subscription-only online publication is designed for residents in Italy and gives detailed information on health, schools, tax, bureaucracy and so on. Also has small ads listings.

Radio

Radio Popolare (107FM, www.radiopopolare.it) is a Milan-based station with a long history of left-leaning political advocacy. There's thoughtful discussion of the issues of the day, and also some lively alternative music shows.

Environmentally conscious Lombard radio station/company **LifeGate Radio** (105.1FM, www.lifegate.it) offers music for tree-huggers.

State-owned stations **RAI 1** (90.6FM, www.radio1.rai.it), **RAI 2** (93.7FM, www.radio2.rai.it) and **RAI 3** (99.4FM, www.radio3.rai.it). feature light and classical music, comedy, chat shows and news bulletins. RAI 3 has some excellent news and culture programmes, including the morning phone-in news Q&A, *Prima Pagina*.

Radio DeeJay (107.0FM, www.deejay.it), **Radio Monte Carlo** (105.3FM, www.radiomontecarlo.net), **Virgin** (104.5FM, www.105.net) and **RTL 102.5 Classic** (102.5FM, www.rtl.it) offer pop music, pop music, pop music – from Italy, the UK and USA. For 1980s and '90s classics, sprinkled with Italian news, there's **Radio Capital** (91.7FM, www.capital.it). Get into the local groove with **RadioItalia** (106.7FM, www.radioitalia.it): '*solo musica italiana*'.

Television

There are seven major networks, three of them owned by state broadcaster RAI.

RAI 1, RAI 2, RAI 3
RAI 1 is the most mainstream of the three state-owned channels, hosting popular shows, comedies, TV dramas and some fairly abominable singing and dancing shows. RAI 3 is the most serious and left-leaning.
Canale 5, Italia 1, Rete 4
Variety, music and talent contests predominate on these three channels owned by Silvio Berlusconi's Mediaset. Canale 5 frequently premieres leading Anglo-American and international films – though these are inevitably dubbed.
La7
Tiny compared to the others, this small, independent channel offers what some consider to be Italy's highest-quality shows.

MONEY

Italy's currency is the euro. There are banknotes of €5, €10, €20, €50, €100, €200 and €500, and coins worth €1 and €2 as well as 1, 2, 5, 10, 20 and 50 cents (c). Euros from any euro zone country are valid in Italy.

Banks & ATMs

Most banks have ATMs (Bancomats), the majority of which accept cards with a Maestro, Cirrus or Visa Electron symbol, and dispense cash to a daily limit of €250. Banks are usually open 8.30am-1.30pm, 2.45-4pm Mon-Fri, and closed on public holidays.

Bureaux de change

The best exchange rates are to be had by withdrawing cash from ATMs. The exchange rates and commissions for currency transactions at banks vary greatly, but most offer more generous rates than private bureaux de change (*uffici di cambio*).

Lost/stolen credit cards

MasterCard and Visa are widely accepted in Italy. American Express is also popular. If your card is lost or stolen, contact the number provided by the issuing bank or the emergency assistance numbers listed below. 800 numbers (freephone) can only be accessed by Italian phones.

American Express *800 874 333 toll-free, 06 4290 4897.*
Diners Club *800 393 939 toll-free, 02 3216 2656.*
MasterCard *800 870 866 toll-free, or call collect 1-636 722 7111.*
Visa *800 819 014 toll-free.*

Tax

For information on reclaiming IVA (VAT or sales tax), *see p67* **Retail Knowledge**.

OPENING HOURS

For information on shop opening hours, *see p67* **Retail Knowledge**. For banks, *see p264*. For post offices, *see pbelow*. Note that the city pretty much closes down for August (*see p267* **When to Go**).

POLICE

For emergencies, *see p262*.

Both the (nominally military) Carabinieri and the Polizia di Stato deal with crimes and emergencies of any kind. So if you have your bag or wallet stolen (or are otherwise made a victim of crime), go as soon as possible to either force to report a *scippo* (bag-snatching). A *denuncia* (written statement) will be signed, dated and stamped with an official police seal. It's unlikely (though not impossible) that your things will be found, but you will need the *denuncia* for making an insurance claim.

There's also the Polizia Locale or Vigili Urbani, the municipal police force, which deals mainly with traffic issues. Below are the most centrally located police stations:

Carabinieri *Comando Moscova Station, via della Moscova 19, North (02 659 5560). Metro Turati, or bus 43, 94.* **Map** p281 E4.
Polizia Locale *Via Beccaria 19, Centre (02 77 271). Metro Duomo, or bus 54, 60, 61, 73, or tram 2.* **Map** p284 E7.
Polizia di Stato (Questura Centrale) *Via Fatebenefratelli 11, North (02 62 261). Metro Turati, or bus 43, 61, 94, or tram 1.* **Map** p281 E5.

POSTAL SERVICES

Italy's postal service (www.poste.it, 803 160) is fairly reliable, but packages do disappear from time to time.

The Italian postal service nominally promises delivery within 24 hours in Italy, three days for EU countries and four or five for the rest of the world, but these times may vary. Postage within Italy starts at 70c, 85c within Europe and €2 for the USA and the rest of the world. Stamps are sold at post offices; some bars selling tobacco products (*tabaccherie*) may sell 70c stamps.

Most postboxes are red and have two slots, one marked *Per la città* (for the city in question, in this case, Milan), the other *Per tutte le altre destinazioni* (all other destinations).

Post offices in Milan can be very crowded: expect to queue. They're generally open 8am-2pm Mon-Fri, and 8.30am-noon Sat and any day before a public holiday. Some stay open until 7pm, including the branch in Piazza Duca d'Aosta, by Stazione Centrale. You need to pick up a numbered ticket for the service you require (postal, banking, etc) and then stand in line.

Posta Centrale (Main Post Office)
Piazza Cordusio 2 & via Cordusio 4, Centre (02 7248 2126). Metro Cordusio or tram 2, 3, 12, 14, 27. **Open** 8am-7pm Mon-Fri; 8am-noon Sat. **Map** p284 D6.

RELIGION

All Saint's Church (Anglican) *Via Solferino 17, North (02 655 2258, www.allsaints.it). Metro Moscova or bus 43, 94.* **Services** usually 7.30pm Wed; 10.30am Sun. **Map** p280 D5.
Central Synagogue *Via Guastalla 19, East (02 551 2029). Bus 60, 77, 94.* **Services** vary; call for details. **Map** p284 F7.
Centro Islamico di Milano e Lombardia *Via Cassanese 3, Segrate (02 213 7080). Metro Cascina Gobba then bus 925.* **Services** times and locations vary; call for details.
Centro Italiano Zen Sôtô (Zen Buddhist) *Via Gaetana Agnesi 18, South (334 140 3396, 334 507 3063, www.centroitalianozen.it). Metro Porta Romana, or bus 62, 90, 91, 92, or tram 9.* **Services** vary; call for details 6-7pm Wed. **Map** p283 F9.
Chiesa del Carmine, San Carlo (Catholic, in English) *Piazza Santa Maria del Carmine 2, North (02 8646 3365, www.chiesadelcarmine.it). Metro Lanza, or bus 57, 61, or tram 3, 12.* **Services** 10.30am Sun. **Map** p284 D6.
Chiesa Evangelica Metodista di Milano (Methodist) *Via Porro Lambertenghi 28, North (02 607 2631, www.protestantiamilano.it). Metro Garibaldi, or bus 70, 82, or tram 2, 4.* **Services** (English) 11.45am Sun; (English/Italian) 11am 1st Sun of mth. **Map** p280 D2.

SAFETY & SECURITY

Milan is, by and large, fairly safe. However, as in any large city, petty crime is a fact of life and tourists who stand out as such are more susceptible. Pickpockets often work in pairs or groups, targeting tourist areas, public-transport routes and the international arrivals area of the airports. Everyone – and lone women especially – should be careful in Stazione Centrale and around parks, especially at night.

Use your common sense, as you would in any large city: keep handbags fastened, don't carry wallets in back pockets, hang on to cameras, etc.

You may also want to keep an eye out for these well-known scams:

- If you see groups of ragged children brandishing pieces of cardboard, walk by quickly, holding on to your valuables. The cardboard is to distract you while accomplices pick pockets or bags.
- If you're waiting with several pieces of luggage and a passer-by drops bits of paper in front of you, hang on to your bags extra-tight. The scammers hope that you will alert the 'careless' pedestrian while his/her accomplice snatches your smallest bag. Give chase, and the 'pedestrian' will run back and grab the rest. This is a common scam outside the car-rental places by the Stazione Centrale, which are located in quiet residential streets.

SMOKING & TOBACCONISTS

Smoking is not permitted in any indoor public place: this includes all public transport, bars, nightclubs and restaurants. The occasional bar or restaurant may have a separate room for smokers. Otherwise, the street – or occasional outdoor terraces and gardens – is the only option. The position on electronic cigarettes is unclear; EU legislation is awaited.

Tabacchi, or *tabaccherie* (identified by a white T on a black or blue background) are the only places to buy tobacco products legally. They also sell stamps, phone top-up cards, individual or season tickets for public transport and lottery tickets. Many *tabaccherie* are attached to bars and thus are open until 7pm. At closing time, an external vending machine starts operating, to keep nicotine-deprived smokers going until they reopen at around 7am.

TELEPHONES

Dialling & codes

Italian landline numbers must be dialled with their prefixes, even if you're phoning within the local area. Numbers in Milan begin with 02 and can have anything from four to eight digits after the prefix.

All numbers beginning with 800 (*numero verde*) are freephone lines. Numbers beginning with 840 and 848 are charged at a nominal rate. 800, 840 and 848 numbers can be called from Italian phone numbers only.

Mobile phone numbers always start with a 3. When calling an Italian landline from outside Italy, the whole prefix must be dialled – including the 0. For Milan, that's 00 39 02 (+ number).

To make international calls from Italy, dial 00, followed by the country code (Australia 61, Canada 1, Republic of Ireland 353, New Zealand 64, South Africa 27, UK 44, US 1).

Mobile phones

There are four main service providers in Italy: Vodafone, Tre (Three), TIM (Telecom Italia) and Wind.

Standard European handsets will work in Italy, but your service provider may need you to activate international roaming to view email. Most US handsets also work; check with your manufacturer.

If your phone is not locked to your home SIM card/service provider, you can buy an Italian pay-as-you go SIM card (*ricaricabile*), available from mobile phone shops for around €10, allowing you to make cheaper calls within Italy. The alternative is to buy an Italian phone plus SIM card. In theory, you have to provide an Italian tax code (*codice fiscale*) to buy an Italian SIM card; in practice, most vendors will waive this requirement. To buy a subscription or a phone, you need to present photo ID.

Roaming charges for mobile phones in the 28-country EU bloc became much cheaper on 1 July 2014 and are expected to disappear completely at the end of 2015. Here are some centrally located mobile phone shops:

TIM *Galleria Vittorio Emanuele II 61, Centre (02 7209 3952, www.tim.it). Metro Duomo, or bus 54, or tram 1, 2, 3, 12, 14, 24.* **Map** p284 E6.
Tre *Corso Buenos Aires 33, East (02 2050 9959, www.tre.it). Metro Lima or bus 60.* **Map** p281 G4.
Vodafone *Corso Buenos Aires 18, East (02 2940 3568, www.vodafone.it). Metro Porta Venezia or tram 5, 33.* **Map** p281 G4.
Wind *Via Cordusio 2, Centre (02 8699 5619, www.wind.it). Metro Cordusio or tram 2, 12, 14, 16, 27.* **Map** p284 D6.

TIME

Italy is one hour ahead of London, six ahead of New York, and eight behind Sydney. As with the rest of Europe, Italy observes Daylight Saving Time (DST): clocks are adjusted forward by one hour, on the same date as the rest of the EU, in early spring and back in late autumn. Check exact time differences at www.timeanddate.com.

TIPPING

There are no hard and fast rules on tipping in Italy, though some Milanese know that foreigners (especially Americans) tip generously back home and expect them to be liberal. Some upmarket restaurants (and a growing number of cheaper ones) will add a service charge of ten to 15 per cent to your bill. A cover charge (*coperto*) for the table and bread is also automatically added – a quasi tip in itself. It's also customary to leave any coinage given as change (minus the coppers). Taxi drivers will be happy if you round the fare up to the nearest whole euro.

TOILETS

Public toilets are few and far between in Milan, though most major tourist sites have them – as do some metro stations and major railway stations; most of these have attendants and you'll have to pay a small fee. In Milan, try one of the very few large department stores, or go to a bar and then ask to use the facilities. You may need to get a key; this is not generally a problem, but it's usual to buy something at the bar in payment – even if just a quick coffee.

TOURIST INFORMATION

At time of writing, the Provincia's (provincial government) main office was about to move – possibly to the **InfoMilano/Urban Centre** (*see right*). Currently, however, the city's most reliable tourist information points are online.

Websites

www.turismo.milano.it
The website of the Comune (city council) provides detailed and generally accurate information about daily events and exhibitions, sites and museums – as well as themed itineraries, on everything from fashion to industrial architecture to Leonardo (see 'Milan & Surroundings/Itineraries'). There's also a burgeoning range of free apps to download – from points of interest along the Navigli to city maps (see 'M14YOU/Download').

www.visitamilano.it
The Provincia (provincial government) website offers practical information on accommodation and getting around, along with opening times of museums and monuments. It also highlights daily events.

Tourist offices

Expo Gate *Piazza Castello, at via Beltrami, North (www.expo2015.org). Metro Cairoli, or bus 50, 57, 61, or tram 1.* **Open** 10am-8pm daily. **Map** p284 C6.
These two triangular pavilions (known to locals as 'the pyramids') will sell tickets for, and provide information on, Expo-related events for the duration of the Universal Exposition (1 May-31 Oct 2015).

InfoMilano/Urban Centre *Galleria Vittorio Emanuele II 11-12, Centre (02 8845 6555). Metro Duomo, or bus 54, or tram 1, 2, 3, 12, 14, 24.* **Open** *Urban Centre* 9am-6pm Mon-Fri. **Map** p284 E6.
This conveniently located office in Milan's famous Galleria (*see p50*) was originally here to help Milanese citizens find their way around bureaucracy. In September 2014, the offices will be expanded and combined with the Comune-run InfoMilano, providing tourist information to the 90,000 visitors anticipated daily during Expo 2015. It's hoped the office will continue after the fair ends.

Ufficio Informazione Turistica Provincia di Milano *In front of platform 21, Stazione Centrale, piazzale Duca d'Aosta, North (02 7740 4318). Metro Centrale FS, or bus 60, 81, or tram 4, 5, 9.* **Open** 9am-5pm Mon-Fri; 9am-12.30pm Sat, Sun. **Map** p281 F3.
This new information kiosk opened in Central Station in May 2014.

Combined tickets

House Museum Card
www.casemuseomilano.it.
This joint ticket gets you into four 'house' museums – for the price of one and a half. Each of the museums – **Museo Bagatti Valsecchi** (*see p64*), **Villa Necchi Campigli** (*see p101*), **Museo Poldi Pezzoli** (*see p64*) and **Casa Museo Boschi-di Stefano** (*see p101*) – was once the home of a private collector (or collectors) and features quirky displays of objets and art. At €15, as opposed to the full price of €27, it's quite a deal. The card is valid for six months from the first visit and can be bought at the first three museums mentioned here. Note, that, although it's included in the circuit, you can visit Casa Museo Boschi Di Stefano whenever it's open – for free.

LOCAL CLIMATE

	Temperature (°C/°F)	Rainfall (mm/in)
Jan	3 / 37	65 / 2.6
Feb	5 / 41	50 / 2
Mar	9 / 48	75 /3
Apr	13 / 55	95 / 3.7
May	18 / 64	120 / 4.7
June	22 / 72	85 / 3.4
July	25 / 77	75 / 3
Aug	24 / 75	85 / 3.4
Sept	19 / 66	100 / 4
Oct	14 / 57	115 / 4.5
Nov	9 / 48	85 / 3.4
Dec	4 / 39	60 / 2.4

Monday Ticket
www.museopoldipezzoli.it.
Sightseeing on Mondays – when Italy's museums close, Milan being no exception – is always an issue. The Monday Ticket points you in the direction of two museums intelligent enough to buck the trend and stay open: **Museo Poldi Pezzoli** (*see p64*) and **Museo Teatro alla Scala** (*see p56*) – and it does so at a very reasonable price. The card is valid for six months from the first visit and can be purchased at either museum. Costing €9, it offers a saving of €4 on the regular price. Added bonus: the card also entitles you to a discount on an ongoing art exhibition at **Palazzo Reale** (*see p50*). The only caveat: you have to visit on a Monday, naturally.

TOURS

Zani Viaggi *Foro Buonaparte 76, North (02 867 131, www.zaniviaggi.it). Metro Cairoli, or bus 94, or tram 1, 12.* **Map** p284 D6.
For those not endowed with the gift of foresight, Zani Viaggi's **Grand Bus Tour** offers one of the few ways to see Leonardo's *Last Supper* (usually requiring pre-booking several weeks ahead; *see p140* **Ticket Tricks**) – at a price. The trip lasts 3.5 hours and includes visits to the **Duomo**, **La Scala** – including the **Museum** – plus tickets (rarer, almost, than a front row seat at an Armani show) to *Il Cenacolo*. It departs from Zani's offices at 9.30am and costs €65; book at least three days ahead.

Alternatively, you can see Milan from the top of an open double-decker bus on the popular hop-on, hop-off **City Sightseeing Milano** tour. This runs from 9.30am to 7.30pm daily; the €25 ticket is valid for 48 hours. You can switch between any of three itineraries: Red (Navigli, 60mins), Blue (Northern Milan, including Garibaldi, 90mins) and Green (San Siro stadium, 90mins). For a list of stops and departure points, consult the website. Three variants are available, including: a ticket to *The Last Supper* (€50); a visit to San Siro stadium (€30); a visit to the Duomo (€35).

Navigli Lombardi *02 9227 3118, same-day bookings 392 707 6412 mobile, www.navigareinlombardia.it.* **Tours** *Apr-Sept* Fri-Sun.
Most of Milan's canal system is not navigable, but you can take a leisurely 55-minute cruise on the Naviglio Grande as far as the 14th-century church of San Cristoforo.

VISAS

For EU nationals, a passport or national identity card valid for travel abroad is sufficient. Non-EU citizens must have full passports. Citizens of the US, Canada, Australia and New Zealand do not need visas for stays of up to 90 days. In theory, visitors are required to declare their presence to the local police within a few days of arrival, unless they're staying in a hotel, in which case this will be done for them. In practice, you will not need to report to the police station unless you're applying for a *permesso di soggiorno* (permit to stay). This is necessary for anyone, including EU citizens, intending to reside in Italy.

WATER

Tap water in Milan is perfectly safe to drink, as is the water in the public drinking fountains you'll find everywhere.

WHEN TO GO

The low-lying Po valley is bordered on the north by the Alps and on the south-west by the Apennines, beyond Pavia. The upside is that windy days in Milan are very rare indeed. The downside is that damp air is kept firmly where it is – hence the fog that can bring traffic in the area around Milan to a halt, and humid summer days. If you're coming to Milan in July or August, ensure your hotel has air-conditioning. September is a very pleasant month, but rain may intrude in late October and November. Snow is uncommon and rarely settles for more than a couple of days. Spring can be variable, alternating brilliant sunshine and temperatures above 20°C (68°F) with cold rainy days. In recent years, this pattern has extended into June.

August is best avoided as, in addition to the heat and humidity, the city pretty much grinds to a halt, with restaurants, museums, bars, cafés and shops shutting for two to four weeks as Milan's working population heads for the beach. Also best avoided: the International Furniture Fair (April) and fashion weeks in January, Febuary/March and September/October. During these periods, hotels are subject to price hikes and restaurants and bars are overcrowded.

Public holidays

For a full list of public holidays (*giorni festivi*), *see p37*.

On these days, public offices, banks and businesses are closed, although – with the exception of Labour Day, Assumption, Christmas Day and New Year's Day – restaurants in the city centre tend to stay open. Public transport is almost non-existent on Labour Day, Christmas afternoon and New Year's Day. Holidays falling on a Saturday or Sunday aren't celebrated on the following Monday. By popular tradition, though, if a holiday falls on a Thursday or a Tuesday, many people will take the Friday or Monday off as well, a practice known as *fare il ponte* (doing a bridge).

WOMEN

Younger foreign women will be the object of attention in northern Italy. You're unlikely to encounter any aggressive behaviour, but avoid outlying areas and don't wander by yourself at night, except in lively zones. Take special care around Stazione Centrale. A taxi (*see p257*) is a good idea if you're crossing the city late at night; most taxi drivers will wait in the street outside until their female passengers are safely inside their front door or hotel lobby.

Further Reference

BOOKS

Classics

Catullus *Poems* Uncannily modern musings from Lake Garda's most famous Roman.
Pliny the Elder *Natural History* Observations of an old Como native.

Fiction

Brown, Dan *The Da Vinci Code* Leonardo da Vinci's *Last Supper* provides vital clues in this somewhat ludicrous pot-boiler of a mystery.
D'Annunzio, Gabriele *The Child of Pleasure* Autobiographical novel by the poet, bon viveur and grand poseur (*see p213* **Poet or Pike?**).
Eco, Umberto *Foucault's Pendulum* Milan takes on a sinister air in this esoteric novel by the renowned author.
Eco, Umberto *The Mysterious Flame of Queen Loana* Following a stroke, a Milanese antiquarian book dealer forgets his family but remembers everything he's read.
Fo, Dario *Accidental Death of an Anarchist* Darkly hilarious play about the fatal 'tumble' of an anarchist from a Milan police HQ window during an interrogation – by the Nobel prize-winning comedian from Lombardy.
Hemingway, Ernest *A Farewell to Arms* Part of this love 'n' war epic is set in Milan and at Lago di Maggiore (*see p191* **Hemingway's Haunts**).
Lee, Andrea *Interesting Women* Elegantly written short stories by an African-American girl-about-town, mostly set in Milan.
Manzoni, Alessandro *I promessi sposi (The Betrothed)* Perhaps Italy's most celebrated novel – focusing on star-crossed lovers in 17th-century Lombardy.
Parks, Tim *Europa* Gripping tale of obsessive love, partly located in Milan.

Non-fiction & Travel

Foot, John *Milan Since the Miracle: City, Culture and Identity* Intriguing study of the city's recent history and culture.
Grundy, Isobel *Lady Mary Wortley Montagu* This 18th-century English traveller spent many years in and around Lovere on Lake Iseo.
Jones, Tobias *The Dark Heart of Italy* Exploration of modern-day Italian culture by a British journalist.
Lawrence, DH *Twilight in Italy* Contains wonderful descriptions of Lake Garda.
Parks, Tim *A Season with Verona* Calcio, Verona FC and much much more, including an account of San Siro Stadium.
Parks, Tim *Italian Ways* Musings on Italian railways, departing from Stazione Centrale – by the Milan-based author.
Severgnini, Beppe *An Italian in Italy* Hilarious account of a journey across Italy by the Lombard-born *Corriere della Sera* journalist.
Wharton, Edith *Italian Backgrounds* A refutation of the 'there's nothing to see in Milan' argument.

FILM

L'Albero degli zoccoli *(The Tree of the Wooden Clogs, Ermanno Olmi, 1978)* This film about subsistence farming at the turn of the century was made with non-professional actors speaking in the *bergamasco* dialect.
Incantesimo Napoletano *(Paolo Genovese & Luca Miniero, 1999)* A Neapolitan girl rejects her heritage and embraces all things Milanese.
Io sono l'amore *(I am Love, Luca Guadagnino, 2010)* Bourgeois morality is thrown out of the window in this stylish film, shot at the Villa Necchi-Campiglio, and starring Tilda Swinton.
Miracle in Milan *(Miracolo a Milano, Vittorio De Sica, 1950)* A magical neo-realist tale about a young orphan who brings light to Milan's beggars.
1900 *(Bernardo Bertolucci, 1976)* This two-part epic on the conflict between Fascism and Communism was shot around Cremona.
Riso Amaro *(Bitter Rice, Giuseppe De Santis, 1948)* Passion and exploitation among Lombardy's rice-paddy workers.
Rocco e i suoi fratelli *(Rocco and his Brothers, Luchino Visconti, 1960)* Five Sicilian brothers and their mother struggle to earn a living in industrial Milan.
Teorema *(Theorem, Pier Paolo Pasolini, 1968)* A young, beautiful stranger (Terence Stamp) engages in rampant sex with all the members of a bourgeois family from the mother to the maid. Not surprisingly, their lives are forever changed.

MUSIC

Mozart, Wolfgang Amadeus (1756-91) Aged 13 when he first visited Milan, Mozart composed several juvenile works and operas here, including: *Mitridate* (1770), *Ascanio in Alba* (1771), *Symphony in F* (1771), *Lucio Silla* (1772), the 'Milanese' String Quartets (1773), and *Exsultate, jubilate* (1773) – still frequently performed today.
Puccini, Giacomo (1858-1924) Though he was born in Tuscany, Puccini studied at the Milan Conservatorio, and several of his operas premiered here, among them: *La Villi* (1885), *Edgar* (1885), *Madame Butterfly* (1904), *Turandot* (posthumously; 1926).
Verdi, Giuseppe (1813-1901) Lombard *per eccellenza*, Verdi gave many of his operas local themes or settings: *The Lombards at the First Crusade* (1843), *The Battle of Legnano* (1849) and *Rigoletto* (1851; set in Mantova). Many more reflect the tribulations of nations oppressed by foreign rulers – a sore point in Milan in Verdi's time.

WEBSITES

www.atm.it Public transport information site (in English and Italian): type in your departure point and destination and it will provide routes.
www.expo2015.org The official website from the organisers of the Milan Universal Exposition (1 May-31 Oct 2015). In Italian, English and French.
www.hellomilano.it City guide – in English – with a daily round-up of English-language films, concerts and other events around Milan.
www.turismo.milano.it The Comune di Milano's official website, listing museums, sites, exhibitions, daily events and more, in various languages including English. Maps and apps available.
www.visitamilano.it The Provincia's official website, with practical information on transport and accommodation, plus details of museums, sites, exhibitions and daily events. The site is in English and Italian.

Vocabulary

Italian is pretty much pronounced as it is spelled. Stresses usually fall on the second-last syllable; a stress on a final syllable is indicated by an accent.

Note that there are three 'you' forms: the formal singular *lei*; the informal *tu* that's used with people you know well or close friends, as well as with children, and animals. The plural *voi* is used to address more than one person.

Masculine nouns and accompanying adjectives generally end in 'o' (plural 'i'), feminine nouns and their adjectives usually end in 'a' (plural 'e').

Vowels

a – as in **a**sk
e – like a in **a**ge or e in s**e**ll
i – like ea in **ea**st
o – as in h**o**tel or in h**o**t
u – as in b**oo**t

Consonants

c before a, o or u – like c in **c**at
c before e or i – like ch in **ch**eck
ch – like c in **c**at
g before a, o or u – like g in **g**et
g before e or i – like j in **j**ug
gh – like g in **g**et
gli – like the lli in mi**lli**on
gn – like ny in ca**ny**on
qu – as in **qu**ick
r – always rolled
s – two sounds, as in **s**oap or ro**s**e
h – silent before a vowel
sc before an e or i – like sh in **sh**ame
sch – like sc in **sc**out
z – two different sounds, like ts or dz

Useful phrases

hello/goodbye (informal) – ciao
good morning – buon giorno
good evening – buona sera
good night – buona notte
please – per favore, per piacere
thank you – grazie
you're welcome – prego
excuse me, sorry – mi scusi (formal), scusa (informal)
I'm sorry, but... – mi dispiace, ma...
I don't speak Italian (very well) – non parlo (molto bene) l'italiano
I don't/didn't understand – non capisco/non ho capito
where's the toilet? – dov'è la toilette/il bagno? (toilets are usually marked 'servizi')
open – aperto
closed – chiuso
entrance – entrata/ingresso
exit – uscita
help! – aiuto!
I need a doctor/policeman – Ho bisogno di un dottore/poliziotto/carabiniere

Times

could you tell me the time, please? – mi sa (formal)/sai (informal) dire l'ora, per favore?
it's x o'clock – sono le (x)
it's half past x – sono le (x) e mezza
when does it open? – a che ora apre?

Directions

(turn) left – (giri a) sinistra
(it's on the) right – é a destra
straight on – sempre diritto
where is...? – dov'é...?
could you show me the way to the Duomo? – mi potrebbe indicare la strada per il Duomo?
is it near/far? – è vicino/lontano?

Transport

bus – autobus
car – macchina, automobile
underground/subway – metro
coach – pullman
taxi – tassì, taxi
train – treno
tram – tram
plane – aereo
bus stop – fermata (dell'autobus)
station – stazione
platform – binario
ticket/s – biglietto/biglietti
one way – solo andata
return – andata e ritorno
(I'd like) a ticket for – (vorrei) un biglietto per...

Communications

phone – telefono
stamp – francobollo
a stamp for England/the United States? – un francobollo per l'Inghilterra/gli Stati Uniti?
can I make a phone call? – posso fare una telefonata?

Shopping

I'd like to try (the blue sandals) – vorrei provare (i sandali blu)
do you have it/them in other colours? – c'é/ci sono in altri colori?
I take (shoe) size... – porto il numero...
I take (dress) size... – porto la taglia...
can you give me a little more/less? – mi dia un po' di più/meno
100 grams of... – un etto di...
300 grams of... – tre etti di...
one kilo of... – un kilo/chilo di...
five kilos of... – cinque chili di...

Accommodation

a reservation – una prenotazione
I'd like to book a single/twin/double room – vorrei prenotare una camera singola/doppia/matrimoniale

Eating & drinking

I'd like to book a table for four at 8pm – vorrei prenotare un tavolo per quattro alle otto
I don't eat meat; what do you recommend? – non mangio carne; cosa mi consiglia?
the bill – il conto
is service included? – è incluso il servizio?
I think there's a mistake in this bill – credo che il conto sia sbagliato

Days & times of day

Monday – lunedì
Tuesday – martedì
Wednesday – mercoledì
Thursday – giovedì
Friday – venerdì
Saturday – sabato
Sunday – domenica
yesterday – ieri
today – oggi
tomorrow – domani
morning – mattina
afternoon – pomeriggio
evening – sera
night – notte
weekend – fine settimana or, more usually, weekend

Numbers & money

0 zero; **1** uno; **2** due; **3** tre; **4** quattro; **5** cinque; **6** sei; **7** sette; **8** otto; **9** nove; **10** dieci; **11** undici; **12** dodici; **13** tredici; **14** quattordici; **15** quindici; **16** sedici; **17** diciassette; **18** diciotto; **19** diciannove; **20** venti; **30** trenta; **40** quaranta; **50** cinquanta; **60** sessanta; **70** settanta; **80** ottanta; **90** novanta; **100** cento; **200** duecento; **1,000** mille
how much is it? – quanto costa?
do you take credit cards? – accettate carte di credito?

Index

INDEX

INDEX

MONTE DEI PASCHI DI SIEN

Maps

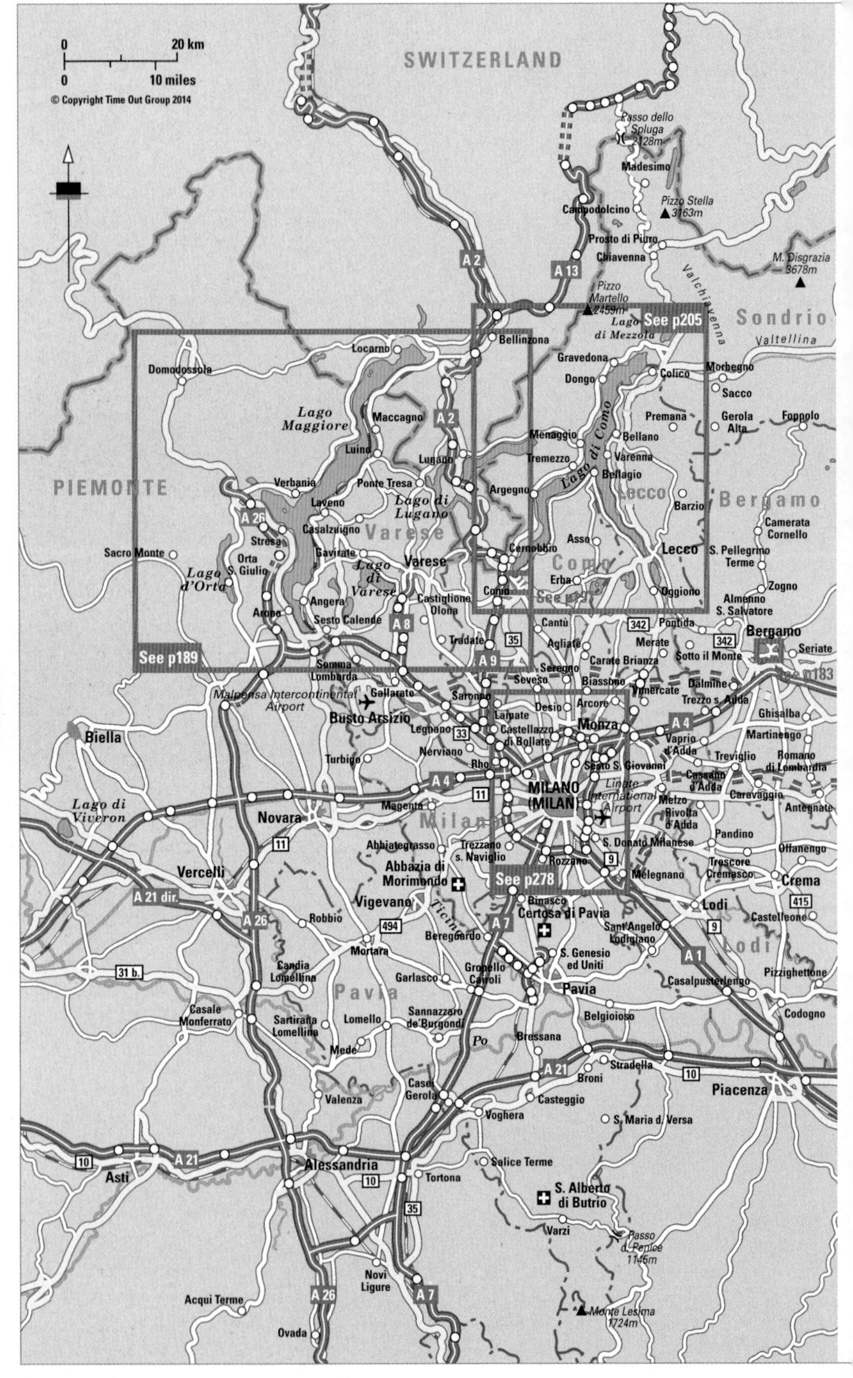

0
20 km
0
10 miles
© Copyright Time Out Group 2014
SWITZERLAND
Passo dello Spluga 2128m
Madesimo
Pizzo Stella 3163m
Campodolcino
Prosto di Piuro
Chiavenna
Valchiavenna
M. Disgrazia 3678m
A 2
A 13
Pizzo Martello 2459m
See p205
Sondrio
Valtellina
Lago di Mezzola
Bellinzona
Locarno
Domodossola
Gravedona
Dongo
Colico
Morbegno
Sacco
Lago Maggiore
Maccagno
A 2
Premana
Gerola Alta
Foppolo
Menaggio
Bellano
Luino
Lugano
Tremezzo
Lago di Como
Varenna
Bellagio
PIEMONTE
Verbania
Ponte Tresa
Argegno
Lecco
Bergamo
Laveno
Lago di Lugano
Barzio
A 26
Casalzuigno
Varese
Camerata Cornello
Stresa
Asso
Sacro Monte
Orta S. Giulio
Gavirate
Lago di Varese
Varese
Cernobbio
Lecco
S. Pellegrino Terme
Lago d'Orta
Como
Erba
Zogno
Angera
Castiglione Olona
Como
Oggiono
Almenno S. Salvatore
Arona
Sesto Calende
A 8
See p205
Cantù
342
Pontida
Tradate
35
Bergamo
Agliate
Merate
342
See p189
A 9
Carate Brianza
Sotto il Monte
Seriate
Somma Lombarda
Seregno
Seveso
Biassono
Vimercate
Dalmine
See p183
Malpensa Intercontinental Airport
Gallarate
Saronno
Desio
Arcore
Trezzo s. Adda
Busto Arsizio
Lainate
Monza
A 4
Ghisalba
Biella
Legnano
33
Castellazzo di Bollate
Vaprio d'Adda
Martinengo
Turbigo
Nerviano
Treviglio
Romano di Lombardia
Rho
Sesto S. Giovanni
Cassano d'Adda
Lago di Viveron
A 4
11
MILANO (MILAN)
Linate International Airport
Melzo
Caravaggio
Antegnate
Novara
Magenta
Milano
Rivolta d'Adda
Pandino
11
Abbiategrasso
Trezzano s. Naviglio
S. Donato Milanese
Offanengo
Vercelli
Abbazia di Morimondo
Rozzano
9
Melegnano
Trescore Cremasco
Crema
A 21 dir.
See p278
Vigevano
Binasco
Lodi
415
A 26
Robbio
Ticino
Certosa di Pavia
Sant'Angelo Lodigiano
9
Castelleone
494
A 7
Bereguardo
A 1
Lodi
Mortara
S. Genesio ed Uniti
31 b.
Candia Lomellina
Gropello Cairoli
Garlasco
Pavia
Casalpusterlengo
Pizzighettone
Pavia
Casale Monferrato
Sartirana Lomellina
Lomello
Sannazzaro de'Burgondi
Belgioioso
Codogno
Mede
Po
Bressana
A 21
Stradella
10
Broni
Piacenza
Casei Gerola
Valenza
Casteggio
Voghera
S. Maria d. Versa
10
A 21
Asti
Alessandria
Salice Terme
10
Tortona
35
S. Alberto di Butrio
Varzi
Passo d. Penice 1146m
Novi Ligure
A 26
A 7
Acqui Terme
Monte Lesima 1724m
Ovada

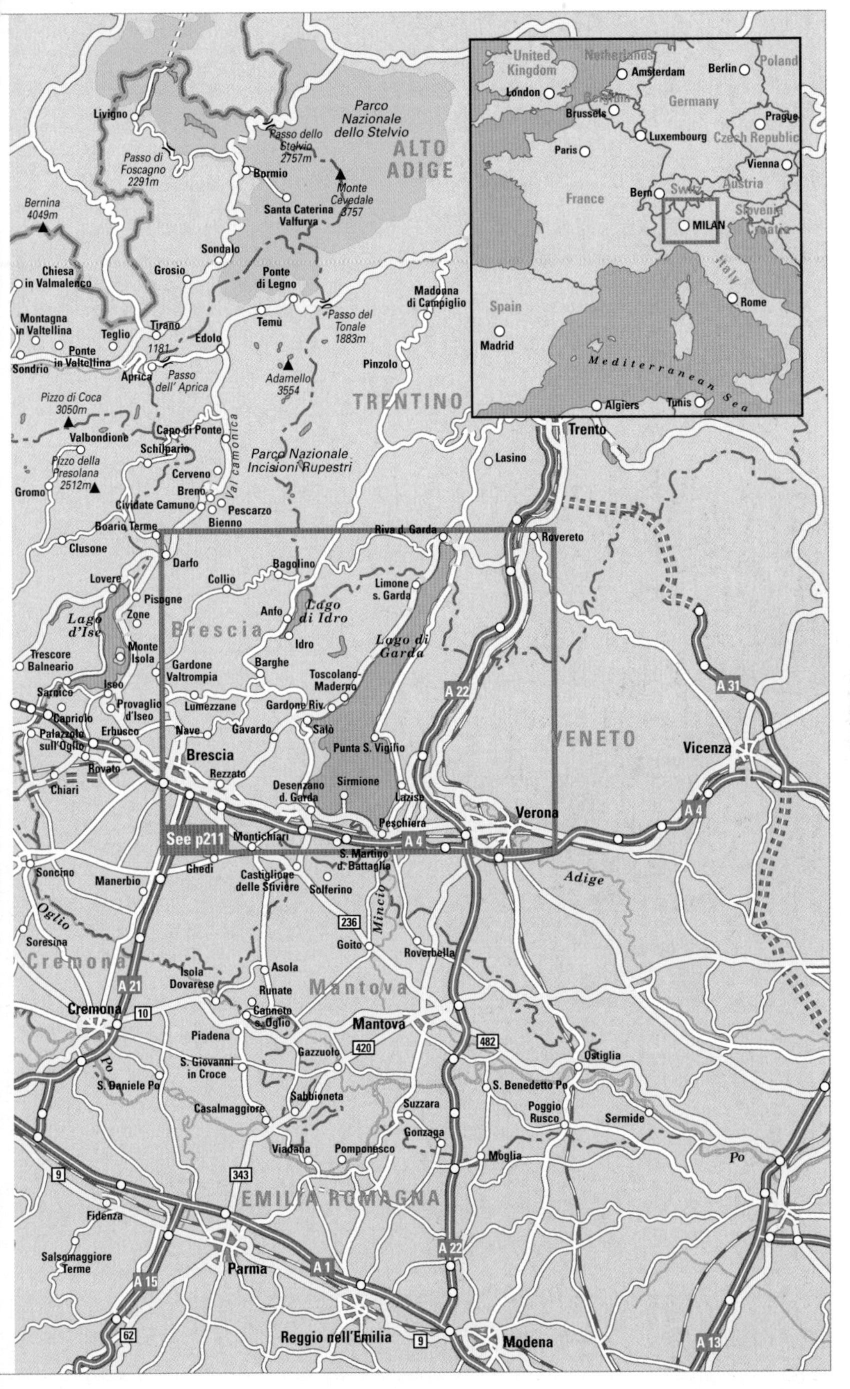

MAPS
Livigno
Passo di Foscagno 2291m
Passo dello Stelvio 2757m
Parco Nazionale dello Stelvio
ALTO ADIGE
Bormio
Monte Cevedale 3757
Bernina 4049m
Santa Caterina Valfurva
Sondalo
Chiesa in Valmalenco
Grosio
Ponte di Legno
Madonna di Campiglio
Montagna in Valtellina
Teglio
Tirano
Temù
Passo del Tonale 1883m
Ponte in Valtellina
Sondrio
1181
Edolo
Aprica
Passo dell' Aprica
Adamello 3554
Pinzolo
Pizzo di Coca 3050m
TRENTINO
Valbondione
Capo di Ponte
Schilpario
Val camonica
Parco Nazionale Incisioni Rupestri
Pizzo della Presolana 2512m
Cerveno
Gromo
Breno
Cividate Camuno
Pescarzo
Bienno
Boario Terme
Clusone
Darfo
Lasino
Trento
Riva d. Garda
Rovereto
Collio
Bagolino
Lovere
Pisogne
Limone s. Garda
Zone
Lago d'Iseo
Anfo
Lago di Idro
Brescia
Idro
Lago di Garda
Monte Isola
Trescore Balneario
Gardone Valtrompia
Barghe
Toscolano-Maderno
Sarnico
Iseo
Provaglio d'Iseo
Capriolo
Lumezzane
Gardone Riv.
A 22
A 31
Palazzolo sull'Oglio
Erbusco
Nave
Gavardo
Salò
Punta S. Vigilio
VENETO
Vicenza
Rovato
Rezzato
Chiari
Desenzano d. Garda
Sirmione
Lazise
Verona
A 4
Peschiera
See p211
Montichiari
S. Martino d. Battaglia
Soncino
Ghedi
Castiglione delle Stiviere
Solferino
Adige
Manerbio
Oglio
Mincio
236
Soresina
Goito
Roverbella
Cremona
Isola Dovarese
Asola
A 21
Mantova
Runate
Canneto s. Oglio
10
482
420
Piadena
Gazzuolo
Ostiglia
Po
S. Giovanni in Croce
S. Daniele Po
S. Benedetto Po
Sabbioneta
Poggio Rusco
Casalmaggiore
Suzzara
Sermide
Gonzaga
Viadana
Pomponesco
Moglia
9
343
EMILIA ROMAGNA
Fidenza
Salsomaggiore Terme
Parma
A 1
A 15
62
Reggio nell'Emilia
Modena
A 13
United Kingdom
Netherlands
Amsterdam
Berlin
Poland
London
Germany
Brussels
Belgium
Prague
Luxembourg
Czech Republic
Paris
Vienna
France
Bern
Switz.
Austria
Slovenia
MILAN
Croatia
Italy
Spain
Rome
Madrid
Mediterranean Sea
Algiers
Tunis

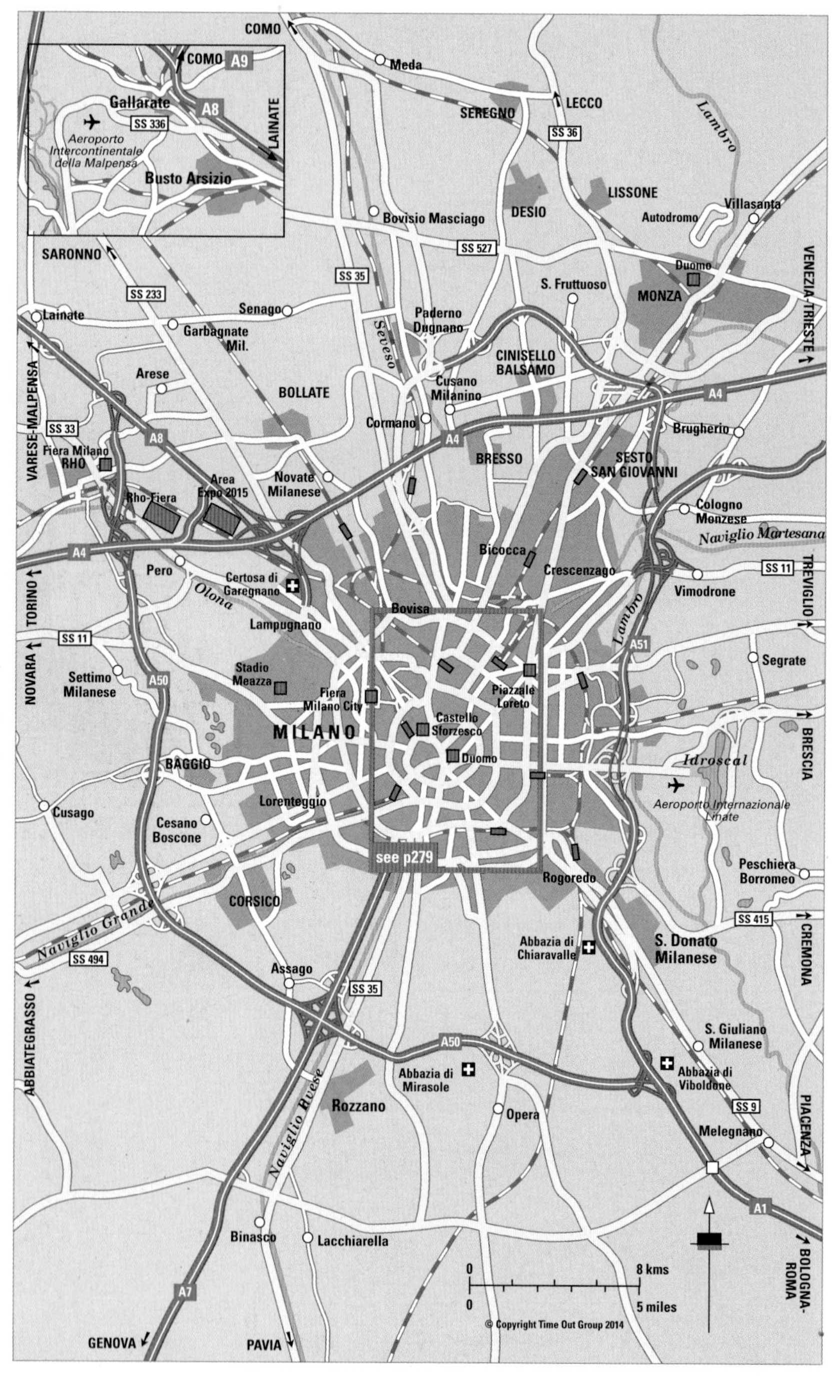
COMO
COMO
A9
Gallarate
A8
LAINATE
SS 336
Aeroporto Intercontinentale della Malpensa
Busto Arsizio
Meda
SEREGNO
LECCO
SS 36
Lambro
LISSONE
Villasanta
Autodromo
Bovisio Masciago
DESIO
SS 527
SARONNO
SS 35
Duomo
S. Fruttuoso
MONZA
SS 233
VENEZIA-TRIESTE
Lainate
Senago
Paderno Dugnano
Garbagnate Mil.
Seveso
CINISELLO BALSAMO
Arese
Cusano Milanino
BOLLATE
A4
VARESE-MALPENSA
SS 33
Cormano
Brugherio
A8
A4
Fiera Milano RHO
BRESSO
SESTO SAN GIOVANNI
Novate Milanese
Area Expo 2015
Rho-Fiera
Cologno Monzese
Naviglio Martesana
A4
Bicocca
Pero
Crescenzago
SS 11
Certosa di Garegnano
TREVIGLIO
TORINO
Olona
Vimodrone
Bovisa
Lampugnano
Lambro
SS 11
A51
NOVARA
Segrate
Stadio Meazza
Settimo Milanese
A50
Fiera Milano City
Piazzale Loreto
Castello Sforzesco
MILANO
BRESCIA
Duomo
BAGGIO
Idroscal
Aeroporto Internazionale Linate
Cusago
Lorenteggio
Cesano Boscone
see p279
Peschiera Borromeo
Rogoredo
CORSICO
SS 415
Naviglio Grande
CREMONA
Abbazia di Chiaravalle
S. Donato Milanese
SS 494
Assago
ABBIATEGRASSO
SS 35
S. Giuliano Milanese
A50
Abbazia di Mirasole
Abbazia di Viboldone
Rozzano
SS 9
Naviglio Pavese
Opera
PIACENZA
Melegnano
A1
Binasco
Lacchiarella
BOLOGNA-ROMA
0
8 kms
0
5 miles
A7
© Copyright Time Out Group 2014
GENOVA
PAVIA

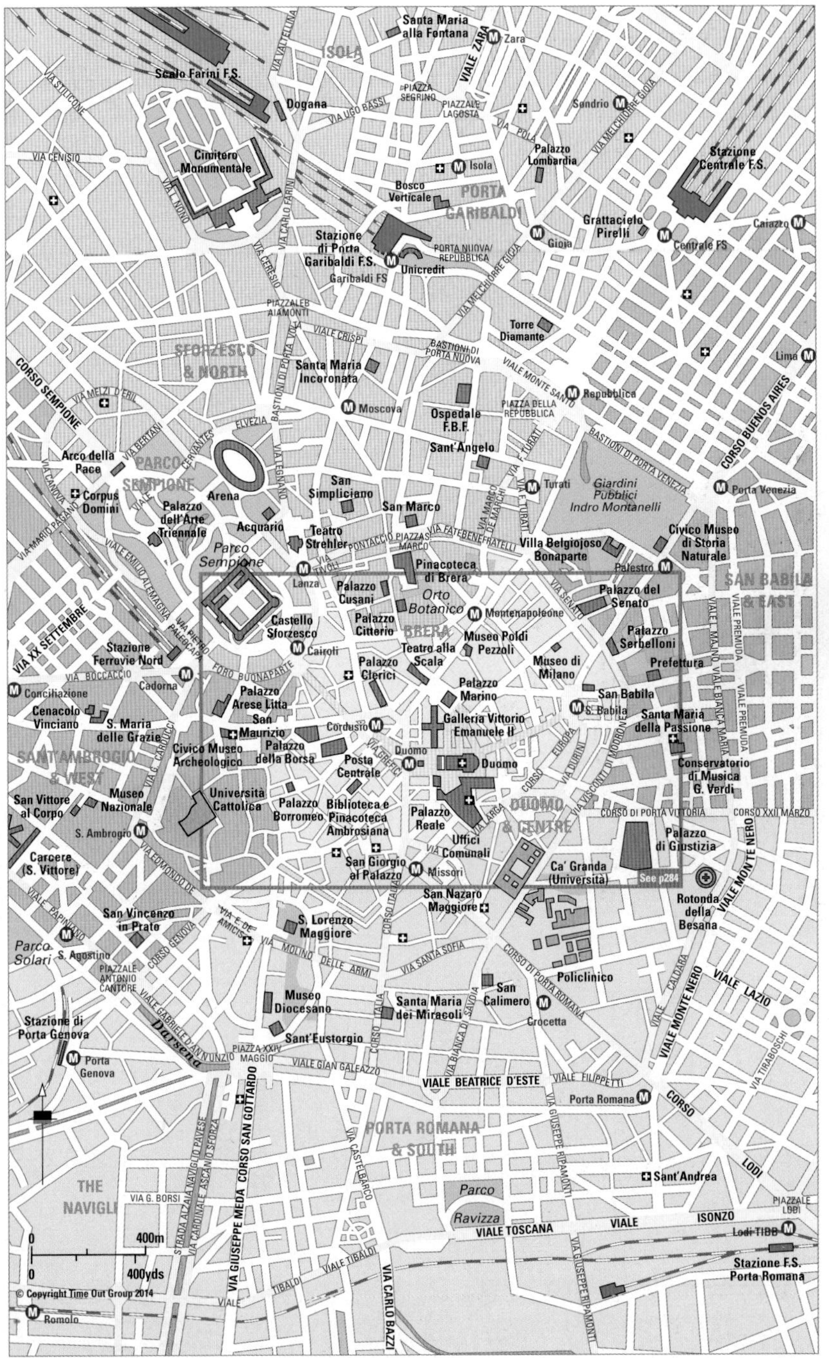

Santa Maria alla Fontana
Zara
ISOLA
VIA VALTELLINA
VIALE ZARA
Scalo Farini F.S.
VIA STILICONE
Dogana
PIAZZA SEGRINO
PIAZZALE LAGOSTA
VIA UGO BASSI
Sondrio
VIA MELCHIORRE GIOIA
VIA POLA
VIA CENISIO
Cimitero Monumentale
Palazzo Lombardia
Isola
Stazione Centrale F.S.
VIA F. NONO
VIA CARLO FARINI
Bosco Verticale
PORTA GARIBALDI
Grattacielo Pirelli
Caiazzo
Stazione di Porta Garibaldi F.S.
Gioia
Centrale FS
PORTA NUOVA/ REPUBBLICA
Unicredit
Garibaldi FS
VIA CERESIO
PIAZZALE B AIAMONTI
VIA MELCHIORRE GIOIA
Torre Diamante
VIALE CRISPI
BASTIONI DI PORTA NUOVA
SFORZESCO & NORTH
Lima
CORSO SEMPIONE
Santa Maria Incoronata
BASTIONI DI PORTA VOLTA
VIALE MONTE SANTO
Repubblica
VIA MELZI D'ERIL
Moscova
PIAZZA DELLA REPUBBLICA
CORSO BUENOS AIRES
ELVEZIA
Ospedale F.B.F.
VIA BERTANI
CERVANTES
VIA TURATI
BASTIONI DI PORTA VENEZIA
Arco della Pace
PARCO SEMPIONE
VIA LEGNANO
Sant'Angelo
VIA CANOVA
Turati
Giardini Pubblici Indro Montanelli
Porta Venezia
Corpus Domini
Arena
San Simpliciano
San Marco
VIA MARCO DE MARCHI
VIA F. TURATI
VIA MARIO PAGANO
Palazzo dell'Arte Triennale
Acquario
Teatro Strehler
VIA FATEBENEFRATELLI
Villa Belgiojoso Bonaparte
Civico Museo di Storia Naturale
VIALE EMILIO ALEMAGNA
Parco Sempione
PONTACCIO
PIAZZA S. MARCO
Pinacoteca di Brera
Palestro
SAN BABILA & EAST
VIA TIVOLI
Lanza
Palazzo Cusani
Orto Botanico
VIA SENATO
Palazzo del Senato
Montenapoleone
VIALE PREMUDA
VIA XX SETTEMBRE
VIA PIETRO PALEOCAPA
Castello Sforzesco
Palazzo Citterio
BRERA
Museo Poldi Pezzoli
Palazzo Serbelloni
Stazione Ferrovie Nord
Cairoli
Teatro alla Scala
Museo di Milano
VIALE L. MAINO
VIALE BIANCA MARIA
FORO BUONAPARTE
Palazzo Clerici
Prefettura
VIA BOCCACCIO
Cadorna
Conciliazione
Palazzo Marino
San Babila
Palazzo Arese Litta
S. Babila
Cenacolo Vinciano
S. Maria delle Grazie
San Maurizio
Cordusio
Galleria Vittorio Emanuele II
Santa Maria della Passione
VIA G. CARDUCCI
Civico Museo Archeologico
Palazzo della Borsa
Duomo
CORSO EUROPA
SANT'AMBROGIO & WEST
Posta Centrale
Duomo
VIA DURINI
Conservatorio di Musica G. Verdi
Museo Nazionale
Università Cattolica
Palazzo Borromeo
Biblioteca e Pinacoteca Ambrosiana
Palazzo Reale
DUOMO & CENTRE
VIA VISCONTI DI MODRONE
San Vittore al Corpo
VIA LARGA
CORSO DI PORTA VITTORIA
CORSO XXII MARZO
S. Ambrogio
Uffici Comunali
Palazzo di Giustizia
Carcere (S. Vittore)
San Giorgio al Palazzo
Missori
Ca' Granda (Università)
See p284
VIA EDMONDO DE AMICIS
VIALE MONTE NERO
Rotonda della Besana
San Nazaro Maggiore
VIALE PAPINIANO
San Vincenzo in Prato
CORSO ITALIA
S. Lorenzo Maggiore
Parco Solari
S. Agostino
CORSO GENOVA
VIA MOLINO DELLE ARMI
VIA SANTA SOFIA
CORSO DI PORTA ROMANA
Policlinico
PIAZZALE ANTONIO CANTORE
VIALE LAZIO
VIALE CALDARA
Museo Diocesano
Santa Maria dei Miracoli
San Calimero
VIA BIANCA DI SAVOIA
Crocetta
VIALE GABRIELE D'ANNUNZIO
Stazione di Porta Genova
Darsena
Sant'Eustorgio
PIAZZA XXIV MAGGIO
VIALE GIAN GALEAZZO
VIA TIRABOSCHI
Porta Genova
VIALE BEATRICE D'ESTE
VIALE FILIPPETTI
Porta Romana
CORSO LODI
CORSO SAN GOTTARDO
PORTA ROMANA & SOUTH
VIA CASTELBARCO
VIA GIUSEPPE RIPAMONTI
THE NAVIGLI
VIA G. BORSI
Parco Ravizza
Sant'Andrea
PIAZZALE LODI
VIALE ISONZO
VIALE TOSCANA
Lodi TIBB
Stazione F.S. Porta Romana
STRADA ALZAIA NAVIGLIO PAVESE
VIA CARDINALE ASCANIO SFORZA
VIA GIUSEPPE MEDA
VIALE TIBALDI
VIA CARLO BAZZI
0
400m
0
400yds
© Copyright Time Out Group 2014
Romolo

MAPS

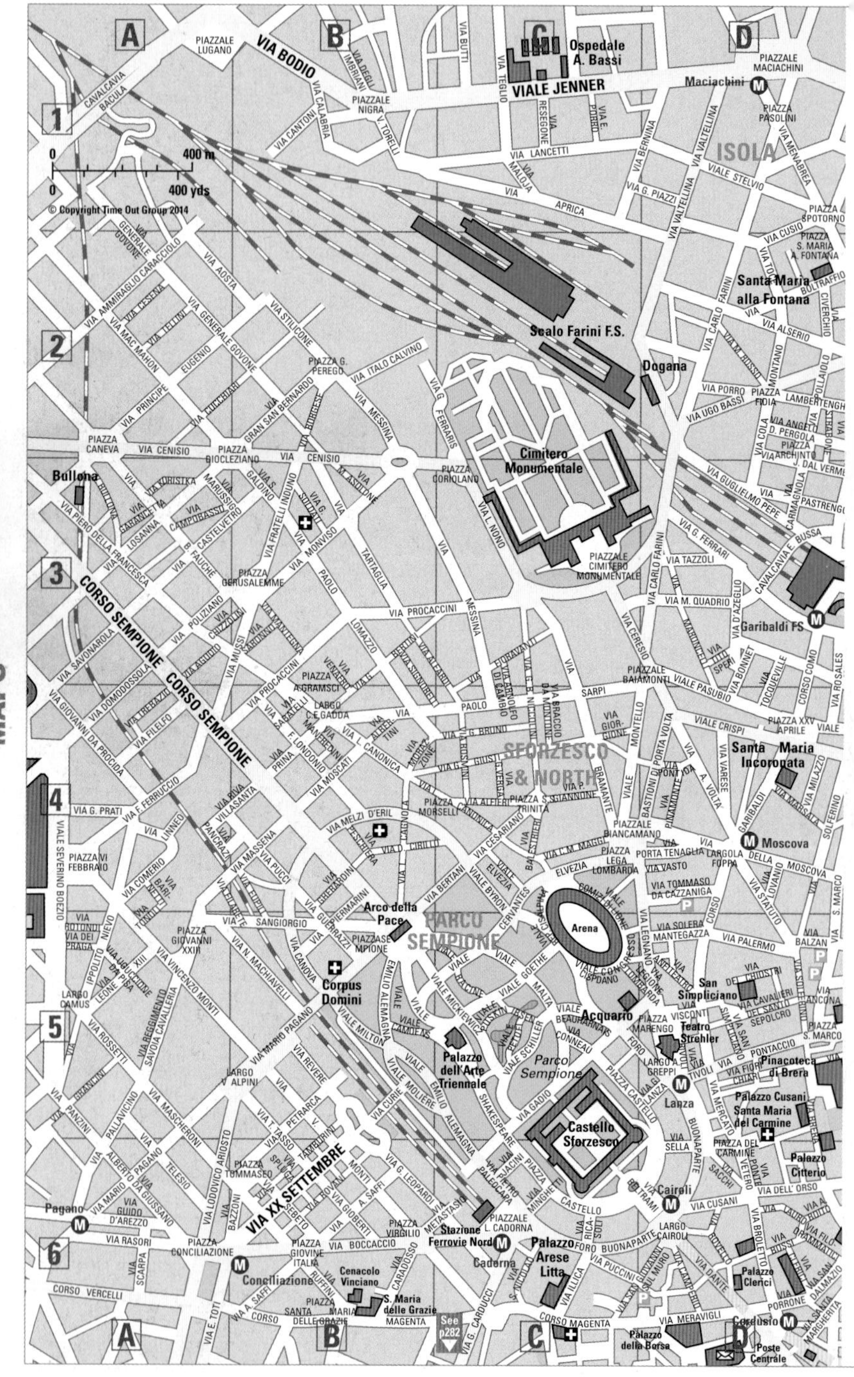
A
B
C
D
1
2
3
4
5
6
0
400 m
0
400 yds
© Copyright Time Out Group 2014
Piazzale Lugano
Via Bodio
Ospedale A. Bassi
Viale Jenner
Piazzale Maciachini
Maciachini
Piazza Pasolini
Isola
Piazzale Nigra
Via Cantoni
Via Calabria
V. Torelli
Via Butti
Via Teglio
Via Resegone
Via Lancetti
Via Maloja
Via Aprica
Via G. Piazzi
Via Bernina
Via Valtellina
Viale Stelvio
Via Menabrea
Piazza Spotorno
Via Cusio
Piazza S. Maria A. Fontana
Santa Maria alla Fontana
Via Boltraffio
Via Civerchio
Cavalcavia Bacula
Via Generale Govone
Via Ammiraglio Caracciolo
Via Aosta
Via Cesena
Via Tellini
Via Mac Mahon
Via Stilicone
Via Eugenio
Piazza G. Perego
Via Italo Calvino
Scalo Farini F.S.
Dogana
Via Carlo Farini
Via Alserio
Via M. Bussi
Via Porro
Via Ugo Bassi
Piazza Fidia
Via Lambertenghi
Via Angelo D. Pergola
Piazza Archinto
J. Dal Verme
Via Cola
Via Principe
Via Cucchiari
Via Gran San Bernardo
Via Borgese
Via Messina
Via G. Ferraris
Cimitero Monumentale
Piazza Caneva
Via Cenisio
Piazza Diocleziano
M. Asolone
Piazza Coriolano
Via Guglielmo Pepe
Via Pastrengo
Via Carmagnola
Bullona
Via Bullona
Via Koristka
Via Marussig
Via S. Galdino
Via G. Sottili
Via Campobasso
Via Piero della Francesca
Via Losanna
Via Castelvetro
Via Fratelli Induno
Via Monviso
Via Tartaglia
Via L. Nono
Via G. Ferrari
Cavalcavia E. Bussa
Via Tazzoli
Piazzale Cimitero Monumentale
Via M. Quadrio
Via D'Azeglio
Garibaldi FS
Piazza Gerusalemme
Via Paolo
Corso Sempione
Via Poliziano
Via Procaccini
Via Mantegna
Via Lomazzo
Via Ceresio
Via Maroncelli
Via Speri
Via Bonnet
Via Tocqueville
Corso Como
Via Rosales
Via Savonarola
Via Domodossola
Via Giovanni da Procida
Via Mussi
Via Arona
Piazza A. Gramsci
Via Bertini
Via Signorelli
Via Alfieri
Via Fioravanti
Via Arnolfo di Cambio
Via Braccio da Montone
Via Sarpi
Piazzale Baiamonti
Viale Pasubio
Via Urbano
Via Filelfo
Via Sebatelli
Largo C.E. Gadda
Via Londonio
Via Manfredini
Via Prina
Via L. Canonica
Via G. Bruno
Via Rosmini
Via G. Giusti
Via G. Verga
Sforzesco & North
Via Giordano
Via Montello
Via Pontida
Via Volta
Via Pianamonte
Viale Crispi
Piazza XXV Aprile
Santa Maria Incoronata
Via Varese
Via Milazzo
Via Moscati
Via Alfieri
Piazza S. Trinità
Via P. Giannone
Via Bramante
Bastioni di Porta Volta
Via G. Prati
Via F. Ferruccio
Via Riva Villasanta
Piazza Morselli
Piazzale Biancamano
Via Garibaldi
Via Solferino
Viale Severino Boezio
Via Linneo
Via Pancrazi
Via Melzi d'Eril
Via Peschiera
Via D. Cirillo
Via Cesariano
Via Balestrieri
Via C.M. Maggi
Piazza Lega Lombarda
Porta Tenaglia
Largo la Foppa
Moscova
Piazza VI Febbraio
Via Comerio
Via Massena
Via Pucci
Via Gherardini
Via Bertani
Viale Elvezia
Viale Byron
Via Elvezia
Via Vasto
Via Tommaso da Cazzaniga
Via Statuto
Via S. Marco
Via Rotondi
Via dei Praga
Via Sangiorgio
Arco della Pace
Parco Sempione
Via Cervantes
Arena
Via Solera Mantegazza
Via Palermo
Via Balzan
Piazza Giovanni XXIII
Piazzale Sempione
Viale Goethe
Viale Malta
Viale Cispano
Via Legnano
Via Anfiteatro
Via del Chiostri
San Simpliciano
Via Cavalieri del Santo Sepolcro
Largo Camus
Via Uguccione da Pisa
Via Vincenzo Monti
Via N. Machiavelli
Via Canova
Corpus Domini
Viale Emilio Alemagna
Viale Mickiewicz
Viale Ruskin
Acquario
Piazza Marengo
Piazza Castello
Teatro Strehler
Via Ancona
Piazza S. Marco
Via Rossetti
Via Reggimento Savoia Cavalleria
Via Mario Pagano
Viale Milton
Viale Camoens
Palazzo dell'Arte Triennale
Viale Schiller
Parco Sempione
Via Pontaccio
Pinacoteca di Brera
Largo V. Alpini
Via Revere
Viale Molière
Via Gadio
Largo A. Greppi
Via Tivoli
Via Fiori Chiari
Lanza
Palazzo Cusani
Santa Maria del Carmine
Via Pallavicino
Via Mascheroni
Via Petrarca
Via Curie
Viale Shakespeare
Castello Sforzesco
Via Mercato
Via Brera
Via Panzini
Via Alberto da Giussano
Via Telesio
Via Lodovico Ariosto
Via T. Tasso
Via XX Settembre
Via Sella
Via Buonaparte
Piazza del Carmine
Palazzo Citterio
Piazza Tommaseo
Via Monti
Via G. Leopardi
Via Paleocapa
Via Minghetti
Via Beltrami
Cairoli
Via dell'Orso
Via Mario Guido d'Arezzo
Pagano
Via Bazzoni
Via Saffi
Via Gioberti
Piazzale L. Cadorna
Stazione Ferrovie Nord
Via Castello
Via Cusani
Largo Cairoli
Via Rasori
Piazza Conciliazione
Piazza Virgilio
Via Boccaccio
Piazza Giovine Italia
Via Ruffini
Via Carducci
Via Caradosso
Cadorna
Palazzo Arese Litta
Foro Buonaparte
Via Puccini
Via San Giovanni sul Muro
Via Dante
Palazzo Clerici
Via Broletto
Via Bossi
Conciliazione
Cenacolo Vinciano
Corso Vercelli
Via E. Toti
Piazza Santa Maria delle Grazie
S. Maria delle Grazie
Corso Magenta
See p282
Via G. Carducci
Via Meravigli
Palazzo della Borsa
Via Porrone
Cordusio
Poste Centrale
Via San Dalmazio

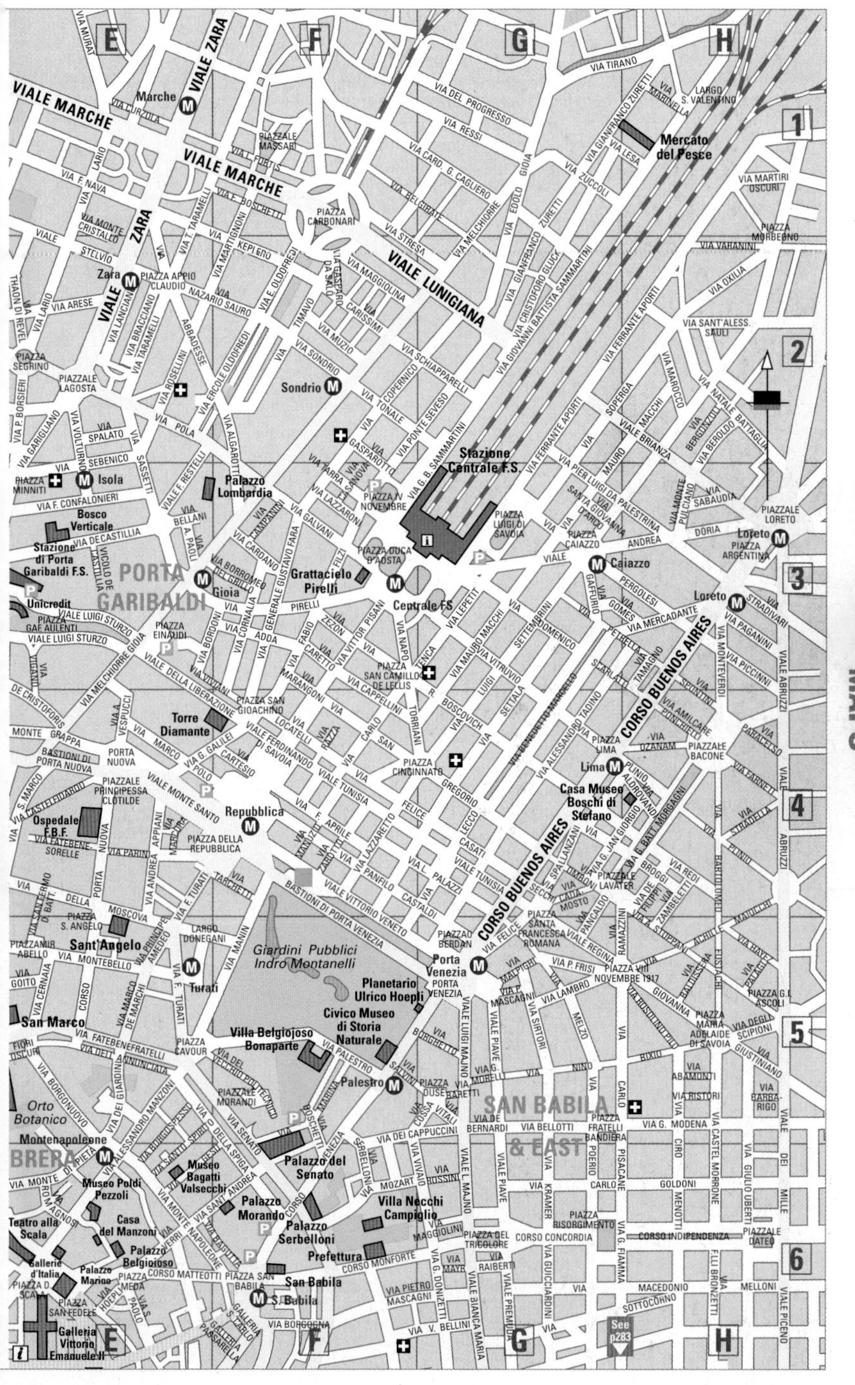

E
F
G
H
1
2
3
4
5
6
VIALE MARCHE
VIALE ZARA
Marche
PIAZZALE MASSARI
PIAZZA CARBONARI
VIA DEL PROGRESSO
VIA RESSI
VIA TIRANO
LARGO S. VALENTINO
Mercato del Pesce
VIA MARTIRI OSCURI
PIAZZA MORBEGNO
VIA VARANINI
VIA OXILIA
VIALE LUNIGIANA
VIA STRESA
VIA MELCHIORRE GIOIA
VIA GIOVANNI BATTISTA SAMMARTINI
VIA FERRANTE APORTI
VIA SANT'ALESS. SAULI
Zara
PIAZZA APPIO CLAUDIO
VIA NAZARIO SAURO
VIA ARESE
PIAZZA SEGRINO
PIAZZALE LAGOSTA
VIA POLA
VIA SONDRIO
Sondrio
VIA TONALE
VIA COPERNICO
VIA SCHIAPPARELLI
VIA PONTE SEVESO
Stazione Centrale F.S.
PIAZZA IV NOVEMBRE
PIAZZA DUCA D'AOSTA
PIAZZA LUIGI DI SAVOIA
PIAZZA CAIAZZO
Caiazzo
VIA ANDREA DORIA
PIAZZALE LORETO
Loreto
PIAZZA ARGENTINA
VIALE BRIANZA
VIA NATALE BATTAGLIA
VIA PIER LUIGI DA PALESTRINA
Isola
PIAZZA MINNITI
VIA F. CONFALONIERI
Bosco Verticale
Palazzo Lombardia
Stazione di Porta Garibaldi F.S.
PORTA GARIBALDI
Gioia
Grattacielo Pirelli
Centrale FS
Unicredit
PIAZZA GAE AULENTI
VIALE LUIGI STURZO
PIAZZA EINAUDI
VIA PIRELLI
VIA VITTOR PISANI
VIA LEPETIT
VIA MERCADANTE
CORSO BUENOS AIRES
VIA STRADIVARI
VIA PAGANINI
VIA PICCINNI
VIALE ABRUZZI
VIA MONTEVERDI
VIALE DELLA LIBERAZIONE
PIAZZA SAN GIOACHINO
PIAZZA SAN CAMILLO DE LELLIS
Torre Diamante
BASTIONI DI PORTA NUOVA
PIAZZA CINCINNATO
PIAZZA LIMA
Lima
PIAZZALE BACONE
Casa Museo Boschi di Stefano
PIAZZALE PRINCIPESSA CLOTILDE
VIALE MONTE SANTO
Repubblica
PIAZZA DELLA REPUBBLICA
VIALE TUNISIA
Ospedale F.B.F.
VIA FATEBENESORELLE
PIAZZALE LAVATER
BASTIONI DI PORTA VENEZIA
VIALE VITTORIO VENETO
PIAZZA S. ANGELO
Sant'Angelo
LARGO DONEGANI
Giardini Pubblici Indro Montanelli
PIAZZA OBERDAN
PIAZZA SANTA FRANCESCA ROMANA
VIALE REGINA GIOVANNA
PIAZZA VIII NOVEMBRE 1917
Porta Venezia
Turati
Planetario Ulrico Hoepli
Civico Museo di Storia Naturale
Villa Belgiojoso Bonaparte
San Marco
PIAZZA CAVOUR
VIA PALESTRO
Palestro
PIAZZA DUSE
PIAZZA MARIA ADELAIDE DI SAVOIA
PIAZZA G.L. ASCOLI
Orto Botanico
BRERA
Montenapoleone
SAN BABILA & EAST
PIAZZALE MORANDI
VIA MANZONI
VIA DELLA SPIGA
VIA MONTE NAPOLEONE
VIA DEI CAPPUCCINI
Palazzo del Senato
Museo Bagatti Valsecchi
Museo Poldi Pezzoli
Palazzo Morando
Villa Necchi Campiglio
Casa del Manzoni
Teatro alla Scala
Palazzo Serbelloni
Prefettura
Palazzo Belgioioso
Gallerie d'Italia
Palazzo Marino
PIAZZA SAN FEDELE
PIAZZA MEDA
CORSO MATTEOTTI
PIAZZA SAN BABILA
San Babila
S. Babila
CORSO MONFORTE
PIAZZA DEL TRICOLORE
CORSO CONCORDIA
PIAZZA RISORGIMENTO
CORSO INDIPENDENZA
PIAZZALE DATEO
VIA VIVAIO
VIALE PIAVE
VIA BELLOTTI
VIA G. MODENA
VIA CASTEL MORRONE
VIA GIULIO UBERTI
VIALE DEI MILLE
VIA MELLONI
VIALE PICENO
Galleria Vittorio Emanuele II
VIA BORGOGNA
See p283

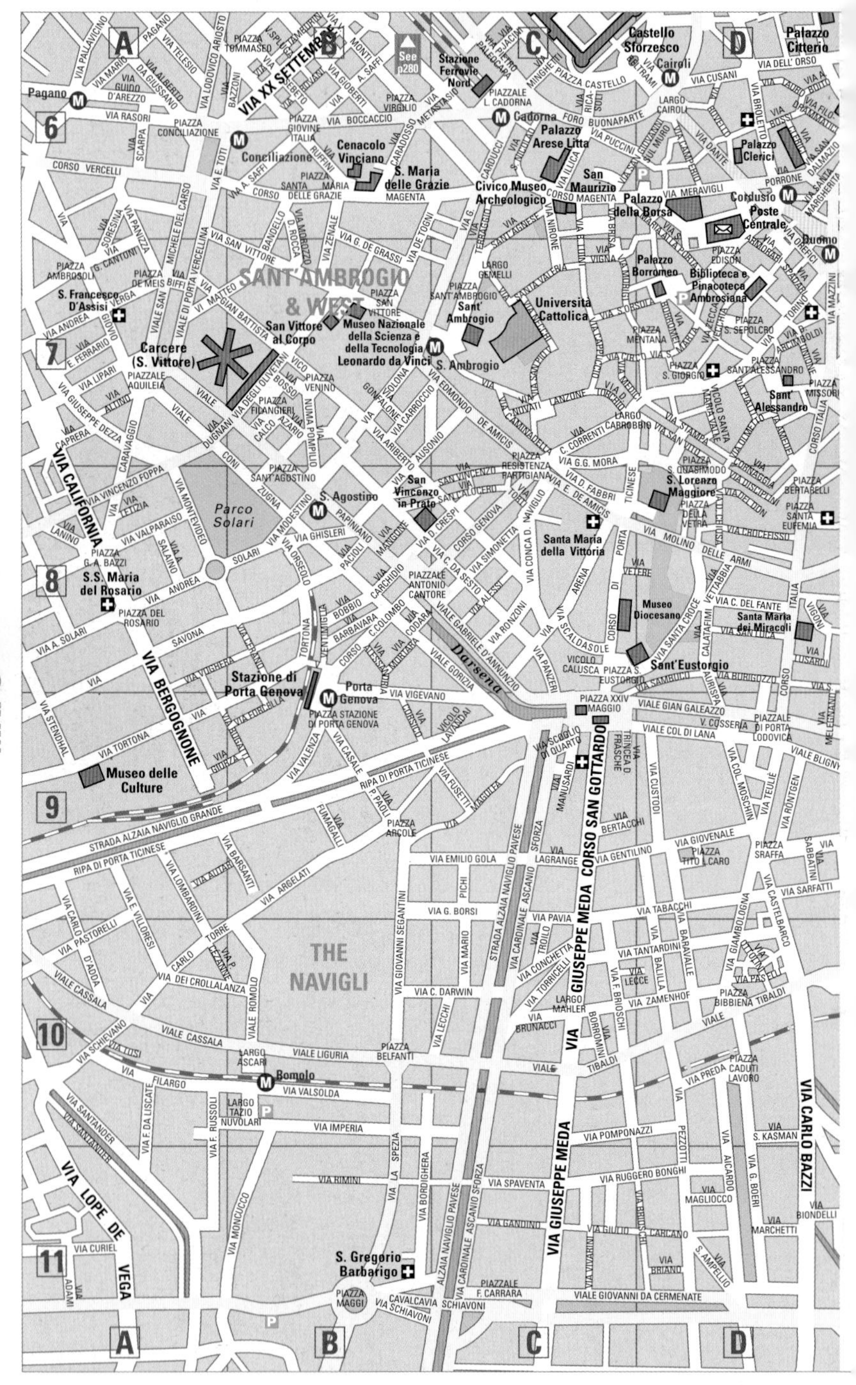
SANT'AMBROGIO & WEST
THE NAVIGLI
Castello Sforzesco
Palazzo Citterio
Stazione Ferrovie Nord
Cenacolo Vinciano
S. Maria delle Grazie
Palazzo Arese Litta
San Maurizio
Civico Museo Archeologico
Palazzo della Borsa
Poste Centrale
Palazzo Clerici
Palazzo Borromeo
Biblioteca e Pinacoteca Ambrosiana
Università Cattolica
Sant' Ambrogio
San Vittore al Corpo
Museo Nazionale della Scienza e della Tecnologia Leonardo da Vinci
Carcere (S. Vittore)
S. Francesco D'Assisi
Sant' Alessandro
S. Lorenzo Maggiore
San Vincenzo in Prato
S. Agostino
Parco Solari
Santa Maria della Vittoria
S.S. Maria del Rosario
Museo Diocesano
Santa Maria dei Miracoli
Sant'Eustorgio
Stazione di Porta Genova
Porta Genova
Darsena
Museo delle Culture
S. Gregorio Barbarigo
Romolo
Cadorna
Cairoli
Cordusio
Duomo
Pagano
Conciliazione
S. Ambrogio
VIA XX SETTEMBRE
VIA CALIFORNIA
VIA BERGOGNONE
CORSO SAN GOTTARDO
VIA GIUSEPPE MEDA
VIA CARLO BAZZI
VIA LOPE DE VEGA
STRADA ALZAIA NAVIGLIO GRANDE
RIPA DI PORTA TICINESE
VIALE GABRIELE D'ANNUNZIO
See p280

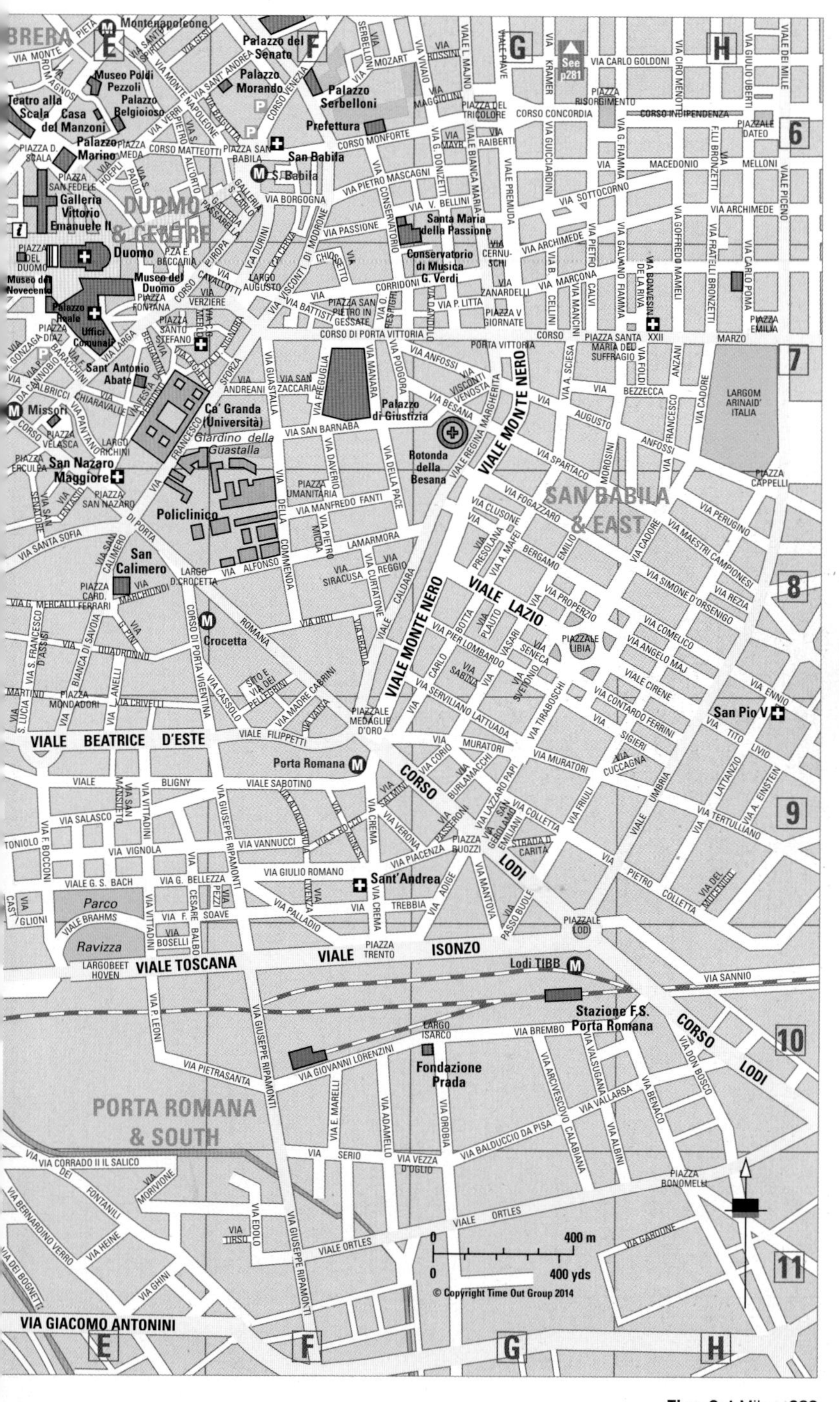
BRERA
E
F
G
H
Montenapoleone
Palazzo del Senato
Museo Poldi Pezzoli
Palazzo Morando
Palazzo Serbelloni
Teatro alla Scala
Casa del Manzoni
Palazzo Belgioioso
Prefettura
Palazzo Marino
San Babila
S. Babila
Galleria Vittorio Emanuele II
DUOMO & CENTRE
Duomo
Museo del Novecento
Museo del Duomo
Palazzo Reale
Uffici Comunali
Santa Maria della Passione
Conservatorio di Musica G. Verdi
See p281
PIAZZA RISORGIMENTO
CORSO CONCORDIA
CORSO INDIPENDENZA
PIAZZALE DATEO
6
CORSO MONFORTE
VIA SOTTOCORNO
VIA ARCHIMEDE
VIA MARCONA
CORSO DI PORTA VITTORIA
PORTA VITTORIA
CORSO XXII MARZO
7
PIAZZA EMILIA
LARGO ARINAID' ITALIA
Sant' Antonio Abate
Missori
Ca' Granda (Università)
Giardino della Guastalla
Palazzo di Giustizia
Rotonda della Besana
San Nazaro Maggiore
Policlinico
VIALE MONTE NERO
SAN BABILA & EAST
PIAZZA CAPPELLI
San Calimero
8
VIALE LAZIO
PIAZZALE LIBIA
Crocetta
San Pio V
VIALE BEATRICE D'ESTE
Porta Romana
CORSO LODI
9
Parco Ravizza
Sant'Andrea
PIAZZALE LODI
VIALE TOSCANA
VIALE ISONZO
Lodi TIBB
VIA SANNIO
Stazione F.S. Porta Romana
10
Fondazione Prada
PORTA ROMANA & SOUTH
VIALE ORTLES
PIAZZA BONOMELLI
VIA GIACOMO ANTONINI
11
0
400 m
400 yds
© Copyright Time Out Group 2014
MAPS

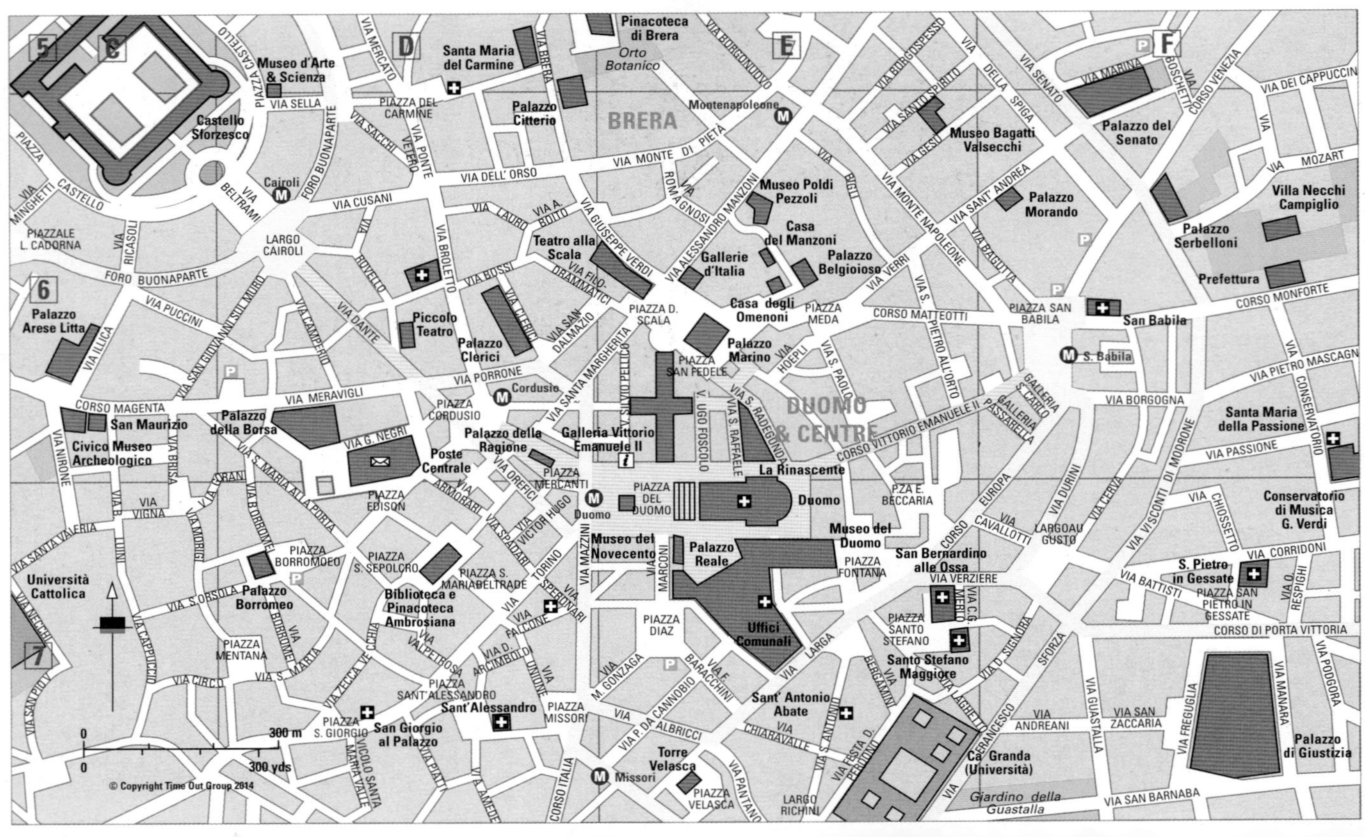
Castello Sforzesco
Museo d'Arte & Scienza
Santa Maria del Carmine
Pinacoteca di Brera
Orto Botanico
Palazzo Citterio
BRERA
Montenapoleone
Museo Bagatti Valsecchi
Palazzo del Senato
Villa Necchi Campiglio
Palazzo Serbelloni
Prefettura
Palazzo Morando
Museo Poldi Pezzoli
Casa del Manzoni
Palazzo Belgioioso
Gallerie d'Italia
Teatro alla Scala
Casa degli Omenoni
Palazzo Marino
Piccolo Teatro
Palazzo Clerici
Palazzo Arese Litta
Cairoli
Largo Cairoli
Piazzale L. Cadorna
Cordusio
San Babila
S. Babila
Palazzo della Borsa
San Maurizio
Civico Museo Archeologico
Palazzo della Ragione
Galleria Vittorio Emanuele II
Poste Centrale
DUOMO & CENTRE
La Rinascente
Duomo
Museo del Duomo
Museo del Novecento
Palazzo Reale
Uffici Comunali
Santa Maria della Passione
Conservatorio di Musica G. Verdi
San Bernardino alle Ossa
S. Pietro in Gessate
Santo Stefano Maggiore
Università Cattolica
Palazzo Borromeo
Biblioteca e Pinacoteca Ambrosiana
Sant'Alessandro
San Giorgio al Palazzo
Sant' Antonio Abate
Torre Velasca
Missori
Ca' Granda (Università)
Giardino della Guastalla
Palazzo di Giustizia
Corso Venezia
Corso Monforte
Corso Matteotti
Corso Vittorio Emanuele II
Via Monte Napoleone
Via della Spiga
Via Alessandro Manzoni
Via Brera
Via Dante
Via Torino
Corso Magenta
Corso Italia
Corso di Porta Vittoria
Foro Buonaparte
Piazza del Duomo
Piazza D. Scala
Piazza San Babila
Piazza Fontana
Piazza Diaz
Piazza Cordusio
0
300 m
300 yds
© Copyright Time Out Group 2014

Street Index

RETE METROPOLITANA E TRATTE FERROVIARIE URBANE
UNDERGROUND NETWORK AND URBAN RAILWAY SYSTEM

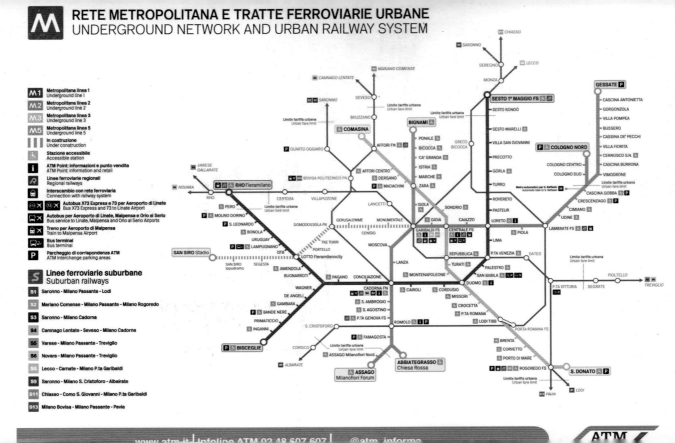

- M1 — **Metropolitana linea 1** / Underground line 1
- M2 — **Metropolitana linea 2** / Underground line 2
- M3 — **Metropolitana linea 3** / Underground line 3
- M5 — **Metropolitana linea 5** / Underground line 5
- **In costruzione** / Under construction
- **Stazione accessibile** / Accessible station
- **ATM Point: informazioni e punto vendita** / ATM Point: information and retail
- **Linee ferroviarie regionali** / Regional railways
- **Interscambio con rete ferroviaria** / Connection with railway system
- **Autobus X73 Express e 73 per Aeroporto di Linate** / Bus X73 Express and 73 to Linate Airport
- **Autobus per Aeroporto di Linate, Malpensa e Orio al Serio** / Bus service to Linate, Malpensa and Orio al Serio Airports
- **Treno per Aeroporto di Malpensa** / Train to Malpensa Airport
- **Bus terminal** / Bus terminal
- P — **Parcheggio di corrispondenza ATM** / ATM interchange parking areas

Linee ferroviarie suburbane
Suburban railways

- S1 — Saronno - Milano Passante - Lodi
- S2 — Mariano Comense - Milano Passante - Milano Rogoredo
- S3 — Saronno - Milano Cadorna
- S4 — Camnago Lentate - Seveso - Milano Cadorna
- S5 — Varese - Milano Passante - Treviglio
- S6 — Novara - Milano Passante - Treviglio
- S8 — Lecco - Carnate - Milano P.ta Garibaldi
- S9 — Saronno - Milano S. Cristoforo - Albairate
- S11 — Chiasso - Como S. Giovanni - Milano P.ta Garibaldi
- S13 — Milano Bovisa - Milano Passante - Pavia

www.atm.it | Infoline ATM 02 48 607 607 | @atm_informa

ATM